Flagship Programmes

Flagship Programmes

Impact, Problems and Challenges Ahead

Editors
K.P. Kumaran, P.K. Nath,
K. Prabhakar and N. Kalpalatha

ACADEMIC FOUNDATION
NEW DELHI

www.academicfoundation.org

First published in 2017
by

ACADEMIC FOUNDATION
4772-73 / 23 Bharat Ram Road, (23 Ansari Road),
Darya Ganj, New Delhi - 110 002 (India).
Phones : 23245001 / 02 / 03 / 04.
Fax : +91-11-23245005.
E-mail : books@academicfoundation.com
www.academicfoundation.org

in association with
National Institute of Rural Development and Panchayati Raj (NIRD&PR), Hyderabad.

Cataloging in Publication Data--DK
Courtesy: D.K. Agencies (P) Ltd. <docinfo@dkagencies.com>

National Seminar on Flagship Programmes: Impact, Problems & Challenges Ahead (2014 : National Institute of Rural Development & Panchayati Raj)
Flagship programmes : impact, problems and challenges ahead / editors, K.P. Kumaran, P.K. Nath, K. Prabhakar and N. Kalpalatha.
pages cm
Papers presented at a National Seminar on Flagship Programmes: Impact, Problems & Challenges Ahead, organized by and held at National Institute of Rural Development (NIRD), Hyderabad during November 19-21, 2014.

ISBN 9789332703711

1. India. Mahatma Gandhi National Rural Employment Guarantee Act, 2005--Congresses. 2. Manpower policy, Rural--India--Congresses. 3. Rural poor--Employment--India--Congresses. 4. Rural development projects--India--Congresses. I. Kumaran, K. P., editor. II. National Institute of Rural Development & Panchayati Raj (India), host institution, organizer. III. Title.

HN690.Z9C6 2014 DDC 307.14120954 23

Typeset, printed and bound by The Book Mint, New Delhi.
www.thebookmint.in

Contents

List of Tables and Figures

Tables

Figures

Foreword

In an unequal society, in terms of asset and skill distribution, market in its functioning differentiates against the segment of population without assets or skill and against the space without adequate infrastructure. This gives a rationale for special government interventions in the form of social security programmes. Such programmes can be classified into two categories: (1) those designed to reduce poverty and vulnerability by way of diminishing people's exposure to risks, and to enhance their capacity to manage economic and social risks such as unemployment, exclusion, sickness, disability and old age, and (2) those that aim at providing rural and urban infrastructure and basic services with the objective of enhancing inclusiveness and human capability.

It is in this perspective that the National Institute of Rural Development and Panchayati Raj (NIRD&PR), Hyderabad, held a seminar on Flagship Programmes. Forty-five papers covering 15 flagship programmes were presented and discussed in the seminar.

One study, at the macro level, estimating multipliers in the social accounting framework highlighted that the flagship programmes like Mahatma Gandhi National Rural Employment Guarantee Act (MGNREGA), Indira Awaas Yojana (IAY) and National Social Assistance Programme (NSAP) have significant impact on output, income, employment and revenue generation when both direct and indirect impacts are taken into account.

Most of the other papers relate to 15 individual flagship programmes. These are intensive studies of the individual programmes using field level primary data to evaluate their impact on the target groups. They have analysed the data carefully and highlighted their important findings in regard to design, stakeholders' participation, manner of implementation, realised outcomes and observed weaknesses and so on.

These studies have observed that these programmes have yielded positive outcomes, to a varying extent, even though realised outcomes have fallen far short of the expected outcomes in terms of reaching out to the targeted segments or the desired level.

Weaknesses highlighted broadly relate to faulty design, lack of the required infrastructure for effective implementation, top down nature of the programmes, lack of people's involvement and participation, poor implementing machinery, inadequate attention to designing instruments for behavioural change. The studies have also suggested how best to address these shortcomings.

The broad message that has emerged from these papers is loud and clear—these flagship schemes have made positive impact even if fallen short of the desired extent. In an economy, such as ours, with widespread poverty, malnutrition and deprivation, particularly in the segments without productive asset and skill base, there is an absolute need for continuing with these programmes; more so, with corrections, by addressing the shortcomings of the respective schemes. After all, these schemes give entitlement/sustenance, even if in the modest way, for the life support and capability enhancement of the vulnerable section of the society. It is, therefore, important that the expenditures on such programme are not viewed as wasteful but as an instrument both for welfare and human capability enhancing and thus their continuance becomes imperative.

I believe the papers would enhance our understanding of the working of the flagship programmes in their various complexities and dimensions, and provide useful insights. Both researchers and policy makers are expected to benefit from these studies—researchers for pursuing more intensively the issues raised and policy makers for learning lessons for policy corrections.

I congratulate Prof K.P. Kumaran, NIRD&PR, for organising this very useful seminar at the current juncture when some rethinking as to the desirability of continuing the flagship programmes is apparently going on at the official level. It is hoped that the findings of the seminar papers incorporated in this volume would serve as useful inputs for the policy makers.

—Atul Sarma

Visiting Professor, Institute for Human Development, New Delhi;
Former Vice Chancellor, Rajiv Gandhi University, Arunachal Pradesh;
Member, Thirteenth Finance Commission

About the Editors/Contributors

Editors:

K.P. Kumaran has more than three decades of professional experience in research and training in the field of rural and urban development. He has to his credit several articles and books published both by the national and international publishers. Currently, he is working as consultant to Centre for Planning, Monitoring and Evaluation (CPME) at National Institute of Rural Development and Panchayati Raj (NIRD&PR), Hyderabad. Prior to this, he held important positions like Prof & Head, CPME and Prof & Head, Centre for Media and Rural Documentation, NIRD&PR, Hyderabad. He has also worked as Professor-Urban Basic Services for the Poor at the Institute of Management in Government, Thiruvanathapuram, Kerala.

P.K. Nath, trained in Economics, was an Administrative Service Officer in Odisha. Since 2008, he has been a Faculty in NIRD&PR. He has contributed in the areas of regional disparity, problems of the marginal (SC/ST and minorities), folklore, monitoring and evaluation of rural development programmes. He has also been a regular columnist in different Oriya dailies and some leading journals like *Mainstream*, *Vidura*, *Grassroots* and others.

K. Prabhakar is Assistant Professor, Centre for Good Governance & Policy Analysis (CGGPA) at NIRD&PR, Hyderabad. His research interests lie in the area of planning, monitoring, evaluation, governance, service delivery, decentralisation, and budget and policy analysis. He is involved in using different social accountability tools like Community Score Cards (CSC), Social Audits, Public Expenditure Tracking Surveys (PETS), Citizen Report Cards (CRC) and CRC+ for different contexts. He is associated with various international and national premier institutes.

N. Kalpalatha is currently working as cartographer in NIRD&PR, Hyderabad. She holds a Master degree in Regional Planning from Indian Institute of Technology, Kharagpur and Doctoral degree from Jawaharlal Nehru Technological University, Hyderabad.

Contributors:

Nilachala Acharya, Senior Research Officer, is working with the Centre for Budget and Governance Accountability (CBGA), a New Delhi based independent public policy research and think tank. He is MPhil in Economics and is pursuing his PhD (Economics) from Jawaharlal Nehru University, New Delhi. His areas of research interest include: financing of agriculture, issues relating to food security, and transparency in government budgets in India. He has contributed a number of articles/papers in journals and books. Apart from research, he has contributed significantly to the training and capacity building programmes on budgets and budgetary processes for the members of civil society organisations, university students, and policy makers, among others.

Michael S. Andrew, is a PhD Research Scholar at Madras Institute of Development Studies, Chennai. He is currently working on rural development with reference to rural development programmes especially employment generation schemes and its impact on the poor, marginalised and women empowerment.

Madhusudan Bhattarai is Principal Scientist—Economics, International Crops Research Institute for Semi-Arid Tropics (ICRISAT), Patancheru, Hyderabad.

Sumit Dadasaheb Bhandari is presently working as Agricultural Finance Officer in Central Bank at Kolkata. Ex-student of Department of Extension Education, Vasantrao Naik Marathwada Krishi Vidyapeeth, Parbhani, Maharashtra, he has completed BSc (Agri) from College of Agriculture, Baramati. He was awarded MSc (Agri) in Extension Education in 2014 with first class.

Narayana Billava obtained his MA and MPhil in Economics from Karnatak University, Dharwad. He is PhD in Economics from Centre for Multi Disciplinary Development Research (CMDR), affiliated with Kannada University, Hampi. He is working as a Researcher for Abdul Nazir Sab Panchayat Raj Chair, CMDR, Dharwad, which is a not-for-profit research organisation affiliated to Indian Council of Social Science Research (ICSSR), New Delhi. His areas of research interest are: decentralisation, public finance, water supply, sanitation and rural development. He has published papers on various aspects related to these issues.

Richa Chintan is a Research Consultant with the CBGA, New Delhi. She has done her MPhil in Economics from Jawaharlal Nehru University, New Delhi. She has earlier worked as a Visiting Research Associate with the Research and Information System (RIS), New Delhi. Her research interest include issues relating to public provisioning on agriculture and healthcare, and other developmental issues in India. She is involved on a campaign on government financing of healthcare being led jointly by Jan Swasthya Abhiyan (JSA) and People's Budget Initiative (PBI).

Sabitribala Das was an MPhil Scholar of the Department of Economics in the year 2013. She is now working in the District Project Office of the Sarva Shiksha Abhiyan (SSA) in Ganjam District.

Sanjukta Das is Reader in Economics, Sambalpur University, Sambalpur, Odisha. She has been a faculty member in the Department of Economics, Arunachal University (presently Rajiv Gandhi University), Arunachal Pradesh and has participated in the preparation of Arunachal Pradesh Human Development Report as a member of the Technical Committee. Presently, she is engaged in a major research project funded by ICSSR, New Delhi. Her areas of interest are: poverty, inequality, social sector development, human development and natural resource management. She has authored *Primary Education in Hills of Arunachal Pradesh: A Micro Study in India* (2011).

Tushar Kanti Das is presently working as a Reader in the Department of Business Administration, Sambalpur University, Odisha. His areas of interest include inclusive growth, social safety nets, financial inclusion, centre state financial relations, environmental economics, finance and marketing. He has around 18 years of teaching and research experience. He has published/presented a number of research papers in various international and national journals/conferences.

Koushik Kumar Hati is Assistant Professor of Economics, Department of Commerce, St. Xavier's College (Autonomous), Kolkata, and a Visiting Research Associate in the CTRPFP unit of Centre for Studies in Social Sciences, Calcutta. He received his PhD in Economics from the University of Burdwan. His research areas include: health, education and public finance. Prior to joining St. Xavier's College, Hati has worked for different research projects of CTRPFP. He has also undertaken research project funded by ICSSR. He is a contributor to the report of 14th Central Finance Commission for the state of West Bengal.

S. Indrakant is presently RBI Chair Professor at Council for Social Development, Southern Regional Office (SRC), Hyderabad. Earlier, he was Head, Department of Economics, Osmania University (2006-2009) and Chairman, Board of Studies, Department of Economics, Osmania University (2004-2006). Prof Indrakant has independently directed 5 research projects and is associated with another 13 research projects. He has 53 publications to his credit which are published in reputed journals like *Economic and Political Weekly*, *Indian Economic Journal*, etc.

K. Jafar is currently working as an ICSSR post-doctoral fellow at Council for Social Development, Hyderabad, after completing his doctoral research from National Institute of Advanced Studies, Bangalore. His research interest broadly falls in the area of development studies and focusing on issues related to education, migration, local finance, decentralisation, human development and gender.

Rajesh Parbhatrao Kadam is presently working as Associate Professor (Extension Education) in Vasantrao Naik Marathwada Krishi Vidyapeeth, Parbhani, Maharasht). He was awarded PhD degree in Extension Education from Marathwada Agricultural University, Parbhani. He has over 10 years of experience in teaching, research and extension in the discipline. He is recipient of Young Scientists Award of GVK Society, Agra and Indira Gandhi Sadbhawana Puraskar of IBC, New Delhi. He has published 6 books, more than 65 research papers in reputed journals and has also contributed book chapters, popular articles, technical bulletins and other extension publications.

T. Sarah Kamala is Professor and Principle Scientist in All India Coordinated Research Project on Home Science. She has vast experience in teaching and extension activities for rural families.

K. Keerthi is a PhD scholar in Prof Jayashanker Telangana State Agricultural University. She did her postgraduation from Acharya N.G. Ranga Agricultural University in 2012. Her specialisation was Home Science Extension and Communication Management. She has successfully managed great events such as Rural Home Science Work Experience Programme, internship with Andhra Pradesh Academy of Rural Development (about Bharath Nirman Volunteers) and has given international and national paper presentations.

M.S. Khan is an Associate Professor and Ex. Head of the Department of the Department of Rural Management under School for Business Management at Babasaheb Bhimrao Ambedkar University,

Lucknow. He has a Doctorate in Management and Masters in Public Administration and Human Rights and Duty Education. He has published 6 books on Management and a good number of research papers in national and international journals. He has been the Editorial Chairperson of *International Journal of Business Management & Research, International Journal of Sales & Marketing Management Research* and *International Journal of Retail Management & Research*. He has been the reviewer of leading national and international journals & books publishers. His area of current research includes International marketing, marketing, international business, general management and rural marketing.

Veeraiah Konduri is pursuing his PhD from Dr K.R. Narayanan Centre for Dalit and Minority Studies, Jamia Milia Islamia, New Delhi under the guidance of Prof Mujtabha Khan. A regular columnist, critique and translator, his field of research includes globalisation and social exclusion, experience of Dalits and Muslims in state of Andhra Pradesh.

P.K. Kulkarni (MCom, DIM) is Assistant Professor, Commerce and Management Department, Government First Grade College, Shahapur, Karnataka.

Nomita P. Kumar, Assistant Professor, Giri Institute of Development Studies, Lucknow, holds MA in Economics from Lucknow University and PhD (Economics) from Kanpur University. She has almost 26 years of research experience and has worked in different research projects at the Institute. Besides research experience, she also has teaching experience at the graduation and post-graduation level. Till now she has 20 research papers, 4 articles in edited books and 2 papers in Government reports to her credit. She has contributed several articles and presented papers in a number of national conferences and seminars. Major areas of her research interest are: women studies, labour market and employment scenario, issues related to family welfare and population policy, situational analysis of Uttar Pradesh, regional development and small scale industry.

V. Mathew Kurian is working as Visiting Professor in School of International Relations and Politics and Joint Director, K.N. Raj Centre of Planning and Centre-State Financial Relations in Mahatma Gandhi University, Kottayam, Kerala. His recent book *Kerala Economy and its Emerging Issues* has been published by SPCS, Kerala.

Aruna Kumar Malik, is currently working as an Assistant Professor of Political Science, Gujarat National Law University, Gandhinagar. He is also associated with several research institutions and universities in India and abroad.

A.D. Manikandan is currently pursuing PhD in Economics from Mahatma Gandhi University, Kottayam, Kerala with the ICSSR Institutional Doctoral Fellowship from Centre for Economic and Social Studies, Hyderabad. He has published number of research articles in national and international journals and has also published chapters in number of books. He has presented research papers in many national and international conferences.

Muktarani Mishra, a Research student, is working under Dr Sanjukta Das in the Department of Economics, Sambalpur University, Sambalpur, Odisha.

Nihar Ranjan Mishra, currently heading the Department of Humanities and Social Sciences, at National Institute of Technology, Rourkela, Odisha, is an Assistant Professor of Sociology. A recipient of University Gold Medal in MA Anthropology Examination, Dr Mishra had his academic training at University of Hyderabad, Hyderabad. He is also the recipient of Jawaharlal Nehru Memorial Scholarship for Doctoral Studies (2005-06), Doctoral Fellowship on Tribal Studies by Ministry of Tribal Affairs, Government of India (2006-07), National Scholarship (1997-2000) and few others. He specialises in natural resource management and sustainable livelihood, displacement issues, tribal and rural development and agrarian studies. He has over 30 publications in professional journals of repute. Along with some monographs, he edited one book on displacement and emerging issues in contemporary India. He has participated in many national and international conferences in India and abroad, and has earned his research and teaching experiences over the years handling various independent and joint projects sponsored by various private and Government departments.

Rudra N. Mishra is Assistant Professor at the Gujarat Institute of Development Research, Ahmedabad.

Soumya Mohanty is a Post Graduate student at Department of Humanities and Social Sciences, National Institute of Technology, Rourkela, Odisha.

Krishna Prasad Mukherjee did his graduation and post-graduation in veterinary sciences. In 2008, he joined the first batch of the Post Graduate Diploma in Rural Development Management (PGDRDM) course of the NIRD&PR, Hyderabad; and was conferred the NIRD Gold Medal for academic excellence. He worked with the NIRD&PR for few months as Training Manager at the Centre for Self-employment & Rural Enterprises. He joined the Government of West Bengal as Veterinary Officer in February, 2010. As in-service candidate in 2015, he completed the Post Graduate Diploma in Agricultural Extension Management from the National Institute of Agriculture Extension Management, Hyderabad. He has contributed to a broad range of research studies in different capacities. He has worked on MGNREGS, livelihood, decentralised planning, mid-day meal, livestock policy, feasibility analysis of livestock enterprises, impact studies on interventions under RKVY, etc. Apart from his stipulated responsibilities, as volunteer, he invests his free hours to the Durgapur Society for development Solutions (DSDS), an organisation which primarily works for promotion of rural livelihood.

Anish Nair is a post-graduate student of the Department of Civics and Politics at the University of Mumbai. With an inclination towards normative and qualitative research, his varied interests include:

understanding modern state and citizenship, the communist movement, and democracy in policy-making processes. He is currently an independent academic based in Trivandrum and a UPSC aspirant.

Nayanatara S. Nayak is Professor in the Centre for Multi Disciplinary Development Research (CMDR), Dharwad, which is a not-for-profit research organisation affiliated to ICSSR, Government of India. She holds a PhD in Economics from Mangalore University. Her research interests includes health economics, environmental studies, decentralisation, water resources and tobacco and alcohol control issues.

S.K. Nayak is working as Professor of Economics at Rajiv Gandhi University, Itanagar, Arunachal Pradesh. At present he is holding the position of Dean, Faculty of Social Science. He is also the Member (Non Official), NSSO 70th Round (a committee appointed by National Statistical Commission, Government of India).

Srikantha Nayaka is Post Doctoral Fellow in Economics (ICSSR) at Centre for Study of Social Exclusion and Inclusive Policy, Mangalore University. Mangalore. He hold an MA, MPhil and PhD in Economics from Mysore. His areas of specialisation are: tribal, caste and social groups, problems of marginalised groups, gender related issues, LAMPCS and cooperative economics and tribal development, forest tribal act, planning, monitoring and evaluation of the developmental programmes. He has more than five years of work experience in the field of Social Science Research and has contributed various papers to national and international journals, and edited volumes.

Bhagabata Patro has been working in the Department of Economics, Berhampur University, Odisha, since 1982 in different capacities. Currently, he is the Head of the Department; Chairman, Board of Studies and Director of Distant Education Centre of the University. He specialises in the area of development economics, public economics and econometrics.

Godawari Shivaji Pawar is presently working as Assistant Seed Research Officer in Vasantrao Naik Marathwada Krishi Vidyapeeth, Parbhani, Maharashtra. She has completed PhD in Crop Physiology from Professor Jayshankar Telangana State Agricultural University, Hyderabad. She has over 8 years of experience in teaching, research and extension in the discipline. She has published 3 books, has authored more than 255 research papers in reputed journals of the country and has contributed book chapters, popular articles, technical bulletins and other extension publications. She is recipient of State Level Agrocare Idol Award 2015 and State Level Sevashree Award 2016.

Floyd Peters is currently working as a Financial Analyst at Verity Knowledge Solutions (Captive KPO to UBS Investment Bank). He has been serving the organisation since April, 2015. He is BA (Economics Honours) from Christ University, Bangalore.

Kiran Prasad is Professor, Department of Communication and Journalism, Sri Padmavati Mahila University, Tirupati. She was Commonwealth Visiting Research Fellow at the Centre for International Communication Research, University of Leeds, UK and Canadian Studies Research Fellow at Carleton University, Canada. She is the youngest ever recipient of the State Best Teacher Award from the Government of Andhra Pradesh, India and recipient of several national awards for academic excellence. She has published over 20 books and over 100 research papers. Her recent books include: *Transforming International Communication: Media, Society and Culture in the Middle East* (2014), *New Media and Pathways to Social Change: Shifting Development Discourses* (2013) and *Media Law in India* (2011). She is Member of the Executive Council and Secretary of Communication Education in the Asian Congress of Media and Communication, Manila, Philippines. She is Series Editor of *Empowering Women Worldwide*.

R.M. Prasad is a retired Associate Director of Extension of Kerala Agricultural University. He served as Advisor, Government of Meghalaya; Agricultural Consultant for the Asian Development

Bank and as Senior Fellow in NIRD&PR, Hyderabad. Dr Prasad had served as Training Specialist in two European Union funded projects (KHDP and KMIP) in Kerala. He was also the National Facilitator of MANAGE, Hyderabad.

V. Ramakrishnappa is Associate Professor, Centre for Study of Social Exclusion and Inclusive Policy, Mangalore University, Mangalore. He holds MA in Economics from Bangalore University and was awarded PhD in Economics from University of Mysore for his thesis entitled "An Economic Analysis of Dairy Enterprise in Southern Karnataka". His areas of specialisation are: studies on social exclusion & inclusive policies, caste and social groups, problems of marginalised groups, informal sector workers, gender related issues, livestock and dairy economics, agriculture and rural development, environmental issues, planning, monitoring and evaluation of the developmental projects. He has more than 13 years of work experience in the field of Social Science Research. A prolific writer, he has authored 4 books and contributed various papers to national and international journals and edited volumes.

Ch. Shankar Rao is an Assistant Professor at Council for Social Development—Southern Regional Centre, Hyderabad. He holds MPhil and PhD in Economics from Centre for the Study of Regional Development, Jawaharlal Nehru University, New Delhi. He did MA in Economics from School of Economics, University of Hyderabad, Hyderabad. His specialisation is in development economics with special focus on agriculture, labour, and institutional dynamics.

P. Punna Rao, Principal Scientist (Agricultural Extension), Directorate of Extension, Acharya N.G. Ranga Agricultural University Hyderabad, Andhra Pradesh, is a highly qualified administrator and agricultural extension professional.

Gaurav Singh is NET-SRF fellow and has already completed his Research work for the award of PhD in Management from Babasaheb Bhimrao Ambedkar University, Lucknow. He has published more than 10 research papers in both national and international journals and also presented research papers in both national and international conferences and seminars.

Mrityunjay Kumar Singh is Assistant Professor (Senior) in the Department of Social Work, Assam University, Silchar. He graduated from Hans Raj College, University of Delhi and completed his MSW and PhD from UGC—Centre of Advanced Study in Social Work, Jamia Millia Islamia, New Delhi. He has published papers in various referred journals and books. He has presented papers in many national and international seminars and workshops. His areas of interest are: social policy, social development, local governance and social entrepreneurship.

Rajani V. Sontakke, Assistant Professor at Department of Economics, Dr. Madhukarrao Wasnik PWS Arts and Commerce College, Nagpur, is MA (Economics), MPhil and was awarded PhD in Economics on the topic "Socio-economic Status of Mahatma Gandhi National Rural Employment Guarantee Scheme (MGNREGA) in Nagpur District". She has 10 years of research experience and 13 years of teaching experience at under graduate and post graduate level. Dr Sontakke has contributed several articles and presented papers in a number of national and international conferences and seminars.

Mamata Swain is currently working as Professor and Head, Department of Economics in Ravenshaw University, Cuttack, Odisha. She obtained her PhD from University of London and MPhil in Economics from Delhi School of Economics. She is recipient of many prestigious international scholarships including Commonwealth Scholarship, Canadian Studies Faculty Research Fellowship, Japan Foundation Japanese Studies Fellowship, Commonwealth Academic Fellowship etc. As a visiting Fellow, she has completed post-doctoral research work in the University of British Columbia, Vancouver, Canada; University of Tsukuba, Japan; University of Thammasat, Thailand and London School of Economics and Political Science. She has completed many research projects in the field of water resources management, environmental economics and gender studies with sponsorship from World Bank, USAID, DFID, SANDEE, ICAR, ICSSR, Planning Commission etc. She has nearly 30 years of experience in teaching, training and research in Agricultural Economics. She has published 7 books and more than 80 research papers in reputed professional journals and edited books.

K.K. Tripathy is an officer of Indian Economic Service (IES), 1999 Batch, and is presently posted in the Ministry of Agriculture, Government of India (GoI). He has received a PhD from Department of Management Studies, Indian Institute of Technology Delhi on "Micro Finance in Rural India". Prior to joining IES, Dr Tripathy served as an officer of a Federal Administrative Service in the state of Odisha where his exposure to grass root level development and later his posting in Ministry of Rural Development, GoI, fostered in him the interest to work on rural development. He has published articles on self-employment and wage employment activities, micro finance and latest agriculture and rural development issues in India, and has presented papers at various state/national and international seminars.

U.R. Rajeshwari is an Assistant Professor in Department of Economics, Christ University, Bangalore. She has an MA Economics and PhD from Karnataka University, Dharwad. Her area of specialisation includes pubic finance and econometrics. She received a Gold Medal for her MA and Nandan Nilekani Scholarship for her PhD. Prior to academics, she worked as research officer at Institute for Social and Economic Change, Bangalore.

Saraswati Unni acquired her MA degree in Political Science from Presidency College, Madras University and her MPhil degree in Politics and Public Administration from the University of Madras. Thereafter she joined NES Ratnam College of Arts, Science and Commerce, Mumbai as lecturer in the Department of Political Science. At present she is an Associate Professor and Head of the Department-Political Science in Ratnam College. She was awarded a PhD for her thesis on "Energy Policy of India" by the

University of Mumbai. She has presented and published a number of papers in national and international fora on related topics such as, decentralised energy and the democratic process, development induced displacement, electricity services and agrarian crisis, impact of electricity on livelihoods.

Vishwanatha is Professor and Chairman, Faculty of Arts, Department of Economics, Mangalore University, Mangalore. His teaching specialisation in Economics includes macroeconomics, development economics, demography, agricultural economics and rural development, micro finance, social exclusion and inclusive policy, Ambedkar studies, Middle Eastern studies. His basic research is in the area of agriculture economics and development studies. Currently, he is engaged with social exclusion, caste discrimination and its impact on Dalits, development of inclusive policies, displacement and rehabilitation and its implications, HIV/AIDS and health issues in Karnataka floriculture and agriculture development, measuring sustainable agriculture income and environmental related issues, micro finance and development of women micro enterprises, food security of marginalised communities, banking reforms and productivity and profitability and affirmative action and policies, labour market discriminations and international labour migration. He has published 4 books and more than 50 research papers in journals, edited books and conference volumes, and has presented more than 50 research papers in both national and international seminars and conferences. So far 7 PhDs have been awarded under his guidance and currently 7 PhD scholars are working under his guidance.

P.K. Viswanathan is Associate Professor at the Gujarat Institute of Development Research, Ahmedabad.

Acknowledgements

With the advent of Eleventh Five Year Plan, special emphasis was made for inclusive growth with social justice and empowerment of weaker sections of the society. This resulted in the introduction of several flagship programmes with focus on welfare of the poor. The ultimate objective behind these programmes is to achieve broad based improvement in the living conditions of the under privileged and to ensure that growth is widely spread and its benefits are adequately shared by all. As flagship programmes have been under implementation for more than one decade, a national seminar "Flagship Programmes: Impact, Problems and Challenges Ahead" was organised[1] to understand the efficacy of these programmes and to improve the process involved in their planning and implementation. This publication is an outcome of this seminar.

The seminar was organised under the guidance of Dr M.V. Rao (IAS), Director-General, NIRD&PR, who provided necessary help and cooperation for the smooth conduct of the programme. We would like to place on record our sincere thanks to him for the encouragement and liberal support extended to us. We also received valuable help from faculties and staff members of the institute particularly from the Centre for Planning, Monitoring and Evaluation, and we express our sincere gratitude to all of them. Similarly, timely help rendered by Ms Chanda Pandit (IAAS), Registrar and Director (Admn) I/C and Financial Advisor, NIRD&PR, and support from the staff members of administration and finance departments is duly acknowledged

1. The seminar was organised by the National Institute of Rural Development and Panchayati Raj, Hyderabad, during 19-21 November 2014.

here. We also take this opportunity to thank Shri S.M. Vijayanand (IAS), Additional secretary, Rural Development Ministry of Rural Development, Government of India, for bringing clarity on the meaning of flagship programmes. The response to this seminar was overwhelming and many scholars and academia contributed papers on various themes selected under the flagship programmes. We profusely thank each one of them.

—Editors

K.P. KUMARAN, P.K.NATH, K. PRABHAKAR and N. KALPALATHA

Introduction

Background

India is a federal republic and the Constitution gives provision for three different levels of governance (at the centre, states and local self governing bodies). The Preamble and the Directive Principle of Indian Constitution made provision to give justice in terms of social, economic and political to the people in general and the weaker sections in particular. To fulfil the above obligations both the Centre and states have been undertaking a number of socio-economic welfare measures for the people. The concept of socialistic pattern of society that the country opted for has generated public demands for various programmes, facilities and services involving huge investments. In consonance with the constitutional obligations, the states have been undertaking many welfare measures of its own. As the financial resources of states are limited, the states have to depend on the Centre for voluntary contributions in the form of grants to implement some of these programmes. At the same time, the Centre has also evolved certain programmes which are implemented with the financial support of the Centre and cooperation and support of the state machinery.

In India, the state legislatures are responsible for making laws, the central and state governments are responsible for the implementation of the laws and policies, and the judiciary interprets the laws. The Centre is responsible for subjects that fall within the union list, the states for state lists and both the Centre and the states are jointly responsible for subjects that fall within the concurrent list. For example, health and education are in the joint list. However, most of the concurrent expenditure on these subjects is undertaken by the state governments. There are several subjects such as health, education, nutrition, water and sanitation for which states are responsible but might not have adequate recourses to address these subjects. In such cases, Centre can provide additional resources to meet the challenges to these sectors. One of the way by which the Centre fulfil the requirements is by establishing CSS (centrally sponsored schemes).

Centrally Sponsored Schemes

CSS are those schemes which are fully or partially funded by the Centre and implemented by the state or state agencies except those which fall under the union list. These schemes were originally instituted to redress development concerns of national importance. For this, through the channels of the CSS, schematic support is provided by the Central government for the subjects that constitutionally fall within the domain of the states. It was in the Fourth Five Year Plan (1969-1974), that Planning Commission had originally classified the development plans sponsored by the Centre as CSS. Accordingly 36 schemes were originally classified as CSS. These schemes were formulated to encourage the states to prioritise in areas which require more attention. By the end of the Fourth Five Year there were 45 CSS, and their number rapidly increased during the Fifth Five Year Plan period and reached to 201 in 1979. Centre's involvement with the state subject started increasing under Mrs Indira Gandhi regime with her focus on "Garibi Hatao" aimed at eradicating poverty in both rural and urban areas. Many schemes in rural development such as Integrated Rural Development Programme (IRDP), creation of employment through public work, rural housing etc., were initiated during this period. Several subjects such as education, population control and forest were brought from the state list to concurrent list through amendment to the Constitution. This enabled the Government of India to pass legislation in these sectors without obtaining states agreement. All this resulted in further increase in the CSS, and particularly in the terminal year of Ninth Five Year Plan, raising the number to as many as 360 schemes.

Funding under the CSS

The Government of India is funding a large number of programmes in sectors/areas such as education, health, labour, skill development etc. that are under the purview of the state list through the operation of CSS and provision of central assistance to the state governments. India's development plan exercises two types of schemes: 1) central sector schemes and 2) CSS. Government of India transfers funds through CSS and Additional Central Assistance (ACA) for state plan schemes. Under the central sector schemes it is 100 per cent funded by the Union Government and implemented by the Central government machinery. Central sector schemes are mainly formulated on subjects from the union list. Under the CSS, a certain percentage of the funding is borne by the states as matching contribution to the Centre in the ratio of 50:50, 75:25 or 90:10, and implementation of such schemes is the responsibility of the state governments. Apart from the matching contributions, the states also provide the human resources and infrastructure required for the successful implementation of such schemes (Saxena, 2007).

Table 1

Funds Transferred through CSS

Plan Period	*Gross Budgetary Support (GBS) (in crores)*	*No. of Schemes*	*CSS (in crores)*	*% of CSS to GBS*	*Centrally Assistance to States & UT's (in crores)*	*Central Assistance to States as % of GBS*
Ninth	3,16,286.00	360	99,001.68	31.3	1,38,394.00	43.75
Tenth	5,94,649.00	155	2,29,763.00	38.6	2,03,117.00	34.02
Eleventh	15,88,273.24	147	6,60,506.00	41.59	39,74,418.93	25.02

Source: Planning Commission.

Over the plan periods there has been a regular increase in number of CSS till the Ninth Five Year Plan, but by the beginning of Tenth Five Year Plan, the number of CSS decreased considerably. Table 1 provides information about the number of CSS under implementation and the budgetary allocation to CSS during the

Ninth, Tenth and Eleventh Five Year Plan period. From the table, it may be noted that although the number of schemes has drastically reduced during these Plan periods, the share of CSS in the total plan expenditure shows a steady increase. At the end of Eleventh Five Year Plan, the percentage share of CSS in the total budget was 42 per cent—an increase of 10.29 per cent over the Ninth Five Year Plan.

Although there was a spectacular increase in CSS till the Ninth Plan, these programmes could not provide the expected results due to faulty implementation without the active participation of the local people. As noted earlier, to meet the various social welfare requirements of the country the number of CSS swelled in 1970s and kept on increasing till 1990s. Though the number of CSS had gone up to 360 by the Ninth Plan, their impact was not up to the expected level. The Comptroller and Auditor General (CAG) studied the implementation of a few CSS and came out with several short comings in the execution of CSS's and some of them are listed below.

1. Inability of union ministers to control the execution of the schemes with a view to ensuring the attainment of stated objectives in the most cost effective manner. The Ministries was concerned about expenditure rather than attainment of the objectives.
2. Misuse of funds provided for vulnerable sections of the society was rampant.
3. The schemes are not being monitored by the central ministries. Funds are released in an indifferent manner without asking for the utilisation certificate.
4. A number of plan schemes are in operation with similar objectives targeting the same population. There are schemes that are no longer productive but still continuing. All this calls for a lot of consolidation and convergence.

Emergence of Flagship Programmes

Ever since India became independent, the country has implemented several Five Year Plans including Annual Plans, by making rapid strides in the economic front. The pace of economic growth further accelerated with the introduction of economic reform measures. All these efforts have resulted in the modernisation of a vibrant economy and India has emerged as a major industrial power. But it has failed miserably in its efforts to alleviate poverty and delivering equitable share of fruits of development particularly among the poor and disadvantaged sections of the society. Although the percentage of population below the official poverty line has come down during 1993-94 to 2004-05, the incidence of poverty among certain marginalised groups such as SCs (schedules castes) and STs (schedules tribes) has hardly declined. India still has some of the lowest indicators of human development. Indicators such as literacy, education, maternal and infant mortality rates, do show steady improvement, but the progress is slow and we continue to lag behind several other Asian countries. Though literacy rate has gone up, the number of illiterate persons is very high, leaving India with the highest number of illiterates in the world. India also suffers from adverse sex ratio. Maternal and infant mortality rates are much higher in India than the countries in East Asia, showing poor access to essential healthcare services. All this has resulted in the increasing the gulf between haves and haves' not. Seeing this, the Government stepped up its efforts for inclusive growth by launching several new schemes and at the same time restructuring and revamping some of the old schemes and programmes. This resulted in emergence of flagship programmes.

Flagship Programmes

According to Twentieth Century Chambers Dictionary (1999) the meaning of flagship is the "ship that carries and flies the flag of the fleet commander." The very terminology flagship derives its origin from geostrategic preparation in naval power. It symbolises the might of the fleet carrying the national flag and leading any attack, followed by other supporting fleets and personnel. In that parlance, the flagship programme/schemes of any ministry/department have to be the lead programme with other programmes following it. In reality this is not the case. Flagship schemes of Government of India are those schemes which are declared so by the union cabinet. There is hardly any clarity about the definition of a flagship programme by any ministry/department. A few selected programmes are named as flagship by individual ministry/department, and are monitored succinctly by the Planning Commission because of the huge allocation and grand geographical coverage.

The Draft Annual Plan 2013-14 of Government of India defines the flagship programmes as the programme that aimed at building rural and urban infrastructure and providing basic services with the objective of increasing inclusiveness and reducing poverty. The ultimate objective behind Flagship Programmes is to achieve broad based improvement in the living standards of people and to ensure that the growth is widely spread so that its benefits, in terms of income and employment, are adequately shared by the poor and the weaker sections of the society, especially the SCs, ST, OBCs (other backward classes) and minorities. Flagship Programmes are CSS which are implemented by the state government agencies but are largely funded by the Central government with the definite state governments share (Planning Commission, 2011).

Masood Ahmed (1999)[1] defines flagship programmes as schemes which are fully funded directly by the Central ministries/departments and implemented by the states and their agencies, irrespective of a pattern of financing (unless they fall under centres sphere of responsibility). Singh (2013) defined flagship programmes as development programmes formulated and launched by the Central government and their agencies. Flagship programmes is not a new phenomena; they have been in operation since independence predominantly for rural development. In short, the concept of flagship programmes is mainly used by the Central government for its schemes and programmes although it is also used to refer some of the schemes/programmes launched by the state governments. It has also been observed that there is no specific number of schemes/ programmes which are treated as flagship and depending on the requirements of the Central ministries the number of flagship programmes may increase or decrease. In this paper, 16 schemes/

1. Advisor, Planning Commission, *http://envfor.nic.in/web/bookpartaiv/a-ino-63htm*

programmes of Government of India have been treated as flagship programmes and the details are given in the following pages.

Flagship Programmes in Tenth and Eleventh Plan

Special emphasis on flagship programmes has been made during the Tenth and Eleventh Five Year Plan periods. In this regard the programmes and schemes focused on two important aspects i.e., poverty alleviation and rural infrastructure. Restructuring rural development schemes started even before the introduction of Tenth Five Year Plan. In the year 1989, the Central government implemented Swarnajayanti Gram Swarozgar Yojana (SGSY), as anti-poverty programme merging and amalgamating six self employment programmes: Training of Rural Youth for Self-Employment (TRYSEM), Cornell Institute for Translational Research on Ageing (CITRA), Development of Women and Children in Rural Areas (DWACRA), Ganga Kalyan Yojana (GKY), IRDP and Million Wells Schemes (MWS). These schemes were primarily aimed at establishing micro enterprises by forming SHGs (self help groups) mostly among women. Further Pradhan Mantri Gram Sadak Yojana (PMGSY) was introduced in 2000-01. The primary objective of the PMGSY is to provide connectivity by way of all weather roads to eligible unconnected habitations in the rural areas. Another important scheme introduced in the plan period was Mahatma Gandhi National Rural Employment Guarantee Scheme (MGNREGS) in the year 2005. The main objective of the scheme is to enhance the livelihood security of people in rural areas by guaranteeing 100 days of wage employment in a financial year to the rural household who volunteers for unskilled manual works. This schemes was formed by merging earlier implemented EGS (employment guarantee schemes) like Sampoorna Grameen Rozgar Yojana (SGRY), National Food For Work programme (NFFWP).

During the Eleventh Five Year Plan, implementation of flagship programmes was centred around rural infrastructure and basic needs, and also to provide opportunities to improve rural livelihoods The major schemes under implementation during this period include rural electrification (Rajiv Gandhi Grameen Vidyutikaran Yojan:

Table 2

Central Government Allocation for Flagship Programmes

No	*Flagship Programme*	*Eleventh Plan (in Rs. Cr)*	*Twelfth Plan (in Rs. Cr)*	*Increase (%)*
1	Integrated Child Development Services	21,882	1,08,503	395.86
2	National Health Mission	66,127	2,50,000	278.06
3	Jawaharlal Nehru National Urban Renewal Mission	34,795	1,01,917	192.91
4	Rashtriya Krishi Vikas Yojana	22,165	63,246	185.34
5	National Rural Livelihood Mission	11,320	29,006	156.24
6	Sarva Shiksha Abhiyan	77,576	1,92,726	148.44
7	Rajiv Gandhi Drinking Water & Sanitation Mission	44,670	1,07,015	139.57
8	Accelerated Irrigated Benefit Programme	38,824	91,435	135.51
9	Mid-Day Meal	38,490	90,155	134.23
10	Backward Region Grant Fund	35,334	76,678	117.01
11	National Social Assistance Programme	24,161	48,642	101.32
12	Accelerated Power Development and Reform Programme	5,697	10,830	90.1
13	Pradahan Mantri Gram Sadak Yojana	65,790	1,24,013	88.5
14	Indira Awas Yojana	41,823	63,585	52.03
15	Mahatma Gandhi National Rural Employment Guarantee act	1,43,042	1,65,500	15.7
16	Rajiv Gandhi Grameen Vidyutikaran Yojana	21,651	23,397	8.07
	Total	6,93,347	15,46,648	123.07

Source: Planning Commission.

RGGVY), urban amenities (Jawaharlal Nehru National Urban Renewal Mission: JNNURM), schemes promoting irrigation facilities (Accelerated Irrigation Benefits Programme: AIBP), drinking water (National Rural Drinking Water Programme: NRDWP). The other flagship programmes that become operational during the Eleventh

Five Year Plan were National Rural Health Mission (NRHM) in 2009, Sarva Shiksha Abhiyan (SSA), Total Sanitation Campaign/Nirmal Bharat Abhiyan (TSC/NBA), Backward Regions Grant Funds (BRGF, in 2007) and Rastriya Krishi Vignan Yojana (RKVY, in 2007). Though Integrated Child Development Services (ICDS) and Mid-Day Meal (MDM) scheme were operational for a long period, they were given special importance and emphasis during this period.

Funding under Flagship Programmes

The major flagship programme implemented during the Eleventh and Twelfth Five Year Plans may be classified under three categorised: 1) poverty alleviation and employment generation, 2) rural and urban infrastructure, and 3) elementary and secondary education. Table 2 shows the list of flagship programmes and the pattern of fund allocation during the Eleventh and Twelfth Plan periods for selected 16 flagship programmes of the Central government.

Poverty Alleviation and Employment Generation Programmes

Under this head, major programmes implemented are MGNREGS and National Rural Livelihood Mission (NRLM). In the Eleventh Plan period, MGNREGA got the highest allocation (21%, 1st position) among the 16 selected flagship programmes, but in the Twelfth Plan, with an increase of 15.7 per cent over Eleventh Plan period it moved to 3rd position (11%). Fund allocation for NRLM was ₹11,320 crore in the Eleventh Plan and ₹29,006 crore in the Eleventh Plan. Both these livelihood schemes together had higher allocations (22.3%) in Eleventh plan among the 16 flagship programme allocations and have come down to almost by half in Twelfth Plan (12.3%).

Rural Urban Infrastructure

Rural infrastructure and development programmes have been designed to achieve a higher degree of rural-urban integration and an even pattern of growth and opportunities for the poor and disadvantaged sections of the society. Some of the important schemes under this category are IAY, PMGSY, NRDWP and BRGF. Budget allocation for these rural infrastructure in Eleventh Plan period was

₹1,87,617 crore (27%), but in the Twelfth Plan the total allocation stood at 24 per cent (with a decrease of 3% over the previous plan period). Under urban infrastructure the major scheme is JNNURM which is implemented in cities with focus on up gradation of urban infrastructure, creation of housing stock, and provision of basic services to the poor through community participation and accountability of urban local bodies. Fund allocation for JNNURM in Eleventh Plan was ₹34,795 crore (5%) and in the Twelfth Plan it was ₹1,01,917 crore (6.6%), showing an increase of 192.9 per cent over the previous plan.

Elementary and Secondary Education

India needs to provide quality education to fully reap the benefits of the demographic dividend. As a percentage of GDP, expenditure on education has gone up from 2.9 per cent in 2008-09 to 3.3 per cent in 2013-14 (BE). SSA and MDM are the major flagship programmes that support elementary and secondary education. In both the plan periods, fund allocation for SSA stood at second position among the flagship programmes with an allocation of 11.2 per cent in Eleventh Plan period and 12.5 per cent in the Twelfth Plan period, indicating an increase of 148.4 per cent over the previous plan. Similarly, MDM scheme also benefitted in Twelfth Plan with an increase of 134.23 per cent (₹90,155 crore) over previous plan period i.e. Eleventh Plan (₹38,824 crore). A comparison of percentage increase in allocation between the two plan periods showed highest change in the case of ICDS followed by National Health Mission and JNNURM.

Issues in Flagship Programmes

Planning and Implementation

From the Tenth Five Year Plan onwards, different new schemes were launched or revamped, and new schemes were added or strengthened to provide education, health, rural infrastructure etc. Some of the study reports regarding programmes like MGNREGS, MDM, IAY, PMGSY, ICDS and SSA showed that they were successfully implemented. But in other schemes like RKVY, AIBP, RGGVY, the awareness level was very low among the public and there is an evidence of under utilisation of funds. Effectiveness of implementation of schemes varies from state to state. Some of the schemes like MGNREGS showed remarkable success in specific areas and social groups, though there were misuse of funds and low quality of durable asset creation. Along with consolidation and strengthening of flagship programmes, there is a need to ensure more financial support and convergence across different schemes to minimise duplication and achieve social inclusion. The effectiveness of the flagship programmes are dependent upon the structure of governance and the extent of people's participation. In addition to this, there should be concerted efforts to ensure participation at the grass roots at the planning and implementation level involving all stake holders. For the success of the flagship programmes and proper utilisation of public money, the Centre and the state governments should work in tandem. Many of the programmes being rights and entitlements based, spatial variation of level of awareness, proportion of people who are poorest among the poor, macro economic growth of the state concerned, have a direct effect on the level of achievement in different flagship programmes.

Monitoring & Evaluation

Provisions have been made with every important project/ programmes of the ministry for the assessment of their performance and outcome. An exclusive Programme Evaluation Organisation (PEO) was set up by the Planning Commission to evaluate schemes/ programmes implemented by the Government of India. Till 1990s, most of the evaluation of the CSS was conducted by the PEO staff. Subsequently, due to lack of staff these works were outsourced to research institutions sponsored by Indian Council of Social Science Research (ICSSR) and to NGOs. (non-governmental organisations). Apart from these agencies on a regular basis some of the flagship programmes are being monitored by the Ministry of Rural Development (MoRD) by engaging national level monitories during the last six years. Let us now examine the status of monitoring and evaluation of flagship Programmes in the country.

A large number of centrally sponsored and central sector schemes are implemented through different ministries in the country. With enormous diversity in implementation and hierarchy across space, it has become all important to have information about physical and financial details about the project in order to monitor its progress. In a paper Awasthi (2013) examines the efficacy of the MIS (management information system) in flagship programmes and check how credible MIS become an effective tool for management. The data and information need to be usable for all the stakeholders including researcher and community at large. It has been noted that in some of the flagship programmes either no feedback system exists or existing mechanism is weak (for example schemes like irrigation, rural telephony, rural electrification, SIA, MDM, ICDS etc.). The paper also revealed that there are no MIS in as many as four flagship programmes worth the name (irrigation, rural telephony, MDM, JNNURM) and also in many cases one is not permitted to visit the MIS on line without a valid authorisation.

Mehrotra et al (2013) carried out an assessment of MIS of 13 central flagship programmes. The programmes were assessed and ranked on the basis of certain criteria. The study found that none of the flagship programmes used a log-frame explicitly, though some have implicit theories of change. All do internal consistency check on the data, but none validate or authenticate the data by conducting a random check. The data are regularly collected and for most of the schemes are available for up to the last financial year, quarter or the latest month. Naturally this is only possible if there is a website. However, the concern is how the data are being used internally by the line ministry for decision-making especially in regard to budget allocation for the following year.

Impact

The role played by the Government of India in poverty removal has resulted in massive investment in social development and physical infrastructure (rural housing, rural roads, rural electrification, irrigation, drinking water, urban infrastructure) and human capital formation under different flagship programmes. The impact of flagship programme though not up to the expectation level, has given some semblance of dignity to a vast majority of the poor in terms of provisioning of rights and entitlement based benefits. Universalisation without ensuring proper quality has resulted in less than optimal achievements in many of the flagship programmes. But there are ample evidences to suggest that in each of the parameters of HRD (human resource development), we are inching forward by reducing the margin of deprivation and arresting abysmally low level of HRD.

A recent study by the Word Bank (2011) indicated that India is spending 1.6 per cent of GDP towards social protection and as much as 59 per cent of social protection spending is on food, fuel and MDM schemes. But their overall impact has fallen short due to method of selection, poor delivery system, and poor accountability. While many schemes have been ineffective in identifying all the needy or even in reaching all the identified beneficiaries, leakages, and corruption have been widely existent too. Further, the study also maintained that development outcomes across sectors are consistently differential and disproportionately worse for certain groups i.e., SCs, STs and minority community when compared with the mainstream and this is attributed to part to the phenomenon of social exclusion which may operate in any of many spheres.

Way Forward

The welfare intention of the flagship programmes continues its relevance even today, but the priority and fund allocation is expected to vary with passage of time. This will be determined by the exigency arising out of the intents of the government. But the core issues like inclusive growth, sustainable development with inter-generational equity of resource use will continue to guide the path of many of these flagship programmes. The primary focus of provisions of basic needs like housing, drinking water and sanitation, basic amenities like universaliation of quality primary education and primary health will continue to dominate the priority agenda of any government. The priority shifting in terms of fund allocation for different flagship programmes may vary. The source of funding for these flagship programmes may take a drastic change with entry of other players like the corporate and industrial sector (in PPP mode). But the issues of addressing the problems of basic needs and basic amenities will continue to bother us.

References

Awasthi, I.C. (2013). *Lessons from Indian Flagship Programmes: The Disconnect Evaluation Framework.*

Mehrotra, Santosh (2013). *The Government Monitoring and Evaluation System in India: A Work in Progress*. World Bank. *www.worldbank.org/ieg/ecd.*

Mehrotra, Santosh et al. (2011). *India Human Development Report: Towards Social inclusion*, Institute of Applied Manpower Research, Planning Commission, Govt. of India. New Delhi: Oxford University Press.

Planning Commission (2011). *Faster, Sustainable and More Inclusive Growth: An Approach Paper to Twelfth Five Year Plan.* Govt. of India.

Saxena, N.C. (2003). *Central Transfers to States and Centrally Sponsored Schemes.*

————. (2007). "Rural Poverty Reduction Through Centrally Sponsored Schemes", *India Journal of Media Research* 126- 381-89, October.

Singh, Nirmal (2013). "The Flagship Programmes in India", *Asia Journal of Research in Social Sciences and Humanities* 3(8), August.

World Bank Report (2011). *Social Protection in a Changing India*. Washington D.C.: World Bank.

1

R.M. PRASAD

Learnings from Success Cases of Rural Livelihood Flagship Programmes

Introduction

Flagship programmes derive their origin from the term flagship, which is the main ship of a country's navy and is symbolic of the main thrust of a nation's development policy. Flagship schemes are declared either by the Union cabinet or Development Evaluation Advisory Committee (DEAC) of Planning Commission. Of the different flagship schemes, three schemes, *viz.*, Mahatma Gandhi National Rural Employment Guarantee Scheme (MGNRES), Rashtriya Krishi Vikas Yojana (RKVY) and National Rural Livelihood Mission (NRLM) were selected for analysis. The often quoted success stories from the websites and published reports on these three flagship programmes from the eight states, *viz.*, Andhra Pradesh, Bihar, Gujarat, Kerala, Madhya Pradesh (MP), Maharashtra, Odisha and Sikkim are presented in this chapter.

An analysis of the success stories of MGNREGS, RKVY and NRLM revealed that most of the projects implemented are NR (natural resource) based and are on convergence mode. The success stories of schemes implemented in eight states highlighted that most of the projects have focused on ensuring food and water security which can enhance livelihood opportunities.

Small farm mechanisation, soil health, water and organic farming were the major concerns addressed by the RKVY scheme. AP had focused attention on community-managed agriculture, Kerala on small farm mechanisation, while Bihar and Odisha on food security. Land and water development schemes were the major focus of RKVY schemes in Gujarat, Maharashtra, Sikkim and MP. Land and water conservation, forest development and eco-restoration were the major focus activities under MGNREGS in all the states. Building a cadre of para-geohydrologists (Sikkim) and individual benefit projects worked upon by the community (Odisha) were innovative initiatives set out under MGNREGS. Innovative institutional arrangements (institutionalisation for the poor in Odisha, dedicated company for implementing NRLM in Gujarat, convergence with NGOs in MP) and innovative projects (elderly self help groups [SHGs] in Kerala, promoting grass-root innovations in Bihar and contract farming in Maharashtra) were implemented as part of NRLM.

Table 1.1

Comparison of the Three Flagship Programmes across States

State	*MGNREGS*	*RKVY*	*NRLM*	*Convergence theme*
Andhra Pradesh	Comprehensive land development of the poor: Fallow land cultivation	Community Managed Sustainable Agriculture (CMSA)	SERP: Knitting Rural Self Help Enterprises (KRuSHE)	Community management and social inclusion
Bihar	Farm development activities for soil and water conservation	Organic farming for promoting sustainable production	Bihar Innovation Forum: linking grass-root innovations with livelihoods	Organic farming and grass-roots innovations
Gujarat	Construction of water tanks and soil conservation works	Taking soil testing labs to farmers, issue of soil health cards	Company to promote multi-crop production, diversified farming (GLPC)	Soil health and farm diversification
Kerala	Natural resource management-Eco-restoration	Food Security Army for addressing labour shortage	Kudumbashree-Elderly SHGs	Food security and social security
Madhya Pradesh	Water conservation structures	Community based water management-Percolation and MMI tanks	Convergence for water conservation and financial inclusion	Water security for increased production, financial inclusion

contd...

...contd...

Odisha	Securing livelihoods of Forest Rights Act beneficiaries	Food for Gods-Cultivation of Tuber crops	Institutionalisation of the poor-TRIPTI, WORLP, OTELP	Forest based livelihoods and tribal development
Maharashtra	Managing water stress with farm ponds	Multi-year farm ponds, Community grower groups	Social inclusion and social entrepreneurship	Contract farming and social entrepreneurship
Sikkim	Reviving springs to mitigate impact of climate change	Organic farming	Ensuring sustainable water resources for livelihoods	Springshed development for water security

Source: Derived from available reports.

How are the Three Flagship Programmes Related?

Land, water and forests are the main life support systems of the rural people. The livelihood security of the majority of Indians relies on land and water based occupations, including crop and animal husbandry, forestry and fisheries. It is interesting to note that all the three flagship programmes give prominence to natural resource based livelihoods.

A critical analysis of the three flagship programmes (MGNREGS, RKVY and NRLM) revealed that there is an organic link among these programmes as presented below:

MGNREGS ⇒	RKVY ⇒	NRLM
Guaranteed support	Enabling support	Empowered support
Wage employment for creating durable assets related to NR	Incentivises states to increase outlays for higher production and productivity of NR	Self and wage employment through sustained NR based livelihood enhancements

Further analysis of the three flagship programmes indicate that there is commonality, convergence and connecting link among these programmes, thereby leading to synergy for rural livelihoods.

State-wise Analysis of the Cases

Andhra Pradesh

Under MGNREGS, the focus was on upgrading natural resources and emphasis was on comprehensive land development of the poor.

It is reported that nearly 14 lakh acres of land have been cleared and brought under cultivation using funds of MGNREGS. Funds from Integrated Wasteland Development Programme (IWDP) were also effectively converged and utilised. Around 70 per cent of works was related to common property resources for strengthening dry land agriculture. At the same time, development works on lands of (scheduled castes) and STs (scheduled tribes) constituted around one-fifth of the tasks. To address the problems of marginalised unproductive lands owned by the poor, the Rainfed Sustainable Agriculture (RFSA) was initiated in collaboration with MGNREGS.

Under RKVY, Community Managed Sustainable Agriculture (CMSA) is one of the successful programmes taken up by Society for Elimination of Rural Poverty (SERP). The programme was approved under 'innovation work' and ₹162 crore was sanctioned under RKVY for five years from 2007-08 to 2011-12. CMSA is a paradigm shift in approach towards the way agriculture is being undertaken, which is aimed at making small farming viable and profitable. The programme has its mandate to eradicate poverty and to improve livelihoods of the poor. The programme is aimed to support the poor farmers to adopt sustainable agricultural practices based on traditional, but scientifically valid practices and using locally available organic materials that reduce the cost of cultivation and increase net incomes. Capacity building is the key component of CMSA and the core investment is on supporting community-managed extension system than on material inputs. CMSA striving to build community best practitioners in technology transfer through Community Resource Persons (CRPs), who provide extension support to farmers. The programme will be adopting Non-Pesticidal Management (NPM) approach for plant protection.

SERP was set up in 2000 by the Government of Andhra Pradesh (GoAP) to implement rural development projects in a professional manner. Based on the experience gained by SERP and various successful interventions made, the society is identified as the implementing agency for NRLM in AP.

To encourage the poor including disadvantaged groups and communities to access the credit facility services seamlessly,

Community Investment Fund (CIF) from project side and linkage from bank's side are provided to the poor women SHG (self help group) members so as to improve their livelihoods. Community Managed Education Services operate early childhood education centres and monitors quality of education in the government schools. Community-managed insurance is also promoted by SERP. Knitting Rural Self Help Enterprises (KRuSHE) under SERP envisages integrated approach of building marketing infrastructure, linking markets and providing access to credit, environment friendly technology, skills, design and institutional development to the rural enterprises. KRuSHE has been conceived to strengthen both forward and backward linkages with marketing as its core component.

Bihar

A vast proportion of MGNREGS works implemented in Bihar are 'green' in nature given their focus on the regeneration and conservation of natural resources and ecosystem, and their main emphasis relate to land, including waste land and water resources. Organic farming has been taken up as one of the priority initiatives by the Bihar government with an amount of ₹256 crore sanctioned for organic farming promotion within a span of five years (2010-11 to 2014-15), which is 100 per cent state plan scheme. The funding under RKVY is in addition to the state scheme.

Organic farming increases the long-term agricultural productivity by the use of advanced techniques of farming, planting methods, quality seeds, use of bio-fertilisers, etc. The government of Bihar (GoB) through MGNREGS works has established 'organic villages'. Organic villages involves: a) applying organic inputs, b) enhancing soil fertility by way of good agronomic practices, c) creating an incentive system for producing organic manure, and d) establishing supply system for capacity building, market linkages and storage facilities.

The piloting of 'Green Opportunities' under RKVY involved the following:

i) Participatory Varietal Selection and Promotion (PVSP): promotion of seeds that cater to the poor farmers' preference for seeds with low input cost, high pest resistance, high drought resistance, etc.

ii) Productivity enhancement technologies: integration of environment-friendly farming practices such as use of organic manure, vermi-compost, bio-fertilisers, bio-control, etc.

iii) Community managed sustainable agriculture: promotion of non-chemical pesticide management.

Confederation of Indian Industries (CII) will be collaborating with the Bihar Government for the promotion of organic farming and skill development. The CII and GoB have been pursuing a joint programme for promotion of farm mechanisation and good agricultural practices. The Bihar Government has taken up several programmes to encourage organic farming with the objective of promoting sustainable production, improving soil organic carbon for sustenance of soil quality and promoting export of quality organic produce. Bio-village concept is one of the key programmes of the state government under NRLM. Integration of organic farming into livelihood intervention will be scaled up through NRLM.

Creating an enabling environment for implementing and scaling up grass-root innovations for rural livelihood development, and service delivery is one of the objectives of Bihar Rural Livelihood Project. One of the components of the project is to support innovations by various institutions, entrepreneurs, NGOs (non-governmental organisations) etc., whose main objective is to improve rural livelihoods. Bihar Innovation Forum is established to build partnerships with various organisations for scouting and promoting innovations and also to complement the activities being undertaken in JEEVIKA (Bihar Rural Livelihood Project).

Gujarat

Gujarat had achieved an average annual growth rate of 11 per cent in its agri-GDP (gross domestic product) in the last 10 years, which is about three times of the national rate (4%). Instead of encouraging low value cereal production in response to successive hikes in MSPs (minimum support prices), the Government of Gujarat

(GoG) encouraged diversification of agriculture towards commercial cropping of fruits, vegetables, Bt cotton, castor, *isabgol* and spices. Promotion of allied activities such as dairy, poultry and fisheries also formed part of the diversification strategy. Under social inclusion, Gujarat has introduced a scheme to promote horticulture in tribal areas through *wadi* (fruit orchard) scheme under RSVY. The funds under MGNREGS were effectively utilised for construction of water tanks and also development of land, including incorporation of soil conservation measures.

Many proactive technical interventions were introduced through RKVY, such as precision farming (banana), cluster cultivation approach (mango, banana, pomegranate), use of drip and mulching (papaya, melon), use of tissue culture plants (banana, dates, flowers), greenhouse cultivation (dutch roses, gerbera, capsicum, tomato), and net house cultivation (capsicum, cucurbits, leafy vegetables) which have resulted in diversified agriculture.

Gujarat is the first state in India to issue soil health card to the farmers for every piece of land. Farmers can test the soil samples with the help of scientists who examine the composition of soil and provide the results. Based on the soil test report, the farmers are provided with appropriate recommendation. This has helped in soil enrichment and also reduced the erosion of land to a large extent. The farmers who used to grow one or two crops are now in a position to grow 3-4 crops with increased income and profit.

In the beginning of 2009-10, the Department of Agriculture had 20 Soil Testing Laboratories (STLs), including two mobile laboratories. Under RKVY project during 2009-10, 61 STLs were sanctioned for various Agricultural Produce Management Committees (APMCs) and during 2010-11, 15 STLs were sanctioned for various sugar cooperatives. The GoG has involved in soil testing programmes, other agencies concerned with agriculture like Land Development Corporation, Sugar Cooperatives and Agricultural Produce Marketing Committees in soil analysis and issue of soil health cards. The state government has also developed software in which soil test analysis report, fertility status, etc., are entered and on online soil test health cards are generated and distributed to the farmers.

Gujarat Livelihood Promotion Company (GLPC) is the executive arm of Mission Mangalam, the implementing agency for NRLM, which is registered under the Companies Act, 1956. GLPC works through strategic partnerships. It promoted the programme titled "Maru Khetar Kare Saat Vakhat Vavetar", focusing on the practice of multi-crop production in an area of land, through the integrated low cost sustainable agriculture multi-tier practices.

GLPC joined hands with Central Salt Marine and Chemical Research Institute (CSMCRI) to encourage sea weed cultivation along the state sea coast. The project named 'Project Sagar Laxmi' has been initiated to provide livelihood opportunities to potential beneficiaries of the coastal belt.

Kerala

There are two important issues addressed in Kerala's MGNREGS works: agricultural productivity and eco-restoration. Soil and water conservation, land development, horticulture, reviving of water bodies, etc., were the major works covered under MGNREGS. One major achievement of Kerala in the context of MGNERGS is the selection of mates (similar to peer leaders), who are now an integral and critical part of all the works executed under the scheme. They are responsible for the maintenance of muster rolls and the work site diary at the work sites. For all works executed under MGNREGS, the mates will be trained to manage work sites during work execution.

In Kerala, over the last four decades, there has been a steady decline in the availability of labour with nearly 12 lakh workers having left the agrarian sector. The primary reason is migration of the younger generation away from the state and from the agriculture sector due to the strenuous nature of the work. As a result, farmers were increasingly opting out of cultivation as it was just not economically viable. In this context, the Government of Kerala (GoK) introduced an innovative idea to address this issue by establishing a corps of highly disciplined and dedicated personnel, similar to the army, to work on farms so as to produce food and ensure food security for the country. This is referred to as Food Security Army (FSA). They are given first-hand experience in operating all agro-machinery in actual field conditions. They are provided with a distinctive dress code and follow good work ethics.

The platform to translate this vision into reality was set out by RKVY. The project had three phases. The first phase comprised putting in place a veritable artillery of new generation agro-machinery that is user friendly, health and life caring and help to remove drudgery and establish a quality training hall. The project was implemented during 2008-2010. The machinery worth ₹100 lakh was procured and used for training. The second phase involved large-scale demonstrations of operations of the FSA in order to convince the farmer of its competence and usefulness. This phase was drawn up and implemented during 2009-2011. The third phase was the actual creation of FSA service centres at village level. The FSA gets first-hand experiential learning of hardware aspects, e.g., repair, service and operation of agro-machinery, and masters the art of crop production using machinery. They are organised to work in groups termed—Agro Machinery Operation Service Centres.

These centres provide agro-machinery operation services on contract basis to the farmers on demand. The service charges are fixed and notified. The services are guaranteed and timely as per contract. The operational services include land preparation, planting, inter-cultivation operations, harvesting and post-harvest handling and several such other operations using agro-machinery for paddy and other crops. The total outlay of ₹250.6 lakh for the three phases was received from RKVY allocation of the state.

Kudumbashree is multi-faceted women based participatory poverty eradication programme initiated by the GoK operating since 1998. The three key concepts of Kudumbashree are economic empowerment, social empowerment and women empowerment. There are various livelihood interventions of Kudumbashree such as individual, group and special projects micro-enterprises, collective farming, consortia, *samagra*, etc. NRLM in Kerala is entrusted to Kudumbashree. Considering the fact that Kerala has the highest proportion of elderly compared to other the states in India, NRLM has drawn in an innovative programme. According to 2011 Census, people above 60 years of age constitute 13 per cent of the state's population (national figure is 8.2%). Two districts in Kerala (Kollam and Ernakulam) have been selected to launch elderly SHGs, which will help generate livelihoods for people who are retired, but able to work. Helpage India will collaborate with this programme.

Madhya Pradesh

Development of water resources for various livelihoods is one of the major interventions under MGNREGS in MP. Labour component under MGNREGS was utilised for construction of farm bunds, farm ponds and irrigation wells and watershed development works like preparation of contour trench, gully plugging, etc. Convergence of funds under Integrated Watershed Management Programme (IWMP) was also effectively utilised for the purpose.

Development of water sources such as percolation tanks and micro minor irrigation tanks for minor irrigation was one of the main projects under RKVY in MP. A percolation tank is an artificially created surface water body submerging a highly permeable land area so that the surface run-off is made to percolate and recharge the ground water storage. The approach adopted was community-based water management for the benefit and progress of the people.

Madhya Pradesh possesses 3.94 lakh ha of water area in the form of large, medium and small irrigation reservoirs, village ponds and private ponds. 3.89 lakh ha (98.12%) of water area has been brought under fish culture, which forms a major livelihood activity for the people. The availability of water has changed the cropping system and increased the cropping intensity. The productivity of wheat and gram in the state has increased significantly. The Kapildhara programme implemented by the state government for small and marginal farmers aims at facilitating land development, and dug wells are provided under MGNREGS, with lifting devices that run on diesel for each farm from the schemes of Swarnajayanti Gram Swarozgar Yojana (SGSY) and Bundhelkhand Package under RKVY.

Water harvesting and water management form an integral part of community life of the people in MP. The practices related to water conservation are performed by the common man and the community as their duty and social responsibility and also as part of good local self-governance. The 'water wisdom' and community-based water management practices of the farmers of MP were effectively utilised in the RKVY project.

Tejaswini Madhya Pradesh was implemented in six rural districts of MP funded by International Fund for Agricultural Development's (IFAD) loan assistance. The programme has made substantial progress to facilitate the SHG members to access entitlements including demanding services for the government departments. The Madhya Pradesh government has recently (2012) launched Samagra Samajik Suraksha Mission (Integrated Social Security Mission) in order to provide social security for the socially weaker sectors such as those under BPL (below poverty line), disabled ones, senior citizens, widows and the destitute. This is a scheme for convergence of financial inclusion and direct benefits transfer. There are different schemes for them under different departments. The mandate of the mission is to simplify the various schemes and provide benefits to the beneficiaries through one single agency as well as to bring about transparency through direct transfer without manual interference.

Maharashtra

Nearly 52 per cent of the cultivated area in Maharashtra is drought prone. Considering this, a massive watershed development plan was conceived for the state and over 30,000 micro watersheds have been developed with state funding by way of constructing check dams, contour bunding, etc. Promoting construction of farm ponds is one of the initiatives taken up under RKVY in Maharashtra with the objective to increase groundwater recharge in water-stressed areas so as to provide protective irrigation to the standing crops during dry period and to improve the groundwater table. During 2007-08, construction of farm ponds was taken up in a massive way, which was continued for the subsequent two years. During 2009-10, an amount of ₹224 crore was allotted under RKVY for multi-year farm ponds project.

The state has also converged the farm pond programme under RKVY, both in terms of scale expansion as well as vertical integration. The state government has taken up the construction of 1 lakh farm ponds under MGNREGS and also other initiatives like Pulse Village programme and State Horticulture Mission. Another initiative under RKVY which has helped the farmers is related to construction of scientific storage structures in Maharashtra for storage of onions. Maharashtra accounts for 25-30 per cent of onions produced in the country. One of the features of onion cultivation in the state is that three crops can be harvested in a year: 10-15 per cent during *kharif*, 30-40 per cent as late *kharif* and 50-60 per cent during *rabi*/summer season. In the absence of scientific and *pucca* storage structures, a significant quantity of onion gets spoiled which had been a major problem faced by the farmers. Maharashtra State Agricultural Marketing Board (MSAMB) utilising the funds from RKVY have effectively intervened to solve the problem of farmers by constructing storage structures for onions for individual farmers, farmer groups and also for the Board.

Maharashtra has successfully implemented supply chain infrastructure and Agri-Business Centres by SHGs through the convergence of schemes under the Agricultural and Processed Food Products Export Development Authority (APEDA), National Horticulture Mission (NHM), RKVY, National Medicinal Plants Board (NMPB) and MSAMB. District Agricultural Marketing Structures (DAMS) have been established for strengthening agricultural marketing system, for creating storage and processing infrastructure and for ensuring better market price to the farmers.

Contract farming is emerging as an important aspect of agri-business, where the products are purchased by multinationals, small companies, government agencies, farmers' cooperatives or individual entrepreneurs. In India, contract farming has considerable potential where small and marginal farmers can no longer compete without access to the services provided by the contract farming companies. Small farmers in India are generally capital starved and cannot make major investments in land improvements and modern inputs. Contract farming can fill up this gap by providing the farmers with quality inputs, technical guidance and management skills. Contract farming can work if there is a collectivisation of small farmers, thereby bringing down the transaction costs, thereby bringing down practiced in Maharashtra.

Maharashtra is in the forefront in the context of contract farming which has helped the small farmers to reap benefits. The success story of contract farming for chipping potato (Satara district) has spread rapidly in Maharashtra since an amendment to Maharashtra's Agricultural Produce Marketing Act in 2006 allowed for companies to establish direct contract relations with farmers. While most of the chipping potato in India is grown as *rabi* (spring harvest), in Satara district, potatoes are grown as *kharif* (monsoon) crop. To ensure year round availability of potato, companies enter into contract with potato farmers. The contract involves a tripartite agreement between the farmers, the contracting firms and a local bank that provides credit to the farmers. Under NRLM, contract farming is proposed to be scaled up in Maharashtra.

Odisha

The land rights settlement under the Forest Right Act (FRA) is still an ongoing struggle at the community level in many states in India. Odisha has taken an initiative to develop the forest lands with the forests under FRA so as to utilise them to the optimum level of production. Under MGNREGS, there was a shift in focus in the land development activities as "community benefited projects worked upon by an individual wage earner to individual benefit projects worked upon by the community." There was also a shift in emphasis from subsistence crops (finger millets, pearl millets) to high value crops. Accordingly, 1,940 ha of forest land belonging to 2,220 MGNREGS households in the tribal areas was developed for raising high value crops like vegetables, ginger, maize, etc.

The tribals of Odisha have a long tradition of collecting and cultivating different roots and tubers to meet their food requirements at times of scarcity. Some tuber crops can withstand long periods of drought and low fertility levels. Orissa Tribal Empowerment Livelihood Project (OTELP) was launched by the Odisha government, which took the responsibility of production and value addition of indigenous tuber crops. Under RKVY, production-cum-seed multiplication programme of tuber crops was taken up during 2011-2012 in the tribal areas covered by OTELP. The state has a tradition of serving meals as *Prasadam* to its deities and its distribution to the devotees at a modest cost. Yam, cassava and other indigenous tuber crops are preferred as raw materials for the preparation of temple food. The production of indigenous tubers thus has a domestic market. The presence of domestic market would ensure the viability of this RKVY project and would provide sustainable livelihoods to the tribals of the state.

NRLM in Odisha is to be implemented in a phased manner. In the first phase, NRLM has been launched in 38 backward poverty stricken blocks of 10 districts, where the World Bank funded Targeted Rural Initiatives for Poverty Termination and Infrastructure (TRIPTI) is being implemented, since the objectives of NRLM and TRIPTI are almost the same. In the second phase, Scheduled Areas, including 4 blocks from 11 districts covered under Western Odisha Rural Livelihood Project (WORLP), JEEVIKA and OTELP and five left wing extremist affected districts will come under its coverage. By the end of 12th Plan, all 30 districts would have come under NRLM. The approach of implementation for NRLM in Odisha will be through institutionalisation of the poor, unlike the earlier approach of implementation by institutionalisation for the poor.

Sikkim

Reviving springs or springshed development—called Dhara Vikas programme—is an initiative to revive and maintain drying springs in Sikkim under MGNREGS with technical support from other organisations. The Dhara Vikas programme was conceptualised and launched by Rural Management and Development Department (RMDD) in partnership with World Wide Fund for Nature (WWF)-India and Peoples Science Institute (PSI), Dehradun, bringing about a paradigm shift in the field of water management in the state. About 80 per cent of the rural households of the state are mainly dependent on springs for drinking water and irrigation needs throughout the year. Although the guidelines of MGNREGS put 50 per cent of the implementation to be taken up by line departments, in Sikkim, the state government devolved 100 per cent implementation of the programme to the *gram panchayats* (GPs). Hence, the Dhara Vikas programme grew on the foundation of strong socio-cultural fabric at the village level and took the form of a community led social movement.

Building a cadre of para geo-hydrologists is one of the important features of this programme. With technical support from PSI, WWF-India facilitated the training of master trainers consisting mainly of field facilitators, who would undertake the programme in their own areas. These grass-roots water engineers received training that taught them the use of GPS (global positioning system), identification of the catchment areas and measuring and monitoring the spring discharge, among other things. Exposure trips to the states of Uttarakhand and Himachal Pradesh, where similar ground water recharge initiatives had been undertaken were also organised. Principles of geo-hydrology, watershed and GIS (geographic information system) were integrated to conceptualise this new initiative in order to revive, restore and rehabilitate water springs, mainly in drought prone areas in view of increasing threat form environmental changes. Four hundred hectares of land was brought under spring-shed development, resulting in an annual groundwater recharge of 90 crore litres. This had led to revival of 40 springs and 4 lakes in 20 drought-prone GPs in the state. Large area was brought under horticulture plants.

Organic farming is promoted by the Government of Sikkim under National Project on Organic Farming (NPOF), NHM and RKVY. The main components under RKVY to assist organic farming are financial assistance to the state for adoption and certification, and for vermicompost production. Sikkim promotes the following certification approach. Firstly, Facilitating certification by third party only for commodities aimed at export outside the state (national or international). Secondly, developing Participatory Guarantee System (PGS) of organic certification for commodities being marketed and consumed within the state urban centres, such as food grains, vegetables, and fruits. Thirdly, developing a concept of niche branding for food items for marketing within state and supporting supply chain formation.

Marketing and infrastructure support will be the primary activities of NRLM in Sikkim. Strengthening the existing SHGs, facilitating greater mobilisation of credit from banks with a higher quantum of internal savings and internal lending will be done under NRLM. Marketing infrastructure is proposed to be strengthened with the creation of 50 additional Rural Produce Marketing Centres (RPMCs). Provisions will be made to create a cadre of service providers, Community Resource Persons (CRPs) and master craftsmen and consequently utilise their services for the training of SHG beneficiaries.

Suggestions on Improvement of the Flagship Programmes

MGNREGS (1995)

Item	*Present Status*	*Remarks/Suggestions*
Focus	Wage employment for only unskilled labour (manual works).	Inclusion of semi skilled workforce may also be considered.
Features	Guarantee scheme, non-negotiable; Social audit.	Strict vigilance is needed to ensure that eligible job card holders are given work. Guidelines on payment of unemployment allowance and delayed payment of wages are yet to be streamlined.
Functions/ Activities	Public/Community works for creating/upgrading durable assets related to natural resources.	Needs to be reoriented to proactively develop improvements on the land holdings of small and marginal farmers for climate-resilient agriculture.
Funding	100 per cent of wages for unskilled manual work, 75 per cent of material costs by the Centre and 25 per cent of material costs by the states.	Norms have to be strictly followed. States have no flexibility in utilising the funds. Proposal for giving freedom to states may be considered.
Observed outcome	Reduced distress migration, enhanced purchasing power of rural labour, and generation of green employment.	Convergence with many other schemes is possible since MGNREGS can provide labour input. Focus on drought hit areas can add value to agriculture labour. More emphasis on green technologies needed.

Source: Author's analysis based on guidelines of MGNREGS (1995).

Way Forward

While MGNREGS provides relative advantage to the rural people in order to get economically empowered, RKVY brings in comparative advantage through technological interventions in terms of improved seeds, innovative practices, etc., thereby enabling higher production and productivity. NRLM brings in competitiveness through the enabling role of institutional factors resulting in better credit linkages and effective market interventions. Although competitive advantage and comparative advantage are used interchangeably, there are certain distinct differences. Comparative advantage is drawn by difference in cost of inputs such as labour or capital, while competitive advantage is drawn by differences in the capacity to transform these inputs into goods and services at maximum profits.

RKVY (2007)

Item	*Present Status*	*Remarks/Suggestions*
Focus	Incentivise states to increase outlays for agriculture and allied sectors for enhanced production and productivity.	Can be effective if the projects are based on District Agricultural Plan (DAP) and State Agricultural Plan (SAP). Should have link with the SAP, which is not insisted at present.
Features	Additional Central Assistance (ACA) scheme, gap filling mode.	Stand alone projects to be avoided. Gap filling projects for scaling up to be given priority.
Functions/ Activities	Integrated development of agriculture and allied sectors, soil health, agricultural mechanisation, market development, infrastructure development for seed, marketing, processing, etc.	Animal husbandry, fisheries and sericulture in some states could perform better with a better infrastructure created under RKVY. This should continue for diversified farming.
Funding	100 per cent Central government grant.	High level of flexibility to states is provided, which will prove very advantageous.
Observed outcome	Increased availability of quality inputs like high yield variety (HYV) seeds, planting materials, bio-inputs and infrastructure facilities like rural godowns, market yards, laboratories, etc.	More emphasis on climate resilient agriculture to be provided.

Source: Author's analysis based on guidelines of RKVY (2007).

Prior to launching of NRLM in 2011, Bihar, MP and Odisha had already implemented poverty reduction/livelihood projects. (MP District Poverty Initiatives Project I (2001) II (2009); Bihar Rural Livelihood Project, JEEVIKA (2007); Orissa Rural Livelihood Project, TRIPTI, 2008). However, with the launching of NRLM, it is possible that more focus can be given to marginalised sections, including tribals. NRLM must address the livelihood needs of 'transient power'. Transient power is defined as those households who move in and out of poverty due to seasonality, life cycle situations, etc. These households have some chances of escaping poverty in a 'good' year, but may step into poverty in a 'bad' year or when exposed to shocks.

NRLM (2011)

Item	*Present Status*	*Remarks/Suggestions*
Focus	Self-employment and wage employment for the rural poor.	Very successful in creating human and social capital. Capacity building may be stressed further.
Features	Creating effective and efficient institutional platforms for rural poor to support sustainable livelihood enhancements and improved access to financial services.	Since NRLM is evolved and is redesigned and restructured based on the SGSY programme, many of the inherent defects of SGSY are corrected. Creation of a dedicated organisation for implementation is a welcome step.
Functions/ Activities	Skill training and placement, capacity building for enterprise development, livelihood activities.	Shift in emphasis from livelihood to entrepreneurship is needed to be addressed properly. Strengthening of delivery of service is needed.
Funding	Centrally sponsored—funding shared between Centre and the state in the ratio of 75:25 (90:10 in Northeast states).	Shift from allocation based funding to demand based funding is a progressive step.
Observed outcome	Functional self-managed SHGs, federated institutions of the poor, support services for marginalised and the poor.	Serious attention to be given to value added agriculture and rural Micro, Small and Medium Enterprises (MSMEs).

Source: Author's analysis based on guidelines of NRLM (2011).

It is observed that NRLM under Ministry of Rural Development (MoRD) has not given serious attention to value added agriculture and rural MSMEs, which has to be addressed. It is necessary that NRLM may implement activities for developing a vibrant ecosystem for agro-MSMEs. NRLM has greater potential for linkages with the agriculture sector to empower women so as to improve nutrition outcomes. NRLM's SHGs can help launch interventions related to homestead horticulture and poultry, micronutrient food fortification, low cost, nutrient dense supplementary foods and primary food processing. Empowering women in agriculture also means ensuring women's legal rights to land and access to inputs. Mahila Kisan Sashaktikaran Pariyojana (MKSP) envisages addressing food and nutrition security of the women farmers and their families. Integration of organic farming into livelihood interventions and scaling up of green technologies may be given a boost under NRLM, which can go a long way in promoting climate resilient farm livelihoods.

References

DAC (2012). *Incentivizing Agriculture: RKVY Initiatives.* Ministry of Agriculture, Government of India. April.

LANSA (2014). *Country Policy Landscape Analysis: A Brief Review of the Agricultural/Nutritional Policy Landscape in India.* UK: IDS.

MoRD (2011). *National Rural Livelihood Project: Social Assessment Report.* Ministry of Rural Development, Government of India. February.

RMDD (2012). *Sikkim Springs: Ensuring Rural Water Security. www.sikkimsprings.org/dv/springshed.php*

SERP (2014). *Andhra Pradesh Rural Inclusive Growth Project: Social Management Framework.* Government of Andhra Pradesh.

Sharma, Aruna (2013). *Mainstreaming of Resource Convergence in Policy making, Programme Design and Execution.* UNDP, India.

Sharma, Rita (2014). "For a Better MGNREGA", *Indian Express. indianexpress.com/article/opinion/columns/For-a-better-mgnrega/*

UNDP India (2012). *Greening Rural Development in India.* Vol I. Ministry of Agriculture, Government of India.

Vicol, Mark (2014). "Potato Contract Farming and 'Privileged Spaces': Preliminary Insights from Rural Maharashtra", *Journal of the Geographical Society of Berlin* 154(3).

2

S. INDRAKANT

Benefit Cost Analysis of MGNREGS in Andhra Pradesh

Introduction

Mahatma Gandhi National Rural Employment Guarantee Scheme (MGNREGS) is a flagship programme launched by the United Progressive Alliance (UPA) government in 2006. Mahatma Gandhi National Rural Employment Guarantee Act (MGNREGA) aims to provide a legal guarantee for at least 100 days of employment in every financial year to adult members of any rural household willing to do public work-related unskilled manual work at the statutory minimum wage. If the government fails do so, it has to pay unemployment relief. The main objectives of the Act were: to enhance the livelihood security of the rural poor by generating wage employment opportunities and to create a rural asset base which would enhance productive ways of employment, and also augment and sustain rural household income.

With the change in power at the Centre, there was a rumour that MGNREGS may be totally scraped. There was a strong protest from the different sections of society. A group of economists wrote a letter to Prime Minister Narendra Modi expressing their deep concern about the future of MGNREGS. They admitted that the scheme could have delivered more benefits, but the gain that have been already achieved are substantial and amply justified further efforts to strengthen it. Therefore, they urged the Prime Minister to reverse the government thinking and to ensure that the scheme receives all the support that it requires to survive and thrive.

Earlier Works

MGNREGS has attracted the attention of many social scientists and social activists. A large number of theoretical and empirical works have been added to the literature over a period of time. Exhaustive review of the literature is out of the scope of the present study. An exhaustive review of works done under MGNREGS, carried out during its initial years, is made by Kumar and Maruthi (2011). Few studies will be referred to give an idea about various aspects covered in the literature.

Dreze (2009) and Ambasta *et al.* (2008) have documented the process followed in the implementation of NREGS. More recently, Abraham (2014) has vividly described the original guidelines of the scheme and the subsequent changes therein. He opines that the present administrative set-up is more tuned to the implementation of top-down policies, but not that of demand-driven policies.

In another study, Narayanan (2008) noted major changes in the lives of women in the form of repayment of debt or retrieval of pawned gold for spending on children education. At the same time, she quotes cases where women workers were turned away when they came with a child.

Banerjee (2011) opines that the right to work in MGNRGES can become a tool in the hands of workers in increasing their wages, creating productive assets and facilitating decentralisation of decision–making which, in turn bring about changes in the power structure of the rural society. He also admits that there can be a gap between rights in theory and rights in practice. Based on his field study in several states in eastern and central India, he concludes that the scheme has positive impact in providing employment, raising wages and deepening democracy in rural area. To make the scheme more effective, he calls for more transparency in the selection of the works and in its implementation. Further, he advocates financial decentralisation at the *panchayat* level to avoid wasteful expenditure.

There is a good number of studies on the working of MGNREGS in Andhra Pradesh (AP). Kareemulla *et al.* (2009) have found that due to NREGA, the migration in Ananthapur District of AP has come down from 27 per cent to only 7 per cent. However, the method of measurement of change in migration is unexplained. Their regression analysis revealed that the number of family members participating in NREGS depends upon family size, land holding and income from other sources. They observed that the additional earnings from NREGS are being spent by the beneficiaries mostly on food, education and health. They have stressed the need to bridge the gap between the envisaged days of employment to be provided and the actual days of employment provided.

In a study of four states, Kareemulla *et al.* (2010) have observed that the NREGS has not only provided wage employment, but also has promoted capital formation in the farmers' land through creation of assets like farm ponds, open wells, land levelling and CPRs (common property resources) like renovation of village tanks, construction of check dams etc. The annual return on such investment works out to be around 3-4 per cent.

Galab *et al.* (2010) have made comparative study of 15 per cent of beneficiary households and 10 per cent non-beneficiary households from each selected *gram panchayat* spread over four districts of AP. They found that the scheme ensured more benefits to the poorest of the poor. They have also offered few policy suggestions for effective implementation of the scheme.

Reddy (2011) in his in-depth study of the Functioning of NREGS in AP has highlighted some of the benefits derived by the wage seekers which include—reduction in distress migration; double benefits derived by de-silting of water-bodies and silt application on the lands belonging to marginal and small farmers in the form of water conservation and higher productivity; extension of cultivated area and; higher wage rate. He also discussed about the unionisation of labour and the role of PRIs (panchayat raj institutions).

In another study of four states, Kareemulla *et al.* (2013) have found that the share of NREGS employment was up to one-third of wage days, while the contribution of NREGS wages to the family income varied in the range of 12-33 per cent. To overcome the problem of labour shortage due to NREGS in irrigated area, they have suggested the practice that is followed Kerala. In Kerala, a cultivator has to pay the difference between NREGS wages and the market wages to the labourer for working on his land.

To make the scheme more effective, Indrakant (2013) based on field experience has suggested for incorporation of IT in the maintenance of attendance of wage seekers and in payment of wages to them, in measurement of work completed and in coordination of MGNREGS works with the cultivation activities in the village, etc.

Some studies have examined the scope for achieving inclusive growth through MGNREGS (Indrakant and Rao, 2010). Another work, based on field study of two villages in Medak District (Indrakant, 2013a), revealed that MGNREGS is likely to increase wage rate in the rural labour market, which in turn may reduce the number of days of employment for the workers. Net effect depends upon relative intensities of these two movements. If a worker loses a part of wage income in open market, then it does not necessarily imply that his total income will decline. Gains from schemes like MGNREGS are likely to promote inclusive growth when they do not adversely affect other components of income in the labour households.

Several studies have revealed that the implementation of MGNREGS has resulted in escalation of the cost of cultivation and some have cautioned that it may endanger the food security of vulnerable sections of the society. Therefore, they have recommended for the coordination of MGNREGS work with the cultivation activities. Generally, it is observed that MGNREGS is labour-friendly, but hurts the cultivators. Indrakant (2013b) has suggested a modification of the scheme in order to make it labour-friendly as well as cultivator-friendly. Under modified scheme, the Government in order to promote food security and to compensate cultivators, permit the cultivators to hire labourers at a relatively lower wage rate, but the farmer pays the differential amount to the labourers, besides providing additional employment to the labourers under the scheme at the government fixed wage rate. There must be coordination between works done under MGNREGS and agricultural activities in the village. This will benefit both labourers and cultivators. At the same time, it will be less burdensome to the government to implement the scheme. It will be a win-win situation.

In a study of two *gram panchayats* in Kadapa District of AP, it was found that beneficiary households experienced an income gain of over ₹9,000 during the year 2008-09 (Shashirekha, 2013).

There are some important studies existing on the working of MGREGS in Tamil Nadu. Based on the percentage of women participants in the scheme, person-days of employment generated and the trend in expenditure on the scheme, Tamil Nadu has been termed as a growing state (Khera and Muthaiah, 2010; Dreze and Oldiges, 2011). The Dalits and women are the major beneficiaries of the scheme (Carswell *et al.*, 2014). Factors for the success of the scheme in Tamil Nadu are: pro-poor commitment by the ruling party whether it is Dravida Munnetra Kazhagam (DMK) or All India Anna Dravida Munnetra Kazhagam (AIADMK); tight supervision by the Chief Minister and other higher officials and; high level of social awareness and collective action among the rural population. However, there are some pockets where the implementation has been slower and remained more partial. The authors have classified the beneficiaries into two categories namely those who are young, strong and willing to work but not getting sufficient work, and those who are old, weak and unable to work on private lands. The first group is unhappy about the relatively low wage rate received under the scheme compared to that earned by working on private lands. But in AP the work under the scheme is allotted to a labour group called Shrama Shakti Sangam (SSS), which consists of both types of beneficiaries who incidentally happen to be relatives.

A study on Tamil Nadu reveals that MGNREGS provides a solid mechanism to overcome the adverse consequences of drought (Suresh Babu *et al.*, 2013). It is also observed that awareness level among the beneficiaries in respect of 'rights and entitlement' is encouraging, but in other aspects like 'social audit' and 'permissible work' is discouraging. It is also noticed that as most of the beneficiaries are very poor, the impact of MGNREGS on poverty reduction is moderate, but the 'poverty gap index' which reflects intensity of poverty has substantially declined. In a critical study of MGNREGS, Shivakumar

(2013) points out that generally no durable assets are created and it has opened a new avenue for corruption. It is worthwhile to mention here that in recent past, *panchayat* buildings have been constructed under the scheme.

In a more recent study, Manikandan (2011) discusses how the MGNREGS can be used for improving food security in a deficit state like Kerala. The labour cost in production of paddy is about 60 to 70 per cent in Kerala. Therefore, he suggests that the MGNREGS programme must be taken up on top priority in small and marginal paddy lands owned by the vulnerable sections like SCs (scheduled castes) or STs (scheduled tribes), and women. This move will reduce the cost of production on one hand and increase food production on the other.

Kumar, and Maruthi (2011) in their extensive study found that the employment per household under MGNREGS in Karnataka during the initial years (2007-2009) varied in the range of 20-40 days. They also observed that the number of employment days under MGNREGS was much lower than that in the open market. The wage seekers, especially females, are substituting MGNREGS works for self-employment.

The findings of various studies reviewed are mixed and to some extent confusing. Most of studies have observed that the scheme is self-targeting as larger proportion of SC/ST households, women workers and poor landless labours are actively participating in the scheme. Another beneficial outcome of the scheme is the increasing wage rate for the works done on private lands. Due to direct and indirect benefits, all the participating households experienced a gain in income. Some could cross the poverty line and some could only manage to more nearer to the poverty line. Consequently, there is some decline in poverty, but sharper decline in the poverty gap. This has resulted in reduction in indebtedness and in improvement in credit worthiness of vulnerable sections of the society. Some studies have found that additional income derived from the scheme is being spent on food, education of the children and health. The scheme has also brought down the magnitude of migration. At the same time, studies have also highlighted the negative elements in the scheme like poor coverage, low level of employment generated, low wage rate received by the workers, delay in wage payments, etc. Some studies have dealt with escalation in the cost of cultivation due to the hike in market wage rate and decline in cultivated area, and this may endanger the food security of the poor. Some studies have touched upon the decline in work ethics among the labourers.

Any welfare scheme can be justified only when the benefits derived by targeted beneficiaries is comparatively more than the expenditure incurred by the government in implementing the scheme. The present paper attempts to analyse the benefits derived and the cost incurred on MGNREGS in AP. It also examines the shortcomings in the process and mechanism of implementation of the scheme.

Implementation of the Scheme

The process and the mechanism of implementation of the scheme are mainly responsible for the observed shortcomings. During the initial years, the emphasis was mainly on providing employment to the wage seekers at a fixed wage rate, while totally neglecting the type of tasks to be carried out and amount of the work done. There was lack of clarity among the functionaries regarding the tasks to be taken up under the scheme. Simple works like bush clearance, pebble collection, etc., which did not result in any durable assets were taken up. Provision of employment to the wage seekers appeared to be the sole purpose of the whole exercise. Some ridiculed it as a means of distributing cash to the labourers. In villages having tanks, de-silting of tanks and strengthening of bunds were another popular work.

The workers were under the impression that their mere presence at the worksite would ensure them a stipulated wage rate, irrespective of the amount of work turned out. So for working on private land, the labourers started demanding a wage rate higher than MGNREGS wage rate. For instance in some villages in Medak District, wage rate for male workers before MGNREGS was only ₹60. After the implementation of the scheme, the labourers started demanding a wage rate of ₹150, which adversely affected the cultivators. With a better planning, one could have obtained a better outcome by way of coordinating the existing cultivation activities in the village with employment provided under the scheme. The cultivators were willing to give ₹60 to the workers for the work done on their land and wanted remaining ₹40 to be paid by the government. If the employment generated by the cultivators in the village was insufficient, then the government could have provided additional work to the wage seekers. This would have prevented the hike in the wage rate and cost of cultivation without lowering the benefits accruing to the labourers. Further, this would also have reduced the burden for the government. It is a lost opportunity and the related discussion will be only of academic interest.

Now that wage rate has increased in the market, the cultivators suggest that a part of the increased wage rate should be borne by the government. For instance, if the market wage rate is ₹150, then the government can pay half of it and cultivators would pay for the other half for the work done on the private land. This will partially compensate the cultivators and reduce the government expenditure.

With passage of time, the guidelines are being revised in order to include more productive, durable and asset–creating tasks. Such tasks are basically of two types—community related and individual related. Important works taken up under community–related works are road formation, digging feeder channels and field channels, digging trenches on hill top and earth bunding, filling up not usable open wells, etc. In some places, construction of *gram panchayat* buildings, de-silting of tanks, and construction of check dams are also taken up. Individual–related works are supposed to benefit only the small and marginal farmers. Important works taken up under this category are land development activities (consisting of bush clearance, stump removal and land levelling), silt application to the fields, construction of farm ponds, digging of open wells, provision of bore well, and horticultural activities (consisting of bund plantation and block plantation). Recently, Individual Households Latrine (IHHL) Scheme is being taken up on a priority basis. Inclusion of all these works in the scheme will make it more effective.

Introduction of biometric attendance of wage seekers and electronic payment of wages on experimental basis in some *mandals* in Nizamabad District of AP have yielded encouraging results. Therefore, to improve the monitoring of the scheme, biometric attendance must be introduced throughout the country. Wage payment must be made through either post-office or bank. The role of *gram panchayat* has to be enhanced.

Trends in Employment Generated and Wage Payment under MGNREGS

The experience of one state may differ from another on the account of manner of implementation, intensity of implementation and local conditions. In this section, the performance of MGNREGS in AP in terms of days of employment generated and wage payment is presented.

MGNREGS was launched in AP on 2 February 2006, in Anantapur district by then Prime Minister Manmohan Singh. On the same day, the scheme was launched in 12 other districts of AP. The scheme was extended to 6 more districts on 1 April 2007. The remaining 3 districts were brought under the scheme in April 2008. In 2006-07, 65 million person days of employment was generated in 13 districts of AP. In the subsequent year, the days of employment generated jumped up to 200 million days due to intensification of Scheme in the districts already included and its extension to six more districts in the state. Since then, employment generated has been steadily increasing with the exception of 2011-12, when there was a marginal decline (Table 2.1 and Figure 2.1). In 2012-13, the employment generated was as high as 338 million person days. As expected, there is a high correlation between the wage payment and days of employment generated under the scheme. The wage payment is about 100 times the days of employment generated. The number of households participated in the scheme increased from 2.1 million in 2006-07 to 5.8 million in 2012-13, thus registering a three-fold increase. The average employment generated per household has also increased from 36 to 57 days. The three indicators *viz.*, number of days of employment generated; number of households participated; and average employment days per household, shows that with passage of time, the programme has intensified. The wage rate per day increased from ₹86 to ₹105. It may be noted that the wage rate is below the norm fixed by the government as workers take more than the stipulated time to complete a work.

The coverage of the scheme is substantial as revealed by the fact that about 40 per cent of the rural households are participating in the scheme. The percentage of households with job cards participating in the scheme exhibited wide fluctuations. In unfavourable agricultural years, many households are compelled to participate in the scheme and in a better agriculture year, they withdraw from the scheme to work on their own fields. At the same time, there are some households who do not participate in MGNREGS works, regardless of having job cards.

Table 2.1

Trends in Employment and Wage Rate under MGNREGS in AP

S. No.	*Year*	*PD*	*W*	*HHP*	*AEMPHH*	*AW PP*	*HHP/ RHH*	*HHP/ JC*
1	2006-07	65	54	2	30.13	81.09	14%	43%
2	2007-08	200	168	4	42.48	82.38	28%	94%
3	2008-09	227	190	5	39.54	82.45	34%	33%
4	2009-10	390	352	6	63.87	89.95	42%	59%
5	2010-11	340	330	6	53.83	96.98	42%	96%
6	2011-12	304	297	5	59.46	97.19	35%	41%
7	2012-13	338	359	6	56.78	105.14	42%	75%

Note: PD=Person days of employment generated in millions, W=Wages in hundred millions, HHP=Households participated in the scheme in millions, AEMPHH=Average employment days per household, AWPP=Average wage rate per person, RHH=Number of Rural Household in 2011, JC=Number of job cards issued, HHP/RHH=Ratio of number of households participated in the scheme to the total number of rural households, HHP/JC=Ratio of number of households participated in the scheme to the number of job cards issued.

Source: *www.nrega.ap.gov.in* and Census 2011.

Comparing with all India performance, the employment provided per household is generally higher in the state. However, wage rate per day per person is marginally lower in the state (Table 2.2 and Figure 2.1 and Figure 2.2).

Figure 2.1

Trends in Employment and Wage Rate under MGNREGS in AP

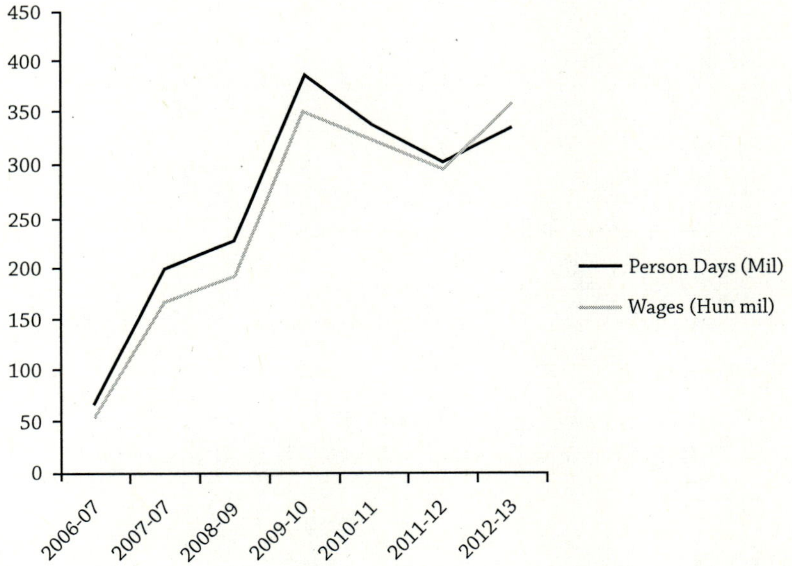

Source: *www.nrega.ap.gov.in* and Census 2011.

Table 2.2

Trends in Employment and Wage Rate under MGNREGS in AP and India

S. No.	*Year*	*AEMPHH*		*AW PP*	
		India	*AP*	*India*	*AP*
1	2006-07	43	30.13	65	81.09
2	2007-08	42	42.48	75	82.38
3	2008-09	48	39.54	84	82.45
4	2009-10	54	63.87	89	89.95
5	2010-11	47	53.83	99	96.98
6	2011-12	42	59.46	113	97.19
7	2012-13	46	56.78	121	105.14

Note: AEMPHH=Average employment days per household, AW PP =Average wage rate per person

Source: *www.nrega.ap.gov.in*

Figure 2.2

Trends in Employment under MGNREGS in AP and India

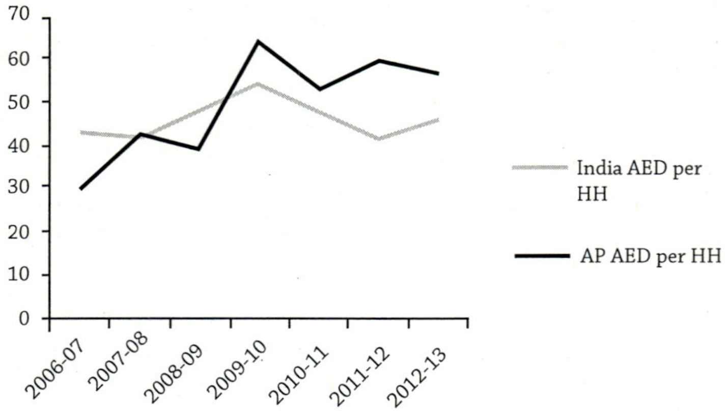

Source: *www.nrega.ap.gov.in*

Figure 2.3

Trends in Wage Rate under MGNREGS in AP and India

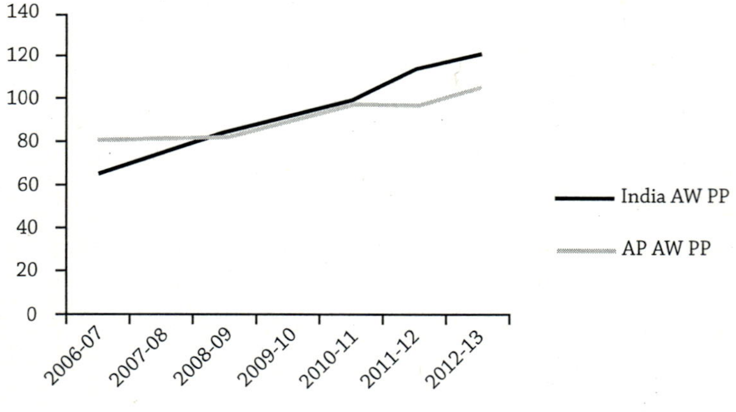

Source: *www.nrega.ap.gov.in*

Wages and Material Components

An analysis of the composition of expenditure on MGNREGS in AP reveals that over the years, the wage component is coming down which reflects the emphasis given on asset creation works during the latter years. In 2006-07, the wage component was as high as 97 per cent which declined to 85 per cent in the following year (Table 2.3). These figures reflect the fact that only labour-intensive works were taken up during the earlier years. In 2010-11, the wage component touched bottom-level of 66 per cent but marginally improved in 2011-12 and 2012-13 to 77 per cent and 74 per cent, respectively. The declining trend in wage component is on account of the inclusion of asset creation works under the scheme. This policy-shift has increased the government expenditure required to generate one-day employment from ₹84 in 2006-07 to ₹144 in 2012-13.

Table 2.3

Wages and Material Components in MGNREGS in AP

No.	Year	Wages (₹ crore)	Material+ Skilled wages (₹ crore)	Total Expend-iture (₹ crore)	Share of wages (%)	Employ-ment Days Generated (crores)	Expenditure/ Person Days (₹)
1	2006-07	540	14	554	97	6.5	84
2	2007-08	1677	299	1976	85	20	99
3	2008-09	1901	573	2474	77	22.7	109
4	2009-10	3522	454	3976	89	39	102
5	2010-11	3301	1690	4991	66	34	147
6	2011-12	2969	883	3852	77	30.4	127
7	2012-13	3587	1290	4877	74	33.8	144

Source: Various years report on *MGNREGS at a Glance*.

Theoretical Framework

Simple demand and supply framework has been used to examine the impact of government intervention scheme in the labour market to assess the benefits derived by the labour households and to estimate BC (benefit-cost) ratio of the scheme.

The likely impact of government intervention schemes in the labour market like MGNREGS can be analysed with simple graphical tools. The demand for labour is basically a derived demand. In backward rural economy, the labour is demanded mostly for agricultural operations by the cultivators of the village. Therefore, the demand for labour is inversely related to the prevailing wage rate. It is true that the demand for labour also depends upon other factors like area under cultivation, price of output, technology adopted by the cultivators, etc. To make the analysis manageable, all such factors are assumed to remain unchanged. The supply of labour, on the contrary, is strongly influenced by wage rate prevailing in the labour market. In general, labour supply is expected to be positively related to the wage rate. In exceptional cases, one may encounter a backward bending supply curve. In the present analysis, such cases are ignored. Therefore, it is not far from reality to assume that demand function for labour is negatively related to the wage rate, while supply is positively related to the wage rate.

In Figure 2.4, DD is the demand curve for labour and SS is the supply curve of labour, when there is no government intervention in the labour market. The point of intersection of these two curves i.e., E gives the equilibrium wage rate (OW) and quantity of labour (OQ) hired in the market.

Figure 2.4

Labour Market

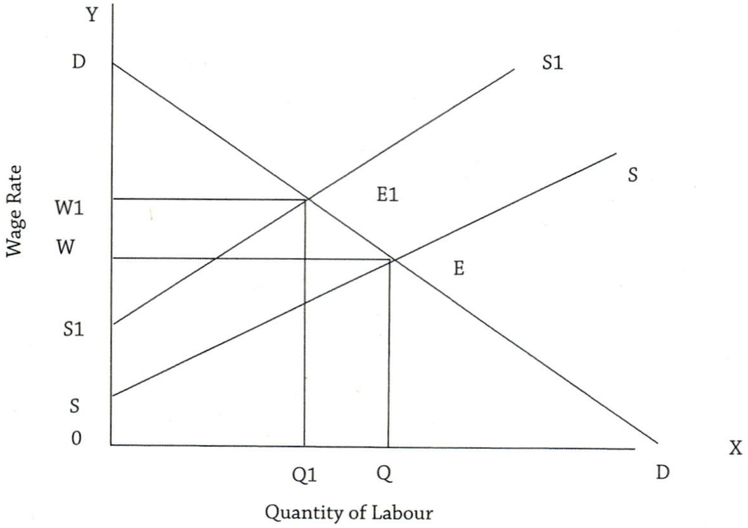

The government intervention schemes in the labour market, like MGNREGS, are likely to shift the supply curve to the left. MGNREGS promises to provide a specified number of days of job (MN) to the registered agricultural labour households at a specified wage rate of MW (which is likely to be higher than the wage rate prevailing in the labour market before the government intervention i.e., OW). Such benefits will tempt the labour to work first in the scheme for available number of days and on the remaining days to work in the fields of private cultivators. The labourers prefer to work in the scheme because of higher wage rate. The actual number of days of work provided under the scheme may be lower than that promised. The behaviour of labourers will restrict the supply of labour in the open market, which can be depicted by a shift in supply curve of labour towards left from SS to S1S1. The equilibrium point shifts from E to E1. Consequently, the wage rate in the market is likely to increase from OW to OW1, but the number of person-days hired may decline from OQ to OQ1. The impact of the scheme on income of the labour households may be estimated in a simple way. It is easy to calculate the workers' income before the implementation of the scheme. The product of number of person-days hired and wage rate will give the income earned by the workers. After implementation of the scheme, the workers will have two sources of income *viz.*, income derived by hiring out their labour in the market, and income earned by working under the scheme. The workers may also benefit when certain tasks on their small piece of land is included in the scheme. In the present analysis, this component is ignored. The procedure of working out the income derived by hiring out labour in the market remains unchanged, while the income derived from the scheme can be obtained as a product of the number of person-days of employment generated under the scheme and the daily wage rate under the scheme. The BC ratio of the schemes is estimated by taking the ratio of change in the income of the beneficiaries to the government expenditure. This ratio has to be carefully interpreted as the increase in market wage rate is likely to have long-term impact on the area under cultivation and agricultural production which are not taken into account in the present analysis. On the contrary, soil and water conservations taken up and the assets created under the scheme are likely to increase the gross cropped area and land productivity which, in turn, may enhance food production.

Income before the intervention	=	Person-days hired in the open market x market wage rate
	=	OQ x OW
Income after the intervention	=	Person-days hired in the open market x market wage rate + number of person-days of work generated under the scheme x government fixed wage rate
	=	OQ1 x OW1 + (MN x MW)
Change in income due to scheme	=	Income after the scheme – Income before the scheme
	=	(OQ1 x OW1) + (MN x MW) – (OQ x OW)
BC ratio	=	Change in income/Government expenditure

Estimation of Benefit–Cost Ratio

To estimate the BC ratio of the scheme, data collected from the field study conducted in six villages spread over the three districts has been utilised. To get a more representative picture, districts with varying levels of performance were selected. The performance indicators used for the present study were average employment per household and average wage rate per person. On the basis of these two performance indicators for the years 2011-12 and 2012-13, three districts—Rangareddy district: a relatively better performing district; Nizamabad district: moderately performing district; and Warangal district: a lagging district—were selected. Two villages were selected from each of these selected districts. Kothlapur and Gottiga Khurd from Rangareddy district, Rudraram and Tujalpur from Nizamabad district, and Kodvatoor and Janakipur from Warangal district were the chosen villages. About 35 households participating in the scheme with due weightage to different categories of beneficiaries were selected from each village. In all, 210 households were included in the sample. It may be noted that many of the beneficiaries had a small piece of land and earned some income by cultivating the same.

Table 2.4

Impact of MGNREGS on Employment per Earner

(in Days)

S. No.	*Item*	*Before MGNREGS*	*After MGNREGS*
1	MGNREGS	—	33
2	Wage Employment	160	144
3	Self Employment	35	35
4	Total (2+3)	195	179
5	Total (1+2+3)	195	212

Source: Field Survey.

Information pertaining to the pattern of employment is presented in Table 2.4. Before MGNREGS, the wage seeker worked for 35 days on his own piece of land and 160 days as wage labourer. Thus, on an average, a wage seeker had 195 days of employment. After the implementation of the scheme, a wage seeker, on an average, got 33 days of work under the scheme. He continued to work for 35 days on his piece of land. But his wage employment in the open market came down to 144 days due to the hike in the market wage rate.

On the whole, after setting out of the scheme, the total days of employment for a wage seeker increased from 195 days to 212 days.

The impact of the scheme on the market wage rate is presented in Table 2.5. It is observed that on an average, market wage rate for men and women in the six selected villages increased from ₹80 to ₹193 and from ₹44 to ₹115, respectively. Hence, average open market wage rate of an earner increased due to the scheme from ₹62 to ₹154.

The data on income from the cultivation was not collected in the field survey. But the value of the days worked by an earner on his own piece of land is imputed at the market wage rate. The computation revealed the income of an earner before implementation of the scheme to be ₹12,090 at current prices (i.e., 2006-07 prices), which increased to ₹31,295 in 2012-13 (at current cost prices) (Table 2.6). Incomes at 2006-07 prices are expressed in 2012-13 prices, using prices inflator of GSDP (gross state domestic product) from the agriculture sector in AP (i.e., 1.84). Therefore, the income of an earner in 2006-07 at 2012-13 prices is estimated to be ₹22,246. Thus, the increase in income of an earner due to the scheme at 2012-13 prices works out to be ₹9,049 (i.e., 31,295–22,246).

Table 2.5

Impact of MGNREGS on Wage Rate

(in ₹)

S.No.	Item	Before MGNREGS	After MGNREGS
1	MGNREGS	-	113
2	Market Wage Rate (Man)	80	193
3	Market Wage Rate (Woman)	44	115
4	AVERAGE	62	154

Source: Field Survey.

Table 2.6

Impact of MGNREGS on Income per Earner

(in ₹)

S. No.	Item	Income per Earner
1	Before MGNREGS at 2006-07 prices	12,090
2	Before MGNREGS at 2012-13 prices	22,246
3	After MGNREGS at 2012-13 prices	31,295

Note: Before MGNREGS=2006-07, after MGNREGS=2012-13.

Source: Field Survey.

Now, let us turn towards the government expenditure. The government under the scheme has provided 33 days of employment to a wage seeker at a wage rate of ₹113 per day. Thus, the wage bill per worker is ₹2,729. In 2012-13, the wage component happened to be 74 per cent of total expenditure. Therefore, the total expenditure per wage seeker works out to be ₹5,039.

Therefore, the benefit derived by a wage seeker from the scheme, on the whole, is ₹9,040; while expenditure incurred by the government is ₹5,039. Hence, the BC ratio is found to be 1.8. In other words, for every ₹1 spent by the government, wage seekers derive benefit of about ₹2.

Conclusion

The three indicators *viz.*, number of days of employment generated; number of households participated; and average employment days per household show that with passage of time, the programme has gradually intensified. The wage rate per day increased from ₹86 to ₹105. It may be noted that the wage rate is below the norm fixed by the government as workers take more than the stipulated time to complete the given task.

Over the years, the wage component in total expenditure on MGNREGS is getting lowered which reflects the emphasis given to asset–creation tasks during the latter years. This policy-shift has increased the government expenditure required to generate one-day employment from ₹84 in 2006-07 to ₹144 in 2012-13.

The BC ratio, based on field study of six villages spread over three districts, works out to be 1.8, i.e., for every ₹1 spent by the government, wage seekers derive a benefit of about ₹2. In short, the benefits derived from the scheme are substantial compared to the expenditure incurred. However, there is a vast scope for improvement.

References

Abraham, Joseph (2014). "MGNREGS: Need for Reforms to Create Productive Rural Employment", *Kurukshetra:* 54-60, October.

Ambasta, Parmatesh, P.S. Vijay Shanker and Mihir Shah (2008). "Two Years of NREGA: The Road Ahead", *Economic & Political Weekly* 43(8): 41-50, 23-29 February.

Banerjee, Kaustav (2011). "Rights in Theory and Practice: A Case Study of the NREGA", in Manoranjan Mohanty (ed.), *Social Development Report 2010: The Land Question and Marginalised.* New Delhi: Oxford University Press. pp.135-46.

Carswell G. and G. De Neve (2014). "MGNREGA in Tamil Nadu: A Story of Success and Transformation?", *Journal of Agrarian Change* 14(4): 564-85.

Dreze, Jean (2009). "NREGA is not Artificial Employment", *Civil Society*: 7-8, May.

Dreze, J. and C. Oldiges (2011). "NREGA: The Official Picture", in R. Khera (ed.), *In the Battle for Employment Guarantee.* Delhi: Oxford University Press. pp.21-39.

Galab S., E. Revathi, P. Prudhivkar Reddy and C. Ravi (2010). "Mahatma Gandhi National Rural Employment Guarantee Programme in Andhra Pradesh: An Assessment", *LBS Journal of Management and Research* 8(1): 14-34.

Indrakant, S. (2013). "Making MGNREGS More Effective", Paper presented at a National Seminar on *Development of Scheduled Castes and Scheduled Tribes: Opportunities, Achievements and Challenges.* Organised by Centre for Planning, Monitoring & Evaluation, National Institute of Rural Development, Hyderabad. 9-11 January.

———. (2013a). *Inclusive Growth through MGNREGS.* 31st Annual Conference Volume of Andhra Pradesh Economic Association. pp.1-15.

———. (2013b). "Making MGNREGS Labour-Friendly and Cultivator-Friendly", Paper presented at *2nd RBI Chair Professors' Conference* held at RBI, Mumbai. 31 May.

Indrakant, S. and R. Nageswar Rao (2010). "MGNREGS and Inclusive Growth: Some Reflections", Paper submitted at National Seminar on *Social Welfare and Inclusive Growth and Development with Special Reference to India* organised by Sri Ramakrishan Degree and PG College, Nandyal, A.P. during 25-26 September.

Kareemulla, K., K. Srinivas Reddy, C.A. Rama Rao, Shalander Kumar and B. Venkateswarlu (2009). "Soil and Water Conservation Works through National Rural Employment Guarantee Scheme (NREGS) in Andhra Pradesh: An Analysis of Livelihood Impact", *Agriculture Economics Research Review* 22 (Conference Number): 443-50.

Kareemulla, K., Shalander Kumar, K.S. Reddy, C.A. Rama Rao and B. Venkateswarlu, (2010). "Impact of NREGS on Rural Livelihood and Agriculture Capital Formation", *Indian Journal of Agriculture Economics* 65(3): 524-39.

Kareemulla, K., P. Ramasunderam, Shalander Kumar and C.A. Rama Rao (2013). "Impact of National Rural Employment Guarantee Scheme in India on Rural Poverty and Food Security", *Current Agriculture research Journal* 1(1): 13-28.

Khera, R. and K. Muthiah (2010). "Slow but Steady Success", *The Hindu*. 24 April. *http://www.thehindu.com/arts/magazine/article409087.ece* (accessed 11 December 2013).

Manikandan, A.D. (2011). "Application of the NREGS in the Food Crop Sector for Improving Food Security in Kerala: A Theoretical Analysis", *The Asian Economic Review* 53(2): 357-68. Hyderabad: The Indian Institute of Economics.

Narayanan, Sudha (2008). "Employment Guarantee, Women's Work and Child Care", *Economic and Political Weekly* XLIII(9): 10-13, 1 March.

Pramod Kumar and I. Maruthi (2011). *Impact of NREGS on Wage Rates, Food Security and Rural Urban Migration with All-India Coverage: Karnataka and a Consolidated Study.* Bangalore: Institute for Social and Economic Change.

Reddy, D. Narasimha (2011). "Functioning of National Rural Employment Guarantee Scheme (NREGS) in Andhra Pradesh", Paper presented at Final workshop under CDS-ASSR project on *Monitoring the Implementation of Social Security for the Working Poor in India's Informal Economy.* Thiruvananthpuram: Centre for Development Studies.

Shashi Rekha, H. (2013). "Socio-Economic Transformation Among Dalit Women Through MGNREGS: An Empirical Study", Paper presented at a National Seminar on *Development of Scheduled Castes and Scheduled Tribes: Opportunities, Achievements and Challenges.* Organised by Centre for Planning, Monitoring & Evaluation, National Institute of Rural Development, Hyderabad. 9-11 January.

Siva Kumar, R. (2013). "An Empirical Analysis of the Working of MGNREGP in Tamil Nadu", Paper presented at a National Seminar on *Development of Scheduled Castes and Scheduled Tribes: Opportunities, Achievements and Challenges.* Organised by Centre for Planning, Monitoring & Evaluation, National Institute of Rural Development, Hyderabad. 9-11 January.

Suresh Babu, V., K. Hanumantha Rao and B. Dhanyashree (2013). "Impact of MGNREGS on Scheduled Castes in Tamil Nadu", Paper presented at a National Seminar on *Development of Scheduled Castes and Scheduled Tribes: Opportunities, Achievements and Challenges.* Organised by Centre for Planning, Monitoring & Evaluation, National Institute of Rural Development, Hyderabad. 9-11 January.

3

K.K. TRIPATHY

In Pursuit of an Effective MGNREGA

Assessing Policy Options

Introduction and Background

The Mahatma Gandhi National Rural Employment Guarantee Act (MGNREGA) is in implementation in all the rural districts (644) of India. The main objective of MGNREGA is to provide for the enhancement of livelihood security of the rural households by ensuring a legal right of at least 100 days of unskilled wage employment to willing adult members. As a safety net for the poor, this Act aims at creating a demand-driven village infrastructure, including durable assets, in order to increase the opportunities for sustained employment.

Rural Unemployment and Work Participation

The employment guarantee programmes in the contemporary world comprise a broad range of goals starting from providing income relief by generating employment, creating productive public infrastructure, ameliorating poverty, cultivating workers' bargaining power in the local labour market, enhancing job opportunity and simplifying job search (Drèze and Sen, 1991; Basu *et al.*, 2009). Further, the employment guarantee in India is quite different from that of the developed nations as the nature of unemployment in countries like India is more complex. The poor in India cannot afford themselves to stay out of work for too long a period. In rural India, the people are not only irregularly employed, but are also largely classified as casual wage earners/labourers.[1]

Table 3.1 indicates that there is a large gap between the rates of current daily status unemployment and the usual principal status of unemployment. While the usual status of unemployment rate indicates chronic unemployment (as all those who are found usually unemployed in the reference year are counted as unemployed), the variation in the usual status and current daily status rates implies the presence of a high degree of intermittent unemployment in rural and urban areas. The intensity of intermittent unemployment is estimated to be higher in rural than the urban areas. This is mainly because of the absence of regular and sustainable employment opportunities for many workers. A low level of literacy highlights the low skill level amongst the employable people.

Besides, National Sample Survey Organisation's (NSSO) 66th Round Survey, 2009-10, and Census data indicate a large rural-urban and male-female divide in employment and attainment of literacy level (Table 3.1).

Table 3.1

Literacy and Unemployment Rates

Status	*Rural*			*Urban*		
	Male	*Female*	*Total*	*Male*	*Female*	*Total*
1	2	3	4	5	6	7
I. Unemployment rate (2009-10)						
Usual-principal status	19	24	21	30	70	37
Current weekly status	32	37	33	36	72	42
Current daily status	64	80	68	51	91	58
II. Literacy, 2011 (%)	77.2	57.9	67.8	88.8	79.1	84.1

Sources: 1. *Key Indicators of Employment and Unemployment in India, 2009-10* (NSS 66th Round Survey); 2. Census of India, 2011.

1. NSSO defines a casual wage labourer as a person who is casually engaged in others' farm or non-farm enterprises and in return receives wages as per the terms of the daily or periodic work contract. In 2009-10, among the three statuses in employment, at the all-India level in the rural areas, self-employment had the dominant share (nearly 54%) in usual status (principal and subsidiary) workforce, while the share of casual labour stood at 39 per cent and the rest (7%) of the workforce was regular wage/salaried employees (NSSO 66th Round).

Estimates of population, labour force and workforce from NSSO data reveal that there has been a reduction of 20.94 million women in labour force and 20.05 million in entire workforce during 2009-10 as compared to 2004-05 (Table 3.2). This had happened when the share of women in the population improved from 48.1 per cent in 2004-05 to 48.4 per cent in 2009-10. Similarly, in case of men, the labour force growth rate was 1.5 per cent as compared to the male population growth rate of 1.6 per cent. While the work participation rate for men between these two periods were more or less stagnant; whereas the female work participation rate reduced by 5.99, from 28.04 in 2004-05 to 22.05 in 2009-10.

Table 3.2

Comparative Estimates of Population, Labour Force and Workforce (in million)

Category	*2009-10*			*2004-05*		
	Male	*Female*	*Person*	*Male*	*Female*	*Person*
1	*2*	*3*	*4*	*5*	*6*	*7*
Population	612.44	575.29	1,187.73	565.79	523.82	1,089.61
Labour Force	340.46	129.90	470.36	315.94	150.84	466.78
Workforce	333.59	126.84	460.43	308.81	146.89	455.70
Unemployed	6.87	3.06	9.93	7.13	3.95	11.08
Labour Force Participation Rate (LFPR)	55.59	22.58	39.60	55.84	28.80	42.84
Work Participation Rate (WPR)	54.47	22.05	38.77	54.58	28.04	41.82

Note: LFPR is the number of persons in the labour force per 1,000 persons/person-days; WPR measures the number of persons employed per 1,000 persons/person-days.

Source: Kanan and Raveendran (2012).

An analysis of data on WPR in the country shows that the rural male WPR during 1983-84 to 2009-10 has remained constant, whereas the decline in female WPR has been relatively steep (Table 3.3).

The low WPR could be ascribed to the non-availability of employment opportunities and the necessary investment needed for job avenues in rural sectors. MGNREGA, in this context, is expected to tap the potential of rural areas for creation of job opportunities by regenerating village economy in the long run (GoI, 2008) and remove demand–side rigidities from the rural scenario.

Table 3.3

Rural Worker Population Ratio during 1983 to 2009-10

(Per 1000 person/person-days)

Category	*1983-84*	*1987-88*	*1993-94*	*1999-00*	*2004-05*	*2007-08*	*2009-10*
1	2	3	4	5	6	7	8
Male	547	539	553	531	546	548	547
Female	340	323	328	299	327	289	261

Source: Statement 32, NSS Report No. 531: *Employment and Unemployment Situation in India*: July, 2007-June, 2008 and July, 2009-June, 2010 (NSS 64th Round of Survey) and *Key Indicators of Employment and Unemployment in India, 2009-10*: July, 2009-June, 2010 (NSS 66th Round Survey).

In this backdrop, implementing an employment guarantee act and considering employability to be a legal right have considerable economic, social and political significance. The state-specific Rural Employment Guarantee Schemes (REGS), which are the consequence of MGNREGA, place a judicially enforceable obligation on the state (GoI, 2013). The REGS is expected to work towards relieving rural households of poverty and hunger by ensuring employment, income and livelihood support.

Literature Review

Several scholars have tried to look into the implementation aspects of MGNREGA since its launch *viz.*, creation of rural assets, rural wage formation and its consolidation processes, attendance of labour in public and private works, shortage of labour in private works and the impact of MGNREGA on agricultural productivity, rural-urban migration, rural poverty, etc.

Ahuja *et al.* (2011) studied the impact of MGNREGA on rural employment and migration in the agriculturally backward and forward districts of Haryana and found that the extent of employment is more pronounced in agriculturally backward district than that in the advanced districts as the farmers owning large size of landholdings and more number of livestock, who are migrating to other places for employment and are indebted, are less likely to work under MGNREGA. The high wage differentials between market wage rate and MGNREGA wage has not been successful in limiting migration from the rural areas.

A study of Channaveer *et al.* (2011) has revealed a significant difference in the use of machine power between fully and partially implemented MGNREGA villages due to higher wage rates in the former category of villages. While the wage rates in fully implemented MGNREGA villages were higher in comparison to the partially implemented ones, the productivity of labour in the former was found to be lower *vis-à-vis* the latter.

Kamath (2010) analysed the design and implementation of MGNREGA and found that, in spite of legal social and livelihood security framework, lack of effective decentralisation and participation of village communities in planning and implementation of the shelf of works[2] under MGNREGA has impacted the programme spread and outreach. Analysing the NSS 62nd round of employment and unemployment data, she argued for a close alignment of agriculture and its seasonal operation with MGNREGA work planning in order to ensure participation of vast underemployed and casually–employed in the rural areas.

Basu *et al.* (2009) analysed labour market implications of the government Employment Guarantee Scheme (EGS) and stated that the EGS can potentially serve two distinct types of purposes: to enhance efficiency in labour markets; and to alleviate poverty by employing workers otherwise left out of the labour market.

Using pooled household level data for the states of Rajasthan and Andhra Pradesh, Jha *et al.* (2009) found that the size of landholding is a negative predictor of National Rural Employment Guarantee Programme (NREGP) participation. Inequity in land holding pattern and higher ratio of NREGP to agricultural wage rate also contributed to the participation rate in MGNREGA works.

Bezu and Holden (2008) studied the public works programme (Food for Work) in Ethiopia and realised that the public works

---

2. Clause 4 of Sub-Section 3 of Section 16, MGNREGA 2005 mandates every *gram panchayat* to prepare a development plan and maintain a series of preferred and projected works for execution under MGNREGA.

encouraged adoption of fertilisers and had no production disincentive effect. They recommended improvement in the planning and distribution of public works through targeting of the poorest as well as through price revision to self-select the needy.

Objective, Data, Methodology and Section Plan

Objective

The objective of this paper is to examine the following research issues:

i) What is the trend/pattern in the implementation of MGNREGA?
ii) What are the factors responsible for effective implementation of this right–based wage employment intervention?
iii) Which policy options should be adopted in pursuit of effective implementation of MGNREGA?

Data and Methodology

The paper analyses secondary data collected from the Ministries/Departments/Agencies of GoI. Besides, data on the implementation of the programme in selected major states have been analysed. This paper also examines the trend in the generation of wage-employment and financial progress under MGNREGA. Although in-house data of Ministry of Rural Development (MoRD) are used for analysing implementation variables of MGNREGA, the study relies on various rounds of NSS employment and unemployment survey so as to shed light on the picture of employment/unemployment, work participation in agriculture and public works.

Section Plan

The following section (Section III) presents a brief review of the progress of implementation of MGNREGA in a few states. Section IV discusses types and nature of tasks taken up under MGNREGA and its linkage with agriculture. Issues responsible for effective implementation of MGNREGA and the possible policy options towards their resolution are deliberated upon in Section V. Section VI presents the concluding remarks.

MGNREGA: The Journey So Far

In this section, the status of implementation of MGNREGA has been reviewed and issues analysed. Due to some missing data, out of the 34 states/Union Territories (UTs) which are implementing MGNREGA, 26 states have been considered here for the analysis.

Expenditure and Employment

During 2007-08 to 2013-14, the expenditure as a percentage of total available funds showed a skewed distribution, ranging between 38.0 (Maharashtra) and 102.5 (Rajasthan) during 2007-08; 54.1 (Karnataka) and 94.4 (Mizoram) during 2008-09; 50.3 (Maharashtra) and 96.1 (Odisha) during 2009-10; 51.5 (Rajasthan) and 105.8 (Manipur) during 2010-11; 43.7 (Manipur) and 105.0 (Maharashtra) during 2011-12; 71.5 (Tripura) and 109.8 (Andhra Pradesh) during 2012-13 and 83.1 (Maharashtra) and 103.6 (Gujarat) during 2013-14 (Table 3.4).

For all the states under reference, the expenditure as a percentage of total available funds witnessed 9.4 percentage points increase, from 82.0 per cent in 2007-08 to 91.6 per cent in 2013-14. The employment (of any duration) provided to jobs demanded under MGNREGA during the reference years were 98.8, 99.1, 99.4, 98.5, 99.1, 96.9 and 92.5 per cent, respectively. The variation in the performance of this parameter between 2007-08 and 2013-14 indicates the prevalence of rationing of demand and weaknesses in the demand management system at the village level. This indicator, however, witnessed a skewed distribution across the states, indicating varying intensity of rightful implementation of the Act. Some states also recorded full employment *vis-à-vis* the demand. However, what remains to be examined is how many people, who have been issued job cards, have actually demanded employment. As per reports (*www.rural.nic.in*), the gap between the number of job cards issued and employment demanded is wide, which could be due to the belief of the applicant that mere registration of application or issuance of a job card ensures unemployment benefits to the job-seeker. Job-seekers may not be aware that after registration, they have to demand employment.

Table 3.4

Expenditure and Employment Performance under MGNREGA (2007-08 to 2013-14)

S. No.	States	% of Expenditure Against Total Available Fund							% Employment (Household) Provided to Demanded						
		2007-08	2008-09	2009-10	2010-11	2011-12	2012-13	2013-14	2007-08	2008-09	2009-10	2010-11	2011-12	2012-13	2013-14
1	Andhra Pradesh	90.9	80.0	83.8	59.7	73.4	109.8	99.9	100.0	100.0	100.0	100.0	100.0	100.0	91.4
2	Assam	68.1	69.8	72.6	72.6	86.0	93.5	90.9	96.9	87.1	99.9	99.5	99.6	99.0	95.5
3	Bihar	69.0	60.2	77.0	83.3	69.2	73.6	87.1	97.6	100.0	100.0	99.5	98.0	95.8	86.6
4	Chhattisgarh	92.4	71.5	81.2	73.2	82.2	82.6	93.7	99.5	100.0	100.0	100.0	99.5	96.6	91.4
5	Gujarat	64.5	69.7	75.3	61.5	72.1	76.7	103.6	100.0	100.0	100.0	99.9	98.2	90.9	90.0
6	Haryana	90.2	66.9	73.8	92.5	93.9	99.8	87.2	100.0	94.8	100.0	99.1	99.7	97.3	89.5
7	Himachal Pradesh	77.8	66.3	89.3	61.2	75.8	87.3	95.9	98.4	98.2	99.6	99.4	95.5	94.2	94.2
8	Jammu & Kashmir	47.3	57.4	72.8	91.6	50.5	87.9	96.1	99.9	92.9	95.4	98.9	97.9	98.2	92.3
9	Jharkhand	84.7	56.8	71.7	78.4	69.3	74.4	92.5	100.0	100.0	100.0	99.9	99.5	98.9	93.5
10	Karnataka	54.2	54.1	81.7	87.6	82.2	77.4	95.6	99.3	98.9	97.5	92.1	99.3	90.6	75.9
11	Kerala	83.6	75.4	79.8	83.5	92.6	95.5	98.9	71.5	99.0	99.8	99.1	99.9	90.1	90.8
12	Madhya Pradesh	87.9	70.0	65.6	65.7	65.2	81.7	107.7	100.0	100.0	100.0	99.1	99.6	99.4	92.1
13	Maharashtra	38.0	58.5	50.3	59.9	105.0	92.6	83.1	100.0	99.8	100.0	99.4	99.0	98.8	90.9
14	Manipur	98.1	90.6	76.9	105.8	43.7	88.4	84.4	100.0	100.0	100.0	99.2	93.6	99.8	100.0
15	Meghalaya	68.9	81.5	72.7	96.2	85.0	87.8	103.5	99.1	93.6	99.3	96.8	99.8	99.7	98.9
16	Mizoram	91.4	94.4	80.2	105.3	60.0	100.2	100.2	100.0	100.0	100.0	100.0	96.0	99.5	100.0
17	Nagaland	53.3	94.2	79.4	95.2	77.2	88.6	90.1	100.0	100.0	100.0	100.0	100.0	99.9	99.9

contd...

...contd...

18	Odisha	71.5	64.5	96.1	85.6	76.1	84.7	94.5	96.6	98.2	98.7	98.8	99.1	90.5	90.5
19	Punjab	59.8	62.4	71.0	71.9	79.8	90.6	99.8	100.0	100.0	99.7	99.8	99.7	97.1	90.7
20	Rajasthan	102.5	85.1	69.1	51.9	70.6	81.1	88.8	99.9	100.0	100.0	95.2	96.1	93.0	91.6
21	Sikkim	82.8	88.9	62.5	102.1	46.8	99.5	92.8	90.3	99.0	100.0	100.0	97.9	99.1	96.8
22	Tamil Nadu	73.7	55.9	73.0	82.2	79.4	90.1	73.2	100.0	100.0	100.0	100.0	99.5	99.4	99.3
23	Tripura	95.5	94.5	75.8	99.0	93.4	71.5	96.3	99.6	100.0	99.8	99.9	99.9	99.8	99.1
24	Uttar Pradesh	85.2	75.8	82.7	78.0	74.6	85.5	87.2	99.8	100.0	96.7	97.7	99.5	94.5	90.8
25	Uttarakhand	62.5	87.2	78.8	94.1	88.0	95.8	93.7	100.0	100.0	100.0	100.0	99.6	99.1	98.2
26	West Bengal	75.4	70.4	87.6	91.1	90.4	89.0	97.2	98.0	100.0	99.7	99.7	99.7	99.5	95.1
	All India	82.0	72.9	76.5	72.7	76.0	87.2	91.6	98.8	99.1	99.4	98.5	99.1	96.9	92.5

Source: MoRD, Government of India (*www.nrega.nic.in*).

Table 3.5

Unskilled Wage and Material Expenditure under MGNREGA (2007-08 to 2013-14)

S. No.	*States*	*Ratio of Expenses on Unskilled Wage to Others*				*% of Expenditure on Material to Total*			
		2007-08	*2009-10*	*2011-12*	*2013-14*	*2007-08*	*2009-10*	*2011-12*	*2013-14*
1	2	3	4	5	6	7	8	9	10
1	Andhra Pradesh	6.1:1	4.7:1	3.2:1	2.4:1	1.8	12.9	23.6	29.3
2	Assam	1.8:1	1.6:1	1.9:1	2.2:1	33.8	32.4	34.9	31.4
3	Bihar	1.4:1	1.6:1	1.2:1	1.3:1	40.7	32.3	45.0	44.4
4	Chhattisgarh	1.8:1	1.8.1	3.0:1	3.5:1	33.9	30.4	25.1	22.3
5	Gujarat	1.9:1	2.4:1	1.4:1	1.8:1	14.6	25.6	41.9	35.3
6	Haryana	1.8:1	1.6:1	1.8:1	2.1:1	33.7	33.1	36.2	32.7
7	Himachal Pradesh	1.1:1	1.2:1	2.0:1	2.3:1	47.2	35.6	33.3	30.4
8	Jammu and Kashmir	1.8:1	1.8:1	1.1:1	1.2:1	33.7	16.6	46.9	45.4
9	Jharkhand	1.4:1	1.4:1	2.0:1	2.1:1	40.8	36.1	33.8	32.3
10	Karnataka	1.5:1	1.7:1	1.6:1	2.5:1	39.3	35.3	38.2	28.2
11	Kerala	7.9:1	6.6:1	26:1	32.4:1	5.0	7.0	3.7	3.0
12	Madhya Pradesh	1.7:1	1.4:1	1.5:1	2.2:1	35.4	35.9	39.8	31.4
13	Maharashtra	17.5:1	4.1:1	2.4:1	2.2:1	4.9	5.7	29.2	31.6
14	Manipur	1.5:1	1.5:1	13:1	2.8:1	40.0	31.7	7.1	26.5
15	Meghalaya	5.1:1	1.7:1	2.0:1	4.2:1	15.2	29.1	33.0	19.4
16	Mizoram	5.1:1	2.9:1	2.4:1	5.2:1	11.6	16.0	29.2	16.1

17	Nagaland	1.5:1	1.4:1	1.5:1	2.5:1	37.3	29.5	40.5	28.8
18	Odisha	1.4:1	1.6:1	1.3:1	3.1:1	41.3	33.9	43.0	24.5
19	Punjab	1.4:1	1.7:1	1.5:1	2.3:1	39.0	29.0	40.2	30.8
20	Rajasthan	2.7:1	2.2:1	1.7:1	3:1	25.5	25.7	37.7	25.1
21	Sikkim	4.2:1	1.8:1	1.8:1	1.3:1	19.3	29.5	35.7	43.2
22	Tamil Nadu	27.3:1	33.9:1	38:1	31.2:1	0.0	0.0	0.3	3.1
23	Tripura	2.0:1	1.7:1	1.8:1	2.1:1	31.5	32.9	36.1	31.8
24	Uttar Pradesh	1.5:1	1.5:1	1.9:1	2.2:1	38.8	33.4	33.9	31.4
25	Uttarakhand	1.5:1	1.7:1	1.5:1	1.7:1	36.1	30.6	39.5	37.0
26	West Bengal	3.6:1	1.9:1	2.0:1	2.4:1	19.4	26.9	33.0	29.7
	Total	2.0:1	2.1:1	2.3:1	2.8:1	30.1	27.1	30.5	26.6

Source: Compiled from data on MGNREGA of MoRD. *www.nrega.nic.in*

Labour-Intensive Unskilled Works

MGNREGA discourages engagement of semi-skilled/skilled workers as the activities taken up under MGNREGA are labour intensive unskilled manual works. Thus, to encourage planning and execution of labour-oriented activities, the expenses incurred under semi-skilled and skilled labour are treated as expenses on material. This has the propensity to limit the material intensity of the total works undertaken under MGNREGA. Under MGNREGA, the ratio of expenses on unskilled wages to other expenses should ideally be 1.5:1.0 (i.e., 60:40). In five states (Bihar, Himachal Pradesh [HP], Jharkhand, Odisha and Punjab), this ratio has been less than the desired minimum during 2007-08 (Table 3.5). During 2013-14, all states under reference conformed to the 60:40 norm, except Bihar (1.4:1) and Jammu & Kashmir (1.1:1). The data on percentage of expenditure made on materials to the total expenditure has been well below 40 per cent ceiling indicating that a large part of the programme funds are directed towards payment of unskilled wages.

The exceptionally high ratio of expenses on unskilled wage to others in some states (Andhra Pradesh, Kerala and Tamil Nadu), may be mainly due to two reasons such as: non reporting or under-reporting of the amount spent on semi-skilled, skilled and other materials; and excessive stress on earth works that require minimal expenses on activities other than the payment made for unskilled wages.

Employment Guarantee: Goal and Achievement

Average person-days employment per household was recorded at 39.8 during 2008-09 (Table 3.6). There was an improvement in the provision of employment under MGNREGA during 2009-10 as the average person–days employment per household increased by 14.3 person-days to 54.1 person–days per household over 2008-09. But this average person-days employment per household declined to 46.8 during 2010-11 and to 45.97 during 2013-14, thereby indicating that MGNREGA did not attract a specific demand pattern in the rural area during the last six years.

Table 3.6

Average Person-days Employment under MGNREGA (2008-09 to 2013-14)

S. No.	States	Average Person-days Employment Per Household					
		2008-09	2009-10	2010-11	2011-12	2012-13	2013-14
1	2	3	4	5	6	7	8
1	Andhra Pradesh	34.55	65.67	54.05	58.81	55.92	49.57
2	Assam	33.76	34.29	26.16	26.14	25.43	23.66
3	Bihar	26.42	27.55	33.82	38.55	45.12	41.87
4	Chhattisgarh	54.95	51.41	44.67	44.28	45.28	51.71
5	Gujarat	20.47	36.65	44.87	38.07	41.39	39.80
6	Haryana	37.35	37.74	35.79	39.37	43.81	36.28
7	Himachal Pradesh	33.53	57.29	49.4	53.44	50.92	52.39
8	Jharkhand	43.37	49.48	41.81	38.72	39.93	38.30
9	Karnataka	81.41	56.62	49.35	42.43	46.38	49.56
10	Kerala	18.26	34.22	40.85	44.70	54.89	56.83
11	Madhya Pradesh	45.67	55.66	49.87	43.53	39.77	42.26
12	Maharashtra	49.26	46.38	44.33	51.31	53.70	45.26
13	Manipur	41.58	73.15	68.14	62.90	62.40	24.86
14	Meghalaya	31.46	49.41	57.72	50.05	52.43	58.98
15	Mizoram	49.61	94.57	97.13	77.41	87.81	75.29
16	Nagaland	49.28	87.4	95.3	79.55	63.47	44.87
17	Odisha	34.08	39.57	48.71	32.91	34.14	41.62
18	Punjab	42.69	28.37	27.11	26.29	27.27	32.68
19	Rajasthan	58.94	68.97	51.64	46.89	52.25	50.86
20	Sikkim	39.17	79.92	85.35	60.13	64.12	69.58
21	Tamil Nadu	32.43	54.67	54.05	47.54	57.80	58.67
22	Tripura	40.03	79.56	67.23	86.41	86.92	88.19
23	Uttar Pradesh	43.01	64.91	52.07	36.48	28.54	35.11
24	Uttarakhand	33.85	34.92	42.44	42.40	43.66	41.67
25	West Bengal	19.4	44.59	31.07	27.12	34.70	37.45
	Total	39.8	54.1	46.79	43.20	46.20	45.97

Note: Due to inconsistency in the data for Jammu & Kashmir, the same was not considered.
Source: Compiled from data on MGNREGA of MoRD, *www.nrega.nic.in*

When one compares the number of households which received the MGNREGA mandated 100 days of employment with the total number of households which demanded employment under the Act, a dismal picture in the performance of the Act emerges (Table 3.7). During 2008-09, out of the total number of households demanding employment, only 3.4 per cent of the households could be assured 100 days of employment. During 2009-10, the MGNREGA performance marked an improvement as 11.1 per cent of households could obtain the promised employment. The performance of this indicator slid down to 10.0 per cent and 9.04 per cent in 2010-11 and 2011-12, respectively. Although there was a slight improvement noticed in 2012-13 (11.34%), it registered a steep decline to 8.99 per cent in 2013-14.

During 2008-09, out of the total household demanding employment, only 9 states (Andhra Pradesh [AP], Assam, Chhattisgarh, Haryana, Madhya Pradesh [MP], Meghalaya, Rajasthan, Tamil Nadu and Uttar Pradesh [UP]) recorded higher than the national average of 3.4 per cent. Similarly, during 2009-10, AP, Karnataka, MP, Nagaland, Rajasthan, Sikkim, Tamil Nadu, Tripura and UP recorded higher than the national average of 11.1 per cent. Similarly, while Andhra Pradesh, MP, Manipur, Mizoram, Nagaland, Odisha, Sikkim, Tamil Nadu and Tripura were above the national average of 10.0 per cent during 2010-11; AP, Chhattisgarh, HP, Kerala, Maharashtra, Meghalaya, Rajasthan, Sikkim, Tamil Nadu and Tripura registered higher than the national average of wage employment during 2013-14.

The employment guarantee under MGNREGA is a legal guarantee provided to each and every rural household. The figure presented in Tables 3.6 and 3.7 also highlights that every rural household is probably reluctant to take up the job offered by the government under the Act due to the prevalence of any one or more limiting factors such as: a) rationing in the programme administration in the rural areas, b) growing wage differentials, c) arbitrary selection of works and award of job offer and d) lack of beneficiary/worker friendly environment at the ground level programme administrative machinery.

Table 3.7

Percentage of Rural Eligible Households Assured 100 Days of Employment under MGNREGA (2008-09 to 2013-14)

No.	*States*	*% of Households Assured 100 Days of Employment to Total Employment Demanded*					
		2008-09	*2009-10*	*2010-11*	*2011-12*	*2012-13*	*2013-14*
1	2	3	4	5	6	7	8
1	Andhra Pradesh	5.5	22.7	15.6	18.98	17.32	11.38
2	Assam	4.9	6.1	2.5	1.16	0.79	1.17
3	Bihar	0.5	6.9	6.0	9.43	8.29	5.19
4	Chhattisgarh	4.8	7.9	7.4	7.58	8.95	12.60
5	Gujarat	2.0	6.5	6.2	4.99	6.98	4.56
6	Haryana	9.0	5.6	3.8	4.93	6.59	3.89
7	Himachal Pradesh	3.0	9.7	4.9	9.08	7.40	9.69
8	Jharkhand	2.5	7.8	6.6	3.67	6.04	5.65
9	Karnataka	1.8	12.3	5.4	2.71	7.10	6.16
10	Kerala	0.4	4.0	5.7	8.80	20.10	24.22
11	Madhya Pradesh	5.3	14.4	10.5	7.82	5.54	5.55
12	Maharashtra	2.0	3.8	6.2	12.97	14.07	9.75
13	Manipur	0.4	0.0	25.0	29.49	0.53	0.00
14	Meghalaya	8.4	4.4	5.5	10.48	16.01	14.88
15	Mizoram	0.0	3.9	77.2	42.99	19.44	0.00
16	Nagaland	0.0	31.8	54.2	22.07	13.92	0.24
17	Odisha	1.5	5.8	10.1	3.42	4.25	8.30
18	Punjab	0.3	2.8	1.9	1.54	1.55	2.72
19	Rajasthan	16.7	23.2	8.1	7.13	9.30	11.30
20	Sikkim	0.7	23.3	45.6	15.66	20.76	21.42
21	Tamil Nadu	7.3	17.4	22.2	9.45	18.98	14.59
22	Tripura	0.1	36.5	14.6	35.18	37.88	47.86
23	Uttar Pradesh	8.1	14.1	9.1	4.20	1.35	2.92
24	Uttarakhand	0.5	4.0	4.7	4.74	5.11	6.92
25	West Bengal	0.1	2.1	2.1	2.16	4.33	4.36
	Total	3.4	11.1	10.0	9.04	11.34	8.99

Note: Due to inconsistency in the data for Jammu & Kashmir, the same was not considered.

Source: Compiled from data on MGNREGA of MoRD (*www.nrega.nic.in*).

MGNREGA Works and Agriculture

Schedule I (Paragraph 4) of MGNREGA 2005 has laid down activities permissible under the Act. These are rural connectivity, flood control/protection and drought proofing, water conservation/ harvesting, minor irrigation, renovation of water bodies and land development. These activities, by its nature and medium of intervention, have important effects on supply conditions, productivity, and sustainability of rural economic activities. Works carried out under MGNREGA not only aim at generating wage employment in rural areas, but also envisage improvements in the agricultural production and productivity. Quite appropriately, Schedule I (Paragraph 3) of MGNREGA 2005 mandates creation of durable assets and strengthening of the livelihood resource base of the rural poor.

The category of works taken up under MGNREGA during 2008-09 and 2013-14 presented in Table 3.8.

During 2008-09 and 2013-14, there is a sharp increase in the number of works taken up under MGNREGA. While 27.75 lakh works were ongoing during 2008-09, during 2013-14, 93.13 lakh of works were under execution. On an average, 73 per cent of total works concerned agriculture–related activities *viz.*, water conservation and water harvesting, micro-irrigation and land development. During 2008-09 and 2013-14, the agriculture related works grew by 124.5 per cent.

Agricultural Statistics at a Glance, 2010 published by Ministry of Agriculture, the Government of India (GoI), explains that out of the country's total geographical area of 329 million hectares, the net sown area is 140.3 million hectares. However, the net irrigated area of the country is only 60.2 million hectares. As much as 174 million hectares of land in the country face degradation problems due to water and wind erosion like water logging, salinity, alkalinity, ravines, etc. In this context, MGNREGA's focus on water and soil conservation, water harvesting, minor irrigation and land development would support the sustainable management of agro-resources in rural areas, besides creating green jobs.

Table 3.8

MGNREGA Works in Terms of Type and Growth

(Works in lakh numbers and growth in per cent)

No.	*Type of Work*	*2008-09*	*2009-10*	*2010-11*	*2011-12*	*2012-13*	*2013-14*	*Growth (%) in 2013-14 over 2008-09*
1	*2*	*3*	*4*	*5*	*6*	*7*	*8*	*9*
1	Water conservation	11.34	20.44	20.81	43.8	44.09	27.49	142.4
2	Micro irrigation	1.45	2.99	3.45	5.01	4.27	4.04	178.6
3	Irrigation facility to individual land owners	5.67	7.73	9.15	9.16	11.92	12.78	125.4
4	Land development	3.98	6.38	7.04	6.32	6.61	6.06	52.2
5	Works with linkage to agriculture	22.44 (81%)	37.54 (81%)	40.45 (79%)	64.29 (80%)	66.89 (64%)	50.37 (54%)	124.5 -
6	Total works	27.75 (100%)	46.17 (100%)	50.99 (100%)	80.76 (100%)	104.6 (100%)	93.13 (100%)	235.6

Note: The difference between the total work and agri-related work is defined as 'Other works', which include rural connectivity, Rajiv Gandhi Seva Kendra, coastal areas, rural drinking water, fisheries, rural sanitation, play ground, *Aanganwadi*, etc.

Source: MoRD, GoI.

MGNREGA: A Few Implementation Issues

The Section 3(1) of the Act guarantees a minimum of 100 days of unskilled wage employment to rural households, irrespective of their poverty status. Every state government is mandated to make Mahatma Gandhi National Employment Guarantee Schemes (MGNREGS) to give effect to the provisions contained in Section 3 of the Act. The responsibility of the implementation of the scheme, however, is vested with the states, as per the Section 18 of the Act. The states implementing the scheme are legally obliged to provide at least 100 days of employment upon demand by opening up asset-creating public works programmes at the stipulated wage rate, as notified under the Section 6(1) of the Act, to the participating rural households.

Undoubtedly, MGNREGA has progressed against the context of persistent poverty and inequality in rural areas and has been embedded into the policy architecture of an all-inclusive growth. However, implementation bottlenecks at the last mile of its execution have turned it into a target–oriented and supply–driven public works programme. An analysis of programme database of MoRD indicates that the average person-days per household have reduced to 46 days (2013-14) from 48 days (2008-09). Although the women participation rate has always been over and above the statutory minimum of 33 per cent, the reduced SC (scheduled caste)/ST (scheduled tribe) participation rate from an all-time high of 61 per cent in 2006-07 to 48 per cent in 2008-09 and to 40 per cent in 2013-14 indicated disinclination of the most disadvantaged sections of our society to opt for public works under MGNREGA. Further, on an average, only about 10 per cent of the total households could complete 100 days of guaranteed job during 2008-09 and 2013-14. Since inception of MGNREGA (2 February 2006), barely 56 per cent of the total works have been completed as on 31 March 2014 (Ministry of Rural Development, 2014). The reduced participation of vulnerable sections of our society in MGNREGA and skewed performance of the programme over the last eight years of its implementation have necessiated examination of a few important implementation issues and contemplation of possible reformative actions.

Fixing Demand-Side Rigidities

The most distinguishing feature of MGNREGA from the earlier rural public works programmes is that it has provided a legal entitlement to work on demand. The Act vests responsibility of planning, execution and monitoring of programme provisions on the community with a view to put in place a demand-driven, self-selecting, right-based, people-centric and bottom-up public works programme. In spite of its in-built demand-driven nature, the implementing states are yet to establish an accurate and systemic infrastructure for timely and accurate capture of the labour demands. Like earlier public works programme, the states have decide to open up tasks without linking those to the work demand of the people.

A case in point is the non-implementation of mandated provisions on unemployment allowance (Section 7 of the Act) due to rampant reported rationing of labour demand. Further, the legality of the provisions relating to payment of unemployment allowance have got restricted and could not be invoked against the implementing states due to non-provision of dated receipt of job applications to the job applicants. In addition, there is low awareness among potential workers about the right-based provisions of the Act. This severely restricts the ability of these rural voiceless poor to demand work, exercise their rights and fully participate to avail of all the entitlements under the Act.

This calls for a deep review of the demand side of the programme implementation in order to put legal entitlements of the rural labour at the heart of the programme. Prior to establishing area-specific robust systems for maintaining accurate record of labour demand, the states need to carry out a detailed survey of all job-card holder households. This attempt would not only help in weeding out duplicate/fake job-cards in circulation and eliminate ghost job-seekers under MGNREGA, but will also throw light on accurate quantum and timing of labour demand. The genuineness of the demand could get reinforced if the state invites work application from the potential workers by organising regular community level *Rozgar Diwas* (employment guarantee days).

Making Decentralised Rural Planning Participative

The Act mandates preparation of Labour Budget (LB)—an essential annual work plan document that entails planning, approval, funding and project execution modalities, in accordance with the provisions made in sections 13–16 of the Act. It was presumed that the participating districts would strictly adhere to the principle of bottom-up approach from planning to approval of the selected shelf of projects for supporting implementation of this people-centric programme. Since the community level self-government institutions were not trained enough to plan, approve and run the programme, the perspective plans were mostly prepared at the district level by the government functionaries, thereby creating disconnect between what is planned and what people needed. Infrequent meetings and low participation at the *gram sabhas* further dampened the spirit of the wage employment programme.

The Act has placed wage employment through active community participation at the centre of the district development planning for rural livelihoods. The *panchayats* are the core planning units, while the district plan is the consolidation and integration of the plans of these units. Thus, the districts should emphasise on participatory decentralised visioning for articulation of goals and outcomes on wage employment initiatives, livelihoods and infrastructure in the district as a whole. The participatory visioning exercise should analyse livelihoods and outcomes, and the potential and resources available at the local levels as well as at the state and national level. It must also focus on capturing the core contents of development and of backwardness, as well as aspirations of the people. This would only be possible when the *panchayat* functionaries are appropriately trained, sensitised and equipped with adequate level of technical expertise in terms of assessing natural resources in the district.

Eliminating Delays in Wage Payments

The Act mandates payment of wage payments within 15 days of completion of the work. However, substantial delays in wage payments have been recorded, which have become enormous disincentives for job-seekers to opt for MGNREGA works. On an average, around 40 per cent of the total wage payments are delayed for more than 15 days. In some cases, the delay is even more than three months. An integrated approach, starting from timely work measurement at the work site to the preparation of payment slips and fund transfer orders, is required to ensure timely disbursement of wages to the workers.

Robust Programme Advisory and Monitoring

The Act mandates the constitution of apex level programme advisory groups—Central Employment Guarantee Council (CEGC) at the national level and State Employment Guarantee Council (SEGC) at the state level—to not only to operationalise the provisions of the

Act as contained in its Operational Guidelines, but also to analyse the policy planning and implementation issues for their possible resolution. The CEGC in the centre and SEGCs in the states need to be established and their meetings convened frequently to identify policy and implementation issues in MGNREGA at the local, state and national levels for focusing on entitlements and livelihoods, covering processes and procedures, systems and institutions, achievement of scheme deliverables, techniques and technologies.

Quality of Assets

MGNREGA is often criticised for generating assets of inferior quality. The quality and durability of assets in MGNREGA have been compromised due to faulty work design, improper selection of project and work site, lack of survey of works, inaccurate work design estimates, inefficient work execution and inadequate supervision. In addition to this, 44 per cent of all works taken up under MGNREGA have remained incomplete. To get the appropriate economic return on the assets created under MGNREGA, we need to frame standardised quality parameters for public works permissible under the Act and raise a cadre of quality monitors both at the national and state levels so as to guide and supervise the quality, usability and durability of the assets so created.

Convergence is the Key

Land and watershed development, water conservation, and flood and drought proofing activities promise to contribute greatly to the economic and ecological development of rural areas, particularly in drought-prone and dry land areas. However, before the extension of MGNREGA to the hitherto untreated regions, efforts should be made to determine the priorities of permissible activities designed for creating durable community assets. Hence, the objective of asset creation should take into account local needs and priorities. Further, activities like irrigation, flood protection, water conservation, etc., should tap the funds budgeted by sectoral departments of the states concerned. Although the MoRD has initiated its effort in converging MGNREGA with other ongoing programmes under them

Ministry of Agriculture, Ministry of Water Resources, Ministry of Environment and Forests, Department of Land Resources, etc., there is an emerging need to devise and implement policy directives on convergence at the district/block/village level with the all-round co-operation of the district/block level sectoral line departments.

Focusing Community Audits

Transparency and accountability have been in-built into the design of MGNREGA in the form of pro-active disclosure and social audits. Although Audit of Scheme Rules 2011 has been notified, yet social audits in most of the states do not take place regularly and often social audits so conducted are not as per the rules outlined. Only a few states have established social audit units and appointed the directors. But these audit units have not been properly staffed and lack requisite funds for regular conduct of social audits. Further, in most of the states, the grievance redressal mechanism such as appointment of ombudsman, help line, kiosks, etc., have not been put in place. The time has come to think about the apt operation of community level audits with the help of the community itself. Information, education and communication in regard to social audit would bring in community ownership of rural assets created under the Scheme and sensitise them to treat the public investment as their own for assets sustainability in the future.

Conclusion

In the recent times, much concern has been conveyed in the country's media on the lack lustre effectiveness of the MGNREGA. Some of the vociferous dissidents have even clamoured for scrapping of the programme by attributing this ambitious right-based rural wage employment initiative to wasteful public extravagance and the harbinger of leakages and widespread corruption. Undeniably, there have been several constraining programme implementation issues and challenges which have failed considerably in adequately assuring the rights and entitlements to the needy job-seekers. However, the importance of MGNREGA in building a whole range of location-specific, nature-based quality and productive community assets cannot be undermined, considering its effective workability in a rural set-up riddled with high incidence of poverty, low work participation, increased casualisation of labour and heavy dependence on the agriculture and non-farm sectors.

MGNREGA broadens occupational choices and assures generation of employment opportunity in the rural areas. Looking at the current momentum in implementation of the scheme, it is expected that this endeavour not only requires a close, dedicated and effective execution at the grass-roots level, but also demands resolution of various demand and supply side rigidities in programme implementation. Further, a synchronised approach is needed to ensure rightful convergence of other ongoing development intervention with the benefits of this employment–generating and rural infrastructure-building initiative.

It is well documented that the present rural India requires sufficient work opportunities to meet the burgeoning demand for casual wage employment in the agriculture as well as rural non-farm sectors (Jatav and Sen, 2013). MGNREGA, through its rights-based and demand-driven approach, can be an effective instrument in absorbing casual wage employment demand and in enriching the rural economy by creating quality and durable community assets. Although public works are prone to leakages and corruption, transparency and accountability provisions are in-built into the rights-based MGNREGA. The real challenge the ways that the states adopt to implement the provisions made in the Act without compromising on the basic spirit of the Act.

References

Ahuja, U.R., D. Tyagi, S. Chauhan and R. Chaudhary (2011). "Impact of MGNREGA on Rural Employment and Migration: A Study in Agriculturally-backward and Agriculturally-advanced Districts of Haryana", *Agricultural Economics Research Review* 24: 495-502.

Basu, A.K., N.H. Chau and Ravi Kanbur (2009). "A Theory of Employment Guarantee: Contestability, Credibility and Distributional Concerns", *Journal of Public Economics* 93: 482-97.

Bezu, S. and S. Holden (2008). "Can Food-for-work Encourage Agricultural Production?", *Food Policy* 33: 541-49.

Channaveer, Lokesha H., L.B. Hugar, J.B. Deshmanya and S.B. Gudappa (2011). "Impact of MGNREGA on Input-use Pattern, Labour Productivity and Returns of Selected Crops in Gulbarga District, Karnataka", *Agricultural Economics Research Review* 24: 517-23.

GoI (2004-05 to 2009-10). *Annual Reports*. New Delhi: Ministry of Labour and Employment.

———. (2006). *The National Rural Employment Guarantee Act 2005 (NREGA).*

———. (2007 to 2011). *Financial and Physical Progress Report on MGNREGA*. Available at *www.nrega.nic.in, Ministry of Rural Development* (accessed on 26 December 2011).

———. (2008). *The National Rural Employment Guarantee Act 2005 (MGNREGA): Operational Guidelines 2008*. 3rd Edition. Ministry of Rural Development.

———. (2010). *Agricultural Statistics at a Glance, 2010*. New Delhi: Ministry of Agriculture.

———. (2011a). *Gazette Notification dated 14.01.2011*. New Delhi: Ministry of Rural Development.

———. (2011b). *Rural Labour Enquiry Report on General Characteristics of Rural Labour Households* (61st Round of NSS, 2004-05). Shimla/Chandigarh: Ministry of Labour (Labour Bureau).

———. (2013). *Mahatma Gandhi National Rural Employment Guarantee Act 2005*. Delhi: Universal Law Publishing Co. Pvt. Ltd.

Jha, R., S. Bhattacharyya, R. Gaiha and S. Shankar (2009). "Capture of Anti poverty Programs: An Analysis of the National Rural Employment Guarantee Program in India", *Journal of Asian Economics* 20: 456-64.

Kamath, R. (2010). "National Rural Guarantee Act: An Effective Safety Net?", *IIMB Management Review* 22: 42-55.

NSSO (1997). *Employment and Unemployment Situation in India: NSS Report No 438*, July 1993-June 1994 (NSS 50th Round Survey).

———. (2001). *Employment and Unemployment Situation in India: NSS Report No 468*, July 1999-June 2000 (NSS 55th Round Survey).

———. (2006). *Employment and Unemployment Situation in India: NSS Report No 516*, July 2004-June 2005 (NSS 61st Round Survey).

———. (2008). *Employment and Unemployment Situation in India: NSS Report No 531*. July 2007-June 2008 (NSS 64th Round Survey).

———. (2011). *Key Indicators of Employment and Unemployment in India: NSS 66th Round Survey*. July 2009- June 2010.

The Hindu (2011). "Is Rs. 25 All that You Need for a Day?"", *The Hindu*, 21 September. Available at: *http://www.thehindu.com/news/national/article2471104.ece* (accessed on 26 December 2011).

Jatav, M and S. Sen (2013). "Drivers of Non-Farm Employment in Rural India: Evidence from the 2009-10 NSSO Round", *Economic & Political Weekly* XLVIII(26 & 27): 14-21.

Kannan, K.P. and G. Raveendran (2012). "Counting and Profiling the Missing Labour Force", *Economic & Political Weekly* XLVII(6): 77-80.

Ministry of Rural Development (2014). *MIS Progress Reports*. Government of India. Available online at *http://164.100.129.6/netnrega/MISreport4.aspx?fin_year=2013-2014&rpt=RP*

4

A.D. MANIKANDAN and V. MATHEW KURIAN

An Assessment of MGNREGS in Attappady Tribal Block in Palakkad District, Kerala

Introduction

An alarming increase in the incidence and intensity of poverty and infant/child deaths due to starvation,[1] malnutrition and related health problems among the tribal groups in Attappady tribal block in Palakkad district of Kerala is a big shame on the facet of the so-called Kerala's towering achievements in social (human) development. Until the 1950s, Attappady had a very high forest cover (nearly 80% of its total geographical area) and shared some major features of the world famous bio-diversity hotspot Silent Valley of Western Ghats. Attappady was inhabited exclusively by hills tribes namely, Irulas, Mudugas (non-primitive group), and Kurumbas (primitive)[2] till the end of 20th century. But, a massive influx of land hungrier non-tribe settlers not only displaced the tribals from the most fertile region (Hoeschele, 1998; 2000; Kalathil, 2004; Valluva, 2006), but also devastated a large part of evergreen forest for agricultural uses (Purushothaman, 2005). Furthermore, during the influx of settlers, Attappady witnessed a tremendous change in socio-cultural institutional mechanisms of governing, conserving and utilising forest and other natural resources, and cultural practices of the tribes due to the influence of settler's socio-economic and political settings. A shift from traditional food crop cultivation to cash crop cultivation

---

1. Starvation deaths are not a new phenomenon in India. Reports of starvation deaths have been coming from other parts of the country, Jharkhand, Rajasthan, and Madhya Pradesh (Khera, 2008b).
2. The term primitive tribal groups (PTGs) replaced by particularly vulnerable tribal groups (PVTGs) (Government of India, 2010; 2013).

of tribal people, resulting in food insecurity and malnutrition problems among the tribes in the region is an example of such a change. The loss of the customary rights of tribes over forest, fertile land and traditional food crop cultivation, and unsustainable land use management of settlers have led to the emergence of wasteland facing desertification (ISA, 2006) and starvation in Attappady. Tribal women and children are the worst victims of it. There has been an alarming increase in the tribal infant/child mortality rate (UNICEF, 2013; Ekbal, 2013a; 2013b; 2013c; 2013d; Manikandan, 2013a; 2014; Suchitra, 2013a, 2013c; Ittyipe, 2013; Narikutty, 2013; Vasanth, 2013a). Government has introduced many developmental schemes, including poverty alleviation schemes, for benefiting the tribal people since 1960s. But, most of these schemes have miserably failed to ensure livelihood security and well-being of the tribal people in Attappady due to carelessness of the officials and exploitation of settlers. It is in this context, we have made an assessment of Mahatma Gandhi National Rural Employment Guarantee Scheme (MGNREGS) in Attappady. The MGNREGS, which assures 100 days of employment to every rural household whose adult members are willing to do unskilled manual works in an year (Manikandan, 2010; 2011; 2012), has not had a major impact on the tribal people in Attappady. It is understood that low awareness, lack of demand for work and delays in providing wages and employment has resulted in low performance of this programme among the tribals in the study area.

Socio-Economic Profile of Attappady

Luiz (1962) found that there were 48 tribal groups in Kerala. In 1965, a study on the SCs (scheduled castes) and STs (scheduled tribes) found that there were 38 tribal groups in the state. As per the study of the Government of Kerala, there were 41 tribal groups in the state (Harijan Welfare Department, 1975). Nai (1976) has brought out a list of 54 tribal groups in Kerala. The Kerala Public Service Commission has stated that there are 36 tribal groups in the state. Vayaleri (1996) has observed that there are 41 to 54 tribal groups in Kerala. From this, it can be inferred that the number of tribal groups varied from 36 to 54 in Kerala. As per the Census of 2001, 1.1 per cent of the total population of the state was tribes as compared to 1.4 per cent in 2011 (Government of India, 2001; 2011). Out of which, 37.4 per cent of the total tribes of the state was from Wayanad district and 13.9 per cent and 10.89 per cent were from Idukki and Palakkad Districts, respectively (Manikandan, 2013b).

As per the Census of 2001, a total of 66,171 persons are there in Attappady, of which, 36,026 belong to General category (54.44%), 3,024 are SCs, and about 27,121 belong to STs. The share of tribal population in the total population was just 41 per cent in 2001 compared to 100 per cent in 1931 and 90 per cent in 1951. Tribal community is divided into three groups viz., Mudugas, Irulas (NPTG) and Kurumbas (PTG). The shares of these groups in the total tribal people were 13 per cent, 77 per cent and 10 per cent, respectively (Table 4.1).

Table 4.1

Population in Attappady Tribal Block, 2001

S.No.	*Population*	*Values*
1	General	36,026 (54.44%)
2	Scheduled Castes	30,24 (4.56%)
3	Scheduled Tribes	27,121 (41%)
4	Irula	20,883 (77%)
5	Muduga	3,482 (13%)
6	Kurumba	2,755 (10%)
7	Total = 1+2+3	66,171 (100%)

Source: *AHADS Status Report 2010.*

Land alienation of the tribes is the highest in Kerala. Alienated land of the tribes is estimated to be more than 10,000 acres in Attappady alone (The Hindu 2013e). A study by Institute for Societal Advancement (2006) has found that more than one-third of the tribal families have less than 10 cent of land and only 23 per cent of the tribal families have above 2 acres of land. Many tribal families are forced to depend on degraded lands for nutrition and income due to alienation of fertile lands. Therefore, tribes are always demanding for their alienated lands (Suchitra, 2013b).

Attappady was once a land of evergreen forest which covered more than three-fourth of the total geographical area of the region. But a massive influx of land hungrier non-tribes, mostly from Tamil Nadu and low and mid lands of Kerala, encroached the evergreen forest for agricultural purposes and cultivated cash crops in Attappady. Immigration of Tamilians into the Attappady[3] region dates back to 15th century while that of non-tribes Malayali settlers goes back to mid-1950s (Kalathil, 2004). The coverage of evergreen forest has come down from more than three-forth to less than two-fourth of the total geographical area. As result, tribes lost immeasurable goods and services of forests such as minor forest produce. Forest law has exacerbated this situation further.

The poverty level in Attappady was 83 per cent, the highest in Kerala in 1997. According to the KILA (2008), there are 8,589 tribal households in Attappady, of which, 6,180 tribal households have ration cards. Only 25.34 per cent among them hold APL (above poverty line) ration cards and rest of them hold BPL (below poverty line) ration card. The literacy rates of male and female among the tribal population were 64 per cent and 56 per cent respectively, while male and female literacy rates of Kerala are 96 per cent and 92 per cent respectively (Government of India, 2011). Only 5.7 per cent of the tribal families have drinking water facilities in their premises. 76.2 per cent of the tribal households do not have any safe sanitation arrangements and 84.0 per cent of tribal households don't have any arrangements for waste water disposal. Electricity and housing facilities of tribes are also precarious in the region (ISA, 2006), resulting in poor quality of life. An increasing infant/neonatal/child deaths due to Asphyxia, Aspiration and Apnoca, Preterm and low birth weight, development growth delay and intrauterime growth retardation (IUGR) are the best example of poor quality of tribal life (UNICEF, 2013; Suchitra 2013a; 2013c; 2013d; The Hindu 2013a; 2013b; 2013c; Vasanth, 2013b; 2013c; 2013d; 2013e).

3. See more details for land use pattern of Attappady (Valluva, 2000; Purushothaman, 2005).

By understanding the higher incidences and intensities of environmental degradation, and livelihood insecurity of tribes in Attappady block, the Attappady Wasteland Comprehensive Environmental Conservation Project (AWCECP) was implemented with the financial support of the Japanese Bank for International Cooperation (JBIC) in Attappady in 1996. In order to implement this project Attappady Hills Area Development Society (AHADS) was constituted. The objective of this project was:

> Ecological restoration of degraded wasteland in Attappady and development of replicable models of participatory eco-restoration so as to prevent further degradation and to promote a sustainable model of livelihood for the local people (with special emphasis on tribal population).

JBIC has sanctioned ₹219 crore, of which, 25 per cent (₹55 crore) need not be repaid, but 75 per cent (around ₹164 crore) needs to be repaid with the interest. The duration of this project was five years, 2000-2005, but, later it extended up to 2010 (Takaki, 2010). AHADS miserably failed to not only restore ecology but also to promote a sustainable livelihood model for the local people, including tribeal people in Attappady. Deaths of 60 tribal children in 2013-14 in Attappady was result of not only failure of AHADS, which deviated from its original concept (The Hindu, 2013d), but also of the so-called Kerala model of development (Manikandan, 2013a; 2014).

In order to promote a sustainable model of ecology and livelihoods of tribes in Attappady, the Government has to handover the governance, conservation and utilisation of forest and other natural resources to the tribal people in the region. Tribal people have their own socio-cultural informal institutional arrangements for regulating, conserving and utilising not only forests but also other natural resources. Socio-cultural informal institutional arrangements of tribes are the most suitable for regulating the access to common resources and are thus successful in creating a balance between use and resource renewal. Apart from this, the government has to ensure the effectiveness implementation of all social security/welfare schemes and laws meant for the tribes in Attappady.

An Assessment of MGNREGS in Attappady

The MGNREGS implemented in India in 2006, is the largest public works employment project in the world (Liu and Barrett, 2013). In 2006 itself, the scheme was implemented in Palakkad and Wayanad districts in Kerala. Attappady is located in Palakkad district. This scheme is being implemented in all 91 *panchayats* under 13 block *panchayats* (Jacob and Varghese, 2006) in Palakkad district. Attappady is one of the largest and most backward tribal settlements in Kerala. It is in this context, we have made an assessment of MGNREGS, as being implemented in Attappady tribal development block since 2006.

Job Card Holders

There was a tremendous increase in the job card issued for various social groups in Attappady block between 2006-07 and 2010-11. During this period, the number of job card holders increased from 9,474 to 18,086. Since then, it has decreased to 9,936 in 2011-12. As per the Kerala Institute of Local Administration (KILA), there were 8,589 tribal households in Attappady in 2008, but the cumulative job card issued for the tribal households in Attappady was only 7,074 in

Table 4.2

Number of Households Issued Job Cards in Attappady Tribal Block

Year	*SC*	*ST*	*Others*	*Total*
2006-07	435	4,113	4,926	9,474
2007-08	558	9,011	6,923	16,492
2008-09	592	9,258	7,363	17,213
2009-10	615	9,555	7,916	18,086
2010-11	615	9,556	7,919	18,090
2011-12	288	4,714	4,934	9,936
2012-13	399	6,705	5,768	12,872
2013-14	451	7,271	6,141	13,863
2014-15*	457	7,469	6,290	14,216

Note: * as on 04-10-2014.

Source: *www.nrega.nic.in*

2013-14, i.e. nearly 15 per cent of tribal households did not received job cards in 2013-14.

Number of Person Days Created

It is a paradox that job card issued for STs is higher than 'Others', but person days generated for STs is less than 'Others' in Attappady. It is largely because of three reasons: i) low awareness among the tribal people; ii) low demand for work; and iii) delays in providing employment and wage. The fact that there is low awareness among tribal communities about the scheme, the officials should have organised more awareness programmes and focused on providing supply-oriented employment and wage to the tribals in the Attappady tribal block; although there are some restrictions in the guidelines of MGNREGS for adopting supply-driven approach. It has been found that a supply-driven approach of proving employment and wage is very effective in the regions where the people are in distress and ignorant about the rights and entitlements of MGNREGS. Therefore, the officials should take a pro-poor approach in MGNREGS when the beneficiaries are in distress or if there are extreme poverty situations.

Table 4.3

Number of MGNREGS Person Days Created in Attappady Tribal Block

Year	*SC*	*ST*	*Others*	*Total*
2006-07	8,172	38,379	88,593	1,35,144
2007-08	11,594	1,53,742	1,44,752	3,10,088
2008-09	10,037	1,38,834	1,57,552	3,06,423
2009-10	13,356	1,66,733	1,72,431	3,52,520
2010-11	15,418	2,03,723	1,96,597	4,15,738
2011-12	9,954	1,70,792	1,95,680	3,76,426
2012-13	16,955	2,85,793	2,66,782	5,69,530
2013-14	19,954	3,35,400	2,74,453	6,29,807
2014-15*	6,867	1,15,731	76,332	1,98,930

Note: * as on 04-10-2014.

Source: *www.nrega.nic.in*

Average Person Days

The average person days of STs is always less than the average person days of 'Others' in a Tribal Block. It is due to: i) demand for works is low; and ii) restricted supply-driven nature of MGNREGS. It is shocking to note that the starvation deaths are increasing among the tribal people, even after the implementation of MGNREGS. What does it mean? MGNREGS has not been to make a considerable effect among the tribal people. It has been found that in 3 villages in Udaipur, Rajasthan, the mean participation was 59 days and that targeting was satisfactory (Jha *et al.*, 2008). But Attappady has never achieved such satisfactory target ever since the scheme was implemented in the block.

Table 4.4

Average Person Days of MGNREGS in Attappady Tribal Block

Year	SC	ST	Others	Total	Kerala
2006-07	27	24	49	37	20
2007-08	31	43	64	50	27
2008-09	27	37	47	41	21
2009-10	50	49	50	49	44
2010-11	56	53	57	55	44
2011-12	42	44	50	47	45
2012-13	42	43	46	44	55
2013-14	44	46	44	45	57
2014-15*	15	15	12	14	15

Note: * as on 04-10-2014.
Source: *www.nrega.nic.in*

Expenditure Incurred for MGNREGS

The expenditure for MGNREGS is increasing every year in Attappady tribal block. Here, the important question is: Whether the benefits of increasing expenditure of MGNREGS are reaching the tribal people in Attappady or not? An alarming increase in the infant/child mortality rate due to malnutrition and related health problems among the tribal people in Attappady shows that MGNREGS has not produced much desirable effects among the tribes in Attappady. Poverty level of the tribal people was more than 57 per cent in 2008.

Table 4.5

Expenditure Incurred for MGNREGS in Attappady Tribal Block

Year	*Expenditure in Lakh*
2006-07	196.51
2007-08	561.02
2008-09	487.28
2009-10	606.55
2010-11	616.26
2011-12	628.24
2012-13	975.24
2013-14	1004.62
2014-15*	685.38

Note: * as on 04-10-2014.
Source: *www.nrega.nic.in*

It is interesting to note that the share of women in person days generated under MGNREGS is exceptionally high in Attappady tribal block. The share of women in person days generated was 82.75 per cent in 2010-11 and 85.80 per cent in 2011-12. Since then the share of women in person days seems fell up to 83.89 per cent in 2013-14. The share of women in person days generated under MGNREGS in Kerala was more than 90 per cent in 2012-13 (Manikandan, 2013). In Kerala, the SHGs (self-help groups) such as Kudumbasree, Janasree, etc., are playing a key role in women participation in MGNREGS. Attappady is alo not an exception to that. The women participation MGNREGS is exceptionally higher than men among the tribal people in Attappady.

Problems and Prospects

The MGNREGS has encountered some problems in Attappady. Major problems include: low coverage of job card issued, average days of person days of MGNREGS is low, not enough awareness about the scheme, low demand for works, delays in providing employment and wage (Suchitra 2013a), initiatives for converging MGNREGS with other programmes, including IAY, horticulture, RKVY, etc., are not sufficient. MGNREGS has miserably failed to understand the specific socio-cultural context of the tribal people. Too much focus on land development works in Attappady is helping non-tribals than tribal people because landlessness and land alienation is very high among the tribal people in Attappady.

Figure 4.1

Share of Women in MGNREGS Person Days in Attappady Tribal Block

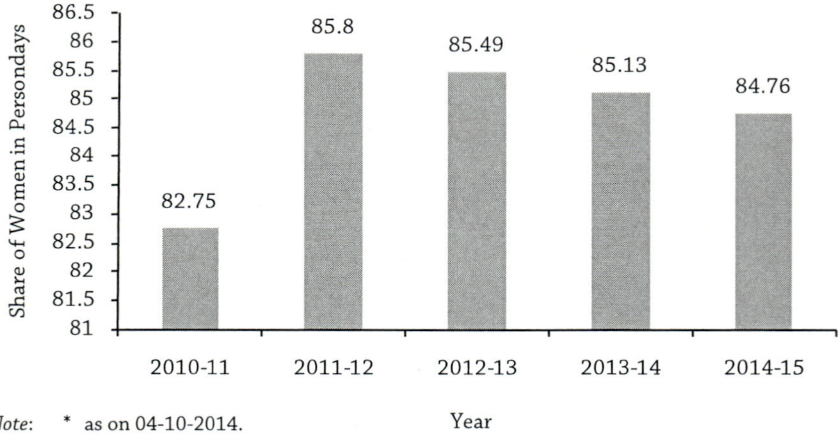

Note: * as on 04-10-2014.

Source: *www.nrega.nic.in*

Policy Suggestions

i) MGNREGS should focus not only on just creating wage employment, but should also focus on ensuring agricultural works, which enhances food self-sufficiency.

ii) There is a clear-cut gender divide in MGNREGS. For instance, among MGNREGS workers most of them are women. But, among the implementing officials/policy/decision makers of MGNREGS most of them are men. This is an important impediment or problem of this scheme. The fact that it is not women-friendly, is affecting the process of understanding problems, strength, weakness or opportunities of MGNREGS to a large extent in the state of Kerala.

Therefore, MGNREGS should be more women-friendly and should be led by *Gram Panchayat* in association with women SHGs (self-help groups).

iii) As MGNREGS is a pro-poor programme, works under the scheme should not be taken on private land belonging to middle and high income families.

iv) Workers, who belong to the middle-income and high-income families should be excluded from the programme.

v) MGNREGS work time can be fixed between 9.30 A.M and 4 P.M.

vi) MGNREGS wage should be revised every three year.

vii) MGNREGS should be implemented as a supply and demand driven scheme in the areas/regions where poverty and low awareness about the programme are high (for instance, tribal areas).

viii) Health security measures for the MGNREGS workers should be ensured (shoes, gloves, mask, medical allowance, etc.).

ix) MGNREGS works should be restricted to food crops only in the agriculture sector

x) MGNREGS works should be taken up in aquaculture also.

xi) Before finalising the works under MGNREGS, public opinion should be collected through participatory method.

xii) After the completion of each work also people's opinion about the work should be gathered through participatory method.

Policy Suggestions for Attappady

In order to ensure effective impact of MGNREGS in Attappady tribal block, some points need to be considered: a) more awareness programmes to be conducted; b) the coverage of job card among the poor households to be ensured; c) the participation of BPL households, especially BPL tribal households, needs to be ensured by the officials; d) delays in providing employment and wage to be avoided; e) works related to drinking water and sanitation should get more priority in the tribal hamlet; f) the tribal hamlet-based planning, execution, monitoring and evaluation of MGNREGS to be promoted; g) the socio-cultural context of tribal people should be taken into MGNREGS works (e.g., bamboo-related works); h) shifting cultivation to be promoted in forest areas under MGNREGS; and i) Mooppan, who is the leader or chief of each tribal hamlet, should get a statutory power under MGNREGS for the governing, executing, planning, monitoring and evaluating of this scheme propogating cultural-friendly approach.

Conclusion

This paper has made an assessment of MGNREGS in Attappady tribal block. Results of the study showed that the performance of MGNREGS is low and particularly, the participation of tribal people and wage employment provided to them is very low. Major causes of low performance of this scheme included low awareness among the tribal beneficiaries, low demand for works, delays in wage and employment provided by the officials, failure in incorporating socio-cultural context of the tribal people and lack of continuous attention from academics and civil society. In order to ensure effectiveness of MGNREGS in Attappady, tribal hamlet based planning, implementing, monitoring and evaluating of MGNREGS should be promoted and Moopan, who is the chief of each tribal hamlet, should be given this responsibility. For ensuring sustainable livelihood and well-being of tribal people in Attappady under MGNREGS, what is needed is the socio-cultural approach.

References

Attappady Hills Area Development Society (2010). *AHADS Status Report 2010.* Attappady, Kerala.

Ekbal, B. *et al.* (2013a). *Report on the Visit to Attappadi by the Medical Team Constituted by the CPI (M) Kerala State Committee.* 18-21 May. Available at *http://www.republicofhunger.org/wp-content/uploads/2013/07/Attapadi-Report-E.pdf* (accessed on 6 January 2014).

Ekbal, B. (2013b). "Attappadiyil Sambhavikkunnath Nishabdha Vamshahathya", in B. Ekbal (ed.), *Attappadiyil Sambhavikkunnathenthu.* Thiruvananthapuram: Chintha Publishers.

———. (2013c). "Attappadiyil Kandathu", *Deshabhimani News Paper*: 6, 30 May.

———. (2013d). "Venam Samagramaya Edapedal", *Deshabhimani News Paper*: 6, 31 May.

Government of India (2001). *Census of Kerala 2001*. Office of the Registrar General India.

———. (2010). *Statistical Profile of Scheduled Tribes in India*. New Delhi: Ministry of Tribal Affairs, Statistics Division.

———. (2011). *Census of Kerala 2011.* Office of the Registrar General India.

———. (2013). *MGNREGA*. New Delhi: Ministry of Rural Development. *www.nrega.nic.in*

Harijan Welfare Department (1975). *Notification No-1 Educational Concessions for Pre-metriculation Studies for Scheduled Castes, Scheduled Tribes, Other Eligible Communities including Kudumbis Other Backward Classes and Converts from them*, Kerala Gazettee, No.20. Kerala: Government of Kerala.

Hoeschele, W. (2000). "Geographic Information Engineering and Social Ground Truth in Attappadi, Kerala State, India", *Annals of the American Geographers* 90(2): 293-321.

Hoeschele, Wolfgand R. (1998). *Land Degradation, State Power and Peasant Livelihood in Attappady (Kerala State, India).* Ph.D Thesis. The Pennsylvania State University, The Graduate School, Department of Geography.

Institute for Societal Advancement (ISA) (2006). *Greening Hills and Empowering the Poor.* Kerala: Thiruvananthapuram.

Ittyipe, M. (2013). "Leeches Fields", *Outlook, Cover Story–Malnutrition Deaths*, pp.28-37, 29 July.

Jacob, A. and Richard Varghese (2006). "NREGA Implementation-I: Reasonable Beginning in Palakkad, Kerala", *Economic and Political Weekly* XLI(48): 4943-45, 2 December.

Jha, R., Raghav Gaiha and Shylashri Shankar (2008). "Reviewing the National Employment Guarantee Programme", *Economic and Political Weekly:* 44-48, 15 March.

Kalathil, M.J. (2004). "Withering Valli: Alienation, Degradation, and Endorsement of Tribal Women in Attappady", *Discussion Paper No.*66. Trivandrum: KRPLLD, CDS.

Khera, R. (2008a). "Empowerment Guarantee Act", *Economic and Political Weekly*: 8-10, 30 August.

———. (2008b). "Starvation Deaths and 'Primitive Tribal Groups'", *Economic and Political Weekly*: 11-14, 27 December.

KILA (2008). *Scheduled Tribe Communities Basic Information–2008 (Palakkad District)*, Thrissur, Kerala.

Liu, Y., and Christopher R. Barrett (2013). "Heterogenous Pro-Poor Targeting in the National Rural Employment Guarantee Scheme", *Economic and Political Weekly*: 46-53, 9 March.

Luiz, A.A.D (1962). *Tribes of Kerala*. New Delhi: Bharatiya Adimajati Sevak Sangh.

Manikandan, A.D. (2010). "Impact of Mahatma Gandhi National Rural Employment Guarantee Scheme on Paddy Cultivation: A Case of Kerala", *The Journal of Rural Development* 37(1): 35-66, January. Bangladesh, Commilla: Bangladesh Academy of Rural Development.

———. (2011). "Application of NREGS in Paddy Field for Improving Food Security in Kerala: A Theoretical Analysis", in R.K Mishra and Jayasree Ravindran (eds.), *Millennium Development Goals and India: Cases Assessing Performance-Prospects and Challenges*. New Delhi: Allied Publishers Pvt. Ltd.

———. (2012). "Mahatma Gandhi NREGS and Women: A Comparative Study of Bihar and Kerala", *Women's Link Journal* 18(3): 27-29, 33, July-Sept, (co-authored with Ch. Sri Laxmi). New Delhi: Indian Social Institute (ISI), Social Action Trust.

———. (2013a). "Keralathile Adivasikal" in Ekbal (ed.), *Attappadiyil Sambhavi-kkunnathenthu.* Chintha Publishers, Thiruvananthapuram, Kerala.

———. (2013b). "An Evaluation of MGNREGS in Kerala". Unpublished.

———. (2014). "A Tragedy unfolding: Tribal Children Dying in Attappady", web exclusives, *Economic and Political Weekly* XLIX(2), January 11, *www.epw.in/web-exclusives-tragedy-unfloding-tribal-children-dying-attappady.html*

———. (2015). "For Sustaining Ecology and Livelihoods in Attappady: Institutions and Governance", in Manjusha (ed.), *Understanding the Tribal Life in India: Issues, Challenges and Alternate Approaches*. New Delhi: ABC Press.

Manikandan, A.D and Che. Sri Lakshmi (2012). "Mahatma Gandhi NREGS and Women: A Comparative Study of Bihar and Kerala", *Women's Link Journal* 18(3): 27-29, 33, July-Sept. New Delhi: Indian Social Institute (ISI), Social Action Trust.

Nair, Somasekharan P. (1976). *Paniyar*. Kottayam: National Book Stall.

Narikutty, J. (2013). "Chelavidunnathu Kodikal: Vizhungunnathum", *Deshabhimani*, 9 May. p.5.

Purushothaman, (2005). "Land Use Strategies for Tribals: A Socio-Economic Analysis", *Economic and Political Weekly*: 5611-19, 31 December.

Suchitra, M. (2013a). "Essential Healthcare Services Failed in Attappady", *Down to Earth*, 10 July.

———. (2013b). "Restore Lands to Tribals: Allow Them to be Self-reliant", *Down to Earth*, 10 July.

———. (2013c). "The Widening Nutrition Gap", *Down to Earth*, 13 July.

———. (2013d). "Infant Deaths Continue in Attappady", *Down to Earth*, 16 July.

Takaki, K. (2010). *Ex-Post Evaluation of Japanese ODA Loan: Attappady Wasteland Comprehensive Environmental Conservation Project*. FASID, India.

The Hindu (2013a). "Malnutrition: One More Infant in ICU", *The Hindu*, 9 April.

———. (2013b). "Addiction Raises a Spectre in Attappady", *The Hindu*, 25 April.

———. (2013c). "Where Grieving Mothers Struggle to Find Answers", *The Hindu*, 3 May.

———. (2013d). "AHADS Project Deviated from its Original Concept", *The Hindu*, 19 May.

———. (2013e). "They want their Alienated Land Back for Cultivation", *The Hindu*, 12 August.

UNICEF (2013). *Problem: Increased Infant/Child Deaths Reported from Attapady Block, Pallakad District*. 28-29 May.

Valluva, S. (2000). *Dynamics of Land Use in Recently Settled Forest Areas: A Case Study of Attappady, Kerala*. Ph.D Thesis. Cochin: Cochin University of Science and Technology.

———. (2006). "Developmental Effects on Livelihood Strategies of Tribes-people in Attappady, Kerala". *Discussion Paper* 99. Thiruvananthapuram: Kerala Research Programme on Local Level Development, Centre for Development Studies.

Varghese, R and Arun Jacob (2006). "NREGA Implementation-I: Reasonable Beginning in Palakkad, Kerala", *Economic and Political Weekly*: 4943-45, 2 December.

Vasanth, M.V (2013a). "Sishumaranangalil Veerppumutty Attappadiyude Hridhayam", *Deepika*, 28 May.

———. (2013b). "Arogyaraksha Sthapanangalere, Vazhunnathu Avaganana", *Deepika*, 29 May.

———. (2013c). "Vattamittu ParannuMaranam", *Deepika*, 30 May.

———. (2013d). "Maranam Perukumbozhum Podichhathulakshangal", *Deepika*, 31 May.

———.(2013e). "Ammamar Parayunnu: Vanabhumi Adivasikalkku", *Deepika*, 1 June.

Vayaleri, K (1996). *Kurichyarude Jeevithavum Samskaravum*. Kottayam: Current Books.

Appendix Table A-4.1

Performance of MGNREGS in India

		FY 2013-14	*FY 2012-13*	*FY 2011-12*
Total no. of Districts		644	636	635
Total no. of Blocks		6,576	6,568	6,378
Total no. of GPs		2,47,643	2,47,643	2,47,643
Total no. of Villages		7,78,134	7,78,134	7,78,133
Total no. of HH Registered (in Cr.)		12.8	12.9	12.6
Total no. of Workers in JC		28.1	28.5	27.8
No. of GPs with NIL exp		40,361	25,711	25,066
No. of Ongoing Works (in Lakhs)		96.4	80.7	53.2
Total no. of Works undertaken (New+Spill Over) (in lakhs)		104.5	106.5	80.8
Total Exp (in Cr.)	Wages (₹ in Cr.)	14612	27129.7	24306.2
	Material and skilled Wages (₹ in Cr.)	4676.4	10379.5	10650.5
	Admn. Exp:			
	GP Level	108.8	307.4	301.8
	Block Level	598.7	1327.4	1191.7
	District Level	234.6	481.9	514.4
	State Level	90.855	32.936	108.055
	Total Adm Expenditure	1,032.9	2,149.6	2,116
	Total Exp (₹ in Cr.)	20,321.3	39,658.7	37,072.7
	Labour Vs Material(%)	75.8	72.3	69.5
	Admin Exp (%)	5.1	5.4	5.7
Wage Employment Provided (in lakhs)	Households	335.6	498.2	506.4
	Individuals	483.1	795.9	820
	Men	242.2	421.4	446.6
	Women	241	374.5	373.3
	SCs	114.1	181	185
	STs	82.8	142.4	147.4
	Persons with Disability	3.1	4.1	4

contd...

...contd...

Person-days (in Cr.)	Total as per LB	255.2	278.7	199.6
	Person-days Generated so far	108	229.9	218.8
	% of Total LB	42.3	82.5	109.6
	% as per Proportionate LB	65	129.8	176.3
	SC person-days	25.4	51	48.5
	ST person-days	16.6	40.8	40.9
Average Wage rate per day per person		126.4	121.4	114.5
Average days of employment provided per Household		32.2	46.1	43.2
Total no. of HHs completed 100 Days of Wage Employment (in Lakhs)		8.1	51.4	41.7
% payments generated within 15 days		68.9	61.4	57.8
% of payments Disbursed through Electronic Fund Management System (EFMS)		12.8	0.9	0

Source: *www.nrega.nic.in*. Date of data extraction is 27-11-2013.

Appendix Table A-4.2

Block-wise Cumulative No. of HH Issued Job Cards (Till the reporting month) in Palakkad District, Kerala

S. No.	*Block*	*2013-14*	*2012-13*	*2011-12*	*2010-11*
		STs	*STs*	*STs*	*STs*
1	Alathur	114	113	88	165
2	Attappadi	7072	6610	4446	9556
3	Chittur	1452	1168	1108	1238
4	Kollengode	1237	1207	877	1341
5	Kuzhalmannam	1	3	0	7
6	Malampuzha	509	493	396	612
7	Mannarkad	414	376	180	656
8	Nemmara	452	421	257	312
9	Ottappalam	0	1	1	1
10	Palakkad	0	0	1	90
11	Pattambi	8	6	0	0
12	Sreekrishnapuram	10	9	1	10
13	Trithala	0	0	1	0
	Total	11271	10405	7356	13988

Source: *www.nrega.nic.in*. Date of data extraction is 27-11-2013.

Appendix Table A-4.3

Block-wise Cumulative Person Days Generated (Till the Reporting Month) in Palakkad District, Kerala

S. No.	*Block*	*2013-14*	*2012-13*	*2011-12*	*2010-11*
		STs	*STs*	*STs*	*STs*
1	Alathur	745	1952	1308	373
2	Attappadi	162989	283863	160750	203723
3	Chittur	11480	24877	17571	13663
4	Kollengode	12475	22575	22720	15058
5	Kuzhalmannam	0	0	0	51
6	Malampuzha	11278	18644	15782	10759
7	Mannarkad	1261	4719	3384	4109
8	Nemmara	1553	4049	2037	1644
9	Ottappalam	0	0	0	0
10	Palakkad	0	0	21	3050
11	Pattambi	0	0	0	0
12	Sreekrishnapuram	38	1	0	0
13	Trithala	0	0	13	0
	Total	201819	360680	223586	252430

Source: *www.nrega.nic.in*. Date of data extraction is 27-11-2013.

Appendix Table A-4.4

Some other Indicators of MGNREGS

S. No	*Block*	*Cumulative No. of HH Completed 100 Days (Till the Reporting Month*	*No. of HH which are Beneficiary of Land Reform/ IAY*	*No. of Disabled Beneficiary Individuals*	*Cumulative No. of HH Completed 100 Days (Till the Reporting Month*	*No. of HH which are Beneficiary of Land Reform/ IAY*	*No. of Disabled Beneficiary Individuals*	*Cumulative No. of HH Completed 100 Days (Till the Reporting Month*	*No. of HH which are Beneficiary of Land Reform/ IAY*	*No. of Disabled Beneficiary Individual*
1	Alathur	1	35	9	1017	37	9	459	32	9
2	Attappadi	56	121	8	2080	207	10	738	11	9
3	Chittur	24	81	14	3434	80	16	940	72	17
4	Kollengode	16	135	5	1805	154	6	618	148	5
5	Kuzhalmannam	6	25	26	471	29	30	92	61	31
6	Malampuzha	17	27	6	1846	31	5	993	70	5
7	Mannarkad	1	78	24	1425	84	27	697	135	24
8	Nemmara	5	3	6	733	5	6	240	79	6
9	Ottappalam	16	39	9	1577	38	6	457	42	5
10	Palakkad	7	190	3	1995	204	5	690	212	8
11	Pattambi	13	56	8	2552	57	8	1315	141	4
12	Sreekrishnapuram	20	35	9	1556	23	8	487	20	5
13	Trithala	4	13	9	1525	36	8	940	110	8
	Total	186	838	136	22016	985	144	8666	1133	136

Source: *www.nrega.nic.in*. Date of data extraction was 27-11-2013.

Appendix Table A-4.5

Works Status in Attappady Tribal Block

Year	*Block*	*Rural Connectivity*	*Flood Control*	*Water Conservation and Water Herversting*	*Renovation of Traditional Water Bodies*	*Drought Proofing*	*Irrigation Canals*	*Irrigation Facilities to SC/ ST/IAY/ LR*	*Land Development*	*Other works*	*Rural Drinking Water*	*Total No of Works*	*Total Approved Work*
		comp.	*comp.*	*comp.*	*comp.*	*comp.*	*comp.*	*comp.*	*comp.*	*comp.*	*comp.*	*comp.*	
2010-11	Attappady	18	67	389	1	9	5	58	63	0	0	610	612
2011-12	Attappady	6	99	14	1	1	0	0	482	0	0	603	1156
2012-13	Attappady	19	131	111	16	10	5	2	1283	0	1	1578	1668
2013-14	Attappady	3	1	11	1	0	1	0	115	0	0	132	1341
Total		46	298	525	19	20	11	60	1943	0	1	2923	4777

Source: *www.nrega.nic.in*. Data is extracted on 28-112013.

5

S.D. BHANDARI, R.P. KADAM and
G.S. PAWAR

Constraints Faced by the Beneficiaries of Mahatma Gandhi National Rural Employment Guarantee Act

Introduction

Employment opportunities in rural areas are only seasonal. Eradication of poverty and hunger through generation of employment opportunities in the community has been one of the main goals of planning in India. The true development of any community or society is only possible when its members learn to help themselves or in other words, when they are being empowered. Empowerment of the deprived begins with their ability to voice their opinion through the process of consensual politics and dialogue. Poverty and unemployment are the twin problem faced by the developing countries. According to the Planning Commission of India, nearly 29.8 per cent population is BPL (below poverty line). Policy makers in India have realised the need for generating employment opportunities on large scale so as to bring the teeming millions of population APL (above poverty line). Majority of the population (72.22%) live in rural areas and many of them suffer owing to seasonal unemployment, under-employment and disguised unemployment.

In India, GDP (gross domestic product) and unemployment rates are going hand in hand, causing fret for any democratic society. Unemployment and poverty are strongly related and hinder the economic growth and development of a country. In India, these two problems are severe in the rural areas, leaving it outside the growth path. Thus the Government of India (GoI), aiming to achieve balanced growth and to overcome above-mentioned weaknesses of past employment programmes, passed the National Rural Employment Guarantee Act (NREGA) on 25 August 2005 in order to empower the rural labourers with the right to get employment of 100 days per year per household during off-season. In accordance, NREGA had been launched in Anantapur district of Andhra Pradesh (AP) on 2 February 2006, with effect from 1 April 2006 in 200 drought-prone and backward districts. This was extended to an additional 130 districts in the financial year 2007-08. The NREGA coverage has been expanded from 330 to 619 districts of India, beginning April 2008.

In Maharashtra the NREGA was implemented during 2006 in 12, of its districts (Dhule, Nandurbar, Ahemednagar, Aurangabad, Hingoli, Nanded, Amravati, Gadchiroli, Yavatmal, Bhandara, Gondhiya and Chjandrapur). Thus NREGA covered the entire country with the exception of districts that have 100 per cent urban population. This programme has been formulated by merging early formulated programmes such as Sampoorna Gramin Rozgar Yojana (SGRY) of 2001 and National Food for Work Programme (NFFWP) of 2004. Again on 2 October 2009, the GoI renamed its flagship rural job guarantee programme—NREGA as Mahatma Gandhi National Rural Employment Guarantee Act (MGNREGA).

The objectives of this paper are:

i. To study the personal, social, and economical characteristics of the beneficiaries of MGNREGA.
ii. To study the constraints faced by the beneficiaries while availing benefit.
iii. To consider the suggestions made by the beneficiaries to overcome the constraints.

Methodology

Keeping in view the objectives, the study was conducted in Parbhani District of Maharashtra during the year 2013-14. Jintur, Selu and Parbhani talukas from Parbhani district were selected. Further, 12 villages from the three *talukas* were selected on the basis of total maximum number of man days work during 2013-14. Ten beneficiaries of MGNREGA were selected randomly from each village.

Taking into consideration the objective of study, the interview schedule was constructed to collect required data from beneficiaries. The data were collected with the help of a structural schedule. The collected data were tabulated and analysed with the help of frequency and percentage to interpret the result.

Results and Discussion

Personal, Social and Economical Characteristics of the Beneficiaries of MGNREGA

It can be seen in Table 5.1 that 37.5 per cent of the beneficiaries had small size family, followed by 33.33 per cent of those who lived in medium size family and 29.17 per cent of beneficiaries living in big size family. It can be observed from the table that 53.33 per cent of the beneficiaries were using medium level of sources of information, whereas 25 per cent and 21.67 per cent used low and high level of sources of information, respectively. As regards to the social participation, 67.5 per cent of beneficiaries had medium social participation, followed by 20.83 per cent with high and 11.67 per cent with low social participation.

Constraints Faced by Beneficiaries of MGNREGA

The results with respect to the constraints faced by the beneficiaries in implementation of MGNREGA are presented in Table 5.2. Here it is observed that constraints perceived by the beneficiaries of the Act during its implementation were: late payment of wages (85%), registration not taking place in the GP (*gram panchayat*) on an ongoing basis (72.5%), delay in allotment of work (60%), and compliant book, registration book and instrument book not easy to access (46.16%).

Poor work site facility was opined by 43.33 per cent, officers not available in the GP for registration (39.16%), non-opportunity to get employment for more than 100 days (38.33%), migration of labour due to non-provision of work under MGNREGA (35%), non-provision of crèche facility (27.5%), non-provision of 100 days' work (26.66%), delay in disposal of beneficiaries complaints (23.33%), same payment provided for all types of work (23.33%), duplicate registration done

Table 5.1

Profile of Selected Beneficiaries of MGNREGA

S. No.	Characteristics	Number	Percentage
1.	**Age**		
	Young	23	19.17
	Middle	78	65.00
	Old	19	15.83
2.	**Gender**		
	Male	81	67.50
	Female	39	32.50
3.	**Education**		
	Illiterate	8	06.67
	Primary education	26	21.66
	Secondary education	73	60.83
	Higher secondary education	12	10.00
	College level education	01	0.83
4.	**Caste**		
	Lower Caste	46	38.33
	Middle Caste	31	25.83
	Upper Caste	43	35.84
5.	**Land Holding**		
	Landless farmer	58	48.34
	Marginal farmer	40	33.33
	Small farmer	18	15.00
	Semi-medium farmer	04	3.33
	Medium farmer	00	0.00
	Big farmer	00	0.00
6.	**Occupation**		
	Landless labourer	58	43.33
	Farming + Labourer	62	51.67

contd...

...*contd*...

7.	**Annual income (₹)**		
	Lower (Up to 21,726)	0	0.00
	Medium (21,727 to 7,056)	99	82.50
	High (70,957 and above)	21	17.50
8.	**Type of family**		
	Nuclear family	55	45.83
	Joint family	65	54.17
9.	**Size of family**		
	Small (Up to 4 members)	45	37.50
	Medium (5 to 7 members)	40	33.33
	Big (8 and above members)	35	29.17
10.	**Sources of Information**		
	Low (Up to 7)	30	25.00
	Medium (8 to 13)	64	53.33
	High (14 and above)	26	21.97
11.	**Social Participation**		
	Low (Up to 0)	14	11.67
	Medium (1)	81	67.50
	High (2 and above)	25	20.83

Source: Based on the original data collected for the present research study from the beneficiaries of Parbhani district during the year 2013-14.

in the registration book (20%), work allotted to relatives and close friends of the contractor and members of GP (20%), non-payment of unemployment allowance (18.33%), long distances of work sites (13.33%), completed work and working site not examined by the officer (9.16%), non-provision of 10 per cent extra travelling expense when work site was more than 5 kms away from village (7.5%) and less payment provided besides the fixed amount (2.5%). These findings are supported by those derived by Argade (2010) and Sarkar *et al.* (2011).

Table 5.2

Distribution of Beneficiaries According to Operational Problem Perceived by Them

(n=120)

S. No.	*Constraints*	*Number*	*Percentage*
1	Late payment of wages	102	85.00
2	Registration was not open in the GPs on an ongoing basis	87	72.50
3	Delay in allotment of work	72	60.00
4	Compliant book, registration book and instrument book are not open to see	53	44.16
5	Poor work site facility	52	43.33
6	Officers are not available in the GP for registration	47	39.16
7	Non-opportunity to get employment for more than 100 days	46	38.33
8	Migration of labour due to non-provision of work under MGNREGA	42	35.00
9	Non-provision of crèche facility	33	27.50
10	Non-provision of 100 days' work	32	26.66
11	Delay in disposal of beneficiaries complaints	28	23.33
12	Same payment was provided to all types of work	28	23.33
13	Duplicate registration made in registration book	24	20.00
14	Work allotted to relatives and close friends of contractor and members of the GP.	24	20.00
15	Non-payment of unemployment allowance	22	18.33
16	Long distances of work sites	16	13.33
17	Completed work and working site was not examined by the officer	11	9.16
18	Non-provision of 10 per cent extra travelling payment when work site was more than 5 kms away from village	9	7.50
19	Less payment was provided besides as per decided	3	2.50

Source: Based on the original data collected for the present research study from the beneficiaries of Parbhani district during the year 2013-14.

Suggestions Made by the Beneficiaries to Overcome the Constraints

An attempt was made to obtain suggestions from the beneficiaries of MGNREGA so as to address the constraints they face for effective implementation of MGNREGA (see Table 5.3).

Table 5.3

Distribution of Beneficiaries of MGNREGA According to their Suggestions to Overcome the Constraints Perceived

(n=120)

S. No.	*Suggestions*	*Number*	*Percentages*
1	Timely payment of wages.	102	85.00
2	Registration should be open in the GP on an ongoing basis	87	72.50
3	Timely allotment of work	72	60.00
4	Compliant book, Registration book and instrument book should be open to see	53	44.16
5	Provision of necessary worksite facility	52	43.33
6	Officers should be available in GP for registration	47	39.16
7	Extend the limit of 100 days employment guarantee	46	38.33
8	Provision of sufficient employment in own village	42	35.00
9	Provision of crèche facility	33	27.50
10	Fulfilment of 100 days employment guarantee	32	26.66
11	Timely disposal of beneficiaries' complaints	28	23.33
12	Payment should be provided in accordance to the work done	28	23.33
13	Correct duplicate registration in registration book	24	20.00
14	Work allotment criteria should be same to all beneficiaries	24	20.00
15	Timely payment of unemployment allowance	22	18.33
16	Provision of the works through GP nearer to the residence	16	13.33
17	Completed work and working site should be examined by the officer	11	9.16
18	Provision of 10 per cent extra travelling payment when work site is more than 5 kms away from village	9	7.50
19	Payment should be provided as per decided	3	2.50

Source: Same as Table 5.2.

Timely payment of wages was mentioned by 85 per cent, registration should be open in the GP on an ongoing basis by 72.50 per cent, timely allotment of work by 60 per cent, access to the compliant book, registration book and instrument book by 44.16 per cent, provision of necessary work site facility by 43.33 per cent, officers should be available in the GP for registration by 39.16 per cent, extension of the limit of 100 days employment guarantee by 38.33 per cent, provision of sufficient employment in own village by 35 per cent, provision of crèche facility by 27.50 per cent, fulfilment of 100 days employment guarantee by 26.66 per cent, timely disposal of beneficiaries complaints by 23.33 per cent, payment should be made in accordance with the work by 23.33 per cent, duplicate registrations to be corrected in the registration book by 20 per cent, work allotment criteria should be same for all beneficiaries by 20 per cent, timely payment of unemployment allowance by 18.33 per cent, provision of the works allotted through the GP should be nearer to the residence by 13.33 per cent, completed work and working site should be examined by the relevant officers by 9.16 per cent, provision of 10 per cent extra travelling payment needs to be in place when work site is more than 5 km away from village by 7.5 per cent, and payment should be provided as per decided vy 2.5 per cent. These finding are supported by that of Sarkar *et al.* (2011) Balu (2000), Argade (2010) and Prasher (2014).

Conclusion

A majority of beneficiaries were from the middle age group, male, literate, lower caste group, landless farmers, farming and labourer were their occupation, medium annual income, lived in joint family, small family size, medium use of information sources and experienced medium social participation. From the above discussion it can be conclude that, the operational problems perceived by majority of the selected MGNREGA beneficiaries were late payment of wages, irregular registration process in the GP, delay in allotment of work, inaccessibility of complaint book, registration book and instrument book. In order to overcome these constraints, they had given curtain suggestions like, timely payment of wages, followed by conducting registration in the GP on an ongoing basis, timely allotment of work, and greater access to complaint book, registration book and instrument book. Regular monitoring and evaluation of any programme or an act was necessary for its successful implementation so that certain modifications, if any needed, for improving the system can be undertaken.

Suggestions and Recommendations

On the basis of fruitful findings of the present study and the personal experiences of the researcher at the time of interviewing the beneficiaries of MGNREGA, the following suggestions and recommendations were drawn,

1) The findings related to personal and social characteristics of the selected beneficiaries of MGNREGA could be effectively utilised by the implementing authorities of the Act for its successful implementation.
2) Majority of the selected beneficiaries was found to be middle and young aged. The middle aged population is participating enthusiastically and with high hopes in MGNREGA works. Hence, the Act should enable empowerment of the rural mass through employment generation.
3) It was found that the women participation in MGNREGA works was less than men. Through employment opportunities, MGNREGA has been bringing them from kitchen to the field, thereby making them self-sufficient. Hence, greater participation of women is required.
4) A considerable portion of the beneficiaries of MGNREGA were landless labourers. Except during the agricultural season, there was no source of employment for them. Hence, nearly for six months in the year they used to migrate to nearby urban areas to get employment. The 100 days of employment guarantee was not sufficient to stop their migration to urban areas. Administration requires to extend the 100 days limit of employment or to create other sources of employment for them in order to restrain this mass migration.

5) Due to temporary appointments of the officials at various levels of implementation of MGNREGA, they are not willing to work carefully and enthusiastically. Hence, sometime they take little care to offer all benefits of the Act to workers. The provision of timely funds at various levels and permanent appointments of officials may be improved for achieving the desired results.
6) The time delay in allotment of work, as well as of the work system should be improved.
7) Payment of through MGNREGA workers' wages should be made promptly through direct transfer in their bank, postal account, etc.

References

Argade, S.A. (2010). "Study on National Rural Employment Guarantee Scheme in Thane District of Maharashtra". M.Sc. (Agri) Thesis. Unpublished. Hyderabad: Acharya N.G. Ranga Agricultural University.

Balu, S. (2000). *Appraisal of Janmabhoomi Programme by Rural People in Mahabubnagar District of Andhra Pradesh*. M.Sc. (Agri.) Thesis. Hyderabad: Acharya N.G. Ranga Agricultural University.

Prattoy, Sarkar, Jagadish, Kumar and Supriya (2011). "Impact of MGNREGA on Reducing Rural Poverty and Improving Socio-economic Status of Rural Poor: A Study in Burdwan District of West Bengal", *Agriculture Economic Research Review* 24: 437-48.

Uma, Prasher (2014). "Mahatma Gandhi National Employment Guarantee Act and its Impact on the Beneficiaries", *Asian Journal of Research in Social Sciences and Humanities* 4(4): 50-60.

6

TUSHAR KANTI DAS

MGNREGA as Social Safety Net

Evidence from Three Districts of Western Odisha

Introduction

Safety nets are only part of the broader strategy of poverty reduction. These interact with and work alongside the social insurance such as health, education and financial services, as well as the provision of infrastructures like roads and various other policies which aim at reducing poverty and managing risks. Safety nets aim to redistribute income to the poorest with an immediate impact on the poverty and inequality reduction (Grosh *et al.*, 2008). They are transfers targeted at the poor.

Social safety nets are transfers targeted to the poor or vulnerable in some manner. They are: a) cash transfers—unconditional or conditional; narrowly targeted to the poor or covering those who belong to the vulnerable categories in the population such as, children, elders and disabled; b) transfers in kind—most commonly school feeding, food rations and other essential goods delivered in kind; c) income support delivered in exchange for participation in work or training activities; and d) fee waivers in essential services such as health or education. Social safety nets are only part of the wider social protection, poverty reduction and development strategies. A full social protection policy will include social insurance, including unemployment insurance, labour and training programmes, and labour regulation. A full social policy will include education and health, housing, access to utilities, as well as social protection (Development Committee, 2012).

Currently, 80 per cent of the developing countries have plans to strengthen their safety nets in order to better respond to future crises (IEG, 2011). Since 2008, dozens of countries have created new safety net programmes, expanded old ones, and improved administrative systems and governance arrangements to modernise their programmes and to make them more efficient. This explosion of policy action assists the clients and countries directly involved in the practice of safety nets.

Safety nets take different forms, encompassing comprehensive programmes like Brazil's Bolsa Familia that assist poor families with cash payments, or Liberia's cash-for-work programme providing access to public works jobs, or school feeding programmes, or academic stipends designed to address temporary nutrition and gender gaps. The safety nets programme like Ethiopia's programme and school feeding in Nicaragua save lives, i.e., providing families with a basic income, and keeping children healthy and in school during the food, fuel and financial crises. Places where such programmes are absent, people have more often faced malnutrition and are forced to sell assets, cut back on food and health care, and pull their children out of school.

India has a long history and experience in implementing wage employment programmes. These programmes provide unskilled workers with short-term employment in public works. They provide income transfers to poor households, especially during the lean periods. The wage employment programmes implemented by state governments with central assistance are self-targeting, and the objective is to provide enhanced livelihood security, particularly to those dependent on casual manual labour. In this regard, MGNREGA is a powerful instrument for ensuring inclusive growth in rural India through its impact on social protection, livelihood security and democratic empowerment. The mandate is to provide at least 100 days of guaranteed wage employment in a financial year to every rural household, whose adult members volunteer to do unskilled manual work.

The present study aims at analysing the development effectiveness of NREGA scheme in three districts of western Odisha. The reason behind selecting districts from the western region is that this region is comparatively less developed from its coastal counterparts. The present section introduces the problem under study. Comparisons of different types of social security schemes are outlined in section 2. Multiplier effect of these schemes/programmes is also discussed in this section. In section 3, the NREGA (2005) scheme as adopted by the Government of India (GoI) is presented. Section 4 deals with data source and methodology. Selection criteria, district profile, sample size and sampling procedure are presented in this section. Findings and analysis of the study are presented in section 5. Issues relating to card holding and working conditions of beneficiaries under NREGA scheme are also presented in this section. The concluding remarks about the study are presented in section 6.

Comparison of the Social Security Schemes

Public works have long been considered a staple of social assistance programmes (Grosh *et al.*, 2008). However they have mostly been designed as short-term 'safety nets' (Subbarao *et al.*, 2013; delNinno *et al.*, 2009). While, in some cases, the focus has been on poverty reduction or on addressing structural unemployment challenges (e.g., those arising from shifts in labour intensity in growth sectors and/or decline in sectors that were relatively better at absorbing labour), they have seldom been implemented on a scale that would allow them to make a substantial impact on in structural poverty (Lal *et al.*, 2010). Most developing countries that followed the dominant development theories to design development policies failed to achieve the goal of narrowing the income gap with developed countries (Lin and Rosenblatt, 2012).

Employment Guarantee Schemes (EGSs) and Cash Transfers (CTs) are social protection programmes which are intended to have a positive impact on the poor, primarily in terms of increased household income—the former through the provision of wage on the basis of work requirement and the latter through the provision of cash transfer (Hagen-Zanker *et al.*, 2011; Prabhu, 2009). EGSs provide a guaranteed amount of employment each year, hence facilitates a guaranteed income, usually by providing payment in the form of cash. Existing EGS programmes have stricter workfare guidelines (Basu, 2013). CTs provide a direct cash payment to households or individuals, which may be unconditional (UCTs), or may have conditions attached such as a requirement for school or clinic attendance by children, in which case they are known as conditional cash transfer (CCTs) programmes. By providing households with additional income, both CCTs and UCTs make it easier for the beneficiaries to access health and educational services among others. The choice between a CCT and a UCT should be driven by what policy makers want to achieve and who they want to target with the programme. EGSs are sometimes considered to be a particular form of conditional cash transfers, where the condition is the work requirement (Zepeda and Alorcon, 2012; Zepeda *et al.*, 2013).

EGSs are a subset of the Public Works Programmes (PWPs), but should not be confused with this broader category of interventions, which typically provide only one type of and short-term employment opportunities. EGSs are distinctive in that they guarantee employment to a specified population over a sustained or indefinite period, in turn representing a form of unemployment or income insurance. They differ from CTs in that receipt of a transfer is conditional on satisfying a work requirement, usually but not exclusively, relating to manual labour. While EGSs are rare, CT programmes are significantly more diverse in conception and execution, far more frequently implemented, and may or may not offer sustained or guaranteed transfers.

The differences in programme design are likely to affect impacts, as is the fact that the two types of intervention may be targeted at different groups—while EGS participation is limited to households with available labour (adequate numbers of working age members), CTs target households or individuals on the basis of a more diverse set of criteria which are often demographic (including the presence of elderly, orphans and vulnerable children or young children within households, or the absence of members of working age). For these reasons, general comparisons of social security schemes may not necessarily be meaningful (Barrientos *et al.*, 2008; Jorgensen and Serrano-Berthet, 2009).

For policy makers it is important to assess the impacts of these social security schemes. EGSs and CTs are often seen as substitutes by policy makers, since only one or the other is accessible by a particular group of beneficiaries. In the few instances they are treated as complements, and implemented in parallel for different population groups, as in the case of the Productive Safety Nets Programme (PSNP) in Ethiopia, which has both CT and EGS components, with the CT component being available for households unable to participate in the EGS. As a consequence, it is not possible to make generalised comparisons between impacts of the two different interventions as they are often implemented in different contexts and target populations (Hagen-Zanken *et al.*, 2011).

Safety Net Programme (SNP) in Indonesia is expected to reach 6.5 million households in extreme poverty. Bolsa Familia in Brazil reaches a further 12 million households. Ethiopia's PSNP reaches 1.7 million households. In South Africa, social assistance grants reach one half of the households, and Progresa/Oportunidades in Mexico and Bolsa Famılia in Brazil reach one quarter of all the households. In low-income countries the growth has been slower, but noticeable. Social transfer programmes have the potential to make a significant contribution to global poverty reduction. Transfer programmes in developing countries show diversity in programme design. Pure income transfers, like South Africa's Old Age Grant, supplement the purchasing power of households suffering from poverty. In other countries, income transfers combined with access to basic services or improvements in infrastructure have been introduced. Mexico's Oportunidades, for example, links transfers to school attendance and primary health care utilisation with the objective of reducing intergenerational poverty persistence. Social transfers conditioned on labour supply link the transfer to local infrastructure development.

Such transfers could strengthen the productive capacity of households in poverty by setting out a basic framework, which would help to collect, organise and assess the relevant findings from existing evaluation studies. The impact of transfer programmes on micro-level growth among the poor and the poorest groups is such that it is unlikely that they could influence aggregate GDP (gross domestic product) growth. The basic framework mapped out the potential linkages existing between social transfers, growth mediating processes and outcomes in relation with the productive capacity of households in poverty (Barrientos, 2012).

Multiplier Effect

The multiplier theory explains the cumulative effect of changes in investment on income via their effects on consumption expenditure. The multiplier measures the response of the economy to change in the demand of a sector. When total output of a sector increases, it has both the direct and indirect effect on the economy. Direct effects are the immediate effects associated with the change in final demand for a particular sector or industry. In addition to the direct effects, the indirect or secondary effects are due to backward linkages of sectors. Public works create labour demand and if they do not prove to be useless, the income or value added multiplier gives an estimate of the direct and indirect employment changes resulting from a change in unit output.

In areas with high poverty incidence, household income growth can be constrained by community-level factors, such as the absence of adequate infrastructure or the scarcity of local liquidity and trade. Transfer programmes conditional on labour supply could in principle have an impact on both these factors, by transferring income to households and improving liquidity, while at the same time upgrading available infrastructure. In practice, the assessment of such programmes has on the whole been very mixed. Many public works programmes transfer only a fraction of their budget to beneficiary households, due to the cost of inputs, equipment and technical advice; and in some cases the value of the newly created infrastructure is marginal. Studies assessing the impact of PWPs find that their impact at the community level depends to an important extent on programme design—especially the level and periodicity of the transfer (McCord, 2007).

Transfer programmes can also improve liquidity and trade at the local economy level by stimulating effective demand. Only a handful of studies have addressed this question. In the context of direct income transfer programmes, existing studies suggest that social transfers could generate multiplier effects, especially in poor rural areas; but evidence on these effects from social transfers must be considered with great care.

MGNREGA (2005) Scheme

On 5 September 2005, the Indian Parliament passed the National Rural Employment Guarantee Act (NREGA) and it came into force with effect from 2 February 2006. On 31 December 2009, the act was renamed by an amendment as Mahatma Gandhi National Rural Employment Guarantee Act (MGNREGA), 2005. The act in effect created India's (and probably the world's) largest anti-poverty programme as measured by the number of beneficiaries. This is the central government's response to the constitutionally manifested right to work and a means to promote livelihood security in India's rural areas. To this end, the Act guarantees 100 days of annual employment at statutory minimum wage rates to any rural household whose adult members are willing to do unskilled manual work (GoI, 2005). The manual work needs to create sustainable assets that promote the economic and infrastructure development of villages.

The act made supplementary livelihood in rural areas by rendering unskilled manual work a legal right. Any rural household seeking unskilled manual work could register its family in the *gram panchayat* (GP) and obtain a job card. With the possession of a job card, the registered rural household could apply for work for atleast 100 days in the GP. According to the Act, any household seeking work must be provided with employment within 15 days or else be paid a daily unemployment allowance until work is found. NREGA has been selectively rolled out in three phases, starting with the 200 most backward districts in India and now is being implemented in all districts nationwide. In 2012, MGNREGS provided employment to 1.63 crore households. Despite its scale, in some states, the scheme appears to fall short of matching demand for work. In Odisha, 7.9

lakh households are provided employment through scheme. The demand for work on MGNREGA scheme tends to be higher in poorer states. This seems to reflect the scheme's built-in self-targeting mechanism, whereby non-poor people find user attractive work on the scheme compared to the poor people (Dutta *et al.*, 2012).

The GoI has taken an 'inclusive growth' approach to poverty reduction, with one of the main flagship programmes being MGNREGA—a public works programme reaching up to 45 million households aimed at supporting a transformation in rural livelihoods and agricultural productivity in India through public works. The Act has two-fold objectives. First, it aims to provide gainful employment and reduce poverty, improving the purchasing power of the rural people, primarily semi-skilled or unskilled ones and those living below the poverty line. Second, it aims to create public assets in the rural areas such as roads, water tanks, and other common property resources that will help residents overcome other hardships associated with poverty.

There are two types of governance challenges facing the large-scale implementation of social safety nets in rural areas. They are the challenge of avoiding elite capture and of actually reaching the poor and the disadvantaged; and the challenge of managing funds allocated to the programme effectively and avoiding leakages and corruption. As a PWP, NREGA uses a self-targeting mechanism to meet the first challenge. In fact, the programme has been remarkably successful in this regard. More than half of its beneficiaries belong to SCs (scheduled castes) and STs (scheduled tribes), and women form a significant majority. Implemented in three phases beginning in 2006, the Act extended to all of rural India in April 2008. NREGA is an innovative answer to the long-standing problem of providing social safety nets in rural areas. Most importantly, it is a rights-based approach (Raabe *et al.*, 2010). In other words, as quoted in UNDP (2009), NREGA exemplifies the features of a "mature democracy", which provides "the poor with the right to demand, the right to know and the right to dignity. Not the right to beg."

The second challenge is more difficult to meet because NREGA involves two features that have been highlighted in the literature as particularly challenging. First, the programme is 'transaction-intensive' in terms of time and space. It requires day-to-day action throughout a country that spans an entire subcontinent. Second, the programme requires discretion, since decision-making on issues such as the type of infrastructure to be created under the programme cannot easily be standardised.

Informed by India's far-ranging experience in managing rural welfare programmes, NREGA has already gone a long way in including innovative design features aimed at overcoming the well-known implementation challenges of such programmes. This scheme is implemented in a decentralised manner and includes consideration of substantial checks and balances as well as oversight and complaint mechanisms. Yet, available evidence indicates that massive implementation problems remain. Farmers have opposed the implementation of the scheme during peak season of agriculture, precisely because of its effect on the wages (Imbert and Papp, 2012). At the same time, there are constant efforts to adjust the implementation procedures so as to resolve these challenges.

The first goal of the millennium development goals (MDGs) is to eradicate extreme poverty and hunger. The target is to achieve full and productive employment and decent work for all, including women and young people. This is one of the most effective routes to eradicate poverty. Suitably designed employment guarantee programmes can contribute to the MDGs in a variety of ways, ranging from the provision of employment *per se* to addressing MDG-related infrastructure and service delivery deficits (Lal *et al.*, 2010). The MGNREGA made supplementary livelihood in rural areas by making unskilled manual work a legal right.

The centerpiece of the 11th Plan's battle against rural poverty was the MGNREGA. The MGNREGA has delivered the largest employment programme in human history, which is unlike any other in its scale, architecture and thrust. Its bottom-up, people-centred, demand-driven, self-selecting, rights-based design is new and unprecedented. Never have in such a short period so many crores of poor people benefited from a government programme (Planning Commission, 2012).

MGNREGA 2.0

As a part of the next level of implementation of MGNREGA, *viz.*, MGNREGA 2.0, GoI has taken up some of the recent initiatives and reforms. The GoI released the revised MGNREGA operational guidelines based on the recommendations of the Mihir Shah Committee (MoRD, 2012). The list of permissible works under MGNREGA has been expanded to strengthen the positive synergy between MGNREGA and agriculture and allied rural livelihoods; to respond to the demands of the states for greater location-specific flexibility in permissible works; and to help improve the ecological balance in rural India.

Some of these works are new but many of them are within the category of works already permitted under MGNREGA. The list was drawn up in response to the demands from states for a more elaborate, specific and unambiguous list of works that could be taken up under the categories currently permissible. While taking up the works under MGNREGA, the following conditions need to be followed. First, only those works are to be taken up that result in creation of durable assets. Second, the order of priority of works is to be determined by the GP. Third, 60:40 ratio to be maintained for labour and material costs should be maintained at the GP level. Lastly, no contractors/labour displacing machinery are to be used.

The expert group has recommended adding 30 agriculture and allied works under the rural job guarantee scheme with the objective of making the programme more effective. These include agriculture, animal husbandry, poultry, drinking water, sanitation and watershed-related works. Besides, the committee also suggested for ensuring demand based character of MGNREGA; effective planning; strict time schedule; deployment of human resources; reducing delays in wage payments; strengthening management information system (MIS); equal opportunity for vulnerable groups; greater role for civil society organisations; and better social audits and vigilance for transparency and accountability (MoRD, 2013).

There is huge governance deficit in the delivery of social development programmes. MGNREGA is directed towards the entire rural adult population without any criteria for getting employment.

As long as one is ready to do hard manual work, one can demand and get work at the notified wage. Now there is a move that the programme be scaled back to just 200 backward districts. This will translate to fewer people/villages benefiting from the programme and to a reduction of fund requirement (Kulkarni, 2014).

Data Source and Methodology

Odisha is situated on the coast along the Bay of Bengal. Odisha stands for its ancient glory and modern endeavour. Endowed with nature's bounty, a 482 km stretch of coastline with virgin beaches, serpentine rivers, mighty waterfalls, forest-clad blue hills of Eastern Ghats with rich wild life, Odisha is dotted with exquisite temples and historic monuments. It has a population of 41,947,358 as per 2011 Census and covers an area of 155,707 square kms. Out of the total population, numbers of male are 21,201,678 and that of female are 20,745,680.

In the present study, beneficiaries of the selected villages are located from the MGNREGA website. Primary data from the beneficiaries are collected using a schedule. The objective behind this is to find out the view of the beneficiaries regarding working of the MGNREGA programme.

Selection Criteria and District Profile

Ten districts of western Odisha lag behind their counterparts of the coastal districts in core sectors.[1] Looking at the degree of development/backwardness of 10 Western Odisha districts, it can be said that out of 87 blocks only 5 blocks are developed, 25 are developing, another 25 are backward and 32 blocks are very backward.

Sample Size and Sampling Procedure

The selected block and sample villages are presented in Tables 6.1 and 6.2. The 3 districts out of these 10 are selected conveniently, i.e.,

1. Eight core sectors include: coal, crude oil, natural gas, petroleum refinery products, fertilisers, electricity, cement and finished steel. "Ten Western Odisha Districts Lag Behind their Counterparts of Coastal Districts in Core Sectors" is taken from the Western Odisha Development Council website (*http://www.wodcorissa.org/about.htm*).

using convenience sampling. These districts are Bargarh, Sambalpur and Sonepur. Out of these districts, one block is selected from each district using simple random sampling. Then out of these three blocks, one village from each block is selected using simple random sampling, except Sambalpur. In Sambalpur, from the selected block Dhankauda, two villages were selected using simple random sampling.

Table 6.1

Demographic Profile of the Districts Under Study (As per 2011 Census)

State/ District	*Total Population (in lakh)*	*Sex Ratio*	*Population Density*	*Literacy Rate*		
				Person	*Male*	*Female*
Odisha	419.47	978	269	73.45	82.40	64.36
Bargarh	14.78	976	253	75.16	84.28	65.84
Sambalpur	10.44	973	158	76.91	85.17	68.47
Sonepur	6.52	959	279	74.42	84.78	63.63

Source: Author's own calculation. Data collected from primary sources.

Table 6.2

List of Sample Village

S. No.	*District*	*Block*	*Gram Panchayat*	*Village*
1	Sambalpur	Dhankauda	Katapali	Katapali
2	Sambalpur	Dhankauda	Kalamati	Budhikhamar
3	Sonepur	Birmaharajpur	Bagbar	Lumurjena
4	Bargarh	Bhatli	Mulbar	Runipali

Source: Author's own calculation. Data collected from primary sources.

Beneficiary schedule was constructed for MGNREGA Scheme based on thematic approach.[2] These include broad categories of

2. Thematic analysis is a method for identifying, analysing and reporting patterns within data. It emphasises pinpointing and examining recording patterns within data. Themes are recording patterns across data sets and are associated to specific research questions. The themes become the categories for analysis. Thematic analysis is performed through the process of coding to create established meaningful patterns. Thematic analysis is most useful in capturing the complexities of meaning within a textual data set.

socio-economic details, awareness, participation, process, monitoring and supervision, payment details, transparency, work site facilities and effectiveness. A robust analytics framework evolved from the objectives with right approach to survey designing, administering, analysing and identifying action items for continual improvements. The size of the sample selected in the four villages—Katapali, Budhikhamar, Lumurjena and Runupali—are 46, 30, 62 and 60 respectively.

Findings and Analysis

The present work is an attempt to make an assessment of the working of MGNREGA in Western Odisha. The households were interviewed by taking their names from the MGNREGA website (*www.nrega.nic.in*) i.e., those households worked under the Scheme in their respective villages.

Issues Relating to Card Holding

In Katapali village, 69.56 per cent of the households do not possess any type of card (Table 6.3). Only 19.56 per cent are found to have BPL (below poverty line) and 8.7 per cent have Antyodaya card. Similarly, in Budhikhamar village, 53.33 per cent, of the individuals, whose names are present in the MGNREGA Scheme list, do not have a ration card and 30 per cent of them have BPL card. About 60 per cent of the

Table 6.3

Types of Card Holders

(in percentage)

S. No.	*Particular*	*Katapali*	*Budhikhamar*	*Lumurjena**	*Runipali*
1	BPL	19.56	30.00	59.68	53.33
2	APL	2.17	6.67	3.22	16.67
3	Antyodaya	8.7	0	17.74	0
4	Control card	0	10.00	0	0
5	Padi card	0	0	0	23.33
6	No card	69.56	53.33	25.81	6.67

Note: *: Indicates a family is being issued two ration cards.

Source: Author's own calculation. Data collected from primary sources.

sample households of Lumurjena village have a BPL card and 25.81 per cent have no card. In Runipali village of Bargarh district 53.33 per cent have a BPL card and 23.33 per cent appear to have padi card.[3]

It is evident that more than half of the beneficiaries in Katapali and Budhikhamar villages do not possess any types of cards. The objective of possessing such cards indicate that the households have access to essential items like rice, wheat, sugar, kerosene, etc., at a subsidised rate. Not possessing these cards debars households from receiving these items at subsidised rate, which is an additional burden for these households.

It can be seen from Table 6.4 that all sample households are aware about the important aspects of MGNREGA in Budhikhamar and Runipali villages. Though the beneficiaries might have heard about the MGNREGA scheme, they are not aware of their entitlements or that they need to ask for work. However, the situation is just the reverse in Budhikhamar and Runipali, i.e., all are aware of the safety nets programme under MGNREGA. This is because the government officials have explained about MGNREGA in these villages. However this is not appropriately explained by the officials in Katapali and Lumurjena villages. To take the full benefit of MGNREGA scheme, it is always advisable to explain the same to beneficiary households by the government officials.

Table 6.4

Awareness of the Households About MGNREGA Amongst Potential Wage Earners

(in percentage)

S. No	*Particular*	*Katapali*	*Budhikhamar*	*Lumurjena*	*Runipali*
1	Households aware of important aspects of MGNREGA	0	100	6.45	100

Source: Author's own calculation. Data collected from primary sources.

There is significant difference among the four villages with respect to job card issued as presented in Table 6.5. The problem is

3. Padi card is a type of ration card which is distributed to poor people by the government. By this card they collect rice, wheat, kerosene etc. from the government at a subsidised rate.

more acute in Katapali village with 39.13 per cent of the households enrolled officially under MGNREGA, but without job cards. Similarly, in Lumurjena village, 14.51 per cent of households do not have job cards. But in the other two villages, all who are working under MGNREGA scheme do have job cards. However, except 3.22 per cent of the households in Lumurjena village, the other selected households have not applied for job cards. The level of awareness about MGNREGA among these potential wage earners is also low in Katapali and Lumurjena villages.

As government officials have explained the usefulness of the Scheme, all sample households in Budhikhamar and Runipali villages have job cards. In the similar manner, most of the households could have job cards too, particularly in Katapali and Runipali villages. Also, most of the beneficiaries of MGNREGA schemes are illiterates in all sample villages. Therefore, the households are innocent about the benefits associated with this Scheme.

Table 6.5

Job Card Status of the Sample Households

(in percentage)

Sl. No.	*Particular*	*Katapali*	*Budhikhamar*	*Lumurjena*	*Runipali*
1	Households who have applied for job cards	0	0	3.22	0
2	Households who had obtained job cards	60.87	100	82.26	100 *
3	Households who had no job cards	39.13	0	14.51	0

Note: * Two households have double job cards.

Source: Author's own calculation. Data collected from primary sources.

Working Conditions

Road construction is the main activity in which the households are engaged. In Katapali and Lumurjena, the households are also engaged in digging of ponds. Some people also work in the dam in Lumurjena village. The average wage rate they are entitled to also varies. In Budhikhamar and Runipali, the workers get ₹125 per day as per the norms, while in Katapali and Lumurjena they receive ₹102.92 and ₹102 respectively (Table 6.6).

Even if the per day wage rate is ₹125, beneficiaries in Katapali and Lumurjena are found to receive lesser amounts as they are unaware about the wage rate. Also, the infrastructure created using MGNREGA scheme is of questionable quality. The workers are basically unskilled or semi-skilled. It is often found that old persons possessing job card do lethargic work.[4]

In the sample villages, the types of infrastructure created are mainly road construction, digging of pond or works in check dam. As mentioned earlier, Mihir Shah Committee had recommended 30 types of infrastructure that can be created under MGNREGA scheme. Clearly, this is not followed in the sample villages. Also, it is interesting to note that as pointed out by the beneficiaries the same work is being repeated in subsequent years. Basic amenities like first-aid box and child care at work site are not found at any of the sample villages. Even drinking water is not provided at the work site in Katapali and Lumurjena.

Table 6.6

Working Conditions of Households under MGNREGA Scheme

S. No.	*Particular*	*Katapali*	*Budhikhamar*	*Lumurjena*	*Runipali*
1	Average wage rate	102.92	125	102	125
2	Type of activity	Road construction and digging of pond	Road construction	Road construction, digging of pond and works in dam	Road construction
3	Facilities available at the work site	No facilities	Drinking water	No facilities	Drinking water

Source: Author's own calculation. Data collected from primary sources.

4. Lethargic work means lazy work. These people, particularly old persons aged more than 55 years do not show any interest in the work. They are very slow in their work.

Then again, in Budhikhamar and Runipali, although the households enrolled under MGNREGA are actually getting jobs at least for some days, in Katapali and Lumurjena, they are failing to get any considerable work (Table 6.7). The situation is worst in Katapali where only 26.08 per cent of the households get the work. So the documentation carried out by government officials is vague.

Basically, the beneficiaries working under MGNREGA for wage employment are illiterate. Taking this advantage, a middleman in Runipali village collects all the job cards from the households. He takes the beneficiaries to the bank/post office to collect their wages, claiming to help them. However, the work of the middleman is suspicious. It is interesting to find that some of the job cards are in the name of individuals who are already dead or have migrated to some other place. The authorities should take necessary steps to identify such cases and cancel their job cards. In Katapali and Lumurjena, the households are not satisfied by the way the Scheme functions.

Table 6.7

Perceptions of Households About MGNREGA Scheme

(in percentage)

S. No.	*Particular*	*Katapali*	*Budhikhamar*	*Lumurjena*	*Runipali*
1	Households who claimed to have got work	26.08	100	83.87	100
2	Average number of days of work obtained	75.42	68.53	53.69	26.15
3	Households who got full payment	100	100	100	100
4	Those satisfied with the functioning of MGNREGA	2.17	100	14.52	100
5	Those who received wage advance	0	10	0	0

Source: Author's own calculation. Data collected from primary sources.

Among those who got the work, the average number of working days noted was far less than 100 days as presented in Table 6.8. It is only 26.15 days in Runipali village. All these shortcomings lead to households losing faith in MGNREGA. However, the good thing is that those who have worked have received their payments and only 10 per cent in Budhikhamar village have taken some wage advance. In almost all the villages, a written format of the application is kept. Persons interested to work under MGNREGA scheme have to collect these formats of application, either put signature or thumb impression and deposit the same in the *panchayat* office. However, the beneficiaries are much ignorant about the benefits associated with these applications and how they are helpful for them. The point to be outlined here is that the beneficiaries are illiterates. They do not know why a written application is required. Government officials should take necessary steps to explain these associated benefits of the scheme. An immediate solution may be to show these to the beneficiaries through documentary/short films.

Issuing of timely payment and regular and adequate amount of work is an critical element for the success of MGNREGA. In these areas, though they are getting the payments in time, the provision of adequate and regular amount of work is the most crucial problem. In Runipali village, those who are interested to work are given employment for a few days and the remaining portion of the work is completed by using machine. It leads to dissatisfaction among the households with the functioning of MGNREGA. Only 2.17 per cent in Katapali and 14.52 per cent in Lumurjena villages are satisfied with the functioning of MGNREGA.

People who applied for work account for 76.67 per cent in Budhikhamar village and 18.33 per cent in Runipali village. In other two villages, they are not aware that a written application needs to be given for work under the Act. In Runipali village, 81.67 per cent of the beneficiaries do not know how to write the application for work. The study clearly indicates that there lies a demand for work via MGNREGA in all these four villages. In three villages except Katapali, people have migrated recently for work. In future, most of the beneficiaries are interested to work under MGNREGA, provided it is properly implemented.

Table 6.8

Awareness Regarding Writing of Application for Employment

(in percentage)

S. No.	*Particular*	*Katapali*	*Budhikhamar*	*Lumurjena*	*Runipali*
1	Households with written work application	0	76.67	0	18.33
2	Households not aware that a written application needs to be given	84.78	0	100	0
3	Cannot write	15.22	23.33	0	81.67

Source: Author's own calculation. Data collected from primary sources.

Conclusions

MGNREGA Scheme has catered to the generic village building initiatives. The programme did not differentiate educated/skilled workers from the unskilled/illiterate ones. The programme remained true to its 'right to work' entailments and did not counsel households with better living standards that approached for works. Lack of awareness is identified in the present study as a severe bottleneck that reflected in poor understanding of minimum wage, unemployment allowance, accident compensation, employment opportunities and overall MGNREGA process. The programme did not have any upper ceiling limit on age. Old people undergo laborious work and instill lethargic work culture among the beneficiaries.

Table 6.9

Migration and Perception of Households Regarding Future Employment

S. No.	*Particular*	*Katapali*	*Budhikhamar*	*Lumurjena*	*Runipali*
1	Whether anyone has migrated in near future for work	0	26.67	3.22	25.00
2	Interested to work in MGNREGA in future	91.31	100	100	100
3	Expect to get work in time	91.31	100	100	100
4	Interested to work in future, if MGNREGA is properly implemented	100	100	100	100

Source: Author's own calculation. Data collected from primary sources.

Safety net programme like MGNREGA scheme was initiated with the strategy of transferring some purchasing power to the hands of poor or marginalised people. The objective is to effectively tackle poverty, enhance growth's effectiveness in reducing poverty and stimulate economic growth. In return, certain infrastructure can be created for the village with the work effort these people provide. However, it is found that these infrastructures which are supposed to be created are of questionable quality. Also, the same work is undertaken at the village level in successive years.

There are a number of constraints in the success of the scheme. The beneficiaries are mostly illiterate. Taking this advantage, middle man take the benefit in the sense that they pay less to the beneficiaries after collecting their dues from either bank or post office. In a low income state like Odisha, money sanctioned under MGNREGA scheme are unutilised and are returned to the Ministry. Therefore, proper implementation of the scheme is a major challenge for the officials at state, district and *panchayat* levels.

With the recommendations of the Mihir Shah Committee, i.e., MGNREGA 2.0, 30 agriculture and allied works were streamlined under public works. But none of these were implemented in the sample villages as evident from our present study. The villages preferred to construct roads or dig ponds. The present research suggests a few changes desired in the Act for better performance. They are identifying village requirements based on secondary research; monitoring the effectiveness of programmes; restricting the use of machines; and creating more opportunities of employment for the rural poor. Multiplier effects of cash transfers by public works can improve the livelihood of beneficiaries, if loopholes and gaps in implementation of the scheme are reduced. This can increase human development of the community.

References

Barrientos, A. (2012). "Social Transfers and Growth: What Do We Know? What Do We Need to Find Out?", *World Development* 40 (1): 11-20.

Barritenos, A. and J. Scott (2008). "Social Transfers and Growth A Review", *BWPI Working Paper* 52. Manchester: Brooks World Poverty Institute, University of Manchester.

Basu, A.K. (2013). "Impact of Rural Employment Guarantee Schemes on Seasonal Labor Markets: Optimum Compensation and Workers' Welfare", *Journal of Economic Inequality* 11(1): 1-34.

delNinno, C., K. Subbarao and A. Milazzo (2009). "How to Make Public Works Work: A Review of the Experiences", *World Bank, Social Protection Discussion Paper* No. 0905. pp.1-78.

Development Committee (2012). *Safety Nets Work: During Crisis and Prosperity.* Joint Ministerial Committee of the Boards of Governors of the World Bank and the International Monetary Fund on the Transfer of Real Resources to Developing Countries, DC2012-0003. 11 April.

Dutta, P., R. Murgai, M. Ravallion and D. de Walle (2012). "Does India's Employment Guarantee Scheme Guarantee Employment?", *Policy Research Working Paper* No.: 6003. pp.1-32.

Government of India (2005). *The National Rural Employment Guarantee Act 2005: Operational Guidelines.* New Delhi: Ministry of Rural Development.

Grosh, M., C. delNinno, E. Tesliuc and A. Ouerghi (2008). "Chapter 5: Benefit Levels and Delivery Mechanisms" and "Chapter 7: Understanding Common Interventions", in *For Protection and Promotion: The Design and Implementation of Effective Safety Nets.* World Bank.

Hagen-Zanker, J., A. McCord and R. Holmes (2011). *Systematic Review of the Impact of Employment Guarantee Schemes and Cash Transfers on the Poor.* London: Overseas Development Institute. June.

IEG (2011). *Social Safety Nets: An Evaluation of World Bank Support, 2000-2010.* Washington, DC: Independent Evaluation Group, World Bank.

Imbert, C. and J. Papp (2012). "Equilibrium Distributional Impacts of Government Employment Programs: Evidence from India's Employment Guarantee", *Working Paper No.*: 14. Paris: Paris School of Economics. pp.1-75.

Jorgensen, S. and R. Serrano-Berthet (2009). "Comprehensive Social Policy for Inclusive and Sustainable Globalization", in Estanislao Gacitúa-Marió, Andrew Norton and Sophia V. Georgieva (eds.), *Building Equality and Opportunity through Social Guarantees: New Approaches to Public Policy and the Realization of Rights.* World Bank, Washington DC. pp.45-68.

Kulkarni, A. (2014). "Is the Proposed Restructuring of MGNREGA Desirable?", *Livemint: Openion.* 20 October.

Lal, R., S. Miller, M. Lieuw-Kie-Song and D. Kostzer (2010). "Public Works and Employment Programmes: Towards a Long-term Development Approach", *Working Paper* No. 66. Brazil: International Policy Centre for Inclusive Growth, Poverty Group, UNDP.

Lin, J.Y. and D. Rosenblatt (2012). "Shifting Patterns of Economic Growth and Rethinking Development", *Journal of Economic Policy Reform* 15(3): 171-94.

McCord, A. (2007). "The Social Protection Function of Short-term Public Works Programs in the Context of Chronic Poverty", in A. Barrientos and D. Hulme (eds.), *Social Protection for the Poor and Poorest: Concepts, Policies and Politics.* London: Palgrave.

Ministry of Rural Development (2013). *Mahatma Gandhi National Rural Employment Guarantee Act, 2005 (Mahatma Gandhi NREGA): Operational Guidelines.* 4th Edition. New Delhi: Government of India.

————. (2012). *MGNREGA Sameeksha: An Anthology of Research Studies on the Mahatma Gandhi National Rural Employment Guarantee Act, 2005, 2006-2012.*Government of India. Edited and compiled by Mihir Shah, Nilakshi Mann and Varad Pande. New Delhi: Orient Black Swan.

Planning Commission (2012). *Report of the 12th Plan (2012-2017): Steering Committee on Rural Livelihoods and Rural Governance.* Rural Development Division, Government of India. January.

Prabhu, K.S. (2009). "Conditional Cash Transfer Schemes for Alleviating Human Poverty: Relevance for India", Discussion Paper 1. 1-28 April.

Raabe, K., R. Birner, M. Sekher, K.G. Gayathridevi, A. Shilpi and E. Schiffer (2010). "How to Overcome the Governance Challenges of Implementing NREGA: Insights from Bihar Using Process-Influence Mapping", *IFPRI Discussion Paper* 00963. Development Strategy and Governance Division. April.

Subbarao, K., C. delNinno, C. Andrews and C. Rodriguez-Alas (2013). *Public Works as a Safety Net: Design, Evidence and Implementation.* Washington D.C.: World Bank. pp.1-403.

United Nations Development Program (UNDP) (2009). *Employment Guarantee Quickening India's March Towards MDGs.* Report on an International Seminar on Rural Poverty: Key Initiatives in Achieving Millennium Development Goals and the Role of NREGA. New Delhi: National Agricultural Science Centre. 21-22 January.

Zepeda, E., S. McDonald, M. Panda and G. Kumar (2013). *Employing India: Guaranteeing Jobs for Rural Poor.* Washington D.C.: Carnegie Endowment and UNDP. pp.1-74

Zepada, E. and D. Alarcon(2012). "Which Way to Reduce Poverty: Cash Transfers or Employment Guarantee Scheme?", in Ashok K. Pankaj (ed.), *Right to Work and Rural India: Working of the Mahatma Gandhi National Rural Employment Guarantee Scheme (MGNREGS).* New Delhi: Sage Publication India Pvt. Ltd. pp.81-97.

7

VEERAIAH KONDURI

Inclusive Potential of MGNREGA

Problems in Perspective

Introduction

The MGNREGA[1] became a turf war between the two streams of economists in India since the Bharatiya Janata Party (BJP) government came to power with full majority. Immediately after the swearing in, the divergent views within BJP government started emerging. The late Rural Development Minister[2] was of the view to implement this Act after strengthening it considerably. We don't have much time or scope to know what would have been his ideas when he referred to the need of strengthening it. But his successor developed a damning criticism by terming this flagship programme as "yet another government program exploited for pure partisan purpose" (Indian Express, 2014a). Terming a programme that purely partisan shows the bent of an incumbent government's mind. The argument against the Mahatma Gandhi National Rural Employment Guarantee Act (MGNREGA) has come into existence, along with the passage of the Act itself. Over a period of time, a broad based campaign was launched discrediting the Act (Patnaik, 2014). Before, the general elections, the free market fundamentalists had lobbied fiercely to reshape the so-called wasteful social sector expenditures. Primary among their targets was the MGNREGA, which according to them

1. The National Rural Employment Guarantee Act 2005 was subsequently rechristened as the Mahatma Gandhi National Rural Employment Guarantee Act 2005 by an amendment passed by the Parliament in 2009.
2. Shri Gopinath Munde died in car mishap immediately after taking over the responsibility as the Minister for Rural Development.

should become UCT (unconditional cash transfer) scheme (Ambasta, 2014). Those who claim that the MGNREGA is a populist scheme, as well as a waste of national resources (Bhalla, 2014) base their understanding in the deep-seated neoliberalism. They don't want to look at the Act and its actual implementation on the ground.

We can identify the two broad themes around which the general discourse surrounding MGNREGA is taking shape. One is the argument extended with the Keynesianist understanding on the multiplier effect and the other represent the opposite pole to it. The Keynesianist understanding seeks an interventionist state, where the second group seeks the withdrawal of state, discharging its duties in the interest of larger public good. The group of economists who petitioned against the proposed changes in the Act and its guidelines, Bardhan *et al.* (Indian Express, 2014b) are of the keyneneslisnist understanding; whereas those who are fiercely batting for whittling down of this Act belongs to the neoliberal camp. Questions are raised on the issues encountered in implementation of the Act (Shah, 2014; NCAER, 2013). These demands were aimed at whittling down the Act and transforming it into an another scheme. If we consider the underlying reason behind the demand for whittling down this Act, we would be able to know the real picture in a better manner.

In the last few years, a plethora of measures have been announced and ushered in to promote financial inclusion, i.e., improving access to finance from formal institutions in rural India. The National Rural Financial Inclusion Plan laid out the road map in this regard. One would have to wait till the data from the next round of All India Debt and Investment Survey (AIDIS) and Situation Assessment Survey of Farmers (SASF) are made available, before realising whether measures to promote financial inclusion are paying off. In this background, in this paper, I shall try to contextualise the debate on financial inclusion and role of MGNREGA in achieving financial inclusion.

Immediate Context for this Debate

To understand why the neoliberal lobby is up its ante against this national flagship programme, we need to look at two powerful expositions made by the economists belonging not truly to anti-reforms camp. One exposition directly links us with the debate about consequences of the economic reforms process; whereas the second one brings out the visible impact at the village level in terms of class power and its authority. Let us consider the basic aims of the objective in order to understand in which context the Act came into being. The primary objective of the Act-based employment guarantee programme is to ensure the transfer of a minimum income to the rural households through self-seeking wage employment—a departure from the existing programmes. This immediate necessity should be seen in the context. The character of pre-NREGA India can be explained as following.

Mosquerira and Fahimi (2014) presents a comparative picture of appropriation and deprivation. According to them, the triumph of neoliberalism in the 1980s across the world and in 1990s in India has resulted in creating significant incomes and in the distribution of wealth worldwide over the past 25-30 years to the detriment of the less privileged. Only the economic and social elite and to a lesser extent, a new middle class, are profiting from this neoliberal surge. The lowest 40 per cent on the income scale are getting very little benefit out of it. On the global scale, Mosquerira and Fahimi (2014) identify three distinct trends in growing economic inequality. The first being the change in terms of income distribution between wages and profits to the detriment of wages. Secondly, the economic growth has been decoupled from material prosperity of the majority of population; and finally, the tax and social transfer policy has had less of a corrective influence on income distribution than in the past. All these trends can be identifiable in the Indian context as well.

The poverty reduction during the reform period did not meet the expectations of policy makers. The rate of poverty reduction has been lower in the post-reform period. This is particularly true in the rural areas which are sustained largely by a small, peasant-based economy. The inequality has increased on several dimensions after economic reforms (Motiram and Vakulabharanam, 2011). This multidimensionality of inequality reflects at three levels, i.e., individual level, sectoral inequality and finally, inter-state and intra-state regional inequalities. The employment- unemployment situation, which plays a key role, deteriorated during the reform period. None other than the former Deputy Chairman of Planning Commission of India, and astute reformist of international reputation, Ahluwalia (2011) himself admitted this. It is also a fact that the condition of the agriculture sector that still provides livelihood to the majority of the population and absorbs about 56.5 per cent of the total workforce, worsened in the reforms process. This inverse dependence of workforce on agriculture eventually resulted in the decline in agricultural productivity, thereby increasing disguised and open unemployment and under-employment as well as low occupational diversification which triggered large scale migration (Pankaj, 2012). With no income and underemployment or unemployment the rural population is faced with the danger of social exclusion. The process of social exclusion and liberalisation-privatisation-globalisation trio are complementary to each other. In the following sections we shall consider this inter-connectivity before proceeding further to consider the inclusive architecture of MGNREGA and this architecture at play in the subsequent sections.

Economic Reforms in India and Social Exclusion

The concept of social exclusion originated in the developed European countries in the early 1970s and for the first time the term came into use in France (Silver, 1994). The then minister for social welfare, Reno Lenoir popularised this notion by applying it for those who were dropping out of the Bismarcian social welfare measures due to peculiar reasons. Since then, the concept got ascendance within the European community and by the time of Tony Blair, it became one of the major concepts around which the welfare policies are designed. Social exclusion is a socially constructed concept and has the flexibility to be adopted so as to suit a country's concrete conditions. By definition, social exclusion is a process in which individuals or an entire community are systematically blocked from being complete members of society. For citizens to participate in their society as full members, access to the various rights and opportunities as well as access to resources should be made available to the citizenery in the normal course of time. Any society can be perceived normal when a citizen of that society in any circumstances shall be in a position to avail the benefits of his share, enjoy the rights guaranteed under the civic administration therein and have access to the national as well as natural resources like any other individual irrespective of his place of birth, origin, caste, creed, colour or by any other means of discrimination. These normal conditions of any nation are usually defined in its statutes and written/unwritten Constitution.

To apply this condition to Indian society, we should have a look at our basic statute book, i.e., the Constitution of India. By law, the Constitution of India provides an equal opportunity for each citizen in all respects of civic life. The fundamental rights, the inalienable basic feature of our constitution, are applicable for all the citizens, irrespective of their separate identities and differences. The right to life, under the Constitution of India, which was expanded to include right to work, by the Supreme Court, stands central in realising the fundamental rights.[3] Even before the Supreme Court intervened to declare the right to work as a fundamental right, the Constitution of India enshrined this right under Chapter IV, Directive Principles of State Policy. Thus right to work and livelihood are constitutional promises to citizens, irrespective of their differences. Article 39(a) reads, "The State shall, in particular, direct its policy towards securing that the citizens, men and women equally—have the right to an adequate means to livelihood", and Article 41 directs the states to make effective provision of securing the right to work to public assistance in case of unemployment.[4] Now let us turn to the implications of neoliberal economic reforms policies on these basic goals and promises of the Constitution to the Indian citizens. There are a number of studies that give a graphic presentation about the impact of economic reforms in India. To be precise, I shall concentrate on the three sources to read into that impact. Firstly, 66th Round Survey of the National Sample Survey (NSS); secondly the Census 2011 data; and finally the findings of Expert Group on poverty estimations headed by the former chairman, Prime

3. Olega Tellis *versus* Bombay Municipal Corporation, *All India Reporter*, 1986, SC 180.

4. Constitution of India.

Minister's Economic Advisory Council. The brief findings of these three data sets imply the following.

The National Sample Survey Organisation (NSSO) data confirms the fact that there are wide-ranging sectoral inequalities in their contribution to GDP (gross domestic product). The share of agriculture in GDP came down from 32.5 per cent in 1984-1995 to mere 15.7 per cent in 2010-11. The contribution of industrial sector stagnated around 26.0 per cent and 29.1 per cent during the same period. The service sector scaled up from 41.5 per cent to 55.2 per cent, an almost 10.0 per cent growth. But as observed in many studies, the dependency of people on agriculture for their livelihood has not declined commensurately. This led to the decline in livelihood opportunities both spatially and temporally during this period. This also in turn resulted in casualisation and contructualisation of workforce—both in agriculture and industry. Of course, the service industry is leading the pack in this regard. The stagnation in employment generation in agriculture and inability of the industry and the service sector to absorb the labour force in the ratio of the growth rate indicate disjunction between growth and employment in the liberalisation period (Pankaj, 2012: 6-7). The second data source on which I relied for deriving my conclusion is the Census 2011. The readings of data from Census 2011 also substantiated the above understanding. The jobless growth, that became the hallmark of economic reforms, now spread to the agrarian sector. The number of farmers that stood at the level ₹10.38 crore in 2001, declined to 9.58 crore. About 80 lakh farmers had quit cultivation as their primary economic activity and became agricultural workers. Similarly, the number of agricultural workers that stood at 26.5 per cent of the total population in 2001, increased to 30.0 per cent by 2011. This fact indicates at the intense and distress conditions that the agrarian sector had encountered during the reforms phase.

Same was the situation in erstwhile Andhra Pradesh (AP). The percentage of farmers declined from 22.52 per cent in 2001 to 16.47 per cent in 2011. Those working in the household industries declined from 4.47 per cent from 2001 to 3.65 per cent in 2011 and joined the ranks of agricultural workers. At the same time, the number of agricultural workers increased phenomenally, from 1,38,32,152 (39.64 per cent of state's population) to 1,69,67,754 (43.04 per cent) in this period. This reflects on the enormity of pressure that was forming on agriculture for employment generation. The number of those who could generate employment in agriculture (the cultivators) declined and that of employment seekers (agricultural workers) increased. Without any further explanation, one can read into the negative impact and factors that contributed to this Patnaik (2014) links this agrarian distress with the propensity of primitive accumulation of capital. He further states:

> Under neo-liberalism however primitive accumulation becomes more pronounced, moe open and more devastating. It takes both a 'stock' form and a 'flow form, 'the former entails a *de facto* dispossession of the peasants by big capital, via obtaining their land at throwaway prices, (and hence an outright destruction of the livelihood of the agricultural labourers) while the later entails a squeeze on the profitability of peasant agriculture, owing inter alia to an increase in input prices supplied by the big capitalists.

He continues to declare that, as a result of this capital's primitive accumulation propensity, the agricultural workers are also falling victims to this agrarian crisis.

This situation has its consequential impact on the wage income of agricultural workers' families. The dwindling work opportunities on farm and changes of manual work patterns from daily wage to contract wage and increasing dependence on non-agricultural wage employment dragging the women workforce as well as forcing them to work even for sub-minimum wages. The findings from Reserve Bank of India (RBI) Working Paper (Misra and Anoop, 2014) corroborated with this understanding. The RBI paper calculates that the employment elasticity was at 2.6 in 1972-73 to 1977-78, when the economy experienced compound annual growth rate of GDP of 4.6 per cent. But in the decade starting from 1993-1994 to 2011-2012, the employment elasticity came down to mere 1.1, when the compound annual growth rate of GDP stood at 6 per cent. Similarly, the employment elasticity in the agricultural sector turned into negative from 1.09 in 1999-2000 to 2004-05 to -0.41 during the period between 2004-05/2011-12. Such a change occurred despite the existence of MGNREGA. One can guess what would have been the situation if there is no MGNREGA! It is a fact that the peasant agriculture, who deploys more manpower in agricultural operations, is the primary source of employment, rather than the capitalist farmer who deploys more and more machines in discharging agricultural operations. This ultimately resulted in curtailment of significant number of work days availability and a cut in their real wages. The cumulative effect of these changes was captured by the Expert Group on poverty estimates, which I had referred to above.

The table given below reflects the variation in the basic details of poverty estimates. Table 7.1 informs about the monthly per capita expenditure, whereas Table 7.2 informs about the absolute number of poor in India, including the absolute poverty decline during the period. As shown in Table 7.1, the per capita monthly consumer expenditure considered by the Tendulkar committee, to be categorised as below poverty, is upwardly revised by the Rangarajan panel from ₹673 to 801 for the rural areas and ₹860 to 1198 for urban areas for the year 2009-10. Similarly for the year 2011-12, the Tendulkar committee fixed minimum monthly per capita expenditure at ₹816 for rural and ₹1000 for urban; whereas the Rangarajan panel pegged these figures at ₹972 and 1407 (respectively) for the same period. The calculations arrived at by the Suresh Tendulkar panel suggests that a person can live on and meet his food and non-food expenditure requirements with mere ₹22.43 per day in rural areas and ₹28.66 per day in urban areas in 2009-10; whereas a person who spent ₹27.20 per day in rural areas and ₹33.33 in urban areas in 2011-12 can be treated as living APL (above poverty line). There is a slight increase in these per day per capita consumer expenditure since the time of Rangarajan panel.

Table 7.2 also reveals similar variations in the number of absolute poor in the country. The Tendulkar committee concluded that only 29.8 per cent of India's population was poor in 2009-10 and it further went down to 21.9 per cent by 2011-12; whereas the Rangarajan panel findings conclude that a 38.2 per cent of Indians were poor in 2009-10 and in 2011-12, the percentage of poor declined to 29.5 per cent. Thus on an average, an additional 10 per cent of the country's people got the BPL tag. Although the number of poor went up with the calculations of Rangarajan panel, the so-called commentariat which expressed its outrage over the Tendulkar committee findings kept silent for its own reasons.

Table 7.1

Monthly Per Capita Expenditure

(Numbers in millions)

	2009-10		*2011-12*	
	Rural	*Urban*	*Rural*	*Urban*
Tendulkar	673	860	816	1000
Rangarajan	801	1198	972	1407

Source: Expert Group to Review the Methodology for Estimation of Poverty, 2005.

Table 7.2

Changes in Absolute Poverty

(Numbers in millions)

	2009-10			*2011-12*			*Decline*		
	Rural	*Urban*	*Total*	*Rural*	*Urban*	*Total*	*Rural*	*Urban*	*Total*
Tendulkar	278.2	76.5	354.7	216.7	53.1	269.8	61.5	23.4	84.9
Rangarajan	325.9	128.7	454.6	260.5	102.5	363	65.4	26.2	91.6

Source: Expert Group to Review the Methodology for Estimation of Poverty, 2005.

When we see the poverty estimates of Rangarajan panel in the light of the NSSO's 68th Round Survey, the incompatibility of both the findings comes out more expressively. According to the 68th Round Survey of NSSO, the total number of workforce increased to 30.9 million by 2011-12. But only 1.5 million workforce could be absorbed by the economy, given its slackening of GDP growth from 8.40 per cent in 2009-10 to 6.88 per cent in 2011-12. Similarly, the labour force participation ratio declined from 392 per 1000 at the time of 61st Round Survey to 364 per 1000 by the time of 68th Round Survey, thereby indicating a stark decrease by 28 per 1000 (Konduri, 2014)· For an economy that is catching up with fast growth rates, one should be concerned about the rate of poverty as we experience in India. No one denies the fact that the slow growth rate in decline of poverty is coupled with the same in employment opportunities and livelihood sources. The cumulative affect all these changes is the slowdown in aggregate demand which will have counter-cyclical effect on the economy. As the large section of people appears to have failed to live up to the daily family needs, it would be impossible to expect from them to be players in the financial services market by availing the plethora of financial products and eventually transform themselves from financially excluded to financially included. Hence, the economic reforms process resulted in overall social exclusion of larger section of people in India.

All these data sources collectively confirm three basic forms of social exclusion in vogue in India arising from the neo-liberal economic reforms. They are economic exclusion, social exclusion and financial exclusion. This damning impact also included political consequences. In the words of Ashok K. Pankaj, the reform phase growth led to some serious social and political implications. Declining employment opportunities for educated rural and rural youth and shrinking sources of livelihood in the rural areas have increased despair and dependency among these population. During this period, India witnessed a series of discontent and unrest. This discontent reflected both in the movements surrounding amelioration of economic distress and at times, this even led to the acceleration of identity-based movements as the excluded seek shelter under the umbrella of natural or constructed identity in order to make the governments listen. Finally, realising from the experiences, the Government of India (GoI), under the pressure from the Left which held considerable influence in the Parliament at that time, came out with a programme of Bharat Nirman that upheld provision for building of rural infrastructure and generation of productive assets. The MGNREGA became a part and parcel of that larger venture. It is in this context the MGNREGA came into being with the basic aims and objectives of creating new employment opportunities for the rural on universal basis. Other objectives include reduction of distress migration, invigorating the civic and community life, as well as strengthening decentralised and participatory development and decision-making process. All in all, the MGNREGA is directed to assure some cushion in terms of income fall. It is with this understanding that some economists have argued in favour of inclusive public spending, as not only desirable but also providing very direct economic benefits as it is much more effective in ameliorating the rural poor from problems such as credit crunch, distress and aggregate demand slow down (Ghosh, 2009).

Social Inclusion and MGNREGA

The approach paper to 11th Five Year Plan categorically stressed on the need of employment generation, more specifically in rural India, as the way to bridge the developmental gaps. For the first time, the country's premier body for developmental planning conceded the fact that during the period of economic reforms, the inequalities between the haves and have-nots, rural and urban, employed and unemployed, and the underemployed are on rise. Perhaps, this kind of realisation dealt a death blow in the hands of neoliberal shenanigans who usurped power through campaign centring on a developmental agenda. This rises a question about the kind and nature of development that the incumbent government is representing. Having said that, let us revert back to the question. The MGNREGA has many firsts in terms of inclusive development goals. The inclusive strategy of MGNREGA lies in its basic objectives. The government listed out four major goals to meet through this Act. They are: strong social safety net for the vulnerable groups by providing a fall-back employment source, when other employment alternatives are scarce or inadequate; strengthen the natural resource base of rural livelihood and create durable assets in rural areas; empowerment of rural poor through the processes of a rights-based law; and finally new ways of doing business, as a model of governance reform anchored on the principles of transparency and grass-roots democracy. All these goals lie at the heart of social inclusion. Moreover, ensuring women participation and inclusion will have far reaching socio-economic consequences. Another major departure lies in the composition of expenditure. The state governments are supposed to meet 25 per cent of the cost including wages of skilled and semi-skilled workers; whereas the central government would bear the remaining cost of material and the whole of wage payments for unskilled labour (Breman and Varinder, 2012). The soul of this Act lies in benefiting the rural unskilled daily wage labour whose prime source of income depends on agriculture. All other existing social welfare programmes and Acts are based on executive discretionary powers and with definitive budgetary allotments. Contrary to such welfare programmes, this is only the welfare programme that is backed by Law and also with provisions for open ended funding pattern. For that matter, it can be said that it is only for this Act the central government came forward to take the financial responsibility, whereas other rights-based Acts such as Right to Education and National Food Security Act warrant the state governments to shoulder considerable responsibility.

MGNREGA is recognised as one of the world's largest publicly-funded employment programme. The implementation has spread all over the country in phased manner. Initially, it took off in 200 districts. In the year 2012-13 alone, according to the report presented by Ministry of Rural Development (MoRD), 230.41 crore man-days were generated; and in 2013-14, it came down to 220.34 crore man-days.[5] The statistics reveal sometimes as well as conceal at other times. The table given below, drawn from the minutes of Performance Review Committee[6] meeting dated 5-6 June 2014, indicates the volume (all figures in crores) both in terms of physical as well as financial execution of the Act. A total of 35.49 crores households were provided employment of 1657.87 crores days, which means that on an average, the households got additional average wage employment for 46.71 days in a year. Although this falls short of the legal mandate, its contribution to the rural economy could not be ruled out. The volume, as the tables given below reveals in terms of budgetary support allocations, hovered around 0.5 per cent of GDP. Of the total amount of ₹243411.4 crores, 70 per cent, i.e., ₹163578.09 is spent on wages—implying that over the last 8 years, this is the amount that have reached directly into the village

5. *http;//mnregaweb4.nic.in/netnrega/all_lvl_details_dashboard_new.aspx.*

6. Performance Review Committee (PRC) meeting 5-6 June, 2014, (MGNREGA Division)

economies. As the data below reveals, during this 8-year period, 1657.87 crores person-days of employment was generated. Also this means each worker earned an additional income of ₹98.66 through MGNREGA. If we considers the total number of households that have benefited under this Act since its inception, the average income accrued to per household stands at ₹4,608.77, which is more than 10 per cent of the total income of an agricultural household. This has its own multiplier effect on the rural economy in particular and the nation's economy in general. It is revealed by several studies, including that done by NSSO, that the workers utilise the majority of their MGNREGA income not only for consumption, but also to meet the needs such as expenditure on education and health. Thus the MGNREGA helped in not only facilitating sustainable asset creation in agriculture, but also the creation of capability enhancing assets that are directly linked to human development—which is again the sole aim of economic development. When we look at the social base of beneficiaries, more than 50 per cent are SC (scheduled caste) and ST (scheduled tribe) beneficiaries in any given year under observation as well as almost 50 per cent of the beneficiaries happened to be women.

Table 7.3

Physical Financial Performance of MGNREGA

(All figures in crores)

	2008-09	*2009-10*	*2010-11*	*2011-12*	*2012-13*	*2013-14*
Job Cards	10.01	11.25	11.98	12.50	12.79	13.13
Employment provided to Households	4.51	5.26	5.49	5.06	4.98	4.76
Person-days	216.32	283.59	257.15	218.76	229.86	218.10
SC Beneficiaries	63.36 (29%)	86.45 (30%)	78.76 (31%)	48.47 (22%)	50.96 (22%)	49.26 (23%)
ST Beneficiaries	55.02 (25%)	58.74 (21%)	53.62 (21%)	40.92 (19%)	40.75 (18%)	37.22 (17%)
Others	97.95 (45%)	138.40 (49%)	124.78 (48%)	129.38 (59%)	138.14 (60%)	131.18 (60%)
Women Beneficiaries	103.57 (48%)	136.40 (48%)	122.74 (48%)	105.27 (48%)	117.93 (51%)	115.15 (53%)

Source: Performance Review Committee (PRC) meeting 5-6 June 2014, (MGNREGA Division).

This is much higher than the stipulations made under the Act, which sought that atleast 33 per cent of the beneficiaries would be women. Pankaj and Tankha (2012) captures the empowerment effects of the MGNREGA on women workers. If we remember the fact that these are the very sections that were deprived of the benefits of growth under neoliberalism, the utility value of the MGNREGA deserves commendation. Thus the Act achieved the unmanageable task of ensuring comprehensive social inclusion.

Survey

The data that I have presented here is part of a larger data set which was collected through field survey aimed at capturing the socio-economic changes in rural AP. The study area spreads across 22 rural districts except Hyderabad. The study was commenced in December 2013 when the state was yet to be bifurcated, and the data are collected for the financial year 2012-13 through the stratified random sample. Four villages have been selected from each district representing different agro-climatic conditions and nature of soil in order to reflect the crop diversity. Also, villages in proximity with the census towns are in considerable proportion, which can give us an understanding about the divergence in livelihood sources. The data are presented for both the parts of states. The questionnaire includes a detailed set of questions on wage labour from the agricultural as well as non-agricultural operations. Three visits were paid to each of the following villages, to collect the primary data as well as to remove the inconsistencies. Next, the variables and the derive values were standardised. The data relating to the total number of job card holders and that of beneficiaries for these villages are collected from the MoRD website. Surprisingly for three villages, the website says there are no beneficiaries under the Act for the survey year; whereas the respondents confirmed that they worked under the Act during the survey year; and this was also cross-checked with the records of field assistants of those villages. Hence, this anomaly is to be considered as a problem in data entry for these villages. Similarly for some villages, the number of job cards issued was far higher than the total population, which indicates embezzlement of records with connivance of the local authorities.

Table 7.4

Financial Performance of MGNREGA

	2006-07	*2007-08*	*2008-09*	*2009-10*	*2010-11*	*2011-12*	*2012-13*	*2013-14*	*Total*
Budget Outlay	11,300	12,000	30,000	39,100	40,100	31,000	30,287	33,000	2,26,787
Central Releases	8,640.85	12,610.39	29,939.60	33,506.61	35,768.95	29,189.77	30,009.96	32,743.68	2,12,409.8
Total Available Fund	12,703.55	19,305.81	37,397.06	49,579.19	54,172.14	48,805.68	45,051.43	42,265.45	
Expenditure in crores against Available Fund (%)	8,823.35 (73%)	15,856.89 (82%)	27,250.10 (73%)	37,905.23 (76%)	39,377.82 (73%)	37,072.82 (76%)	39,657.04 (88%)	37,468.65 (89%)	2,43,411.4
Expenditure on Wages (%)	5,842.37 (68%)	10,738.47 (70%)	18,200.03 (69%)	25,579.32 (70%)	25,686.53 (68%)	24,306.2 (70%)	27,128.36 (72%)	26,096.81 (74%)	1,63,578.09 (70%)
On Material	2,758.77 (32%)	4,617.47 (30%)	8,100.89 (31%)	11,084.49 (30%)	11,891.09 (32%)	10,650.48 (30%)	10,403.31 (28%)	9,159.32 (26%)	68,665.82 (30%)

Source: Performance Review Committee (PRC) meeting 5-6 June 2014, (MGNREGA Division).

Table 7.5

Data on Village Sampling

District		*Name of the Village*	*Total No. of Households in village*	*Sample size*	*% of Sample Size to Households*	*Sample of Agricultural Workers*	*% in total sample*
Anantpur	Gandlapenta	Katarupalle	412	42	10.19	6	14 %
Kurnool	Pattikonda	Juturu	357	34	9.05	6	17%
East Godavari	Kirlampudi	S. Timmapuram	394	36	9.13	6	16.66 %
Krishna	Ghantasala	Kottapalli	278	30	10.79	6	20%
Vishakapatnam	S. Rayavaram	Pettugollapalli	376	27	7.18	6	22%
Karimnagar	Ramagundam	Akenaipalli	288	31	10.76	6	19.35%
Nizamabad	Bansuwada	Budimi	309	35	11.32	6	17.14
Khammam	Dummugudem	Ramarao Pet	325	28	8.16	6	21.48
Total		8	2739	263	9.25	48	18.45

Wage Income of agricultural workers and percentage of MGNREGA income in the total wage income.

Source: Data from Field Survey by Sodhana, Hyderabad during 2012-13 agricultural year.

The MGNREGA has a place of prime importance in the survey. For this paper, we have culled out some data of agricultural labourers and their wage income, both from agricultural operations and MGNREGA. This income is presented here in comparison with the basic living cost of the family as per informed during the enumeration. A total of 9.25 per cent of the sample was selected for a detailed interview; of which, nearly 18.5 per cent of agricultural workers have been chosen so as to compare their income from agricultural wage and that from employment under MGNREGA.

Preliminary Readings of the Data

The broad readings from the above two tables reflect that in almost all the villages, except one from East Godavari district, the percentage of MGNREGA income in the total wage income stands out above 15 per cent and even went up to 33 per cent. Of the above districts, agricultural workers' income from MNREGA in Vishakapatnam stands out highest with 33 per cent. For an agricultural worker's household, the income from MGNREGA provides a critical support for the family. Had this critical support not been there for these families, they would have landed up in the debt trap. There is a need for more work on this data to present a more rigorous analysis and also a disaggregate analysis of women as well as male agricultural workers earnings. This minimum income assurance also resulted in bargaining for the better wages. This is what the study by D. Mukherjee and U.B. Sinha imply when they say, "the possibility of alternative source of income raises the reservation age all workers in the rural sector, and implicitly confers some bargaining power to rural workers." This critical income support that the MGNREGA is providing is being used to repay hand loans and pay for expenses such as education, health and other immediate necessities, thereby helping the family to stay off from the clutches of the usurious rural lending market. Had this not been there, their per capita annual wage income would be too low. Literally, the MGNREGA is helping the agricultural workers' families to stay away from the threat of economic exclusion. The number of working days when compared to the average days of wage labour by that family, stands out to be almost 20-25 per cent.

This is the key momentum in providing basis for economic and social inclusion. As we argued above, under the pressure from neoliberal economic policy dynamics, the rural poor are faced with the threat of dwindling employment opportunities. But the MGNREGA could help those families who are on the verge of economic exclusion.

The increased income aided by MGNREGA is creating a positive impact on the household economy as well. In all these eight villages, though it is a snapshot study and we don't have the advantage of a comparison, it is evident that this added income has led to enhanced spending on food and other articles as well. A comparison between the expenditure on basic family needs by an agricultural worker-cum-MGNREGA worker and a lone agricultural worker is yet to be developed to assert this point. Nonetheless, a similar study was already done by the Institute of Applied Manpower Research under, now defunct, Planning Commission confirms the same. Despite its cake of problems in ensuring the widest possible reach, it is the only programme under GoI till now which provides equal opportunities for anyone to be employed under the Act provided he/she chooses to

Table 7.6

MGNREGA Performance in Selected Villages in 2012-13

Name of the Village	*Number of Job Card Holders*	*No of Beneficiaries under MGNREGA*	*Average Agri-Wage Income*	*Average Income from MGNREGA*	*% of MGNREGA Income in Total Agri-Wage Income*
Katarupalle	1,193	370	33,718	3,916	11.60
Juturu	2,385	1261	17,071	2,300	13.47
S. Timma-puram	604	530	31,766	1,353	4.25
Kottapalli	217	216	36,975	4,516	12.21
Pettugol-lapalli	447	464	15,625	5,165	33.00
Akinapalli	418	0	24,841	5,968	24.00
Budimi	558	0	28,068	4,875	17.36
Ramarao Pet	1,117	0	31,476	6,635	21.07
Average			27,445	4,341	15.81

Source: First two columns, Number of Job Cards and No of Beneficiaries is collected from MNREGA website and remaining data is compiled from field data analysis..

do so. Hence, we can overcome the basic exclusionary frame, denial or lack of access to work in this manner. This has its consequential impacts on the other two frames of social exclusion, i.e., social and financial inclusionary aspects. The MGNREGA is helping the agricultural workers' families not only from the view point of increased income and wage rates, but has also become one of the major money flow channels through institutional mechanism such as post office or bank accounts. Thus the MGNREGA is playing a bigger role in achieving financial inclusion—one of the pet project of governments. The *Briefing Book 2013* reveals the potential of financial inclusion with its 8.71 crore post office/bank accounts.

Problems in Perspectives

The remaining section of this paper considers the ongoing debate which is directly linked to the survival of this Act. So far in the year 2014-15, against the proposed employment generation of 227 crore man-days, only 103.8 crore man-days were generated. According to the government data itself, the average days of employment generated per household drastically came down from 46 days to 31.4 days in this year. But the MoRD had repeatedly modified the guidelines of MGNREGA. The main aim were is to dilute the right to work enshrined by law in this Act. The new guidelines also dis-empowers local bodies and Gram Sabha, attacking both decentralisation and democratic functioning that was included in the Act especially at the request of agricultural workers unions. From universal application of the Act, the new guidelines proposes a restrictive application. The guidelines issued on 24 July 2014 mandate the implementing authorities to select only 60 per cent of the works that are directly linked to agriculture and allied activities. Those issued in September 2014 increased the material component from 40 per cent to 49 per cent and reduced the labour component from 60 per cent to 51 per cent. These new guidelines automatically reduce the net wage labour income by 10 per cent, which will have a serious impact on the earnings of agricultural labour who are already getting only a fourth of what is their due. In the name of linking agriculture and allied activities, the government intends to introduce more and more machinery against the letter of the law. This is going to further reduce the wage earnings of those who are employed under this Act. With the proposed changes in guidelines, this figure is going to reduce further. To execute all these measures, the central government initiated an "Intensive Participatory Planning Exercise". As part of this, the authorities are supposed to visit all *gram panchayats* (GPs) to ascertain the amount of work to be taken up during the upcoming MGNREGA season. Thus, the most democratic element in the implementation of this Act, which is the right of GPs in selecting the work, is transferred to the bureaucrats. All these moves, when they came into effect, are going to be fatal not only for the MGNREGA but also for the over all project of social inclusion. The reasons expounded by the supporters of these amendments indicate that a huge quantum of nation's resource is being wasted. For all of them, here is my straight question. As explained above, with mere 0.5 per cent of expenditure from the coffers of annual budget over the last 8 years, 1657.87 crore working days has been generated which helped in accruing an additional income of ₹163565.45 crore in the rural India. This has a direct multiplier effect on the nation's economy. When we compute the multiplier effect on the economy by including the community assets created under this Act over the last 8 years, it would reach enormous proportions.

During this same period, which also happened to be the period of global crisis of capitalism, the government handed out 34 lakh crore concessions to the industrial houses. When we refer to the budget speeches of successive finance ministers, they state that these dole-outs are given in anticipation of employment creation and sustaining the growth. The economic growth faltered as it is evident from the monthly data released by the Central Statistical Organisation. But no government agency took any pain to compute the employment generation by the beneficiaries of these tax concessions and their multiplier effect on the economy. When a transparent allocation and expenditure of mere 0.5 per cent of budget could generate more than 220 crore person-days annually benefiting near about 5 crore of households, how many person-days ought to be generated by utilising nearly 5 per cent of the budget (which is 10 times of MGNREGA allocations!) In layman's logic, this would have created 2200 crores of person-days benefiting 50 crore of households annually! But such benefits are not visible in the field. It won't be a problem for the neoliberal critics who harps on the result orientation and utility of welfare expenditure as these concessions are catering the interests and enriching the class to which they naturally belongs to.

Here one thing is clearly visible. The multiplier effect of MGNREGA only sustained the momentum of economic growth, as opposed to the tax concessions enjoyed by the corporate houses. The income generated through MGNREGA reached the economy, whereas the income from the tax concessions reached the tax heavens, which in turn returned to India in form of FIIs (foreign institutional investors) and FDIs (foreign direct investments) in order to claim further concessions. And the argument against MGNREGA often comes from the fiscal fundamentalists as well those who argue that such subsidies are considerably to widening the current account deficit and fiscal deficit. It is the amount of revenue forgone that is feeding the fiscal deficit rather than the income generated from MNRGA. This is the problem with the perspectives of an incumbent government which took on to its heart the task of whittling down the MGNREGA and squeezing the budgetary support for other similar social safety and security programmes. This problematic perspective is already at play. The central government recently announced a flat 25 per cent cut in the budgetary allocations of MoRD on the pretext of controlling the fiscal deficit. Those vocal critics of MGNREGA should respond to and provide answers to this single question that is being put forward here. It is no secret that these problems in perspectives are also the issues arising from deep-seated neoliberalism. Thus the impending attack on the country's social security is not any other general attack. It is the socio-political-ideological attack of those who enjoyed the fruits of power and growth under the globalisation.

Conclusion

As have been referred a number of times, the national flagship schemes and programmes are being designed, constantly monitored and evaluated by the Planning Commission. The Planning Commission has played a key role in assessing the need for Acts like MGNREGA and designed those from the viewpoint of national economy. Also, it had a whole chapter on MGNREGA in the Twelfth Five Year Plan document suggesting ways to improvise the implementation of Act. For this, the Planning Commission has drawn inferences and experiences from a large number of independent research organisations. The Twelfth Plan document in fact draws a blue print to improve this Act by undertaking more productive and inclusive works. When the time is apt to attempt for the much-needed changes, the Planning Commission itself will become a defunct body. With the two decades of experiences even when we had state-owned think-tanks such as Planning Commission, the consequences of neoliberal economic reforms have been prominent. When the governments are moving ahead with the packaged reforms, and with the demise of Planning Commission, all these national flagship programmes will become rudderless and face the danger of withering away in the tsunami of the capital's propensity to primitive accumulation.

References

Ahluwalia. M.S. (2011) . "Prospects and Policy Changes in the Twelfth Plan", Economic and Political Weekly XLVI(21): 88-105.

Ambasta, Pramatesh (2014). "Telling the Right Reform from the Wrong", *Indian Express,* 16 October.

Breman. J and J. Varinder .J (2012). "Implementation of NREGA in India: A National Overview", *Hivos Knowledge Programme Paper* 9. Center for Developmental Studies, Trivandrum and University of Amsterdam.

Bhalla, K. Surjit (2014). " ", *Indian Express,* 2 November.

Ghosh. J. (2009). "Equity and Inclusion through Public Expenditure: The Potential of the NREGA", Paper presented at the *International Conference on NRERGA*. New Delhi.

Indian Express (2014a). "Gadkari Ministry Writes Note Thrashing NREG Purely Partisan Plan", *Indian Express*, 17 October.

Indian Express (2014b). "Economists Ask PM Not to Dilute NREGS; Gadkari Says Focus on the Needy Areas", *Indian Express*, 15 October.

Konduri, Veeraiah (2014). "Has the Poverty Decreased ?", *Power Politics*, November. New Delhi.

Mosquerira, Victor Baez and Yasmin Fahimi (2014). *Economic Inequality or Social Justice for Everybody?* Progressive Alliance.

Misra, Sangita and Suresh. K Anoop (2014) Estimating Employment Elasticity of Growth for the Indian Economy, RBI Working Paper Series W P S (DEPR) : 6/2014.

Motiram, Sripad and Vamsi Vakulabharanam (2011). "Poverty and Inequality in the Age of Economic Liberalization", in D.M. Nachane (ed.), *India Development Report 2011*. New Delhi: OUP. pp.59-69.

NCAER (2013). "Is the MNREGA Benefing the Rural Poor?", *Macrotrack*. NCAER.

Pankaj, Ashok K. (2012). *"Guaranteeing Right to Work in Rural India: Context, Issues and Policies"*, in Ashok K. Pankaj (ed)., *Right to Work and Rural India: Working of the Mahatma Gandhi National Rural Employment Guarantee Scheme (MGNREGS)*. New Delhi: Sage Publications. p.7.

Pankaj, Ashok K. and Rukmini Tankha (2012). "Empowerment Effects of the MGNREGS on Women Workers", in Ashok K. Pankaj (ed)., *Right to Work and Rural India: Working of the Mahatma Gandhi National Rural Employment Guarantee Scheme (MGNREGS)*. New Delhi: Sage Publications.

Patnaik. Prabhat, (2014) *Inaugural Address at AIAWU 8th All India Conference*. Warangal.

Shah, Mihir (2014). "How to Reform and How Not To", *The Hindu*, 4 November.

Silver, Hillary (1994). Social Exclusion and Social Solidarity. International Labour Review. p.133.

8

K. JAFAR[1]

MGNREGS, SHGs and Women Empowerment

The Dynamic Role of Migration and Culture in Kerala

Introduction

Among others, higher educational status of the workforce, level of human development and incidence of migration directly affect the employment situations and functioning of the rural employment guarantee programme, Mahatma Gandhi National Rural Employment Guarantee Scheme (MGNREGS) in the state of Kerala. The Mahatma Gandhi National Rural Employment Guarantee (MGNREGA) Act aims at enhancing the livelihood security of people in rural areas by guaranteeing 100 days of wage employment in a financial year to a rural household whose adult members volunteer to perform unskilled manual work. In the first phase, the Act (first notified as the National Rural Employment Guarantee Act—NREGA—on 7 September 2005) was notified in 200 districts and later extended to other districts (Pani and Iyer, 2012). Unlike in other states in India, the participation of male workers in various activities of the MGNREGS, in Kerala is very low. Given the high incidence of migration in the state, the present paper looks into the pattern of women's participation in MGNREGS, and tries to understand the implications of migration and cultural factors that affect the process of women empowerment study, considering three *gram panchayats* (GPs) from Malappuram district of Kerala.

---

1. I am thankful to Dr Narendar Pani, professor at NIAS- Bangalore for his valuable guidance and insights at various stages of the study. The discussion with other faculty members and friends has been helpful. None of them are responsible for any errors that remain.

Method: Study Area and Data

The findings are primarily drawn from a larger study conducted during 2008-2013 in Malappuram district in Kerala. In terms of occupational pattern, its share of cultivators and agricultural labourers in its total main workers declined from 47.1 per cent in 1991 to 21.2 per cent in 2001, but Malappuram remained one of the least urbanised Kerala districts (Census of India, 1991; 2001). The district-wise distribution of remittances shows that Malappuram is ranked first in the terms of proportion of total remittances and per household remittance (Centre for Development Studies, 2005: 46). Thus the district economy is largely remittance driven. At the same time, the district-wise per capita income figures in the state and its Human Development Index (with HDI value 0.749 against 0.773 Kerala as a whole) posited Malappuram in the lowest ranks in Kerala (GoK, 2012; Centre for Development Studies, 2005: 60). Culturally, 68.5 per cent of Malappuram's population is Muslim and the remaining is accounted for by Hindus (29.2%), Christians (2.2%) and other religious groups (GoK, 2006). At one level, it has followed the same macroeconomic patterns, especially the non-agrarian and mass-education based development pattern, that the whole of Kerala experienced in recent decades (Pani and Jafar, 2010). Yet on the contrary, it remains low or lags behind other districts in human development and makes as a lower-end case of Kerala. These factors, especially the pattern of migration and cultural composition, provide new insights into ways in which they affect women's participation in MGNREGS and process of women's empowerment.

Broadly, the economic transition, international migration and the diverse geography of the district across coastal areas, high-lands and agrarian hinterlands make the district an interesting case. The study selected three regions (taking *talukas* as the administrative units) from the coastal, midlands and highlands areas. The three *talukas*, namely Tirur, Perinthalmanna and Nilambur, were chosen accordingly. As a reflection of the difference in geographic and environmental conditions of the district, the occupational structure of these region shows sharp differences. For conducting the detailed study, three GPs representing each of the three regions were selected in such a way that their occupational structure was similar to the modal values of the coastal, agrarian plain land (midland) and highland areas. The primary data was collected through questionnaire surveys and detailed interviews (during 2011 and 2012). The household survey was carried out in two GP-wards selected on the basis of their geography and occupational pattern being close to the other three respective ones. Detailed information was collected by administering a structured questionnaire survey among 750 sample households selected from the three GPs (125 households from each of the representative wards). This was supported with qualitative information collected through regular observation and detailed personal interviews with senior family members, elected members and authorities of the respective GP offices, and also local leaders engaged in social-political and religious activities. This was very helpful in understanding the different practices and institutions in their everyday life.

Background: Women's Employment and Gender Relations in Kerala

Women's employment status and earning can be considered as a key factor in empowering them. Although Kerala is known for high educational status among the women and remarkable progress in social development, the work participation rate among women remains very low. Many studies point out that the state has failed in translating its improvement in women's educational status so as to ensure a higher status to them and, in turn, women remain excluded from benefits associated with the celebrated Kerala model of development (Devika, 2002; 2006a; 2006b; Devika and Thampi, 2011; Jeffrey, 1987; 2001; 2004-05; Kodoth and Eapen, 2005; Mukhopadhyay, 2007; Saradamoni, 1994; 2006). Studies expect a positive correlation between education and female labour force participation. Compared to the non-working/non-earning women, working women with independent incomes have a decisively greater role in household decision-making (Devi, 2002). In this sense, the poor gender relations in Kerala can be seen in the light of low work participation rate among the women. Malappuram district also experiences a very low female work participation rate (6.63%, far below of 15.38% across Kerala), even with a high literacy rate (73.8% in 2001). There are various socio-cultural reasons that have contributed to this poor performance.

The Distribution of Adult Females

The samples from three regions consist of a total of 1543 adult females (includes 16 females below 18 years old but married). Their marital status shows that 73.17 per cent of them are currently married and the rest are either unmarried (10.95%) or widowed or divorced or separated or missing (15.88%). Based on the status of migration, the married women are classified into three groups—married women from non-migrant households (34.2%), married women from migrant households (28.1%) and Gulf-wives [2] (10.9%). Thus, the study classifies the total adult females into five groups and looks at the pattern of their participation in selected spaces outside their homes.

There are differences in the way the three sample regions experience the pattern of migration and therefore, the distribution of these groups varies across regions. Coastal region has a large number of married women from migrant households (49.4%), while midland region has more Gulf-wives (48.2%). It may be noted that a large number of the migrant households in the coastal region (35.9%) have returned migrants[3] (against 11.4% and 25.9% in highland and midland regions respectively). Midland has more migrant households with current migrants (32.7% against 17.7% and 21.2% households in coastal and highland regions respectively). The other groups are distributed across the three regions, with an exception that the coastal region has a larger share of total unmarried and widows or divorcees (46.2% and 40.8% respectively). The distribution across

2. Studies often consider 'Gulf-wives' (GWs) as a subset of 'women left behind' (WLB). The distribution of our sample shows that more than 95 per cent of the total married women left behind are Gulf-wives. Therefore, the present study use 'Gulf-wives' as a common category which includes all women left behind.

3. At least one member ever migrated out of Kerala and now returned back to his/her birthplace or last place of residence.

the religions shows that share of Muslim women in the total (75.6%) as well as in the five groups remains very high (68%, 72.7%, 65.1%, 88.7% and 86.3% respectively in unmarried, widows or divorcees, married women from non-migrants and migrants, and Gulf-wives). Across the caste-groups, the concentration of married women from migrant households and Gulf-wives is among the forward and backward castes (except 0.5% married women from migrant households who belong to SCs [scheduled castes]).

These groups are endowed with a different set of means (like education, occupation, and family background) and therefore, experience difference in their capabilities. The average age of the females in the five groups indicates that among the married ones, the Gulf-wives are relatively young. Their average total years of education points out the unmarried women and Gulf-wives have spent more years on their education, followed by married women from the non-migrant and migrant households.

Table 8.1

Educational Status of Adult Females (Share in %)

			Married Women		
	Unmarried	*Widow/ Divorced*	*Non-Migrant HHs*	*Migrant HHs*	*Gulf-wives*
Illiterate	8.3	38.4	8.7	5.5	0.0
Up to class IX	18.3	50.6	50.1	52.9	31.6
X- SSLC	24.3	7.8	26.6	26.1	40.5
PUC or Diploma	18.3	2.0	10.8	9.4	16.7
Graduation and above	30.8	1.2	3.8	5.9	11.4

Note: HHS- Households; SSLC- Secondary School Leaving Certificate; PUC: Pre-University.
Source: Primary Survey 2011-12.

It is very interesting to see that there are no illiterate Gulf-wives, whereas other groups have many illiterate members (Table 8.1). Majority of the widows or divorcees (50.6%) as well as the married women from non-migrant households (50.1%) and migrant households (52.9%) had their highest education below SSLC. Overall, the unmarried women and Gulf-wives have higher educational qualification, while mean years of total education for the widows and divorcees remains very low. The educational pattern across the regions shows that married women from highland are more educated; whereas the women from coastal region are the least educated ones. Across the religions, married women from Christian families have higher educational qualification, followed by the Hindu and Muslim women. Among the Hindus, married women from STs (scheduled tribes) and SCs are the least educated ones.

The occupational pattern shows that majority of the unmarried women are either unemployed (36.1%) or students (30.2%) and only a small share is employed. In other groups, house-wives[4] constitute the largest share (respectively 73%, 82.2%, 91.9% and 93.5% among widows/divorcee, married woman from non-migrant and migrant households and Gulf-wives) (Table 8.2). Among the workers, share of the monthly salaried workers in unmarried (8.3%) and Gulf-wives (4.2%) are higher that of other groups (1.2%, 2.8% and 1.8% respectively from widows/divorcee, married women from non-migrant households and migrant households. A significant number of widows/divorcees and married women from non-migrant households (6.5% and 9.5% respectively) are engaged in agricultural and MGNREGS allied works, whereas only 1.8 per cent of unmarried and married women from the migrant households (none from Gulf-wives) are engaged in such jobs.

The employment status across the regions shows that highland has more married women from non-migrant households working as wage labour. Married women from other groups remain either unemployed or work as monthly salaried worker, and the pattern persists across the three regions. The share of non-working women is

4. Women whose work is to maintain and organise the household and look after their husbands and children, including washing, cleaning, cooking and full–time care of pre-school children (Bhaskar, 1997). A housewife's occupational duties "usually include cooking, dishwashing, housecleaning, laundry work, child care, and a 'personal relations' component, which includes sexual relations" (Bergmann, 1981). There exist a wide range of discussion that criticise the economic idea of considering 'housewife' as 'unproductive' or not considering the occupation of housewife at all (Folbre, 1991).

highest among Muslims. The pattern of migration suggests that only a small share of females has ever migrated out of the state. Among them, education was the reason for the migration of unmarried women, while others migrated for personal and family preferences.

Table 8.2

Employment Status of Adult Females (Share in %)

			Married women		
	Unmarried	*Widow/ Divorced*	*Non-Migrant HHs*	*Migrant HHs*	*Gulf-wives*
Unemployed	36.10	0.0	0.20	0.0	0.0
Agricultural and MGNREGS workers	1.80	6.50	9.50	1.80	0.0
Other wage workers	1.80	2.40	1.70	0.20	0.0
Trade and service workers	2.40	0.0	0.0	0.0	0.0
Monthly salaried workers	8.30	1.20	2.80	1.80	4.20
Family labourers	1.20	1.20	0.60	0.0	0.0
Fisherman	0.0	0.0	0.0	0.20	0.0
Others	10.10	14.70	2.30	3.20	0.0
Migrant out of the state	0.60	0.0	0.0	0.20	0.0
Student	30.20	0.0	0.80	0.50	2.40
Home-maker	7.70*	73.90	82.20	91.90	93.50

Note: * They are not married, but do household works and belong to the category of home-maker or housewife.

Source: Primary Survey 2011-12.

Women's Engagement in MGNREGS and Process of Empowerment

Apart from the financial stability, women's access to employment and earning has its impact on their social, political and personal life. The fact that local governments use the wide network of Kudumbashree and other SHGs (self-help groups) to coordinate the activities of MGNREGS can be seen as a good example to realise the way in which the participation in MGNREGS and SHGs transform the rural women in Kerala. Women's engagement in various SHGs enables them to enter into a wide range of activities that takes place outside their home. Studies have pointed out that their engagement in Kudumbashree activities has gradually empowered them to participate in the process of development (Chirayath and Chirayath, 2010; Devika, 2012; Devika and Tampi, 2007; Oommen, 2008; Williams *et al.*, 2011). The SHG members act as the agency to implement various welfare programmes and local campaigns that enable them to build a strong social network among the local people. Women's entry into Kudumbashree activities and its leadership can be seen as a way to enter into local politics and leadership. It has been reported that a large number of Kudumbashree members have been drafted into the women's wing of the Communist Party of India-Marxist (CPI-M) (Devika, 2012). This engagement has helped many of the active SHG members with basic education make inroads into politics. When Kerala implemented 50 per cent reservation for women in the local self-governing bodies, political parties found the active SHG members to be potential candidates and thus they found their way into local politics and leadership (Jafar, 2013).

Migration of men[5] (only a few male migrants are joined by their womenfolk) leads to situations where the women from migrant households play multiple roles (Gardner, 2011; Gardner and Osella, 2003; Gulati, 1993; Zachariah and Rajan, 2012). Unlike other married women, the ones from migrant households miss the support of their husbands that forces them to undertake multiple roles, but might render them more 'independent and autonomous'. They face various handicaps, but the ways in which they cope with such situations and deal with tasks that they have traditionally been excluded from are remarkable (Gulati, 1993: 145). Among them, 'Gulf-wives—married women in Kerala whose husbands are migrants to the Gulf—are particularly known for facing the new challenges and opportunities (Zachariah *et al.*, 2003; Zachariah and Rajan, 2009). One of the

5. Compared to men, the number of migrant women is very small; except those of nurses migrating to developed countries and big cities in India (Nair, 2011; Percot and Nair, 2011). Similarly, studies identify migration of women as domestic workers and 'marriage migration' (women migrate for family or marriage, not for job) as the two common forms of female migration (Neetha, 2011; Varghese and Rajan, 2011).

recent studies estimated that Gulf-wives account for about 10.8 per cent of the currently married women in the state (Zachariah and Rajan, 2012: 194).

Table 8.3

Women's Participation in SHGs (Share in %)

	Married Women			
	Non-migrant Household	*Migrant Household*	*Gulf-wives*	*Total*
Not engaged	64.8	77.8	85.1	72.8
Kudumbashree SHG	24.2	13.4	9.5	17.9
Other SHGs	3.2	2.3	2.4	2.7
Member but not active	4.5	4.4	1.8	4.1
Member in multiple SHGs	3.2	1.8	1.2	2.4
Not Available	0.0	0.2	0.0	0.1
Total	100	100	100	100

Source: Primary Survey 2011-12.

It is very interesting to note that 30.6 per cent of the married women from non-migrant households are actively engaged in different SHGs (with Kudumbashree SHGs, other SHGs and multiple SHGs together). Compared to this, only 13.1 per cent of Gulf-wives and 17.5 per cent of married women from migrant households have active engagement with these SHGs (Table 8.3). The pattern across the regions shows that the share of women engaged in various activities related to SHGs are relatively high in the highland region (56%, 37% and 20% for married women from non-migrant households, migrant households and Gulf-wives respectively).

Across religions, the share of married women from the non-migrant households engaged in SHG activities (64.4%) is high among Christians. The share of married women from migrant households engaged in such activities is high among Hindus (47.1% against 34.4% from Christians and 20.1% from Muslims). Though a majority of them are not engaged in any activities promoted by the SHGs, the share of married women from non-migrant households engaged in SHG activities is higher than their counterparts (except in the coastal region, where this share of married women from the migrant households is higher than other groups). Overall, married women from the non-migrant households are very active in SHGs, whereas the married women from migrant households, especially the Gulf-wives, are not active in such activities.

The low level participation of women in various meetings (organised by political parties, religious, educational institutes etc.) and public spaces related to their everyday life also reflect these factors. For instance, the share of married women who attend political meetings alone is low in all groups (2.7%, 1.2% and 0.6% for married women from non-migrant households, migrant households and Gulf-wives respectively). The share of married women attending such programmes alone is high among Hindus (7.2% and 11.8% respectively from non-migrant and migrant households) and Christians (8.9% and 3.1% from non-migrant and migrant households respectively). Overall, the Gulf-wives do not attend political meetings. The dynamic nature of politics seems to keep many women away from the local politics. For those who are actively attend such meetings, their husbands or some family members are found to be actively involved in local politics. The absence of married women from migrant households and Gulf-wives in political meetings (only 1.8% and 0.6% respectively) confirms the findings drawn on the *panchayat* election held in 2010. The fact that none of the candidates (198 candidates contested to three GPs) were migrants suggests that migration inversely affects the candidature as the migrant households have very little role in local politics (Jafar, 2013).

Majority of the women in all the five groups are not engaged in work promoted through the MGNREGS. The results show that 8 per cent of married women from non-migrant households and a very small proportion from the migrant households (1.4%) are actively involved in such works. It is very interesting to note that none of the Gulf-wives (except 0.6% who hold the card but never worked) are engaged in MGNREGS work (Table 8.4). The results show that only 16.8 per cent of the married women from non-migrant households in the highland region (against less than 5% in other groups in any region) are involved in MGNREGS work.

Table 8.4

Women's Participation in MGNREGS Work (Share in %)

Nature of Engagement	*Married Women*			
	Non-migrant Household	*Migrant Household*	*Gulf-wives*	*Total*
Not engaged	91.7	97.9	98.8	95.1
Active	8.0	1.4	0.0	4.3
Card–holder, never worked	0.4	0.5	0.6	0.4
Not Available	0.0	0.2	0.6	0.2
Total	100	100	100	100

Source: Primary Survey 2011-12.

Relatively, the married women from non-migrant households in the highland region (16.8% against less than 5% in other groups in any region) are active in such works. A large number of married women from non-migrant households who are Hindus and Christians (18% and 20% respectively against 2.9% of Muslims) are very active. Among the married women from migrant households, only Hindu women (11.8%) are active. Overall, the coastal region has the least share of women engaged in such activities and hence Muslim women are largely absent from MGNREGS related works.

Table 8.5

Religion and Women's Participation in MGNREGS Work (Share in %)

Nature of Engagement	*Hindu*	*Muslim*	*Christian*	*Total*
Not Engaged	220 (14.9)	1143 (77.6)	109 (7.4)	1472 (100)
Active	35 (54.7)	18 (28.1)	11 (17.2)	64 (100)
Card–holder, never worked	2 (28.6)	5 (71.4)	0 (0)	7 (100)
Total	257 (16.7)	1166 (75.6)	120 (7.8)	1543 (100)

Source: Primary Survey 2011-12.

The nature of participation across total adult women belonging to the three major religions shows that majority of the non-participating women (77.6%) are Muslims. More than half of the total women who actively engage in MGNREGS (54.7%) are Hindus (against 28% from Muslims and 17% from Christians). The count of women who have registered for work under MGNREGS, but never worked, remain high among the Muslims (Table 8.5). A large number of married women from non-migrant households that are Hindus and Christians (18% and 20% respectively against 2.9% of Muslims) are very active. Among the married women from migrant households, only Hindu women (11.8%) are active in MGNREGS work. Overall, the coastal region has the least share of women engaged in such activities. Muslim women are largely absent from MGNREGS related works.

Table 8.6

Caste and Women's Participation in MGNREGS Work (Share in %)

Nature of Engagement	*No Caste*	*Forward Caste*	*OBCs*	*SCs*	*STs*	*Total*
Not Engaged	2 (0.9)	33 (14.9)	120 (54.3)	54 (24.4)	12 (5.4)	221(100)
Active	0 (0.0)	4 (11.4)	11 (31.4)	19 (54.3)	1 (2.9)	35 (100)
Card-holder, never worked	0 (0)	1 (50)	1 (50)	0 (0)	0 (0)	2 (100)
Total	2 (0.8)	38 (14.7)	132 (51.2)	73 (28.3)	13 (5.0)	258 (100)

Source: Primary Survey 2011-12.

It is very striking to note that only one ST woman (out of 13 covered under the study) engages in MGNREGS work (Table 8.6). The non-tribal women members engaged in MGNREGS works in the tribal areas are not very keen about including the tribal women into their groups. The concerned authorities seem to have failed to organise similar groups exclusively for tribal women. Some of the earlier experiences of poor performance of the various development programmes and lack of accountability were cited as the cause of such reluctance.

The relative absence of married women from the migrant households and Gulf-wives in SHG activities and jobs carried out through MGNREGS reflects the options available to them. It may be argued that they receive remittance money and therefore may be reluctant to opt for such jobs or the family may discourage them from doing so. In general, community pressure, especially from the family and relatives of Gulf-wives, is very high in the absence of their husbands. Such pressures are very crucial in influencing any decision taken by the Gulf-wives. The active presence of married women from the non-migrant households in these activities can be seen as a reflection of their livelihood options. Beyond offering new options of jobs and loans, these two programmes seem to empower the 'under-privileged women' in different ways.

Conclusion

Beyond providing access to income, women's participation in the MGNREGS can be used in understanding the local factors which affect the process of women empowerment. Factors like education, occupation, and participation in other public spaces may contribute to this pattern. For instance, women's involvement in SHGs or MGNREGS demands their participation in *gram sabha*[6] meetings and in turn in their presence other programmes organised by the political parties.

The overall pattern suggests that there are differences in the way women from different migration statuses and cultural backgrounds participate in MGNREGS works. Overall, the active participation in various works organised under the MGNREGS remain low. Compared to 8 per cent of married women from the non-migrant households, a very small proportion from the migrant households is actively involved in the same. None of the Gulf-wives (except 0.6% who hold the card but never worked) are engaged in MGNREGS work. Similarly, very few Muslim women (who constitutes the majority of the sample) actively engage in these activities. The relative absence of Gulf-wives and Muslim women from these activities clearly indicate the role that male migration and cultural factors play.

By guaranteeing 100 days of wage-employment in a financial year, the MGNREGS enhances the livelihood security of people in

6. *Gram sabha* is the lowest decision–making unit in decentralised local governance.

rural areas. It is expected that the people living in poor economic conditions and the under-privileged sections would benefit from this programme. As a women-centred poverty alleviation programme, Kudumbashree activities provide employment for women dwelling in poor financial conditions. The active presence of married women belonging to the poor SC and OBC families in the different SHGs confirms this assumption, while the absence of women from STs remains an exception. The relative absence of ST women from the MGNREGS works and SHGs in fact raises concerns regarding the exclusionary nature of development in Kerala.

References

Bergmann, B.R. (1981). "The Economic Risks of Being a Housewife", *The American Economic Review* 71 (2): 81–86.

Bhaskar, M. (1997). "Women Panchayat Members in Kerala: A Profile", *Economic and Political Weekly,* 32 (17): WS13–20.

Census of India (1991 & 2001). Office of the Registrar General and Census Commissioner, Government of India.

Centre for Development Studies (2005). *Human Development Report 2005 Kerala.* Prepared for Government of Kerala. Thiruvananthapuram: State Planning Board.

Chirayath, S. and D. Chirayath (2010). "Reaching amilies Through Women and Reaching Community Through Families: A Success Story of Women Empowerment in Kerala—The Case of Kudumbashree", *Management and Labour Studies* 35 (4): 455-68.

Devi, K.R.L. (2002). "Education,Eemployment, and Job Preference of Women in Kerala: A Micro-level Case Study", *Discussion Paper* No. 42. Kerala Research Programme on Local Level Development. Thiruvananthapuram: Centre for Development Studies

Devika, J. (2002). "Family Planning as 'Liberation': The Ambiguities of 'Emancipation from Biology' in Keralam", *Working Paper* No. 335. Thiruvananthapuram: Centre for Development Studies.

———. (2006a). *Engendering Individuals: The Language of Re-forming in Early Twentieth Century Keralam.* Hyderabad: Orient Longman

———. (2006b). "Negotiating Women's Social Space: Public Debates on Gender in Early Modern Kerala, India", *Inter-Asia Cultural Studies* 7(1): 43-61.

———. (2012). "The Beauty of Unintended Consequences", *Seminar* (Gods Own Country: A Symposium on Kerala in Transition) 637: 83-87, September

Devika, J, and B.V. Thampi (2007). "Between 'Empowerment' and 'Liberation': The Kudumbashree Initiative in Kerala", *Indian Journal of Gender Studies* 14 (1): 33-60.

———. (2011). "Mobility Towards Work and Politics for Women in Kerala State, India: A View from the Histories of Gender and Space", *Modern Asian Studies* 45 (5): 1147-75.

Folbre, N. (1991). "The Unproductive Housewife: Her Evolution in Nineteenth-century Economic Thought", *Signs* 16 (3): 463-84.

Gardner, A.M. (2011). "Gulf Migration and the Family", *Journal of Arabian Studies: Arabia, the Gulf, and the Red Sea* 1(1): 3-25

Gardner, K. and F. Osella (2003). "Migration, Modernity and Social Transformation in South Asia: An Overview", *Contributions to Indian Sociology* 37(1&2): v-xxviii.

Government of Kerala (2006) *Panchayat Level Statistics, Malappuram District*. Thiruvananthapuram: Department of Economics and Statistics, Government of Kerala.

Government of Kerala (2012). *Economic Review*. Thiruvananthapuram: State Planning Board.

Gulati, L. (1993). *In the Absence of Their Men: The Impact of Male Migration on Women*. New Delhi: Sage Publications

Jafar, K. (2013). "Reservation and Women's Political Freedom: Candidates' Experience from Three Gram Panchayats in Kerala, India", Social Change 43(1): 79-97.

Jeffrey, R.(1987). Governments and Culture: How Women Made Kerala Literate. *Pacific Affairs* 60 (3): 447-72.

———. (2001). *Politics, Women and Well-being: How Kerala Became 'a model'*. Oxford India Paperbacks. New Delhi: Oxford University Press

———. (2004/05). "Legacies of Matriliny: The Place of Women and the 'Kerala Model'", *Pacific Affairs* 77 (4): 647-64.

Kodoth, P. and E. Eapen (2005). "Looking Beyond Gender Parity: Gender Inequities of Some Dimensions of Well-being in Kerala", *Economic and Political Weekly* 40 (30): 3278-86.

Mukhopadhyay, S. (2007). "Understanding the Enigma of Women's Status in Kerala: Does High Literacy Necessarily Translate into High Status?", in S. Mukhopadhyay (ed.), *The Enigma of the Kerala Woman: A Failed Promise of Literacy*. New Delhi: Orient Longman. pp.3–31

Nair, S. (2011). "Multiple Identities and Migratory Dynamics of Nurses", in S.I. Rajan (ed.), *India Migration Report 2011: Migration, Identity and Conflict*. New Delhi: Routledge. pp. 213-18.

Neetha, N. (2011). "Closely Woven: Domestic Work and International Migration of Women in India", in S.I. Rajan (ed.), *Migration Report 2011: Migration, Identity and Conflict*. New Delhi: Routledge. pp. 219-35.

Oommen, M.A. (2008). "Micro Finance and Poverty Alleviation: The Case of Kerala's Kudumbashree", *Working Paper* No. 17. Kochi: Centre for Socio-economic & Environmental Studies

Pani, N. and C.G. Iyer (2012). "National Strategies and Local Realities: The Greenfield Approach and the MGNREGS in Karnataka", *India Review* 11 (1): 1-22.

Pani, N. and K. Jafar (2010). "Mass Education-led Growth and Non-agrarian Villages: Long-term Results of the Kerala Model", *Oxford Development Studies* 38 (1): 25-42.

Percot, P. and S. Nair (2011). "Transcending Boundaries: Indian Nurses in International Migration", in S.I. Rajan and M. Percot (eds.), *Dynamics of Indian Migration: Historical and Current Perspectives*. New Delhi: Routledge. pp.195-223.

Saradamoni, K. (1994). "Women, Kerala and Some Development Issues", *Economic and Political Weekly* 29(9): 501-09.

———. (2006). "Women and the Changed Family in Kerala: Some Masked Realities", in J. Tharamangalam (ed.), *Kerala: The Paradox of Public Action and Development*. New Delhi: Orient Longman. pp.169-87.

Varghese, V.J. and S.I. Rajan (2011). "Governmentality, Social Stigma and Quasi-citizenship: Gender Negotiations of Migrant Women Domestic Workers from Kerala", in S.I. Rajan, and M. Percot (eds.), *Dynamics of Indian Migration: Historical and Current Perspectives*. New Delhi: Routledge. pp.224-48.

Williams, G., B.V. Thampi, D. Narayana, S. Nandigama and D. Bhattacharyya (2011). "Performing Participatory Citizenship: Politics and Power in Kerala's Kudumbashree Programme", *Journal of Development Studies* 47 (8): 1261–80.

Zachariah, K.C., E.T. Mathew and S.I. Rajan. (2003). *Dynamics of Migration in Kerala: Dimensions, Differentials and Sonsequences.* New Delhi: Orient Longman

Zachariah, K.C. and S.I. Rajan (2009). *Migration and development: The Kerala Experience.* Delhi: Daanish Books

———. (2012). *Kerala's Gulf Connection, 1998-2011: Economic and Social Impact of Migration.* New Delhi: Orient BlackSwan.

9

MRITYUNJAY KUMAR SINGH

MGNREGA and Participatory Planning in Rajasthan

Introduction

The National Rural Employment Guarantee Act (NREGA), 2005, is a landmark legislation in Indian history of social security legislation after Independence. Enacted after a successful struggle for an employment guarantee legislation, this legislation is a partial victory towards a full-fledged right to employment in the context of any developing country.

For the first time, right to work has been made a legal compulsion and entitlement for unemployment allowances in the case of non-allotment of employment assured through this act. What is considered to be crucial is the empowerment of the poor through the provision of a right-based law, which would act as a strong safety net in the lack of alternative employment opportunities for poor people. The other key attributes of this scheme are time-bound guarantee, labour-intensive work, decentralised participatory planning, women empowerment, work site facilities, and above all, transparency and accountability through the provision of social audits and right to information. NREGA is a unique and unprecedented effort in strengthening grass roots democracy in India. For the first time, the Indian state has legally mandated the implementation of a mechanism that strengthen transparency and accountability at every step of the delivery chain, by creating a platform for citizens to articulate their voice and directly engage with the state. This legal mandate has been the catalyst for state governments across the country in order to innovate with different tools to strengthen accountability (Aiyar and Samji, 2009).

Salient Features of NREGA

Evolving the design of the wage employment programmes to more effectively fight poverty the Federal Government had formulated the NREGA in 2005—a paradigm shift from earlier wage employment programmes. With its legal framework and rights-based approach, NREGA provides employment to those who demand it. This is the largest ever public employment programme visualised in human history. The successful implementation of NREGS can improve the safety nets and eliminate hardcore poor (Rao, 2007).

Major objectives of NREGA are:

i) To enhance livelihood securities through the provision of minimum 100 days of employment to a rural household based on their demand.
ii) To create durable assets and strengthen the livelihood resource base of the rural poor.
iii) Strong social safety net for the vulnerable groups by providing a fall-back employment source, when other employment alternatives are scarce or inadequate.
iv) Growth engine for sustainable development of an agricultural economy.
v) Empowerment of rural poor through the processes of a rights-based law.
vi) New ways of doing business, as a model of governance reform anchored in the principles of transparency and grass roots democracy.

The design of the NREGS programme is unique in being largely demand driven and through the introduction of entitlement of unemployment allowances in case of non-allotment of employment. Undoubtedly, the NREGA has addressed many of the weaknesses of the earlier programmes through introduction of the rights-based framework, time bound accession to fulfil guarantee, incentive and disincentive structures, demand based resource availability and accountability.

The rights-based design of MGNREGA has a genesis in the preceding wage employment programmes. Almost all the rights-related features of MGNREGA are inherited from previous wage employment programmes. The rights-based framework was inherited from the Maharashtra Employment Guarantee Act 1977. Under MGNREGA, apart from guaranteeing 100 days of wage employment, the PRIs (panchayati raj institutions) have been vested with the responsibility of planning, implementation and monitoring of activities taken up under the scheme. MGNREGA made the demand factor a conscious strategy as a right to obtain employment. Financial obligations, both of the Centre and the State, are part of the legal framework. The MGNREGA guidelines also detail administrative modalities of implementation seeking to address the limitations of the earlier wage employment programmes, placing greater emphasis, for example on planning processes, and MIS for improving data management.

Gram Panchayats (GPs) are also one of the most responsible stakeholders in successful implementation of the NREGS programme. It is responsible for creating awareness about the scheme, receiving applications, registering names, issuing job cards, providing employment to the job seeker and also keeping records of the works conducted under NREGS. Along with this, GP has to prepare self-schemes to provide employment within the stipulated 15 days of demand, and to provide timely wage. It also has to make arrangement for adequate amount of funds for wage payment. GP is also responsible for redressing complaints lodged by people. It has to publish and update the data related to implementation of NREGA in the specified hoarding in a pro-active disclosure format.

Participatory Planning

From its roots in needs-based development in the 1970s and 1980s, to its wide-spread adoption by mainstream agencies and policy-makers during the global shift from governing to governance in the 1990s (Marsh and Rhodes, 1992; Kooiman, 1993), participation has emerged as a core concept underpinning local and national development policies and strategies alike. Its ascension to the mainstream in international development circles is possibly best exemplified by its adoption by the World Bank and other donors as a central concept underpinning national-level poverty reduction strategies. For proponents of participation, its advantages lie in its capacity to foster a sense of shared purpose, ownership and responsibility among fractured communities—in the process, building social capital and enhancing state legitimacy (DFID, 2006; Brinkerhoff, 2007; World Bank, 2011).

Some are strident in their criticism, notably the contributors to the provocatively entitled *Participation: The New Tyranny?* (Cooke and Kothari, 2001), who focusing largely on micro-level participatory rural appraisals, argue that so-called participatory approaches often fail to engage with issues of power and politics, thereby depoliticising local development processes.

Objectives of the Study

This paper is based on an empirical study done in two districts of Rajasthan—Dungarpur and Karauli. These two districts were selected because they were included in the phase one of implementation of NREGA in the state. NREGA is operational in these districts since its beginning in February 2006. The other reason for selecting these districts was that in both of them, STs (scheduled tribes), SCs (scheduled castes) and OBCs (other backward castes) has a very high count in the total population of the district. Dungarpur is a tribal majority district. One of the objectives of the NREGA is to strengthen local democracy at the grass-roots level. *Gram sabha* will decide the type of work that will be done in the *panchayat*, also will prepare the labour budget and Annual budget. As brought out by several studies, caste and patriarchy are quite entrenched in the traditional society of Rajasthan. So in this background, the objectives of the study were to describe participatory planning in the implementation of NREGA, to find out the level of participation of women, SCs, STs and differently abled in *gram sabha* for preparation of annual plan and labour budget and to find out strategies for better planning and implementation of NREGA.

Findings of the Study

Socio-economic Profile of the Workers

i) In Dungarpur, men constituted 28.7 per cent and women constituted 71.3 per cent of the total respondents. In

Karauli, men constituted 29.3 per cent and women constitute 70.7 per cent of the total respondents. Together in both the districts, women constituted 71 per cent and men constituted 29 per cent of the total respondents.

ii) In Dungarpur, respondents from the general category constituted 9.3 per cent of total respondents, constituted 4 per cent of them are from backward class, SC constituted 13.3 per cent and ST constituted 73.3 per cent of the total respondents. In Karauli, none of the respondents are from the general category, 26.7 per cent were from OBC, 44 per cent were from SC and 29.3 per cent were from ST. Together in both the districts, general respondents constituted 4.7 per cent, OBC constituted 15.3 per cent, SC comprise 28.7 per cent and ST comprise 51.3 per cent of the total respondents.

iii) Differently-abled respondents constituted 6 per cent and 0.7 per cent of the total respondents in Dungarpur and Karauli, respectively. So participation rate of the differently-abled was very less in both the districts.

iv) In Dungarpur, 83.3 per cent of the total respondents were illiterate, 12 per cent have primary education and 4 per cent have middle school education. In Karauli, 94.7 per cent of the total respondents were illiterate, 3.3 per cent had primary education and 1.3 per cent had secondary education.

v) In Dungarpur, 100 per cent respondents from general category, 100 per cent from OBC and 93.6 per cent of the respondents from ST own land, whereas 100 per cent respondents from SC do not own land.

vi) In Karauli, 97.5 per cent respondents from OBC owned land, 98.5 per cent from SC did not own land, and 90.9 per cent from ST owned land.

MGNREGA and Participatory Planning

i) In Dungarpur, for 92 per cent of the respondents, member of *panchayat* are the source of awareness about NREGA. In Karauli, for 74 per cent of respondents, member of *panchayat* are the source of awareness about NREGA and 26 per cent of the respondents have learnt about NREGA from community people.

ii) In Dungarpur, 61.3 per cent of the respondents submitted written application for work and 38.7 per cent of them verbally demanded it. In Karauli, 15.3 per cent of the respondents submitted written application for work and 84.7 per cent verbally demanded the same.

iii) In Dungarpur, 98.7 per cent of respondents did not get a dated receipt for their application. In Karauli, 100 per cent of respondents did not get a dated receipt for their application.

Hence, they do not give a dated receipt, then they are not obliged for unemployment allowance. This is done deliberately. During focus group discussion, it came out that the mates take worker's thumb impression for 100 days in advance, without writing a date on the application. So whenever there is work, they give them some as per their wishes. This is done to show that they are given work within 15 days of applying but in actual practice, it never happens.

i) In Dungarpur, 91.3 per cent of the respondents are not aware about the official wage rate. In Karauli, 98 per cent of the respondents were not aware about the official wage rate.

ii) In Dungarpur, 92.9 per cent of the respondents from general category, 100 per cent respondents from OBC, 100 per cent from SC, and 89.1 per cent from ST were not aware about the official wage rate. In Karauli, 100 per cent respondents from OBC, 100 per cent respondents from SC and 93.2 per cent respondents from ST were not aware about the official wage rate.

So they are never paid full wages.

i) In Dungarpur, 46.7 per cent respondents mentioned presence of discrimination in getting work while in Karauli, 52.7 per cent respondents mentioned the same discrimination in getting work.

ii) In Dungarpur, 76 per cent respondents were not satisfied with the measurement of work at the work sites. In Karauli, 57 per cent respondents were not satisfied with the measurement of work at the work sites.

Since the measurement of work was not done properly, they were never paid full wages. They were paid less than half of the official wage rate.

i) In Dungarpur, 98.7 per cent respondents were not aware about the Right to Information (RTI) Act and in Karauli, 100 per cent respondents were not aware about the same. In Dungarpur, only 7 per cent respondents from general category are aware about the RTI; whereas 100 per cent respondents from OBC, SC and 99.1 per cent from ST were not aware about RTI. In Karauli, 100 per cent respondents from OBC, SC and ST were not aware about RTI.
ii) In Dungarpur, 54.7 per cent of respondents have been paid wages after more than one month of completion of work. In Karauli, 98.7 per cent of the respondents were paid wages after more than one month of completion of work.
iii) In Dungarpur, 99.3 per cent respondents did not get compensation for delayed payment of wages. In Karauli, 98.7 per cent respondents did not get any compensation for delayed payment of wages.

Participation of Women, SC and ST in Planning in MGNREGA

i) In Dungarpur, 11.6 per cent men and 9.3 per cent women participated in *gram sabha* meeting, while in Karauli 4.5 per cent men and 0.9 per cent women participated in *gram sabha* meeting.
ii) In Dungarpur, 28.6 per cent respondents from general category, 16.7 per cent respondents from OBC, none from SC and 9.1 per cent from ST participated in meeting of *gram sabha*. In Karauli, none from OBC and SC and 6.8 per cent from ST participated in the meeting of *gram sabha*.

Hence, the participation of workers in *gram sabha* meeting is very less that and of SC in *gram sabha* was nil in both districts.

i) In Dungarpur, 39.5 per cent men and 22.4 per cent of women respondents participated in the discussion related to the annual plan of NREGA in *gram Sabha*. In Karauli, 2.3 per cent men and 2.8 per cent women participated in the discussion of annual plan of NREGA in *gram sabha*

ii) In Dungarpur, 50 per cent respondents from General category, 33.3 per cent of respondents from OBC, 15 per cent from SC and 26.4 per cent from ST participated in the discussion of annual plan of NREGA in *gram sabha*. In Karauli, 5 per cent respondents from OBC, 1.5 per cent from SC and 2.3 per cent from ST participated in the discussion on annual plan of NREGA.

iii) In Dungarpur, 25.6 per cent of men respondents are allowed a to speak in the discussion-making on NREGA and 16.8 per cent of women respondents were allowed to speak in the discussion. In Karauli, 2.3 per cent of men respondents were allowed to speak in the discussion on NREGA while 1.9 per cent of women respondents were allowed to speak in the discussion on NREGA in *gram sabha*.

iv) In Dungarpur, 35.7 per cent of respondents from General category, 33.3 per cent from OBC, 0 per cent from SC and 20 per cent from ST were allowed to speak in the discussion on NREGA. In Karauli, 5 per cent from OBC, 0 per cent from SC and 2.3 per cent from ST were allowed to speak in the discussion on NREGA in *gram sabha*.

v) In Dungarpur, 51.2 per cent of respondents were given awareness on NREGA when they participated in *gram sabha* and 55.8 per cent of respondents who were given awareness did not participate in *gram sabha*. In Karauli,75 per cent of respondents who were given awareness in the *gram sabha* participated in the discussion on annual plan and 28.3 per cent of respondents who were given awareness did not participate in the discussion.

vi) In Dungarpur, respondents got an average of 80 days of work in 2012-13 and 81 days of work in 2013-14. In Karauli, respondents have got 27 days of work in 2012-13 and 26 days in 2013-14.

vii) In Dungarpur, respondents who participated in the discussion on annual plan of NREGA got 84 days of work, whereas those who did not participate got 76 days of work. In Karauli, respondents who participated in the discussion on annual plan of NREGA got 32 days of work and those who did not got 23 days of work.

viii) In Dungarpur, 51.2 per cent of respondents who replied that work from NREGA has improved their sources of livelihood, participated in the annual plan discussion of NREGA. In Karauli, 96.7 per cent of those who claimed that work from NREGA has not improved their source of livelihood were found to not participate in the discussion on annual plan of NREGA.

So from the above findings, it is clear that compared to Karauli, because of pressure from the district administration, there is some participation of people in planning of NREGA work in *gram sabha* in Dungarpur. Tribes constitute 65 per cent of the total population of Dungarpur. It is at the bottom of the Human development Index (HDI) of Rajasthan. Agricultural productivity is very less due to lack of irrigation facilities. So programmes like NREGA is highly required in the district. The focus group discussion (FGD) revealed that this participation is also token participation. Since the *panchayat* has to fulfill the rule of required quorum of attendance in *gram sabha*, they ask people to participate in it. In the name of discussion, they ask people to write their demands on a piece of paper and submit. Participation of women is very less and that of SC is nil. When they attend *gram sabha* with their demands, they are asked to leave for being ignorant in nature.

Conclusion

In both the districts, participatory planning is only symbolic, awareness about key features of NREGA is very low among people, and they are not aware that it is a rights-based programme. For making the annual plan, although some people are called for *gram sabha*, the said discussion never happens and they are told to write submit their demand on paper to the *panchayat* office. But *panchayat* never looks into these demands. Therefore, people have lost interest in *gram sabha* meetings.

Participation of women, SCs and STs is very low and they are asked to attend *gram sabha* for solely the quorum. As a result, it is the *panchayat* members and secretary, and the local elite who decide on the work that will be done under NREGA in the *panchayat*, contrary to the provisions of NREGA. Although they are providing average of 80 days of work to people, some *panchayats* do maintain the 100-days, but it is happening under pressure from the district administration. Since incidence of poverty is high in the district, income from NREGA has provided food security to the workers. Therefore, against the provisions of the act, workers (100%) never filled a Form to demand work, it is the mates who filled the form of personally selected people and ask them to come for work. Effectively, planning is still top-down and not bottom-up. There is a lot of corruption in measurement of work and attendance is also given to selected people even of they miss work. So there is forgery while filling of muster rolls; In the process, people do not get full wages, mostly less than half of the official wage rate and majority of them are not even aware about the official wage rate. Even if people get 100 days, of work this does not render the programme successful because they are not given full wages which are also often are paid late.

In Karauli also, *gram sabha* is not called regularly and participation of women and particularly the SC therein is very low. Although participation rate of women as workers is very high, they are not given adequate opportunity to participate in the annual plan discussion and preparation of labour budget which takes place in a highly patriarchal environment. Caste system is quite entrenched and people fear speaking to the dominant caste. Therefore, in both these districts, no one has ever filed any complaint officially, fearing the displeasure of the dominant *panchayat* functionaries who threaten to deprive them of the benefits of any government programme in the future.

One of the solutions is the formation of an association of workers as provided in the NREGA. But the association of workers has not been formed yet. Majority of the people were of the opinion that if there is an association of workers, then they can forcefully put up their due demands in the *gram sabha* meetings, which will enable them to get work when they needed. Another strategy which has been successfully adopted by states like Andhra Pradesh (AP) is for *panchayats* to voluntary seek cooperation of the non-governmental organisations (NGOs) in planning, implementation and social audit of NREGA. In Rajasthan, NGOs like Mazdoor Kisan Shakti Sangathan (MKSS) and Aastha, which did social audit in 2006 in Dungarpur, found several irregularities and instances of corruption done by *panchayat* functionaries. Therefore, *panchayat* presidents violently oppose their participation in NREGA. In Rajasthan, the association of *panchayat* presidents opposed the involvement of NGOs in NREGA and the state government bowed to their pressure. Thus, social audit is done by a team selected by district administration. Social audit is only symbolic and is done to complete the formality.

Although instances of corruption are rampant, no action has been taken so far against any official. The people have thus lost faith in the authorities implementing NREGA and this is also a major reason why people do not want to participate in *gram sabha* and social audit. There is an urgent need to involve NGOs like MKSS and Aastha who have expertise in planning, doing social audit, conducting need-based assessment and creating awareness among people aobout NREGA and RTI. For successfully implementing NREGA and for ensuring participatory planning, NGOs and SHGs (self-help groups) should be involved, and the state government should take steps and give direction to the district administration in this respect.

To ensure broad-based representation of people in need-based assessment and planning, planning of NREGA work should be done at ward sabha level, which is not happening. There is a also a need to create awareness among people on the key aspects of NREGA as well as about the RTI Act, which is an integral part of NREGA, by NGOs, SHGs and People's Organisation. In a block, where there is a People's Organisation supported by Aastha, there the participation of women and tribals there is high in *gram sabha* meetings in the context of preparing the annual plan. Appointing leaders of the women SHGs, as well as people from SC as members of vigilance and monitoring committees and as mates, will also help in enhancing their confidence and ensure greater participation in planning in *gram sabha*. There is an urgent need to do capacity building of *panchayat* functionaries on NREGA and its implementation on regular basis. In many *panchayats*, adequate staff to implement NREGA has not been provided. Further, at block level, BDO is also programme officer and man power at block level and district level is also not adequate for successful implementation of the programme.

References

Aiyar, Y. and S. Samji (2009). *Guaranteeing Good Governance: Understanding the Effectiveness of Accountability Mechanism in NREGA*. NREGA e-Knowledge Network. New Delhi: UNDP.

Bagchi, K.K. (n.d.). *Good Governance and Sustainable Local Development: A Case Study of GPs in West Bengal. www.ignou.ac.in*

Brinkerhoff, D.W. (2007). "Governance and Intrastate Conflict: Contributions, Challenges and Caveats", Paper presented at the *Global Effects and Local Dynamics of Intrastate Conflict*. International Workshop. Jerusalem. May.

DFID (2006). "States in Development: Understanding State-building", *DFID Working Paper*.

Ghatak, Maitreesh and Maitreya Ghatak (2002). "Recent Reforms in the Panchayat System in West Bengal: Toward Greater Participatory Governance?", *Economic and Political Weekly* 37(1): 5-11, January.

HSS Department (2009). *The Appraisal of Procedures and Processes of NREGA in ORISSA: A Case Study of Balasore and Mayurbhanj District*. IIT Kharagpur. Sponsored by MoRD, Govt. of India.

Islam, Nazrul Md (2004). "Decentralised Governance Transparency and Accountability: Empirical Evidence from West Bengal", *ISEC Working Paper* 144. Bangalore: Institute for Social and Economic Change.

Marsh, D. and R.A.W. Rhodes (eds.) (1992). *Policy Networks in British Government*. Oxford: Clarendon Press.

North, Douglass C. (2005). *Understanding the Process of Economic Change*. Princeton, NJ: Princeton University Press.

Kooiman, J. (ed.) (1993). *Modern Governance. New Government-Society Interactions*. Newbury Park: Sage.

Panchayats and Rural Development Department (2008). *Panchayati Raj*. Government of West Bengal, May.

Rao, V.M. (2007). "Making Safety Nets Effective for Hardcore Poor", *Economic and Political Weekly*, 18 August.

Rotberg, Robert (2004). "Strengthening Governance", *Washington Quarterly* 28(1): 71-81 (Winter).

Sharma, Shailendra. D (2007). "Democracy, Good Governance, and Economic Development", *Taiwan Journal of Democracy* 3(1): 29-62.

State Institute of Panchayat and Rural Development (2008). *NREGA Sahayika* (in Bengali) Panchayats and Rural Development Department, Government of West Bengal.

UNDP (1997). *Governance for Sustainable Human Development*. A UNDP policy paper.

World Bank (2011). *World Development Report 2011: Conflict, Security, and Development*. Washington DC: The World Bank, forthcoming.

Table 9.1

Gender-wise Distribution of Respondents

	Male		*Female*		*Total*	
	N	*%*	*N*	*%*	*N*	*%*
Dungarpur	43	28.7	107	71.3	150	100.0
Karauli	44	29.3	106	70.7	150	100.0
Total	87	29.0	213	71.0	300	100.0

Table 9.2

Caste/Category-wise Distribution of Respondents

	General		*Backward Class*		*Scheduled Caste*		*Scheduled Tribe*		*Total*	
	N	*%*	*N*	*%*	*N*	*%*	*N*	*%*	*N*	*%*
Dungarpur	14	9.3	6	4.0	20	13.3	110	73.3	150	100.0
Karauli	0	.0	40	26.7	66	44.0	44	29.3	150	100.0
Total	14	4.7	46	15.3	86	28.7	154	51.3	300	100.0

Table 9.3

Ability-wise Distribution of Respondents

	Disabled					
	Yes		*No*		*Total*	
	N	*%*	*N*	*%*	*N*	*%*
Dungarpur	9	6.0	141	94.0	150	100.0
Karauli	1	.7	149	99.3	150	100.0
Total	10	3.3	290	96.7	300	100.0

Table 9.4

Education-wise Distribution of Respondents

	Educational Qualification													
	Illiterate		Primary		Upper Primary		Secondary		Higher Secondary		Graduate		Total	
	N	%	N	%	N	%	N	%	N	%	N	%	N	%
Dungarpur	125	83.3	18	12.0	6	4.0	1	.7	0	.0	0	.0	150	100.0
Karauli	142	94.7	5	3.3	1	.7	2	1.3	0	.0	0	.0	150	100.0
Total	267	89.0	23	7.7	7	2.3	3	1.0	0	.0	0	.0	300	100.0

Table 9.5

Caste-wise Distribution of Respondents Holding Land in Each District

		Land holder					
		Yes		No		Total	
		N	%	N	%	N	%
Dungarpur	General	14	100.0	0	.0	14	100.0
	Backward Class	6	100.0	0	.0	6	100.0
	Scheduled Caste	0	.0	20	100.0	20	100.0
	Scheduled Tribe	102	93.6	7	6.4	109	100.0
	Total	122	81.9	27	18.1	149	100.0
Karauli	General	0	.0	0	.0	0	.0
	Backward Class	39	97.5	1	2.5	40	100.0
	Scheduled Caste	1	1.5	65	98.5	66	100.0
	Scheduled Tribe	40	90.9	4	9.1	44	100.0
	Total	80	53.3	70	46.7	150	100.0
Total	General	14	100.0	0	.0	14	100.0
	Backward Class	45	97.8	1	2.2	46	100.0
	Scheduled Caste	1	1.2	85	98.8	86	100.0
	Scheduled Tribe	142	92.8	11	7.2	153	100.0
	Total	202	67.6	97	32.4	299	100.0

Table 9.6

Distribution of Respondents as per their Source of Awareness About NREGA

	Source of information about MNREGA									
	Members of the Panchayat		Radio/T.V./ News Paper		Non-Governmental Organization (NGOs)		Community People		Total	
	N	%	N	%	N	%	N	%	N	%
Dungarpur	138	92.0	0	.0	0	.0	12	8.0	150	100.0
Karauli	111	74.0	0	.0	0	.0	39	26.0	150	100.0
Total	249	83.0	0	.0	0	.0	51	17.0	300	100.0

Table 9.7

Distribution of Respondents as per the Mode of their Application for Job in NREGA

	Mode of Application for work in NREGA					
	Written		Verbal		Total	
	N	%	N	%	N	%
Dungarpur	92	61.3	58	38.7	150	100.0
Karauli	23	15.3	127	84.7	150	100.0
Total	115	38.3	185	61.7	300	100.0

Table 9.8

Distribution of Respondents as per the Dated Receipt for their Application for Job in NREGA

	Provision of dated receipt in NREGA							
	Yes		No		Do not know		Total	
	N	%	N	%	N	%	N	%
Dungarpur	0	.0	148	98.7	2	1.3	150	100.0
Karauli	0	.0	150	100.0	0	.0	150	100.0
Total	0	.0	298	99.3	2	.7	300	100.0

Table 9.9

Distribution of Respondents as per their Awareness About Official Wage Rate

	Awareness about official wage rate					
	Yes		*No*		*Total*	
	N	*%*	*N*	*%*	*N*	*%*
Dungarpur	13	8.7	137	91.3	150	100.0
Karauli	3	2.0	147	98.0	150	100.0
Total	16	5.3	284	94.7	300	100.0

Table 9.10

Distribution of Respondents as per their Satisfaction About Measurement of Work

	Satisfaction with the measurement of work					
	Yes		*No*		*Total*	
	N	*%*	*N*	*%*	*N*	*%*
Dungarpur	36	24.0	114	76.0	150	100.0
Karauli	65	43.3	85	56.7	150	100.0
Total	101	33.7	199	66.3	300	100.0

Table 9.11

Gender-wise Distribution of Respondents as per their Participation in Discussion on Annual Plan of NREGA in Gram Sabha

		Participated in discussion of annual plan of NREGA in gram sabha							
		Yes		*No*		*Not Applicable/Do not know*		*Total*	
		N	%	*N*	%	*N*	%	*N*	%
Dungarpur	Male	17	39.5	14	32.6	12	27.9	43	100.0
	Female	24	22.4	29	27.1	54	50.5	107	100.0
	Total	41	27.3	43	28.7	66	44.0	150	100.0
Karauli	Male	1	2.3	19	43.2	24	54.5	44	100.0
	Female	3	2.8	41	38.7	62	58.5	106	100.0
	Total	4	2.7	60	40.0	86	57.3	150	100.0
Total	Male	18	20.7	33	37.9	36	41.4	87	100.0
	Female	27	12.7	70	32.9	116	54.5	213	100.0
	Total	45	15.0	103	34.3	152	50.7	300	100.0

Table 9.12

Distribution of Respondents as per their Response Against Time Gap Between Completion of Work and Payment of Wages

	Time gap between completion of work and payment of wages									
	Within one week		*Within 15 days*		*Within one month*		*Beyond one month*		*Total*	
	N	*%*	*N*	*%*	*N*	*%*	*N*	*%*	*N*	*%*
Dungarpur	1	.7	4	2.7	63	42.0	82	54.7	150	100.0
Karauli	0	.0	0	.0	2	1.3	148	98.7	150	100.0
Total	1	.3	4	1.3	65	21.7	230	76.7	300	100.0

Table 9.13

Gender-wise Distribution of Respondents Having Say in Decision-making

		Allowed to speak in the discussion							
		Yes		*No*		*Not Applicable/ Do not know*		*Total*	
		N	*%*	*N*	*%*	*N*	*%*	*N*	*%*
Dungarpur	Male	11	25.6	12	27.9	20	46.5	43	100.0
	Female	18	16.8	16	15.0	73	68.2	107	100.0
	Total	29	19.3	28	18.7	93	62.0	150	100.0
Karauli	Male	1	2.3	1	2.3	42	95.5	44	100.0
	Female	2	1.9	4	3.8	100	94.3	106	100.0
	Total	3	2.0	5	3.3	142	94.7	150	100.0
Total	Male	12	13.8	13	14.9	62	71.3	87	100.0
	Female	20	9.4	20	9.4	173	81.2	213	100.0
	Total	32	10.7	33	11.0	235	78.3	300	100.0

Table 9.14

Caste-wise Distribution of Respondents Having Say in Decision-making

		Allowed to speak in the discussion							
		Yes		*No*		*Not Applicable/ Do not know*		*Total*	
		N	*%*	*N*	*%*	*N*	*%*	*N*	*%*
Dungarpur	General	5	35.7	2	14.3	7	50.0	14	100.0
	Backward Class	2	33.3	0	.0	4	66.7	6	100.0
	Scheduled Caste	0	.0	7	35.0	13	65.0	20	100.0
	Scheduled Tribe	22	20.0	19	17.3	69	62.7	110	100.0
	Total	29	19.3	28	18.7	93	62.0	150	100.0
Karauli	General	0	.0	0	.0	0	.0	0	.0
	Backward Class	2	5.0	0	.0	38	95.0	40	100.0
	Scheduled Caste	0	.0	4	6.1	62	93.9	66	100.0
	Scheduled Tribe	1	2.3	1	2.3	42	95.5	44	100.0
	Total	3	2.0	5	3.3	142	94.7	150	100.0
Total	General	5	35.7	2	14.3	7	50.0	14	100.0
	Backward Class	4	8.7	0	.0	42	91.3	46	100.0
	Scheduled Caste	0	.0	11	12.8	75	87.2	86	100.0
	Scheduled Tribe	23	14.9	20	13.0	111	72.1	154	100.0
	Total	32	10.7	33	11.0	235	78.3	300	100.0

10

P.K. VISWANATHAN, RUDRA N. MISHRA and
MADHUSUDAN BHATTARAI

Gender Impacts of MGNREGA

Evidence from Selected ICRISAT Villages in India

Introduction

One of the unique features of the MGNREGA, launched in 2005, has been its impact on gender empowerment across states irrespective of their overall status of economic development. At the aggregate level, the share of women in the total 'MGNREGA (NREGS hereafter) work force' had increased from 41 per cent during 2006-07 to almost 53.41 per cent during 2013-14, indicating an overall increase of 13.41 per cent during the eight year period with an annual average increase of 1.641 per cent. In absolute terms, the employment generated for women increased by more than 57.41 per cent from 16 million during 2009-10 to 25.2 million during 2013-14, registering an annual average increase of 11.541 per cent during the reference period. More importantly, the most crucial and socially beneficial outcome of this increased work participation in the NREGS has been the decline in the gender wage gap across states. Besides the decline in the gender wage gap, other benefits, like flexible working hours, less hazardous nature of work undertaken as well as the proximity to the work sites (as work is provided within 5 km radius of the worker's residence) have resulted in increased women participation in this nation-wide flagship programme. Further, reduced influence of work contractors and the formation of social groups within work sites reduced the fear of exploitation and encourage women to participate in large numbers (Viswanathan and Mandal, 2012).

In fact, the high levels of GWP (gender work participation) in the NREGS assumes relevance especially in a context when the aggregate (national) level rural work participation by women has been hovering around 35-37.41 per cent as per the various NSSO surveys between 2005-06 and 2010-11. A comparison of GWP rates in the rural labour market (as observed from the primary census abstract) *vis-à-vis* the NREGS reveals (Figure 10.1) that in most states, the GWP rates in the NREGS is well above that of GWP in the rural labour market and this underscores that the flagship programme has certainly boosted greater women participation in it, enabling them to be an important stakeholder in the process of rural transformation. In fact, the outcome of increased women participation in the NREGS and the resultant women empowerment is considered to be an unintended (or incidental) benefit of the MGNREGS across states in India (Pankaj and Tankha, 2010).

NREGS was conceptualised as a national flagship programme that would provide employment to the unskilled rural poor in the slack season, thereby protecting them from extreme poverty and deprivation. As the proportion of unemployment in India kept increasing, the government had to resort to strategies and actions to arrest the growing unemployment and ensure growth of the economy. It was believed that NREGS would help revive the economy as it was formulated on Keynes' famous principle of 'providing employment to people by letting them dig pot holes and fill it'. The basic idea was that NREGS will provide short term employment to people in rural areas; but at the same time, it will also help physical asset creation in these areas. These assets will generate employment in the long run through multiplier effects. Thus, initial investment and support by the government will provide the necessary stimulus required for reviving the economy from prolonged levels of depression and stagnation.

MGNREGS was launched in 2006, and since then, many researchers have taken keen interest in studying the progress of the scheme till date. While there were some obvious outcomes that were envisaged by the founders of the MGNREGA, there were many unintended positive benefits also that came along the way, which became a matter of great discussion among the scholars. One such unintended positive outcome is the 'increased participation of women in the NREGS. MGNREGA mandated that one-third of the beneficiaries must be women and wages for males and females will be uniform. Although not initially expected, NREGS created many direct and indirect benefits for the rural women in the country, including employment awareness generation, knowledge about rights, increased bargaining power and stronger role in decision-making at the local level. So far, numerous studies have been carried out at the regional, national as well as international levels to analyse the specific impacts of NREGS on women and their household and suggest suitable measures to improve the nexus so that women employment becomes a strong objective and outcome of NREGS (Kelkar, 2011).

Figure 10.1

Gender Work Participation in NREGS and Rural Labour Market across Major States

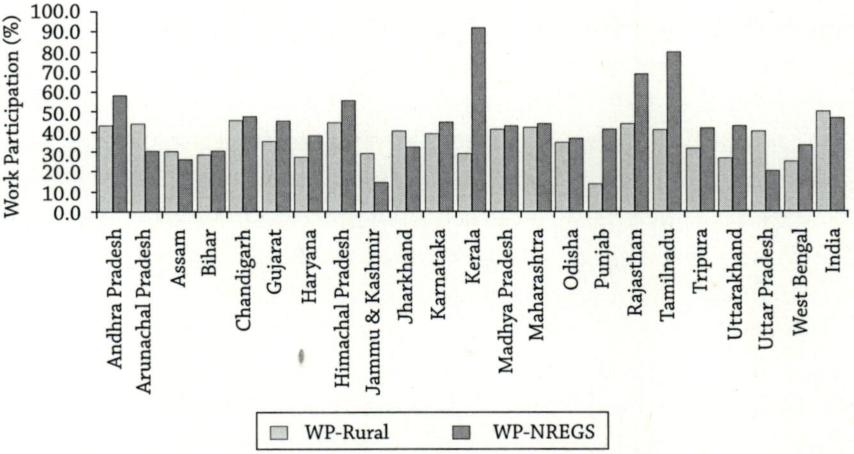

Note: The figures are averages for the period 2009-10 to 2013-14. FWPR (female work participation rate) has been interpolated from the Primary Census Abstract data of 2001 and 2011. Post 2011 gender work participation data has been extrapolated using CAGR method.

Source: *http://nrega.nic.in/Netnrega/stHome.aspx* (for NREGS data).

NREGS design ensures that it is suitable for women, especially as work is given in a radius of 5 kms, contractors and intermediaries are absent, same wages has to be paid to both men and women, crèches, drinking water and other facilities are also to be provided at the work site, and women are given the freedom to participate in the decision-making and implementation of the programme (Chhabra et al., 2009). Studies have shown that the participation of women in NREGS related activities had increased since its inception. In majority of the states, the proportion of women is seen higher than the 33 per cent as mandated in the Act. This is more evident from the proportion of women person days generated under NREGS, particularly in the states of Kerala (93%), Tamil Nadu (84%), Rajasthan (68%), Andhra Pradesh (59%) and Madhya Pradesh (63%), the national average being 53 per cent during 2013-14. Nevertheless, some northern and eastern states still fall way below the stipulated 33 per cent reservation for women in the NREGS. Such inter-state variations in women participation are observed due to social restrictions faced by women as well as administrative discrimination against them (Narayanan and Das, 2014).

The fact that the proportion of women working in NREGS is higher than the proportion of women in the total rural workforce signifies the greater opportunity and willingness on part of women to work in the NREGS. Consequently, they do enjoy many benefits. Case studies and primary surveys conducted for different states of India have brought out many interesting gender outcomes of NREGS implementation. One such outcome is reduction in distress migration due to improvement in family incomes as a consequence of women working in NREGS (Ghosh, 2009).

Another study on the impact of NREGS on women participation in three states, namely Himachal Pradesh, Kerala and Rajasthan revealed that women were introduced to outside work for the first time in their life. Furthermore, local governance institutions, such as *Gram Panchayats* and SHGS (self-help groups) like Kudumbashree (in Kerala) helped women increasingly participate in the NREGS and manage their earnings even by saving a portion of their income (Sudarshan, 2011). It was also observed that increased involvement of women in NREGS help women increase the total household income and add to the improved consumption levels of the family (Tripathi, 2013).

Evidence also suggests that NREGS has increased incomes and credit worthiness of the household; the women respondents felt they could save more. Women also felt that their earning ensured two regular meals every day for their family. NREGS has played an important role in improving the social status of women by involving them in various social audit programmes, encouraging them to participate in the management and monitoring aspects and providing satisfaction in the form of guaranteed 100 days wage employment (Arora et al., 2013). A case study on NREGS in Kerala reveals that the programme has increased the bargaining power of women as they demand more wages in non-NREGS activities as well, which has augmented the general wage level in the rural areas. Dependent women like widows and elderly who were considered a burden could now work in NREGS and earn, with an overall improvement in their social status (Poonia, 2012; Kelkar, 2011).

Another major advantage of NREGS is that it has freed women from working under contractors of intermediaries who can be extremely exploitative or discriminative. Women find it difficult to work in activities involving heavy physical work or longer hours of work, and NREGS gives a relaxation on both these aspects. Widows, single mothers and women in the families with male out-migration can take care of their household responsibilities and work under less stress in NREGS. Many women have used their NREGS income to buy essential items for their family and also invest in productive inputs and tools (Khera, 2009). As NREGS considers 'household' as the unit of entry into the scheme and allows more than one person from a family to participate, women are able to have greater control over their earnings as they are paid separately. This gives them freedom to avail paid employment at their doorstep, which increases a sense of confidence among them and their role and importance in the family. These factors could also be responsible for increased participation of women in NREGS (Pankaj and Tankha, 2010; Hirway et al., 2010). As NREGS offers paid work, women felt they could channelise their income to repay old debts, invest more on the education of their children and health of the family members. They also felt a sense of economic independence due to NREGS. Moreover, it also helped bring down the extent of poverty in any region and improve the living conditions of the beneficiaries (Borah and Bordoloi, 2014).

Thus, the empowerment of rural women has emerged as an unintended consequence of the MGNREGA. Women have benefited more as workers than as a community. Women as individuals have gained because of their ability to earn independently, made possible due to the paid employment opportunity under MGNREGA. Independent and monetised earnings have increased consumption choices and reduced economic dependence. This has helped women in registering their tangible contribution to the household's income. The overall effects of these have translated into an increased say for women in household affairs. Their increased presence in the *gram sabha*, the increasing number of women speaking out in the *gram sabha*, frequent interactions with government officials and PRI (panchayati raj institution) representatives, and access to banks and post offices are new developments. Additionally, the participation of women in MGNREGA has reversed the traditional gender roles, albeit in a limited manner (Pankaj and Tankha, 2010: 54).

However, although NREGS has ensured that women earn special benefits, its performance is not flawless as it emerges from many studies. For instance, many women respondents felt that they could not participate in NREGS due to family responsibilities and other social obligations. Special facilities related to child care and sanitation are not provided at all NREGS work sites, hence lactating mothers face problems in keeping their infants at home and coming to work (Kar, 2013). Poor awareness regarding their rights and powers within the NREGS setup further constrain their ability to participate. Some women also felt that they did not get any support from their husbands for household work; hence they could not work in NREGS. There have been delays in payment of wages and women are discouraged to continue working due to future payment uncertainties. NREGS has also drawn much flak for its inability to provide 100 days of employment to the workers; workers are not interested in working for irregular days and hence, opt out of NREGS. Another important statistic with regard to NREGS is that proportion of women seeking work is very low because women are never considered when deciding about the nature of work. There may be certain types of work that women are not comfortable performing, if such works are provided under NREGS. As many evidences reveal, in many typical rural villages, women do not have a say in household level decision-making, they do not own any asset or property, even accounts are opened in the name of the male members; thus their choices or preferences are not respected with regard to NREGS as well (Holmes *et al.*, 2011).

Nevertheless, the ultimate success of the programme depends on the local settings as well as the specific socio-economic contexts of the rural villages in which the schemes are being implemented. While the positive impacts as well as the multiplier effects of the employment programme could be more pronounced in the highly backward rural areas, the outcomes may not be that much impressive in villages, which are reasonably developed with the households enjoying relatively better socio-economic status.

Against this backdrop, this chapter tries to explore some of the important gender-specific impacts of the NREGS as they emerge from few selected villages that form part of the Village Dynamics South Asia (VDSA) project implemented by the International Crops Research Institute for Semi-Arid Tropics (ICRISAT), Hyderabad. The empirical analysis presented in the chapter is based on the village level data (information) gathered during the period September 2013-May 2014. The analysis covers a sample of 486 women NREGS beneficiaries (326 households) drawn from 10 villages located in three states, viz., Gujarat (4 villages), Madhya Pradesh (2 villages) and Maharashtra (4 villages). The sample represented small farm (with holdings less than 5 acres per household) and landless labour households. The sample women were selected from all the households in the study villages representing the categories (small farm and landless labour) for which a separate questionnaire was administered. Thus, the study covered a reasonable number of households, where only women participated in the programme.

Rest of the chapter is organised into three sections. While section 2 discusses about methodology in brief, section 3 presents the results of the empirical study of the various gendered impacts of NREGS in the study villages. Section 3 concludes the chapter by highlighting the key messages and policy relevant points that emerge from the study.

Methodology

The objective of the study was to understand 'what changes that NREGS has brought to the women in the household and for themselves?' The survey was conducted with semi-structured questionnaire during Sepetmber 2013 to May 2014. The villages selected are part of the ICRISAT-VDSA project. All together 10 villages were selected, 4 each from Gujarat and Maharashtra and 2 from Eastern Madhya Pradesh. In Gujarat, out of the 4 villages, 2 were from tribal dominated Panchamahal district and the other 2 villages were from non-tribal areas of the Junagadh district. From Maharashtra, the 4 villages selected included 2 each from South-Western Maharashtra (Solapur district) and Vidarbha region (Akola district). From Madhya Pradesh, the 2 villages selected were from Raisen district from Eastern part of the state. The villages predominantly depend upon agriculture, but some of them are closer to industrial areas. In 3 of the 10 villages located near industrial areas, we found no takers for NREGS work. These villages are: Makhiala from Junagadh district in Gujarat and Kalman and Shirapur in Solapur district of Maharashtra. In Chhattha village from the tribal district of Panchamahal and Kinkhed village of Akola district, the status of work implementation was very little or totally absent.

Hence, the information about the performance and gender impacts of the NREGS as presented in the chapter are mostly drawn from the Babrol village in Panchamahal district (representing tribal region) and Karmdi-chingariya village in Junagadh district (representing non-tribal region) in Gujarat. In the case of Maharashtra, the results are drawn from the Kanzara villages in the Vidarbha, as the other villages did not report any NREGS activity being undertaken. In total, 326 households were visited in the survey consisting 486 women, who worked in the programme at least once. These households were drawn through systematic random sampling method from the list of all the households in that village. A house listing was done before drawing the sample in order to identify the households who had effectively worked in the programme. The sample was drawn in such a way that it represents the social-occupational structure of the given village. Approximately 20 per cent households were surveyed from the prominent socio-economic groups in the village. In what follows, we present the major highlights and findings as they emerge from the data analysis.

Gender Impacts of MGNREGA in the ICRISAT Villages

A brief overview on the profile of the sample respondents is presented here in order to understand the socio-economic status of the households. The largest number of the sample households with job cards belonged to the tribal village (Babrol) of Gujarat (47%). From among the total 326 sample households, we found a total number of 486 women having the job card. Out of the total sample of 486 women surveyed, Gujarat reported the largest coverage of 76 per cent (54% from Tribal region and 22% from non-tribal region), followed by 17 per cent in case of Maharashtra (South-West Maharashtra 12%; Vidarbha 5%) and 7 per cent in Madhya Pradesh (Table 10.1).

The sample households differ in terms of social categories. For instance, majority of the households from three of the four Gujarat villages belong to ST (scheduled tribe) category; larger proportions of households from Madhya Pradesh belong to SC (scheduled caste) and OBC (other backward class) categories, while Maharashtra villages report a mix of SC and OBC categories (Table 10.1). While majority of the respondents are married in all the villages, the proportion of widows is reported to be relatively high in Kinkheda village (17%) in Maharashtra, followed by Papda village (12%) in Madhya Pradesh and Chattha village (8%) in Gujarat.

The average age of the women participants range between 35-40 years (Table 10.1). Nearly half of them are illiterate. However, at least 5-10 per cent of the women across the villages reported to have studied till 12th standard. It was found that in the absence of other job options, educated women were not hesitant to take up the NREGS work. The proportion of women having studied at least 10th or more was found higher in Maharashtra villages. Nearly 90 per cent

Table 10.1

Socio-Economic Profile of Sample Women Respondents

Characteristics	*Categories*	*Gujarat-Tribal Region N=153*	*Gujarat-Non-Tribal Region N=70*	*Madhya Pradesh-Eastern Belt N=29*	*Maharashtra-South-West N=53*	*Maharashtra-Vidarbha N=21*	*Total N=326*
1. Total number of women who had job cards		261	110	35	57	23	486
2. Average number of women per household		1.7	1.6	1.2	1.07	1.09	1.5
3. Social group of sample women (% of total women)	SC	0.0	59.1	51.4	24.6	34.8	21.6
	ST	100.0	30.9	5.7	0.0	0.0	61.1
	OBC	0.0	10.0	42.9	43.9	52.2	13.0
	Others	0.0	0.0	0.0	28.1	13.0	3.9
	Not responded	0.0	0.0	0.0	3.5	0.0	0.4
4. Marital status (% of total women)	Married	85.8	88.2	85.7	94.7	91.3	87.8
	Unmarried	10.7	9.1	5.7	1.8	0.0	8.4
	Widow	3.4	2.7	8.6	3.5	8.7	3.9
5. Mean age of sample women (St. Deviation)		38.0 (14)	39 (14)	38 (12)	39 (10)	39 (8)	38 (13)

contd...

.contd...

Characteristics	*Categories*	*Gujarat-Tribal Region N=153*	*Gujarat-Non-Tribal Region N=70*	*Madhya Pradesh-Eastern Belt N=29*	*Maharashtra-South-West N=53*	*Maharashtra-Vidarbha N=21*	*Total N=326*
6. Education status (% of total women)	Uneducated	60.2	44.5	54.3	42.1	34.8	52.9
	Primary	9.6	23.6	25.7	28.1	34.8	17.3
	Secondary	14.9	28.2	17.1	24.6	21.7	19.5
	Higher secondary & above	15.3	3.6	2.9	5.3	8.7	10.3
7. Primary occupation of women ((% of total women)	Farming	76.2	10.9	22.9	19.3	13.0	47.9
	Farm labour	1.1	59.1	0.0	52.6	34.8	21.8
	Non-farm work	0.4	5.5	68.6	28.1	52.2	12.1
	Housewives	22.3	24.5	8.6	0.0	0.0	18.2
8. Average annual income of the household (St. Deviation)		8841 (6024)	9253 (6844.7)	18530.5 (22553.4)	28035.7 (20540.8)	27165 (18873)	1349 (14315)

Note: The 'N' referes to number of households in which the women were interviewed.

Source: Field Survey of ICRISAT villages (2013-14).

of women in Gujarat's Panchmal village were engaged in farming as the main occupation, while in the villages of Junagadh (Gujarat), Maharashtra and MP, almost half of the women respondents worked as farm labour or casual labour. The average annual earnings of these women from NREGA work varied from ₹9,000 in Gujarat (lowest) to ₹27,000 for Maharashtra, while in MP the same was ₹18,000. However, significant variations observed in the annual wage earnings across beneficiaries (Table 10.1).

As regards the benefits from the different safety net programmes provided by the three states, most of the beneficiaries agreed that PDS (public distribution system) is very important for their households, while the help from relatives and neighbours also mattered a lot. Very few households hardly received any benefit from state provisioning for agriculture, credit, health systems and other developmental schemes.

Participation in the NREGS

All the villages report a reasonably higher share of economically active women members (58-91% across villages), with an exception in case of Chattha village (Gujarat), where, the proportion of economically active members was only 47 per cent. Four of the Maharashtra villages reported the highest proportion of economically active women members (average being 91%). The participation of economically active women members in the NREGS was reported to be almost complete in all the villages, with a minimum of more than one member per household (Figure 10.2). The reasons indicated by members in Chattha for non-participation in NREGS were: a) generally women do not go for work outside (34%); b) NREGS work being strenuous (32%); c) customs in the village prevent daughters and sisters working outside (25%); and d) engagement in domestic activities, including caring of children (9%).

When asked about the average days these women got work from MGNREGA, the responses varied across the states (Table 10.2). In Gujarat's tribal region the average days of work has gone up from 20 odd days in initial years (2006-2009) to 26 odd days till 2011, after which there were no works in the villages. In non-tribal region of

Gujarat representing 2 villages in Junagadh, the average number of days women get work has gone up from 20 days to 34 days in same period, but the number of women participating in the work had declined.

Figure 10.2

Mean Number of Women who Worked in NREGS Per Household

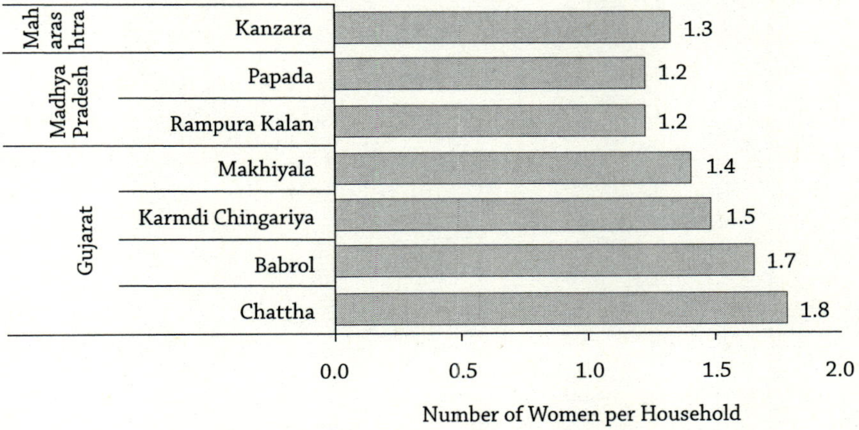

Source: Field Survey of ICRISAT villages (2013-14).

In Madhya Pradesh, the average number of days work available to women respondents rose from 16 days to 32 days between 2006-2009, while it came down in 2010-2012 and after that it is mostly around 30 days (see Table 10.2).

In Solapur (from south-western region) in Maharashtra, there was no work participation reported mainly due to the reason that alternative work options were available for both men and women, while in Vidarbha (Akola district consisting Kanzara as in Kinkhed there were no NREGS works), the average working days have increased from 25 days in 2010 (when the programme started in the village) to 45 days in 2012-13.

Except for Kanzara in all other villages, women beneficiaries informed that they received equal wages, while in Kanzara women reported that they get less wages than men. Even then, the annual income has gone up for the households. However, these figures are to be considered in the light of the fact that the number of women whoc participated in each year in NREGS varied considerably.

Table 10.2

Participation in NREGS for Sample Women

Characteristics	*Year*	*Gujarat-Tribal Region N=153*	*Gujarat-Non-Tribal Region N=70*	*Madhya Pradesh-Eastern Belt N=29*	*Maharashtra-South-West N=53*	*Maharashtra-Vidarbha N=21*	*Total N=326*
1. Total number of women who had job cards		261	110	35	57	23	486
2. Total number of women who actually worked at least once in NREGS (%)		152 (58.0)	70 (63.0)	25 (71)	0.0	18 (78.0)	265 (62.0)
3. Mean number of days women got work in NREGS (no. of women)	2006	25.0 (21)	0.0 (2)	0.0 (0)	0.0	0.0	26.0 (23)
	2007	29.0 (83)	0.0	0.0 (0)	0.0	0.0	29.0 (83)
	2008	41.0 (11)	0.0	17.0 (6)	0.0	0.0	33.0 (17)
	2009	32.0 (24)	15.0 (30)	31.0 (21)	0.0	0.0	25.0 (75)
	2010	32.0 (13)	38.0 (14)	31.0 (14)	0.0	25.0 (2)	34.0 (43)
	2011	31.0 (9)	42.0 (32)	26.0 (13)	0.0	34.0 (5)	36.0 (59)
	2012	0.0 (0)	30.0 (25)	36.0 (15)	0.0	37.0 (11)	34.0 (51)
	2013	0.0 (0)	25.0 (23)	33.0 (18)	0.0	46.0 (6)	31 (47)

contd...

.contd...

Characteristics	*Year*	*Gujarat-Tribal Region N=153*	*Gujarat-Non-Tribal Region N=70*	*Madhya Pradesh-Eastern Belt N=29*	*Maharashtra-South-West N=53*	*Maharashtra-Vidarbha N=21*	*Total N=326*
4. Women receive wage equal to men (%) - Those reporting Yes		100.0	100.0	100.0	100.0	12.5	95.1
5. Average number of days women got work in MGNREGS	2006	20.0	32.0	0.0	0.0	0.0	20.0
	2007	20.0	0.0	0.0	0.0	0.0	20.0
	2008	25.0	0.0	17.0	0.0	0.0	22.0
	2009	11.0	12.0	26.0	0.0	0.0	17.0
	2010	16.0	34.0	24.0	0.0	25.0	26.0
	2011	24.0	34.0	24.0	0.0	35.0	32.0
	2012	0.0	26.0	35.0	0.0	42.0	33.0
	2013	0.0	20.0	32.0	0.0	49.0	30.0
6. Average daily wage earned by the women	2006	66.0	65.0	0.0	0.0	151.0	88.0
	2007	70.0	0.0	0.0	0.0	161.0	79.0
	2008	74.0	0.0	89.0	0.0	129.2	94.0
	2009	90.0	65.0	86.0	0.0	136.5	87.0
	2010	78.0	64.0	104.0	0.0	148.0	97.0
	2011	102.0	64.5	114.0	0.0	187.0	113.0
	2012	0.0	67.0	114.0	0.0	144.0	120.0
	2013	0.0	68.7	127.0	0.0	148.0	121.0

contd...

.contd...

Characteristics	*Year*	*Gujarat-Tribal Region N=153*	*Gujarat-Non-Tribal Region N=70*	*Madhya Pradesh-Eastern Belt N=29*	*Maharashtra-South-West N=53*	*Maharashtra-Vidarbha N=21*	*Total N=326*
7. Average household earnings from MGNREGS*	2006	2753.0	4250.0	0.0	0.0	3108.0	2906.0
	2007	2151.0	0.0	0.0	0.0	3223.0	3180.0
	2008	4306.0	0.0	1633.0	0.0	4150.0	2436.7
	2009	2336.0	1607.0	26823.0	0.0	5260.0	2605.8
	2010	2636.0	4187.0	3458 .0	0.0	4766.7	3601
	2011	5729.0	4667.0	3602.4	0.0	6686.9	4643.8
	2012	0.0	3433.0	3602.0	0.0	7224.06	5641.9
	2013	0.0	2397.4	5267.7	0.0	11246.8	6129.0

Note: % calculated from total number of women who reported having job cards. Since job cards are issued in name of the household head the total wage amount is deposited in the account holder's name. It was difficult for women to say how much was the women's share in the total income received by the household.

Source: Field Survey of ICRISAT villages (2013-14).

Use of MGNREGA Money by Women or Their Households

The major head of expenditure for the income from NREGS was for domestic expenses followed by education of children and health needs of the family members (Table 10.3).

Table 10.3

Use of Money Earned from NREGS for Sample Women

Major Heads on which Money is Spent by Women	*Gujarat-Tribal Region N=153*	*Gujarat-Non-Tribal Region N=70*	*Madhya Pradesh-Eastern Belt N=29*	*Maharashtra-South-West N=53*	*Maharashtra-Vidarbha N=21*	*Total N=326*
1. Domestic expenses	30.4	62.4	60.5	0.0	43.8	38.4
2. Education of children	21.5	19.3	16.3	0.0	31.3	21.2
3. Health needs	20.8	13.0	16.3	0.0	21.9	19.3
4. Agricultural expenses	22.9	5.3	2.3	0.0	0.0	17.5
5. Gives to husband	2.1	0.0	0.0	0.0	0.0	1.5
6. Wages not received	2.3	0.0	2.3	0.0	0.0	1.8
7. To pay interest	0.0	0.0	2.3	0.0	0.0	0.1
8. For making home	0.0	0.0	0.0	0.0	0.0	0.3
Total no. of women who responded	480	114	43	0	33	670

Source: Field Survey of ICRISAT villages (2013-14).

When asked about their participation in *gram sabha* meetings to decide about the work to be taken under NREGS for a given year, the participation of women in Gujurat's tribal region was the highest (80%) in terms of responses (the participation was better in Babrol than Chhatha) where as for Vidarbha it was 100 per cent (for Kanzara only). In non-tribal region of Gujarat only 50 per cent of women responses were found to be affirmative. In Madhya Pradesh, the women's participation was lowest (see Table 10.4).

It is evident from Table 10.5 that most of the women have expressed lack of basic facilities as mandated under the MGNREGA at work site.

Table 10.4

Participation of Women in Decisions Regarding Works to be Undertaken in MGNREGA

Participation in Decision-making (%)	*Gujarat-Tribal Region N=153*	*Gujarat-Non-Tribal Region N=70*	*Madhya Pradesh-Eastern Belt N=29*	*Maharashtra-South-West N=53*	*Maharashtra-Vidarbha N=21*	*Total N=326*
1. No idea about their role	8.5	3.8	18.8	0	21.4	9
2. They are not consulted	11.2	44.9	43.7	0	78.6	24
3. (%) of women who say they are part of decision making process	80.3	51.3	37.5	0	100	67
Total responses	224	78	32	0	14	348

Source: Field Survey of ICRISAT villages (2013-14).

Table 10.5

Facilities for Women at Work Site

(% Responses)

Responses (%)	*Gujarat-Tribal Region N=153*	*Gujarat-Non-Tribal Region N=70*	*Madhya Pradesh-Eastern Belt N=29*	*Maharashtra-South-West N=53*	*Maharashtra-Vidarbha N=21*	*Total N=326*
1. No facilities	74.2	19.2	15.9	0.0	7.1	47.9
2. Drinking water available	23.2	68.5	50.0	0.0	92.9	42.3
3. Place for resting available	1.9	0.0	6.8	0.0	0.0	2.4
4. First aid available	0.0	12.3	11.4	0.0	0.0	4.9
5. Child care facilities available	0.0	0.0	9.1	0.0	0.0	2.4
Total responses	155	73	44	0	14	286

Source: Field Survey of ICRISAT villages (2013-14).

Women's Responses About the Difficulty in NREGS Work

In general it was found that women consider NREGS work easier than the farm work or any other work (Table 10.6). One reason could be that the NREGS work is flexible in terms of working hours and in many cases the work is paid on piece rate basis.

Table 10.6

Women's Responses About the Difficulty in MGNREGA Work

Responses (%)	*Gujarat-Tribal Region N=153*	*Gujarat-Non-Tribal Region N=70*	*Madhya Pradesh-Eastern Belt N=29*	*Maharashtra-South-West N=53*	*Maharashtra-Vidarbha N=21*	*Total N=326*
1. Work under NREGA is strenuous	6.5	15.7	20.7	0	7.1	10.4
2. It is manageable	14.4	8.6	27.6	0	7.1	13..8
3. Easier compared to farm work	79.1	75.7	48.3	0	85.7	75.7
Total responses	153	70	29	0	14	266

Source: Field Survey of ICRISAT villages (2013-14).

Management of Household Affairs versus NREGS Work Participation

Table 10.7 shows that the NREGS work does put additional work burden on women across all study areas, as they have to get up early and also prepare children for school. Thus, overall burden on women has increased due to NREGS work.

However, most of the women reported having received support of some kind from their family members to fulfil their routine household tasks, so that they could participate in MGNREGA. As Table 10.8 shows, in-laws and spouse were the major source of support as most of the participating women in our sample are married (only exception being the non-tribal region in Gujarat). Some of these households where women do not get any support are smaller households or households having old age members who can not help them.

Table 10.7

Management of Household in View of MGNREGA Particpation

Impact on Women's Work Burden and Coping Strategy	*Gujarat-Tribal Region N=153*	*Gujarat-Non-Tribal Region N=70*	*Madhya Pradesh-Eastern Belt N=29*	*Maharashtra-South-West N=53*	*Maharashtra-Vidarbha N=21*	*Total N=326*
1. Has to get up early	72.8	82.9	67.8	0	72.2	74.7
2. Difficulty in managing children	14.5	2.9	9.7	0	0	10.3
3. Have to send children for school early	6.3	0	3.2	0	0	4.1
4. More work has to be done	1.73	5.7	3.2	0	22.3	4.8
5. No additional burden	4.6	8.5	9.7	0	5.6	6.2
Total responses	173	70	31	0	18	292

Source: Field Survey of ICRISAT villages (2013-14).

Table 10.8

How Other Members in the Household Play a Role in Supporting Women

Support Received from the Household (%)	*Gujarat-Tribal Region N=153*	*Gujarat-Non-Tribal Region N=70*	*Madhya Pradesh-Eastern Belt N=29*	*Maharashtra-South-West N=53*	*Maharashtra-Vidarbha N=21*	*Total N=326*
1. Get help from in-laws and other family members	63.4	42.9	42.9	0	64.3	55.4
2. Found spousal support	0.0	5.7	21.4	0	14.3	4.5
3. From neighbours	0.0	0.0	0.0	0.0	7.1	1.1
4. No household support	36.6	51.4	35.7	0	14.3	39.0
5. Total responses	153	70	28	0	14	265

Source: Field Survey of ICRISAT villages (2013-14).

Changing Status of Women in the Family and Society

Table 10.9 shows that the working in NREGS and earning money has definitely improved the status of the women in the family and the community across the states.

Table 10.9

Women's Perception About Changing Status in the Family and Community

Changes in Status	*Gujarat-Tribal Region N=153*	*Gujarat-Non-Tribal Region N=70*	*Madhya Pradesh-Eastern Belt N=29*	*Maharashtra-South-West N=53*	*Maharashtra-Vidarbha N=21*	*Total N=326*
1. Change in status of women in the family (%)						
(a) Had gained respect in family	53.3	85.5	82.8	0.0	84.2	66.9
(b) Cooperation from other members have increased	44.1	14.4	13.7	0.0	15.8	31.2
(c) Cannot say, if my status has changed	2.6	0	3.4	0.0	0	1.9
Total responses	152	69	29	0	19	269
2. Change in status of women in the community (%)						
(a) Honour and respect increases in community	71.0	15.5	77.3	0.0	75.0	76.3
(b) Gender discrimination reduced	12.9	2.8	9.1	0.0	5.0	10.0
(c) Opportunity to take decisions	3.9	0.0	0.0	0.0	10.0	2.9
(d) No change in status	12.3	2.8	13.6	0.0	10.0	10.8
Total responses	155	71	22	0	20	272

Source: Field Survey of ICRISAT villages (2013-14).

Positive Impacts on Children Education and Household Welfare

NREGS seems to have shown positive impact on education of children in the family. The sample women does tell that additional income has helped them to ensure education of their children (Table 10.10). A major spillover benefit in this regard was the increased trend of educating the girl children. However, this could also be due to the impact of other dedicated programmes in recent years to encourage the parents to send their girls to schools. Our data and the interactions show that 40 to 70 per cent of the sample women respondents were highly appreciative of the fact that the households were able to send their girl children to schools using the wage earnings realised from working in NREGS (Table 10.10).

Table 10.10

Impact of MGNREGA on Education of Girl Children

Impact on Education/ Enrolment (%)	*Gujarat-Tribal Region N=153*	*Gujarat-Non-Tribal Region N=70*	*Madhya Pradesh-Eastern Belt N=29*	*Maharashtra-South-West N=53*	*Maharashtra-Vidarbha N=21*	*Total N=326*
1. No improvement	58.0	53.6	55.6	0	30.8	54.8
2. Proportion of girls in the school has increased	42.0	46.4	44.4	0	69.3	45.2
Total responses	150	69	27	0	15	261

Source: Field Survey of ICRISAT villages (2013-14).

Perception of Women on Various Impact of NREGS on Household

When asked about whether the NREGS has improved the overall welfare of households for sample women, the response was mostly 'no significant change' (Table 10.11). But 33 per cent respondents in non-tribal region of Gujarat, 24 per cent in Eastern Madhya Pradesh and 50 per cent of women in Vidarbha does report that NREGS has helped improving the general welfare and status of their households. However, the respondents were unable to reflect upon the specific welfare impacts attributable to the NREGS work participation.

Table 10.11

Impact of MGNREGA on Welfare of the Household

Responses (%)	*Gujarat-Tribal Region N=153*	*Gujarat-Non-Tribal Region N=70*	*Madhya Pradesh-Eastern Belt N=29*	*Maharashtra-South-West N=53*	*Maharashtra-Vidarbha N=21*	*Total N=326*
1. General welfare has improved (%)	5.9	32.9	24.1	0.0	50.0	18.2
2. The welfare has not changed (%)	94.1	67.1	75.9	100.0	50.0	81.8
Total respondents	152	70	29	0	16	267

Source: Field Survey of ICRISAT villages (2013-14).

Table 10.12

Impact of MGNREGA on Economic Condition of Household in Women's Own Perception

Responses (%)	*Gujarat-Tribal Region N=153*	*Gujarat-Non-Tribal Region N=70*	*Madhya Pradesh-Eastern Belt N=29*	*Maharashtra-South-West N=53*	*Maharashtra-Vidarbha N=21*	*Total N=326*
1. Economic situation in general has improved	57.8	50.7	33.3	0.0	33.3	52.4
2. Household is financially stable with additional income	16.3	7.5	16.7	0.0	11.1	13.6
3. Cash availability has improved	14.3	20.9	0.0	0.0	27.8	19.2
4. Difficulty in purchasing food items lessened	9.5	16.4	44.4	0.0	5.6	10.8
5. Overall dignity of the household has improved	2.0	4.5	5.6	0.0	0.0	4.0
Total responses	147	67	18	0	18	250

Source: Field Survey of ICRISAT villages (2013-14).

From the point of view of the respondents, NREGS have beneficial impact on economic status of the household in general, especially for sample households in Gujarat and Vidarbha. In Madhya Pradesh, 44 per cent of responses indicated that NREGS helped in improving purchase of food items. Another major impact reported was the availability of cash in the household, highest being in Vidarbha and non-tribal region of Gujarat (Table 10.12).

In terms of social impact on households participating in the NREGS, women respondents view that the programme has given an identity to most of these households and their general status in their respective communities across villages. In the villages in Madhya Pradesh and Maharashtra, which are traditionally male dominated societies, the women appreciate the fact that they can work with men and get same wage as that of men (Table 10.13).

Table 10.13

Impact of MGNREGA on Social Condition of Household in Women's Own Perception

Responses (%)	*Gujarat-Tribal Region N=153*	*Gujarat-Non-Tribal Region N=70*	*Madhya Pradesh-Eastern Belt N=29*	*Maharashtra-South-West N=53*	*Maharashtra-Vidarbha N=21*	*Total N=326*
1. New identity to the household	47.9	28.4	23.5	0.0	25.0	39.3
2. Respectability in the neighbourhood has improved	21.8	55.2	35.3	0.0	25.0	32.2
3. Participation in the activity of the community has improved	30.3	16.4	0.0	0.0	0.0	22.3
4. It enables men and women to work together and earn equal wage	0.0	0.0	41.2	0.0	25.0	4.5
5. Could not say	0.0	0.0	0.0	0.0	25.0	1.7
Total responses	142	67	17	0	16	232

Source: Field Survey of ICRISAT villages (2013-14).

In terms of institutional impact, we found women acknowledging the fact that the earnings from NREGS has given new identity to them in the village set-up dominated by patriarchy for a long time. In case of Madhya Pradesh, 80 per cent of women acknowledges this fact. In Gujarat, the women acknowledge that the programme has helped to create a sense of identity among them, the response being highest (57%) in the non-tribal region of Gujarat followed by 47 per cent in the tribal region (Table 10.14). As noted, the programme is also beneficial to women in enabling them to send their children to school. This may be due to the fact that the households get additional income source with which they could support the education of their children.

Table 10.14

Institutional Impact of MGNREGA for Households in Women's Own Perception

Responses (%)	*Gujarat-Tribal Region N=153*	*Gujarat-Non-Tribal Region N=70*	*Madhya Pradesh-Eastern Belt N=29*	*Maharashtra-South-West N=53*	*Maharashtra-Vidarbha N=21*	*Total N=326*
1. It gives new identity to women in the society as they also earn for their household	47.5	55.6	80.0	0.0	33.3	39.1
2. Able to send children to the school	44.6	44.4	20.0	0.0	33.3	36.7
3. Part of village dairy	7.9	0.0	0.0	0.0	0.0	4.3
4. Cannot say	0.0	0.0	0.0	0.0	66.7	19.9
Total responses	139	54	10	0	6	256

Source: Field Survey of ICRISAT villages (2013-14).

In terms of environmental impact, the increase in ground water level in respective villages across the 3 states gets highest response from women, most notably in non-tribal region of Gujarat followed by Madhya Pradesh. Improvement in green cover in the villages including forests was also confirmed by the respondents. In Karmdi-Chingariya village of the non-tribal region of Gujarat, we found the deepening of the village pond has improved the ground water level to an extent that the bore wells in the village gives water through out the year. Reduction in soil erosion is also highlighted by the sample women because of check dams, farm bonds and check holes (Table 10.15).

A large number of sample women reported that the additional income from the NREGS helps them during medical treatment. This corroborate the finding from Table 10.3, where women reported that the third major head of expenditure for the wage they received from the work was to meet the health needs of the family. It also helps the households to purchase non-cereal food items like pulses and vegetables to supplement their staple food mainly consisting of cereals. In other words, these households are now able to get a more balanced diet (Table 10.16). Nearly 18 per cent of households in Gujarat (both the regions) also reported that they feel that their physical ability to do manual work has increased in the post NREGS period. The pathway in this case may be the intake of better diet that helps the families to get healthier and increase their ability do manual labour.

Despite the positive picture that emerges from Table 10.11 through Table 10.16 about various aspects of impact of the programme on households from which the sample women were interviewed, the major drawbacks noted were lesser participation of women in deciding the works to be undertaken, increase in work burden for women and the lesser availability of work, especially in Gujarat and Madhya Pradesh. In none of the states we found any sample household which has received 100 days of work as per the mandate of the Act. Another disturbing finding from the study is that in Barol village from Gujurat's tribal region there were no works from 2012 onwards; Chhattha the other village has not got any substantial work all these years. Similar is case for Eastern Madhya Pradesh and Vidarbha. In Vidarbha, the Kinkhed village is yet to get any work even after 8 years of the launch of the programme.

Field surveys also revealed that women hardly know about how much amount they earned as wages, as many of them depends upon their male family members to operate the bank accounts. Many

Table 10.15

Environmental Impact of MGNREGA for the Community in Women's Own Perception

Responses (%)	*Gujarat-Tribal Region N=153*	*Gujarat-Non-Tribal Region N=70*	*Madhya Pradesh-Eastern Belt N=29*	*Maharashtra-South-West N=53*	*Maharashtra-Vidarbha N=21*	*Total N=326*
1. Ground water level rose	30.7	47.8	44.4	0.0	26.7	36.1
2. Natural environment improved	29.3	23.3	0.0	0.0	20.0	25.8
3. Soil erosion reduced	16.4	17.4	11.1	0.0	0.0	15.5
4. Growth of village forest	16.4	4.3	22.2	0.0	13.3	12.9
5. Helps trees in village to survive and grow	5.7	1.4	0.0	0.0	0.0	3.9
6. Water level in well rises	0.0	0.0	0.0	0	13.3	0.9
7. Water scarcity in the village came down	1.4	5.8	0.0	0.0	0.0	2.6
8. Due to construction of road air pollution due to dust came down	0.0	0.0	11.1	0.0	0.0	0.4
9. Construction of school sanitation facilities help better environment for children	0.0	0.0	11.1	0.0	0.0	0.4
10. Cannot say	0.0	0.0	0.0	0.0	26.7	1.5
Total responses	140	69	9	0.0	15	233

Source: Field Survey of ICRISAT villages (2013-14).

of the women also could not tell us whether they are part of the decision-making in the household regarding the spending of the money. Also, on many of the responses on various impacts of the programme, we could not quantify the impacts, as the responses were mainly based on perceptions of women respondents. This is one of the limitation of this study. The NREGS has one crucial objective, which is to reduce gender disparity in the society and to provide them opportunity to participate in meaningful economic activities. Unless adequate number of days are provided under the act, the impact of the programme on women and their household will remain partial. It is evident from the analysis that the women or their households had hardly purchased any durable household asset from their wage income.

Conclusions and Policy Imperatives

The analysis bring out an important aspect of inability of women in decision-making as regards NREGS works undertaken in the villages. It was found that except for Babrol in Panchamahal, in all other villages women complained of their limited or no role in deciding about the works to be undertaken in NREGS. The *gram sabhas* hardly listen their voices or even in most cases they were not informed about the meetings related to NREGS. Most of these women respondents also deny of getting any facility other than the provision of drinking water at the work sites. The water is mostly collected by few women members whose houses are nearby. Nearly 75 per cent women in Gujarat appreciates that the NREGS work is easier than the routine farm work, while in Maharashtra (for Kanzara alone) the satisfaction is 88 per cent. In Madhya Pradesh, the satisfaction level was only 43 per cent for women, as the NREGS work mostly consisted of digging well in individual farms under 'Kapildhara' scheme of the Madhya Pradesh government. The work sites in this case were reported to be having the presence of hard black granite blocks, which made their tasks harder and tougher.

As far as the impact of NREGS on women households is concerned, nearly 90 per cent of the respondents reported that there is no marked improvement in their household economic status

Table 10.16

Impact of MGNREGA on Health and Nutrition of Women in their Own Perception

Responses (%)	*Gujarat-Tribal Region N=153*	*Gujarat-Non-Tribal Region N=70*	*Madhya Pradesh-Eastern Belt N=29*	*Maharashtra-South-West N=53*	*Maharashtra-Vidarbha N=21*	*Total N=326*
1. Additional income helps women to take care of health needs of themselves and their household	49.4	47.9	38.1	0.0	15.0	45.7
2. Additional income has helped in better food consumption which improves general health of the family	19.8	17.8	19.0	0.0	25.0	19.6
3. Family getting more pulses and vegetables to eat	12.3	17.8	33.3	0.0	30.0	16.7
4. Physical energy increased	18.5	16.4	9.5	0.0	10.0	16.7
5. No effect	0.0	0.0	0.0	0.0	20.0	1.4
Total responses	162	73	21	0	20	276

Source: Field Survey of ICRISAT villages (2013-14).

(despite acknowledging that the total income of the household has increased) as the wage is very low compared to the prevailing farm wages in the village and the wages are often paid late. Majority of women respondents also acknowledged that the work load on them had increased after they choose to work in NREGS and the main coping mechanism is to get up early to finish the routine household chores, though many of them acknowledge help they get from their spouses and in-laws. The money earned is controlled by the husband as in most cases the job card is issued in the husband's name, in whose name, bank account was also opened. This is further evident, as many of the women failed to recall how much money were paid against the number of days they had worked. The overall impacts of the programme tend to be bleak, as there were hardly any woman out of 486 respondents, who had acquired any durable asset, like land or live-stock from the money earned from NREG work.

As it emerges from the present study and several others, as discussed in the earlier section, the ambit of NREGS has to expand to include healthcare, nutrition, sanitation and literacy related programmes which will encourage women to participate more effectively. Another major lacuna concerning NREGS is lack of awareness and information regarding the benefits associated with it. One such initiative in Rajasthan aims at collaborating ICT (information and communication technology) with NREGS implementation. They developed many kiosks, tracking tools and community radios to ensure spread of NREGS to the villages. The pilot has been successful in creating awareness among the beneficiaries and minimising exploitation and corruption at various levels (Sharma et al., 2013). Similar structures can be adopted in other states to reduce information asymmetries and aid effective implementation.

The study also reveals that NREGS still has a long way to go to accommodate women in the decision-making process for jobs to be taken up under the programme, mostly benefiting them. In the three states where patriarchy rules the roost, women opening the account in their name seemed to be a remote possibility. In most cases, account was in the name of the eldest male member, who is also enrolled as the job card holder. This nullifies the objective of empowering women through interventions like NREGS. It is also found that women were hardly aware of the provisioning of the programme and merely obey the decisions by the household elders to go or not to go for work under the programme. We came across that in most cases the young daughters and daughters-in-law hardly participated in NREGS. There were also hardly any noticeable facility in the ongoing work sites for women or their children. These loopholes definitely need to be plugged to realise the goal of women empowerment as envisaged by the proponents of the NREGS.

References

Arora, V., L.R. Kulshreshtha and V. Upadhyay (2013). "Mahatma Gandhi National Rural Employment Guarantee Scheme: A Unique Scheme for Indian Rural Women", *International Journal of Economic Practices and Theories* 3(2): 108-14.

Borah, K. and R. Bordoloi (2014). "MGNREGS and its Impact on Daily Waged Women Workers: A Case study of Sonitpur District of Assam", *IOSR Journal of Economics and Finance 4(4): 40-44.*

Chhabra, S., R.L. Raina and G.L. Sharma (2009). *A Report on the Management of National Rural Employment Guarantee Scheme*. New Delhi: LBSIM.

Ghosh, J. (2009). "Equity and Inclusion Through Public Expenditure: The Potential of the MGNREGS", Discussion paper presented at *International Conference on NREGA*. Ministry of Rural Development and ICAR. 21-22 January.

Hirway, I. and S. Batabyal (2011). *MGNREGS & Women's Empowerment*. Report prepared for UN Entity for Women Equality and the Empowerment of Women.

Hirway, Indira, M.R. Saluja and Bhupesh Yadav (2010). *Employment Guarantee Programme and Pro-Poor Growth*. New Delhi: Academic Foundation. p.225.

Holmes, R., N. Sadana and S. Rath (2011). "An Opportunity for Change? Women Analysis of the Mahatma Gandhi National Rural Employment Guarantee Act", *Project Briefing* no. 53. Project conducted by Overseas Development Institute and Indian Institute of Dalit Studies.

Kar, S. (2013). "Empowerment of Women through MGNREGS: Issues and Challenges", *Odisha Review*: 76-80, February-March.

Kelkar, G. (2011). "MGNREGS: Change and Continuity in Women Relations", *Journal of Economic and Social Development* 7(2): 11-24.

Khera, R. (2009). *Group Measurement of NREGA Work: The Jalore Experiment*. Delhi: Delhi School of Economics.

Khera, R. and D. Jean (2009). "The Battle for Employment Guarantee", *Frontline* 26(1).

Narayanan, S. and U. Das (2014). "Employment Guarantee for Women in India: Evidence on Participation and Rationing in the MGNREGS from the National Sample Survey", WP-2014-017, Mumbai: Indira Gandhi Institute of Development Research.

Pankaj, A. and R. Tankha (2010). "Empowerment Effects of the NREGS on Women Workers: A Study in Four States", *Economic and Political Weekly* 45(30): 45-55 (July).

Poonia, J. (2012). "Critical Study of MGNREGS: Impact and Women's Participation", *International Journal of Human Development and Management Sciences* 1(1): 35-55.

Sharma, A. and S.A. Vincent (2013-14). "ICT for Women: Creating Women Sensitive Spaces for Mahatma Gandhi National Rural Employment Guarantee Act (MGNREGS)". Case study by OneWorld Foundation India as part of *Case Studies on e-Governance in India*.

Shome, S., R. Shetty, T.J. Joseph and M. Dash (2012). "Impact of Workfare Programmes on Quality of Life: A Case Study of National Rural Employment Guarantee Act in India", *Stirling International Journal of Postgraduate Research* 1.1: 17-45.

Sudarshan, R. (2011). "India's National Rural Employment Guarantee Act: Women's Participation and Impacts in Himachal Pradesh, Kerala and Rajasthan". CSP (Centre for Social Protection) Research Report 06.

Tripathi, R. (2013). "MGNREGS: A Ray of Hope for Women or a Myth", *International Journal of Advanced Research in Management and Social Sciences* 2 (6): 146-50.

Viswanathan, P.K. and Amit Mandal (2012). "NREGS as Instrument of Gender Mainstreaming: An Exploratory Analysis", *Man and Development* 34(3): 17-36 (September).

11

MICHAEL ANDREW

Impact of MGNREGS on Rural Development in Tamil Nadu

Introduction

Rural development has been given prime importance since the inception of Planning Commission. A vast majority of people (69%) reside in the rural areas and depend on agriculture and allied activities in India (Census 2011). But their living condition is rather backward and entangled with a number of socio-economic problems like illiteracy, unemployment, poverty, malnutrition, inadequate access to safe drinking water, health and sanitation. Hence, changing these conditions and developing the rural society is imperative for development of the nation. And therefore, strenuous efforts were taken by the Planning Commission to improve the living standard of the rural people and to bring sustainable development at the grass-roots level. There were several community development projects and programmes that have been initiated to develop the rural areas since Independence. This is because, public actions play a crucial role in improving the living standards of the people by providing food security, gender equality and reducing poverty (Guhan, 2001). And this would eventually lead to the eradication of poverty and bring about development in the rural society. One among such latest and flagship initiatives was the launch of Mahatma Gandhi National Rural Employment Guarantee Scheme (MGNREGS).

It is a wage employment programme with legal entitlement. It ranks among the most powerful initiatives ever undertaken for the transformation of rural society in India. The assumption behind implementation of the scheme is that it would transform the rural lives by improving living conditions, increasing sustainable agrarian activities and finally empowering the economic aspect of lives (NFIW, 2008). It gives the legal right to the rural poor to get 100 days of employment in a financial year. MGNREGS has made significant contribution in improving the rural society since its inception. MGNREGS is a scheme with decent wage, statutory provisions like right to demand for work, work duration, work site facilities, unemployment allowance, etc. There were a number of rural development programmes introduced for raising the socio-economic growth of rural areas, but MGNREGS is unique. It provides livelihood security, creates productive assets and reduces rural-urban migration. It has substantially reduced the rate of rural unemployment along with making significant contribution to the independence and social empowerment of the rural poor (Patnaik, 2005). The scheme has been introduced in 200 most distressed and backward districts in India under phase-I, wherein six among them were from Tamil Nadu. It has been doing well in Tamil Nadu and brought about remarkable changes in the lives of the rural people. Hence, this paper focuses on the impact of the scheme on employment generation, livelihood and food security and infrastructure development in rural Tamil Nadu.

Objectives of the Study

1) To study the quantum of employment that the scheme has created in the lives of the rural poor.
2) To examine the impact of the scheme on livelihood and food security.
3) To explore infrastructure development that has taken place in implementation of the scheme.

Methodology and Sources of Data

The scheme has been introduced in 200 most distressed and backward districts of the nation under its phase-I. Six among them are from Tamil Nadu and has been chosen for the study as these have been successful in implementing the scheme with active participation of the people. It is a macro (state) level quantitative-qualitative study, which attempts to capture and describe the impact of MGNREGS on the lives of the rural people. It primarily relies on secondary data sources like MGNREGS website, articles, journals, etc., in order to study the stated objectives.

The Need for Wage Employment Programme

One of the most important and influential factors that determines one's standard of living and status in the society is employment. Some experts like Bishiho viewed employment as a state of being engaged in production. Whereas Amartya Sen argues employment as one which gives income to the employed, yields output and gives the person recognition of being engaged in something worthwhile (in Palanichamy, 2011). Hence, employment gets the prime importance in everyone's life. However, employment in rural areas is seasonal and irregular in nature. As a vast majority of the people reside in the rural areas depending on agriculture and allied works which are dependent on monsoon, any changes in them affect its dependents. As the result, it causes unemployment. As unemployment breeds poverty, it in turn deprives the poor and the marginalised of the basic amenities like food, shelter, clothing, education, etc. Therefore, employment is seen as the fundamental component of economic empowerment (West, 2006).

The Tenth Five Year Plan (2002-2007) viewed wage employment programmes as an important component of the anti-poverty strategy, sought to achieve multiple objectives. It provides employment opportunities not only during lean agricultural seasons, but also in times of floods, droughts and other natural calamities. The works that are taken up create further infrastructure development in the rural areas that support and hasten the economic activity. These programmes also put an upward pressure on market wage rates by attracting people to public works programmes, thereby reducing labour supply and pushing up demand for labour. Such an assurance would ensure a minimum level of employment and stability to the incomes of the poor, giving them an opportunity to develop their collective strength. It would improve their economic position, reduce vulnerability and discourage migration (Naomi, 2008).

Rationale for the Emergence of MGNREGS

The enactment of Mahatma Gandhi National Rural Employment Guarantee Act (MGNREGA) is the culmination of a long and hard struggle since Independence. The scheme emanates to redeem the rural poor suffering amidst the wide-spread distress and growing unemployment and poverty (ISWSD, 2006). Mihir Shah (2007) enumerated five reasons for the emergence of MGNREGS which are noteworthy.

- First, following the Depression, many Western capitalist countries introduced different forms of unemployment insurances. By the 1980s, the constitutions of 30 countries, including 18 developing nations, had incorporated the right-to-work scheme. In 25 countries, this right is specified as a work guarantee.
- Second, the 61st round (2004-05) employment surveys of the National Sample Survey (NSS) provided clear evidence of a rise in rural unemployment in India. There was a steady fall of employment growth from 2.04 per cent during 1983-94 to 0.98 per cent during 1994-2000 (ISWSD, 2006). Additionally, the 61st round NSS data of the National Commission for Employment in the Unorganised Sector (NCEUS) report showed that about 77 per cent of the people in India had per capita consumption expenditure of less than or equal to ₹20 per day.
- Third, the World Bank's (2005 in Shah, 2007) estimates showed that 80 per cent of the people in India were living below the international poverty line of $2 a day.
- Fourth, for the first time since the mid-1960s, foodgrain production grew slower than the population in 1990s. As a result, both per capita foodgrain production and its availability have fallen below their 1960 levels by 2001.
- Finally, in the backward regions of India, returns to private investment were low. Agriculture production plummeted from 3.5 per cent in 1980s to 2 per cent per annum in 1990s, and real income growth fell from 4.5 to 2.5 per cent

per annum over the same period (ISWSD, 2006). A major reason for this was that many 'public goods', such as healthy watersheds or basic infrastructure that govern this rate of return, were missing in these areas. In addition, the NSSO data showed that majority of the agricultural labour families have some land, but with little or no productivity. So they supplement their income by hiring out as labourers.

In order to get out of this trap, a 'Big Push' was needed (Rosenstein and Rodan, 1943 in Shah, 2007). An individual act can not give such a huge intervention. This necessitated government's intervention. Thus MGNREGA came in as a big push in the regions of distress (Shah, 2007) for generating employment opportunities in the rural areas and enhancing livelihood security. These are a few major reasons and contexts owing which the Act achieves its significance.

MGNREGS: An Overview

The MGNREGA is an act, enacted by legislation on 25 August 2005. The Act became effective at the state level since February 2006 in 200 selected districts. It was extended to another 130 districts in the following year and eventually extended to all the rural districts in India by March 2008. The scheme provides a legal guarantee of 100 days of employment in every financial year to the rural adult members of every household at the statutory minimum wage.

The Act was introduced with the twin objectives of employment generation to improve the purchasing power of the rural people and to create productive assets for the community for developing as self-sufficient. It is a socio-economic inclusive programme, which intends to develop specific rural development activities such as, water conservation and harvesting, afforestation, rural connectivity, flood control and protection such as construction and repair of embankments, etc. Digging of new tanks/ponds, percolation tanks and construction of small check dams are also given importance. MGNREGA marks a paradigm shift from the previous programmes as it is a demand-driven programme rather than a supply-driven one. It is one of the first tangible commitments to the poor by which they can earn their living with dignity and as a right (Mathur, 2007).

Ever since it was launched, there has been almost tenfold increase (from ₹4,050 crore in 2005-06 to ₹40,100 crore in 2010-11) in the financial allocations for MGNREGS in India. It has occupied almost 50 per cent of the allocations for rural development in the country (Viswanathan and Mandal, 2012).

Uniqueness of MGNREGS

MGNREGS is a multifaceted programme with its uniqueness. First and foremost, uniqueness of MGNREGS is that it is a legal right and demand-driven scheme, unlike the previous schemes which were supply driven. Second, it is an inclusive approach that caters to every rural household in the rural society who are willing to take up unskilled work. Third, it is envisaged as a gender-sensitive scheme providing equal wage for both men and women. Moreover, it gives one-third reservation for women and has some special provisions that attract women for higher participation. Some of its other unique aspects are outlined below:

1) It is a bottom-up and people-centred approach.
2) Availability of work site facilities.
3) Work is available in their village itself.
4) It has a better pay than other works.
5) Legal provision of unemployment allowances.
6) Provision of social auditing which creates unprecedented accountability and transparency.
7) Less chance of work conditions being exploitative.
8) Work is considered socially acceptable and 'dignified' (MGNREGA Sameeksha, 2012; Khera and Nayak, 2009).

By generating employment for women at fair wages in the village, MGNREGA can play a substantial role in economically empowering women and laying down the basis for greater independence and self-esteem (Jandu, 2008).

MGNREGS in Tamil Nadu

The Tamil Nadu Rural Employment Guarantee Scheme (TNREGS) was launched in the first phase (2006-07) itself, covering six most backward districts (Villupuram, Cuddalore, Tiruvannamalai,

Nagapattinam, Dindigul and Sivagangai) therein. It was then extended to four more districts in the second phase (2007-08) in the state and the remaining 21 districts in the third phase (2008-2009), except Chennai as being urban. Hence, it has spread to all 385 blocks in which about 12,524 *gram panchayats* (GPs) benefit. It has given prime importance to works such as formation of new ponds, renovation of existing ponds, *kuttais, kulams, ooranies*, temple tanks, etc., desilting of channels, desilting and strengthening of bunds of irrigation tanks, formation of new roads and other water conservation/soil conservation measures/flood protection measures.

Tamil Nadu has been doing very well in terms of the implementation of MGNREGS. Following are the significant features of MGNREGS in the state:

1) Stands first in the country with 33 per cent work completion rate during 2012-13.
2) Occupies 2nd place in the country in women participation rate (84%) in 2013-14, next to Kerala.
3) Tamil Nadu is one among the three states in India to exceed the projected man-days target. Tamil Nadu has exceeded the projected man-days target of 38.91 crore with the achievement of 38.99 crore man-days as on 13 March 2013.
4) Tamil Nadu is one among the four states in India to exceed the national average in relation to provision of employment per household. The average person days per household is 59 days as against the national average of 46 for the year 2013-14.
5) Of the seven districts in the country, two of them from Tamil Nadu (Thanjavur and Tiruchirappalli) have received the best performing award for the year 2011-12.
6) Similarly, of the 10 village *panchayats* from all over the country, Kadambadi, from Coimbatore district, have been selected for Best Village *Panchayat* Award.

MGNREGS is expected to generate employment that would enhance the purchasing power, quality of life, economic prosperity and strengthen rural infrastructure, which in turn regenerate natural resource, promote agricultural production and reduce distress migration (ISWSD, 2006).

Impact of MGNREGS in Tamil Nadu

The scheme has been implemented in the last nine years. It is a multifaceted programme that caters to different aspects of the rural living. On one hand, it has created employment opportunity in the rural areas so that the poor can avail it and earn their livelihood. On the other hand, the works that are taken up under the scheme are inclined towards infrastructure development, which has the potency to strengthen the rural resource base. Besides providing employment, it has also ensured gender equality in rural Tamil Nadu. As the former Union Minister for Rural Development and *Panchayati Raj*, Dr C.P. Joshi said, “the Government will not lag behind in providing adequate livelihood security to the poor, down trodden, and members of SC [scheduled caste] and ST [scheduled tribe] communities,” the same has been ensured in Tamil Nadu. The programme employed a very good proportion of SC and backward caste people (RTBI, IITM, 2009).

A social audit on MGNREGS in Villupuram district revealed that despite many problems, it enhances transparency and accountability in governance and offers a lifeline to the rural poor. Perhaps Jean Dreze, one of the exponents of the scheme viewed that regardless of its shortcomings, the programme does provide jobs and wages for the poor and deprived (Lakshman, 2007). It has brought significant changes in the rural society.

Quantum of Employment Generation

Indian population has been broadly stratified as workers and non-workers in terms of employment. These workers are further classified into main workers and marginal workers, comprising four sub-groups, namely cultivators, agricultural labourers, household industry workers and other workers. The main workers are those who work at least for six months (180 days) and above in a year. And the marginal workers are those people who work for less than six months (180 days) in a year (Census 2011). It is evident from the above that people get work for about six months in a year and in the remaining six months, they have no work opportunity which causes unemployment and food insecurity, resulting in acute poverty. So the government came up with an alternative employment strategy—MGNREGS—to assist them during the lean season.

Since its inception, MGNREGS has generated ₹1,764.49 (in crore) person days of employment, incurring ₹26,6707.40 crore as expenditure at the national level (*www.nrega.nic.in*). The national average employment generated per household was 46 for the last two financial years (2012-13 to 2013-14). In case of Tamil Nadu, the government was able to generate 38.99 crore person days as against the target of 38.91 crore person days during 2012-13, and 33 crore person days as against the target of 30.02 crore during 2011-12 . It is said to generate an average of 1.25 crore person days of employment per district in a financial year. Table 11.1 gives the total number of households who are registered and have got employment under the scheme since 2006 in Tamil Nadu.

Table 11.1

Employment Generation in Tamil Nadu (2006-07 to 2013-14)

Year	*Total HHs applied for JC*	*Total JCs (SC)*	*Total JCs (ST)*	*Total JC (non-SC/ST)*	*Total persons demanded work*	*Total households allotted work*
2013-14	9,790,811	2,690,368	152,886	6,798,433	8,782,133	6,309,096
2012-13	9,344,972	2,672,006	145,815	6,410,597	10,742,196	7,104,257
2011-12	8,419,826	2,239,028	133,854	5,998,425	9,807,662	6,373,922
2010-11	7,347,187	3,008,384	144,170	4,194,633	4,969,140	4,969,140
2009-10	6,535,710	2,700,881	111,852	3,720,977	4,373,257	4,373,257
2008-09	5,512,827	2,354,280	91,016	3,067,531	3,345,648	3,345,648
2007-08	2,200,437	980,500	37,856	1,182,081	1,234,818	1,234,818
2006-07	1,157,525	572,102	32,727	552,696	683,708	683,481
Total	50,309,295	17,217,549	852,176	31,925,373	43,938,562	34,393,619

Note: HHS: Households; JC: Job card.

Source: Compiled from *nrega.nic.in*

It is evident from Table 11.1 that the scheme has been generating a substantial number of person days of employment in the rural society. Moreover, the beneficiaries of MGNREGS are both men and women belonging to the most disadvantaged groups namely, the SCs and STs and the rural poor (Khera and Nayak, 2009). The state average person days employment generated per household was 59 and 58 for the last two financial years (2012-13 to 2013-14), respectively. The average person days for SC and ST households were 60 and 54 respectively in the financial year 2013-14. The total number of households to have completed 100 days of employment is 9,20,784 (10.48%) against the 87,82,133 households who demanded in the financial year 2013-14 (*www.nrega.nic.in*).

The empirical study revealed that Cuddalore district has been successful in providing 100 per cent employment on demand. In Kurinjipadi block, almost 58 per cent of the workers belong to SC and ST groups and the rest belongs to OBC (other backward classes) and general categories. Then again, in Melbhuvanagiri, SCs and STs represented about 75 per cent. It is a dalit dominated area. Both are dalit populated areas and almost 90 per cent of them live below poverty line (BPL). Hence, MGNREGS has been a boon for these poor households (NFIW, 2008). MGNREGA work is treated as government work without involvement of private landlords or contractors and is associated with 'dignity'. Owing to this Scheme, these rural individuals are able to avoid working at a stone quarry, which was hazardous (Khera and Nayak, 2009). The employment opportunity has subsequently influenced the food security of these rural poor.

Although it has generated a large quantum of employment opportunity which apparently give a positive figure, in reality it is an eye-wash atleast in three aspects. They are as follows.

a) Manipulated Person days

Manipulated person days here refers to the systematic process of increasing the number of persons in a household and decreasing the number of person days of employment for each adult in the family. For an example, it was found in the analysis of job cards of the households that there is an unknown adult person who does not belong to the household, but is included nevertheless. The same kind of manipulation was also found in the number of households. It is a dynamics through which we can show higher person days of employment to a household, *panchayats*, blocks and state, etc.

How does it take place? For instance, it has been noted in a random cross-verification of the number of adult members registered for MGNREGS work as per the MIS (management information system) data available on the website, that at least one fake name is added in a household. If the real household is given 30 days of employment in a year, the fake adult is also given 30 days or less than that of employment. Finally, when it comes to account the person days generated per household, apparently it will be an attractive figure of 60 days per household, but it is 30 days only in reality. Hence, it is clear that merely half of the figure is fake or fudged. This manipulation in person days generated leads to the next step of manipulation in payment.

b) Manipulated Payment

The empirical studies conducted in the northern regions (Khera and Nayak, 2009; Vanaik and Siddhartha, 2008; Adhikari and Bhatia, 2010) have brought out different types of malpractices at different stages in the scheme. Tamil Nadu is not an exception to it. Here also we find such kind of manipulation and malpractice in terms of muster roll, person days of employment and wage. Manipulation in payment takes place in different ways. Though money is paid through bank, the implementing agency has an invisible hand in it. For example in the above case, there is firstly a greater possibility to open a fake account in the name of the unknown person and accordingly money can be deposited and withdrawn. Secondly, the implementing agency may collide with workers and manipulate the number of working days getting his share after paying through the banks. Thirdly, payment is made to accounts of the family members and kith and kin of the implementing authorities, high caste people who have never visited the work site. Since GP acts as both implementing and wage payment agency, there are chances and tendencies in manipulating the payment system. Moreover, Tamil Nadu was the only state where cash payment was in practice until recently, on the grounds that it is able to control leakages within the system and that cash payments help to ensure timely disbursal of wages (Khera, 2011). There are lots of chances for manipulating the payment in fake names or real workers. Although payment through banks was brought about to curb corruption and malpractices, the loopholes continue to persist. It is based on the assumption that the first problem naturally leads to the second.

c) Supply Based and Not Demand Driven

Although MGNREGS work is demand driven, there is delay in providing work as per demanded due to the lengthy bureaucratic process. Moreover, in the survey area, there was not even a single work site where demand-driven approach has been put into practice. For example, Maharashtra experience where All India Agricultural Workers Union has submitted applications for work in March (1,330 applicants), in April (1,267 applicants) and May (655 applicants) from several villages in the *tehsil*, and even received an acknowledgment in Nanded district. Yet all those who had applied for work remain unemployed so far (ISWSD, 2006). The same situation is found in Tamil Nadu. The role of PRIs (panchayati raj institutions) is to take initiative in providing employment on demands. But employment in general under MGNREGS is not demand driven, but supply driven. It is totally against the guidelines of the Act. Moreover, rationing is used in justifying the supply-driven district as backward in nature with large number of poor and illiterates, only 25 days of employment was provided to majority (75%) of the people. It is not a good sign of success for the programme. Only a negligible proportion of have worked about 75-100 days and nearly three-fourth of them have worked less than 50 days (NFIW, 2008).

Food Security and Livelihood

Employment brings income and income meets the needs. MGNREGA ranks among the most powerful initiatives ever undertaken for facilitating the transformation of rural livelihoods in India. Although a number of employment generation and poverty alleviation programmes were in practice, nothing brought about significant changes. But it was momentous that MGNREGS has facilitated a noteworthy relief in the lives of the poor. As the study

(Khera and Nayak, 2009) conducted in the North revealed that the earnings from MGNREGS has enhanced food security in a variety of ways (like cash in hand allows households to buy food in larger quantities which is generally cheaper than buying on a daily basis and to buy productive assets, sewing machine, etc.), even in Tamil Nadu, over 80 per cent women participated in the programme and earned a daily minimum wage of ₹80 (Nirmala, 2007).

It has helped the people to ensure food security, which is why they no more borrow for purchasing food. The study conducted in four districts of Tamil Nadu revealed that villagers consider MGNREGS as a boon for improving rural livelihood. Provision of job within the village is greatly encouraging to the villagers (RTBI, IITM, 2009) and has positive effect on rural-urban migration. A case study in the state indicates that the scheme has been a ray of hope by way of ensuring a minimum livelihood. It has also enabled women to contribute substantively to their household livelihood. Almost 81 per cent of the earnings from MGNREGS is spent on food and consumer goods in Cuddalore district, as well as for children's education and setting debts (NFIW, 2008). A study conducted in Thiruvannamalai districtt shows that about 59 per cent of the respondents had more than ₹1,001 expenditure before joining work under MGNREGS work. But it has increased to 81 per cent after joining MGNREGS (Palanichamy, 2011). It is a clear indication that the scheme has enhanced the purchasing power of the people. Women workers were found to take pride in their increased contribution to the family expenditure on food, clothing and consumer goods. In Kurinjipadi, 87 per cent and 76 per cent in Melbhuvanagiri said to have spent their NREGA earnings on food, consumer goods and clothing for their family. These expenses were followed by healthcare, children's education and religious activities (NFIW, 2008).

Problems in Attaining Food Security

Though it has been life line to the poor, it has not achieved its intended goal of providing enough food security at least in two ways as envisioned.

a) Problem of Bigger Household and Joint Family

The empirical study in Tamil Nadu shows that more than 55 per cent of the households are joint families, and the PRIs in Odisha and Tamil Nadu have undermined the joint family. If a joint family has four adults, then the work supply is rationed as 25 days per person and calculated to 100 days. Moreover, the joint family households in Tamil Nadu consists of 6-10 adults. In such a case, you may find reduction of entitlements. This can also be related to the average number of employment days given to the household. Tamil Nadu at the most has reached 53 days of employment per household. If 2-3 adults per household are provided employment of 50 days, it would serve the people to obtain a minimum standard of living. If a household which has more than 5-6 members and are provided the same number of employment days, then it would not serve or help the family for their livelihood and food security (ISWSD, 2006). Therefore, 100 days of employment per household is inadequate to remove poverty and curb migration in the rural society. Perhaps, the dependency ratio is very high (ISWSD, 2006).

b) Inadequate Income to Ensure Food Security

It is more authentic to discuss the issue with a case study chosen from the study conducted.

> Earlier my family used to go to neighboring villages and towns for works. Life has become relatively stable with the coming of NREGA as our family can stay in the village and do some work under EGA. I have so far worked for 24 days under EGA and have earned ₹1,512 as wage i.e., around ₹63 per day. No longer is our family forced to migrate for reasons of searching job (NFIW, 2008: 29).

Although this case study may convince some, in my opinion it may not so. Twenty-four days of work in a year with ₹1,512 may not be sufficient for a household to live. If we calculate this amount with the minimum stated in the recent BPL report by Rangarajan committee, the result may not reach even half of it. According to the report, the BPL mark for rural is ₹32 and urban it is ₹47. The new poverty line thus works out to monthly per capita consumption expenditure of ₹972 in rural areas and consequently a monthly consumption expenditure of ₹4,860 therein for a family of five (GoI, 2014). Even according to the report, ₹11,680 is needed for per person per annum. The average size of a rural household is four (Census 2011). Therefore, there must be minimum of ₹46,720. Even according to the report, `11,664 is needed for a person per annum. The average size of a rural household is four in Tamil Nadu (Census 2011). Therefore, there must be minimum of `46,656 is necessary for the survival. If this is so, then the above stated case study may become illogic and may not curb migration. Moreover, if a household is happy with the 24 days of employment per annum and it could contain migration, then naturally when more than 75-100 days of employment is provided, a household could have become rich and crossed BPL. If so, this scheme would have increased the APL households and decreased the BPL households in the rural India. There is nothing as such has taken place. However the status of poverty remains the same (NFIW, 2008).

Infrastructure Development

The villages are lagging behind in attaining the basic infrastructure facilities and the PRIs take it as an opportunity to provide the statutory services (Rural Development & Panchayat Raj Development Department, Policy Note: 2009-10). MGNREGS mainly covers two aspects; one is to create local employment opportunities for the rural poor and the second is to invest on building rural sustainable assets through works such as water conservation, irrigation facilities, rural connectivity, land improvement on land owned by STs/SCs, etc. (NFIW, 2008). Perhaps all the works undertaken in MGNREGS is watershed approach, which would enhance water retention and used for community purposes (ISWSD, 2006).

Rural sanitation has been given prime importance which also forms a base for more than 50 per cent of the works that have been undertaken in the financial year 2013-14. Besides developing the water bodies in the rural areas, the second major task that was taken up under MGNREGS was renovation of traditional water bodies. Thirdly, rural connectivity gained its priority and therefore road construction was also given equal importance. Moreover, the works that are conducted under the scheme have tremendous potential to enhance the livelihood sources in the villages like ponds, canals, irrigation canals, drainage, road construction and improve of land activities in the land of SC/STs. Tangible assets that the scheme has created are road construction which connected market areas, water facility and increment in wages. Furthermore, the MGNREGS works have improved the local drainage system, prevented the adverse effects arising from minor floods and safeguarded the crops as well (NFIW, 2008).

However, there is a notion that the assets that are said to be created under MGNREGS are poor in its quality and therefore its durability is questionable. Also, of the works taken up were quality oriented, then by this time there could have been a strong resource base in the rural society. Hence, roads constructed under the scheme are washed out by the simple rain. Both quantity and quality are an eye-wash under the scheme.

Conclusion

Being one of the poverty alleviation programmes, the scheme was initiated to improve the standard of living of the rural people and develop the rural infrastructure, creating employment opportunity for at least 100 days in a year and reducing distress migration. Immense amount of money is invested towards the rural development. People certainly have greatly benefited from the same. One of the empowerment strategies is to assist the marginalised people with employment opportunity and enable them to be empowered by themselves (Jandu, 2008). As it's objectives, on one hand, it has enabled the rural people to improve their socio-economic standard, especially that of women. On the other hand, it has created productive assets at the village level for supporting sustainable development. Transparency and accountability is maintained to a certain extended. However, its effectiveness depends on the people's participation and strict functioning of the PRIs and other related functionaries.

MGNREGS is not only an act that came about with benevolence of United Progressive Alliance (UPA) government, rather it should be looked as a promise of the Constitution which upholds the directive principles of state policy that the state shall in particular direct its policy toward securing... that the citizens, men and women equally have the right to an adequate means of livelihood (in NFIW, 2008, Directive Principles of State Policy, Indian Constitution: Part-IV). More than 82 per cent of the women have found employment and are found to earn ₹80 per day as opposed to the largely arbitrary and discriminatory wages that they earned previously (Lakshman, 2007). The state now is also an employer, providing employment and wage income; the landowners are no longer the sole employment providers. Thus, the sense of loss for the landed is multifaceted. The gain for the working class is phenomenal, both in qualitative and quantitative terms. Thus, MGNREGA and the public distribution system have engineered much deeper and wider social changes in the study village (Jeyaranjan, 2011).

One of the major objectives of the wage employment programme is to develop the deprived social groups, along with their women. In case of Tamil Nadu where women participation in MGNREGS in terms of person days is quite high, powerful prospects are queued for bringing about major changes in the lives of women (Narayana, 2008). Hence MGNREGS, the employment guarantee scheme has the potency to facilitate socio-economic and livelihood development. NREGA, despite all its critical aspects, has brought about some relief to the state of destitution, poverty, hunger, livelihood and joblessness (NFIW, 2008).

References

Adhikari, Anindita and Kartika Bhatia (2010). "NREGA Wage Payments: Can We Bank on the Banks?", *EPW Economic & Political Weekly* XLV(1): 30-37.

Ambasta, Pramathesh, Vijay Shankar and Mihir Shah (2008). "Two Years of NREGA: The Road Ahead", *Economic & Political Weekly,* 23 February.

Bhatia, Bella and Jean Dreze (2006). Employment Guarantee in Jharkhand: Ground Realies, *Economic and Political Weekly* 41(29): 3198-202.

Dev, S.M. (1996). *"Food Security: PDS vs ECS: A Tale of Two States", Economic and Political Weekly*, 6 July.

Dreze, J. and A. Sen (1989). *Hunger and Public Action*, Oxford.

Government of India (2014). *Report of the Expert Group to Review the Methodology for Measurement of Poverty.* New Delhi: Planning Commission.

Government of Tamil Nadu (2013). *Statistical Handbook of Tamil Nadu 2013*. Chennai: Dept. of Economics and Statistics.

Guhan, S. (2002). "Rural Poverty Alleviation in India", in S. Subramanian (ed.), *India's development Experience: Selected Writings of S Guhan*. OUP India.

Hirway, Indira. M.R.Saluja and Bhupesh Yadav (2010). *Employment Guarantee Programme and Pro-Poor Growth: The Study of a Village in Gujarat*. New Delhi: Academic Foundation. p.225.

Indian School of Women's Studies Development (2006). *Monitoring and Evaluation of National Rural Employment Guarantee Scheme with Special Focus on Gender Issues*. New Delhi.

Jandu, Navjyoti (2008). *Employment Guarantee and Women's Empowerment in Rural India*.available: *http://www.righttofoodindia.org/data/navjyoti08_employment_guarantee_and_women%27s_empowerment.pdf* (accessed on 10/10/2014)

Jeyaranjan, J. (2011). "Women and Pro-Poor Policies in Rural Tamil Nadu: An Examination of Practices and Responses", *Economic & Political Weekly* (43), October 22.

Khera, Reetika (2008). Empowerment Guarantee Act, *Economic & Political Weekly*, 30 August.

————. (2009). "Right to Food Act: Beyond Cheap Promises", *Economic & Political Weekly* XLIV(29): 40-44.

————. (2011). "The UID Project and Welfare Schemes", *Economic & Political Weekly* xlvi(9): 38-43.

Khera, Reetika and Nandini Nayak (2009). "Women Workers and Perceptions of the National Rural Employment Guarantee Act", *Economic & Political Weekly* XLIV(43): 49-57.

Lakshman Nirmala (2007). "The Hundred Days Basket", *The Hindu*, 14 August.

Mathur, L. (2007). "Employment Guarantee: Progress so Far", *Economic & Political Weekly* 29 December.

MGNREGA Sameeksha (2012). *An Anthology of Research Studies on the Mahatma Gandhi National Rural Employment Guarantee Act, 2005, 2006–2012*. Edited and compiled by Mihir Shah, Neelakshi Mann and VaradPande. Ministry of Rural Development, Government of India. New Delhi: Orient Black Swan.

Naomi, Jacob (2008). "The Impact of NREGA on Rural-Urban Migration: Field Survey of Villupuram District, Tamil Nadu", *CCS working paper* 202.

Narayanan, Sudha (2008). "Employment Guarantee, Women's Work and Childcare", *Economic and Political Weekly*.

National Federation of Indian Women (NFIW) (2008). A *Study On Socio-Economic Empowerment Of Women Under National Rural Employment Guarantee Act (NREGA)*.

Palanichamy, A.P. (2011). "A Study on Mahatma Gandhi National Rural Employment Guarantee Program (MGNREGP) in Thuinjapuram Block Thiruvannamalai District in Tamilnadu", *International Multidisciplinary Research Journal* 1(3): 37-46.

Patnaik, Prabhat (2005). "On the need for providing Employment Guarantee", *Economic and Political Weekly*, 15 January.

RTBI, IITM, (2009). *Evaluation of National Rural Employment Guarantee Act (NREGA) in Tamil Nadu, PIN, Chennai.*

Sankaran, Kamala (2011). "NREGA Wages: Ensuring Decent Work", *Economic & Political Weekly* XLVI(7): 23-25.

Shah, Mihir (2007). "Employment Guarantee, Civil Society and Indian Democracy", *Economic & Political Weekly*: 45-51, 17 November.

———. (2008). "Structures of Power in Indian Society: A Response", *Economic & Political Weekly:* 78-83, 15 November.

Siddhartha and Anish Vanaik (2008). "CAG Report on NREGA: Fact and Fiction", *Economic & Political Weekly:* 39-45, 21 June.

Swaminathan, S. Anklesaria Aiyar (2013). "Rising Rural Wage May Boost UPA's Chances", *Times of India*, 7 July. Chennai. p.16.

Vanaik, Anish (2008). "NREGA and the Death of Tapas Soren", *Economic & Political Weekly:* 8-10, 26 July.

Vanaik, Anish and Siddhartha (2008). "Bank Payments: End of Corruption in NREGA?", *Economic & Political Weekly*: 33-39, 26 April.

Viswanathan and Amit Mandal (2012). "NREGS as Instrument of Gender Mainstreaming: An Exporatory Analysis", *Man & Development* 3(xxxiv): 17-35.

West, S. Brooke (2006). "Does Employment Empower Women? An Analysis of Employment and Women's Empowerment in India". Unpublished thesis. Cornell University.

Websites:

http://en.wikipedia.org/wiki/Viluppuram_district

http://www.tnrd.gov.in/schemes/cen_nrega_13.html

Five Year Plans on Rural Development and Employment (1952-2012).

12

K. KEERTHI, MADHUSUDAN BHATTARAI,
T. SARAH KAMALA and P. PUNNA RAO

MGNREGA Impact on Rural Asset Creation

A Study in Two Villages of Prakasam District of Andhra Pradesh, India

Introduction

Out of total population of 1.21 billion people in India, 833 million people live in rural areas (Census of India, 2011), which accounts for nearly 70 per cent of India's population. Rampant poverty is more prevalent in rural India over the urban area. These rural populations can be characterised by mass poverty, low levels of literacy and income, high level of unemployment, and poor nutrition and health status. Currently said to be around 7.8 per cent, unemployment has been rising in India. This has led to migration of huge numbers of people from rural to urban areas. With over 65 per cent of India's population under the age of 35, the country needs to create 60 million jobs over the next five years to prevent the unemployment rate from gaining unmanageable proportions

When employment expands along with production, the benefits of growth are widely shared. Better employment opportunities provide people with new, and often improved, sources of income. In this way, improving the quality and quantity of employment opportunities directly links economic growth to poverty reduction. Low income households possess few assets of their own. Instead, the most abundant resource the poor have at their disposal is their labour (Islam, 2004; Squire, 1993). A development strategy that fully employs a country's human resources and raises the returns to labour becomes a powerful tool for reducing poverty. To realise this potential and to meet the twin challenges of reducing poverty and creating employment, the Government of India enacted the Mahatma Gandhi National Rural Employment Guarantee Act (MGNREGA), the largest employment-generating programme in the world, ensuring the right to work in a country with a population of over one billion in 2005. To operationalise this act, the Government of Andhra Pradesh has formulated the Scheme called Andhra Pradesh Rural Employment Guarantee Scheme, which has come into force with effect from 2 February 2006.

Employment Programmes in India

In the post independence period, the Government of India placed increasing emphasis on taking up schemes for providing additional employment opportunities and various special schemes of employment generation were implemented right from 1960s. During the Second Five Year Plan, employment to the rural manpower primarily during the lean seasons was emphasised, while the Third Five Year Plan focused on creation of additional employment in the traditional hand industries and wage employment in development works. The basic assumption in all such programmes has been better utilisation of unemployed or underemployed manpower in the rural areas till employment potential is augmented on a permanent basis over a period of years. These programmes are being continued since then in one form or the other. However, there is one very significant difference i.e., the programmes initiated during the Third to the Fifth Five Year Plans were ad hoc in nature and since the Sixth Five Year Plan, rural works programmes have been given an important place in the overall strategy of poverty alleviation.

Thus, MGNREGA has come after almost 56 years of experience of other rural employment programmes to address the twin challenges of reducing poverty and creating employment, which include both CSS (centrally sponsored schemes) and those launched by State governments. These comprise the National Rural Employment Programme (NREP) 1980-1989; Rural Landless Employment Guarantee Programme (RLEGP) 1983-1989; Jawahar Rojgar Yojana (JRY) 1989-90; Employment Assurance Scheme (EAS) 1993-1999.

Jawahar Gram Samridhi Yojana (JGSY) 1999-2002; Sampoorna Grameen Rojgar Yojana (SGRY) 2001; National Food for Work Programme (NFFWP) 2004. Among these programmes, the SGRY and NFFWP have been merged with MGNREGA in 2005. Jean Dreze, a Belgian economist, who is currently with the Delhi School of Economics, is the chief author of the scheme MGNREGA which is also known as National Rural Employment Guarantee Scheme (NREGS) before 2009, when it was first introduced in 2005. The National Rural Employment Guarantee Bill features important innovations. First, it establishes a legal right for households to be employed for up to 100 days per year; in fact, individuals who apply but do not receive work within a period of two weeks are entitled to unemployment compensation. Second, the minimum wage rate, set at the state level, applies equally to males and females, making the programme particularly attractive to women, who normally receive significantly lower wages than men (Deininger et al., 2013). Amenities such as crèches, which by law must be provided at the work sites to encourage women's participation, can further reduce gender discrimination. Third, to improve productive capacity of rural areas in the long term and thus make the programme sustainable, there is a desire to focus work on productive infrastructure such as irrigation systems, minor roads, and land improvement.

Maharashtra Employment Guarantee Scheme (MEGS) an Inspirational Source for MGNREGA

Unlike the other wage employment programmes of India placed above, the MEGS is a programme launched by the provincial Government of Maharashtra in early 1970s. It was one of the most researched and discussed programmes both at the national and the international levels. Compared to the programmes in other countries, the MEGS had been in existence for a long time—more than three decades. Organisations like World Bank and International Labour Organization (ILO) have organised studies to learn from the scheme's success, particularly its sustainability over time. The United Nation Development Programme's *Human Development Report* (1993) commends MEGS as one of the largest public programmes in the development world. The MEGS is an especially interesting example of a universal public works programme for poverty alleviation because it guarantees employment at a defined wage—an unprecedented feature in a public works programme. It is considered a model because of this underlying philosophy of guarantee and because of its approach towards fulfilling this guarantee (Braun, 1995).

MGNREGA—Asset Creation and Sustainability

One of the most distinguishing features of MGNREGA programme is the creation of environmentally sound productive assets under the decentralised administration of *panchayats*. Generally, the village and intermediary *panchayats* manage the implementation activities, while coordination of activities is done at the district level. However, at every level, the concerned agencies and institutions are accountable to local people.

During 2007-08, MGNREGA programme created more than half a million productive assets, mostly water and soil conservation structures. Water conservation has been accorded top priority and accordingly 49 per cent of works taken up under MGNREGA relate to water conservation. The performance of MGNREGA programme in March 2008, as shared with the Parliament by the Union Minister for Rural Development, showed, reviewed an average of 42 days of employment during the year so far. Out of a total of 141.62 crore (1416 million) person days, the share of SCs (scheduled castes) is 38.70 person days (27.3%) and STs (scheduled tribes) is 41.36 crore person days (29.2%), which together comes to a total of 56.53 per cent person days. Priya (2008) showed that the share of women beneficiaries is 60.39 crore person days, which is 42.60 per cent.

MGNREGA promises a revolutionary demand-driven, people-centred development programme. Some of the provisions given under MGNREGA for the durability and maintenance of the MGNREGA assets, thereby sustainability are:

i) Convergence of the MGNREGA funds with funds from other sources for the creation of durable assets.
ii) The maintenance of assets created under, will be considered as permissible work under MGNREGA.

iii) To ensure sustainable assets and holistic approach to planning, a project approach should be adopted towards defining a work.

iv) Funds available with PRIs (panchayati raj institutions) from other sources can also be dovetailed with MGNREGA funds for the construction of durable community assets/works permissible under MGNREGA.

Institute of Human Development (IHD) (2009) as part of NREGS works with the village *Gram Sabha's* have taken up development of lands, thereby ensuring that such land owners would be able to cultivate hitherto barren and uncultivable lands. This particular 'work' is more popular in the villages of Andhra Pradesh (such works accounted for over 20% of total works in the state in 2009) as that enabled small and marginal cultivators to engage in crop cultivation, in several cases for the first time in their life and families who earned from NREGS works were able to invest in children's education, health, repayment of old debt, and for other such useful purposes.

Prabeena Kumar Bebarta (2013) studied the impact of MGNREGA on the lives of tribal people and concluded that the tribal households in the Rayagada block in Gajapati district of Odisha have benefited from MGNREGA as it has increased their income thus having multiple impacts on their social and economic life.

Gupta(2009) study revealed that the recent learning from Bihar shows that social afforestation programme undertaken by the State forest department is extremely successful in six participating districts not only from the point of developing wastelands but also from the point of view of providing gainful employment to the rural landless families.

> MGNREGA is a valuable and valued opportunity for the rural poor, and particularly for women, to earn a living wage in a dignified manner, (Dreze, 2008).

Materials and Methods

The research design adopted for this study was ex post facto since the phenomenon had already occurred. According to the Kerlinger (1964), ex post facto research is a systematic empirical enquiry in which the scientists do not have direct control of the independent variables, because their manifestation have already occurred or because they are inherently not easy to manipulate. Hence, this design was considered appropriate to address the kind of issues noted earlier, as planned in this study. The study was conducted in Prakasam district and accordingly, the sample was selected in Janapala Cheruvu Agraharam (JCA) and Pamidipadu (PMD) of Bestavaripeta and Korisapadu mandals respectively. A total of 120 respondents were selected, out of these 60 respondents who are involved in farming from each village were selected randomly. Stratified random sampling procedure was adopted in the selection of the respondents at two villages.

Findings and Discussion

The present study consists of two major types of assets: a) individual assets, and b) community based assets. The individual assets consists of three major categories like wage and man days, land development, and material procurement; and the community based assets included activities that successfully created useful assets in both the villages.

Individual Asset Creation

It was operationalised as creation of assets that the respondent secured in terms of wage employment, land development and purchase of materials due to participation in MGNREGA works. While wage employment was an earning, land development and purchase of materials were the indicative of purchasing capacity of the respondents.

Wage Employment

Wage employment was the amount earned for the work performed under MGNREGA. The data obtained for five years, i.e., from 2008 to 2012 is depicted in Table 12.1 in terms of mean scores of man days and amount paid.

Table 12.1

Individual Asset Creation of the Respondents: Wage Employment (n1= 60, n2= 60)

Village	Wage Man Days/Amount									
	2008		2009		2010		2011		2012	
	Days	₹	Days	₹	Days	₹	Days	₹	Days	₹
JCA	92.25	99.67	74.58	79.58	59.17	67.25	59.88	66.33	58.23	61.33
PMD	86.6	100.0	78.8	92.8	68.9	92.9	—	—	—	—

Note: nl = JCA, n2 = PMD.

Land Development

The respondents spent some amount to make the land cultivable after partnership in MGNREGA. We collected the information on household expenditure and the mean expenditure across the households sampled and the same is presented in Table 12.2.

Table 12.2

Amount Spent on Land Development (n1= 60, n2= 60)

(₹ *in lakhs)*

Village	2008	2009	2010	2011	2012	Total
JCA	4.23	8.23	7.4	5.92	5.22	31.0
PMD	6.6	9.82	8.99	8.91	7.98	42.3

Note: nl = JCA, n2 = PMD.

It is clear from Table 12.2 that most of the farmers were small, followed by medium. Substantial amount was spent by these participants during the five years of study on land development to bring the assigned land which is otherwise barren and unusable, under cultivation. MGNREGA has acted as an initiative and also motivator to make maximum use of available land for cultivation which will give them additional long lasting results. Developed land has thus become the created asset because of participation in MGNREGA and promoted the cultivators to engage in crop cultivation and also stopped migration to other areas for want of employment to some extent. It was observed that PMD village spent more than JAC village. There were also more umbers of medium and large farmers in PMD village compared to JAC village. Per capita investment might be claimed as ₹0.5 and ₹0.7 lakhs in JAC and PMD respectively.

Shah (2008), in his study explored that the emphasis on creation of public productive assets under MGNREGA, such as land development, water conservation and water harvesting structures, drought proofing, irrigation facilities etc., has significant bearing on development of smallholder productive assets, land, livestock, tree covers, irrigation works all related to agriculture and its productivity. The development of barren and uncultivable lands including assigned lands by the SCs (scheduled castes) taken up land owners is more popular in the villages of Andhra Pradesh (such works accounted for over 20% of total works in the state in 2009) as that enabled small and marginal cultivators to engage in crop cultivation, in several cases for the first time in their life (IHD, 2009a). The present results were also in accordance with it.

Material Procurement

Due to some returns from land and earnings from wage employment, the purchasing capacity of the respondents has increased, which they spent on purchase of certain items. The details of the same presented in Table 12.3.

Table 12.3

Amount Spent by the Respondents on Material Procurement (n1= 60, n2= 60)

(₹ *lakhs)*

Village	*House Repairs*	*Livestock*	*Electrical and Electronic Goods*	*Transport Vehicles*	*Payment of Education Fee*	*Total*
JCA	1.47	1.55	5.47	0.05	0.24	8.78
PMD	1.46	0.6	0.81	1.81	0.17	4.99

Note: n1 = JCA, n2 = PMD

The earnings were utilised for procurement of materials is evident from the data. The respondents attained varied benefits. House, the basic amenity of life, was attended and its repairs were carried to make the living better. Livestock like buffalos increased their alternative livelihoods and enriched the irregular diet as well as provided additional income by selling the milk and its products. Major electrical and electronic goods reduced the drudgery of hard work, besides owning these goods are seen as a status symbol in the society, for example owning at least a mobile in a house has almost became a necessity in the present day living in all rural India. Transport vehicles purchased saves time as well as facilitated comfort and status. It can be observed that high expenditure, almost 50 per cent more, could be seen in JCA compared to PMD, because they purchased electronic and electrical goods. Some families spent amount on payment of educational fee for children as they joined them in private English medium schools. As NREGS aims to increase the productivity of resource use and small-scale works on participants' own land that is eligible for programme support, investment on marginal lands to enhance agricultural productivity is another avenue for programme impacts to materialise, though these would not directly benefit the landless but provide interest to develop the unused land.

Community Asset Creation

In the present study, community asset creation was operationalised as activities undertaken to develop the resource base of the village to enhance the livelihood of the community. The data was descriptively narrated.

Community Asset Creation in JCA

Community works taken-up under MGNREGA programme in JCA were de-silting of village ponds, jungle cutting and canal works. De-silting of tanks in JCA, was done almost every year since the initiation of programme. The pond was 4 km away from the village and it occupies 200 acres of land. At the time of investigation it was reported that for about 10 years there was no water in this tank and it became dry and unused. After taking up de-silting and jungle cutting works through MGNREGA, there is an increase in water level and the village community is able to use it for agriculture and other purposes which is a welcome asset for the entire village across all sections of the villagers. Ierepalle pond is another pond which is also 4 km away from the village on another side and it occupies about 25 acres of land. With bush and jungle cutting, this water body was also made available to the entire village. Another pond by name Sitaiah was about 3 km from the village. De-silting and pond bunding activities saved the pond and increased the water level. Apart from this, Ooragunta and Dapillegunta were very close to village, about 1 km. De-silting and jungle cutting activities in this area activated groundwater bodies of the village. Jungle cutting on the sides of the road cleared the road of 40 kms joining JCA with other villages, viz., Pitikikavala, Kottapeta, Gantapuram and Kazzipuram. Otherwise it was a very problematic road for two wheelers and cyclists. Now auto rickshaws and heavy vehicles like tractors and trucks could be driven safely. Over all the infrastructure facilities increased with the MGNREGA.

Community Asset Creation in PMD

In PMD village, MGNREGA was in operation from 2008. But, due to some political interference and misuse of field assets, no execution work was carried from 2011 onwards. However, de-silting of two ponds popularly called as *Vuricheruvulu* (village ponds) which occupies 10 and 5acres respectively was done. One pond which is very close to the village, aided in increasing the groundwater level. Second pond is presently functional for agricultural and animal husbandry activities. Other ponds Gopasamudramo f 35 acres wide, Kanakaiyagunta of 20 acres and other *kuntas* like Kateruvenkanna, Sheshaiya occupying 20 acres were also brought under use for agriculture purpose. Yalamvarigunta and Ravivarigunta of 10 acres wide is used for animals. In all these ponds de-silting activities were undertaken and thus became very useful for community and for their livelihoods.

Conclusion

Most of the sample households surveyed were small, followed by medium households. In spite of that, some substantial amount was spent during the five years of study on land development from the wages as well as other land development activities. MGNREGA has acted as an initiative and also motivator to make maximum use of available land for cultivation. Developed land has thus become the created asset because of participation in MGNREGA by the deprived communities like Dalits and backward classes. It was observed that PMD village spent more than JAC village. Per capita investment drew ₹0.5 and ₹ 0.7 lakh in JAC and PMD respectively.

Community works taken under MGNREGA programme in JCA were de-silting of village ponds, jungle cutting and canal works. De-silting of tanks in JCA village was done regularly almost every year since the initiation of programme. Overall the study revealed that the programme has positive impact in creation of individual as well as community assets in the surveyed sampled two villages in Prakasham district of Andhra Pradesh. In fact, the study also suggests that impact of the MGNREGS programme on asset creation also greatly vary by the location specific factors, and kind of activities performed in each of the locations.

References

Bebarta, Prabeena Kumar (2013). *Impact of MGNREGA in the Lives of Tribal People: A Study of Rayagada Block in Gajapati District Odisha*. Review February–March.

Braun, J. V. (ed.) (1995). *Employment for Poverty Reduction and Food Security*. Washington DC: International Food Policy Research Institute. pp.108-138.

Deininger, K., S. Jin, and H. K. Nagarajan (2013). "Wage Discrimination in India's Informal Labor Markets: Exploring the Impacts of Caste and Gender", *Review of Development Economics* 17(1); 130-147.

Deshingkar, P., and C. Johnson (2003). "State Transfers to the Poor and Back: The Case of the Food for Work Programme in Andhra Pradesh", *ODI Working Paper* 222. London: Overseas Development Institute.

Dreze, Jean (2004). "Employment a Social Responsibility'", *The Hindu*, 22 November.

———. (2008). "NREGA: Ship Without Rudder?", *The Hindu*, 19 July.

Gupta, Alok Kumar (2009). "Money Growth Policy for Bihar: Social Forestry Project Links Rural Employment with Growing Saplings", *Down To Earth*, 31 October. *http://southasia.oneworld.net/features/money-growth-policy-for-indian-villages#.U6acBJSSw3k*

Institute of Human Development (IHD) (2009). *Processes, Institutions and Mechanisms of Implementation of MGNREGA: Impact Assessment of Bihar and Jharkhand*. New Delhi.

———. (2009a) Processes, Institutions and Mechanisms of Implementation of NREGA: Impact Assessment of Bihar and Jharkhand, Institute for Human Development, New Delhi.

Islam, Rizwanul (2004). *The Nexus of Growth, Employment, and Poverty Reduction: An Empirical Analysis*. Geneva: Recovery and Reconstruction Department, International Labour Office.

Kerlinger, K.N. (1964). *Foundation of Behavioral*. New York: Holt Rinchart and Winstan, Inc. p.275.

Priya (2008). *National Study: Phase III. Role of Panchayati Raj Institutions in Implementation of NEREGA*. New Delhi.

Shah, Amita and Sunny Jose (2008). "Asset Creation and Local Economy Under NREGS: Scope and Challenges", Paper presented at International Seminar on *National Rural Employment Guarantee Scheme in India*. 16-17 September. New Delhi.

Squire, Lyn (1993). "Fighting Poverty," *American Economic Review* 83(2): 377-82.

United Nation Development Program (1993). *Human Development Report. http://hdr.undp.org/en/reports/global/hdr1993*

13

NIHAR RANJAN MISHRA and SOUMYA MOHANTY

Development Programmes and Tribal Livelihoods

A Case of MGNREGA in Western Odisha

Introduction

The Government has initiated several development programmes and social welfare schemes in an effort to enhance the livelihood pattern of tribal communities and to stem the extremist' allure in tribal areas. The most significant is the National Rural Employment Guarantee Act (NREGA, now re-titled to MGNREGA), the government's flagship employment development programme. NREGA was launched in 2006 to enhance livelihood security in rural and tribal areas beset by chronic joblessness and falling agricultural productivity by guaranteeing at least 100 days per year of wage employment to every rural household. It offers a remarkable prospect to India as a State to do justice with a vast section of its people in rural areas who confront a myriad of problems including access to adequate cash to meet the basic needs for survivals. By the end of 2011, almost all the districts of our country were covered under this scheme to provide sustainable development to the marginal communities. Using anthropological techniques, the present paper attempts to see to what extent MGNREGS has given justice in sustaining the livelihoods of poor tribal communities in Sundargarh district of Western Odisha. It also critically examines the process of implementation of this programme.

It is observed in our study that the MGNREGS has failed in sustaining the rural livelihoods and checking migration. The faulty implementation strategy has ruined the spirit of this programme.

Showing favouritism towards the villagers belonging to the same religion and living in the same street of the Sarapancha while distributing the job cards have discouraged the other villagers.. The culture of ignorance, drinking alcohol, feeling marginal, poverty, illiteracy, dominance of powerful families, defective leadership and the improper coordination among the stakeholders have stood as major hurdles in this programme.

Since independence, the Government of India has initiated several development programmes and social welfare schemes to enhance the livelihood pattern of tribal communities and to stem the extremist' allure in tribal areas. Since then, much emphasis was given on public investment in environmental regeneration that could not only improve the environment and water supplies, it will also make a quantum increase in agricultural productivity of small and marginal farmers in the neglected regions of India a possibility. Much emphasis was given on raising the purchasing power of the poor which can help lower the burden of food subsidies by raising PDS (public distribution system) off take and thereby reducing the carrying cost of grain. This will also enable government to continue to provide price support to farmers. Later it was thought that the best way of undertaking the necessary public investment is by enshrining it as a constitutional right.

NREGA, enacted in the Parliament in 2005 by Government of India, offers legal entitlements to households in rural India of at least 100 days of wage employment in a year. It is one of the flagship schemes of Government that guarantees wage employment on an unprecedented scale. Since its implementation in 2006, the scheme has attracted wide attentions both at national and international level. It is one of the few experiments in the world to provide alternative source of livelihood which will have an impact on reducing migration, growth in education and healthcare spending and for these reasons it has been considered as the largest anti-poverty programme in the world. Providing decent wages to job seekers, bringing poorest, marginalised, SCs (schedule castes) and STs (scheduled tribes) households who have been sidelined from the mainstream development process under its purview by offering them a secure source of income, empowering rural women and PRIs (panchayati raj institutions) are some of the noteworthy features of the Act. The primary objective of the Act is augmenting wage employment. Its auxiliary objective is strengthening natural resource management through works that address causes of chronic poverty like drought, deforestation and soil erosion and thus encouraging sustainable development. The process outcomes include strengthening grass root processes of democracy and infusing transparency and accountability in governance. Some of the unique features of the Act include, time bound employment guarantee and wage payment within 15 days, incentive-disincentive structure to the State governments for providing employment as 90 per cent of the cost for employment provided is borne by the Centre or payment of unemployment allowance at their own cost and emphasis on labour intensive works prohibiting the use of contractors and machinery. The Act also mandates 33 per cent participation for women. Other key attributes of this scheme are time bound guarantee, labour-intensive work, decentralised participatory planning, women's empowerment, work site facilities and above all, transparency and accountability through the provision of social audits and right to information. The unprecedented use of information technology in this programme is considered to bring about greater transparency through intensive monitoring and faster execution. The payment of wages through bank and post office accounts is another innovative step that is likely to reduce fudging of the muster rolls on the part of the implementing agencies since the actual payments are beyond their reach. There is an effort to separate payment agencies from implementing agencies and thereby preventing embezzlement of wages (Vanaik and Siddhartha, 2008).

The NREGS came into effect, on a pilot basis, in February 2006 in 200 economically disadvantaged districts of the country. In the second phase of implementation, it was extended to 130 additional districts and the remaining districts were covered in the third phase on 1 April 2008. In the context of Odisha, all the tribal dominated districts were covered from the very beginning.

With the above background the present paper attempts to understand the implementation procedures of NREGS and its impact on tribal livelihoods in a tribal dominated *panchayat* of Sundargarh district, Odisha. It tries to understand the role of *gram panchayat* (GP) to generate sufficient employment opportunities? Are the procedures for registration, issuance of job cards, and application for employment followed properly so that people are not demotivated to work under the scheme? What should be done to bring more people under the ambit of the scheme to make it a successful poverty alleviation programme? What determines the awareness level? Given this backdrop, there is thus a need to make an appraisal of the processes and procedures of NREGA. This would enable us to understand and examine the institutional mechanisms under which the entire programme is being implemented. The problems and prospects of NREGA can then be better understood and accordingly, necessary measures can be devised to make the programme realise its set objectives.

Methodology

This study is based on information gathered through an in-depth fieldwork. Purposively Santoshpur GP of Bisra block in Sundargarh district was selected. A sample of 150 households was selected randomly from Santoshpur GP. Both quantitative and qualitative information on the details of processes and procedures of NREGS implementation were gathered using questionnaires. *Sarpanch* and investigator questionnaires were designed to elicit information at the GP and/or work level. Job card and non-job card holder questionnaires were designed to elicit information at the household level. Excepting investigators' own questionnaires, in all other cases, study was carried out on the basis of personal interviews. In addition, qualitative methods such as FGDs (focus group discussions) among different groups such as lower castes, women, and landless households were held. Transect walks into the NREGS work sites were conducted to have first hand experience on the NREGS works at the community/ village level. Discussions with local GP officials as well as government officials both at the local and block level were held on the issues related to implementation and functioning of the NREGS.

Discussion

NREGA is distinctive for its unique vision to redefine avenues of providing employment opportunities to the deprived in rural India. But the possibility and efficient chances of employment largely comes with the better level of awareness as it marks the level of accessibility. This issue of awareness emerges as one of the hindrances to the local community. It thus necessitates sufficient awareness amongst the intended beneficiaries regarding provisions like guaranteed days of employment, unemployment allowance, minimum wages, availability of complaint register, etc. However, the situation in this front is not very encouraging in the study areas. As most of the worker respondents are illiterate and belong to the economically poor class, the extent of awareness about NREGA has emerged out to be a major concern in all the hamlets. Around 93 per cent of the villagers are aware about the NREGS. But workers' awareness on how to apply for job cards, awareness about minimum wages and demand for work was reportedly very low. Around 7 per cent villagers are not at all aware about NREGS. Out of those who are aware about it only 41 per cent of the respondents are aware of the number of minimum days of employment guaranteed to each household under the scheme. Only 54 per cent households in this *panchayat* are having job cards.

The procedural and implementation aspects of NREGA have never been free from confronting some basic challenges like general awareness, understanding policy nitty-gritty, sufficient access etc. Having given the socio-economic background of the respondents, the structural issues such as transparency, maintenance of documents and accountability were difficult things to actualise from the workers' point of view. When asked whether beneficiaries knew about the time span of getting employment from the date of the submission of applications under the NREGA, only 20 per cent respondents revealed that they were aware of such guidelines like getting employment within the 15 days from the date of application for jobs.

More strikingly, the unemployment allowance for the failure to provide employment within 15 days of application as per the guidelines of NREGA was not followed. One way to look at this failure is the issue of low awareness among the beneficiaries to claim for such provision under the Act. Two ways of fighting it can be suggested: one, unless there is awareness and understanding of the whole idea of the programme there will be lesser participation in the programme and second, transparency and accountability of the programme cannot be ensured unless the beneficiaries are made efficient enough to raise issues concerning the programme. Around 80 per cent of the respondents were not aware about the unemployment allowances. During our field visit it was found that all most all the villagers are confused about the wages they are supposed to receive under NREGS Therefore, there is a great deal of work that needs to be carried out as far as awareness, fair implementation and assurance of accessibility is concerned.

The major source of information for the villagers regarding NREGS is reported to be PRIs including *sarpanchs*, ward members, *gram sathis*, and GP officials. Around 77 per cent of the villagers (Table 13.1) claimed that they got the news about NREGS from GP office.

Table 13.1

Community-wise Source of Getting Information on NREGS

Source of Information	*Community of the Respondent*				*Total*
	SC	*ST*	*OBC*	*GC*	
Panchayat office	4	67	26	10	107
Media-radio	1		1		1
Neighbour		17	4	3	25
Any other		3	2	1	6
Total	5	87	33	14	139

Provisions for safeguard of transparency and accountability are incorporated into the Act and also in the NREGA guidelines. For instance, the NREGA guidelines require muster rolls to be available in the *panchayat* office and also at work sites. This can go a long way to preventing corruption in wage payments, since it makes the muster rolls available for public scrutiny and social audit. But the reality is somewhat else.

Interestingly, a large section of the respondents (40.7%) across *panchayats* report that they hardly see notifications in advance regarding the NREGS meetings. This perhaps indicates that notices are not widely circulated by the *panchayats*. The place and mode of notification may also cause hindrance. This is so because the notifications are generally put in the government offices and villagers hardly visit these offices. They visit such offices only when they desperately feel to do so. Further, most of the job seekers being illiterate do not have the ability and inclination to read the notification even when it is written in vernacular language. This is likely to restrict not only the job seekers' participation in the scheme but also incorporation of their needs and views in works.

While more than 85 per cent of the respondents, having job card, reported that they had free and easy access to job cards, rest claimed that they paid for it. Around 70 per cent of the non-job card holders claimed that their demand for job card is not addressed by *sarpanch*. The respondents of general category or with education of higher secondary level or above have distinct advantages over others in terms of registering for job cards easily and freely. As regards issuance of job cards, about a third of the respondents have reported that they received their job cards after a month or more. Some interesting things were found in the initial days during 2006. It was revealed that few villagers first got employment without job card and after working some days, got their job card at the work place. Bribe was also taken from Government employees, rich families, by the *sarpanch*, *gram sathi* and GP secretary in order to give one or two job cards to a single household.

Some of the Muslim women claimed that as the *sarpanch* belongs to ST community, he has ignored their demand for card in many times. However, after intervention by the Block Development Officer, a few of them got the card.

As per the guideline of the scheme, pasting of photographs on job cards is mandatory without any charge. However, not a single job card with photograph was found in the field.

While large majority of the job card holders reported that they keep the cards in their own custody, few respondents (20%) have reported that their cards are normally kept in the custody of the ward members or *sarpanchs* or *gram sathis*. This may largely be due to the ignorance of the job seekers about the custody of the cards. The main purpose of job card was to enable MNREGA labourers to "verify their own employment and wage details". But there is no such column to mention about the wage paid in the job card. This creates a great problem for the villagers to became conscious.

The average number of respondents applied for employment is very low in the study area (10%). Those who applied for job are mostly non-tribal beneficiaries. However, this does not necessarily mean that there is low demand for employment in the study areas. The poor tribals have not much courage to go to the GP office and claim for job. Still most of them feel that the job they used to get through NREGS is nothing but mercy of *sarpanch*. In some cases it was even found that those who really needs the cards have not received the card. Whereas few villagers who are working in public sectors have taken job cards and are not at all applying for job. During the field work it was also observed that some households are giving their cards to other households from whom they are receiving benefits. Even in few cases it was observed that villagers mortgaged their cards to contractors and money lenders.

There is no proper execution of works. Hence, it is a matter of concern that throughout the GP, the approved works are not always publicly displayed. It was revealed by the villagers that there was no *Gram Sabha* meeting regarding the activities of NREGS. The villagers used to work in any work assigned by the contractor or *sarpanch*. The internal understanding between contractors, *sarpanch* and JE (junior engineer) used to confine the work in papers only. Site account registers in respect of receipt and issue of materials to the work and temporary advance register in respect of advance availed for payment of wages had not been maintained, despite their mandated requirement for departmental execution. Materials were not purchased on tender/quotation basis and purchase bills/ payment receipts were not treated as expenditure document. Instead, work bills were paid to the JE based on item and volume of works executed in similar manner as allowed in the case of work done by the contractors. Measurement for these works was also made by the same JE, shown as departmentally executing the work. This is indicative of execution of works by the contractors in the guise of *sarpanch* and in the name of departmental execution. NREGA guidelines permit execution of road projects providing all weather connectivity in rural areas. However, it was observed during field work that the roads are not up to mark even after improvement.

Wage payment on the basis of piece rate is gaining momentum throughout the *panchayats*. However, the daily wage labour activities are still higher. As villagers are gaining little more in case of piece work, they are giving it importance. The data from the field reflected that there is huge irregularity in payment of wages. While only 28 per cent beneficiaries claimed that they received the wages within a month the rest claimed that there is no certainty in getting wages. But they received it mostly after 2 months. The contractors were quite conscious while paying the wages. They used to delay in paying wages to those labourers who are illiterate and thus had no voice. Those who received wages after 2 months are mostly illiterate (32%). It is observed from the field that around 81 per cent of the beneficiaries are not receiving the minimum wages fixed by the centre. While the MNREGA guidelines permit equal wages for equal work, it is not happening in reality. As per the views of few villagers, widows and old women are receiving lesser wages in comparison to men.

Around 71 per cent of the beneficiaries have not opened their account either in bank or in post office. Around 32 per cent of the beneficiaries have received their wages directly through cash. Reading out of the muster roll at the time of payment is mandatory under the NREGA. However, the situation is not very encouraging in this regard. All the respondents have pointed out that the muster rolls are not read out. Majority (70%) of the farmers are not aware about the muster rolls. There are reported discrepancies between the labour statement, muster roll entries and the job card entries. With respect to average days of employment provided to the households, it is 50 man days according to muster roll, while according to job card entries and labour statement it is 60 and 15 man days respectively. The cross checking of job cards during the field visit showed that there are large number of fake entries in the cards, highlighting the fact that this system is highly corrupted and officials are not worried about the poor tribals. Regarding up-dation of the job card, no such initiative is being taken by GP.

Redressal of grievances is an integral part of the NREGS. Majority of the respondents did not know that there is provision for grievance redressal and the officials do not educate the villagers about the same.

Around 45 per cent of the households are not having job cards (Table 13.2). This may be due to their lack of interest to work under the NREGS as they have greater mobility for alternative lucrative job opportunities even at a distant place. Amongst the sample non-job card holding households, around 50 per cent households have already applied for job cards. The waiting time after the applications for job cards as reported by the respondents vary between 5 to 24 month. The reasons for non-issuance of job cards may be attributed to several factors. Among them, the prominent ones are the relative socio-political and economic strength of the households in the village, awareness level, proximity with the PRI functionaries, political affiliation etc. Those who have not applied for job cards have cited procedural ignorance, lack of interest and lack of awareness about the scheme as common reasons. Regarding employment, respondents shared that they have not availed complete 100 days in a year. Even in last 5 years altogether nobody got 100 days of employment. The villagers of Santoshpur GP worked under NREGS for around 15 days in last 5 years. Only 10 per cent of households received around 50 days of work in last 5 years. As per the rules, the labourers are entitled to get their wages within 15 days of completion of work, but this was not true in most of the cases. The villagers submitted their application at the *panchayat* office to do unskilled manual work, however, they did not received any reply from the *panchayat* office. On many occasions, inconsistencies are observed, especially, in respect of number of days of employment entered in the job cards in comparison with that stated by the job seekers. There are reported inconsistencies between the muster roll entries and the entries in the job cards. In course of the survey, it is also found in some cases that workers were working at the work sites without any job cards and more importantly some such workers were suspected to be minors. To make the NREGS activities more vibrant Government of Odisha launched the Gaon Sathi scheme. Under the Goan Sathi scheme launched by Odisha Government (letter number 4323 dated 30/01/2008 GoO), two persons in each village were recruited to assist the implementation of NREGA especially organise cardholders to start a job, write muster rolls, help check measurement, make payments of labourers etc. However, most of the Goan Sathis were not much trained and aware about the policies. Even their recruitment has not brought much change in the situation. The muster roll was not found at the work site; even attendance was not recorded. In some cases it was observed that the muster roll) records only job card number leaving the name of the actual worker; it creates a scope for proxy/ghost worker at the site.

Table 13.2

Job Card Holders as per Educational Qualification

Having Job Card	*Educational Qualification of the Respondent*						*Total*
	Illiterate	*Lower Primary*	*Upper Primary*	*High School*	*Intermediate*	*Graduate*	
Yes	41	3	3	11	4	—	82
No	31	4	18	11	2	2	68
Total	72	7	41	22	6	2	150

The respondents of general category or with education of higher secondary level or above are better placed in terms of registering for job cards easily and freely, whereas it takes comparatively more time for the socially backward and aged respondents. This implies that issuance of job cards largely depends on the pursuance by the applicants. However, the female job-seekers are issued job cards at a relatively faster pace as compared to their male counterparts.

Although there are provisions and guidelines, the scheme suffers from the problem of requisite transparency during the course of implementation. The works are not always notified nor are the muster rolls read out on a regular basis. Further, even when the works are notified, the notification is not always made in vernacular language. The practice of open sharing of information on decisions and execution is hardly followed. This not only creates confusion in the minds of the people, but also leaves enough scope of malpractices and leakages of resources.

There are two types of risks associated with working under NREGS. First, in most of the cases, the wages are paid on piece rate basis and depending on his/her performance, a worker may get even less than the minimum prevailing market wage rate. This, in fact, encourages many job seekers (especially, the risk averters) to concentrate on works other than that under the NREGS to ensure a minimum wage earning. Second, as per the provisions under the scheme, a household should get minimum 100 days of employment. But, the GP fails to provide 100 days employment to a job-seeking household. Such limited and irregular supply of works creates uncertainty in the minds of the job-seekers and thereby enhances opportunity costs of working under the NREGS, especially when there is scope for regular works outside the purview of NREGS though at lower wage rate. This undoubtedly restricts the job-seekers from working under NREGS. Regular employment opportunities also motivate many of them to migrate to other states like Gujarat and Maharashtra.

Work Site Conditions

Any study on NREGS would sound incomplete if it does not talk about work site facilities. A proper working condition is a primary necessity for ensuring safety for workers which is particularly important in the case of women workers. According to NREGS guidelines, it is mandatory to have basic facilities of safe drinking water and first-aid kits. Child care facility at the work sites is also of great importance since many of the women being their children with them when they go for work. It was observed during field work that except drinking water no other facilities were arranged near the work site. Even some respondents claimed that in some cases drinking water was also not available. While discussing work site facilities like shade, some of the respondents narrated that the trees adjacent to work sites were used and treated as shady shelters. It is an interesting point of contradiction and manipulation of actual purpose and meaning of work site facilities to be created for the workers. In the face such manipulations by the local implementing agencies and absence of any monitoring mechanism at the same time have resulted in the creation of unsafe and sub-standard working conditions.

The issue of work site facility was further taken up and it was found that majority (90%) of the workers said that there was no crèche facility at the work site. The women workers reportedly complained that they were facing difficulties in taking their children to work sites. Regarding the provision of first-aid kit at the work sites, 75 per cent respondents said no first aid or medical help was available in the case of injuries at the work sites. In addition to the above challenges, there was a negligible display of work site boards with basic information, no monitoring groups have been formed in all the areas and no social audits seemed to have been taken up in the study area. Thus, with the exception of drinking water, the availability of other facilities like first-aid kit, shade and crèche facility, at respective work sites under NREGA, were virtually negligible.

The *sarpanch* is the most important agents of implementation of the NREGS as he works at the local level with the help of Gram Sathi and Village Level Workers (VLW). As the GPs are authorised to spend 50 per cent of the NREGA fund, the *sarpanchs* need to play a pivotal role in this regard. They are involved in the planning, designing and implementation of NREGS. Awareness of the *sarpanchs* regarding different aspects of the scheme and their integrity are thus crucial for its successful implementation. The observation from the field reveals that the *sarpanch* is not much aware about the scheme. A tribal lady who is *sarpanch* in the *panchayat* is not much active. Her husband acts as dummy. Though she attended some of the training programmes on NREGS at the block level, she is not quite aware. Her husband who acts as a contractor is misleading about the entire programme. While distributing work and cards he is taking care of those who voted for him. Even though he is well aware about some rules and regulations, he is not ready to share it with the villagers.

Livelihood

The data from the field reflected that there is not much impact of MNREGA on rural livelihoods. As villagers are not able to get the work as per the rules, it is difficult to claim that any change in field area is due to NREGS. It has failed to achieve its aims as there is no proper and regular work which is the direct result of poor implementation.

On the issue of asset creation, nothing much is observed from the field. Except road work no other works are being taken up here. Recently some initiations have been taken by *sarpanch* for the SC/ST land development. In all these hamlets people had expressed their disappointment with the NREGA works.

Rural women in India have got the constitutional right to be able to earn. EGA is significant for womenfolk not only for the economic opportunities generated but also for the mobility that is created for the women's labour. In addition, the economic opportunities generated under EGA have also increased the efficiency of women taking decisions in the family matters and also their participation in the public sphere. For example, when asked 'was it your own decision to work', 70 per cent respondents said that it was their own decision to come for NREGA works. This perhaps is a new found identity for women in rural India as there is a positive growth in the ability to take decisions.

This trend has snowballing effect in various aspects of women's strengthening identity both in the sphere of family and society. For example, women have started asserting their voices in the family matters and nature of spending money as far as the hard earned wages from EGA is concerned. Though awareness still continues to be a stiff challenge, women in study area have become pro-active learners and participants in the schemes and programmes operating in the villages.

Conclusion

Though NREGA is a well thought-out legislation, a powerful tool in the hands of the common people to get their basic livelihood, its poor execution, deprives them of their basic rights. The study reveals that despite numerous problems, NREGA is a programme that has begun to make a difference in the lives of women. Furthermore, it is popular among the workers, who routinely ask if more work could be made available to them under the NREGA. Clearly, there is a massive demand for NREGA work, and the administration should respond to it by increasing the scale of employment.

A proper working condition is a primary necessity for ensuring safety and efficient condition for workers which particularly in the case of women is much more important.

References

Baisakh, Pradeep (2007). *Has NREGA Reduced Poverty in Orissa*? 23 July. *www.orissadiary.com*

Dey, Subhasis and Arjun Bedi (2010). "The National Rural Employment Guarantee Scheme in Birubham", *Economic and Political Weekly* 41.

Indian Institute of Technology, Madras, Chennai (2009). *Evaluation of National Rural Employment Guarantee Act: In Districts: Cuddlore, Dindugal, Kanchipuram, Nagai, Thiruvalallur: State: Tamil Nadu.* May.

Jain, S.P. (2001). *Emerging Institutions for Decentralised Rural Development.* Hyderabad: NIRD&PR.

Karalay, G.N. (2005). *Integrated Approach to Rural Development: Policies, Programmes and Strategies.* New Delhi: Concept Publishing Company.

Kashyap, Chaman Lal (1989). *Management and Planning of Rural Development in India.* New Delhi: Sterling Publishers.

Khan, Amir Ullah and M.R. Saluja (n.d.). *Impact of MNREGA on Rural Livelihoods. www.idfresearch.org*

Mohsin, Nadeem (1985). *Rural Development Through Government Programmes.* New Delhi: Mittal Publications.

Roy, Sen., Dipjoy and Debabrata Samanta (2009). "Good Governance and Employment Generation through MNREGA: A Case Study of Gram Panchayat in West Bengal", Presented a paper in Conference entitled *Infrastructure, Finance and Governance: Push for Growth.* November. New Delhi.

Shah, Mihir (2004). "National Rural Employment Guarantee Act: A Historic Opportunity", *Economic and Political Weekly* 39(50): 5287-91.

Vanaik, A. and Siddhartha (2008). "Bank Payments: End of Corruption in NREGA", *Economic and Political Weekly* 43(17): 33-39.

Websites:

http://www.gov.in

http://www.nrega.net

http://www.nrega.nic.in

http://www.righttofoodindia.org

14

RUDRA N. MISHRA, P.K. VISWANATHAN and
MADHUSUDAN BHATTARAI

Impacts of MGNREGA Programme on Income, Assets and Food Security of Poor and Vulnerable Groups

Evidence from Selected Semi-Arid Tropic (SAT) Villages in India

Introduction

India is a country with a vast majority of the workers depending on the informal sector for livelihood. About 86 per cent of the total workers belong to the informal sector. However their share in national output is only 50 per cent approximately. Most of these workers are either casual in nature or are self-employed. These workers have no security, no legal contract, no health facilities and other benefits extended to those of the formal sector (Kannan and Breman, 2013: 1). Their vulnerability is extended by the necessity to remain mobile due to the saturation and lack of demand in the primary agricultural sector. They generally have to work outside the place of their birth and face many uncertainties due to unfamiliar conditions, work expectations and job profile. Further, they are, by and large, paid much less than the nominal wage for any particular job owing to basic limitations like lower education, poor skills and dearth of capital. The lean seasons or failure to produce sufficient agricultural output due to the vagaries of nature force many of these rural households (with no land or with smaller and marginal holdings) to migrate under distress so as to sustain their families; especially from areas where agriculture is essentially rainfed. Often these migrants end up in city slums, live in unhygienic conditions and supply the bulk of unskilled and semi-skilled labour to the manufacturing and service sectors in urban areas, often at lower wages than that prescribed under law. Those who fail to migrate, depend upon meagre assets which they sell or mortgage, as well as cut back on their consumption including that of food, health care and education of their children (Kannan and Breman, 2012: 3).

To address these issues discussed above, the Government of India (GoI) came up with Mahatma Gandhi National Employment Guarantee Act (MGNREGA) in 2006. The twin objectives of the programme were to create employment opportunity for the rural population for certain minimum days in a year as a matter of right, and tap the vast reserve of underemployed and unemployed labour force in rural India, particularly women, in time of agricultural crisis in particular and non-agricultural seasons in general (Viswanathan and Mandal, 2012). It was anticipated that the programme will particularly benefit the rural population in lean seasons and reduce distress migration, increase the purchasing power in general and create necessary physical assets in rural areas using the otherwise untapped labour potential therein.

Targeting poverty alleviation through employment generation using rural works has had a long history in India that had begun in the 1960s. There were few notable precursors to the MGNREGA, which were based on the theme of alleviating rural poverty by way of creating employment in rural areas. These were Food for Work Programme (FWP) of 1977 and three years later National Rural Employment Programme (NREP) was introduced in 1980. In 1989, the above programmes were merged as Jawahar Rozgar Yojana (JRY) that was implemented through *panchayats* for the first time; in 1999, the programme was revamped and rechristened as Jawahar Gram Swarojgar Yojna (JGSY), reinforcing the role of *panchayats* with greater autonomy as the sole implementing authority. In 1993, another programme with the same objective was launched—Employment Assurance Scheme (EAS)—specifically targeting job creation for rural areas in lean agricultural months. This programme was implemented through *zila parishads* or district level elected bodies as the sole implementing authority. In 2001, the government merged the EAS and JGSY to converge employment generation, infrastructure development and food security in rural areas. The government integrated EAS and JGSY into a new scheme—Sampoorna Grameen Rozgar Yojana (SGRY), with the village *panchayats* as sole implementing authority. Over these years the above programmes often overlapped and were administered by different government departments. Of course, all these programmes suffered from poor coverage, wrong targeting and lack of coherence among the multiple agencies. Even entrusting these activities to *panchayats* yielded little desired results. In 2006, the government integrated SGRY and FWP of 2001 into a new scheme called Mahatma Gandhi National Employment Guarantee Act (MGNREGA). The innovative feature of the scheme was that of ensuring employment for a certain number of days in a year, which became a matter of right to the people [keeping in view the spirit of directive principles of Indian Constitution (Article 41), which direct all the states in India to ensure all citizens living in their jurisdiction right to work in line with the fundamental right to life guaranteed under Article 21 of the Constitution]. Originally, the law was proposed in September 2005 and implemented in the 200 most backward districts in February 2006, which later was made a universal programme.

It has been argued that the provision of employment to the rural poor is not an exclusive step; but has multifaceted effects on the economy. Unemployment is strongly correlated with poverty; thus, provision of gainful employment will help reduce the number of poor. Also, the provision of income facilitates livelihood security, decision—making and bargaining power to the poor. The socially marginalised and deprived communities are rejuvenated to fight for themselves. Local savings are boosted, adding to local capital formation. Even the women folk has started to realise its true potential and are willing to accept newer roles and responsibilities in the process of rural development. Distress migration, constituting a significant proportion of migration in India, was thought to be brought down considerably thereby helping to overcome its ill effects on the society. Besides, there are positive effects on physical and mental health of the households as well. By absorbing the surplus labour in productive activities, pressure on agriculture gets reduced considerably which further boosts agricultural productivity. Thus, it was believed that the provision of gainful long-term employment can result in many constructive spillover effects on the society.

In this backdrop, this paper examines the local level impacts of the national flagship programme that has gained global attention. The local level impacts are captured through an empirical survey covering 10 villages that form part of the International Crops research Institute for Semi-Arid Tropics (ICRISAT)-Village Dynamics in South Asia (VDSA) project. Following an overview of the important aspects and the status of implementation of the MGNREGA at the national level, the paper discusses the specific village level implications with respect to their outcomes on household income, asset creation and food security and also poverty reduction with particular reference to the socio-economically vulnerable groups. Following the presentation of the major impacts as pointed above, the paper concludes by highlighting some of the policy relevant aspects that need serious attention in the future for making the programme yield sustainable results in the rural scenario.

MGNREGA: An Overview

As mentioned earlier, MGNREGA is a wage employment scheme, enacted by the GoI in 2005, with the aim of providing 100 days of guaranteed employment to every rural household willing to perform unskilled activities. In a sense, it creates legal entitlements to work as a fundamental right of individuals. If the state fails to keep that 100 days' contract, it will have to pay an unemployment allowance as compensation. If the state fails to pay the allowance, the complainant can even go to the courts. Wages paid under MGNREGA would correspond to the minimum wages paid in the particular state, revised from time to time. It is a decentralised programme involving the *gram panchayats* (GP) and other local authorities in the implementation and supervision of the scheme. Initially implemented in 200 most backward districts of the country in 2006, the programme covers the entire country today. Nearly 619 districts covering all states had been included in MGNREGA.

The MGNREGA was envisaged as a demand-driven programme, where the work in a particular village is undertaken based on the demand created from a number of households asking for such work in a given year, the upper cap being 100 days per household per year. The costs are to be shared by both the centre and the states, even though larger part of the fiscal burden is to be borne by the former. The centre provides 100 per cent funding of the wages for unskilled manual work and 75 per cent of material cost of the schemes, including payment of wages to skilled and semi-skilled workers, while the states fund 25 per cent of material including payment of wages to skilled and semi-skilled workers. It was also decided that in case the states are unable to provide the required employment opportunities within the stipulated time, they will be entitled to pay an unemployment allowance to the beneficiaries. This was considered as a deterrent for possible lags in implementing the scheme on the part of state governments.

The main provisions of the Act are:

i) Employment to be given within 15 days of application for work.
ii) If employment is not provided within 15 days, daily unemployment allowance is to be paid in cash.
iii) Employment within 5 kilometres radius, else extra wages to be paid.
iv) At least one-third of the beneficiaries have to be women.
v) *Gram sabha* will recommend works.
vi) *Gram panchayat* to execute at least 50 per cent of works.
vii) Panchayat Raj Institutions (PRIs) have a principle role in planning and implementation.
viii) Transparency, accountability and social audit would be ensured through institutional mechanism at all levels.
ix) Grievance redressal mechanism to be put in place for ensuring a responsive implementation.

The other intended benefits from MGNREGA, apart from job creation and improving livelihood conditions of the rural poor, are:

i) To reduce distressed migration from rural to urban areas and also from one part to another of rural areas.

ii) Creation of durable assets in rural areas.
iii) Invigorate civic and community life and enliven PRIs as they have been entrusted to formulate, implement and monitor the scheme.
iv) Empowerment of rural women by providing opportunity to earn income independently and to participate in social groups.
v) Overall development of rural economy.
vi) Promotion of inclusive growth and development.
vii) Multiplier effects on the economy.

Implementation Process

MGNREGA was enacted to be implemented mainly in the rural and semi-urban areas. It was applied in three phases. In the first phase, the 200 most backward districts in the country were included in the purview of MGNREGA. In the second phase, another set of districts who are slightly better off than the first phase districts were included. In the last phase, all remaining districts were covered. MGNREGA has a list of activities that can be undertaken for providing jobs, mostly focusing on creation of physical assets in rural areas through construction of public infrastructure, construction and restoration of canals, tanks, check dams, protection walls, open wells and tube wells, building and restoration of village roads and land development. A job card had to be issued to the household after systematic registration of all the workers, noting down the necessary details. The official structure and functioning of MGNREGA is discussed below.

At the Central level, the Department of Rural Development, GoI, is in charge of the implementation of MGNREGA in rural areas. It formulates policies and provides guidelines to the states and local governments to implement the scheme. At the state level, there is MGNREGA council headed by Chief Minister as the chairman and the Minister for Rural Development as the vice chairman. Further, the state government is responsible for fixing rates to different works every year in consultation with the MGNREGA State Council. The district is the nodal unit for implementation of MGNREGA.

The collectors-cum-district magistrates are the District Program Coordinators (DPCs) of MGNREGA works. The project directors of District Rural Development Agency (DRDA) work as nodal officers of the programme. Moreover at the district level, the most important institution is the *zilla panchayat,* which acts as a nodal agency for the preparation of five year perspective plan based on the village level plans as well as the annual plan of MGNREGA activities. At the block level, the block or *panchayat samiti* lies between the GP and *zilla panchayat* in implementation of MGNREGA works and plays a crucial role. The block/*taluka* level set-up consists of Program Officer (PO), who is invariably the Block Development Officer (BDO). His chief responsibility is to ensure-employment for anyone who applies for work within 15 days. The GP is the root of the three-tier *panchayati raj* system in India and is the nodal implementing body in successful execution of MGNREGA. The GP is responsible for many activities including registration of households, issue of job cards, creation of awareness, planning and execution of works and maintenance of records. A coalition of all these, especially the GP, is necessary to for a successful planning, execution, monitoring, evaluation and grievance redressal mechanism of MGNREGA.

Performance of MGNREGA

There have been some significant achievements owing to MGNREGA. Since its inception in 2005, the performance of MGNREGA has been somewhat wavering. In some states and in certain indicators, it has performed above potential; whereas in others, it is found lacking in many respects. Overall, its performance cannot be considered to be flawless. There are some revisions in the act as per the need of the hour. But in spite of these, there have been many areas where the act is found wanting. However over the years, as the studies show, the experience gathered from working under MGNREGA varies across states and within a given state.

Table 14.1 gives a statistical account of the performance of MGNREGA in different aspects and across different classes of society. Asset creation and utilisation of allocated funds have also been used as an indicator to measure the success of MGNREGA. Table 14.1

Table 14.1

Performance of MGNREGA Across Different Indicators

Descriptives	*2006-07*	*2007-08*	*2008-09*	*2009-10*	*2010-11*	*2011-12*	*2012-13 (P)*	*2013-14 (till 13 December)*
	1	*2*	*3*	*4*	*5*	*6*	*7*	*8*
Number of HHs provided employment (in crore)	2.10	3.39	4.51	5.3	5.5	5.06	4.98	3.81
Person–days (in crore) [% of total person days]								
Total	90.5	143.59	216.32	283.6	257.2	218.76	229.86	134.80
SC	22.9 [25]	39.4 [27]	63.4 [29]	86.5 [30]	78.8 [31]	48.47 [22]	50.96 [22]	31.53 [23]
ST	32.9 [36]	42.1 [29]	55.0 [25]	58.7 [21]	53.6 [21]	40.92 [19]	40.75 [18]	38.3 [16]
Women	36.8 [40]	61.2 [43]	103.5 [48]	136.4 [48]	122.7 [48]	105.27 [48]	117.93 [51]	73.33 [54]
Others	34.6 [38]	62.2 [43]	97.9 [45]	138.4 [49]	124.8 [48]	129.38 [59]	138.14 [60]	82.18 [61]
Average person–day per household	43	42	48	54	47	43	46	35
Funds Allocated and Utilised (in ₹ crore)								
Budget outlay	11,300	12,000	30,000	39,100	40,100	40,000	33,000	33,000
Central release	86,40.8	12,610.3	29,939.6	33,506.6	35,768.9	29,189.7	30,009.	29,885.9
Total available fund (including OB)	12,073.5	19,305.8	37,397.1	49,579.2	54,172.1	48,805.7	45,051.4	37,084.7
Expenditure	8,824	15,857	27,250	37,905	39,377	37,072.8	39,657.0	24,848.7

contd...

.contd...

	1	*2*	*3*	*4*	*5*	*6*	*7*	*8*
Average wage per day (₹)	65	75	84	90	100	111	9.	10.
Average cost per day (₹)	97	110	126	134	153	169	11.	12.
Works detail (in Lakh)							13.	14.
Total works taken up	8.4	17.9	27.8	46.2	51.0	80.8	106.51	111.64
Works completed	3.9	8.2	12.1	22.6	25.9	27.6	25.60	11.17
Water conservation	4.5 [54]	8.73 [49]	12.79 [46]	23.4 [51]	24.3 [48]	48.81 [60]	49.26 [46]	45.41 [41]
Works on individuals land	0.81 [10]	2.63 [15]	5.67 [20]	7.73 [17]	9.15 [18]	9.16 [11]	11.81 [11]	12.62 [11]
Rural connectivity	1.80 [21]	3.08 [17]	5.03 [18]	7.64 [17]	9.31 [18]	13.86 [17]	13.04 [12]	12.62 [11]
Land development	0.89 [11]	2.88 [16]	3.98 [15]	6.38 [14]	7.04 [14]	6.32 [8]	6.58 [6]	5.78 [5]
Any other activity	0.34 [4]	0.56 [3]	0.28 [1]	0.98 [2]	1.06 [2]	2.31 [3]	9.87 [9]	9.65 [9]

Note: Data in [ ] brackets represent percentage figures; HH - Households; OB - Outcome Budget

Source: Compiled and computed from the official report of MGNREGA 2013. *http://nrega.nic.in/netnrega/WriteReaddata/circulars/Report_to_the_people_English2013.pdf*

shows that the participation of different vulnerable groups—women, SC (scheduled caste) and ST (scheduled tribe)—have increased until 2009-10 and shows decline in following years. The funds in terms of nominal figures increased all these years, except for 2012-13. The nominal figure for average wage paid also increased over time. However in terms of physical assets created, the programme shows an upward trend over the years. But a caution of words here will be appropriate—it may be because some of these works are taken over to the next year.

The remainder of the paper tries to address the following aspects of implementation and outcomes of the MGNREGA in the context of 10 study villages, that are part of the ICRISAT-VDSA study.

i) How is MGNREGA functioning across study villages?
ii) The participation of village housheholds in the programme.
iii) Status of employment and wage across study villages in MGNREGA from the year of implementation in therein until 2012-13, i.e., the survey year.
iv) The benefits enjoyed from MGNREGA by respective villagers.

Data and Methodology

In 2012-13, ICRISAT, Hyderabad and Gujarat Institute of Development Research (GIDR), Ahmedabad had undertaken a survey of households spread across the states of Madhya Pradesh, Gujarat and Maharashtra in order to assess the impact of MGNREGA on income, assets and food security of poor and vulnerable groups in 10 villages (all ICRISAT villages). Out of these 10 villages, these were 2 villages each from Panchmahal (constituting mostly tribals) and Junagadh (mostly backward classes) in Gujarat, 2 villages from eastern Madhya Pradesh (MP) and 2 villages each from south-western Maharastra (Solapur distrcit) and Vidarbha (Akola district, with households mostly from back-ward classes). All these villages are of semi-arid climatic condition. In total, 1678 households from small farmers (with holding of less than 5 acres per household) and landless labourers were surveyed. However in this particular study, information from 891 households belonging to small farmer groups and landless labour households who had job cards were considered.

The sample households were selected through a random sampling approach from the list of all the households in each village. The studied households constitute approximately 20 per cent of the households in these social groups for any given village selected for the study.

Results and Discussion

Socio-Economic Profile of Sample Households

Table 14.2 shows that among the sample households, male headed over are predominant in any given region. In Gujarat, among the MGNREGA beneficiaries, 65 per cent were BPL (below poverty line) (in the tribal region), while 45 per cent in Junagadh were found to belong to BPL households (2 villages). In MP, 72 per cent of all the beneficiaries belonged to BPL households, while in Maharashtra for Vidarbha and South Maharashtra, the figures were 88 per cent and 65 per cent respectively. However when asked about the self-assessment of their economic status within the village context, the figures appear to be contradictory. It may happen in a village setting where the households determine their social-economic status in the given micro-setting which may go contrary to the official norms. In MP and Maharashtra, beneficiaries were basically from OBC (other backward classes) (more than 60%); for Gujarat, in Panchmahal 90 per cent of beneficiaries were from ST and in Junagadh 62 per cent were from SC groups. As given in Table 14.1, the majority of sample households in non-tribal region of Gujarat (consisting of 2 villages in Junagadh district), eastern MP (consisting 2 villages of Raisen district) and in Vidarbha (consisting 2 villages of Akola district) were from landless households—mostly from SC communities. Remaining households in these areas as well as other study areas who have land, are mostly small farmers (see Table 14.2).

Participation of Sample Housheolds in MGNREGA

On an average in case of the households in Gujarat, little more than two members participated in the job, while for the other two states, it is only one member who had participated in the MGNREGA

Table 14.2

Socio-economic Profile of Sample Households (%)

No.	*Characteristics*	*Categories*	*Gujarat-Tribal Region N=127*	*Gujarat-Non-Tribal Region N=70*	*Madhya Pradesh-Eastern Belt N=122*	*Maharashtra-South-West N=434*	*Maharashtra-Vidarbha N=138*	*Total N= 891*
1.	Sex of the respondents	Male	92.9	92.9	98.4	97.2	95.7	96.2
		Female	7.1	7.1	1.6	2.8	4.3	3.8
2.	Socio-economic status	APL	34.6	51.4	17.2	25.6	8	25.0
		BPL	65.4	45.7	72.1	62.4	88.4	66.9
		Antyodaya	-	2.9	9	11.8	-	7.2
		Ration card not available	-	-	1.6	0.2	2.9	1.8
3.	Social group	SC	7.1	62.9	24.6	13.1	26.1	19.5
		ST	90.6	1.4	4.9	-	0.7	13.8
		OBC	0.8	34.3	69.7	45.2	62.3	44.0
		Others	1.6	1.4	0.8	31.6	2.9	16.3
		Nomadic Tribes (NT)	-	-	-	10.1	8	1.8
4.	Economic status of the sample households (self–assessment)	Very rich	0.0	0.0	0.0	0.7	0.7	0.4

contd...

.contd...

		Rich	0.0	0.0	1.6	6.7	14.5	5.7
		Medium	50.4	45.7	56.6	85.0	66.7	70.3
		Poor	46.5	45.7	59.3	7.4	18.1	22.0
		Very Poor	3.1	8.6	2.5	0.2	0.0	1.6
5.	Ownership of land (%)	Those who possess land	86.6	28.6	45.9	59.0	44.2	56.5
6.	Size of the land holding (those owning land)*							
	Less than 1 acre		1.8	0.0	0.0	1.1	0.0	0.8
		1-5 acres	98.2	84.8	96.4	80.7	94.2	87.9
		5-10 acres	0.0	8.9	1.8	12.5	4.4	7.9
		More than 10 acres	0.0	5.3	1.8	5.7	1.4	3.4

Note: In case of Panchamahal 96.1 per cent of 127 total sample have worked at least once in NREGA, for Junagadh the corresponding figure is 100 per cent for a total of 70 households, and for Raisen in MP the figure is 100 per cent for 122 sample households from Papada and Ramura Kalan. For Maharashtra in Solapur, None of the study villages have a single household which has participated in MGNREGA. In Kinkhed only one household has participated, so the figure for Akola district is presented mainly from Kanzara where 68.8 per cent of sample household has at least worked once in MGNREGA. We did this analysis because, as per the above table, the responses for various impacts could be affected whether the household has actually participated in MGNREGA or not. In MP and Gujarat, almost every household barring the Chattha, had worked at least once of MGNREGA. In case of Maharashtra, only Kanzara has reported participation of MGNREGA, the figures reported for Akola is in reality the findings from this village.

Source: Sample Survey.

Table 14.3

Participation in MGNREGA in the Sample Villages in Three States of India, 2006-2012

Characteristics	*Gujarat-Tribal Region N = 127*	*Gujarat-Non-Tribal Region N = 70*	*Madhya Pradesh-Eastern Belt N = 122*	*Maharashtra-South-West N =434*	*Maharashtra-Vidarbha N = 18*	*Total N = 891*
No. of households reported to participate in MGNREGA at least once in between 2006 and 2013 (%)	125 (98.4)	70 (100.0)	122 (100.0)	0 (0.0)	97 (70.3)	414 (46.5)
No. of households worked in each year (% of the total households mentioned above)						
2006	35 (27.6)	2 (2.9)	0 (0.0)	0 (0.0)	13 (9.4)	50 (5.6)
2007	93 (73.2)	0 (0.0)	0 (0.0)	0 (0.0)	11 (8.0)	104 (11.7)
2008	11 (8.7)	0 (0.0)	51 (41.8)	0 (0.0)	13 (9.4)	75 (8.4)
2009	7 (5.5)	31 (44.3)	82 (67.2)	0 (0.0)	10 (7.2)	130 (14.6)
2010	9 (7.1)	15 (21.4)	56 (45.9)	0 (0.0)	6 (4.3)	86 (9.7)
2011	6 (4.7)	35 (50.0)	57 (46.7)	0 (0.0)	26 (18.8)	124 (13.9)
2012	0 (0.0)	26 (37.1)	52 (42.6)	0 (0.0)	49 (35.5)	127 (14.3)
2013	0 (0.0)	23 (32.9)	52 (42.6)	0 (0.0)	17 (12.3)	93 (10.4)
Average no. of days males who got work (total number of males)						
2006	20.7 (35)	30.0 (2)	0.0 (0)	0.0 (0)	20.8 (13)	21.6 (50)
2007	21.8 (93)	0.0 (0)	0.0 (0)	0.0 (0)	20.0 (11)	21.6 (104)

contd...

.contd...

2008	24.2 (11)	0.0 (0)	16.4 (51)	0.0 (0)	36.5 (13)	21.0 (75)
2009	13.2 (7)	12.3 (31)	24.7 (82)	0.0 (0)	47.3 (10)	22.9 (130)
2010	19.7 (9)	34.2 (15)	27.3 (56)	0.0 (0)	37.5 (6)	28.4 (86)
2011	24.3 (6)	37.8 (35)	24.6 (57)	0.0 (0)	46.5 (26)	32.9 (124)
2012	0.0 (0)	26.8 (26)	32.8 (52)	0.0 (0)	42.2 (49)	35.1 (127)
2013	0.0 (0)	20.5 (23)	33.4 (52)	0.0 (0)	65.6 (17)	36.1 (93)
Average no. of days that the females got work (total number of females)						
2006	19.9 (35)	32.5 (2)	0.0 (0)	0.0 (0)	0.0 (0)	20.5 (37)
2007	20.0 (93)	0.0 (0)	0.0 (0)	0.0 (0)	0.0 (0)	20.0 (93)
2008	25.1 (11)	0.0 (0)	16.9 (7)	0.0 (0)	0.0 (0)	21.9 (18)
2009	11.5 (7)	12.5 (31)	26.0 (21)	0.0 (0)	0.0 (0)	17.4 (56)
2010	16.2 (9)	33.9 (15)	24.2 (15)	0.0 (0)	25.0 (1)	26.3 (39)
2011	24.0 (6)	35.9 (34)	24.5 (13)	0.0 (0)	35.3 (8)	32.2 (61)
2012	0.0	26.5 (26)	35.0 (16)	0.0 (0)	42.3 (14)	32.9 (56)
2013	0.0	20.5 (23)	32.3 (17)	0.0 (0)	49.4 (9)	29.6 (50)

Source: Sample Survey.

for the above-mentioned year (table not shown separately). The average working days per household was highest in the tribal region of Gujarat, which had fallen over time from 38 days in 2006-07 to 10 days in 2012-13, while in Junagadh it has fallen from 69 days to 41 days during the same period. In MP during the same period, the average number of days when work is available to the household has gone up from 18 to 42 days. In Maharashtra's Vidarbha region, the number of working days have gone up from 20 to 41 days during the same period (in Kanzara only). In South Maharashtra, i.e., Solapur region, in both the villages, none of the households despite having a job card, had worked in MGNREGA as the opportunity for work is plenty in agriculture activities within the villages and nearby industrial areas (table not shown separately).

Table 14.3 gives the figures of participation for sample households in MGNREGA from the year of implementation in their respective villages. It shows in Gujarat's non-tribal region and MP that all the sample households had at least worked once in the programme. However in Vidarbha, only 70 per cent of those with job cards had worked at least once in the programme. Apart for Vidarbha, the number of households participating in the programme are falling or has remained stagnant over the years, except for the initial couple of years. The average working days over the given years are similar for both male and female participants. In Vidarbha region, the average number of days available for work has increased for both males and females, while in other areas it is declining for both the sexes.

The average wage earned by the hosueholds from the MGNREGA varied widely in the three states. In Gujarat for both the region, the average household earning was below ₹2,000; in MP it is around ₹3,200; and in for Maharashtra, it is more than ₹6,000 (for Kanzara in Vidarbha region). The rates for the work done were fixed on 'per piece' basis in Gujarat and MP, whereas in Kanzara the workers are paid around ₹145-160 on per day basis.

Wage from MGNREGA for Sample Households

Table 14.4 indicates that the daily average wage for the beneficiary households have gone up in each of the regions during

Table 14.4

Income Received from MGNREGA in the Sample Villages in Three States of India, 2006-2012

Characteristics	*Gujarat-Tribal Region N = 127*	*Gujarat-Non-Tribal Region N = 70*	*Madhya Pradesh-Eastern Belt N = 122*	*Maharashtra-South-West N =434*	*Maharashtra-Vidarbha (Eastern Maharashtra) N = 138*	*Total N = 891*
Average daily wage earned by the household in ₹ (total number of households)						
2006	66.0 (35)	65.0 (2)	0.0 (0)	0.0 (0)	150.8 (13)	88.0 (50)
2007	69.7 (93)	0.0 (0)	0.0 (0)	0.0 (0)	160.9 (11)	79.4 (104)
2008	73.6 (11)	0.0 (0)	88.8 (51)	0.0 (0)	129.2 (13)	93.8 (75)
2009	90.0 (7)	65.0 (31)	86.3 (82)	0.0 (0)	136.5 (10)	87.3 (130)
2010	78.0 (9)	64.0 (15)	103.8 (56)	0.0 (0)	148.0 (6)	96.9 (86)
2011	102.0 (6)	64.5 (35)	113.8 (57)	0.0 (0)	186.6 (26)	112.69 (124)
2012	0.0	67.0 (26)	113.8 (52)	0.0 (0)	144.1 (49)	119.9 (127)
2013	0.0	68.7 (23)	127.5 (52)	0.0 (0)	148.4 (17)	121.0 (93)
Average annual income earned by the household in ₹ (total number of households)						
2006	2753.7 (35)	4250.0 (2)	0.0 (0)	0.0 (0)	3107.7 (13)	2905.6 (50)
2007	2151.0 (93)	0.0 (0)	0.0 (0)	0.0 (0)	3222.7 (11)	3180.0 (104)
2008	4306 (11)	0.0 (0)	1633.3 (51)	0.0 (0)	4150.0 (13)	2436.7 (74)
2009	2335.7 (7)	1607.1 (31)	2682.9 (82)	0.0 (0)	5260.0 (10)	2605.8 (130)
2010	2636.2 (9)	4187.3 (15)	3458 .1 (56)	0.0 (0)	4766.7 (6)	3601 (86)
2011	5729.0 (9)	4667.7 (35)	3602.4 (57)	0.0 (0)	6686.9 (26)	4643.8 (124)
2012	0.0 (0)	3433.4 (26)	3602.4 (52)	0.0 (0)	7224.06 (49)	5641.9 (127)
2013	0.0 (0)	2397.4 (23)	5267.7 (52)	0.0 (0)	11246.8 (17)	6129.0 (93)

Source: Sample Survey.

the initial couple of years, while later it started to decline. The average annual income for the households in respective areas also shows an upward trend. But this increasing trend should be viewed in context of the declining number of households participating each year. The increasing average duration of work and rising wage rate in MGNREGA has boosted the average annual income for sample households in Vidarbha region, more than three-folds, but the number of households participating, has fallen drastically.

In most of the sample villages, the primary nature of MGNREGA implementation is related to the creation of community assets like check dams and road construction, except for eastern MP where 60 per cent of the work were related to digging up farm ponds in the private fields under 'Kapildhara Yojana' of the state government (see Table 14.5).

Issues Related to Payment

One of the major dissatisfaction of the sample households who had worked in MGNREGA is that of delay in payment of wages. Most of these works take place in non-agricultural season, when small farmers and landless labourers face difficulty in meeting their daily needs. However, the wage is paid after at least a month or more. Even if the wage rate under MGNREGA remains less than that prevailing in these villages, the people wants the wages to be paid within a week, which will help them to meet their consumption needs (see Table 14.6). Most of the beneficiaries receive their wages in their accounts, but this has not been able to prevent the leakage completely as they nevertheless have to pay a proportion of their wages to local leaders and officials so as to ensure their continued participation in the following year.

Table 14.5

Name of the Activities Undertaken by the Sample Households who had at least Worked Once in MGNREGA

S. No.	*Name of the Activities in which the Household Worked*	*Gujarat-Tribal Region N = 127*	*Gujarat-Non-Tribal Region N = 70*	*Madhya Pradesh-Eastern Belt N = 122*	*Maharashtra-South-West N = 434*	*Maharashtra-Vidarbha N = 138*	*Total N=891*
1.	Closed embankments	8.3	0.0	0.0	-	4.6	2.9
2.	Check dam	18.6	0.0	1.6	-	0.0	4.9
3.	Well construction	1.3	0.0	59.6	-	7.9	29.6
4.	Construction of pits	1.3	0.0	0.0	-	0.0	0.3
5.	Farm ponds	5.8	0.0	0.0	-	7.2	3.6
6.	Deepening of ravines	1.9	0.0	0.0	-	0.0	0.4
7.	Road construction	60.2	0.0	34.9	-	67.1	43.1
8.	Clay work	2.6	0.0	0.0	-	0.0	2.3
9.	Deepening/desiltation of lake	0.0	58.6	0.3	-	7.9	6.1
10.	Bori Dam work	0.0	41.4	0.0	-	0.0	4.2
11.	Tree plantation	0.0	0.0	1.0	-	4.6	1.3
12.	Sanitation work	0.0	0.0	0.3	-	0.0	0.1
13.	Build a school	0.0	0.0	1.3	-	0.0	0.6
14.	Agriculture work	0.0	0.0	1.0	-	0.0	0.1
15.	Canal construction	0.0	0.0	0.0	-	0.7	0.4
	Total responses	156	70	304	0	152	682

Source: Sample Survey.

Table 14.6

Payment Related Issues

Variables	*Categories*	*Gujarat-Tribal Region N = 127*	*Gujarat-Non-Tribal Region N = 70*	*Madhya Pradesh-Eastern Belt N = 122*	*Maha-rashtra-South-West N = 434*	*Maha-rashtra-Vidarbha N = 138*	*Total N = 891*
Delay in receiving wages	Within 15 days	72.0	15.2	25.0	0.0	13.5	30.7
	15-30 days	19.3	31.8	56.8	0.0	62.8	46.0
	31-60 days	0.0	35.6	9.7	0.0	19.6	13.8
	61-90 days	0.0	0.0	3.1	0.0	3.4	4.9
	91 day onwards	0.0	0.0	2.6	0.0	0.0	1.1
	Not received	6.8	17.4	2.8	0.0	0.7	2.9
Mode of payment	Bank	75.8	97.0	63.9	0.0	40.5	53.5
	Post office	8.7	3.0	28.5	0.0	56.1	24.9
	Cash	8.1	0.0	4.2	0.0	2.7	18.2
	Not received wages	6.8	0.0	3.4	0.0	0.7	3.4
Total number of responses		158	132	352	0	148	790

Source: Sample Survey.

Use of Earnings from MGNREGA by Sample Households

It is clear from Table 14.7 that the cash-starved households in our sample who are mostly small farmers and labourers spent a major part of their earning from MGNREGA on the purchase of food articles and necessary household consumption, especially in non-tribal region of Gujarat and Vidarbha. In the tribal region of Gujarat, 30 per cent of the responses indicated the use of MGNREGA money to meeting agricultural expenses. Some of the households also use this money to purchase the raw materials for their handicraft/other small businesses.

Table 14.7

How NREGA Wage is Spent by the Households (%)

S.No.	*Heads on which the Money has been Spent*	*Gujarat-Tribal region N = 127*	*Gujarat-Non-Tribal region N = 70*	*Madhya Pradesh-Eastern belt N = 122*	*Maharash-tra-South-West N = 434*	*Maha-rashtra-Vidarbha N = 138*	*Total N=891*
1.	Domestic expenses, mostly food consumption	55.6	81.4	68.2	-	86.6	63.5
2.	Agricultural expenses	30.1	8.1	-	-	-	11.5
3.	Wages not received	4.6	0.0	1.73	-	0.80	2.2
4.	To buy raw materials	7.1	1.2	13.3	-	-	2.6
5.	Educational expenses	2.6	9.3	0.57	-	4.5	12.2
6.	Debt paying	-	-	6.4	-	0.9	2.7
7.	Health expense	-	-	4.6	-	2.7	2.2
8.	House repairing	-	-	5.2	-	4.5	3.0
	Total responses	231	88	190	-	116	625

Various Impacts of the Programme from Beneficiary's Point of View

None of the beneficiaries in the studied villages (except for Babrol and Karmdi-Chinagariya in Gujarat and Kanzara in Maharashtra) enjoy any direct material benefit to their household from the MGNREGA work. However they do acknowledge that the assets created are beneficial to the community as a whole, especially check dams, roads, and renovation of large ponds. Then again in Gujarat, the construction of check dams, wells and deepening of local ponds, and in Maharashtra, the construction of village roads, had directly benefitted the surveyed beneficiaries (see Table 14.8). However, we did not come across any example of beneficiaries acquiring land, live stock or any other income generating assets by themselves from the wage earnings. Among the studied villages, the migration is substantial in those of Gujarat and Vidarbha region of Maharashtra. It is seen among the sample households that they still send someone from their family to work outside because the remuneration is high. Over the years, MGNREGA opportunities has fallen (in Gujarat) and so has the strenuous physical work involved in the works of the scheme.

Table 14.8

The Benefits Received by the Households from the MGNREGA Work

Categories	*Gujarat-Tribal Region N = 127*	*Gujarat-Non-Tribal Region N = 70*	*Madhya Pradesh-Eastern Belt N = 122*	*Maharashtra-South-West N = 434*	*Maharashtra-Vidarbha N = 138*	*Total N = 891*
% of households did not respond	19.9	0.0	62.4	0.0	43.2	15.
No direct material benefit from the asset to the household	78.3	37.9	0.8	0.0	19.6	37.9
Economic benefit	18.6	58.3	73.7	0.0	19.6	47.7
Roads came closer to houses	3.1	0.8	7.5	0.0	3.4	4.2
Bath facility	0.0	2.3	0.0	0.0	0.0	0.6
Well recharge	0.0	0.8	3.0	0.0	2.7	1.9
Get employment	0.0	0.0	9.8	0.0	10.8	6.1
Construction of well for irrigation	0.0	0.0	3.0	0.0	0.0	0.8
Well construction	0.0	0.0	0.8	-	0.7	0.4
Sanitation work	0.0	0.0	1.5	-	-	0.4
Total number of responses	129	132	133	-	84	478

The economic impacts from the beneficiaries' point of view (in terms of responses) largely concentrated on increase in household income and improvement of overall economic conditions (see Table 14.9). Another major benefit as reported by the beneficiaries especially in case of Gujarat was that the additional wage income earned enabled them to purchase food grains.

Table 14.9

Economic Impacts of MGNREGA as Perceived by the Respondents

Heads on which the Money has been Spent	*Gujarat-Tribal Region N = 127*	*Gujarat-Non-Tribal Region N = 70*	*Madhya Pradesh-Eastern Belt N = 122*	*Maharashtra-South-West N = 434*	*Maharashtra-Vidarbha N = 138*	*Total N = 891*
Household income has increased	52.3	44.6	51.7	-	58.7	53.2
Improvement in overall economic conditions	33.8	41.9	32.8	-	35.6	31.5
Children's educational expenses	1.5	0.0	-	-	-	0.5
Purchasing food grains	7.7	5.4	1.7	-	1.0	3.3
Savings in the household	0.9	6.7	-	-	-	3.1
No need to go out for employment	3.8	1.4	2.5	-	4.7	6.4
Debt paid	-	-	11.3	-	-	3.1
Total responses	126	79	116	0	104	425

Source: Sample Survey.

The additional amount brought in the household has improved the economic condition, which in turn has a direct bearing on social status of the household. Table 14.10 does show for 70 per cent of households in the study areas the additional income has improved their social status. The opportunity for women to participate in public work is next major social gain from the programme.

Table 14.10

Social Impact of MGNAREGA as Perceived by the Sample Respondents

S. No.	*Social Impacts*	*Gujarat-Tribal Region N = 127*	*Gujarat-Non-Tribal Region N = 70*	*Madhya Pradesh-Eastern Belt N = 122*	*Maharash-tra-South-West N = 434*	*Maha-rashtra-Vidarbha N = 138*	*Total N=891*
1.	Social status has increased	85.8	89.5	59.4	-	80.8	61.2
2.	Equal status for males and females	5.5	0.0	10.6	-	0.0	4.0
3.	Women of the house started working outside	3.1	6.6	9.5	-	2.9	2.7
4.	Accepted as a member of the society	1.6	0.0	4.5	-	1.5	1.6
5.	Unique identity was created in the society	3.1	2.6	4.9	-	14.8	5.9
6.	Helpful in domestic expenses	0.9	1.3	6.1	-	0.0	12.0
7.	Asses to loan or debt	0.0	0.0	3.0	-	0.0	1.6
8.	Asses to borrowing	0.0	0.0	1.5	-	0.0	0.3
9.	Debt is paid	0.0	16.	1.5	-		
	Total responses	128	76	122	0	68	394

Source: Sample Survey.

The programme was helpful in providing greater benefits for the rural households in terms of increased school enrolment of their children, dairy units as well as banks. The exact pathway of the institutional link of households and MGNREGA in our study still needs further exploring. However, as per the data given, the additional income has helped the households to send their children regularly to the school. It has given them the job card which also doubles up as an identity card for the poor households who lacked any recognition from the government machinery. In some of the sample households, it is the only official identity card available.

Table 14.11

Institutional Impacts of MGNREGA as Perceived by the Sample Respondents

Institutional Impacts	*Gujarat-Tribal Region* N = 127	*Gujarat-Non-Tribal Region* N = 70	*Madhya Pradesh-Eastern Belt* N = 122	*Maharashtra-South-West* N = 434	*Maharashtra-Vidarbha* N = 138	*Total* N = 891
Entry in schools	67.2	62.3	54.7	-	21.4	56.8
Connected to milk producing dairies	11.4	3.3	0.0	-	0.0	5.8
New identity with the institution created	21.4	34.5	35.8	-	50.0	31.3
Knowledge about bank activity	0.0	0.0	9.4	-	2.4	2.2
Not perceived any social impact	0.0	0.0	0.0	-	26.2	4.0
Total responses	122	61	53	-	42	278

Source: Sample Survey.

As far as the environmental impact of MGNREGA is concerned, construction of check dams has helped to increase or at least stabilise the ground water level in these villages. The expansion of greenery surrounding these water bodies has improved the village atmosphere. Soil erosion has minimised and drinking water availability has improved in some areas (see Table 14.12).

However, people perceive that the overall food security concerns have not been properly addressed by the MGNREGA so far although earlier, some of the households were found to use the money earned to purchase food grains. It implies that the money earned from the activity is still inadequate to ensure food security for the households (Table 14.13).

Table 14.12

Environmental Impacts of MGNREGA as Perceived by the Sample Respondents

Environmental Impacts	*Gujarat-Tribal Region N = 127*	*Gujarat-Non-Tribal Region N = 70*	*Madhya Pradesh-Eastern Belt N = 122*	*Maharashtra-South-West N = 434*	*Maharashtra-Vidarbha N = 138*	*Total N = 891*
Water level rose due to check dams	44.4	64.2	11.7	0.0	2.3	24.2
Natural atmosphere improved	22.8	17.1	0.0	0.0	16.2	15.3
Due to road, less dirtiness	0.0	0.0	40.2	0.0	28.0	25.2
Soil erosion decreased	8.1	11.4	1.4	0.0	4.8	6.7
Water was utilised for farming	1.5	0.0	0.0	0.0	2.3	0.6
Well construction led to water storage	0.0	3.0	19.5	0.0	25.6	3.1
Used as drinking water	0.0	0.0	25.9	0.0	0.0	6.1
Forest development	17.6	2.9	1.3	0.0	20.8	15.6
Seedlings properly matured	6.6	1.4	0.0	0.0	0.0	3.4
Total responses	136	70	78	0	43	326

Source: Sample Survey.

Table 14.13

Impact of MGNREGA on Status of Food Security

Impact on Food Security	*Gujarat-Tribal Region N = 127*	*Gujarat-Non-Tribal Region N = 70*	*Madhya Pradesh-Eastern Belt N = 122*	*Maharashtra-South-West N = 434*	*Maharashtra-Vidarbha N = 138*	*Total N = 891*
Any change in food availability in the household due to working for NREGA						
(a) Increase	8.7	18.6	15.6	0.0	0.7	4.9
(b) Decrease	0.0	1.4	0.0	0.0	0.0	0.1
(c) No change	91.3	80.0	84.4	100.0	99.3	95.0
Change in food consumption in village due to work done for NREGA						
(a) Increase	7.9	17.1	14.8	0.0	9.4	5.9
(b) Decrease	0.8	0.0	0.0	0.0	0.0	0.1
(c) No change	91.3	82.9	85.2	100.0	90.6	93.9

Source: Sample Survey.

Table 14.14 shows that MGNREGA has otherwise no impact on agriculture or agriculture practices in studied villages, be it agricultural wages, labour supply and on poverty, indebtedness or general welfare. Given the inadequate availability of days of work under MGNREGA and a lower wage rate these macro variables in a village context can hardly show any improvement.

Conclusions and Policy Suggestions

Overall we found that the MGNREGA had varied experience across the three states. While in Gujarat the work opportunities had significantly gone down over the years, in other two states the work opportunity had increased. But in none of the states we found any household where one has worked for 100 days in reference year 2012-2013. The payment of wages were advertently delayed which discourage people to demand work from the scheme (exception being Kanzara where people work on daily wage rate). In all the 10 villages, the participation of women is very low compared to the national average. This is because women found the work very hard. In Maharashtra, the two villages of south Maharashtra had barely undertaken any work in MGNREGA for all these years as plenty

Table 14.14

Impact of MGNREGA on Cropping Pattern, Availability of Labour, Labour Wage, Cost of Agriculture, Poverty, Indebtedness, Purchasing Power, and General Welfare

Impact on Food security	*Gujarat-Tribal Region N = 127*	*Gujarat-Non-Tribal Region N = 70*	*Madhya Pradesh-Eastern Belt N = 122*	*Maharash-tra-South-West N = 434*	*Maharashtra-Vidarbha N = 138*
Has cropping pattern changed					
Yes	0.8	0.0	2.5	0.0	0.0
No	90.6	95.7	97.5	0.0	72.5
No idea	8.6	0.3	0.0	0.0	27.5
Availability of labour					
Increased	3.9	1.4	13.1	0.0	0.0
Decreased	3.1	4.3	2.5	100.0	0.0
No change	93.0	94.3	84.4	0.0	100.0
Increase in labour wage					
Yes	5.5	8.6	15.6	0.0	0.0
No change	93.7	91.4	84.4	100.0	100.0
No idea	0.8	0.0	0.0	0.0	0.0
Increase in production per unit of principal crop					
Yes, increased	1.6	0.0	5.7	0.0	0.0
Yes, decreased	3.9	0.0	0.0	0.0	1.4
No change	94.5	100.0	94.3	100.0	97.1
No idea	0.0	0.0	0.0	0.0	1.4
Protection against extreme poverty					
Yes	4.7	17.1	19.7	0.0	13.8
No	94.5	82.9	80.3	0.0	65.9
No idea	0.8	0.0	0.0	0.0	20.3
Indebtedness					
Yes	3.1	12.9	23.0	0.0	10.1
No	96.9	87.1	77.0	0.0	70.3
No idea	0.0	0.0	0.0	0.0	19.6
Additional purchasing power					
Yes	3.1	14.3	14.8	0.0	8.7
No	96.9	85.7	85.2	0.0	72.5
No idea	0.0	0.0	0.0	0.0	18.8
General welfare					
Yes	6.3	24.3	18.0	0.0	18.8
No	92.8	75.7	82.0	0.0	62.3
No idea	0.9	0.0	0.0	0.0	18.8

Note: Above questions are asked to all the sample households who had participated in MGNREGA at least in one year between 2006-07 and 2012-13.

Source: Sample Survey.

of alternative livelihood options and employment opportunities are available with the villagers in and around their residences. The governance of MGNREGA seems to be an issue with the respondents who are reportedly not aware of the process and had decided to take the work. Very few of them had knowledge of *gram sabhas* who are authorised to suggest the work to be undertaken in the village. People are also not satisfied with the delay of payments, lack of supervision and lack of transparency in the implementation. In the light of the empirical evidence shown here, the whole scheme undoubtedly needs to be reoriented. The focus must be on those regions where such intervention is needed. The role of institutions at grass-roots level must be improved with more accountability, and the leakages must be checked so as to revive the confidence of the people on MGNREGA as a social safety net, as was the case during it's incpetion.

References

Kannan, K.P. and Jan Breman (2013). *The Long Road to Social Security: Assessing the Implementation of National Social Security Initiatives for the Working Poor in India.* Oxford University Press.

Pankaj, A. and R. Tankha (2010). "Empowerment Effects of the NREGS on Women Workers: A Study in Four States", Economic and Political Weekly 45 (30): 45-55 (July).

Viswanathan, P.K. and Amit Mandal (2012). "NREGS as Instrument of Gender Mainstreaming: An Exploratory Analysis", *Man and Development* 34 (3): 17-36 (September).

Ministry of Rural Development Department of Rural Development, Government of India, New Delhi (2005). *Mahatma Gandhi Rural Emplyment Act, 2005: Report To the People*', Accessed on 22 February 2014 from: *http://nrega.nic.in/netnrega/WriteReaddata/circulars/Report_to_the_people_English2013.pdf*

Acknowledgements: This paper is work in progress and forms part of a larger study undertaken by the authors with support from the ICRISAT-VDSA project. The first and second authors gratefully acknowledge the support received from the ICRISAT for undertaking this study. We also acknowlegde the efficient research support rendered by the GIDR research team, particularly, Ms. Hema Iyengar and Mr. Ramnik Chavda. Authors are solely responsible for the errors and omissions that remain.

15

RAJANI V. SONTAKKE

Flagship Programmes: Impact, Problems and Challenges Ahead

With Special Reference to MGNREGA in Nagpur District

Introduction

Poverty is one of the main problems for the developing countries like India, especially at that time when we are globalised. After globalisation, India on one hand is experiencing 8 per cent growth rate since last decade, but on the other, the country is suffering from poverty and unemployment. Poverty indicates a condition in which a person fails to maintain his quality life along with physical and mental efficiency due to lack of livelihood opportunities. According to 2010 data from the United Nations Development Programme (UNDP), an estimated 37.2 per cent of Indians are living below the poverty line. A recent report by the Oxford Poverty and Human Development Initiative (OPHI) stated that eight Indian states (Assam, Bihar, Chhattisgarh, Jharkhand, Madhya Pradesh (MP), Odisha and Uttar Pradesh [UP]) have more poor than 26 poorest African nations combined, which totals to more than 410 million poor in the poorest African countries.

The Global Hunger Index (GHI) Report 2011, ranked India 45th amongst leading countries, where the GHI between 1996 and 2011 went up from 22.9 to 23.7 per cent, while 78 out of the 81 developing countries studied, including Pakistan, Nepal, Bangladesh, Vietnam, Kenya, Nigeria, Myanmar, Uganda, Zimbabwe and Malawi, succeeded in improving their hunger index. India ranked 136th in Medium Human Development Index (HDI) among 187 countries with 0.554 value in 2012, the average annual HDI growth being 0.64 in 2010-2012.

Governments world-wide have implemented various schemes for overcoming the problem of poverty and improving the welfare of the poor people. Although huge amounts have been spent on these programmes, the target have not been achieved.

The Government of India (GoI) in this respect took a historical step and launched Mahatma Gandhi National Rural Employment Guarantee Act (MGNREGA) on 1 April 2006, in 200 most backward districts in India, with the dual objective of poverty alleviation and employment generation. MGNREGA not only creates a right to work, but is also demand-driven and has an in-built target mechanism.

MGNREGA is the first tangible commitment to the poor wherein they can expect minimum wage without loss of dignity and can demand 100 days of guaranteed unskilled manual work per family. This is the first scheme in our history where the government has a statutory obligation to provide employment to every household, or if unable to do so, to provide unemployment allowance.

MGNREGA is the largest and most ambitious social security and public works programme in the world. MGNREGA came into action by merging National Food for Work Programme (NFFWP) (2004), Sampoorna Grameen Rozgar Yojna (SGRY) (2001), Jawahar Swarojgar Yojana (JSGY) (1999), Employment Assurance Scheme (EAS) (1993), Jawahar Rozgar Yojana (JRY) (1989), National Rural Employment Programme (NREP) (1980) and Rural Landless Employment Guarantee Programme (RLEGP) (1983).

The MGNREGA, 2005, provides right to work with dignity and a means to promote livelihood security in India's rural areas. In reality, the idea of MGNREGA is taken from Maharashtra's Employment Guarantee Scheme which was implemented in 1972-73 in order to fight acute drought in Maharashtra. This Act has a demand-driven framework and was first implemented in 200 most backward districts in 2006, and was later extended to all of the rural India in 2008. The Act provides 100 days of guaranteed unskilled manual work, and is supposed to have generated 12 billion person-days of work at a total expenditure of ₹166,760 crore since 2006 (MoRD, 2013: 288).

The provision of expenditure on MGNREGA was ₹39,100 crore, ₹40,000 crore, ₹33,000 crore, and ₹33,000 crore during the financial years 2009-10, 2010-11, 2011-12, 2012-13 and 2013-14 respectively (Yojana, 2013: 66). The provision for expenditure is around 1 per cent of the total budget.

Review of Literature

Both the positive and negative sides of the scheme have been explained by the researchers—some criticise it, whereas some have appreciated its success in reducing poverty and preventing acute distress during the times of drought. The Twelfth Five-Year Plan document says that there are problems in the MGNREGA because it involves huge expenditure that could have been spent more productively.

Since it was implemented across India, MGNREGA has been marked by a huge diversity in implementation and impact, and there is an extensive review of literature on the scheme. Research has been conducted on the patterns of uneven implementation (Dreze and Oldings, 2011), on the process of monitoring and auditing (Aiyer, 2010), on the effects of NREGA on wages (Berg et al., 2012); and on the scheme's poverty alleviation potential (Dreze and Khera, 2009), etc.

Shah (2008) emphasises that anti-poverty programmes to succeed demands more than cash transfers (whatever the degree of their directness). It requires that many challenges to be addressed simultaneously—strengthening people's institutions, extension of appropriate technology, skill development, leveraging markets for the poor and wise, and adequate public investment. Only then can sustainable livelihoods be generated and an end can be visualised for both poverty and anti-poverty programmes.

Ghosh (2009) stated that MGNREGA tends to be more socially inclusive as in that it involves women, SCs (scheduled castes) and STs (scheduled tribes) as workers in the scheme. Greater participation of women in the NREGS, particularly in some states, is clearly a positive indicator of the inclusive potential of the programme. However, NREGA's potential has still not been achieved completely. He suggested that capacity building and administrative support at local government levels are key elements for better implementation of NREGS.

Birner *et al.* (2010) indicated the problems of NREGA—governance issues in the NREGA such as implementation, elite capture on planning of projects, exclusion in issuing of job cards, lack of awareness and capacity among rural citizens, misappropriation of funds, lack of capacity due to staff shortages and absence of training—are creating obstacles in fulfilling the objectives of NREGA.

Research Methodology

Statement of the Problem

The present research study analyses and discusses the impact, problems and challenges of MGNREGA with regard to rural livelihood in Nagpur district.

Objective of the Study

i) To study socio-economic background of the respondents working under MGNREGA.
ii) To analyse how MGNREGA is helpful in economic redistribution and social equity, and also the usefulness of this scheme for women.
iii) To analyse employment generation opportunities in Nagpur district arising out of the implementation of MGNREGA.
iv) To study asset creation through MGNREGA.

Hypotheses

i) It is hypothesised that the poor rural people are not utilising MGNREGA employment opportunities due to their non-competence.
ii) Women are not participating in works conducted under MGNREGA due to contractor's dominations.

Methodology

Universe of the Study

The present research study was carried out in the rural area of Nagpur district.

Sampling Procedure

Nagpur district is divided into 14 blocks. However, under MGNREGA only rural area are covered, therefore, 13 blocks in rural Nagpur were selected for the study.

This study is based on the impact of MGNREGA on the rural area's of the Nagpur district. Though urban Nagpur is well developed, the people in the rural Nagpur area are still struggling for their livelihood. This study is based on the primary data collected by conducting survey and interview across the 13 rural blocks of the Nagpur district. This data is analysed to understand the reasons for the improving performance of NREGA scheme.

Nagpur district has Bhivapur, Hingna, Kamptee, Katol, Kuhi, Kalameshwar, Mouda, Nagpur (Rural), Narkhed, Parsheoni, Ramtek, Savner and Umred blocks, and the total number of *gram panchayats* (GPs) are 795. Ten (10) per cent of the GPs were selected. For this present study, stratified sampling method is used.

Sample Size

A sample of 837 MGNREGA beneficiaries from the 13 rural blocks of Nagpur district were selected through multistage stratified sampling method. Questionnaire and relevant questions were framed for the survey.

Data Collection

To satisfy the objectives, the primary data was collected from the 13 blocks, with the help of a structured questionnaire. Structured informal interviews were also conducted with selected beneficiaries and the observation method was used. Statistical tool (percentage) has been used to draw meaningful inferences from the study.

Performance Evaluation of MGNREGA Scheme in the Study Area

In its third phase, MGNREGA was introduced in Maharashtra to tackle the problem of poverty. This was done to help the poor families cross over the poverty line by raising their income level with the assistance of income generating assets provided under the scheme. But independent evaluation studies conducted in Nagpur district revealed some glaring deficiencies in the implementation of this scheme. An analysis of the findings of present study has been made for the performance evaluation of MGNREGA scheme.

Discussion and Analysis

Nagpur district has 14 blocks. Responses were obtained from 837 respondents across 13 blocks of the district. When NREGA was launched in the financial year (FY) 2008-09, the labourers did not respond to this scheme because of low wages being offered as well as lack of relevant information. Therefore, its performance was very poor. Only Umred and Bhivapur *talukas* had taken up few works, but those projects were not completed. Presently, NREGA work has been taken up—even though it is at a small level—in all the 795 GPs under the 13 rural blocks.

The study was carried out to observe the impact and effectiveness of this scheme on the lives of respondents, by the way of using questionnaire, in-depth interview method and observation. Socio-economic characteristics of selected respondents were assessed.

A survey was conducted with 837 MGNREGA respondents which included information on their occupations, incomes, caste, education, debt and sources of credit.

Block-Wise Sample Size in Nagpur District under MGNREGA

Across 13 blocks of the Nagpur district, 837 respondents were selected. There were 112 respondents from Bhivapur block, 42 from Hingna block, 88 from Kalameshwar block, 47 from Kamptee block, 59 from Katol block, 37 from Kuhi block, 66 from Mouda block, 39 from Nagpur (Rural) block, 49 from Narkhed block, 81 from Parsheoni block, 62 from Ramtek block, 25 from Savner block, and 130 from Umred block. Out of the total respondents, 556 were male and 281 were female.

Table 15.1 depicts the spread of the respondents across the blocks. It was found that four blocks—Bhivapur, Kalameshwar, Parsheoni and Umred—have most respondents as the works taken up under NREGA was at large scale therein. Katol, Mouda and Ramtek have middle-level work, whereas Hingna, Kamptee, Kuhi, Nagpur (rural), Narkhed and Savner had very few works taken up under NREGA.

Table 15.1

Block-wise Break Up of the Sample

Sr. No.	*Name of the Block*	*Total No. of Respondents*	*Male*	*Female*
1	Bhivapur	112	70	42
2	Hingna	42	19	23
3	Kalameshwar	88	65	23
4	Kamptee	47	29	18
5	Katol	59	37	22
6	Kuhi	37	28	09
7	Mouda	66	48	18
8	Nagpur (Rural)	39	19	20
9	Narkhed	49	34	05
10	Parsheoni	81	66	15
11	Ramtek	62	26	36
12	Savner	25	14	11
13	Umred	130	91	39
	Total	837	556	281

Source: Primary data collected from the field as on 2011-12 and 2012-13.

Socio-economic Background of the Respondents

A total of 837 respondents from 77 GPs were selected across 13 blocks of the Nagpur district. Out of these total respondents, 556 (66%) were male and 281 (34%) were female. Since males and females form equal parts of the economic development process and provisions made, i.e., one-third reservation for women under MGNREGA, the overall picture shows that Nagpur district is giving full opportunity to the women respondents. Age-wise break-up of the respondents shows that highest number of respondents, i.e., 321 (38.35%) under the age group of 36-45 were working under MGNREGA. Out of these, 214 (38.51%) were males and 101 (35.94%) were females. The lowest number of respondents were under the age group of 56 and above—23 (2.74%) were men and 3 (1.01%) were women. The research study points out that of the 837 respondents, 97 per cent were labourers and 3 per cent (25) were marginal farmers. The marginal farmers were doing daily wages work due to lack of irrigation facilities available in their area. As Nagpur district is a part of Vidarbha region that has always faced drought and flood situation, the respondents were involved with MGNREGA as the last resource because of unavailability of no other jobs in the region. During the survey, the joint family system has been seen to persist and 39.9 per cent families were found in the size of 5-8. Caste and category always play an important role in rural lives. Category-wise share of the respondents presents the number of 213 SCs (25.45%), 33 STs (3.94%), 190 OBCs (22.70%) and 331 General category (39.55%). The most surprising fact that showed up was that 70 respondents (8.36%) who were adivasis had participated under MGNREGA, because no other livelihood opportunities were available in rural Nagpur. MGNREGA had a positive impact on all the categories in way of giving them job opportunities in their village. All sample beneficiaries under the research study had their own house on their own land, although their houses were *kuchha*, semi-*pucca* and hut-like, yet, they felt safe in their own house.

Eighty per cent of the land owners have land of 2 acres or smaller in size. Therefore, even with their own land they found it very difficult to meet the daily needs as most of the land was non-irrigated.

Findings

Debt Burden

A positive impact that has been noticed on the field is that the respondents wants to be free from the debt trap. Five years earlier, respondents were taking loan even for their daily needs from *savkar*. But NREGA has changed this picture. Out of the 837 respondents, 287 (34.29%) have taken loan from public sector banks. Since they have opened their account in the bank or post offices, it has become easy to take a loan from these branches. Hence, the dependency for loan on *savkar* is totally diminished. Table 15.2 illustrates the debt burden of the respondents.

Table 15.2

Loan Burden of the Respondents

Loan Burden	Yes %	No. of Respondents	No %	No. of Respondents
	34.29	287	65.71	550

Source: Primary data

General Information about MGNREGA

During the field survey, it was found that 100 per cent of the respondents knew about MGNREGA, but not right from its beginning. MGNREGA was implemented in Nagpur district from 1 April 2008. But villagers were not aware about this scheme. Those who knew about this scheme, had registered their names under MGNREGA, but could not get any work. Consequently, they lost their hopes of getting work under NREGA. After two years of its performance, the Government of Maharashtra woke up and started pressurising the GPs to enrol maximum number of workers under the scheme. *Gram Sevaks* were easily escaping their responsibility by saying that labourers were unwilling to work under NREGA at lower wage rates. Therefore, the performance of NREGA could not be improved. This is the tragedy of other Indian social welfare schemes too and as a result, these schemes are rolled down after some time, or remain on paper only.

Source of Information

During the survey, the question: How do you get information about MGNREGA? was asked to the respondents to know the sources of information for MGNREGA, and it was found that 395 (47.19%) respondents got the information from the *Panchayat Samiti*, 412 (49.22%) from the GPs and 30 (3.58%) from their neighbours and friends. It has been observed that media is not playing a leading role in making people aware about NREGA. In reality, media can play a vital role in enhancing public awareness about the government schemes. It was found that people themselves went to the *Panchayat Samiti* or GP office, where they are able to get information about the scheme. But it is the responsibility of the GPs and Blocks to make the villagers aware of various schemes being offered. Unfortunately, the same has not happened in the study area (See Table 15.3).

Table 15.3

Source of Information about MGNREGA

Sr. No.	*Source of Information*	*No. of Respondents*	*% of Respondents*
1.	*Panchayat Samiti*	395	47.19
2.	*Gram Panchayat*	412	49.22
3.	Media	—	—
4.	Neighbour/Friend	30	3.58
	Total	837	100

Source: Primary data.

Sabhas and *Melawas* can be arranged by *Panchayat Samities* and GPs to make the villagers aware about NREGA. This can ensure that maximum number of villagers can be benefitted and the target of poverty alleviation can be achieved.

Time Taken for Getting Information About NREGA

Timely information regarding any government scheme given to the poor effectively leads to better implementation of the scheme, which allows them to reap the associated benefits. While implementing NREGA, it was expected that the relevant information will be sent door to door to each and every poor household. But during the survey, it was found that out of 837 respondents, 186 (22.22%) respondents got information about NREGA just after its implementation but could not get work, 253 (30.23%) respondents got information about NREGA in the next successive year i.e., 2011-12, and 237 (28.32%) respondents got information in 2013-14 and the remaining 161 (19.24%) got information in the year 2013-14 (see Table 15.4).

Registration for Work Under NREGA

The implementation of NREGA begins with the registration of a household/family and distribution of a job card. According to the guidelines of NREGA (section no. 5.1.3), every individual/household has the right to get a job card.

To register under NREGA, a household has to mention the names of all the adult members of the family who are willing to work under the scheme, including age, sex and category, in an application. A prescribed format is to be followed. But even on a plain paper, a household can apply for registration. An oral application can also be accepted and his or her name will be registered like other applicants.

In the study area, 837 (100%) respondents have registered their names to work under NREGA. Thirty-four (4.1%) respondents took others' help to register their names and large number of respondents (803 or 95.94%) registered their names by themselves (see Table 15.5).

Table 15.4

Time Taken to Gather Information About NREGA

Time Taken	*No. of Respondents*	*Percentage*
2010-11	186	22.22
2011-12	253	30.23
2012-13	237	28.32
2013-14	161	19.24
Total	837	100

Source: Primary data.

Table 15.5

Ways taken to Register Names under NREGA

Registration done by	*No. of Respondents*	*%*
Self	803	95.94
Mediator	34	4.1
Total	837	100

Source: Primary data by field survey.

Job Cards After Registration

It is government's responsibility to issue a job card within 15 days after verification of the application and the same is valid for five years. Job card is a very important document through which transparency can be maintained. Hence, the job card should stay with the beneficiary. It is an offence on the part of the beneficiaries to keep the job card with anybody else. But it was seen that more often, the beneficiaries did not have their job cards with them. The time taken to issue a job card is illustrated in Table 15.6

Table 15.6

Time Taken for Issuing Job Card

Sr. No.	*Time taken for issuing job card*	*No. of Respondents*	*%*
1.	8 to 15 days	364	43.49
2.	16 days to 1 month	345	41.22
3.	More than 1 month	103	12.35
4.	No job cards	25	2.99
	Total	837	100

Source: Primary Data

During the survey, the most interesting thing found was that, 43.49 per cent respondents got their job cards within 15 days. Although they were issued a job card, not a single respondent was found with her/his job card. Their job cards were in the GP office. As a result, no entry of working days could be made on the cards. 41.22 per cent respondents got their job cards within 16 days to 1 month, and 12.35 per cent of them received their cards after more than 1 month. It was also seen that no rules and regulations were followed by the GPs.

Types of Works Under NREGA

Unskilled manual labour work is given under NREGA. The main aim of the model of this scheme was to create infrastructure and permanent assets in the rural area. Keeping this in view, nine types of works were allotted under this scheme. In the surveyed area, only six types of works were done under this scheme from 2011-12 to 2012-13. Table 15.7 shows the work done under NREGA.

In the survey area, majority of the workers (419 or 50.06%) were working on road construction that is called *Pandhan Rasta*. All-weather road construction is to be conducted under this scheme. But there was no monitoring agency to monitor the construction of these roads. These were 249 (29.75%) respondents doing nursery work, 35

(4.18%) were engaged in the construction of *shouchalay* (toilets), etc., 8 of them (0.96%) were engaged in building the Rajiv Gandhi Seva Kendra, 123 (14.69%) were working on constructing irrigation wells and only 03 (0.36%) respondents were doing forestry work.

Nursery work had been undertaken in every GP because it can be showcased whenever the government authorities enquired about NREGA work. The government has targeted 100 crore tree plantation in the year 2011-12 in Maharashtra, but because of poor implementation, many plants and nurseries were left low on oxygen.

Table 15.7

Types of Work Under NREGA

Sr. No.	*Type of Work*	*No. of Respondents*	*Percentage*
1	Nursery	249	29.75
2	Road Construction (*Pandhan Rasta*)	419	50.06
3	Construction	35	4.18
4	Rajiv Gandhi Seva Kendra	08	0.96
5	Irrigation Wells	123	14.69
6	Forestry work	03	0.36
	Total	837	100

Source: Primary data.

Time Taken for Getting Work after Registration and Application for Demanding Work

During the survey, it was found that beneficiaries did not know about the application process for demanding work and that the GP is liable to give work within 15 days from the submission of the work application. A count of 93.18 per cent respondents (780) were below SSC (secondary school certificate) educated. Mostly primary educated, the respondents were unknown of all these rules. Rojgar Sewak took disadvantage of their ignorance.

It is mandatory that after registering household names under NREGA, work must be provided within 15 days. And if it is not possible to provide work within 15 days, the GP is liable to pay an unemployment allowance. Unemployment allowance is the right of NREGA worker (*www.nrega.nic.in*).

On overall basis in Nagpur district, only 21 per cent (176) respondents got work within 15 days, 49.7 per cent (416) got work in 16 days to 1 month and 30.5 per cent (255) respondents got work within 3-6 months. There is a big gap in the time taken for registration, getting a job card and getting work in the survey area (see Table 15.8). Since a large number of respondents (97%) are daily wagers, care should be taken to provide them with job under NREGA well in time so as to save them from starvation or taking loan.

Table 15.8

Time Taken for Getting Work

Sr. No.	*Time Taken For Getting Work*	*No. of Respondents*	*% of Respondents*
1.	Within 15 days	176	21
2.	16 Days to 1 month	416	49.7
3.	More than 1 month (nearly 3-6 months)	255	30.5
	Total	837	100

Source: Primary data.

Time Taken for Getting Wages

Of the total 837 respondents, 306 (36.56%) received wages within 2-4 weeks of work taken and remaining 531 (63.44%) reported that it took them more than 4 weeks to receive wages.

Delay in payment of wages is the main reason for quitting NREGA works. It was found that respondents left their jobs even before completing 100 days of work.

NREGA payments are made in cash through banks and post offices. Therefore, 100 per cent respondents have opened their accounts in public sector banks. It was expected that transparency will be maintained if the wages are paid through banks or post offices. Yet, it was found that bank accounts were opened by the mediators who also withdraw their amount. Some of the respondents did not even know about their balance amount or the amount of wages that was deposited. The mediators took their signatures on the withdrawal slip and only a little amount from the whole payment was given to the respondents.

The respondents were happy that their earnings were deposited in bank and bank officials could not do any mismanagement with their accounts.

Table 15.9

Time Taken for Payment of Wages

Time	*No. of Respondents*	*%*
2-4 weeks	306	36.56
More than 4 weeks	531	63.44
Total	837	100

Source: Primary Data.

Wages Paid for Other Works (Except NREGA Work)

According to the survey, if the labourers work outside NREGA, they can get more than ₹150 per day as wages. 44.32 per cent respondents claimed to get ₹170 to ₹225 per day. 370 respondents (44.21%) got wages less than ₹145 per day and 96 (11.47%) respondents got wages equal to or less than ₹140 (see Table 15.10).

Table 15.10

Wages Outside NREGA

Amount in ₹	*No. of Respondents*	*Percentage*
₹ 127	96	11.47
₹<145	370	44.21
₹ 150 and above	371	44.32
Total	837	100

Source: Primary data.

Income Expenditure of the Respondents

Most of the respondents spend their money on daily needs. Eighty per cent of the total income of the respondents is spent on daily needs as they have the burden of dependents. Nearly 3-4 persons are dependent on the respondent including mother, father and widow or unmarried sisters. A very small proportion (5%) spend on their children's education and things like stationary, school bags, uniform, etc. Male respondents spend 15 per cent of the wages on their habits, like liquor, tobacco, *bidi*, *matka*, etc. Sometimes they borrow money from their wives or forcefully snatch away cash or gold ornaments. These poor people have ration cards, but they stated those to be useless as in spite of presenting the cards at the shops, they often return empty-handed. They have to purchase grains from open market, which is not affordable for them. The government run PDS (public distribution system) facility is to facilitate the poor to purchase grain at lower prices, but they have not benefitted from this system. Therefore, much amount is spent on their daily needs. If the PDS scheme is properly implemented in villages, people can save a considerable amount of their wages and the saved money can be spent in making their lives easier and better.

Table 15.11

Income Expenditure of the Respondents

Sr. no.	*Items*	*Money Spent (%)*
1.	Daily Needs (Kirana, grain, vegetables, cloths, relative functions, festivals, deaths of related persons, etc.)	80
2.	Education of children (stationery, uniform, etc.)	5
3.	Respondents habits(liquor, tobacco, *bidi, pan, cigarette, mutka, jua*, etc.)	15
	Total	100

Source: Primary Data.

Unemployment Allowance

It is strictly mentioned in NREGA section 7(5) that, "The unemployment allowance shall be made no later than 15 days from the date on which it becomes due for payment."

The following provisions are made under unemployment allowance:

- Unemployment allowance should not be less than one-fourth of the wages for first three days and after that not less than half of the wages.

- It is the main responsibility of Block Development Officer (BDO) to pay unemployment allowance on time and it is paid by the state government.
- Unemployment allowance also should be paid within 15 days of the expected day.

In the case of delay in payment of unemployment allowance, ₹1,500-₹3,000 should be paid as compensation under Wages Distribution Act, 1936.

Then again, it at times takes nearly 2-6 months to get a job. But since the respondents were not aware of the unemployment allowance, they did not dare to complain against any officials. During the survey, it has been noticed that neither at GP level nor at Block level, was a single *sabha* who was responsible for spreading knowledge about unemployment allowance.

According to the MGNREGA Guidelines 7.3.1, if a person has been registered and applied for work under MGNREGA, and he or she could not get work within 15 days from the date on which work is requested, he or she has a right to get unemployment allowance. This provision is only made in the NREGA. No other scheme has this provision of providing unemployment allowance for lack of work. Yet, irrespective of such a provision, not a single beneficiary was aware it.

Wages to Female Workers under NREGA

According to the section 7.1.2 of NREGA operational guidelines, equal wages shall be paid to both men and women workers and the provisions of the Equal Remuneration Act, 1976, shall be complied with (*www.nrega.nic.in*).

As a rural wage employment programme, MGNREGA recognised the relevance of incorporating gender equity and empowerment in its design. Various provisions under the Act and its guidelines aim to ensure that women have equitable and easy access to work, decent working conditions, equal payment of wages and their representation in decision-making bodies is assured (*www.nrega.nic.in*).

Through the survey, a positive impact of MGNREGA on women respondents was found. In a survey area, women specially widows and *paritaktyas* stated that MGNREGA was helping them to avoid hunger or starvation. A proportion of 33.6 per cent women had participated under NREGA.

Women were willing to work under NREGA throughout the year because that would allow them to help their family, regardless of inappropriate working conditions and unequal payment of wages. When the survey was conducted in March 2012, 78.65 per cent (221) women used to get wages of ₹145 and in April 2013, 21.35 per cent (60) women were getting wages of ₹162 per day (see Table 17.12) Although equal wages were said to be paid to women, reality was that less wages were paid to women in the surveyed area.

Table 15.12

Wages to Women Respondents under NREGA

Wages in ₹	*No. of Women Respondents*	*Percentage*
₹ 127	—	—
₹ 145	221	78.65
₹ 162	60	21.35
Total	281	100

Source: Primary Data.

Work Site Facilities

According to the MGNREGA guidelines, it is mandatory to have basic facilities such as safe drinking water, first-aid kits, shades during the period of rest and crechē facility near the work sites. But during the survey, no such facilities were found to be arranged near the work site. Even drinking water was not available at work site. While discussing work site facilities like shade, some of the respondents claimed that the nearby trees were treated as shade shelters. Thus, the manipulation done by the local implementing agencies, as well as absence of any monitoring mechanism, resulted in the prevalence of unsafe and sub-standard working conditions.

Social Audit

The operational guidelines detailed the procedure of social audit forums to be held by *Gram Sabha* on NREGA works on a six months basis. But social audit was never held in the villages. Nearly all the villagers were not even aware about the concept of social audit.

Role of Gram Rojgar Sevak

Besides the GP Head and Panchayat Secretary, there is a provision under NREGA guidelines to appoint a *Gram Rojgar Sevak*, in order to make the NREGA activities more effective. *Gram Rojgar Sevak* has the only responsibility of creating NREGA work. In this scheme, two persons from each village are recruited to assist the implementation of MGNREGA. Organising cardholders to start a job, writing muster rolls, checking measurement, payment of labours, etc., are the duties assigned to the *Gram Rozgar Sevak*. However, these selected persons are neither trained nor made aware about the policies of NREGA.

Gram Rojgar Sevak is an important link between villagers and NREGA. As the *Rojgar Sevak* gets 2 per cent commission, he brings more labourers from villages for NREGA work without making them aware about entry in job cards, signing in muster roll, payment of wages, measurement of the work etc.

Poor Quality of Works

There was no proper execution of works. Hence, it was a matter of great concern that throughout the GP, the approved works were not publicly displayed. It was revealed by the villagers that there was no *gram sabha* meeting regarding the activities of NREGA. A majority of the people were ignorant about *gram sabha* meetings, which reflected non-participation of villages or community in decision-making. NREGA guidelines permit the execution of road project providing all-weather access in rural areas. However, during field work, it was observed that the road remained *kaccha* and incomplete, and was not able to provide all-weather access.

Conclusion

A very slow rise in the number of respondents under this scheme in 2012-13 proves that, in rural Nagpur, MGNREGA is being implemented with a low degree of success. Even then it has had a positive impact on the rural poor, and poor women in particular.

The state level policy decision include the imposition of top-down implementation targets, the development of administrative support structures, the issuing of job cards in individual workers' name, the continuation of weekly payments in cash, the relaxation of work loads over time, and the ban on the use of materials and contracts. This study suggest that the respondents should have their job cards (including their name, photograph and job card number) so as to identify them properly and avoid payment to fake workers. For proper implementation of this scheme, political will is needed so that productive assets can be created. MGNREGA works have led to enhanced productivity and regeneration of the natural resource base, thereby further strengthening its potential for generating environmental benefits. The transparency and accountability in the system is greater. MGNREGA has great potential to reduce poverty and create permanent assets. There is no denying that MGNREGA is conceptually a very important national programme. But at the implementation stage it is mired with widespread corruption and low level of fund utilisation. It has not succeeded in creating sufficient productive assets for strengthening rural infrastructure. The scheme is losing its enthusiasm and momentum. Proper implementation and timely monitoring of the projects or works and inclusion of transparency and social audit must be done time to time, thereby ensuring that MGNREGA can change the lives of rural poor as well as rural India as a whole. With proper implementation and regular auditing, the scheme can become a positive step towards alleviating poverty from India.

Suggestions

i) The provision of daily wage payment should be made so that more respondents choose to join MGNREGA.

ii) A proper monitoring agency should be involved.

iii) More and more work should be added, so that greater number of people is covered under this programme, which will help in developing rural areas.

iv) Awareness level should be increased by involving National Service Scheme (NSS) students, post graduation students, teachers, Anganwadi sevika, ASHAs (accredited social health activists) and SHGs (self-help groups).

v) Social audit should be strictly conducted from GP to Central level.

References

Aiyer, Y. and S. Samji (2009). "Guaranteeing Good Governance: Understanding the Effectiveness of Accountability in NREGA", in *NREGA: Design, Process and Impact.* New Delhi: MoRD, GoI.

Berg, Erlend, Sambit Bhattacharyya, Rajasekhar Durgam and Manjula Ramachandra (2012). "Can Rural Public Work Affect Agriculture Wage:Evidence from India", *Working Papers* WPS/2012-15. Centre for the Study of African Economies (CSAE).

Birner et al. (2010). "How to Overcome the Governance Challenges of Implementing NREGA", *Discussion Paper* 00963. International Food Policy Research Institute (IFPRI)

Dreze, Jean (2011). "Breaking the Nexus of Corruption", in R. Khera (ed.), *The Battle for Employment Guarantee.* New Delhi: Oxford University Press. pp.241-50.

Dreze, J. and K. Oldings (2011). "Employment Guarantee and the Right to Work", in R. Khera (ed.), *In the Battle for Employment Guarantee.* New Delhi: Oxford University press. pp.21-43.

Dreze, J. and R. Khera (2009). *Group Management of NREGA Work: The Jallor Experiment.* New Delhi: Delhi School of Economics.

Ghosh, J. (2009). "Equity and Inclusion through Public Expenditure: The Potential of the NREGS", Paper for *International Conference on NREGA.* 21-22 January. New Delhi.

Hirway, I. *et al.* (2012). *NREGA & Women's Empowerment.* New Delhi: UN Women South Asia.

Khera, R. (2008). "Employment Guarantee Act", *Economic & Political Weekly* 43(30), 30 August.

Khera, R. and N. Nayak (2009). "Women Worker's Perception of the National Rural Employment Guarantee Act", *Economic & Political Weekly* 44(43), 29 October.

Raabe, Katharina, Regina Birner, Madhushree Sekher, K.G. Gayathridevi, Amrita Shilpi and Eva Schiffer (2010). "How to Overcome the Governance Challenge of Implementing NREGA: Insights from Bihar Using Process-Influence Mapping'", *Discussion Paper* 00963. Development Strategy and Governance Division. International Road Policy Research Institute (IFPRI).

MoRD (2013). *Annual Report. New Delhi:* GoI. *www.rural.nic.in*

Rizwan, Islam (2013). "Economic Growth, Employment and Poverty Reductions: Evidence and Lessons", *Yojna* 57: 29, October.

Shah, Mihir (2008). "Direct Cash Transfer No Panacea by Itself", *The Hindu.* 20 September.

Shah, Mihir, D. Banerji and P.S. Vijayshankar (1998). *India's Drylands: Tribal Societies & Development through Environmental Regeneration.* New Delhi: Oxford University Press.

Tapliyal, Nivedita (2013). "Land Management Can Improve Rural Economy", *Kurukshetra* 6(5), March.

Others:

Daily Lokmat, 28 June 2012.

India Human Development Report 2011: Towards Social Inclusion. New Delhi, Oxford University Press.

Yojana 57: 66, March 2013.

Sameeksha, MGNREGA (2006-2012), *A Collection of Research of NREGA*, 2005. GoI, MORD. Orient Black Swan. *www.nrega,nic.in*

16

ARUNA KUMAR MALIK

Participatory Process to Implement Backward Regions Grant Fund (BRGF)

Critical Analysis of Institutional Arrangements

Background

The BRGF was launched in 2006-07. Implemented by the Ministry of Panchayati Raj and the Planning Commission, it subsumes the Rashtriya Sam Vikas Yojana (RSVY), which was launched in 2003-04 and was being administered by the Planning Commission. BRGF covers 250 districts in 27 states, of which 232 districts fall under the purview of Part IX and Part IX-A of the Constitution dealing with *panchayats* and the municipalities respectively. The remaining 18 districts are covered by other local government structures, such as Autonomous District and Regional Councils under the Sixth Schedule of the Constitution and state-specific arrangements as in the case of Nagaland and the hill areas of Manipur. The fund has two components:

i) The districts component covering 250 districts (including 147 RSVY districts), implemented by the Ministry of Panchayati Raj

ii) Special plans for Bihar and the Kalahandi, Bolangir, and Koraput (KBK) districts of Orissa, implemented by the Planning Commission

The districts component of BRGF has the following objectives:

i) To fill critical infrastructure gaps and other development needs not adequately met through existing programmes.

ii) Capacity building and professional support for promoting participatory planning, decision-making, implementation, and monitoring at *panchayat* and municipality levels that reflect local felt needs.

iii) Converge through supplementary infrastructure and capacity building, the substantial existing developmental inflows into these districts.

The districts component of the BRGF has two funding windows:

i) The Capability Building Fund (CBF).

ii) A substantial Untied Grant (UG).

The CBF of ₹250 crore per annum (at ₹1 crore per district) is to be used primarily to build capacity in planning, implementation, monitoring, accounting, and improving accountability and transparency, which would include arrangements for contracting and outsourcing.

The UG is to be used by *panchayats* and ULBs (urban local bodies) for filling critical gaps which are vital for development and which remain even after other major interventions, identified through the participative planning processes have been implemented. The Plan prepared by *panchayats* and ULBs and consolidated by DPCs (district planning committees) is to be considered and approved by a high powered committee headed by the State Chief Secretary and consisting of, *inter alia*, the Development Commissioner, Planning Secretary, State Secretary of Panchayati Raj, State Urban Development Secretary, state secretaries incharge of sectors concerned, a representative of the Ministry of Panchayati Raj, and State Plan Adviser of the Planning Commission as well as other Government of India nominees.

The allocation criteria of the UG across districts is as follows:

i) Every district receives a minimum of ₹10 crore per annum as UGs.

ii) Fifty per cent of the balance allocation under the scheme is allocated on the basis of the share of the population of the district in the total population of all the backward districts.

iii) The remaining 50 per cent is distributed on the basis of the share of the area of the district in the total area of backward districts.

iv) RSVY districts continue to receive funds as per RSVY norms till the entire amount of ₹45 crore (plus the existing monitoring fee) is released to each district. However, by 31

December 2009, all the 147 RSVY districts had received their total entitlement of ₹45 crore each.

Each state is to indicate the normative formula that will be used for the allocation of BRGF funds to each *panchayat* and ULB (excluding capital cities/cities with a population of 1 million). The components that go into the formula may include the following:

i) Any index prepared by the states to measure backwardness.
ii) Addressing specific district-wise priorities identified as described by the guidelines of the Planning Commission on district planning.
iii) A reasonable percentage of funds may be earmarked as performance-based incentives

Shrimati Pratibha Patiba, the erstwhile President of India, in her address to Parliament on 4 June 2009 spoke of "restructuring the Backward Regions Grant Fund, which overlaps with other development investment, to focus on decentralised planning and capacity building of elected *panchayat* representatives." The government is currently engaged in this exercise. Meanwhile, a World Bank study on BRGF across eight states has just been completed.

Drawing on these sources and based on the short experience of the implementation of BRGF across the country, certain issues need to be highlighted:

i) The volume of funds provided under BRGF is insufficient to bridge development gaps and address backwardness. Most *gram panchayats* (GPs) get ₹ 2-6 lakh per annum. Increasing the BRGF allocation is desirable because the distribution of the amount allocated leads to very small amounts for each unit and these amounts lead to 'disinterest' and lack of attention to the other two objectives of improving district planning and capacity building.
ii) BRGF districts with large populations are at a disadvantage since they get very low per capita funding. This is primarily a result of the large proportion of the development grant, which is allocated equally to all districts regardless of their size.
iii) The best way to improve the targeting of BRGF is to move the focus of intervention downwards towards the block. There

are many instances of relatively advanced districts with pockets of backwardness within. This is especially the case with tribal blocks.

iv) The BRGF guidelines speak of a performance-based funding system but this has rarely been followed as a result of which there are few incentives for improved performance. What appears to have happened is that in a quest for flexibility, outputs have been compromised badly. The ideal approach would be to lay down nationally, in consultation with states, the outcomes of a given number of parameters in each district, provide the funds as untied, and periodically monitor and later evaluate the implementation.

v) In many states, PRIs have become 'petitioners' to the DPCs, which carry ultimate discretion. Most of the time, the DPC technical secretariat is very weak or non-existent. Most examples of convergence are of PRIs using BRGF funds as bandages to fix deficiencies of other schemes, rather than as a relationship of positive synergy. PRIs/ULBs are unlikely to play a leading role in integrated planning when the discretionary budget is dwarfed by other players. DPCs should focus on technical support and not control PRI/ULB priorities. The best way would be to specify a list of non-eligible expenditures (negative list) prior to the start of planning and then allow PRIs/ULBs full discretion to allocate BRGF funds within the provided menu (positive list). It may be prudent to specify that investments should be in public services and infrastructure, rather than in private projects, which benefit only a few individuals. It would be better to undertake an ex-post monitoring of compliance and audit, rather than an ex-ante approval in each instance, which undermines PRI/ULB autonomy. An earlier start to the planning process with a clear budget envelope and planning calendar would be of great help to PRIs/ULBs.

While these issues are important, a major bottleneck in the planning and budgeting processes is the flow of funds, which is impeding utilisation of BRGF funds. There is backlog of one financial year (in some places two years) in releases from the Centre to the states due to the layers of 'approval or review/veto' of development plans. Subsequent disbursements are further delayed by the current requirement of submission of Utilisation Certificates (UCs) (100% for year T-2 and 75% for year T-1).

A major complication is created by the fact that well-functioning PRIs/ULBs, which utilise and account for funds speedily, have to wait for full compliance by their slower peers. Requiring 100 per cent UC for any year means that even one laggard can affect the release for the entire district. Table 16.1 shows significant delays in some states, while others show that timely disbursals are indeed possible down the line.

Table 16.1

Delay in Getting Funds

State	*From Centre to State*	*From State to PRIs/ULBs*
Andhra Pradesh	January 7, 2008	March 2008 (1st release); March 2009 (2nd release)
Assam	Release only for one district, (Morigaon) only during 2009-10	No release yet
Bihar	January 2008	Madhubani: March 2008 Samastipur: May 2008 (1st instalment)
Chhattisgarh	December 12, 2008	February 16, 2009 and March 7, 2009
Madhya Pradesh	October 31, 2007	December 7, 2007
Orissa	Ganjam: December 27, 2007 Dhenkanal: May 8, 2009	Ganjam: January 29, 2008 Dhenkanal: July 3, 2009
Rajasthan	March 2008 (90%) + March 2009 (10%)	May 27, 2008 (90%) + July 2009 (10%)
West Bengal	February 2008 (90%)	Bankura: February 21, 2008 Purulia: February 28, 2008

Source: *The First Independent Review of BRGF*, World Bank, 2009.

The current disbursement system based on UC submission could be changed to a replenishment system, involving front-loading of funds with regular replenishments and allowing a higher level of unspent funds. It would be best to directly transfer funds from the state to PRIs/ULBs using electronic bank transfers.

Resources and mandates should be allocated to the different tiers as per the principle of subsidiarity and not retained at the district level. Given resource constraints and the presence of relative backwardness even within a district, the focus should be on the block level.

Restructuring BRGF

In the light of the experience gained, BRGF is proposed to be restructured so that it has the following components:

i) Development grant to 250 districts or identified blocks based on the following non-negotiable principles:
   - Preparation of participatory district plans as per the guidelines issued in the Planning Commission Manual for Integrated District Planning.
   - Consolidation of the plans of lower tiers by District Planning Committees.
   - Priority to backward blocks within the districts.

ii) Giving a Capability Building Grant to all the districts in the country with a view to building the capabilities of local governments in terms of basic core staff and infrastructure, including ICT and *panchayat ghars*, and providing adequate training to PRI functionaries to enable them to discharge their responsibilities effectively and efficiently.

iii) Strengthening PRIs to make them effective institutions of local government. This component would include infrastructure, training and capacity building and e-enablement. Each *panchayat* would first make an effort to get funds for infrastructure from other sources and use this component only as a last resort since the outlay per *panchayat* is likely to be relatively modest.

iv) Incentivising states to transfer functions, functionaries, and funds as per the Eleventh Schedule and other matters related to *panchayats*/PESA. The states may also be asked to sign MoUs on the reforms that they would undertake within a specified time frame. This may not necessarily be a separate component but fund release under the first two components could be made conditional upon states undertaking reforms as per the MoUs signed.

Special Plan for Bihar and KBK Districts of Orissa

As mentioned earlier, the special plans for Bihar and the Kalahandi, Bolangir, and Koraput (KBK) districts of Orissa are an important components of the BRGF. The Special Plan for Bihar (SPB) has been formulated to bring about improvement in sectors like power, road connectivity, irrigation, forestry, and watershed development. Some of the programmes taken up under SPB are restoration of the Eastern Gandak Canal, development of state highways, strengthening the sub-transmission system in south Bihar, and renovation and modernisation of Barauni and Muzaffarpur thermal power stations.

The KBK programme covering Koraput, Bolangir, and Kalahandi districts of Orissa is also being given funds as part of the process for developing backward areas. These districts have since been reorganised into eight districts. The state government had started preparing a special plan from 2002-03. An allocation of ₹250 crore per year has been made during the Eleventh Plan for these districts, which includes ₹120 crore under the district component of BRGF and ₹130 crore as special plan for KBK districts. A participatory bottom-up planning process has been initiated starting with meetings at *Gram Sabha* level. Notwithstanding the differences in the quality of participation, it was reported that the introduction of the BRGF as the first time plans have been generated from the *Gram Sabha* level. The priorities were reported to be scrutinised at the PS and ZP levels to establish whether they are filling the gaps and meeting the sector norms.

In ULBs, however, it was reported that there are no Ward Sabhas and the Ward Councillors bring the priorities to the municipal level following informal consultations with community members. There are also cases where the community members submit their proposals directly to the Municipality.

Given the above background of the scheme, it is significant to refer to Article 243G of the Constitutions of India which is the operational aspect of the 73rd Amendment to the Constitution and says that:

> The legislature of a State may, by law, endow the *Panchayats* with such powers and authority as may be necessary to enable them to function as institution of self-government and such law may contain provisions for the devolution of powers and responsibilities upon *Panchayats* at the appropriate level, subject to such conditions as may be specified therein, with respect to (a) the preparation of plans for economic development and social justice; and (b) the implementation of schemes for economic development and social justice as may be entrusted to them including those in relation to the matters listed in the Eleventh Schedule.

Article 243W of the Constitution contains similar provisions for urban local bodies. It says that:

(1) There shall be constituted in every State at the district level a District Planning Committee to consolidate the plans prepared by the *Panchayats* and Municipalities in the district and to prepare a draft development plan for the district as a whole.

(2) The Legislature of a State may, by law, make provision with respect to:

   (a) The composition of the District Planning Committees.

   (b) The manner in which the seats in such Committees shall be filled. Provided that not less than four-fifth of the total number of members of such Committees shall be elected by and from amongst the elected members of the *Panchayat* at the district level and of the Municipalities in the district in proportion to the ratio between the population of the rural areas and of the urban areas in the district.

   (c) the functions relating to district planning which may be assigned to such Committees.

   (d) the manner in which the Chairpersons of such Committees shall be chosen.

(3) Every District Planning Committee shall, in preparing the draft development plan:

(a) have regard to:

(i) matters of common interest between the *Panchayats* and Municipalities including spatial planning, sharing of water and other physical and natural resources, the integrated development of infrastructure and environmental conservation.

(ii) The extent and type of available resources whether financial or otherwise.

(4) The Chairperson of every District Planning Committee shall forward the development plan, as recommended by such Committee, to the Government of the State.

Above mentioned Constitutional provisions are designed to enable the State Governments to make *panchayats* viable institutions so that they can prepare economic and social planning with people's participation at various levels of decentralised governance.

Keeping above views, it is expected that for the purpose of formulation of the decentralised plan, the first step is that it should be discussed in the *Gram Sabha* (GS) for onward consideration in the *Gram Panchayat* (GP). The plans prepared by all GPs falling under the jurisdiction of the *Panchayat Samiti* are to be assembled at its level with the purpose to have detailed discussion on the plan proposals received by various GPs and if there is any gap or lacunae in the plans prepared by various GPs, they should be sorted out. The prepared plans by all the *Panchayat Samitis* of the district will be sent to the *Zilla Parishad* with the purpose for the discussion at its level and if there are some gaps still persisting it can be solved through discussion. In this way, plan for the entire rural areas of the district will be prepared by the *Zilla Parishad*. In a similar way, plans of the urban areas would be prepared by the Urban Local Bodies of the District. These prepared plans by the urban local bodies would integrate by the District Planning Committees. These Committees are expected to prepare the plan for the entire district and will send a draft plan to the State Government. This is the constitutional provision for the decentralised planning.

Conclusion

The BRGF, supported and implemented by Ministry of Panchayati Raj, aims at redressing regional imbalances in development. The BRGF is anchored in a participatory district plan and has provisions for additional funding for capacity building as well as untied funds for development schemes. For preparation of participatory plans, the guidelines issued by the Planning Commission apply. The BRGF guidelines mention that baseline surveys need to precede the planning exercise. The BRGF is currently operational in 250 backward districts. Technical Support Institutions (TSI) facilitate the conduct of baseline surveys and the preparation of district plans. In districts where DHDRs (District Human Development Reports) are prepared, the DHDRs themselves could be the baseline surveys necessary for preparation of District Plans. They could be excellent tools for situation analysis and the visioning exercise envisaged in the district planning guidelines.

References

Accountability Initiative (2010a). *Budget Briefs: Rural Drinking Water and Sanitation, 2009-10.* New Delhi: Government of India.

Acharya, S. S. (2010). "Caste and Patterns of Discrimination in Rural Public Health Care Services", in S. Thorat and K.S. Newman (eds.), *Blocked by Caste: Economic Discrimination in Modern India.* New Delhi: Oxford University Press. pp.208-29.

Ahluwalia, M. (2011). "Prospects and Policy Challenges in the Twelfth Plan", *Economic and Political Weekly* 46(21): 88-105.

Alok, K. (2010). *Squatting with Dignity: Lessons from India.* New Delhi: Sage Publications.

Baraik, V.K. and P.M. Kulkarni (2006). "Health Status and Access to Health Care Services: Disparities among Social Groups in India", *Indian Institute of Dalit Studies Working Paper Series* 1(4): 1-37.

Borooah, V. K. (2010). "Inequality in Health Outcomes in India: The Role of Caste and Religion", in S. Thorat and K.S. Newman (eds.), *Blocked by Caste: Economic Discrimination in Modern India.* New Delhi: Oxford University Press. pp.179-207.

Comptroller and Auditor General of India (2010). *Performance Audit of the National Rural Health Mission (Ministry of Health and Family Welfare)*, Report of the Comptroller and Auditor General of India Union Government (Civil) No. 8 of 2009-10. Government of India. pp.1-115.

De Haan, A. (1998). "Social Exclusion: An Alternative Concept for the Study ofDeprivation?", *IDS Bulletin* 29(1): 10-19.

———. (1999). *Social Exclusion: Towards an Holistic Understanding of Deprivation.* Background paper prepared for the *World Development Report 2001* Forum on "Inclusion, Justice and Poverty Reduction". pp.1-19.

Deshpande, A. (2011). *The Grammer of Caste: Economic Discrimination in Contemporary India.* New Delhi: Oxford University Press.

17

KIRAN PRASAD

Innovation and Technologies in Livelihoods

Recasting Strategies for Empowerment of Rural Women

Introduction

India has the world's largest rural population (857 million) and is home to the widest rural-urban disparities leading to skewed development. The United Nations' *Human Development Report* (HDR) (2010) has calculated that South Asia is home to half of the world's multi-dimensionally poor population accounting to 844 million. Eight states of India are home to 421 million multi-dimensionally poor people, which is more than the 410 million people residing in the 26 poorest African countries. South-Asia including India houses the largest rural-urban disparities. It is estimated that India will be among the least urbanised countries in 2050 and will account for a quarter of the world's rural population then, as it does now (UN, 2014).

In India, women constitute a population of 586.5 million, with 405.2 million (48.6%) in the rural areas and 181.2 million in the urban areas (Census, 2011). The states with a high population of rural women (over 20 million) include Bihar, Uttar Pradesh (UP), Madhya Pradesh (MP), Andhra Pradesh (AP), West Bengal and Maharashtra; followed by Rajasthan, Tamil Nadu, Karnataka, Gujarat, Odisha, Kerala, Assam and Jharkhand with a population of over 10 million rural women. The vast majority of rural women continue to be at the periphery of development of India. Bringing rural women into the mainstream of development is a major concern for the Government of India (GoI) through several flagship programmes.

The GoI in its National Policy for Empowerment of Women in 2001 sought to bring about the advancement, development and empowerment of women. These goals are also regarded as one of the important Millennium Development Goals (MDGs) to be achieved in 2015. The very slow gains in nutrition, education and poverty alleviation over the last decade suggest that India is passing through an era of growth marked with widening inequalities and development gaps. This paper will analyse the interrelations between innovation and technologies in livelihoods to recast strategies for empowerment of rural women in India. The flagship programmes of the government must develop appropriate policies for skill development; creation, maintenance and modernisation of assets; financial management; and participation in innovation and technology design which will be key to bridge the development divide and narrow the gender gap for shaping a new paradigm of inclusive and sustainable development.

Growth without Equality

India has been a welfare state since Independence and government policies and programmes were designed with the aim of alleviation of rural poverty. It was realised that a sustainable strategy of poverty alleviation had to be based on increasing the productive employment opportunities for the rural poor and providing a better and higher quality of life. Rural development is defined as the process of sustained growth of the rural economy and improvement of well-being of the rural population. Thus the flagship programmes for rural development have twin goals; the economic betterment of people as well as greater social transformation. Initially, the main thrust of rural development was laid on agriculture and allied industry, communication, education, health and allied sectors.

Despite rapid economic growth in the post-reform period, India has over 250 million below the poverty line and lags behind in providing access to food and drinking water to all the people, which is the most basic goals of development. India recorded a high economic growth of 9 per cent per annum during 2005-06 to 2008-09. In 2011, India's human development index (HDI) was 134 out of 169 countries in 2011 (same as in 1980—32 years ago). The

United Nations International Children Education Fund (UNICEF) estimates in 2011 show that there are 55 million out of 102 million underweight children under five in the world, which is 54 per cent of the global total live in India. It is estimated that nearly 37 per cent of the world's stunted children live in India.

It is widely reported that agricultural production is on an all-time high and India has food stocks needed to ensure food security for all. In spite of such a huge surplus, it is estimated that 20 per cent of rural Indians do not get even a single meal a day and 14 per cent of Indians get less than the minimum calorie intake required to survive. The coexistence of surplus grain and extensive endemic hunger in India is a cold reminder that despite our top position in agricultural production, farmers continue to commit suicide and people continue to die of hunger (Prasad, 2009). There is a dire need to strengthen nutrition and health programmes such as the Integrated Child Development Services (ICDS), Public Distribution System (PDS), Mid-Day Meal Schemes (MDMS) and the National Rural Health Mission (NHRM) in order to address the health needs of rural women and children.

The dismal status of women at present is reflected in the Gender Inequality Index which ranks India at 132 out of 146 countries. In rural India where fertility rates are higher and teenage marriages are common, women face insecurity regarding a regular income, food, shelter and access to health care and other essential services. It is an understatement to say that violence against women is multidimensional—it is structural, brutal and a part of everyday life (Ravi and Sajjanhar, 2014). Indian women marry at a median age of just 17 years, and 16 per cent of women aged 15-19 have already started bearing children, according to the 2005-06 National Family Health Survey (IIPS, 2007). India ranks among the countries with the highest maternal mortality rates; the MMR (maternal mortality rate) in India stood at 212 per 100,000 live births in 2007-2009 (Registrar General of India, 2009).

Gender discrimination and violence against women have had a profound effect on the sex ratio in India. The sex ratio (the percentage of female children per 1000 male children under five years of age) has been dropping steadily for the past 50 years, with a steep decline from 962 girls to 1000 boys in 1981, to 945 in 1991 and to 927 in 2001. In 2011, the sex ratio of females stood at 940 females per 1000 males (Census, 2011).

Education is regarded as an important catalyst, especially in women's development and reducing gender discrimination. The status of women and children are interconnected in a great measure. As Sen (1999) observes:

> There is considerable evidence that women's education and literacy tend to reduce the mortality rates of children. The influence works through many channels, but perhaps most immediately it works through the importance that mothers typically attach to the welfare of the children, and the opportunity the mothers have when their agency is respected and empowered, to influence family decisions in that direction. Women's empowerment appears to have a strong influence in reducing the much observed gender bias in survival (particularly against young girls).

The female literacy rate was estimated to be 65 per cent in the 2011 Census with the female literacy rate being 58.8 per cent in rural areas and 79.9 per cent in urban areas. Rural women in Rajasthan, Bihar, Jharkhand, Jammu and Kashmir, UP and Arunachal Pradesh have low levels of literacy, where around half of them are illiterate.

The poor existing social and living conditions have had a negative impact on the lives of rural women. The type of housing and space available is crucial in ensuring good health, particularly of women who require greater privacy to manage their health. The last national Census (2011) revealed that 37.1 per cent of Indian families (325 million) live in one-room houses. Small houses with hardly any ventilation and lack of privacy to manage personal sanitation can also worsen the already morbid conditions of inhabitants, more often women and children who are home bound. The 2011 Census data indicated that two-third of the households continue to use firewood, crop residue, cow dung cakes or coal for cooking—exposing women to significant health hazards and hardship.

The access to water and sanitation in the rural areas is a daily struggle for rural women. According to the Census (2011) data in India, only 32 per cent of the households use treated water for drinking. Seventeen per cent households do not have access to water at home and fetch drinking water from a source located more than 500 metres away in rural areas or 100 metres away in urban areas. But much of it is not potable and the supply is not adequate to meet the daily requirements. Women are the water providers for families and the disappearance of water sources present consequential burdens and drudgery. The increasing time spent on collection of water has direct effect on their health and opportunities for other fruitful activity (Prasad, 2014).

The Census (2011) also revealed that less than half of the households (46.9%) have toilet facilities and less than 50 per cent of the waste-water is collected and treated. The shortage of water leads to poor sanitation, especially among women, who are in the reproductive age group. Lack of toilet facilities also increases the chance of infections and related diseases. Women and children are particularly vulnerable to diseases due to poor sanitation and insufficient water to manage personal hygiene and health care (Rao and Somayajulu, 2004). It seems absurd that families walk for miles from their homes to bathe and attend to nature's call, but would watch television within the confines of their homes (Saran, 2003). Health initiatives, providing rural women with access to safe water and to basic sanitation facilities, along with education and livelihood opportunities are needed for empowering them. The answer to sustainable development of India lies not in economic growth alone; it must be accompanied by a more robust analysis of social interventions, such as flagship programmes, to eradicate social inequalities and disparities among the rural women.

Livelihoods and Work Participation

It is widely accepted that the primary sector is the main source of livelihood for the rural population. But employment in agriculture in the rural areas has fallen sharply over the last decade and a combination of farm-oriented and non-farm work has become the most common form of rural employment. The findings of the nationwide representative sample survey conducted by the National

Council for Applied Economic Research (NCAER), which covered 42,000 households across the country, documented the fall in agricultural employment (NCAER, 2014). In 2004-05, half of all the rural men (50%) and 83 per cent of rural women worked only on farms, making it the major type of rural employment. In 2011-12, exclusive farm-oriented work continued to be the most prevalent form of employment among over two-third of the rural women (66%), while only 35 per cent of men engaged in farm work.

In 2004-2005, while 25 per cent of men were engaged in farm and non-farm work, less than one-tenth of the rural women (9%) were employed in the same. In 2011-12, over one-third of the rural men (35%) were engaged in farm and non-farm work, while less than a quarter of the rural women (22%) were employed in these economic activities. The distribution of rural workers further shows that while 29 per cent of the rural men were engaged in non-farm jobs, only just over one-tenth of the rural women (12%) were employed in non-farm work. The states of Kerala, Tamil Nadu, Punjab, Haryana, Assam and the north-eastern States have been the main providers of non-farm work to rural men and women.

There is an alarming fall in the participation of women in workforce of the country and it is found that less than 15 per cent of the women are engaged in any form of paid work. While the fall in non-farm employment of rural men can be explained by rising education and migration to urban areas for jobs, the fall in work participation rates for women have several reasons including the spate of violence against them. The female work participation data often hides the tasks that women performed before an article or a product entered the market (Jain, 2011). Jain in her time-use studies from 1974 to 1986 found many such instances where the women's work was never accounted for in macro data, such as the cocoon rearers of Karnataka, or *tussar* cocoon gatherers of MP, the hardships faced by the prawn peelers of Kerala who went as migrants to Gujarat, the contractors who cheated the *bidi* rollers of Mangalore, the patriarchal hold over the tea pickers of the Nilgiris, and the exploitation of *chikan* workers of Lucknow.

Jain (2011) has argued for attention to women in these invisible roles, for wage, skill development and prevention of occupational hazards. According to Jain (2011), in macroeconomic data collection and policy formulation in India, women were considered secondary bread winners (with males being the primary ones). Thus, they are more in need of social welfare, especially maternity and child care services. Women were rarely identified as principal contributors in the main economic sectors like agriculture or industry and in turn, did not receive credit or technical services or protection from occupational hazards in employment.

There is an avowed strategy of women's empowerment that focuses on their employment. But what is shocking is that studies indicate a link between women's employment and domestic violence. NHFS-3 (IIPS, 2007) data report that there is much higher prevalence of violence against women who were employed at any time in the past 12 months (40%) in comparison to women who were not employed (29%). This reality contradicts the widely held global perception that better economic status of women lowers their risk to violence.

In the light of persistent inequality of rural women, the gender equality survey of the World Economic Forum places India at 114 out of 142 countries in the Global Gender Gap Index. While India ranks 126 on educational attainment, it is ranked 134 on economic participation and opportunity, and the lowest at 142 on the health and survival of women. Despite all the flagship programmes of the government, India ranks very low on narrowing the gender gap in education, health, economic participation and equal pay for equal work. At present, India is among the few countries of the world where female labour force participation is shrinking. This brings us back to the critical question whether the solution to the development divide lies not principally in increasing investments in low-skill employment, but in other area such as free and compulsory education and skill training that could change priorities, save money, and deliver better results.

Innovation and Technologies in Sustainable Livelihoods

The foregoing discussion points to the argument that economic growth and human development in India have not coincided or even shown positive correlation. When income inequalities continued to rise, it was often thought that the benefits of development would trickle down and reduce the development gaps. Development paradigms have relied heavily on top-down approaches with information, knowledge and expertise flowing from scientists, development planners, policy makers and bureaucrats, who advocated from the lab-to-land approach, symbolised by the green revolution in India. As Shiva (2009: 25) puts it:

> The so-called green revolution was neither green, nor revolutionary. It has dispossessed small peasants, pushed our rich agro-biodiversity to extinction, mined our aquifers, desertified our soils and undermined our nutrition and health...It was supposed to create prosperity, but it left farmers steeped in debt. Both in financial and ecological terms, industrial agriculture and chemical farming is based on a negative economy—it uses more inputs than it produces. The consequence is impoverished ecosystems and impoverished and indebted farmers.

Buttressing the above argument is the case of Punjab. Once regarded the cradle of the Green Revolution, the prosperity of Punjab was the success story across urban and rural India for decades. Punjab now has 7,000 farmers who have committed suicide with 11 villages put up for sale and a phenomenal debt of farmers estimated to a tune of over ₹9886 crore (Dey, 2014). While it is well documented that over a quarter million farmers have committed suicides from 1995 to 2010 in Maharashtra, AP and Odisha, more and more farmers across India are being pushed to the brink of debt and suicide.

Under such an unprecedented agricultural crisis, rural women are particularly vulnerable as an increasing number of them must take charge of their families after the suicides of male members and other social crisis. According to the 2011 Census, about 27 million households, constituting 11 per cent of total households in the country, are headed by women. The highest number of female-headed households is in Lakshadweep at 43.7 per cent and in Kerala at 23 per cent. There were about 49 lakh single-member female households, of which three-fourth were in rural areas. In seven states—Chhattisgarh, MP, Tamil Nadu, AP, Maharashtra, Odisha and Gujarat—the proportion of single-member female-headed households was more than 20 per cent (Census, 2011). Insights into the growing nature of female-headed households particularly in the rural areas are needed to help the government plan programmes accordingly to their specific needs for facilitating equitable and inclusive development.

Agricultural productivity suffers due to lack of innovative approaches, such as sustained access to institutional credit facilities, remunerative support prices for crops, cooperative farming, efficient irrigation and energy sources, value-addition and an integrated marketing system. Farmers groups in different villages in Kerala have formed into marketing groups called the Swasraya Karshaka Samiti (SKS) under the Vegetable and Fruit Promotion Council (VFPCK) of the Kerala Government. The SKS consisting of 20-25 farmers as members is responsible for sourcing and marketing farm produce. They run their own markets and have been successful in eliminating middlemen to get a better price for their produce (Prabhu, 2013). Traders are informed by the Market Information Centre (MIC) on the daily prices and they also inspect the produce. Presently, 600 farmers are members of the SKS and about 150 non-member farmers also make use of these facilities. Farmers, tribals and rural women previously viewed at the fringes of the top-down approach have emerged as innovative farmers who challenge many mainstream notions of commercial agriculture. Agricultural innovation has entered a new phase with organic farming and a reverse strategy from the land-to-lab where agricultural scientists go to the field and often return to the lab to understand the regenerative power of nature and knowledge inherent in communities (Prasad, 2013a).

Women in the rural areas have been practising integrated soil and water management technologies leading to a rise in organic farming (Chauhan, 2006). Rural women can benefit from a range of technologies like solar cookers, biogas plants, fuel-saving cooking techniques, appropriate community water solutions, rural housing technologies, technologies that lighten the drudgery of agricultural tasks, battery-operated vehicles, and many intermediate technologies that aid value-addition of farm products, which can be scaled to micro-enterprises (Chauhan, 2006).

The Narmada Bachao Andolan (NBA) led by Medha Patkar has been able to drive home the message that 'There are Many Alternatives' as against the global media refrain that 'There is No Alternative' (TINA). Intermediate technologies in the form of check dams, rain water collection tanks and mini water projects, along with the active involvement of the local people in several states, have evinced greater support and participation rather than large dams involving massive funds with heavy costs of submergence, environmental impact, rehabilitation and resettlement of the affected people.

The Mission 2007 with the concept of Providing Urban Facilities in Rural Areas (PURA), backed by technology, is seen as a major strategy to bridge the rural-urban divide. The concept of PURA was backed by former President Dr A.P.J. Abdul Kalam to create a network of information kiosks in 600,000 villages in India. The VKCs (village knowledge centres) in the *panchayat* would enable the villages to receive information on agriculture, weather and economic opportunities for fishermen, craftsmen, traders, entrepreneurs, rural women, unemployed youth and students. The year 2005 was also titled 'The Year of Micro-Credit' and the International Fund for Agricultural Development (IFAD) supports several women's development projects using the SHG (self-help group) strategy. The micro-enterprises of SHGs built over the decade can be integrated into the national market and connected at low cost to other markets within the country and across regions. There is a need to plan skill development and continuous training programmes for rural women according to the demands of a vast domestic market like India.

India's MSMEs (micro, small and medium enterprises) sector recorded more than 10 per cent growth in recent years and has contributed nearly 8 per cent to the national GDP (gross domestic product). MSMEs have employed over 8 crore people in nearly 4 crore manufacturing and service enterprises. It has also accounted for 45 per cent of the manufactured output and 40 per cent of exports made from India. The policy of the government to step up their potential to create employment and provide economic growth should envisage the inclusion of rural women who have traditional skills in textile, arts and crafts manufacture and design. Exclusive women's cooperatives and markets as in many European countries can be incorporated to expand entrepreneurship. Such innovative initiatives will lead to renewed creation, maintenance and modernisation of the assets; financial management; and participation in innovation and technology design by rural women entrepreneurs.

The Nagoya Protocol, a new international treaty, is seen as one of the victories for India and other developing nations, to ensure that the benefits of natural resources and their commercial derivatives are shared with rural communities. Rural women play a significant role in the management and protection of natural resources. The Nagoya Protocol includes a sweeping plan to protect bio-diversity by setting targets for 2020. Nations agreed to turn 17 per cent of the globe's land area and 10 per cent of coastal and marine areas into protected regions, as opposed to the current levels of 13 and 1 per cent, respectively. They also agreed to bring 'natural capital' into national accounting systems so that the trillions of dollars worth of benefits that nature provides to economies are valued. This agreement is a result of almost two decades of UN negotiations, where India leads a group of 17 mega diverse countries with rich reserves of exploitable natural resources.

The new Access and Benefit Sharing (ABS) rules advocate that multinational companies will have to share their profits with local communities not only for using the original resource, but also any derivative products developed from it. For example, a pharmaceutical company which develops a new drug from ingredients found in an Indian plant will now have to give a fair share to the Indian communities that nurtured the plant in the first place. International drug firms will also have to pay for awaiting human genetic material such as pathogens—the germs responsible for virus pandemics which are used to develop lucrative vaccines. This is the consequence of the previous practice of companies who used to simply take the pathogens from the developing countries, make the vaccine, and then sell it back to them for billions of dollars. However, the flip side is that the US—one of the largest users of such resources—is not among the nearly 200 signatories of the rules of the Nagoya Protocol (Jebaraj, 2010).

Despite India's efforts to pursue several policies and flagship programmes for empowering rural women, violence against women is widespread, irrespective of their education, social class or public status. The development discourse rarely extends to equal rights and safety, which remain just out of reach for many women across the country (Prasad, 2013b). Gender justice is not only about achieving social justice, it is also about creating a space which allows women to become more than they have been traditionally defined by men (Prasad, 2013b). Women, against the odds, are attempting to balance autonomy and dependence; self-fulfillment; and a desire and obligation to care for others. Basic education, quality healthcare and innovative livelihoods can transform the lives of rural women and put India on the road to gender equality.

Bridging the Development Divide

The National Mission for Empowerment of Women (NMEW), which was announced on 8 March 2010, works with all the States and Union Territory governments and has 14 Ministries and Departments of GoI as its partners with the Ministry of Women and Child Development as the Nodal Ministry. The mandate of the Mission is to bring in convergence and facilitate the processes of ensuring economic and social empowerment of women with emphasis on health and education, reduction in violence against women, generate awareness about various schemes and programmes meant for women, as well as empowerment of vulnerable women and those in difficult circumstances (*www.nmew.gov.in*). The Mission aims to engage in strategic communication for inter-ministerial convergence of gender mainstreaming of programmes, policies, institutional arrangements and processes of participating ministries, which have largely hitherto operated independently and in a stand-alone manner.

There is a growing emergence of webs and networks of the relations among individuals, groups, communities, states, international organisations and transnational actors in the contact of rural development. This is in turn creating a challenge to global corporations focused on merely economic growth that attempt to have a homogenising impact on lifestyles and consumption patterns. The right to information campaign led by Aruna Roy, struggle for natural resources led by Medha Patkar, the sustainable agriculture movement led by Vandana Shiva, and a host of local agitations led by women like C.K. Janu and Mayilamma have converged and have played a stellar role in grounding sustainable development in India. Those who were long neglected and silenced in the development processes, particularly women, have been awakened by people's movements like the Nirmal Bharat Abhiyan (NBA). Owing to the networking with the NBA, rural women in the local collectives/ federations have been able to maintain better contact with the bureaucracy in the government offices. Prior to the networking with the National Alliance for People's Movements (NAPM), many women were unaware of where the government offices were located and played a minimal role in the political life of the country. Now women representatives elected to the local government bodies visit the state offices and interact with officials, and are also informed by them about various rural development programmes. In addition to greater interaction with government officials, networking with national organisations like the NAPM helps rural women to take up leadership roles in their own neighbourhoods, communities and villages (Prasad, 2013a).

Nevertheless, the degree of power that autonomous women's organisations can exert within the political process often determines the outcome in the form of appropriate policy changes for development. However, women's empowerment is generally perceived as a matter of 'low politics', and policy reforms and strategies are therefore influenced primarily by the extent to which they are likely to influence political stability (Heise, 1994). Now there is a growing acceptance within the women's movement that any strategy to achieve significant policy reforms at the state, regional or local level must engage the state and demand reform. Women who attempt to reform the process of development by resistance against bureaucratic structures often find that an alliance of politicians and vested interests have an almost impregnable hold on the central institutions of the society. The increasing poverty of these women allows them neither to enjoy leisure time nor realise that the rise of popular protest which can bring in change must be built from the fringes of society to the centre, until this becomes the dominant socio-political organisation in the country (Chakravarty, 2003: 638).

Further, rural women's extreme poverty and their pseudo-enfranchisement in the developing countries sometimes make them realise that their powerlessness will not easily change their circumstances. This situation is complicated by policy makers who often ignore a world in which women are seldom leaders, doers and supporters of families, and where women's concerns like poverty and lack of health care are absent or trivialised (Prasad, 2008). But the struggle of women is strongly founded on the hope that status and legitimacy will be bestowed on their issues. It does give an indication as to the realisation of women of the changes in themselves as they prepare to raise difficult questions regarding the sustainability of development projects. If satisfactory answers are not forthcoming, women will be gradually moving towards a position of adopting alternative models of development that place people's welfare on the top of the agenda, even though they still have a long way to go.

References

Census (2011). *Census of India*. New Delhi: Registrar General of India, Government of India,

Chakravarty, Meera (2003). "Communication for Women's Empowerment: New Dynamics and Priorities", in Kiran Prasad (ed.), *Communication and Empowerment of Women: Strategies and Policy Insights from India*. Vol.2. New Delhi: The Women Press. pp.627-41.

Chauhan, Narendrasinh, B. (2006). "Environment Friendly Technologies for Farm women" In Kiran Prasad (Ed.). Women in Rural Development: Contemporary Social Policy and Practice, New Delhi: The Women Press.

Dey, Soumik (2014). "Cradle. Now. Grave", *The Week*, 24 August. pp.24-32.

Heise, et. al. (1994). "Violence Against Women: A Neglected Public Health Issue in Less Developed Countries", *Social Science and Medicine* 39(9): 1165-79.

IIPS (2007). *National Family Health Survey (NFHS-3), 2005-06: India: Volume II*. Mumbai: International Institute for Population Sciences (IIPS) and Macro International.

Jain, Devaki (2011). "Sexual Division of Labor: What Transformative Policies", Paper presented at the *ECLAC Conference*. Santiago Chile. October.

Jebaraj, Priscilla (2010). "Nagoya Protocol a big victory for India, says Jairam Ramesh" retrieved 1 November 2010 from *http://www.hindu.com/2010/11/01/stories/2010110153950300.htm*

Ministry of Women and Child Welfare (2009). *Gendering Human Development Indices: Recasting the Gender Development Index and Gender Empowerment Measure for Index*. New Delhi: Government of India.

NCAER (2014). *Most Rural Population Now Not Solely in Agriculture*. NCAER survey available at *http://www.ncaer.org/news_details.php?nID=49*.

Prabhu, M. J. (2014). "Farmers Groups in Kerala Run their Own Markets, Eliminate Middlemen", *The Hindu*, 21 February. p.17.

Prasad, Kiran (2014). "Strategic Health Communication", in Charles Okigbo (ed.), *Strategic Urban Health Communication*. USA: Springer.

————. (2013a). "Environment Communication from the Fringes to the Mainstream: Creating a Paradigm Shift in Sustainable Communication", in Jan Servaes (ed.), *Sustainable Development and Green Communication: Asian and African Perspectives*. USA: Palgrave MacMillan.

————. (2013b). "Burdened by Shame: Women, Media, Culture and Identity Crises in India" in M. Moshe and N. Corbu (eds.), *The Walk of Shame*. New York: Nova Science Publishers Inc.

————. (2009). *Communication for Development: Reinventing Theory and Action*. Vol. 1: *Understanding Development Communication*; and Vol 2: *Advanced Development Communication*. New Delhi: B.R. Publishing Corporation.

————. (2008). "Gender Sensitive Communications Policies for Women's Development: Issues and Challenges" InKatharine Sarikakisand Leslie Regan Shade (Eds.) Minding the Gap: Feminist Interventions in International Communication. USA: Rowman and Littlefield.

Rao, Prakash A. and Somayajulu U.V (2004). "Health Status of Women Living in the Slums of Bangalore", in *Women, Health and Development*. Tirupati: Dept. of Population Studies-UGC SAP (Phase-1) Sri Venkateswara University.

Ravi, Shamika and Anuradha Sajjanhar (2014). "Beginning a New Conversation on Women", *The Hindu*, 21 June.

Registrar General of India (2009). *Maternal Mortality Rates*, New Delhi: Government of India.

————. (2011). *Maternal and Child Mortality and Total Fertility Rates*. New Delhi: Government of India.

Saran, Rohit (2003). "How We Live", *India Today*, 28 July.

Sen, Amartya (1999). *Development as Freedom*. New York: Alfred. A.Knopf, Random House, Inc.

Shiva, Vandana (2009). "Food Meets Media", *Opening Address, Media and Global Divides, IAMCR World Congress*, Stockholm, 2008, *Nordicom Review* 30: 11-31, June.

UN (2014). *World Urbanization Prospects*. New York.

UNICEF (2011). *The State of the World's Children: Adolescence-An Age of Opportunity*. New York.

United Nations Development Programme (2010), Human Development Report 2010, UNDP: Oxford/New York.

World Economic Forum (2014). *The Global Gender Gap Report 2014*. Geneva, Switzerland.

18

MAMATA SWAIN

Implementation of Rashtriya Krishi Vikas Yojana in Odisha

Tasks Ahead

Introduction

Odisha is predominantly an agrarian economy with more than 60 per cent of its workforce depending on agriculture to earn their livelihood. The mission of the state government is to improve agricultural production and productivity with sustainable agricultural practices and foster inclusive growth to strengthen agricultural economy and income of the farmers with higher investment, efficient production technology, post-harvest solutions, effective value addition and remunerative market options. The Rashtriya Krishi Vikas Yojana (RKVY), a state plan scheme fully funded by the Government of India (GoI), has been under implementation in Odisha from 2007-08 with the objective of providing incentives to the state to increase public investment in agriculture, achieve the goal of reducing the yield gaps in important crops, maximise returns to the farmers and bring about quantifiable changes in the production and productivity of various agriculture and allied sectors.

The National Development Council (NDC), in its meeting held on 28 May 2007, resolved to initiate a special Additional Central Assistance (ACA) scheme *viz.*, RKVY. The purpose behind this programme was to encourage States to draw up district and state agricultural plans, as well as increase their own spending on the sector so as to reorient agricultural development strategies for rejuvenating Indian agriculture during the Eleventh Plan (2007-2012). RKVY aimed at achieving 4 per cent annual growth in agriculture and the allied sector during the Eleventh Plan period. RKVY targets at achieving and sustaining the desired annual growth during Twelfth Plan period by way of ensuring holistic development of agriculture and allied sectors.

This paper attempts to evaluate the strengths and weaknesses of the RKVY scheme, under implementation in Odisha, by using secondary data collected from various official reports and publications. The paper highlights the deficiencies in its implementation and suggests measures for increasing its effectiveness so as to achieve the targeted agricultural growth rate and for promoting integrated and holistic development of agriculture and allied sectors.

Salient Features of RKVY Scheme

Objectives

Main objectives of RKVY as listed in the scheme guidelines (GoI, 2007; 2014) are:

i) To incentivise the states so as to increase public investment in agriculture and allied sector.
ii) To provide flexibility and autonomy to the states in the process of planning and executing the schemes.
iii) To ensure preparation of agriculture plans for the districts and states based on agro-climatic conditions, availability of technology and natural resources.
iv) To ensure that the local needs/crops/priorities are better reflected in the agriculture plan of the state.
v) To achieve the goal of reducing yield gaps in important crops through focused intervention.
vi) To maximise returns to the farmers in agriculture and allied sector, and
vii) To bring about quantifiable changes in the production and productivity of various components of agriculture and allied sectors by addressing them in a holistic manner.

The Department of Agriculture and Cooperation (DAC), GoI, has stated that the RKVY scheme has been formulated with two strategic objectives in mind—to incentivise states to allocate more funds for agriculture and allied sectors; and to ensure that states focus on additional growth in agriculture and allied sectors by better planning and undertaking appropriate growth-oriented projects. This is to be done by drawing up effective plans more comprehensively, by integrating livestock, poultry and fisheries, thereby reflecting needs/crops/priorities taking into account their agro-climatic conditions, natural resources and technology. Funds under the scheme are provided to the states as 100 per cent grant by the central government.

Eligibility Criteria for Allocation of Funds

Allocation of funds to the states is dependent upon additional resources committed by them for agriculture and allied sectors in their state plans and the growth projected and generated. There are no prescriptions about the projects, schemes and other programmes to be undertaken by states under RKVY. The scheme provides complete flexibility to the states to choose what is best suited to their conditions in order to generate growth for enabling the country to achieve the national target of 4 per cent growth in agriculture and allied sectors during Eleventh and Twelfth Plan period. Each state will become eligible to receive RKVY allocation, only if

i) The base line share of agriculture and allied sectors in the total state plan (excluding RKVY funds) expenditure is maintained.

ii District Agriculture Plans (DAPs) and State Agriculture Plans (SAPs) have been formulated.

Base line level of expenditure will be determined on the basis of the average percentage of expenditure incurred under agriculture by a state government in the state plan during three years prior to the previous year (excluding RKVY funds). During introduction of the scheme, the base line was to be a moving average of the previous three years. However, since October 2007, the base line was operated to be the minimum of last three years in order to ensure larger participation of states in RKVY.

Fund Allocation Criteria

The states are allocated funds based on following three parameters:

i) Percentage share of net unirrigated area in a state to the net unirrigated area of the eligible states—20 per cent.
ii) State's projected growth in its GSDP (gross state domestic product) for agriculture and allied sectors over the base year—30 per cent.
iii) Increase in the total Plan expenditure in agriculture and allied sectors in the previous years over the year prior to that year—50 per cent.

RKVY funds are available to the states in two streams:

i) Stream I accounts for at least 75 per cent of the allocation for specific projects/schemes/programmes as approved by the State Level Sanctioning Committee (SLSC) and in line with the priorities defined in the district and state plans.
ii) Stream II accounts for the remaining 25 per cent of the allocation for strengthening the existing state schemes and for filling resources gaps under the state plans.

Based on feedback received from the states, experiences garnered during implementation in the Eleventh Plan, and inputs provided by stakeholders, operational guidelines of RKVY were revised to not only enhance efficiency and efficacy of the programme, but also its inclusiveness during the twelfth Plan period. Restructured RKVY, which is operational from 2014-15, has four streams of funding:

i) RKVY (Production Growth) with 35 per cent of annual outlay,
ii) RKVY (Infrastructure and Assets) with 35 per cent of annual outlay;
iii) RKVY (Special Schemes) with 20 per cent of annual outlay; and
iv) RKVY (Flexi Fund) with 10 per cent of annual outlay (the states can undertake either Production growth or infrastructure and assets projects, where allocation depends upon state-specific needs/priorities).

Funds under the above schemes would be made available to the states as determined by DAC in two instalments of 50 per cent each.

Sanctioning Procedure

Projects are sanctioned by a SLSC under the chairmanship of the Chief Secretary and with representation of all concerned departments, including agriculture universities. The SLSC is responsible for:

i) Sanctioning the projects under Stream I of RKVY.
ii) Monitoring the progress of the sanctioned projects.
iii) Ensuring that no duplication of efforts and resources takes place.
iv) Commissioning or Undertaking field studies to monitor implementation of the projects.
v) Initiating evaluation studies from time to time, as may be required.
vi) Undertaking any other project of importance to the state's agricultural growth.
vii) Eliminating inter-district disparities with respect to financial patterns/subsidy assistance in the projects.

SLSC can meet as often as required, but at least once in a quarter.

Areas of Focus under RKVY

An indicative list of focus areas have been provided for in the RKVY guidelines. Some of the areas covered are:

i) Integrated development of major food crops such as wheat, paddy, coarse cereals, Minor millets, pulses and oilseeds.
ii) Agricultural mechanisation.
iii) Activities related to enhancement of soil health.
iv) Development of rainfed farming systems.
v) Support to state seed farms.
vi) Integrated pest management.
vii) Strengthening of market infrastructure.
viii) Extension services.
ix) Animal husbandry and fisheries.
x) Promotion of horticulture.

The states are, however, free to choose other components/ activities, but must ensure that they are reflected in the district and the state plans.

Schemes of National Importance

Though not provided for in the original guidelines, schemes of national importance, commonly known as sub-schemes, were introduced in RKVY since 2010-11. These schemes are formulated and monitored by the concerned subject divisions in DAC, but are implemented through the states more or less on the Centrally Sponsored Scheme (CSS) mode with 100 per cent central grant. The implementations of sub-schemes have helped in focusing efforts of the Centre and the states in areas that require special attention.

The sub-schemes implemented so far are the following:

i) Oil seeds and Pulses villages.
ii) National Mission for Protein Supplements.
iii) Palm Oil (Oil Palm Area Expansion; OPAE).
iv) Vegetable clusters.
v) Nutri-cereals (Intensive Millet Production; INSIMP).
vi) Accelerated Fodder Development Programme (AFDP).
vii) Rainfed Area Development Programme (RADP).
viii) National Saffron Mission.
ix) Vidarbha Intensive Irrigation Development Project (VIIDP).

Public-Private Partnership for Integrated Agricultural Development (PPPIAD)

To augment the current government efforts made in agricultural development by leveraging the capabilities of the private sector, Public Private Partnership for Integrated Agriculture Development (PPPIAD) has been recently launched under RKVY. The scheme envisages facilitating large scale integrated projects, led by private sector players in the agriculture and allied sectors, with a view to aggregate farmers, and integrate the agriculture supply chain with financial assistance through RKVY.

Corporates are supposed to propose integrated agricultural development projects across the spectrum of agriculture and allied sectors, taking the responsibility of delivering all the interventions. Each project must target at least 5000 farmers, spread over the project life of around 3-5 years. There is complete flexibility in design, but ensures an integrated value chain approach, covering all aspects from production to marketing. Average investment per farmer is to be quantified with an average of ₹1 lakh per farmer as a desirable benchmark. Government support through RKVY is to be limited to 50 per cent of the overall per farmer investment proposed, with a ceiling of ₹50,000 per farmer through the project cycle. Key interventions must include mobilising farmers into producer groups, technology infusion, value addition and marketing solutions.

Activities Undertaken under RKVY

State governments, keeping in view their priorities, have approved project proposals for implementation under RKVY in wide-ranging sectors, which include crops, horticulture, organic farming, farm mechanisation, micro-irrigation, watershed development, marketing, storage, dairy development, fisheries, etc. Critical infrastructure such as state seed farms, soil and fertilisers testing labs, etc., have received substantial support under RKVY.

Implementaion of RKVY in Odisha

In Odisha, the agriculture sector provides employment and sustenance, directly or indirectly, to more than 60 per cent of the population. The agriculture sector is still the mainstay of the state's economy. It suffers from frequent natural shocks like cyclones, droughts and flash floods. Due to susceptibility of the state to natural calamities, the food grains production generally fluctuates from one year to another. The food grain production was 102.10 lakh tonnes in 2012-13, as compared to 63.16 lakh tonnes in 2011-12 and 76.19 lakh tonnes in 2010-11. Paddy still constitutes more than 90 per cent of total production of food grains and continues to be the dominant crop in Odisha; although in terms of acreage, there has been a gradual shift from paddy to cash crops. Though rice productivity has been slowly increasing and was of the order of 23.61 quintals/ha in 2012-13, it is less than the national average of 24.61 quintals/ha.

The cropping intensity of Odisha has increased from 166 per cent in 2011-12 to 167 per cent in 2012-13.

One major constraint in improving agriculture and agricultural production in a sustained manner in the state is the inadequate and erratic irrigation facilities. Irrigation intensity in the state was only 31 per cent in 2006-07 in comparison to the all-India average of 44 per cent. However, the situation has been gradually improving. The rate of fertiliser use and other inputs in the state still remains lower than the national average.

Agriculture in Odisha is characterised by low productivity on account of various factors. These factors include problematic nature of soil (acidic, saline and waterlogged), lack of assured irrigation, low seed replacement rate, low level of fertiliser consumption, low level of mechanisation, etc. These factors, which lead to low investment, trap agriculture in a negative spiral by bringing about lower returns that leave lower funds for investment, thus increasing risk in agriculture. RKVY is expected to play a positive role in boosting agricultural productivity by increasing public investment in agriculture. RKVY is a demand-driven scheme based on bottom-up approach.

Since inception of RKVY in the state, i.e., from the year 2007-2008 to 2013-14, a total number of 399 projects have been executed by 18 implementing agencies as shown in Table 18.1 During this period, 207 projects was completed and the project details have been uploaded in the RKVY Data Management Information System (RDMIS). The yearwise breakup of projects sanctioned and completed is shown in Table 18.2 The number of projects sanctioned has increased from only 21 in 2007 to 108 in 2013. The funds received from GoI has also increased substantially from ₹3,660 lakh in 2007 to ₹52,942 lakh in 2013 as shown in Table 18.3.

RKVY has also helped to restore the ruined economy of farming community in Odisha caused by the cyclone Phailin, during October 2013. The GoI had sanctioned additional fund of ₹30 crore for this purpose. The SLSC sanctioned few projects for Phailin-affected farmers, which were implemented on priority basis. The projects sanctioned included paddy demonstration, replanting coconut and palm, strengthening milk union and cooperative activities, assistance to fishermen, natural resource management activities, organisation of animal health camp, renovation of damaged seed processing plant, etc.

Department of agriculture has been designated as the nodal agency to implement RKVY in the state. Some of the important projects undertaken by the Directorate of Agriculture and Food Production (DA & FP) during 2013-14 are discussed below.

Bringing Green Revolution to Eastern India (BGREI)

To increase the production of rice crop by enhancing the productivity, BGREI is being implemented in the state from the financial year 2011-12. This project was initially implemented in 15 districts of the state, but has been extended to all the 30 districts during 2013-14 with a provision of ₹19,930 lakh. 140,577 hectares of demonstrations were conducted in different rice ecosystems of the state. Beside block demonstrations, 32,000 pump sets and 700 transplanters were supplied to the farmers under site-specific interventions; and 509 community threshing floors and 1,192 farm-cum-fish ponds were taken up by the farmers under asset building activities with a total expenditure of ₹16,194.84 lakh against a project cost of ₹19,930 lakh.

Nutri-Cereals

Millet crops have more nutritional value and can be cultivated under marginal condition. To create demand for millet crops, a new scheme, Initiative for Nutri-cereal Security through Intensive Millets Promotion (INSIMP) has been introduced in the state during 2011-12. Among the millets, *Ragi* occupies the major area in the state. *Ragi* is grown in about 1.85 lakh hectares in 8 districts, namely Koraput, Ganjam, Rayagada, Gajapati, Malkangiri, Kalahandi, Nawarangpur and Bolangir. During 2013-14, an amount of ₹120.95 lakh has been utilised for conducting demonstration in 4,240 ha of farmers' fields. Beside that, 42 farmers' training programmes were organised under the scheme during 2013-14.

Vegetable Initiative for Urban Cluster

This scheme had been introduced in the state during 2011-12 to increase vegetable production in nearby areas of the state capital so as to meet the vegetable requirement. After noticing the encouraging response from farmers, the area of operation has presently been expanded to cover villages located within a radius of 100 kilometers from the state capital covering 5 districts, namely Puri, Khurda, Nayagarh, Cuttack and Jajpur. Subsequently during 2012, 3 more clusters namely Sambalpur (to cover Sambalpur, Bargarh, Deogarh and Jharsuguda districts), Berhampur (to cover Ganjam district) and Rourkela (to cover Sundargarh and Keonjhar districts) were added to the programme. These clusters have been linked with Bhubaneswar through a cool chain operated by an aggregator (Surendra Agritech Pvt. Ltd.) which has opened Aggregation Centres in these clusters and retail outlets in Bhubaneswar city (Udyan Fresh). Further, another Odissi Exports Pvt. Ltd. has been selected as Aggregator-cum-Developer for the clusters of Sambalpur, Berhampur and Rourkela. Surendra Agritech Pvt. Ltd. (SAPL) has developed a modified temperature cold storage with mechanised sorting and grading facilities at Trisulia. During 2013-14, an amount of ₹1,200.00 lakh has been provided for implementation of the scheme; ₹858.97 lakh was utilised for formation of 220 farmers' association/groups; and 1,190.15 hectares each were covered under open pollinated and hybrid vegetables cultivation in the farmers' field. This programme will be continued during 2014-15 with the proposed outlay of ₹1,500 lakh.

Incentivising Hybrid Maize Cultivation for Increasing Production and Productivity of Maize under PPP Endeavour

This project is being implemented by DA and FP. To popularise hybrid maize cultivation in the state, incentives were provided to hybrid maize growers at the rate of 50 per cent cost of the inputs, limiting to ₹3,750 per ha. During 2013-14, a sum of ₹1,700.00 lakh had been utilised against the total project cost of ₹2,010.00 lakh.

Popularisation of Agricultural Machineries/ Implements in the State

The DA and FP (Odisha; O) has been executing the project for popularisation of farm machineries such as tractors, power tillers, combine harvester rotavator, power driven equipment, power operated paddy threshers, etc., in order to address labour shortage and reduce drudgery as well as cost of cultivation, and in turn enhance agricultural productivity by providing subsidies under RKVY. During 2013-14, an amount of ₹6,004.21 lakh has been utilised against the total project cost of ₹7,538.40 lakh.

Establishment of Gene Bank at SSTL

A Gene Bank with controlled atmospheric condition has been established at State Seed Testing Laboratory (SSTL), Bhubaneswar, with a project cost of ₹200.00 lakh with an objective to preserve local germ plasm of different crops. After completion of this project, the state will be able to preserve 897 farmers' varieties of paddy. This project is registered under Protection of Plant Variety and Farmers Right Authority (PPV & FRA) New Delhi, which has awarded the DA & FP, Odisha, for being the first state in India to submit large numbers of farmers' varieties of paddy for registration. So far, 514 local paddy varieties have been registered and certificates have been issued by the PPV & FRA, New Delhi, to the concerned farmers. An additional fund of ₹250.00 lakh has been provided under RKVY for establishment of a freezing chamber with temperature of -100^0 C to -200^0 C in Gene Bank, which provides facility for maintaining the germ plasm for a longer period.

e-Pest Surveillance and Pest Management

This project is implemented by DA & FP (O) with an objective to take up pest surveillance (fixed/roving survey) for eliminating the major pests of paddy and non-paddy crops (pulses and groundnut) by farmers' friends in 1,835 *gram panchayats* (GPs) covering 14,680 villages. By successful execution of this project, the incidence of pest and diseases was minimised in the state to a great extent. During

2013-14, a sum of ₹100.00 lakh has been utilised against the total project cost of ₹189.55 lakh.

Establishment of Block Level Training and Extension Centres

Block level training and extension centres will be established in 176 blocks each so as to provide training to the farmers of horticulture sector. These block level centres will act as the farmers' training and extension centres for enhancing horticultural activities. During 2013-14, an amount of ₹1143.00 lakh has been utilised for establishing of these extension centres.

Establishment of Centre of Excellence in Horticulture at Deras

The Centre of Excellence for horticultural crops—first of its kind in the state of international standard with latest technologies—is an innovative project under RKVY established at Deras, a suburb of Bhubaneswar over 25 acres of land, has become a centre of attraction for farmers, agro-entrepreneurs, researchers as well as students. During 2013-14, an amount of ₹1,960.76 lakh has been utilised against the total project of ₹2067.93 lakh. There are 5 poly-greenhouses of 4,160-5304 sq m, 24 Polytunnel houses of 990-1,020 sq m and 7 shade net houses of 4,092 Sq m sizes for the production of different HYV (high yielding varieties) of vegetables and flowers. The cultivation is supported with drip, micro-sprinkler and boom irrigation as per requirements for various crops. The crops grown at Centre of Excellence, Dera, include, brinjal, tomato, capsicum, chillies, cucumber, lettuce, coriander and mint under vegetables; and rose, gerbera, bird of paradise, chrysanthemum, lilium, gladiolus, tuberose and marigold under flowers. Besides, semi-perennial fruit crop, papaya is being taken up under protected cultivation.

For 2014-15, GoI have allocated ₹50,413.00 lakh under RKVY, which include ₹29,093.00 lakh for normal RKVY and ₹21,320.00 lakh for 3 sub-schemes of RKVY. The allocation under sub-schemes constitute ₹1,8400.00 lakh for BGREI, ₹1,400.00 lakh for Vegetable Initiatives for Urban Clusters (VIUC) and ₹1,520.00 lakh for National Mission for Protein Supplements (NMPS). A Budget provision of

₹55,000.00 lakh has been proposed for 2014-15 under scheme RKVY against the government's total allocation of ₹50,413.00 lakh.

Achievements of RKVY

RKVY has been preferred by the states for its inbuilt flexibility in selecting state-specific interventions. One of the objectives of RKVY during the Eleventh Five Year Plan was incentivising states to increase expenditure on agriculture and allied sectors. State plan expenditures (excluding RKVY receipts) as percentage of GDP (gross domestic product) in agricultural and allied sectors increased from 1.0 per cent in the tenth Plan to 1.4 per cent in the Eleventh Plan. State plan expenditures on agriculture and allied sectors (excluding RKVY) have also increased as the percentage of total plan spending by states, from about 5 per cent during the tenth Plan to over 6 per cent during Eleventh Plan, thereby indicating some success in motivating states to pay greater attention to agriculture, besides providing increased central assistance for the sector. RKVY as assistance was particularly useful for the funds-starved animal husbandry, dairy and fisheries sectors. Projects amounting to over ₹5,000 crore were sanctioned under RKVY for these sectors during the Eleventh Plan, which is about 20 per cent of the total sanctioned RKVY projects. As per the latest estimates that have been released by the Central Statistics Organisation (CSO), India achieved 4.1 per cent growth in the agriculture and allied sectors during the Eleventh Plan period. It surpasses the objective of RKVY scheme of achieving 4 per cent growth rate.

RKVY has imparted definite momentum to the agriculture sector in the state of Odisha. Regular activities starved of resources, promising strategies languishing for lack of support, and limited opportunities for experimentation and innovation, have found a new hope in RKVY. Government of Odisha (GoO) is now allocating more funds to agriculture so as to incorporate schemes of agriculture development. This is reflected in additional plan allocation made to the agriculture sector. Agriculture, which had lagged behind, is making a comeback.

The projects under RKVY cover the entire gamut of activities in the agriculture and allied sectors. RKVY supplements and complements ongoing schemes and projects in these sectors. The Yojana emphasises on convergence through DAPs and SAPs so as to eliminate overlap of resources and efforts ,thus ensuring optimal utilisation of funds available through various Centrally Sponsored/State Plan Schemes.

The state government of Odisha, keeping in view the priorities, has approved project proposals for implementation under RKVY in wide-ranging sectors which include crops, horticulture, organic farming, agriculture/farm mechanisation, micro/minor irrigation, watershed development, agriculture marketing and storage, seed farms and soil/fertiliser testing laboratories, animal husbandry, dairy development, fisheries, extension and research, etc. Critical infrastructure such as state seed farms, and soil and fertiliser testing laboratories that have been starved over the years due to paucity of funds, got a much-needed dose of assistance under RKVY in the state. RKVY has definitely emerged as a principal instrument of development for agriculture and allied sectors in Odisha and has indeed accelerated agricultural growth.

The state government of Odisha received two awards from GoI under National Food Security Mission (NFSM) scheme *viz.*, a) Best performing state in the eastern region for 2007-08 and 2008-09; and b) Krishi Karman Award as best performing state in food grain production during 2010-2011.

Critical Evaluation

National Institute of Rural Development and Panchayati Raj (NIRD&PR), Hyderabad, was commissioned in 2008 to undertake concurrent evaluation of RKVY. Some of the salient findings of the implementation and monitoring study conducted by NIRD&PR, Hyderabad, are : a) States have preferred RKVY for its in-built flexibility in selecting state-specific interventions; b) RKVY succeeded in motivating states to pay greater attention to agriculture, besides providing greater Central assistance for the sector; c) RKVY assistance was particularly useful for the funds-starved animal husbandry, dairy and fisheries sectors.

However, the report revealed that states have not been able to balance investments in growth-oriented projects and those for development of agricultural infrastructure. Infrastructure development, if any, by the states was not found to be based on any definite vision or plan. Further, there has been thin spread of RKVY resources across all sectors and amongst all districts of the state.

The DAC in their background note (GoI, 2013) has mentioned their observations on the performance of RKVY based on interactions made with the states. These are as follows:

i) States have not been able to balance investments in growth-oriented projects and projects for development of agricultural infrastructure. Infrastructure development, if any, by the states was not found to be done according to any definite vision or plan. One of the reasons could also be the annual budget utilisation framework which is not very suitable for financing infrastructure projects.
ii) Increasing number of special schemes within the RKVY window, where the states' flexibility is compromised, need a relook to determine the percentage of RKVY funds, if any, that should be committed to the same.
iii) There is a lack of focussed approach; priority areas are given a miss due to thin spread of resources across all sectors and amongst all districts of the state.
iv) Comprehensive district agriculture plans (C-DAPs) and comprehensive state agriculture plans (C-SAPs) were prepared by all the states to determine priorities and identify gaps in development of agriculture and allied sectors. It was assumed that States would prepare projects under RKVY in line with the identified gaps and priority areas of development. In many instances, these were not adhered to.
v) Flow of funds to the implementing agencies was found to be a tedious and lengthy process despite state governments receiving the funds well within time.

vi) Quality of Detailed Project Reports (DPRs) leaves much to be desired. Often the implementing agencies are unable to quantify outputs and outcomes of a project.
vii) SLSC functioning under the Chief Secretary is unable to devote adequate time for holding detailed discussion of the projects before presenting it for approval. In many states, prior scrutiny of the projects is not done, thus compromising on quality of the project sanctioned by the SLSC.
viii) Some states have used RKVY funds without exhausting provisions available under different schemes of GoI. This may be because states find it less tedious accessing RKVY funds in comparison to the GoI funds under other schemes. States are thus losing out on additional finance available from GoI.
ix) Despite a robust web-based MIS (management information system) put in place by the Ministry, state governments have faltered in providing real time report on the progress made, especially physical progress and impact.
x) Research also indicates that there is a clear lack of vision about the institutional support required to turn activities into real livelihood opportunities. Even if the opportunity exists, there is lack of innovation within organisations to realise the potentials. Thus opportunities remain unchallenged and unexplored.
xi) Despite repeated emphasis on collaborative extension efforts involving public and private agencies, this approach is yet to receive adequate attention. There are very few successful partnerships in the country.

The Agricultural Development and Rural Transformation Centre (ADRTC) under Institute for Social and Economic Change (ISEC), Bengaluru, has been entrusted with the task of evaluating RKVY over the Eleventh Plan period. The preliminary findings of ADRTC's report suggest that RKVY has been making a significant impact in rejuvenating agriculture and allied sectors in the country. The preliminary report findings are as follows:

i) The macro-level impact measured using three indicators: a) growth in GDP, overall GSDP and agricultural GSDP; b) growth in agricultural production; and c) growth in the percentage of agricultural spending out of state plan and agricultural GSDP—indicates that RKVY has been playing a major role in catalysing growth in agriculture and allied sectors.

ii) Empirical data indicates that there is a strong correlation between RKVY spending and private GCF (gross capital formation).

iii) States are giving more emphasis on infrastructure projects. During the Eleventh Plan, the states implemented 1,584 infrastructure projects under RKVY, absorbing about 30 per cent of the total expenditure; of which 566 were flagship projects of the States absorbing 17 per cent of total expenditure made.

iv) Very high expenditure allocation ratio for these infrastructure projects (up to 0.85) also points to the growing emphasis by the states for timely completion.

v) Out of these projects, major focus was directed at minor and micro irrigation projects (about 32%) that has significantly helped to enhance agricultural productivity.

vi) Increased irrigation coverage has also led to greater expenditure for agricultural input like fertiliser use (positive correlation between RKVY expenditure and fertiliser use [kg/ha] has been noted), mechanisation, high quality seeds, etc.

The primary objectives of launching RKVY in the Eleventh Plan, among other things, were to reduce the yield gaps in important crops and to ensure that states increase their plan allocation to the agriculture and allied sectors, as GCF in the sector was unsatisfactory. The Lok Sabha Committee on Agriculture (GoI, 2013-14) finds that no substantial headway has been made in this regard during the Eleventh Plan. Admittedly, there are huge yield gaps across the country and in certain crops, the gaps are relatively bigger. The Committee has gladly noted that despite two major droughts, the overall growth of the agriculture and allied sectors during the Eleventh Plan, is in the vicinity of 4.1 per cent, thus surpassing the target of 4 per cent. The Committee would, however, like to caution the government that there should be no complacency in sustaining the growth momentum achieved in the Eleventh Plan, and all efforts must be made to further accelerate agricultural growth during the Twelfth Plan.

The CAG (Comptroller and Auditor General of India) report on implementation of RKVY in Odisha points out several shortcomings in execution of the schemes as follows:

i) Submission of inflated utilisation certificates (UCs).
ii) Non-utilisation of RKVY funds.
iii) Shortfall in profiling of secondary and micro nutrients in soils.
iv) Belated training.
v) Absence of soil testing before and after demonstration.
vi) Absence of information on sector-wise fund flow including (SC), (ST) and women categories.
vii) Incomplete agriculture market infrastructure.

Keeping in view the above shortcomings in implementation of the RKVY scheme, there seems to be great need for monitoring and impact evaluation.

Monitoring of RKVY

Monitoring the implementation of RKVY is an area of concern. At the central level, there is hardly any monitoring except taking stock of the progress and receiving utilisation certificate at the time of release of second instalment of allocation. The DAC, GoI, has put in place a web-based MIS for RKVY—called RKVY Database and Management Information System (RDMIS)—to collect and disseminate relevant information and data related to each of its project and also to collect the progress and completion details over its life cycle. The states are entering data on the approval and implementation of projects under RKVY online in its website. It is expected that this system will provide all stakeholders with updated data. The RKVY is a broad spectrum scheme and it covers every part of the agriculture and allied sectors, except forestry. Hence, it is difficult to have a cohesive or unified or integrated physical target approach. So, each project under RKVY has to be monitored separately. The difficulty or the challenge involved in

RKVY's monitoring was that the projects sanctioned by the state level committees were too diverse in nature to be categorised easily.

The monitoring mechanism, the coordination mechanism and the supervision mechanism—all needs to be strengthened at various levels. Timely spending of money and correct utilisation of funds are to be monitored. Whether or not the funds are being spent on the appropriate interventions and the desired outcomes are achieved, need to be monitored. Sometimes diversion of funds take place due to flexibility in utilisation of funds. Therefore, 2013 onwards, the CAG had started auditing RKVY. The CAG audit will help in the long run to streamline the system.

Tasks Ahead

Although RKVY schemes are demand driven and based on bottom-up approach aiming at integrated and holistic development of agriculture and allied sectors, there are some grey areas in the implementation process as discussed in the previous sections, which need to be rectified. To increase efficacy and effectiveness of the RKVY schemes in Odisha, the following measures are necessary.

Preparation of Comprehensive District Agriculture Plans

Preparation of C-DAPs has been a weak area in the state, partly due to lack of trained manpower and database at the district/state level. At least 25 per cent of projects sanctioned by SLSCs should originate from the district level, preferably approved by District Planning Committees. For this purpose, suitable units can be formed involving Agricultural technology management Agency (ATMA)/Krishi Vigyan Kendra (KVK)/State Agriculture University (SAU) and any other technical support unit. It is necessary to see decentralised planning as an iterative planning-doing-learning-planning cycle rather than simply a one-time activity. The challenge is to institutionalize this process and ensure that the agency facilitating planning is also accountable for the outcome. The state will be required to revisit and modify the agriculture plans for the districts and the state so as to maintain its vision of agriculture development over the next plan period.

Selection of Infrastructure Projects

Infrastructure projects will be selected and executed on the basis of the normative requirement of infrastructure, actual availability thereof and the gap in agriculture infrastructure in the state.

Screening of Projects

A SLSC headed by an officer nominated by Chief Secretary of the State will screen all project proposals prepared by the various departments for consideration in terms of its suitability, its linkage to DAP and SAP and its adherence to the RKVY guidelines. The Screening Committee will also certify that funds available under other schemes of the state government and/or GoI for the proposed projects have been accessed and utilised, before they are brought under the RKVY umbrella.

Monitoring of Schemes and Impact Assessment

For administrative convenience and ease of implementation, the state governments may identify or create an exclusive agency to set the scheme on the fast-track. To ensure proper implementation of the schemes and compliance with the norms laid down, 25 per cent of the projects sanctioned by the state each year under the two streams shall be taken up for third-party monitoring and evaluation. A detailed impact assessment of the scheme is imperative for further gaining experience and learning.

Convergence of Programmes

Although several new schemes are introduced and more funds are contributed for overall agricultural and rural development, the overall performance of these schemes has suffered due to absence of complementary linkages among different agencies and lack of convergence of schemes. Even though efforts are currently being made to support the development of locally relevant schemes through district and state level plans, staff shortages, fear of loss of power and control on resources, and lack of capacity in designing locally relevant programmes, are constraining real convergence. The GoI is keen to achieve convergence among these different programmes, and

Table 18.1

Physical Status of Project Implementation in Odisha under RKVY (2007-08 to 2013-14)

Sl. No.	*Name of the Implementing Agencies*	*No. of Projects Sanctioned*	*No. of Projects Completed and Entered in RDMIS*	*No. of Ongoing Projects*
1	Animal Husbandry and Veterinary Services (VS)	23	10	13
2	The Orissa State Cooperative Milk Producers' Federation Limited (OMFED)	28	5	23
3	Fisheries	18	7	11
4	Agriculture	109	82	27
5	Horticulture	86	27	59
6	Soil Conservation	12	4	5
7	Odisha State Seed & Organic Products Certification Agency (OSSOPCA)	9	7	2
8	IMAGE	6	6	0
9	Orissa University of Agriculture and Technology (OUAT)	29	25	4
10	Orissa State Seeds Corporation Limited	11	10	1
11	Department of Cooperation	9	2	7
12	Odisha State Agricultural Marketing (OSAM) Board	22	13	9
13	Department of Water Resources	28	4	24
14	Odisha Agro Industries Corporation (OAIC)	1	1	0
15	Textiles & Handlooms	2	1	1
16	Odisha Tribal Empowerment & Livelihoods Programme (OTELP)	3	3	0
17	Directorate of Research on Women in Agriculture (DRWA)	1	0	1
18	Odisha State Cashew Development Corporation	2	0	2
	Total	339	207	192

Source: GoO (2014).

consequently, a number of relevant initiatives are currently being taken.

RKVY encourages convergence with other programmes such as National Rural Employment Guarantee Scheme (NREGS), Swarnajayanti Gram Swarozgar Yojana (SGSY) and Backward Regions Grant Fund (BRGF). The state has initiated attempts to bring about convergence, but the progress is less than satisfactory, mainly due to the apparent reluctance of different departments to share resources, lack of adequate consultations and lack of empowered authority to coordinate and facilitate convergence at the district level. This problem needs to be resolved to increase effectiveness of the scheme.

Table 18.2

Year-wise Physical Status of Project Implementation in Odisha under RKVY (2007-08 to 2013-14)

Year	*Projects Sanctioned*	*Projects Dropped/ Desanctioned*	*Projects Completed*	*Projects Ongoing*
2007-08	21	0	20	1
2008-09	52	0	47	5
2009-10	12	0	12	0
2010-11	89	3	76	10
2011-12	65	1	35	29
2012-13	56	0	14	42
2013-14	108	0	3	105
Total	403	4	207	192

Source: As in Table 18.1.

Table 18.3

Financial Position under RKVY for 2007-08 to 2013-14

Financial Position (₹in Lakh)

Items	*2007-08*	*2008-09*	*2009-10*	*2010-11*	*2011-12*	*2012-13*	*2013-14*
Funds received from GoI	3660.10	11544.00	12149.00	27440.00	35696.00	46828.00	52942.00
Amount Released to Implementing Agencies	3660.10	11543.93	12018.56	27440.00	35917.35**	50392.00**	58617.37**
Expenditure	3660.10	11543.93	12018.56	27440.00	35381.35	46117.51	45029.76
UCs Submitted to GoI	3660.10	11543.93	12018.56	27440.00	35381.35*	46117.51	45029.76

Notes: *: Unspent amount of ₹314.65 lakh for 2011-12 have been carried over to 2012-13 and the account of 2011-12 is squared up; **: Excess amount has been released out of total budgeted allocation of the state and refunded amount of previous year.

Source: As in Table 18.1.

References

GoI (2007). *Guidelines for National Agriculture Development Programme (NADP), Rashtriya Krishi Vikas Yojana (RKVY).* New Delhi: Department of Agriculture and Cooperation, Ministry of Agriculture.

———. (2013). *Agenda Notes for the Meeting to Discuss Implementation of The Rashtriya Krishi Vikas Yojana During 12th Five-Year Plan*, held on 18th April 2013 at Shinde Symposium Hall, NASC Complex, Dev Prakash Shastri Marg, Pusa, Delhi.

———. (2013-14). *Rashtriya Krishi Vikas Yojana: An Evaluation, Department of Agriculture and Cooperation, 61st Report.* Committee on Agriculture, Fifteenth Lok Sabha.

———. (2014). *Rashtriya Krishi Vikas Yojana: Operational Guidelines for XII Five Year Plan.* New Delhi: Department of Agriculture and Cooperation, Ministry of Agriculture.

GoO (2013-14a). *Odisha Economic Survey.* Planning and Coordination Department.

———. (2013-14b). *Activity Report of Agriculture Department.* Odisha.

———. (2014). *RKVY Odisha News, RKVY Cell.* Agriculture Department Government of Odisha..

19

NILACHALA ACHARYA AND RICHA CHINTAN

Utilisation of Funds under RKVY
Issues and Challenges

The Constitution of India provides for a clear division of the functions of the Union and State governments, which has translated into a division of expenditure responsibilities and taxation powers between them. The Constitution also specifies exclusive functions of the Centre in the Union list and the exclusive functions of states in the State list. The Concurrent list captures all other subjects falling under the Union's and States' joint jurisdiction. Further, all residual expenditures, functions as well as residual powers of taxation have been assigned to the Centre. In such a federal set up, arrangements of powers, functions and responsibilities between the Union and State governments has always been a crucial issue. Over the years, it has been observed that the legislative, administrative and financial powers are disproportionately assigned in favour of the Union Government, whereas the states have crucial responsibilities without adequate financial power either to augment resources or autonomy in spending the resources received as grants from the former.

However, since the early 1990s, with significant twists and turns in the socio-economic and political arena, important changes have been noticed in the sphere of Centre-State relations. It has been commonly noted that during the era of economic reforms, followed by the legislation of Fiscal Responsibility and Budget Management (FRBM) in 2003, the fiscal health of the states in India has come under serious stress, particularly in terms of provisioning for their development needs.

Given the crisis in their fiscal health since then, most states have become heavily dependent on the Central grants for financing new and targeted interventions for facilitating socio-economic development. Agriculture, even though a state subject, receives a sizeable chunk of resources from the Union budget under Centrally Sponsored Schemes (CSSs) and Central Sector Schemes. However, in 2007, the National Development Council (NDC) approved the proposal for implementing Rashtriya Krishi Vikas Yojana (RKVY), a flagship programme of the Union Government of India (GoI). The RKVY has been implemented as part of Additional Central Assistance (ACA) Scheme of the Union government, but primarily as a State Plan Scheme, and was rolled out in 2007-08. Under RKVY, states have been given adequate flexibility to design programmes appropriately to accommodate local needs. However, it has been observed that the states were unable to spend the proposed amount fully under the Scheme during the Eleventh Five Year Plan (FYP), even after introduction of a couple of sub-schemes in the later years of the Plan. Although the proposed allocation for RKVY in the Twelfth FYP period (2012-2017) increased substantially over the Eleventh FYP, utilisation of funds has remained a serious concern.

Further, it has also been noticed that inadequate awareness programmes about the scheme for the beneficiaries has resulted in low levels of fund utilisation. One of the major constraints in effective utilisation of allocated funds is the shortage of required human resources at different levels of programme implementation. This field level study reveals that a high percentage of vacant posts, as against the sanctioned strength and contractual nature of the deployed staff, has made the implementation difficult and tardy. Despite the scheme being devised so as to follow a bottom-up approach, budgets, planning and selection of beneficiaries in most of the cases have been observed to be a top-down exercise. A lack of need-based budgeting and rigorous analysis of the unit costs required have resulted in poor outcomes and failure in achieving the core objectives of the scheme. Moreover, a lack of coordination among different government agencies/institutions/departments and poor convergence of existing similar schemes/programmes have made matters worse.

In this context, this research study attempts to collate evidences on major underlying issues and concerns regarding poor fund utilisation under RKVY in four districts across three states of India since its inception. In order to contextualise the issue and to highlight the gravity of the problem, a brief introduction with relevant literature is placed in the next section. Apart from this, a snapshot of the performance of the Indian agriculture sector has also been highlighted in this section. In section II, relevant trends and patterns of fund allocation and utilisation under RKVY have been discussed. Section III presents specific case studies on the concerns relating to planning, budgeting and utilisation of funds under RKVY. Section IV concludes the paper with a few policy pointers.

Introduction

Balanced growth with development is one of the pre-requisites for long-term economic progress. In India, the planning process has striven to strike a balance between different sectors of the economy. The Independent India had inherited a weak economy with almost stagnant agriculture and industrial sectors, and the first FYP accordingly laid emphasis on the development of both agricultural and industrial sectors, with a focus on the primary sector. Gradually, the base was built as Indian economy progressed from one Plan to the other. At the time of Independence, with more than 80 per cent of the population dependent on agriculture, it was obvious that this sector acquired importance for planned policy intervention.

With the introduction of Green Revolution (GR) during the mid-1960s, the agriculture sector paid substantial dividends, and the period from 1980s until mid-1990s stands out as the most prosperous era for India's agriculture in terms of growth performance compared to all other decades since Independence. In fact, the annual average growth rate of primary sector (which comprises agriculture, forestry and fishing, mining and quarrying) in the decade of 1980s was 4.74 per cent compared to 2.78, 2.65 and 1.35 per cent during the 1950s, 1960s and 1970s, respectively. For the last decade, the relevant figure stands at 2.68 per cent (Table 19.1). In fact, growth performance of the primary sector during the 1980s was not too far behind the overall growth (decadal) of GDP (gross domestic product), which stood at 5.59 per cent, the highest since Independence until then. However, in the decades of 1990s and 2000s, the gap between the overall GDP growth rate and that of the primary sector has increased substantially (Table 19.1).

Table 19.1

Decade-wise Annual Average Growth Rates of the Primary Sector and of GDP (at 2004-05 Prices, in Per cent)

Period	*For Primary Sector*	*For GDP*
Annual Average (1951-52 to 1959-60)	2.78	3.59
Annual Average (1960-61 to 1969-70)	2.65	3.95
Annual Average (1970-71 to 1979-80)	1.35	2.95
Annual Average (1980-81 to 1989-90)	4.74	5.59
Annual Average (1990-91 to 1999-2000)	3.39	5.81
Annual Average (2000-01 to 2009-10)	2.68	7.26

Source: Computed by the authors from the base date given in the *Economic Survey, 2012-13*, GoI.

As noted, Indian agriculture received a shot in the arm with introduction of the HYVs (high yielding varieties) during the phase of GR and in fact this was instrumental in making India self-sufficient in the production of foodgrains. No doubt, with HYVs and better technology in use over the decade of 1980s and until mid-1990s, like the development of primary sector, growth in the agriculture sector also performed in tandem with that of the overall economy. After witnessing fairly high growth rate of GDP for agriculture and allied sectors of about 4.8 per cent over the Eighth FYP, there was a sharp fall during the Ninth FYP to 2.5 per cent. Although during the Tenth FYP the growth rate of overall economy improved to reach 7.8 per cent per annum, compared to only 5.52 per cent in the previous FYP, the agriculture and allied sectors recorded a growth rate of as low as 2.4 per cent per annum. However in the recent period, there has been a spurt in growth rate of agriculture and allied sectors, which was estimated to be 4.1 per cent per annum (Table 19.2).

Table 19.2

Average Growth Rates of GDP, Overall Economy and for Agriculture and Allied Sector (Percentage Per Annum, at 1999-2000 Price)

Period	*Years*	*Overall Economy*	*Agriculture and Allied Sectors*
Pre-green revolution	1951-52 to 1967-68	3.69	2.54
Green revolution	1968-69 to 1980-81	3.52	2.44
Wider technology dissemination period	1981-82 to 1990-91	5.4	3.52
Early reforms period	1991-92 to 1996-97	5.69	3.66
Ninth FYP period	1997-98 to 2001-02	5.52	2.5
Tenth FYP period	2002-03 to 2006-07	7.77	2.47
Post RKVY			
Eleventh FYP period*	2007-08 to 2011-12	8.0	4.1

Note: * at 2004-05 prices.
Source: Eleventh FYP document, Planning Commission, GoI.

Anecdotal evidences show that the recent growth of agriculture sector owes much to the implementation of RKVY, along with other push factors. It is true that performance of Indian agriculture has been well below its potential almost consistently since Independence (other than the decades of 1980s and until mid-1990s), and it may be argued that the problems have become more serious in the neo-liberal era largely because of the change in overall macro-policy regime. In this regard, it is important to note that in the 1950s, the annual growth average rate of total foodgrains was 5.08 per cent, which tended to decline during the next few decades before picking up in the 1980s (4.96%) awing to spread and deepening of the GR package. However, this was halved to 2.18 per cent in the 1990s and in the subsequent period, it nose-dived to about 1 per cent. On the whole, 1980s was the best decade in terms of yield growth rates since Independence; and the last decade (2000-01 to 2009-10) clearly stands out for its worst performance (both with respect to yield as well as output) (Table 19.3).

Hence, it may be said that much of the growth in agriculture and allied sectors during the Eleventh FYP period was contributed by the allied sectors (largely with a spurt in growth from the animal husbandry sub-sector and to some extent due to increased pulses production).

The stagnancy in the growth of agriculture sector for almost a decade (during Ninth and Tenth FYP) raised concerns, especially so because a large percentage of rural population of the country continued to depend on this sector for their livelihood. The situation in the agriculture sector and the rural areas was so deplorable that it was termed as a crisis period for Indian agriculture. The Mid-Term Appraisal (MTA) for the Tenth FYP had noted that there was a loss of dynamism in agriculture and allied sectors after the mid-1990s (Eleventh FYP document: 3-4).

Table 19.3

Growth Rates of Production of Cereals, Pulses and Total Foodgrains since 1950s

Year	*Annual Average Growth Rates*					
	Rice	*Wheat*	*Coarse Cereals*	*Total Cereals*	*Pulses*	*Total Foodgrains*
Annual Average (1951-52 to 1959-60)	5.52	6.02	5.00	5.19	4.83	5.08
Annual Average (1960-61 to 1969-70)	3.13	8.15	2.32	3.62	1.62	3.25
Annual Average (1970-71 to 1979-80)	1.53	5.30	0.71	1.99	-1.99	1.58
Annual Average (1980-81 to 1989-90)	6.56	4.91	3.26	4.98	4.90	4.96
Annual Average (1990-91 to 1999-2000)	2.09	4.52	-0.08	2.29	0.94	2.18
Annual Average (2000-01 to 2009-10)	0.68	0.77	2.47	0.87	1.99	0.93

Source: Computed by the Authors based on the data available on *Handbook of Statistics on Indian Economy*, RBI, 2011-12.

It has been well established that public investment has a positive impact on the growth in agriculture sector. As can be seen from Table 19.4, the overall investment in agriculture (public and private) witnessed a considerable decline, which remained below 10 per cent of the agricultural GDP until 2000-01 and increased only marginally thereafter. There was also a consistent decline in public investment in agriculture from mid-1980s to 2000-01, with the GCF (gross capital formation) in agriculture as the percentage of agricultural-GDP reaching a meagre 1.8 per cent in 2000-01. The public investment has remained low throughout, with private investment surpassing the public investment by substantial margins. It was only during the Eleventh FYP that the investment in agriculture consistently maintained a double-digit figure, reaching about 20 per cent of the agricultural-GDP in 2010-11 (Table 19.4).

Table 19.4

Gross Capital Formation (GCF) in Agriculture as percentage of Agri-GDP

Year	*GCF in Agriculture as Per cent of GDP Originating from Agriculture Ssector*		
	Public Sector	*Private Sector*	*Total*
1980-81 to 1984-85	5.0	5.5	10.5
1985-86 to 1989-90	3.5	5.2	8.7
1990-91 to 1994-95	2.4	5.9	8.4
1995-96 to 1999-2000	2.0	5.9	7.9
2000-01	1.8	7.8	9.6
2010-11*	3.0	17	20.1

Note: * at 2004-05 prices.

Source: Compiled from Eleventh and Twelfth FYP document,Planning Commission, GoI.

Thus, the impact of various structural inadequacies, e.g. low public investment, adverse terms of trade, slow pace of research and minimal technological up-gradation, and lack of dynamism contributed to low growth and low productivity in Indian agriculture. During the initial years of the decade of 2000, i.e. from 2002-03 to 2004-05, the growth rate in agriculture was below 1.0 per cent. This low growth started manifesting in increased rate of hunger and malnutrition and an upsurge in farmers' suicides. While in 1999-2000, the share of agriculture in total employment was 59.9 per cent and the share of agriculture in GDP was 23.2 per cent, in 2013-14, the share in employment decreased to 54.6 per cent (Census, 2011), and that of GDP dropped down to 13.9 per cent. Therefore, despite the sharp

Table 19.5

State-wise Annual Average Share of Expenditure on 'Ag and RD' Out of Aggregate Expenditure of the Respective States (in %)

State/Year	*Annual Average Share (1991-92 to 1999-2000)*	*Annual Average Share (2000-01 to 2009-10)*
Andhra Pradesh	21.27	21.88
Arunachal Pradesh	19.02	16.26
Assam	15.47	13.3
Bihar	18.05	16.27
Chhattisgarh	NA	20.13
Goa	9.15	7.62
Gujarat	22.88	14.96
Haryana	14.58	12.11
Himachal Pradesh	11.46	8.47
Jammu and Kashmir	13.2	11.38
Jharkhand	NA	18.91
Karnataka	23.32	17.83
Kerala	18.11	10.58
Madhya Pradesh	18.36	15.31
Maharashtra	26.01	20.26
Manipur	15.68	13.86
Meghalaya	16.09	14.94
Mizoram	19.25	14.36
Nagaland	15.04	13.09
Odisha	19.78	13.29
Punjab	12.53	7.92
Rajasthan	17.48	12.3
Sikkim	6.78	7.88
Tamil Nadu	17.73	11.53
Tripura	17.03	12.23
Uttar Pradesh	20.46	14.13
Uttarakhand	NA	16.65
West Bengal	16.34	9.07
All States	19.35	14.89

Note: 'Ag and RD' refers to 'Agriculture and Rural Development'.

Source: Jha and Acharya (2011).

fall in its contribution to GDP of the economy, the agriculture sector continued to support nearly 55 per cent of the country's population for their livelihood (*Economic Survey*, 2013-14).

Agriculture and agricultural practices across India are diverse in nature, owing to different agro-climatic conditions. The policies and priorities of different states, accordingly, differ in this sphere. A comparison of the annual average share of expenditure through annual budgets on agriculture and rural development (combined), as a percentage of aggregate expenditure in different states between two decades—1991-92 to 1999-2000 and 2000-01 to 2009-10—shows that there was a temporal decline in this share across almost all the states (except Andhra Pradesh [AP] and Sikkim). For all states combined, the annual average share of expenditure on agriculture and rural development declined from 19.35 per cent between 1991-1992 and 1999-2000 to 14.89 per cent between 2000-01 and 2009-2010 (Table 19.5). This indicates a pervasive neglect of agriculture and structural bottlenecks in the sector across states in India.

Analysing the state-wise growth rate in agriculture and allied sectors in the pre-RKVY and post-RKVY period, it is found that as an outcome of this general neglect of the sector and decreasing public investment, both in the Union and State government budgets, the growth of agriculture sector stagnated and even tended to decline during the latter half of 1990s and early 2000s (period prior to the introduction of RKVY). The post-RKVY period has seen better growth rates across most of the States. This can be seen from the data presented in Table 19.6.

This substantiates the argument that with the implementation of RKVY, the agriculture sector has tended to grow considerably well in almost all the States barring a few. It may be seen that states like AP, Arunachal Pradesh, Assam, Chhattisgarh, Jharkhand, Karnataka, Madhya Pradesh (MP), Odisha, Tripura, Uttar Pradesh (UP), Uttarakhand and West Bengal, have been performing better in terms of growth of the agriculture sector during the post-RKVY period as compared to the pre-RKVY period. At the all-India level too better performance of the agriculture sector can be seen during the post-RKVY period. However, during the post-RKVY period, states like

Bihar, Gujarat, Haryana, Punjab and Rajasthan have been performing way below compared to their performance in this sector during the pre-RKVY decade.

Table 19.6

State-wise Growth Rates of Agriculture and Allied Sector since 1996-97

States	*Annual Average 1996-97 to 2006-07 (Pre -RKVY)*	*Annual Average 2007-08 to 2013-14 (Post-RKVY)*
Andhra Pradesh	4.00	5.41
Arunachal Pradesh	0.96	4.11
Assam	0.22	4.05
Bihar	7.04	3.60
Chhattisgarh	2.52	6.09
Goa	0.43	0.63
Gujarat	6.65	3.70
Haryana	3.29	2.97
Himachal Pradesh	4.07	4.96
Jammu and Kashmir	3.19	2.28
Jharkhand	5.57	8.30
Karnataka	1.38	3.40
Kerala	0.90	-0.48
Madhya Pradesh	3.25	10.94
Maharashtra	4.27	3.55
Manipur	4.31	2.95
Meghalaya	5.04	3.99
Mizoram	3.19	4.40
Nagaland	10.97	4.56
Odisha	2.04	2.78
Punjab	2.33	1.34
Rajasthan	6.72	5.66
Sikkim	3.88	4.59
Tamil Nadu	3.30	2.05
Tripura	4.72	8.80
Uttar Pradesh	2.41	3.44
Uttarakhand	1.93	3.33
West Bengal	2.26	2.90
All India	3.07	3.78

Source: Computed from the data tables from the Planning Commission website.

To summarise the section, it would be worth highlighting the findings noted in the Twelfth FYP document (Vol. II: 10):

> ...the Eleventh Plan architecture, with the RKVY as core, appears to have delivered despite adverse weather, a public investment shortfall and implementation gaps. The strategy of spreading known technology wider had paid.

Trends and Patterns of Fund Allocation and Utilisation under RKVY

As discussed above, a period with slow pace of public investment resulting in poor growth performance of the sector, and in the wake of a serious crisis (often termed as rural crisis manifested in large number of farmers' suicides), the Eleventh FYP set out to rejuvenate the sector with a massive boost in public investment. Hence, the year 2007-08, the first year of the Eleventh FYP, saw major policy initiatives being undertaken to address the concerns. The adoption of the National Policy for Farmers, launch of National Food Security Mission (NFSM) and implementation of RKVY were among the measures initiated to give a boost to the long-ailing agricultural sector.

In conjunction with the objectives of the National Policy for Farmers and the Eleventh FYP, the RKVY aimed at achieving a 4 per cent annual growth in the agriculture sector during the Eleventh FYP period by ensuring a holistic development of the agriculture and allied sectors. Thus, as per the National Development (NDC) resolution, RKVY was introduced as a "special Additional Central Assistance Scheme (ACA) to incentivise States to draw up comprehensive agriculture development plans taking into account agro-climatic conditions, natural resources and technology for ensuring more inclusive and integrated development of agriculture and allied sector" (RKVY Operational Guidelines: 1). The stated objectives of the RKVY were:

i) To incentivise the states so as to increase public investment in agriculture and allied sectors;

ii) To provide flexibility and autonomy to States in the process of planning and executing agriculture and allied sector schemes;

iii) To ensure the preparation of agriculture plans for the districts and the States based on agro-climatic conditions, availability of technology and natural resources;
iv) To ensure that the local needs/crops/priorities are better reflected in agricultural plans of the States;
v) To achieve the goal of reducing the yield gaps in important crops through focused interventions;
vi) To maximise returns to the farmers in agriculture and allied sectors; and
vii) To bring about quantifiable changes in the production and productivity of various components of agriculture and allied sectors by addressing them in a holistic manner.

Thus, RKVY was designed to give more flexibility to States, and incentivise them to spend more on agriculture on the basis of properly designed district and state plans. As noted in the Eleventh FYP document, the RKVY requires that every district should draw up a district plan that fully utilises an initial resource envelope available from all existing schemes, State or Central, including resources at district level from Central schemes such as those of Rural Development, Ministry of Panchayati Raj, Ministry of Water Resources, and other ministries. The District Agricultural Plan (DAP) should include livestock and fishing and be integrated with minor irrigation projects, rural development works, and other schemes for water harvesting and conservation. The State Agricultural Plan (SAP) should be based on these initial DAPs, subject to reasonable resources from its own plan and adding those available from the Centre, aimed at achieving the state's agricultural growth objective, keeping in view the sustainable management of natural resources and technological possibilities in each agro-climatic region (Eleventh FYP: 39)

As noted earlier, the RKVY is implemented as a State Plan scheme with 100 per cent grant from the Union government. However, a state becomes eligible to receive RKVY fund if and only if:

i) The base line[1] share of agriculture and allied sectors in its total state plan (excluding RKVY funds) expenditure is at least maintained; and

ii) DAPs and SAPs have been formulated.

Further, the objectives of the Comprehensive District Agriculture Plan (C-DAP) are:

i) To prepare a C-DAP through participatory process involving various organisations and stakeholders;

ii) To enable optimum utilisation of scarce natural, physical and financial resources;

iii) To assess and plan for the infrastructure required to support agriculture development;

iv) To establish linkages with the required institutional support services, like credit, technology transfer, ICT (information and communication technology), research, etc., and

v) To evolve an action plan for achieving sustainable agricultural growth with food security and cropping system that will improve farmers' income.

However, in many instances, it has been found that preparation of C-DAP has remained merely a technical exercise and consultation with stakeholders, particularly with farmers (the beneficiaries) at the district level have largely been ignored. Further, it has also been observed that proposals given in C-DAP were not included in SAP and a number of stakeholders (including the implementing personnel) were of the view that targets have been dictated from above.

Table 19.7 shows that over the Eleventh Plan period, the release of funds as percentage of allocation and the expenditure out of these releases were quite satisfactory, recording more than 97 per cent under each. It should be noted here that this 97 per cent of expenditure against the release of funds under RKVY could be achieved due to the introduction of a couple of sub-schemes during

1. The base line level of expenditure is the "minimum of the percentage expenditure incurred on agriculture and other identified sectors during three years preceding to previous year." For states to become eligible "average percentage share of expenditure in agriculture and other identified related sectors during last three years" should be at least equal to base line level of expenditure. (*Source*: *Rashtriya Krishi Vikas Yojana (RKVY) Operational Guidelines for XII Five Year Plan*. Government of India, 2014).

the latter part of the Eleventh FYP. On the other hand, one must also note here that the proposed allocation for RKVY during this FYP was ₹25,000 crore. While comparing the actual expenditure of funds with that of the proposed allocation under RKVY during the Eleventh FYP, there is a shortfall of around 11 per cent.

Table 19.7

Funds Allocated, Released and Expenditure under RKVY since 2007-08

(in ₹crore)

Years	*Total Allocation*	*Total Release*	*Total Expenditure*	*Release as % of Total Allocation*	*Expenditure as % of Total Release*
2007-08	1489.7	1246.9	1246.8	83.7	100.0
2008-09	3165.7	2886.8	2880.9	91.2	99.8
2009-10	3806.7	3760.9	3756.5	98.8	99.9
2010-11	6722	6720.1	6720.1	100.0	100.0
2011-12	7810.9	7794.1	7715.2	99.8	99.0
11th FYP Period	22995	22408.8	22319.5	97.5	99.6
2012-13	9217	8400	8318.5	91.1	99.0
2013-14 RE	9954	7052.5	5172.8	70.9	73.3
2014-15 BE	9954	4741.4	538.5	47.6	11.4

Source: Collated from the RKVY website *http://rkvy.nic.in/*, accessed on 17 October 2014.

From Table 19.8 it is observed that as in September 2014, the total amount spent and Utilisation Certificates (UCs) furnished under RKVY were to the tune of ₹21,226.31 crore against the fund released, i.e., ₹27601 crore. The amount spent during the period stands at just 77 per cent of that released (Table 19.8) for all the states combined. Such low levels of utilisation of funds under RKVY have been a serious concern, especially with regard to achievement of the targeted objectives in the sector.

Further, a disaggregated analysis of RKVY data on expenditure as percentage of release across states shows that the proportion of funds utilised under RKVY against the amount released varies from one state to the other. While Mizoram records 100 per cent expenditure against fund released under RKVY, merely 55 per cent of funds were spent by Punjab. Only three states, namely AP, Kerala and Mizoram, have been able to spend more than 90 per cent of funds against the amount released under RKVY. States like Arunachal Pradesh, Chhattisgarh, Himachal Pradesh (HP), Manipur, Nagaland, Odisha, Sikkim and Uttarakhand have been able to spend between 80-90 per cent, and others show less than 80 per cent of funds-spent under RKVY against the release (Table 19.8).

Table 19.8

Release and Expenditure of Funds under RKVY (as Reported by States) including Sub-schemes (as on 30 September 2014)

States	*Release*	*Expenditure*	*UCs Received*	*Expenditure as % of Release*	*UCs as % of Release*
Andhra Pradesh	1839.23	1688.69	1688.69	91.8	91.8
Arunachal Pradesh	68.66	60.39	60.39	88	88
Assam	1051.92	829.81	829.81	78.9	78.9
Bihar	1824.32	1440.77	1440.77	79	79
Chhattisgarh	1208.74	1001.51	1001.51	82.9	82.9
Goa	70.48	49.01	49.01	69.5	69.5
Gujarat	1769.92	1279	1279	72.3	72.3
Haryana	698.16	489.26	489.26	70.1	70.1
Himachal Pradesh	279.65	235.98	235.98	84.4	84.4
Jammu and Kasmir	330.02	236.73	236.73	71.7	71.7
Jharkhand	694.19	489.43	489.43	70.5	70.5
Karnataka	1928.03	1388.04	1388.04	72	72
Kerala	731.25	672.01	672.01	91.9	91.9
Madhya Pradesh	1390.84	1097.71	1097.71	78.9	78.9
Maharashtra	3252.69	2155.01	2155.01	66.3	66.3
Manipur	115.39	93.88	93.88	81.4	81.4
Meghalaya	115.49	81.07	81.07	70.2	70.2
Mizoram	298.77	298.77	298.77	100	100
Nagaland	179.74	153.36	153.36	85.3	85.3
Odisha	1606.73	1362.7	1362.7	84.8	84.8
Punjab	716.49	393.77	393.77	55	55
Rajasthan	2145.78	1703.47	1703.47	79.4	79.4
Sikkim	59.54	49.95	49.95	83.9	83.9
Tamil Nadu	1365.77	1073.77	1073.77	78.6	78.6
Telangana	90.45	0	0	0	0
Tripura	192.7	152.56	152.56	79.2	79.2
Uttar Pradesh	1969.74	1491.99	1491.99	75.7	75.7
Uttarakhand	181.08	150.25	150.25	83	83
West Bengal	1425.62	1107.42	1107.42	77.7	77.7
Total	27601.38	21226.31	21226.31	76.9	76.9

Source: Collated from the RKVY website *http://rkvy.nic.in/*, accessed on 17 October 2014.

Before getting into the details of noting concerns relating to fund utilisation under RKVY, it would be pertinent to briefly discuss about nature and number of projects (sub-sectors in which funds have been spent) that have been undertaken under RKVY. Data presented in Table 19.9 shows that bulk of the investment under RKVY between the period 2007-08 and 2013-14 has been made in the horticultural sector, followed by crop development, micro and minor irrigation, animal husbandry, agriculture mechanisation and on seed sectors. Further, in terms of number of projects taken up in each of these sectors over this period, the animal husbandry sector (1463) tops the list, closely followed by the horticulture sector (1272). In total, there are as many as 20 sectors that have received funds under RKVY to the tune of ₹48,912 crore having 8941 projects (Table 19.9). The Twelfth FYP document notes that RKVY assistance was particularly useful for the funds-starved animal husbandry, dairy and fisheries sectors (Twelfth FYP document: 48). Almost 30 per cent of the total sanctioned projects have been implemented in these three sectors during the Eleventh FYP period.

In this paper, which undertakes a district-specific analysis of the RKVY, the districts chosen are spread across three predominantly agricultural states of India, *viz.*, MP, Rajasthan and UP. Table 19.10 traces the quantum of funds allocated, released and the expenditure incurred under the RKVY scheme, since its inception, in these three select states.

In all the three states, barring the initial year of RKVY's launch, the percentage of expenditure to the amount allocated was 100 per cent during 2008-09 to 2011-12. However, in 2012-13, the expenditure was less than the amount allocated in all the three states. The worst performance was that of UP where fund utilisation was only 68 per cent of the amount allocated. It may also be noted that in this very year (2012-13), there was a substantial fall in the allocated amount itself under RKVY in both Rajasthan and UP, allthough in MP it was higher than the previous year. One of the probable reasons for low allocations in the year 2012-13 may be related to the delays in finalising the Twelfth FYP, and it marks the first year of ongoing plan period. This reflects the fact that under RKVY, grants from the Centre are contingent upon each state's own contribution to the sector in their respective annual budgets. At the end of the Eleventh FYP, there were already apprehensions regarding whether RKVY would be continuing in the next FYP and if continued, in which form. Thus, allocation and expenditure under RKVY during 2012-13 mark this break.

Table 19.9

Sector-wise total Number of Projects Taken up and Costs Approved under RKVY

Sectors	*2007-08 to 2013-14*		*2014-15**	
	Total Cost	*Total No. of Projects*	*Total Cost*	*Total No. of Projects*
Agriculture Mechanisation	4271.3	407	346.0	56
Animal Husbandry	4915.0	1463	554.6	160
Cooperatives and Cooperation	1106.4	143	119.1	26
Crop Development	6118.7	675	1506.7	66
Dairy Development	1830.7	387	94.6	22
Extension	1981.2	442	273.1	37
Fertilisers and INM	810.1	159	48.1	14
Fisheries	1622.4	831	165.7	74
Horticulture	7615.1	1272	516.4	177
Information Technology	133.2	42	3.8	1
Innovative Programmes/Training/Capacity Building/Others	2174.3	241	284.1	53
Integrated Pest Management	611.8	152	24.7	9
Marketing and Post-Harvest Management	2163.1	422	289.3	34
Micro/Minor Irrigation	5177.7	383	686.5	61
Natural Resource Management	2582.8	373	185.9	33
Non-Farm Activities	283.4	117	276.1	35
Organic Farming/Bio-Fertiliser	1015.4	227	59.2	29
Research (Agriculture/Horticulture/Animal Husbandry, etc.)	1040.4	600	120.6	108
Seed	3247.5	438	511.9	54
Sericulture	211.7	167	46.8	32
Total	48912.1	8941	6113.2	1081

Source: RKVY website-Year-wise/sector wise summary of projects http://*rkvymis.dacnet.nic.in/(S (std5n5k1yxeuyupmjimc4505))*/-reports/SectorSummary.aspx, accessed on 17 October 2014.

Table 19.10

Fund Allocation, Release and Expenditure under RKVY for Select States since 2007-08

Year	Madhya Pradesh			Rajasthan			Uttar Pradesh		
	Allocation	Release	Expenditure	Allocation	Release	Expenditure	Allocation	Release	Expenditure
2007-08	110.01	101.62	101.62 (92.4)	71.68	55.76	55.76 (77.8)	116.15	103.9	103.9 (89.5)
2008-09	146.05	146.05	146.05 (100)	233.75	233.76	233.76 (100)	316.57	316.57	316.57(100)
2009-10	247.44	247.44	247.44 (100)	186.12	186.12	186.12 (100)	390.97	390.97	390.97 (100)
2010-11	589.09	559.18	559.18 (94.9)	572.47	628.01	628.01(109.7)	635.92	695.36	695.36 (109.3)
2011-12	398.37	398.37	398.37 (100)	685.04	692.08	692.08 (101)	757.26	762.83	762.83 (100.7)
2012-13	448.13	448.13	434.12 (96.9)	363.09	348.18	348.18 (95.9)	432.26	294.52	294.52 (68.1)
2013-14	545.15	276.25	265.22 (48.7)	735.24	735.24	663.21 (90.2)	746.69	561.09	434.64(58.2)
2014-15*	547.55	268.09	-	740.55	370.28	133.66 (18)	704.93	351.3	-

Note: Figures in parentheses are expenditure as per cent of amount allocated; *: Figures available upto 30 September 2014.

Source: Compiled from base data given on RKVY website.

Concerns Relating to Planning, Budgeting and Utilisation of Funds under RKVY

While analysing the design, timing and structure of fund releases under RKVY, a number of studies (CBGA, 2014) point out that low utilisation of funds may be due to delay in their release. During the initial years of RKVY, although there were inter-state variations in the pattern of releases, most of it were done in the second and third quarters. Regardless of proving beneficial in providing agriculture with the required impetus, there are still a number of problems encountered in implementation of RKVY. As reported in one of the specific study for MP,[2] some of these issues include lack of long-term clarity on fund flows, overlap of CSS pre-dating RKVY, lack of clarity on convergence with other development programmes, planning capacity at district level needs a considerable and higher overhead costs 5% instead of 1%).

Further, while highlighting on the functioning of RKVY, a parliamentary committee[3] noted that one of the primary objectives of the Yojana in the Eleventh Plan was to reduce the yield gaps in important crops and to ensure that states increase their plan allocation to the agriculture and allied sectors, as GCF in the sector was unsatisfactory. The Committee concludes that not much headway has been made in this regard during the Eleventh Plan and huge yield gaps continue to persist across the country. It also notes that in certain crops, the gaps are bigger than the others.

The Report cites the findings of National Institute of Rural Development and Panchayati Raj (NIRD&PR)[4] and notes that:

> The States have not been able to balance investments in growth oriented projects and projects for development of agricultural infrastructure. Infrastructure development, if any by the States was not found to be based on any definite vision or plan. Further, there has been thin spread of RKVY resources across all sectors and amongst all districts of the States.

---

2. For further details, please see *http://agricoop.nic.in/rkvy/mp.ppt.*
3. For details refer to the 61st Report of the Committee on Agriculture (Lok Sabha) entitled, "Rashtriya Krishi Vikas Yojana—An Evaluation".
4. The study was commissioned by the DAC, GoI, in 2008 to undertake concurrent evaluation of RKVY during the Eleventh Plan period.

The Committee also cautioned the government on the Public Private Partnership for Integrated Agriculture Development (PPPIAD) launched under RKVY, saying that PPPIAD must not result in exploitation of farmers. The PPPIAD envisages facilitating large scale integrated projects led by private sector players in the agriculture and allied sectors. Each project is to target at least 5,000 farmers with an average investment of ₹1 lakh per farmer through a project cycle of 3-5 years. The intervention also aims to include mobilisation of farmers into producer groups, technology infusion, value addition and marketing solutions.

Further, a need to strengthen the monitoring mechanisms must be noted for better implementation of the scheme.[5] At the Union level, there is hardly any monitoring except taking stock of the progress and receiving UCs at the time of release of second instalment of the RKVY fund. According to the officials, the difficulty in monitoring RKVY is that the projects undertaken are so diverse in nature that it is difficult to group them. This directly points to a lack of convergence across schemes and underlines a need for developing synergy in their implementation, aiming at overall development of the agriculture sector. Thus, there are certain structural problems inherent in the RKVY scheme, which need to be addressed.

There have been some interventions under the RKVY which have turned out to be successful. Here, we note some of the successful interventions[6] made in three states, namely MP, Rajasthan and UP. These are the select states from which four of the districts have been chosen for the district-specific analysis of relevant data in the present study.

In MP, rice is the main crop covering nearly 76 per cent of its net cultivated area. The results of the initiatives taken under RKVY, particularly with regard to Seed Replacement Rate (SRR) in paddy, show an overall increase in area, production and use of quality paddy seeds. Lack of infrastructural facilities have been a major constraint under the SRR and under RKVY construction of new seed processing

5. Ibid.

6. For details please refer to *http://rkvy.nic.in/Index_for_success_stories.html.*

centres, strengthening of old processing centres, construction of seed warehouses, and subsidy on seed production and distribution have been undertaken. Similarly, the Kisan Call Centres (KCCs) were established in MP under RKVY during 2008-09, which to some extent facilitates an interface between the farmers and the engineers and promotes better agriculture practices in the field. Under the RKVY, another initiative taken up in the state was inclusion of percolation tanks and micro/minor irrigation tanks. The overall status of production and productivity of the major crops in MP has recorded significant improvement since the Yojana intervention.

Rajasthan ranks third in milk production in India. The Dairy Cooperative Societies (DCSs) collect milk from the small dairy owners. The milk is retained in a DCS until the milk tanker reaches its collection centre. In many cases, the milk is transported in raw form to the district level milk processing plants in simple plastic/aluminium milk cans, and the time between milking and its delivery to the milk processing plant is at times long enough to adversely affect the quality of milk. The installation of Bulk Milk Coolers (BMCs) at village level DCSs, despite being done before RKVY, received a significant boost after RKVY funds became available in 2007-08. Installation of BMCs has substantially boosted the process of dairy development in Rajasthan.

In western UP, an attempt has been made to enhance area and production of pulses by inter-cropping with sugarcane, with funding from RKVY. For increasing the area and production of pulses, inter-cropping with sugarcane is considered as one of the potential possibilities because of crop compatibility and timing. A scheme for increasing area and production of pulses through inter cropping with spring sown sugarcane has been implemented under RKVY in major sugarcane growing areas of UP since February 2011. This project has promoted efficient use of cultivated land, and created soil fertility has further resulted in increased production of sugarcane. In another experiment, the area affected by the floods in the river Ramganga, which had gradually been converted into wasteland and where the occurrence of perennial weeds had stopped agricultural activities, has been taken up for land reclamation and turned into cultivated land.

This has been made possible with the usage of funds available under RKVY.

However, these success stories are only one side of the picture. There are a number of problem areas in implementation of RKVY, like those pertaining to inadequate human resources and lack of proper monitoring mechanisms. In this context, it is worth referring to the observations noted in the Twelfth FYP, which stressed for a detailed impact assessment of the scheme for further learning, and also suggested some modifications. It has made two specific suggestions. One, constituting a proper committee to examine and vet all projects proposed to State Level Sanctioning Committee (SLSC); and two, that this committee or the SLSC must work closely and be coterminous with state level bodies for better convergence and project selection (Twelfth FYP document: 48).

District-specific Analysis of RKVY: A Case of Four Districts in Three States

In order to assess RKVY in greater details, the Centre for Budget and Governance Accountability (CBGA), a New Delhi-based public policy research and think tank, undertook a study in collaboration with its state level partner organisations. The study covered three States—MP, Rajasthan and UP, and four districts were chosen from these three states—Rajgarh in MP, Alwar and Jhunjhunu in Rajasthan and Hardoi in UP.

The performance of RKVY was analysed in these select districts on three counts: a) assessment of the extent and quality of fund utilisation, b) factors constraining the extent and quality of fund utilisation, and c) concerns related to planning and budgeting. The findings of the study in each of the districts are summarised below. The study also captured the perceptions of various stakeholders in the scheme. The field study was conducted over a period from November 2012 to September 2013. The data analysis was undertaken for three consecutive financial years—2010-11, 2011-12 and 2012-13.

Assessment of Extent and Quality of Fund Utilisation under RKVY

It has been found that the extent and quality of fund utilisation under RKVY, in all select districts, has been very poor. Quality of fund utilisation under RKVY was measured in terms of three broad parameters, namely fund utilisation across geographical area (such as districts and sub-districts), across various components of the programme, and across quarters in a financial year.

With regard to the extent of fund utilisation across various components of the programme, a higher percentage of funds was found to be utilised under the components like salary, administrative expenses, etc. It was generally observed that components under which beneficiaries can be selected easily reflect better implementation and higher quantum of expenditure; while utilisation of funds is poor on components where beneficiary selection process is long drawn and cumbersome. It has also been observed that much of the RKVY funds have been disbursed in the third and fourth quarters of a financial year, which makes it difficult to properly and timely implement of the scheme for achieving the desired outcomes.

In the Rajgarh district of MP, fund utilisation as percentage of available funds increased over the three year period with 74 per cent in 2010-11 and increasing to 92 and 91 per cent in 2011-12 and 2012-13 respectively. Priority components with higher allocation have been demonstration and seed treatment, while popularisation of seed treatment, purchase of breeder seeds and seed production, hybrid seed distribution and tube wells are those with lower priority. Schemes like support for organic certification for small and marginal farmers, project for sugarcane development and projects to support tribals and families of malnourished children were also being poorly implemented. Funds were released in many instalments, on the basis of demands received from different blocks. It was found that although RKVY funds were being released from state to the district in many instalments, no data had been maintained regarding timeliness of fund disbursal.

In the Alwar district of Rajasthan, there were huge unspent balances noticed during the period 2010-11 to 2012-13. Expenditure as percentage of the proposed budget then ranged between 51-75 per cent only. However, expenditure as the percentage of released amount was 87-97 per cent during the study period. Direct beneficiary schemes, with long beneficiary selection process, were found to have low level of expenditure; expenditure was delayed in schemes like farm pond, water tank, etc. Physical progress (completion of projects on time) was very low—22 per cent in 2010-11 and 37 per cent in 2011-12. However, in 2012-13 this rose to 91 per cent. Schemes like material supply for quality control, and Gypsum distribution reflect higher expenditure because of the ease of selecting beneficiaries. It was observed that hardly any amount was spent until June (end of the first quarter), and most of the expenditure was incurred only in the fourth quarter of the financial year.

In the Jhunjhunu district of Rajasthan, there were huge unspent balances under RKVY at the district level during 2010-11 to 2012-2013. Expenditure as percentage of the proposed budget was 64-89 per cent; however, expenditure as percentage of the amount released was to the tune of 81-98 per cent during the study period. As in the case of Alwar, in Jhunjhunu the direct beneficiary schemes with a long beneficiary selection process were found to have low expenditure. Physical progress of certain projects undertaken under RKVY was very high, e.g., in Gypsum distribution programme. However, in 2010-11, physical progress was only 28 per cent increasing to 96 per cent in 2012-13. During the financial year, there was again a last quarter rush for incurring expenditure under RKVY.

In the Hardoi district of UP, under six heads (irrigation, agriculture, SIMA (Rahman Khera), administrative and animal husbandry), the percentage of expenditure ranged between 20 and 40 per cent leading to huge unspent balances during the study period. Under the other six heads (Sericulture, cooperative dairy farming, etc.), expenditure recorded was between 50 and 100 per cent. Overall, only 29 per cent of the total funds released by the state were spent.

Factors Constraining Quality of Fund Utilisation

Across all these districts, factors leading to low levels of fund utilisation under RKVY were found to be largely similar. Among others, shortage of human resources is prominent, particularly the posts of frontline service providers like Rural Agriculture Extension Officers (REAOs) in MP have been ideal. It was found that in Rajgarh district, there was a shortage of staff (overall) to the tune of around 43 per cent of the sanctioned posts and REAO posts were also lying vacant to the tune of around 46 per cent against the sanctioned posts.

Further, many officials who are involved in implementation of the scheme at the ground shared that the targets are dictated from the top, whereas ground level demands and priorities are completely different. This many a times results in poor fund utilisation under various sub-schemes and components of the programme. Most of the beneficiaries were not even aware about the scheme. Lack of monitoring mechanisms to ensure effective utilisation of funds has been another factor contributing to in appropriate fund utilisation. Lack of convergence among schemes has been a major factor in quality fund utilisation, along with failure to reflect state-specific problems and huge gaps in internal coordination among line departments at the district level, coupled with lack of accountability at almost all levels.

In Alwar district, it was found that bottom-up approach in planning and budgeting is missing. Slow process of beneficiary selection has been a major constraint in fund utilisation. Further, delay in fund allocation to the districts with no budget for administrative and management purpose at the sub-district levels resulted in parking of funds at the district level, even though availability of funds was expanded.

Problems Relating to Planning and Budgeting

Following the top-down approach of planning and budgeting and lack of adequate flexibility in the scheme, along with inadequate unit costs, have been a major hindrance in quality fund utilisation in all the four districts. The study captured perceptions from various stakeholders, and the study team recorded these perceptions. It is noted that although in most cases a fair system was being followed in beneficiary selection, the field officers were generally apathetic towards linking more farmers with the scheme. Also, in many instances, selection of beneficiaries was done on a lottery basis, which is an ad hoc exercise and erratic in nature. Small and marginal farmers were not interested in programmes like farm pond because it required a land of about 1-2 *bigha*, that they did not possess.

There were no sub-schemes or components addressing the needs of the disadvantaged sections of the population. The study also found that the data was available only up to district level; no financial and physical data was available at the sub-district levels. Even if the data and other information is collected and compiled by the officials at the sub-district level, there is no mechanism of keeping such information ready for easy dissemination.

The problem of poor and inadequate infrastructure had been shared by the officials implementing the programme at the grass-roots level. It was shared that sometimes political influence in selection of beneficiaries led to delay in project implementation and hence, failure in achieving the desired outcome and even accomplishing the targets. Due to shortage of human resources, particularly at the sub-district level, the quantum of work had increased over the years leading to poor monitoring of the programme, which ultimately affects the quality of fund utilisation.

There are a number of agencies who are involved in implementing various schemes funded through RKVY at the district level. Even though Agriculture line department has been working as the nodal agency itself at the district level, many other line departments often do not report to the district level nodal agency. An important observation noted by the study team was that in many line departments, RKVY funds were being spent on old schemes that were already being financed by the states, prior to RKVY. Further, there is no system of accountability to check incorrect reporting. Projects are scattered over the district with a huge number of beneficiaries and low unit costs, across departments. Hence, physical verification of the project outcomes becomes a huge task and sometimes it is nearly to impossible to verify whether the projects have even been completed.

Thus, despite RKVY bringing about improvements in the agricultural sector, there still are a number of areas which are a cause of concern. Although the scheme is devised so as to follow a bottom-up approach, the budgets, planning and selection of beneficiaries in most of the cases has been observed to be a top-down exercise. One of the most telling observations with regard to the preparation of C-DAP was a visible lack of capacity among the officials. This has been acknowledged in the Twelfth FYP (p.48) also that "...preparation of C-DAPs has been a weak area in many States, partly due to lack of capacity at district/State level." A lack of need-based budgeting in the scheme, which are also carried out without rigorous analysis of the unit costs on the ground, defeats the very purpose of strengthening the grass-roots in the policy-making and implementation process. Further, inadequate human resources and lack of awareness among the beneficiaries as well as the functionaries/implementing staff about intricacies of the scheme prove to be a hindrance in its proper execution.

Concluding Observations and Policy Pointers

In Indian economy, the agriculture sector still holds a place of significance, even though its contribution to the economy's share has dwindled to 13.9 per cent in 2013-14, and accounts for about 54.6 per cent of total employment. Due to the rainfall-dependant nature of Indian agriculture and tardy public investment, growth rates in the sector have been widely fluctuating. Given the dependence of a sizeable proportion of population on agriculture for livelihood, time and again, there have been efforts to revitalise the sector. In the wake of decade long condition of extremely low growth rates in agriculture over the period 1997-2007, and even negative growth rate in 2002-03, the latest efforts to resuscitate the sector were made in the form of schemes like the RKVY with the beginning of the Eleventh FYP in 2007-08. As discussed earlier in the paper, these efforts have yielded results and the target of 4 per cent growth rate in the agriculture sector for the Eleventh FYP was met. The RKVY has come about as a much-needed intervention by the Union government to support investment made by states in their respective agriculture and allied sectors. A number of success stories and the modest revival of the sector points to a successful intervention. However, there are a number of lacunae identified in the design and implementation of RKVY, which need to be addressed urgently.

This research study, with an in-depth analysis of the RKVY scheme across four districts in three states, further finds evidence pointing to less than optimal fund utilisation, skewed nature of expenditure across geographical region (district and sub-district level), components, and quarters in a financial year. The study also identifies the constraints in proper implementation of the scheme, which include issues like the absence of a bottom-up approach in planning and budgeting, lack of proper convergence across schemes, shortage of human resources for scheme implementation, lack of proper knowledge about the scheme and capacity to formulate C-DAPs among the functionaries, inappropriate monitoring and accountability mechanisms, ad-hoc and biased selection of beneficiaries, and inefficient maintenance of proper accounts and information at the district and sub-district level, among others. Thus, in order to ensure that the progress made by the agriculture sector during the Eleventh FYP is continued and is strengthened further, a thorough review of the structural and implementation bottlenecks in the RKVY must be carried out.

References

Centre for Budget and Governance Accountability (2014). *What Ails Utilisation of Funds in Development Schemes*. New Delhi.

Government of India (2013). *Census of India 2011*. New Delhi: Registrar General of India.

———. (2014). "Rashtriya Krishi Vikas Yojana: An Evaluation". *61st Report of the Committee on Agriculture (LokSabha)*.

———. (2014). *Economic Survey, 2013-14*. New Delhi: Ministry of Finance.

———. (2008). *Eleventh Five Year Plan*. Vol. II. New Delhi: Planning Commission.

———. (2008). *Twelfth Five Year Plan*. Vol. II. New Delhi: Planning Commission.

Jha Praveen and N. Acharya (2011): "Expenditure on the Rural Economy in India's Budget since the 1950s: An Assessment", *Review of Agrarian Studies* 1(2): 134-56

Websites:

http://rkvy.nic.in/

http://www.rbi.org.in/

20

CH. SHANKAR RAO

Performance of Indian Agriculture under RKVY

A State Level Analysis

Introduction

Rapid and sustainable growth of agriculture and allied sectors is critical for inclusiveness and balanced development pattern in India. But this crucial sector was caught under severe crisis during 1990 and early 2000s, mainly because of gross negligence by the government in terms of declining public investment. In order to address this, Government of India (GoI) has started a massive public support and holistic sustainable agricultural development scheme called Rashtriya Krishi Vikas Yojana (RKVY) in 2007-08, which aims at incentivising states into making higher expenditure on agriculture and allied sectors on the basis of district and state agricultural plans prepared with considerable flexibility according to local resources and needs through participation of the local people. This scheme is expected to have significant positive influence on public investment in agriculture, agricultural growth rates and instabilities, cropping pattern and yield levels, cost, revenue and profits of cultivation of the crops.

Schultz (1964) noted that "transforming traditional agriculture" requires investment in physical and human capital. Schultz (1967) and Hayami and Ruttan (1971) argued that a continuous stream of new technical knowledge as well as institutional inputs are a necessary condition for facilitating modern agricultural development. According to them, this flow of new technical inputs must be complemented by investments made in general and production education for farmers. Nelson (1964) and Feder *et al.* (1985) noted that public investment is necessary to promote technology adoption, stimulate complementary on-farm investment, input use and market the agricultural produce. Antholt (1994) justified public investment in basic infrastructure, human capital formation and research and development of agriculture as necessary conditions for private investment. According to Chakravarty (1993), Indian agriculture requires different types of investment including irrigation, fertilisers, better seeds, etc., and some of these capital inputs often require to be organised on a very large scale, which makes state intervention essential. The private investment is significantly induced by the behaviour of public investment.

Chand (2000) observed a significant positive relationship between public investment and agricultural productivity across the states. But he refuted any complementarity between public and private investments. Later, with another set of data, Gulati and Bathla (2002) have observed that, in India, public capital formation in agriculture explained more than 90 per cent of the variations observed in private investment, and also these two have significant impact on agricultural GDP (gross domestic product). According to them, public sector investments in canals and power are important for their inducement effect on private investment. They found that public outlay in agriculture had significant positive effect on growth rates of the real value of output of cereals and pulses. Roy and Pal (2002), in their study on investment, agricultural productivity and rural poverty, observed that both public and private investments have positive relationship with agricultural productivity and also that the effect of investment on productivity is stronger than that of subsidies.

It is understood from the literature that the public expenditure in agriculture has multiple direct and spillover effects on overall performance of the sector. While there is an anecdotal evidence of early successes of RKVY which is evident in accelerating growth rates, a detailed state level analysis of this scheme will have to be undertaken in order to allow for further experience and learning. In this context, one must examine the performance of Indian agriculture under major public expenditure programme in the agricultural sector—RKVY in India. The main objectives of the present paper is to study the trends and patterns of allocation of the funds in RKVY under various sub-sectors across the states in India and critically examine the status of public investment in agriculture, agricultural growth rates and instabilities, cropping pattern and yield levels, cost, revenue and profits of crop cultivation during RKVY period. The analysis in this paper is based on the available secondary data from government reports and data provided by the Ministry of Agriculture, GoI and used simple statistics, average growth rates, coefficient of variation for instabilities, and trend analysis to assess the data.

The scope of the study is based on all India and major states, except six minor North-East states because of their distinct nature of agriculture. The study period is from 2002-03 to 2011-12, which has been divided into two quinquennium periods—2002-2006 as pre-RKVY period or the Eleventh Five Year Plan (FYP) period and 2007-2012 as the ongoing RKVY period or Twelfth FYP period. This demarcation will help us to examine the performance of various indicators of agriculture pre and during RKVY program period.

YThis paper is divided into five sections. After the introduction, section II contains the analysis of expenditure amount, pattern and important heads of spending under RKVY programme. Section III deal with the analysis of public outlay and capital formation in agriculture. Section IV examines the issues of agricultural growth rates and instabilities, cropping pattern and yield and also the cost, revenue and profitability of crops. Finally, section V provides the summary and conclusion.

Trends and Patterns of Expenditure under RKVY

The expenditure under RKVY has been gradually increasing in India since its beginning in 2007-08. It varies across the states over the time. The admiring point is that historically, agriculturally backward states where the green revolution was initially absent, such as Himachal Pradesh (HP), Jharkhand, Chhattisgarh, Odisha, Bihar and Assam except Kerala and Tamil Nadu, have received and spent more funds per hectare net sown area (NSA) (Table 20.1). The erstwhile green revolution states have got relatively less funds per se.

The data shows that the amount of money spent per hectare since its inception is very less, varying from ₹1,012 in Punjab to ₹6,156 in HP which needs to be enhanced. In other dimension, the actual amount under RKVY is less than approval among many states especially Punjab, Jharkhand, Uttarakhand, Andhra Pradesh (AP), Madhya Pradesh (MP), Jammu & Kashmir, etc., as most of them are below 75 per cent of total allocation.

Another point to be mentioned here is that this spent proportion for approval at all-India level has been gradually falling from 93.6 per cent in 2007-08 to 70 per cent in 2012-13 (Table 20.2), which needs to be addressed by specifically looking at the institutional mechanism to spend the allotted money for agricultural development among states and yield the specific outcomes.

The Components of RKVY Spending

At all-India level, irrigation development (15%) receives a higher proportion of funds from RKVY, followed by animal husbandry, horticulture, crops, seeds, agricultural machinery etc (Table 20.3). Extension services, an important issue of agricultural development to reduce the potential yield gaps, receives less money and must be upgraded in the future by increasing overall allocation and prioritisation of spending.

This spending pattern varies across the states under the categories. Crops development received better share in the states of Bihar, Chhatishgharh, Kerala, Odisha, Tamil Nadu and Jharkhand. Horticulture received fair treatment in the states of AP, Chhattisgarh, Haryana, HP, Jammu & Kashmir, Uttarakhand, Punjab and Rajasthan. Animal husbandry got priority in states of West Bengal, AP, Chhattisgarh, Haryana, HP, Jammu & Kashmir, Kerala, MP, Maharashtra, Punjab and Uttarakhand. The amount spent on improving fisheries is significant only in Kerala and not even in other coastal states where fishing potential is high. AP and MP have spent a fair amount on seeds. The states of Odisha, Tamil Nadu, Karnataka, Kerala, Assam and Bihar have spent more on agricultural machinery.

Table 20.1

Expenditure Incurred under RKVY

(in ₹ crore)

Sl. No.	*State*	*2007-08*	*2008-09*	*2009-10*	*2010-11*	*2011-12*	*2012-13*	*2013-14*	*Total Expenditure RKVY ₹ Cr*	*RKVY Expenditure per Ha (₹)*
1	Himachal Pradesh	11	12	42	76	56	74	61	331	6156
2	Jharkhand	54	8	89	143	86	168		548	5054
3	Kerala	55	59	111	175	260	238	75	972	4764
4	Chhattisgarh	63	160	87	353	647	584	234	2128	4550
5	Odisha	62	223	58	359	298	497	423	1919	4368
6	Bihar	58	149	111	370	517	624	325	2152	3988
7	Tamil Nadu	176	132	127	216	314	609	273	1846	3703
8	Assam		135	78	200	199	215	203	1030	3665
9	Uttarakhand	23	24	46	4	102	35	22	256	3588
10	Karnataka	195	703	425	317	625	743	505	3514	3534
11	Maharashtra	131	314	421	1132	1025	2366	493	5882	3383
12	Jammu & Kashmir			54	100	58	17	3	233	3118
13	Gujarat	44	319	336	339	766	470	25	2299	2231
14	Andhra Pradesh	74	272	340	336	538	462	324	2346	2102
15	Haryana	17	36	200	187	164	63	1	667	1900
16	Uttar Pradesh	100	309	416	656	652	530	294	2958	1779
17	WestBengal	66	83	149	89	222	101	118	828	1592
18	Madhya Pradesh	73	156	223	547	408	460	228	2095	1375
19	Rajasthan	106	369	790	534	164	69	90	2120	1176
20	Punjab	52	98	45	37	49	122	16	419	1012
21	India	1381	3611	4229	6356	7267	8690	6781	38316	2721

Source: Ministry of Agriculture, GoI.

Table 20.2

Proportion of Approval of Funds under RKVY Allocation

Sl. No.	*State*	*2007-08*	*2008-09*	*2009-10*	*2010-11*	*2011-12*	*2012-13*	*2013-14*	*All 2007-2013*
1	Andhra Pradesh	82	85.1	94	49.2	85.5	52.5	84.4	76.1
2	Assam		97.7	100	97.5	83.4	53.7	49.8	80.4
3	Bihar	100	85.5	53.1	92.9	52.9	74.6	64.7	74.8
4	Chhattisgarh	93.8	121.7	81.7	74	301	103.4	67.6	120.5
5	Gujarat	93.5	90.6	101.8	72.4	93.3	46.9	10.1	72.7
6	Haryana	94.8	44.6	164	79.9	87.2	23.3	0.3	70.6
7	Himachal Pradesh	100	107.2	95.6	102	97	113.7	37.4	93.3
8	Jammu & Kashmir			116.4	82.5	111	35.3	2.7	69.6
9	Jharkhand	37.9	28.7	76	48.2	26.9	24.4		40.4
10	Karnataka	128.5	154.9	98.9	117.8	108.8	124.5	71.3	115.0
11	Kerala	99.2	99.3	85.6	79.9	86.5	102.4	27.4	82.9
12	Madhya Pradesh	89.3	73.2	80.7	75.4	77.6	60.4	15.2	67.4
13	Maharashtra	101.6	69.6	76.8	94.6	118.9	216.1	77.6	107.9
14	Odisha	99.7	94.6	99.4	93.5	73.6	78.5	46.3	83.7
15	Punjab	98.1	59.2	49.4	21.7	25	8.4	4.5	38.0
16	Rajasthan	106.2	80.2	95.7	51.7	262.3	13.1	56.6	95.1
17	Tamil Nadu	96.2	90.9	99.1	71.5	73.1	96.2	82.6	87.1
18	Uttar Pradesh	91.2	90.1	76.9	88.7	59.2	69.1	30.1	72.2
19	Uttarakhand	84.4	84.6	43	53.3	82	61.9	29.4	62.7
20	West Bengal	99.3	70	132.4	61.7	70.2	36	41.7	73.0
21	India	93.6	90.6	89.1	75.8	82.5	70.6	74	82.3

Source: Ministry of Agriculture, GoI.

None of the states have spent fair share of funds on extension development, which is crucial for conducting better farm practices, achieving potential yield gaps and materialising the much-acclaimed concept of Lab to Land. Uttarakhand and Gujarat have spent more on marketing. Only Punjab, Karnataka and Kerala have allotted adequate amount for agricultural and education. Only Gujarat has spent a higher share on natural resource management, that is, soil health and watershed development. Irrigation has received a lion share in majority of the states. Dairy development got fair share only in Punjab.

This description of spending among different components shows that states have followed the allotment of funds under RKVY as per regional priority needs and plans which was envisaged in the programme. But the question arising here is whether or not such allocation pattern followed by the states is appropriate to realise the agro-climatic, economic potentials of agriculture in the region. Some states fail to allocate the funds as per their agro-climatic conditions. Coastal states which have high potential in fishing allocate less funds to fisheries. Similarly, the states like Madhya Pradesh and Odisha who have high potential in fruit & vegetables allocate less funds to Horticulture.. Hence, there is a need for the state to change the priorities of allocation as per their agro-climatic, economic potentials.

Figure 20.1

Proportion of Expenditure Heads under RKVY (2007-2013) in India

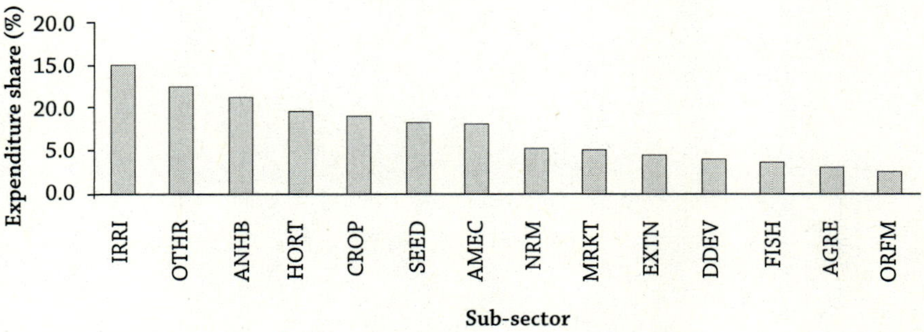

Source: Ministry of Agriculture, GoI.

Table 20.3

Heads of Components of Spending under RKVY

Sl. No.	State	Crop	Horti-culture	Animal hus-bandry	Fish	Seed	Agri-cultural Mech-anisa-tion	Exten-sion	Mar-keting	Agri-cultural Research and Edu-cation	Natural resource manage-ment	Irriga-tion	Organic farming	Dairy devel-op-ment	Oth-ers
1	Andhra Pradesh	6.0	17.9	15.7	2.2	21.5	8.8	1.2	2.7	5.9	0.0	3.1	2.4	3.7	8.8
2	Assam	6.5	6.7	10.3	8.3	5.0	14.5	1.9	3.9	4.7	2.3	23.1	2.0	2.7	8.0
3	Bihar	17.0	3.4	8.8	2.5	10.4	12.5	7.7	1.9	5.6	0.4	0.1	7.8	5.0	16.9
4	Chhattisgarh	15.2	19.7	13.7	6.4	11.0	4.1	6.1	2.9	0.3	1.5	2.8	1.8	0.1	14.3
5	Gujarat	7.2	5.5	6.5	2.0	3.1	8.6	0.9	10.6	2.5	25.9	3.9	5.7	6.2	11.3
6	Haryana	4.7	4.9	21.3	2.0	11.5	6.8	0.2	2.9	2.1	1.0	29.0	1.4	2.6	9.8
7	Himachal Pradesh	9.7	18.5	16.1	5.0	6.8	1.6	0.8	6.2	1.8	4.0	11.0	13.4	1.8	3.2
8	Jammu & Kashmir	2.1	29.2	15.5	3.6	6.2	3.0	4.2	8.4	0.0	3.6	14.4	2.3	0.0	7.6
9	Jharkhand	13.5	7.6	7.2	3.8	7.7	6.0	8.1	3.3	0.1	4.1	17.6	0.5	12.7	7.7
10	Karnataka	5.0	9.7	9.0	3.0	6.9	15.0	7.4	6.6	8.3	1.3	2.9	3.6	0.2	21.1

contd...

...*contd*...

11	Kerala	19.5	10.5	17.4	15.8	0.7	13.8	3.8	1.4	9.3	2.7	1.5	0.3	2.0	1.5
12	Madhya Pradesh	8.0	2.9	15.8	3.9	16.0	8.3	5.7	2.2	1.3	2.1	23.3	1.4	1.5	7.6
13	Maharashtra	4.5	7.0	14.6	2.8	3.3	7.3	2.7	9.1	0.0	2.8	37.8	0.0	2.2	5.9
14	Odisha	18.4	3.3	7.7	5.9	4.4	18.9	4.5	4.9	2.8	9.2	8.1	1.5	4.8	5.7
15	Punjab	4.7	12.7	16.2	1.0	1.0	3.2	1.9	6.7	11.3	15.1	6.2	2.0	10.8	7.1
16	Rajasthan	8.5	12.0	5.2	0.7	9.1	1.5	7.8	2.3	2.8	1.0	29.7	1.3	8.0	10.0
17	Tamil Nadu	16.8	9.2	7.9	2.7	3.4	15.6	2.5	11.3	0.2	0.1	2.4	2.2	4.1	21.6
18	Uttar Pradesh	8.0	6.0	6.2	1.3	9.9	1.3	5.0	0.2	0.3	5.6	25.5	2.0	2.6	26.1
19	Uttarakhand	4.7	19.5	15.3	1.9	1.3	1.0	4.1	16.1	0.5	6.7	6.9	11.0	4.3	6.8
20	WestBengal	0.1	8.0	24.0	7.8	9.9	9.1	1.4	7.9	0.6	12.1	2.5	0.2	2.0	14.4
21	India	9.0	9.4	11.2	3.6	8.1	8.0	4.3	4.9	2.8	5.1	15.0	2.5	3.8	12.3

Source: Ministry of Agriculture, GoI.

Plan Outlay, Public Spending and Capital Formation in Agriculture

It is important to investigate whether the expenditure made under RKVY has induced the plan outlay and capital formation in the agriculture and allied sectors in India. The data shows (Table 20.4) the plan outlay for agriculture and allied sectors at all-India level in absolute number, which has increased 2.7 times from pre-RKVY period—Eleventh Plan (2002-2006) to during RKVY period—Twelfth Plan (2007-2011), which is higher from total plan outlay for the whole economy that stands at 2.3 times for the same period. In terms of the share of plan outlay for agriculture and allied sectors to the total plan outlay too, it has increased from 3.8 per cent before RKVY period to 4.4 per cent during RKVY period.

Table 20.4

Actual Expenditure in Agriculture and Allied Sectors in India

(in ₹ crore)

Year	*Plan Outlay for Agriculture and Allied Sectors*	*Total Plan Outlay*	*% Share of Activities in Agriculture and Allied Sectors*
2002-03	7655	210203	3.6
2003-04	8776	224827	3.9
2004-05	10963	263665	4.2
2005-06	12554	247177	5.1
2006-07	16573	309912	5.3
Before RKVY (2002-2007)	60702	1618460	3.8
2007-08	20014	371809	5.4
2008-09	27087	477263	5.7
2009-10	29498	717035	4.1
2010-11	40369	826268	4.9
2011-12	16194	508596	3.2
During RKVY (2007-2012)	163105 (2.7 times rise)	3676936 (2.3 times rise)	4.4

Source: National Account Statistics, CSO, GoI.

In case of the proportion of agricultural gross capital formation (AGCF) in total AGDP (Table 20.5), there is a significant improvement from 14 per cent during pre-RKVY period to about 19 per cent during RKVY period which was largely contributed by the private sector—a positive development in Indian agriculture where public investment is inducing private investment in the agricultural sector also which was thought to be otherwise.

Table 20.5

Gross Capital Formation (GCF) in Agriculture and Allied Sectors (2004-05 Prices)

	GDP from Agriculture and Allied Sectors (₹ crore)	*GCF in Agriculture and Allied Sectors (crore)*			*AGCF as % of GDP from Agriculture and Allied Sectors*		
		Public Sector	*Private Sector*	*Total*	*Public Sector*	*Private Sector*	*Total*
2002-03	5,14,208	12,807	60,842	73,989	2.5	11.8	14.4
2003-04	5,65,653	15,845	55,787	71,560	2.8	9.9	12.7
2004-05	5,65,426	16,187	59,909	76,096	2.9	10.6	13.5
2005-06	5,94,487	19,940	66,664	86,604	3.4	11.2	14.6
2006-07	6,19,190	22,987	69,070	92,057	3.7	11.2	14.9
Before RKVY (2002-2006)	28,58,964	87,766	3,12,272	4,00,306	3.1	10.9	14.0
2007-08	6,55,080	23,255	82,484	1,05,741	3.5	12.6	16.1
2008-09	6,55,689	20,572	106,555	1,27,127	3.1	16.3	19.4
2009-10	6,60,987	22,693	1,10,469	1,33,162	3.4	16.7	20.1
2010-11	7,13,477	19,918	1,11,306	1,31,224	2.8	15.6	18.4
2011-12	7,39,495	22,095	1,24,483	1,46,578	3	16.8	19.8
During RKVY (2007-2011)	34,24,728	1,08,533	5,35,297	6,43,832	3.2	15.6	18.8

Source: National Account Statistics, CSO, GoI.

Hence, the above discussion shows that although there is a little amount of expenditure per hector under RKVY, it has a noticeable and significant effect in inducing both public and private investment in the agricultural and allied sectors in India. These evidences also encourage us to advocate enhancement of the funding done under RKVY for faster development of agriculture and allied sectors.

Agricultural Output, Growth and Instability

The expenditure incurred under RKVY as per the needs of regional agricultural plans is expected to have significant influence on agricultural output, growth and instability (measured by the method of co-efficient of variation [CV]) in the region.

The following data (Table 20.6) shows the average agricultural output per hectare among the states. At all-India level, it has increased by 15 per cent which shall be appreciable. Except Kerala, all

Table 20.6

Value of Output of Agriculture in India

(per Ha)

Sl. No.	*State*	*RKVY Expenditure per Ha (₹)*	*Before RKVY (2002-2006)*	*During RKVY (2007-2011)*	*Growth in Output*
1	Andhra Pradesh	2102	52959	63683	20.2
2	Assam	3665	46593	52478	12.6
3	Bihar	3988	39434	47103	19.4
4	Chhattisgarh	4550	21833	27094	24.1
5	Gujarat	2231	36136	39397	9.0
6	Haryana	1900	60999	71000	16.4
7	Himachal Pradesh	6156	108416	111669	3.0
8	Jammu & Kashmir	3118	94096	100443	6.7
9	Jharkhand	5054	60688	95545	57.4
10	Karnataka	3534	29536	36962	25.1
11	Kerala	4764	80619	78502	-2.6
12	Madhya Pradesh	1375	20583	24226	17.7
13	Maharashtra	3383	26413	32546	23.2
14	Odisha	4368	31006	40065	29.2
15	Punjab	1012	72031	77896	8.1
16	Rajasthan	1176	18686	21847	16.9
17	Tamil Nadu	3703	49962	58883	17.9
18	Uttar Pradesh	1779	44055	48718	10.6
19	Uttarakhand	3588	65170	72529	11.3
20	West Bengal	1592	91031	100741	10.7
21	India	2721	42200	48616	15.2

Source: Directorate of Economics and Statistics, Ministry of Agriculture, GoI.

the states in India have shown significant improvement during RKVY period from the pre-RKVY period. Jharkhand has registered a highest growth of 57 per cent, which may be because of large spending of RKVY funds therein. The states of HP and Jammu & Kashmir have the highest output because of their fruits cultivation, and West Bengal also have more output because of its high cultivation of vegetables. Finally, these data imply that the agricultural sector has been boosted with better performance during the RKVY period owing to fund spending.

The data (Table 20.7) shows that at all-India level, the average growth of agriculture and allied sectors has increased from 2.7 per cent during pre-RKVY period to 4.1 per cent during RKVY period, and that growth exhibits lesser instability where it has come down from 208 to 78.5 for the same period.

Among states, this picture is with mixed results, where the states of AP, Assam, Chhattisgarh, Jammu & Kashmir, Jharkhand, Karnataka and MP have improved their growth rates, while rest have shown a fall. But in case of growth instability, majority of the states (except few—HP, MP, Uttarakhand and West Bengal) have a shown drastic fall.

It is also important to study whether this positive growth is led by factors like the change in cropping pattern towards high value crops, increase in yield levels etc. This issue is addressed in the foregoing analysis.

Figure 20.2

Annual Growth Rate of Agriculture and Allied Sectors in India

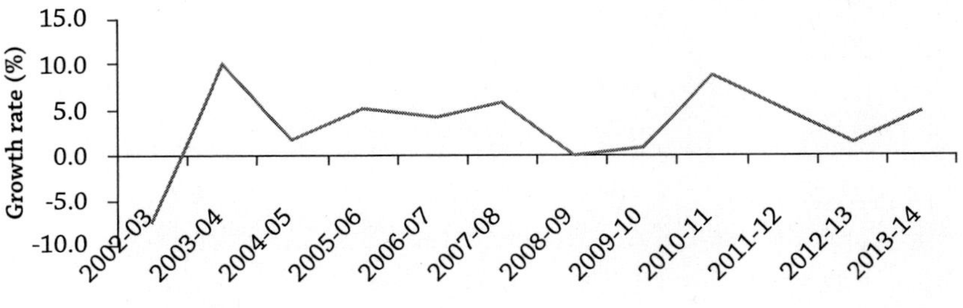

Source: Ministry of Agriculture, GoI.

Table 20.7

Growth Rate and Instability (CV) in Agriculture in India

Sl. No	State	Before RKVY(2002-2006)		During RKVY (2007-2011)	
		Average Annual Growth Rate	CV	Average Annual Growth Rate	CV
1	Andhra Pradesh	4.0	185.0	4.8	134.2
2	Assam	1.2	114.3	3.9	46.7
3	Bihar	7.7	208.1	3.9	280.0
4	Chhattisgarh	4.0	582.8	6.2	165.4
5	Gujarat	9.7	191.9	5.5	176.5
6	Haryana	4.5	133.1	3.7	101.4
7	Himachal Pradesh	4.2	101.9	2.4	434.6
8	Jammu & Kashmir	2.8	112.6	2.9	107.6
9	Jharkhand	2.7	408.4	8.4	116.3
10	Karnataka	2.1	633.0	5.0	178.9
11	Kerala	0.9	492.2	-1.5	-190.0
12	Madhya Pradesh	4.6	392.2	6.9	101.8
13	Maharashtra	6.0	117.6	4.3	267.5
14	Odisha	2.9	442.8	2.3	172.1
15	Punjab	2.1	109.2	1.7	76.3
16	Rajasthan	8.4	464.8	7.9	184.0
17	Tamil Nadu	4.3	330.1	3.3	167.9
18	Uttar Pradesh	1.5	114.0	3.2	57.9
19	Uttarakhand	3.3	100.0	3.0	144.7
20	West Bengal	1.6	109.8	1.9	208.1
21	India	2.7	208.2	4.1	78.5

Source: Directorate of Economics and Statistics, Ministry of Agriculture, GoI.

In case of yield level of crops, at all-India levels, all the crops have registered impressive positive growth during RKVY period in comparison to pre-RKVY period (Table 20.9). Among all, the yield of cotton has grown by 41.5 per cent, followed by coarse cereals (27%), oilseeds (18.5%), pulses (11.4%) paddy and wheat (11% each). This trend is appreciable for the spending of RKVY on crops development for their rise in yield. The state level tables are given in Appendix

A-20.2 for a detailed understanding of the effect of RKVY on crop yields.

Table 20.8

Cropping Pattern in India (Area Share in GCA)

Sl. No.	*Crop*	*Before RKVY (2002-2006)*	*During RKVY (2007-2011)*	*Growth in Area Share*
1	Rice	23.6	22.0	-6.6
2	Wheat	14.1	14.7	4.3
3	Coarse cereals	15.4	14.2	-7.5
4	Cereal	52.2	51.4	-1.5
5	Pulses	11.9	12.3	3.2
6	Food grain	64.2	63.7	-0.6
7	Fruits and Vegetables	5.1	5.0	-1.9
8	Total Food crops	74.3	73.4	-1.2
9	Oilseeds	13.5	13.8	1.9
10	Cotton	4.5	5.4	20.9
11	Sugarcane	2.3	2.4	5.8
12	Total non-food crops	25.7	26.6	3.4

Source: Directorate of Economics and Statistics, Ministry of Agriculture, GoI.

Table 20.9

Yield Level of Crops in India

(per Ha in Kg)

Sl. No.	*Crop*	*Before RKVY (2002-2006)*	*During RKVY (2007-2011)*	*Growth in Yield*
1	Rice	2008	2228	10.9
2	Wheat	2650	2943	11.0
3	Coarse cereals	1139	1445	26.9
4	Cereals	1925	2216	15.1
5	Pulses	593	661	11.4
6	Food grain	1677	1915	14.2
7	Oilseeds	912	1081	18.5
8	Cotton	320	453	41.5
9	Sugarcane	64730	69042	6.7

Source: Directorate of Economics and Statistics, Ministry of Agriculture, GoI.

Cost, Revenue and Profits of Cultivation of Crops

It is also crucial to investigate whether the spending under RKVY has any influence over the cost of cultivation, output value and profit of crops. The data (Table 20.10) shows that although there has been an increase in cost and value of output during RKVY period compared to pre-RKVY period, growth of the latter is higher than the former (R>C2) among all the major crops in India, except wheat which resulted in significant rise in positive profits. The state level tables are given in Appendix 3 for a detailed understanding of the effect of RKVY on costs, value of output and profits of crops.

Summary and Conclusion

The historically agriculturally backward and non-Green Revolution states such as HP, Jharkhand, Chhattisgarh, Odisha, Bihar and Assam have received and spent more funds per hectare, while the developed and erstwhile Green Revolution states have got relatively less funds per se under RKVY. The amount of money spent per hectare since its inception is very less varying from ₹ 1,012 in Punjab to ₹ 6,156 in HP, which needs to be enhanced. The actual proportion of the spent money to approval has been gradually falling from 93.6 per cent in 2007-08 to 70 per cent in 2012-13.

Irrigation development (15%) receives higher proportion of funds from RKVY, followed by animal husbandry, horticulture, crops, seeds, agricultural machinery, etc. An extension service which is an important issue of agricultural development to reduce the potential yield gaps receives less money. It varies widely across states as per their local priorities which is an essential aspect under RKVY, but these allocations are not as per their agro-climatic, economic potentials. Fishing which has the high potential for growth in coastal states, got less money. Also the horticulture which has high potential for growth in the states of Madhya Pradesh and Odisha, got less funds under RKVY.

The plan outlay for agriculture and allied sectors at all-India level, both in absolute number and in proportionate share in AGDP, has increased. The proportion of AGCF (agricultural gross capital formation) in total AGDP has also substantially increased during

Table 20.10

Cost of Cultivation, Value of Output and Economic Profit of Crops in India

(Per Ha in ₹ at 2004-05 Prices)

Crop	*Before RKVY (2002-2006)*			*During RKVY (2007-2011)*			*Growth Rate*		
	Cost of Cultivation (C2)	*Output Revenue (R)*	*Economic Profit (VOR-C2)*	*Cost of Cultivation (C2)*	*Output Revenue (R)*	*Economic Profit (VOR-C2)*	*Cost of Cultivation (C2)*	*Output Revenue (R)*	*Economic Profit (VOR-C2)*
Paddy	22873	23888	1015	23947	28989	5042	4.7	21.4	396.7
Wheat	18958	23864	4906	18377	25861	7483	-3.1	8.4	52.5
Maize	13009	12514	-495	14576	15745	1169	12.0	25.8	-336.2
Gram	9902	13270	3369	11656	16456	4800	17.7	24.0	42.5
Groundnut	19685	19729	44	20139	21470	1331	2.3	8.8	2925.0
Cotton	25550	28043	2493	26682	33923	7241	4.4	21.0	190.5
Sugarcane	59045	77714	18669	73158	110038	41715	23.9	41.6	123.4

Note: VOR: Value of Output Revenue.

Source: Various reports of "Cost of Cultivation of Crops in India", Directorate of Economic and Statistics, Ministry of agriculture, GoI.

RKVY period, which was largely contributed by private sector. This shows that public investment is inducing private investment in the agricultural sectors which is a positive development in Indian agriculture.

The agricultural output per hectare and average annual growth have significantly increased at both all-India and state (except Kerala) levels during RKVY period, and the growth is relatively very high in dry land states like Jharkhand, Chhattisgarh, Bihar, Odisha, MP, Karnataka, Maharastra, AP and Rajasthan. Interestingly, instability, in the agricultural growth rate has declined during RKVY period.

There has not been any remarkable change in cropping pattern in India during RKVY period, where the share of area under non-food crops has improved by just 1 per cent. Individually, the crops of rice and coarse cereals have registered a small fall, while that of pulses and cotton have shown a small rise. But not much change is registered in fruit and vegetable.

All the major crops in India have registered impressive positive growth during RKVY period. Among all, the yield of cotton has grown by 41.5 per cent, followed by coarse cereals (27%), oilseeds (18.5%), pulses (11.4%) paddy and wheat (11% each). There has been a hike in cost and value of the output of major crops during RKVY period, but the growth of revenue (R) is higher than the cost (C2)—(R>C2)—among all the major crops in India, except wheat, which brought about greater profits.

Therefore, it can be concluded that the money under RKVY has been allotted more to dry land states, which is appreciable. But the amount of money is still inadequate which needs to be improved. The allocation pattern of RKVY funds needs to be improved since the extension facilities still receive very little money and states will plan this funding as per their agro-climatic potentials. The RKVY has induced public outlay and capital formation in agriculture and this trend of private investment inducement by public spending encourage allocation of more money for RKVY. Although there has not been much change in cropping pattern, the yield level of major crops had increased in India during RKVY period. There has been a significant rise in profits from the cultivation of crops during the RKVY period. These positive trends like inducement of capital investment in agriculture, increase in agricultural growth, yield and profit level and lesser instabilities in Indian agriculture during RKVY period (2007-2011) were possible with very a meagre allocation of money per hectare under RKVY. Hence, RKVY has the potential to improve the performance of agriculture and strengthen this programme by making greater allocation and providing clear guidance, which could take the Indian agriculture to the greater heights. This paper advocates for strengthening of this scheme for the purpose of holistic sustainable development of agriculture and allied sectors by increasing the funding for decentralised local planning process, development and transfer of cost effective technology, while keeping the small farmers in mind, supporting the participatory group approach, emphasising on extension facilities and developing and regulating the markets from their failures.

References

Antholt, C.H (1994). "Getting Ready for the Twenty-First Century: Technical Change and Institutional Modernisation in Agriculture", *World Bank Technical Paper* 217. February.

Chakravarty, Sukhamoy (1993). *Selected Economic Writings.* New Delhi: Oxford University Press.

Chand, Ranesh (2000). "Emerging Trends and Regional Variations in Agricultural Investments and their Implications for Growth and Equity", *Policy Paper* 11. National Centre for Agricultural Economics and Policy Research.

Feder, G., R.E. Just and D. Zilberman (1985). "Adoption of Agricultural Innovations in Developing Countries: A Survey", *Economic Development and Cultural Change* 33: 255-98.

Gulati, Ashok and Seema Bathla (2002). "Capital Formation in Indian Agriculture: Trends, Composition and Implications for Growth", *NABARD, Occasional Paper* 24.

Hayami and Ruttan (1971). *Agricultural Development: An International Perspective.* Baltimore, MD: The Johns Hopkins University Press.

Nelson (1964). "Aggregate Production Functions and Medium-Range Growth Projections", *American Economic Review* 54(5): 575-606

Roy, B.C and Suresh Pal (2002). "Investment, Agricultural Productivity and Rural Poverty in India: A State-Level Analysis", *Indian Journal of Agricultural Economics* 57(4) Oct-Dec.

Schultz, T.W. (1964). *Transforming Traditional Agriculture.* New Haven and London: Yale University Press.

Appendix A-20.1

Table A-20.1.1

Area Share of Food Grains

Sl. No.	State	RKVY Exp per Ha (₹)	Pre–RKVY (2002-2006)					During RKVY (2007-2011)				
			Rice	Wheat	Coarse Cereals	Pulses	Food Grains	Rice	Wheat	Coarse Cereals	Pulses	Food Grains
1	Himachal Pradesh	6156	8.5	38.0	35.9	3.2	85.7	8.2	37.8	34.5	3.4	83.8
2	Jharkhand	5054	83.8	4.1	14.4	16.5	118.8	88.8	7.7	17.2	28.2	141.9
3	Kerala	4764	9.6	0.0	0.1	0.2	10.0	8.3	0.0	0.1	0.3	8.7
4	Chhattisgarh	4550	66.4	1.7	6.3	16.0	90.4	65.8	1.8	5.0	15.0	87.7
5	Odisha	4368	51.5	0.0	1.9	8.1	61.6	67.2	0.1	2.9	13.0	83.2
6	Bihar	3988	44.0	26.8	8.8	8.5	88.1	43.7	28.7	9.1	7.7	89.2
7	Tamil Nadu	3703	30.9	0.0	13.9	9.7	54.4	32.5	0.0	11.6	10.3	54.4
8	Assam	3665	61.7	1.6	0.7	2.8	66.8	61.2	1.3	0.6	2.9	66.0
9	Uttarakhand	3588	0.0	32.6	23.3	4.1	84.1	15.6	33.1	22.0	5.3	85.2
10	Karnataka	3534	10.4	2.0	30.2	17.0	59.6	11.7	2.1	28.8	19.0	61.6
11	Maharashtra	3383	6.9	3.9	30.8	16.0	57.6	6.8	4.9	26.3	15.8	53.7
12	Jammu & Kashmir	3118	22.8	22.8	32.7	2.6	80.9	22.8	25.1	30.9	2.5	81.4
13	Gujarat	2231	4.8	7.1	14.5	7.1	34.3	6.3	9.7	12.5	7.0	35.6
14	Andhra Pradesh	2102	26.8	0.1	11.3	15.8	54.0	30.2	0.1	9.2	14.5	53.9
15	Haryana	1900	15.9	36.5	11.5	2.7	66.6	18.5	38.6	11.5	2.6	71.2
16	Uttar Pradesh	1779	22.2	36.2	8.7	10.8	78.0	22.4	37.4	7.9	9.3	77.0
17	West Bengal	1592	61.0	4.1	0.8	2.4	67.8	62.1	3.4	1.1	2.0	65.0
18	Madhya Pradesh	1375	8.5	19.7	11.1	22.1	61.5	7.4	19.6	8.6	22.3	57.9
19	Rajasthan	1176	0.5	10.9	33.4	15.8	60.7	0.6	10.9	30.8	17.2	59.4
20	Punjab	1012	33.2	43.8	2.3	0.5	79.8	35.0	44.6	2.0	0.3	81.8
21	All India	2721	23.6	14.1	15.4	11.9	64.2	22.0	14.7	14.2	12.3	63.7

Source: Directorate of Economics and Statistics, Ministry of Agriculture, GoI.

Table A-20.1.2

Area Share of Fruit and Vegetables and Food Crops

Sl. No.	State	RKVY Exp per Ha (₹)	Pre–RKVY (2002-2006)			During RKVY (2007-2011)		
			Fruits	Vegeta-bles	Total Food crops	Fruits	Vegeta-bles	Total Food crops
1	Himachal Pradesh	6156	6.8	3.8	96.8	8.0	3.9	96.8
2	Jharkhand	5054	0.3	5.4	97.1	0.3	6.6	96.9
3	Kerala	4764	13.9	5.8	44.0	12.8	5.2	39.5
4	Chhattisgarh	4550	0.2	1.8	94.6	0.2	2.0	94.4
5	Odisha	4368	3.7	7.6	89.3	1.4	3.0	93.6
6	Bihar	3988	1.4	4.0	95.5	1.2	4.1	95.5
7	Tamil Nadu	3703	6.1	3.6	72.0	6.7	3.9	73.5
8	Assam	3665	2.7	6.9	81.3	2.8	7.9	81.9
9	Uttarakhand	3588	1.3	2.5	94.2	1.3	2.8	94.6
10	Karnataka	3534	2.2	2.3	69.7	2.6	2.5	73.7
11	Maharashtra	3383	3.2	2.1	67.0	3.1	1.6	62.8
12	Jammu & Kashmir	3118	5.6	1.4	89.0	6.1	1.7	89.2
13	Gujarat	2231	1.4	2.0	44.2	1.4	2.4	44.4
14	Andhra Pradesh	2102	5.4	1.8	67.1	5.7	1.8	66.5
15	Haryana	1900	0.2	0.8	70.0	0.2	0.8	73.6
16	Uttar Pradesh	1779	1.2	2.7	92.0	1.2	3.0	91.4
17	West Bengal	1592	1.8	12.8	83.8	2.3	14.0	83.1
18	Madhya Pradesh	1375	0.2	0.9	64.6	0.2	1.1	62.5
19	Rajasthan	1176	0.1	0.5	63.9	0.1	0.6	63.5
20	Punjab	1012	0.7	1.4	83.4	0.7	1.4	85.1
21	All India	2721	2.1	3.0	74.3	2.1	2.9	73.4

Source: Directorate of Economics and Statistics, Ministry of Agriculture, GoI

Table A-20.1.3

Area Share of Non-Food Grains

Sl. No.	State	RKVY Exp per Ha (₹)	Pre–RKVY (2002-2006)					During RKVY (2007-2011)				
			Ground-nut	Total Oilseeds	Cotton	Sugar-cane	Total Non-Food crops	Ground nut	Total Oilseeds	Cotton	Sugar-cane	Total Non-Food crops
1	Himachal Pradesh	6156	0.0	1.7	0.0	0.3	3.2	0.0	1.5		0.2	3.2
2	Jharkhand	5054	0.0	2.8	0.0	0.2	2.9	1.4	11.6	0.0	0.4	3.1
3	Kerala	4764	0.0	0.1	0.1	0.1	56.0	0.0	0.1		0.1	60.5
4	Chhattisgarh	4550	0.6	5.2	0.0	0.1	5.4	0.5	6.0		0.2	5.6
5	Odisha	4368	0.9	3.6	0.5	0.2	10.7	1.2	4.5	1.1	0.2	6.4
6	Bihar	3988	0.0	1.8	0.0	1.4	4.5	0.0	1.8	0.0	2.1	4.5
7	Tamil Nadu	3703	10.0	11.7	1.9	5.0	28.0	7.7	9.1	2.0	5.6	26.5
8	Assam	3665	0.0	7.1	0.0	0.6	18.7	0.0	6.6		0.7	18.1
9	Uttarakhand	3588	0.2	2.8	0.0	9.7	5.8	0.1	2.4	0.0	9.3	5.4
10	Karnataka	3534	7.2	19.8	3.3	2.2	30.3	6.5	15.0	3.7	2.8	26.3
11	Maharashtra	3383	1.9	14.5	13.0	2.6	33.0	1.5	16.8	15.9	4.1	37.2
12	Jammu & Kashmir	3118	0.0	5.7	0.0	0.0	11.0	0.0	5.6	0.0	0.0	10.8
13	Gujarat	2231	17.3	25.9	16.7	1.7	55.8	15.1	24.5	21.3	1.6	55.6
14	Andhra Pradesh	2102	12.8	20.6	7.7	1.8	32.9	11.4	17.0	11.4	1.5	33.5
15	Haryana	1900	0.0	10.5	8.7	2.4	30.0	0.0	8.3	8.0	1.5	26.4
16	Uttar Pradesh	1779	0.4	4.5	0.0	8.4	8.0	0.4	4.7		8.3	8.6
17	West Bengal	1592	0.5	6.8	0.0	0.2	16.2	0.7	7.3		0.2	16.9
18	Madhya Pradesh	1375	1.1	28.6	3.0	0.3	35.4	0.9	31.5	3.0	0.3	37.5
19	Rajasthan	1176	0.0	20.6	2.1	0.0	36.1	0.3	19.5	1.6	0.0	36.5
20	Punjab	1012	0.1	1.1	6.5	1.4	16.6	0.0	0.7	6.9	1.0	14.9
21	All India	2721	3.3	13.5	4.5	2.3	25.7	3.0	13.8	5.4	2.4	26.6

Source: Directorate of Economics and Statistics, Ministry of Agriculture, GoI.

Appendix A-20.2

Table A-20.2.1

Yield of Food Grains

Sl. No.	State	RKVY Exp per Ha (₹)	Pre–RKVY (2002-2006)					During RKVY (2007-2011)				
			Rice	Wheat	Coarse Cereals	Pulses	Food Grains	Rice	Wheat	Coarse Cereals	Pulses	Food Grains
1	Himachal Pradesh	6156	1398	1585	1985	602	1696	1565	1405	2213	933	1734
2	Jharkhand	5054	1395	1690	1292	635	1280	1853	1690	1243	765	1563
3	Kerala	4764	4756		742	818	2183	2514		655	838	2445
4	Chhattisgarh	4550	1203	965	516	498	1024	1401	1111	729	602	1219
5	Odisha	4368	1355	1366	873	397	1210	1575	1500	1370	469	1396
6	Bihar	3988	1259	1761	2259	760	1466	1441	2068	2307	862	1684
7	Tamil Nadu	3703	2668		1201	402	1896	3105		2598	386	2476
8	Assam	3665	1453	1086	665	552	1399	1680	1154	674	563	1612
9	Uttarakhand	3588		1884	1203	634	1637	2022	2177	1280	773	1813
10	Karnataka	3534	2699	674	1314	376	1271	2626	941	1853	500	1550
11	Maharashtra	3383	1591	1305	840	565	886	1701	1614	1107	689	1106
12	Jammu & Kashmir	3118	2007	1809	1409	494	1662	2050	1549	1554	504	1659
13	Gujarat	2231		2466	1159	638	1426	1917	2847	1328	791	1741
14	Andhra Pradesh	2102	2928	826	2180	618	2088	3167	1141	3383	735	2540
15	Haryana	1900	2941	3993	1261	722	3140	2985	4483	1774	787	3519
16	Uttar Pradesh	1779	1938	2648	1402	819	2052	2159	2978	1572	841	2338
17	West Bengal	1592	2528	2200	2132	753	2442	2596	2659	3315	785	2557
18	Madhya Pradesh	1375	835	1688	1127	726	1124	1037	1884	1197	749	1239
19	Rajasthan	1176	1390	2771	781	391	1042	1853	3028	943	467	1194
20	Punjab	1012	3775	4203	2696	812	3960	3924	4573	3492	860	4255
21	All India	2721	2008	2650	1139	593	1677	2228	2943	1445	661	1915

Source: Directorate of Economics and Statistics, Ministry of Agriculture, GoI.

Table A-20.2.2

Yield of non-Food Grains

Sl. No.	State	RKVY Exp per Ha (₹)	Pre–RKVY (2002-2006)					During RKVY (2007-2011)				
			Ground-nut	Rapeseed and Mustard	Total Oil-seeds	Cotton	Sugar-cane	Ground-nut	Rapeseed and Mustard	Total Oil-seeds	Cotton	Sugar-cane
1	Himachal Pradesh	6156	833	512	509	-	16853	866	423	434	252	20337
2	Jharkhand	5054	-	496	319	-	35120	880	612	596	-	58693
3	Kerala	4764	684	244	96514	858	219	105182	-	-	-	-
4	Chhattisgarh	4550	1110	369	432	270	2549	1349	409	577	198	2507
5	Odisha	4368	1119	175	510	381	59377	1182	203	616	487	61271
6	Bihar	3988	522	854	909	-	42347	961	994	1023	45284	-
7	Tamil Nadu	3703	1674	230	1521	258	98999	2235	292	1995	438	106981
8	Assam	3665	-	499	503	120	37552	546	545	87	38006	-
9	Uttarakhand	3588	1133	668	834	-	57133	1418	765	1040	-	58882
10	Karnataka	3534	615	304	523	203	80453	723	360	637	351	88622
11	Maharashtra	3383	1039	310	942	193	69592	1170	359	1095	316	82896
12	Jammu & Kashmir	3118	-	665	647	-	3800	-	835	803	-	-
13	Gujarat	2231	1252	1335	1189	449	72458	1522	1497	1475	600	71646
14	Andhra Pradesh	2102	679	303	648	332	74433	930	571	871	451	78894
15	Haryana	1900	770	1269	1266	476	61837	906	1571	1566	662	67343
16	Uttar Pradesh	1779	730	1018	859	186	58076	792	1143	827	159	57020
17	West Bengal	1592	1643	876	924	372	73109	1794	932	986	356	84209
18	Madhya Pradesh	1375	1005	953	891	184	42278	1270	1058	1087	342	40992
19	Rajasthan	1176	-	1123	1063	288	52580	-	1167	1135	418	62284
20	Punjab	1012	842	1072	1076	629	58585	1262	1260	1323	688	62075
21	All India	2721	1025	1053	912	320	64730	1269	1127	1081	453	69042

Source: Directorate of Economics and Statistics, Ministry of Agriculture, GoI.

Appendix A-20.3

Table A-20.3.1

Cost of Cultivation, Value of Output and Economic Profit of Food Grains

(Per Ha in ₹ at 2004-05 Prices)

State	Before RKVY (2002-2006)			During RKVY (2007-2011)		
	Cost of Cultivation (C2)	Output Revenue (R)	Economic Profit (VOP-C2)	Cost of Cultivation (C2)	Output Revenue (R)	Economic Profit (VOP-C2)
			Paddy			
Andhra Pradesh	28540	32309	3769	32916	38620	5704
Assam	13978	12145	-1833	14892	13451	-1441
Bihar	13964	13155	-809	13509	15410	1901
Haryana	30030	34353	4323	31298	45342	14044
Karnataka	29124	33424	4300	27434	36528	9094
Kerala	26640	26707	67	26980	34687	7707
Madhyapradesh	11464	10178	-1285	14444	17891	3446
Odisha	17611	15958	-1653	18733	19085	352
Punjab	29292	37829	8536	30997	44954	13957
Tamilnadu	31062	30327	-736	30853	33698	2844
Uttar Pradesh	18602	18750	148	20523	24156	3634
West Bengal	24172	21524	-2648	24786	24043	-743
All India	22873	23888	1015	23947	28989	5042
			Wheat			
Bihar	14784	16198	1415	13374	18332	4958
Gujarat	17781	24692	6910	16554	26484	9930
Haryana	24218	31144	6926	25810	37381	11571

contd...

...contd...

Himachal Pradesh	14500	14662	162	12568	12093	-474
Madhya Pradesh	15300	18407	3108	14863	20712	5849
Punjab	24080	31003	6923	22459	32387	9928
Rajasthan	20742	31058	10315	20255	31819	11564
Uttar Pradesh	20257	23750	3493	21134	27675	6541
All India	18958	23864	4906	18377	25861	7483
			Maize			
Andhra Pradesh	18284	17540	-744	23571	24130	560
Bihar	14572	18374	3802	14042	23119	9077
Himachal Pradesh	11503	11320	-183	11062	10658	-405
Karnatakataka	12721	14689	1968	14569	19046	4477
Madhya Pradesh	9062	6465	-2597	9953	8639	-1314
Rajastan	12802	10427	-2375	14254	14286	32
Uttar Pradesh	12118	8781	-3338	14582	10335	-4247
All India	13009	12514	-495	14576	15745	1169
			Gram			
Bihar	9666	14366	4700	9640	18180	8540
Haryana	8463	9205	742	9150	9776	626
Madhya Pradesh	10862	14187	3325	13509	19641	6132
Rajasthan	8821	12518	3696	10592	14785	4193
Uttar Pradesh	11696	16076	4380	15386	19895	4509
All India	9902	13270	3369	11656	16456	4800

Source: Various reports of "Cost of Cultivation of Crops in India", Directorate of Economic and Statistics, Ministry of agriculture, GoI.

Table A-20.3.2

Cost of Cultivation, Value of Output and Economic Profit of Non-food Grains

(Per Ha in ₹ at 2004-05 Prices)

State	Before RKVY (2002-2006)			During RKVY (2007-2011)		
	Cost of Cultivation (C2)	Output Revenue (R)	Economic Profit (VOP-C2)	Cost of Cultivation (C2)	Output Revenue (R)	Economic Profit (VOP-C2)
			Groundnut			
Andhra Pradesh	17774	15618	-2156	24606	24495	-112
Gujarat	18231	24368	6137	20058	25155	5098
Karnataka	12435	11480	-955	13286	13230	-56
Maharashtra	22365	18868	-3497	22698	21849	-849
Odisha	21369	24325	2956	18714	22133	3420
Tamil Nadu	25933	23716	-2218	21470	21958	488
All India	19685	19729	44	20139	21470	1331
			Cotton			
Andhra Pradesh	33214	38030	4816	31464	36895	5432
Gujarat	25213	33722	8509	28072	39487	11415
Haryana	26383	27944	1560	31340	39681	8341
Karnataka	12888	15961	3073	17014	21949	4936
Madhya Pradesh	25661	24442	-1219	20948	28765	7817
Maharashtra	22044	20699	-1344	24656	26398	1742
Punjab	34499	38745	4246	35035	43620	8585
Rajasthan	18509	25766	7257	22675	37313	14638
Tamil Nadu	31538	27080	-4458	28935	31202	2267
All India	25550	28043	2493	26682	33923	7241
			Sugarcane			
Andhra Pradesh	59100	71610	12510	85936	101191	16854
Haryana	53349	71303	17954	61655	101899	44856
Karnataka	62209	97617	35408	68436	122343	58861
Maharashtra	74643	81355	6712	91227	123369	37457
Tamil Nadu	67910	86468	18558	85480	129915	51548
Uttar Pradesh	37058	57931	20873	46216	81513	40715
All India	59045	77714	18669	73158	110038	41715

Source: Various reports of *Cost of Cultivation of Crops in India*, Directorate of Economic and Statistics, Ministry of Agriculture, GoI.

21

U.R. RAJESHWARI AND FLOYD PETERS

Evaluation of National Rural Health Mission in Bangalore Rural District

Introduction

The National Rural Health Mission (NRHM) was introduced in the year 2005. It is a flagship programme of the United Progressive Alliance (UPA) government, to revitalise the public system of healthcare in the country. The thrust of this mission is on establishing a fully functional, community owned, decentralised health delivery system with inter-sectoral convergence at all levels, to ensure simultaneous action on a wide range of determinants of health such as water, sanitation, education, nutrition, social and gender equality. Institutional integration within the fragmented health sector was expected to provide a focus on outcomes, measured against Indian Public Health Standards (IPHS) for all health facilities. Although it is difficult to measure the full scope of NRHM's impact on the status of healthcare, evaluation study of any programme is a fundamental part of the planning process. In assessing the performance of a programme, an evaluation study plays a key role. It provides necessary feedback to the implementing agencies about implementation of the scheme and bottlenecks experienced in achieving the scheme objectives. In this context, this study focuses on regional disparities and analysis of the role of fund allocation, expenditure on physical and human infrastructure and development indicators on the health measures of the region. In the first section, we have analysed the secondary data including allocation and expenditures. Further, in the second section, field analysis has been done.

NRHM was first implemented in Karnataka in 2005. But the full-fledged activities began in 2007-08. In Karnataka, the implementation plan for NRHM had been developed by integrating different strategies suggested by the state health policy and the core strategies of NRHM. The district health action plans from all the districts of the state are integrated to form the state Program Implementation Plan (PIP) with emphasis on the backward districts and high-focused districts. The PIP mainly gives an overview of the present health status, situational analysis of the infrastructural facilities of the state and the plan of implementation for the current year.

It highlights the strategies and activities to be undertaken by different components of the programme in detail so as to meet its goals and objectives. As evident in the next sections, the mission has been able to improve health status of the state in terms of the health indicators such as decreased MMR (maternal mortality ratio), IMR (infant mortality rate), higher number of institutional deliveries, etc.

The vision of the Mission consists of the following main elements:

- To provide effective healthcare to rural population throughout the country;
- Commitment of the central government to raise public spending on health from 0.9 per cent of GDP (gross domestic product) to 2 to 3 per cent of GDP;
- Undertake architectural correction of the health system so as to effectively handle increased allocations;
- Promote policies that strengthen public health management and service delivery in the country;
- Revitalise local health traditions and mainstream Ayurveda, Yoga, Unani, Sidha and Homeopathic (AYUSH) treatments into public health systems;
- Decentralise programs for district management of health;
- Define time-bound goals and report publicly on their progress; and
- Improve access of rural people, especially poor women and children, to equitable, affordable, accountable and effective primary healthcare.

Objectives of U/C

- Reduction in IMR and MMR.
- Universal access to public health services, such as women's health, child health, water, sanitation and hygiene, immunisation and nutrition.
- Prevention and control of communicable and non-communicable diseases, including locally endemic ones.
- Access to integrated comprehensive primary healthcare.
- Population stabilisation, gender and demographic balance.
- Revitalise local health traditions and mainstream AYUSH treatments.
- Promotion of healthy lifestyles.

The NRHM mission document proposes 10 core strategies for realising the proposed objectives.

- Enhance capacity of PRIs (panchayat raj institutions) to own, control and manage public health services through continued training;
- Place a female health activist at the village level to ensure household level access to improved healthcare;
- Strengthen sub-centres through an Untied Fund for local planning, action and induction of more Multi-Purpose Workers (MPWs);
- Implement an inter-sectoral District Health Plan (DHP), encompassing drinking water, sanitation, hygiene and nutrition, prepared by the District Health Mission (DHM);
- Integrate the vertical health and family welfare programs at block, district, state and national levels;

There are 10 components of the action plan of NRHM. They are:

i. Accredited Social Health Activists (ASHA).
ii. Strengthening sub-centres.
iii. Strengthening PHCs (primary health centres).
iv. Strengthening CHCs (community health centres) for FRU (first referral unit).
v. District health plan.
vi. Converging hygiene and sanitation under NRHM.

vii. Strengthening disease control programs.
viii. Public-private partnerships (PPP) for public health goals.
ix. New health financing mechanisms.
x. Reorienting medical education.

Important Demographic Indicators of Bangalore Rural District

Below table presents the comparison of important health indicators at the state levels and Bangalore Rural District.

Table 21.1

Important Demographic Indicators

Indicators	*Bangalore Rural*		*Karnataka*	
	2005	*2010*	*2005*	*2010*
Crude Death Rate	5.6	5.4	6.5	6.6
Crude Birth Rate	16.1	14.2	18.1	19.3
Infant Mortality Rate	45	30	-	41

Source: Field Survey.

Human Resources

The following table presents the comparative picture of the status of infrastructure and key grass-roots personnel in Bangalore Rural District. It helps to the trend in rural health infrastructure and human resources through the period of implementation of NRHM.

Table 21.2

Staff Position of Bangalore Rural District 2012

Staff	*Sanctioned*	*No. Position*	*No. of Vacancies*
Regular ANM	207	175	32
Health Assistant (M) (S+J)	133	66	67
Lady Health Visitor	24	14	10
ASHA	785	580	205
Drivers	31	21	10

Note: ANM-Auxillary Nurse Midwive, ASHA-Accredited Social Health Activist.

Source: Department of Medical and Public Health and Family Welfare, Government of Karnataka (GoK).

Objective of the Evaluation Study

The principal activity under this objective was to conduct a systematic evaluation of the performance of NRHM in Bangalore Rural District, relying on empirical analysis of the primary and secondary data; along with detailed interviews of health functionaries at the village, block and district levels.

Methodology

Since NRHM primarily represents architectural improvements in the public health system in the rural areas, we review performance of the Mission at different levels starting from the bottom. Thus, we have the major components of NRHM as: a) village level-ASHAs (20); b) sub-centre level-ANM (10); c) PHC level-24 hours PHCs (4); d) CHC level-FRU (2); and e) District level-NRHM fund.

For each of the category of participants, separate semi-structured questionnaires were prepared. The questionnaire covered the following aspects:

- The role of the ASHAs.
- The existing infrastructure and human resources at the SCs (sub-centres) and the PHCs.
- Planning related processes being followed.
- Issues relating to ANMs.
- HR issues, reporting activities.
- Community participation and involvement.
- Fund and expenditure related aspects.
- Implementation patterns and issues in NRHM activities.
- Supply of drugs.

In order to collect the necessary data and information, we utilised a set of questionnaires for ASHAs, ANMs, and medical officers in charge of the PHCs and CHCs. Qualitative information was collected in a subset of such institutions, using open-ended semi-structured questionnaires. These questionnaires were devised to capture qualitative information regarding planning, implementation and expenditure processes and community involvement related issues. For this purpose, personnel within the health department were individually interviewed. The participants of these interviews were: District Health Officers (DHOs)/District Programme Management Officers (DPMOs), Taluk Health Officers (THOs), Medical Officers (MOs), ANMs, ASHAs and Village Health and Sanitation Committee (VHSC) representatives.

The following sections present the analysis of quantitative information collected during the field visits. The quantitative analysis provides a broad representative picture of the general utilisation levels of PHCs (using the monthly OPD, in-patient registrations and monthly deliveries), along with comparative analysis of the current status of infrastructure and its utilisation.

Results of Field Analysis

Functioning of CHCs

A structured schedule was canvassed at the CHC level and information was elicited primarily from its Medical Officer In-charge (MOIC). Apart from background information of the respondent the structured schedule intended collection of information on the background of CHC, medical and paramedical human resource, and availability of specialist services including emergency services. Further information of diagnostic equipments, facilities and services, physical infrastructure, furniture, drugs/medicines as per checklist of IPHS, etc. was elicited by canvassing the schedule.

The two CHCs have own buildings with the necessary equipment for delivery, pharmacy and the medicines. But medicines are available only to some extent. As far as availability of emergency obstetric care, emergency care for sick children, safe abortion services, etc. are concerned,we find the situation is awful in both the CHCs. Both the CHCs have separate wards for males and females. In case of Vijayapura, there are 10 wards each for males and females, whereas in case of Thyamgondlu, only two wards exist. Vijayapura CHC has equipped labour room like that in Thyamgondlu, which also does not have a minor OT (operation theatre). In both the CHCs, electricity supply is available for 6-8 hours only and the generators are not functioning. One of the noteworthy aspects is that both the CHCs are not connected with any blood banks. Availability of specialists/ doctors comprising surgeons, gynaecologists, paediatricians, and even physicians is poor in both the CHCs (See Table 21.3).

Table 21.3

Available Staff for CHCs

	IPHS Norm	*Vijayapura*	*Thyamgondlu*
General Surgeon	1	0	0
Physician	1	0	0
Gynaecologist	1	0	1
Paediatrician	1	1	0
Anaesthetist	1	0	0
Public Health Manager	1	0	0
Dental Surgeon	1	0	0
General Duty Medical Officers	6	0	1
AYUSH	1	1	1
Staff Nurse	15	2	2
Lady Health Visitor	1	0	2
Public Health Nurse	1	-	-
ANM	1	3	5
Pharmacist/Compounder	3	1	1
Lab Technician	3	1	1
Radiographer	2	1	0
Dresser	2	0	0
Ward boys	5	3	3
Clerk	2	1	1
Accountant	1	2	2
OT Technician	1	0	0
Driver	1	0	1

Source: Field Survey.

According to IPHS norms, a CHC should have one general surgeon, one Physician, and one dental surgeon. But in both the CHCs visited, none of these specialists were found in position.

Functioning of PHCs

In order to provide optimal level of quality healthcare, PHC is universally recognised as the most effective intervention to achieve significant improvements in the health status of population in the locality. For study purposes, four PHCs have been surveyed in our sampled district under the sampling criteria of two PHCs under every selected CHC in the district.

All the four PHCs surveyed were reported to be functioning in own buildings. All the four PHCs have drinking water facility, but Dabaspet and Manne PHCs has only 2-4 hours of water availability. In all the four PHCs, pharmacy is available but adequate medicines are absent. However, all the PHCs have OPD rooms but none of them has minor OT or general OT. In all the PHCs, only 6 hours of electricity is available and none of them had a functioning generator. Only two PHCs have functional vehicles. None of the PHCs are linked with blood banks. The following table shows human resource shortage in all the four PHCs.

Functioning of SCs and ANMs

Sub-centre is a bridge between rural community and public primary healthcare system. A sub-centre is responsible for providing all kind of primary healthcare and makes the services more responsive and sensitive for the rural community. This section provides information on the SCs and ANMs based on our sample survey. It can be seen that on an average, there is one ANM per SC. The number of villages covered per ANM is in the range of 5-8. Quality of healthcare at SC therefore obviously suffers. The number of ASHAs per ANM also varies substantially in these SCs. The average number of rooms in the SCs also varies considerably from 1-4. Only 30 per cent of SCs have their own buildings. In terms of the physical infrastructure, about 50 per cent SCs did not have delivery tables, 40 per cent SCs did not have medical equipments, 30 per cent SCs did not have electricity connection, 50 per cent SCs did not have water supply for 24 hours per day, and only 5 per cent SCs had a two wheeler. NRHM funds have not succeeded so far to remove this deficiency of physical infrastructure prevailing at the SCs.

Table 21.4

Available Staff for PHCs

	IPHS Norm	*Dabaspeth*	*Avathi*	*Manne*	*Budigere*
Medical Officer	2	1	1	1	1
AYUSH	1	0	1	1	0
Pharmacist	1	1	1	1	1
Staff Nurse	1	2	3	2	2
Health Worker Female	1	-	-	-	-
Health Assistant Male	1	1	1	1	0
Health Assistant Female	1	1	1	0	0
Clerks	2	1	0	0	1
Data Assistant	1	0	0	0	1
Lab Technician	1	1	1	0	0
Driver	1	1	1	0	0
Class IV Employees	4	6	2	1	3

Source: Field Survey.

Seventy per cent of ANMs are involved in the selection of ASHAs with whom they have to work closely. However, 60 per cent of the ANMs felt that ASHAs had reduced their workload. Almost all ANMs received the NRHM untied Grant of ₹10,000 per year. All ANMs had joint bank account with *sarpanch* of the *panchayat*. Eighty per cent ANMs used the fund for repairs and renovations; 10 per cent for buying medicines; and 10 per cent for obtaining electricity supply. In short, the funds were mostly used for overcoming the infrastructural shortcomings. However, utilisation of the NRHM fund by the ANMs also ran into problems reported by 30 per cent of the ANMs. This happened largely because of the joint account opened with the *sarpanch*, where the NRHM funds were made available. The *sarpanch* used to demand his commission for signing the cheque that would be in the range of 20-50 per cent of the amount. As a result, some

ANMs would not spend the money and others may be simply unable to properly spend it. However, 80 per cent of the ANMs felt that the funds given under NRHM were not adequate, since the physical infrastructure continued to be in the bad shape as found above.

The ANMs get their drug kits refilled, as reported to us, regularly. Sixty per cent of them get it weekly; 30 per cent fortnightly; and 10 per cent rarely. Yet, the refill of drug kits still remains a problem and AYUSH medicines are largely missing. None of the ANMs conducted deliveries, which were mostly referred to either a PHC or CHC. At the SC level, NRHM has started making some difference particularly by providing some discretionary fund for improving the infrastructure and getting some equipment; but there is still a huge gap in these matters before quality of the healthcare is improve significantly. Problems encountered by ANMs in utilising this fund need to be particularly addressed to promptly achieve better progress.

Results of Household Survey

An important objective of this study is to assess the availability, adequacy and utilisation of health services in the rural areas; the role played by ASHAs and AYUSH in creating awareness of health, nutrition, sanitation and hygiene among the rural population; and to identify the limitation and mechanism in implementation of NRHM.

The household schedule comprised mainly socio-economic and demographic characteristics of the household, details about utilisation of ANC by the pregnant women, and utilisation of the delivery and PNC (postnatal care) for children aged 0-5 years. In addition to this, information was obtained over the benefits of Janani Suraksha Yojana (JSY), sources of health services, etc. in the surveyed villages. Further, we gathered information about the prevailing awareness about NRHM, ASHA, existence of VHSC, etc. and also people's satisfaction with the health services.

Therefore, selection of villages was to facilitate purposive selection 40 households with the objective criterion of selecting households having respondents under pregnant women, and lactating women with new born children of less than one year.

Table 21.5

Sample Design Background Characteristics of Households

Village	*Frequency*	*Per cent*
Dabaspeth	15	37.5
Thyamagondlu	15	37.5
Vijayapaura	10	25.0
Total	33	100.0

Source: Field Survey.

Background Characteristics

Table 21.5 reveals that 33 per cent of the households belong to SC (scheduled castes), 12 per cent household belongs to ST (scheduled tribes) and 55 per cent belongs to OBCs (the other backward classes) category. Overall, about 69.7 per cent of households reported total annual income less than ₹25,000 and around 30.3 per cent households reported the income to be over ₹50,000.

Table 21.6

Background Characteristics of Households

Social Category	SC	33.3
	ST	12.1
	OBC	54.5
Total Income of HH	Less than 25,000	69.7
	Between 25,000-50,000	30.3

Source: Field Survey.

Antenatal Care Utilisation

Information on utilisation of antenatal care has been depicted in Table 21.7. Around 94 per cent of pregnant women had registered within the first trimester. Of all respondents, 60.6 per cent said that they are going for ANC. Majority of the antenatal checkups are being reported to be done either at CHCs or SCs (sub-centres). Barely around 12 per cent pregnant women reported opting for antenatal checkups at DHs. Further, only 9 per cent of the pregnant women have reported depending upon private doctors or health facilities for the ANC checkups.

Knowledge about ASHA, NRHM and VHSC

The NRHM envisages that every village will have a female ASHA to act as an interface between the community and the public health system. Secondly, under NRHM, GPs (gram panchayats) have been called upon to constitute VHSC. These committees shall steer the preparation of village health and sanitation plans. Such committees are essential for applying broad approaches to health improvement that involve a wide range of activities.

Table 21.7

Information about ANC

Pregnancy registration	<3months	93.9
	3-6months	6.1
Whether going for any ANC	Yes	60.6
	No	39.4
Whether going for prenatal check up/place of check up	ASHA	15.2
	ANM	27.3
	CHC	36.4
	District Hospitals (DH)	12.1
	Private Hospital	9.1
Whether ASHA/ANM helps in any pregnancy related problems	Yes	78.8
	No	21.2

Source: Field Survey.

Data collected through field surveys indicate the extent of respondents' knowledge regarding NRHM, ASHA and VHSC. The data show that only 30.3 per cent of people have heard about ASHA and 54.5 per cent of people have heard about NRHM.

A proportion of 44.4 per cent of respondents have heard about NRHM through newspapers, followed by ASHAs/ANMs. Thirty-six per cent of the respondents said that ASHA visits weekly, and 33 per cent households said bi-weekly in the respective village. Thirty-one per cent of the households reported that ASHAs will not visit their village. On an average, only 30 per cent ASHAs had kits and in 27 per cent of the cases they provide common medicines to people as reported by the surveyed individuals. Even though VHSCs are one of the important components of NRHM, 93 per cent of the respondents told that these committees do not exist in their village. A proportion of 75.8 per cent of the households replied that no health camps were conducted in the village. Only 42.4 per cent people have spoken about improvement after the launch of NRHM.

Of all respondents, 42.4 per cent said to have seen some improvement in health facilities and infrastructure after the launch of NRHM. After introducing this scheme, improvements have been noticed in the availability of medicine and the quality of treatment.

Table 21.8

Information about ASHA and NRHM (in %)

	Response	*Percentage*
Have you heard about ASHA?	Yes	30.3
Have you heard about NRHM?	Yes	54.5
Source of information?	ASHA/ANM	38.9
	TV	11.1
	NewsPaper	44.4
	Other	5.6
How often does ASHA visit your house?	Every Week	36.4
	Bi-Weekly	33.3
	Never	30.3
Does ASHA carry a kit?	Yes	30.3
Does ASHA provide common medicines free of cost?	Yes	27.3
Does ASHA tell about health practices like good sanitation/ hygiene?	Yes	33.3
Is any health day at Aanganwadi or at any other place organised in your village?	Yes	12.1
Is there any village health and committee (VHSC) in your village?	Yes	6.1
Are any health camps organised at village/community/ block level?	Yes	24.2
Are you aware of the timings of the doctor's visit at SC?	Yes	57.6
Is there any improvement after launching of NRHM?	Yes	42.4

Source: Field Survey.

Functioning of ASHAs

Under NRHM, introduction of ASHA as a link between the community and the rural health system had aimed to motivate and help vulnerable sections like poor, women and children to improve their accessibility to basic health services at the time of their need. The facility survey elicited information about functioning of ASHAs in the selected villages through structured schedule as well as focus group discussions in order to highlight their knowledge and awareness about their roles and responsibilities under the programme.

Our survey provides information on the different aspects of ASHA's background, selection, training, and interface with community and rewards. To analyse the functioning of ASHAs, we interviewed 20 of them. Out of these, 70 per cent of the ASHAs have joined in the year 2009 and 80 per cent of them stay in the serving village.

About the selection procedure, 55 per cent ASHAs said that focused group discussions were conducted before selection and candidates were accordingly short listed. Forty per cent of them said that gram sabha meeting was held during the selection process. Fourty-five per cent of the ASHAs had worked as community-based workers earlier. Almost all of them had received training after joining. Almost 95 per cent ASHAs received some formal training for 10-31 days during the first year of their work. Almost all ASHAs felt that the training was very useful in solving doubts and in refilling supplies. About 90 per cent ASHAs received a compensation of ₹500 for attending the training. About 95 per cent ASHAs had received drug kits. Medicines for fever, pain killers, etc., were the part of the drug kits given to 20 per cent of the ASHAs. More than 90 per cent ASHAs interviewed informed us about their active involvement in creating awareness in the community about health, hygiene and nutrition; mobilising community to utilise healthcare services such as ANC, PNC, immunisation, sanitation, counselling women on birth preparedness and safe delivery; new born care, breast feeding and complementary feeding, infant immunisation, use of contraceptives and family planning measures, escorting pregnant women and sick children to the nearest healthcare facility and informing SC/PHC/CHC about births and deaths in the village. However, 35 per cent of the ASHAs did not participate in promoting construction of household toilets. The preferred destination of ASHA escorting a pregnant woman was a sub-centre. There is a marked variation in the reported average amount received for accompanying a pregnant woman to a healthcare facility by ASHA. It varied from ₹100 to ₹400. About 90 per cent ASHAs complained about the money being inadequate since they had to spend extra money out of their pockets. Only 15 per cent ASHAs received performance-based incentives. About 75 per cent ASHAs received proper support from the ANMs or AWWs (Anganwadi Workers) for refilling the drug kits, on the job training, for guidance regarding use of various medicines, doses and side effects of contraceptive pills, and danger signs of pregnancy and labour pain. Only 60 per cent of the ASHAs were actively involved with PRIs and VHSCs. Almost 75 per cent ASHA felt that institutional deliveries have increased after the implementation NRHM, which implies positive mind set and optimistic attitude of the activists.

Insights from the Field

Field-level experiences from in-depth discussions with the state health officials provided an insight into the policy environment for implementation of the NRHM programme. Although the programme was initiated quite late, it seems to be making considerable progress.

i. Serious shortage of medical doctors and specialists and paramedical staff, especially staff nurses and lab technicians, was extended as a serious reason for not getting good results, despite facing no financial constraints under NRHM. It was clearly expressed that postings and availability of qualified doctors in the rural areas would not be possible because of nearly absent social facilities, like educational infrastructure for children, irregular supply of electricity as well as potable water, safety of females in certain rural tracts in most of the states, and unhygienic and unsanitory conditions, not only in rural neighbourhood or villages, but also in the vicinity of health facilities.

ii. Some suggestions like higher transport allowance or transport facilities from the nearby towns to rural areas can help in availing services from qualified doctors, as well as the better educational facilities for their children in the nearby towns.
iii. Further, certain financial incentives like enhancement of non-practising allowance for doctors and other paramedical staff can help in proper implementation of the statutory requirements, like no permission for private practice, etc. Health officials at PHCs and SCs also clearly expressed similar serious constraints, like political interference in terms of transfers of ANMs, safety and security of female medical staff, irregular supply of electricity, non-availability of water in general and potable water in specific, irregular supply of drugs and equipments, etc.
iv. Because of the lack of properly equipped laboratories, it becomes difficult to diagnose even minor ailments and thus most of the patients get referred to higher level secondary and tertiary health facilities, which unnecessarily get crowded. This hampers effective delivery of healthcare.
v. The ASHA scheme seems to work quite effectively as we find that almost all the deliveries get registered under the JSY scheme and have enhanced institutional deliveries, which in turn would reduce infant and maternal mortality and morbidity. However, these incentives irrespective of the birth order may have some pro-natalist effects. Involvement of ASHAs in organising family planning camps, routine immunisations, DOTS distribution etc., seem to have gone up.
vi. Training of the grass-roots health functionaries, like ASHA, needs to be taken up seriously.
vii. Effective ambulance system at the PHC and SC level for movements of patients referred to health facilities and also for emergency services at the doorsteps would definitely help in rendering the prompt delivery of healthcare in rural areas. Improvement in the ambulance system, especially at the CHC and PHC levels, along with the upgrade as per the IPHS standards, should be taken up seriously.

22

KOUSHIK KUMAR HATI*

State Intervention for Safe Motherhood

Reflections from the Field

Introduction

Health is considered to be one of the key ingredients of human development for an economy as it helps in enhancing the quality of human capital and thereby improves the state of human development. Health is also perceived to be the promoting' factors to an economy (Dreze and Sen, 1995). In spite of accepting the primacy of health sector in augmenting the development process, access to basic health services has continued to remain poor in developing countries. The Millennium Development Goals (MDGs) adopted and ratified by India also speaks of reducing child mortality by two third between 1990 and 2015, indicated by under-5 mortality rate and IMR (infant mortality rate). In addition to child health, maternal health is also targeted to be improved by reducing the MMR (maternal mortality ratio) by three quarter during the same period. Safe delivery by way of encouraging proportion of births attended by skilled personnel is also strategised as a part of the programme. In India, despite substantial investment in health infrastructure, both access to and use of services remain suboptimal and varies considerably across states and regions. As a consequence, yet today every second young child in India is malnourished, less than one

* This research article is a part of a broader study on "Impact Evaluation of Janani Suraksha Yojna in Burdwan District" financed by the Eastern Regional Centre of Indian Council of Social Science Research. The author would like to express his gratitude to Prof Rajarshi Majumder of the University of Burdwan for his suggestions, which has contributed much to this paper. Remaining errors are solely the author's responsibility.

fourth of rural population use toilets and only 4 out of every 10 girls who enrol in formal schools complete elementary schooling. According to the MDG Report, the target regarding health is to reduce the IMR and MMR to 109 per 100,000 live birth by 2015.[1] In reality however, both IMR and MMR are still way above the target. The IMR for India stands at 44 for the year 2011. While that of MMR stands at 212. Several indicators of health status show that India is still lagging behind the global standard. Comparing with global average, according to a recent report by United Nations Children's Fund (UNICEF) the global IMR decreased from 61 deaths in 1990 to 37 deaths in 2011. Annual infant deaths declined from 8.4 million in 1990 to 5 million in 2011. According to the report, India's IMR showed a minor decline in 2012 compared to 2011. IMR decreased from 44 deaths for every 1,000 live births in 2011 to 42 deaths for every 1,000 live in 2012. To discuss more regionally, as released in the latest report of Register General of India (RI), Kerala has done a remarkable job by reducing her IMR to 12 while Assam stood at worst in India with IMR of 55. The performance of West Bengal at 32 is also not good. The lagging states like Uttar Pradesh and Odisha showed improvement with IMR in both the states declining from 57 in 2011 to 53 in 2012. The main causes for such high IMR in India are said to be the low awareness of health and reproductive rights, maternal anaemia and the burden of malnutrition.

Under such circumstances, the National Rural Health Mission (NRHM) launched in India in 2005 aimed to provide accessible, affordable and quality healthcare to the rural population, especially the vulnerable groups. The NRHM programme includes specific schemes with the objective of reducing maternal and neonatal mortality by promoting institutional delivery among poor pregnant women. These objectives are targeted to be fulfilled through Janani Suraksha Yojna (JSY) programme, a flagship programme under the NRHM.

In this study we seek to examine the effectiveness of the scheme in spreading awareness about maternal and child health, participation

1. Millennium Development Goals, UNDP; Accessed from *http://www.in.undp.org/content/india/en/home/mdgoverview/overview/mdg5/* (accessed on 20 October 2014).

in the scheme and its impact on the extent of institutional delivery as well as on infant mortality. We also look at the role of Accredited Social Health Activist (ASHA) workers in the successful implementation of JSY. The study was conducted in Burdwan district of West Bengal during the period 2013-14.

Background of the Scheme

In an attempt to make promotive and preventive healthcare services available, especially to the poorest and the most vulnerable segments of the rural society, JSY forms a crucial component of the NRHM. JSY is a safe motherhood intervention initiated to reduce maternal and neo-natal mortality. It is a conditional cash transfer scheme that ensures quality maternal care during pregnancy, delivery and in the immediate post-delivery period along with appropriate referral and transport assistance. This is a CSS (centrally sponsored scheme) which links cash assistance with delivery and post-delivery care. The scheme has made special provisions for states having low institutional delivery rates. Further to improve accessibility to health facilities, the scheme has made provisions for engaging the private sector.

Eligibility Criteria

Under this scheme, the states are first classified into two categories, viz., LPS (low performing states) and HPS (high performing states). States having institutional delivery rate of 25 per cent or less of the total delivery were termed as LPS and those which have institutional delivery rate more than 25 per cent of the total were classified as HPS. Uttar Pradesh, Uttaranchal, Bihar, Jharkhand, Madhya Pradesh, Chhattisgarh, Assam, Rajasthan, Odisha and Jammu and Kashmir come under the LPS category, while rest of the states come under the HPS category. Tables 22.1 and 22.2 describe the details about the eligibility for receiving cash assistance and the amount of money provided to the JSY beneficiary.

Sample Survey and Methodology

The methodology followed in this paper is in accordance with the standard requirements for the impact evaluation studies - monitoring about 50 per cent of the beneficiaries in the selected village as samples. The survey has been conducted in 10 villages with representation from each of the surveyed CD (community development) Blocks. Detailed frame of the survey is portrayed in Table 22.3. A Stratified Random Sampling Technique was adopted to identify the sample villages. Thereafter, a purposive random sampling technique was adopted to identify the beneficiaries who are to be surveyed.

Table 22.1

Eligibility for Cash Assistance

Low Performing States	All pregnant women delivering in Government health centres like Sub-centre, PHC/CHC/FRU/general wards of District and State hospitals or accredited private institutions.
Other States	BPL (below poverty line) pregnant women, aged 19 years and above. All SC and ST women delivering in a government health centre like Sub-centre, PHC/CHC/FRU/general ward of District and State hospitals or accredited private institutions.

Source: Ministry of Health and Family Welfare, Government of India (GoI).

Table 22.2

Scale of Cash Assistance for Institutional Delivery

	Rural Area		*Urban Area*	
Category	*Mothers*	*ASHA Workers*	*Mothers*	*ASHA Workers*
Low Performing States	1,400	600	1,000	200
Other States	500	—	500	—

Source: Ministry of Health and Family Welfare, GoI.

Table 22.3

Survey Coverage

Indicators		*Existing*	*Surveyed*	*No. of Women Surveyed*
No. of CD Blocks (Rural)	Aggregate	14	10	279
	East	4	3	86
	Central	5	4	115
	West	5	3	78

Source: Office of Chief Medical Officer of Health (CMOH), Burdwan District and Field Survey, 2013-14.

Based on the purpose of the study, our target was to select households within a village having at least one woman who has given birth to a baby in last two years or a pregnant woman. As is the norm in any monitoring activity, our random survey method sought to ensure that the findings are representative of the reality. In total 279 beneficiaries were interviewed. As per our objective of the study we looked at the indicators related to awareness about the scheme, its components and participation the scheme; finally, if the scheme has been able to put a mark on the institutional delivery in the district. Along with this, we also intended to see the role of ASHA workers in implementing JSY schemes. Two sets of questionnaires were designed accordingly—one is for the beneficiaries and the other for the ASHA workers.

At a spatial level, the district has a varied geography and socio economic conditions—amply reflected in the three sub-regions—East (CD Blocks: Kalna-I, Kalna-II, Katwa-I, Katwa-II, Ketugram-I, Ketugram-II, Mongalkote, Monteswar, Purbasthali-I, Purbasthali-II), Central (CD Blocks—Ausgram-I, Ausgram-II, Bhatar, Burdwan-I, Burdwan-II, Galsi- II, Jamalpur, Khandoghosh, Memari-I, Memari-II, Raina-I, Raina-II) and West (CD Blocks—Andal, Barabani, Durgapur-Faridpur, Galsi-I, Jamuria, Kanksa, Pandabeswar, Raniganj, Salanpur). Wherever possible, we have tried to bring out the relative situation in these three sub-regions so that policies may be streamlined according to local conditions. It must be noted here that the Eastern and Central sub-regions are predominantly agricultural in nature, while the Western sub-region is dominated by mining, quarrying, and manufacturing activities with sparse agriculture. Keeping these economic characteristics in mind will help us understand the results better.

Awareness, Participation and Impact of JSY

Awareness about the scheme among women, especially among pregnant women and mothers, and to have their participation is the key to successful implementation of the programme. The ultimate goal of safe motherhood and consequent reduction of maternal mortality can be achieved only by such consciousness involvement.

In this section of the study, we bring out the level of awareness among the women about the secure motherhood procedures provided under JSY programme and the extent of participation in the programme by looking at the utilisation of the services. However, before going into that, we look at the background characteristics of the surveyed women in terms of their socio, economic and demographic physiognomies.

Background Characteristics of Surveyed Women

The socio-economic profile of the women surveyed indicates that majority of them are Hindu. However, Eastern part of Burdwan has substantial number of Muslim representatives (Table 22.4). In rest of the zones, Muslims were less than 10 per cent. In aggregate, out of every 100 surveyed women, around 91 belonged to Hindu religion and rests were from the Muslim community. Truncating the sample across caste, a large number of people are from SC (scheduled caste) community. Number of ST (scheduled tribe) women are less in number and are absent in the Eastern zone. 'Other' category includes the General Caste and the OBC (other backward classes). The reason why the General and OBCs are combined is because of the rationale to get JSY benefit. To avail the benefit, either your economic status has to lie below the poverty line irrespective of whatever caste/religion you belong to or be a SC/ST irrespective of whatever is your economic status. East Burdwan has highest number of women belonging to General Caste and OBC.

The proportion of women belonging to BPL category is higher in Central zone followed by East and West. Nearly half of the population in our study in almost all the zones belongs to BPL category. Focusing on the level of education among women, more than 50 per cent are primary graduate in all three zones of the district. However, a significant number of women are illiterate, ranging from 17 per cent to 24 per cent.

The probability of finding highly educated women or educated at least up to a certain reasonable level is scanty. Only 9 in every 100 women were found to have completed their higher secondary schooling. Though we found a significant number of women to be primary graduate but knowledge among such mothers about the mechanisms of safe motherhood is a questionable issue. Poor education has to have an adverse impact on the maternal and neonatal mortality. Along with mother's schooling, edification among rest of the family members is also desirable. That too in our study is found to be significantly low in all three stratums. The average years of schooling of the family members is hovering between Class III to IV in the regions.

Table 22.4

Background Characteristics of Surveyed Women

	Burdwan			
	West	*Central*	*East*	*Aggregate*
Aggregate Sample Size	86	115	78	279
Religion				
Hindu (%)	98.8	93.0	78.2	90.7
Muslim (%)	1.2	7.0	21.8	9.3
Caste				
SC (%)	75.6	63.5	43.6	61.6
ST (%)	5.8	14.8	NA	7.9
Others (%)	18.6	21.7	56.4	30.5
Economic Status				
APL (%)	58.1	53.0	57.7	55.9
BPL (%)	41.9	47.0	42.3	44.1
Years of Schooling of eneficiary				
Illiterate (%)	23.3	24.3	17.9	22.2
Below Primary (%)	2.3	1.7	NA	1.4
Primary Passed (%)	55.8	51.3	56.4	54.1
Secondary Passed (%)	10.5	13.0	17.9	13.6
Higher Secondary and Above (%)	8.1	9.6	7.7	8.6
Average Years of Schooling of the Family	4.0	3.9	3.7	3.8
Age of Mothers				
Under 20 Years (%)	9.3	14.8	15.4	13.3
20–25 Years (%)	67.4	67.8	69.2	68.1
Over 25 Years (%)	23.3	17.4	15.4	18.6

Source: Field Survey, 2013-14.

Another important factor in this context is the age of mothers. An interesting point found in the study was that around 9-15 per cent of mothers delivering in the reference period were younger than 20 years of age. This basically increases the chance of premature delivery and causes severe health disorder to both mother and child, sometime even leading to death. 68 per cent of the mothers have delivered between 20 to 25 years of age, while 18 per cent at the age of 26 years and above. There is not much variation in figures across zones in this regard. Only point is, delivery under 20 years is lesser in West, which can be a noted success of the programme.

While socio-economic condition helps in being aware about promotive healthcare service on maternal care, preventive healthcare mechanism depends a lot on the dwelling condition of the new born baby and the mother. A *kaccha* house (made of soil) with poor sanitisation system and no proper source of safe drinking water definitely would be unhygienic for a child making him/her vulnerable to be affected by diseases. To start with, a major number of women are residing in *kaccha* house in almost all regions of the district. People residing inWestern region are little bit better off in this respect. Among the regions, only about 30 to 38 in every 100 women are fortunate enough to be residing in *pucca* house (made of concrete), rest are dwelling either in *kaccha* or in semi-*pucca* house at the most (Table 22.5).

Drinking water, known to be transferor of germs of many diseases, is a big issue in the surveyed areas. Nearly 50 per cent of women as well as the child don't have access to tap water. They are bound to drink water either from tube well or from dug well. Though the incidence of using dug well as source of drinking water is less in number, but is still there and is dominant in West Burdwan. Overall, Western part has the acute problem in providing safe drinking water compared to the other two regions.

Having toilet is another component of sanitation and is useful to maintain hygienic condition both within the house and the premises. On the average, 42 in every 100 household in the district don't have a toilet in their house. Central Burdwan has maximum such households. Only 40 per cent of the households have managed to build *pucca* toilet for them in the district so far. However, the ratio varies a lot across regions.

Table 22.5

Dwelling Condition of Surveyed Women

	Burdwan			
	West	*Central*	*East*	*Aggregate*
Aggregate Sample Size	86	115	78	279
Type of House				
Kaccha (%)	33.7	50.4	46.2	44.1
Pucca (%)	38.4	29.6	35.9	34.1
Semi-*Pucca* (%)	27.9	20.0	17.9	21.9
Source of Drinking Water				
Tap Water (%)	43.0	61.7	44.9	51.3
Tube Well (%)	51.2	38.3	53.8	46.6
Dug Well (%)	5.8	0.0	1.3	2.2
Toilet Type				
Nil (%)	41.9	45.2	38.5	41.9
Kaccha (%)	7.0	7.8	1.3	5.7
Semi *Pucca* (%)	22.1	9.6	3.8	12.2
Pucca (%)	29.1	37.4	56.4	40.1
Number of Family Members				
Up to 5 (%)	69.8	66.1	57.7	64.9
Between 6 to 8 (%)	27.9	24.3	33.3	28.0
More than 8 (%)	2.3	9.6	9.0	7.2

Source: Field Survey, 2013-14.

Lastly, we focus on the size of the family. Maximum number of women are from families with a size of 5 or even less family members. Only 7 per cent of the households are found to be having large family with number of family members exceeding eight, rest of the women are staying in a 5 to 8 member family.

Awareness About JSY

After looking at the socio-economic background and the dwelling condition of women, we now focus on those who are entitled get the

JSY benefit. Burdwan being a district belonging to a state which does not fall under the preview of 'LPS' in terms of institutional delivery, namely, West Bengal, to get the JSY scheme benefit, the resident women either has to belong from SC/ST community or her economic status has to lie below the poverty line. In other words, while looking at the awareness about some exclusive scheme benefit like cash incentive, provision of transportation cost, etc., we don't look at those women who are from General Caste and/or from OBC with economic status lying above the poverty line.

Awareness Among Eligible Mothers and Pregnant Women

It has been nearly eight years since JSY has been in effect. Therefore, people have become aware about the programme. In our study area, 83 per cent of Hindus and 96 per cent of Muslims were aware about the scheme. The proportion of aware women seems to be more than 90 per cent in all regions except for Hindus in the West. 29 per cent of Hindu eligible women still haven't heard of JSY in the region. Discussing across various social groups, awareness within SC community is low compared to the other communities (Table 22.6).

However, on the average, more than 80 per cent of the people do have information about JSY, irrespective of whatever caste they belong to. Notable awareness is there among the STs, where the proportion is close to 100 per cent in all regions. However, we could not find any eligible woman from ST community in the East. West zone has once again been found to be the worst performer in spreading information about the scheme. More than 30 per cent of women from SC community and 25 per cent of General and/or OBC eligible women don't know about the scheme in the West.

To avail the benefit of the JSY scheme, one has to possess a JSY card. Upon registration, the card is issued to the pregnant woman from the nearest SHC (sub health centre) if she is entitled to the scheme benefit based on her socio/economic background. It was observed that in terms of possessing JSY card, Muslims are in a better state compared to Hindus except in Eastern region where the percentage of Muslim beneficiaries is substantially lower compared to that of Hindus (Table 22.7). Number of Hindu beneficiaries in the

West Burdwan is a cause of concern as the figure has fallen to less than half of the total eligible women in that area. As in other criterion, SC women are lagging behind in terms of having JSY card also.

Table 22.6

Percentage of Eligible Women Aware About JSY

Percentage of Mothers Aware About JSY	*Burdwan*			
	West	*Central*	*East*	*Aggregate*
Across Religion				
Hindu	71.4	88.3	92.1	82.8
Muslim	100.0	100.0	94.1	96.2
Across Caste				
SC	69.2	87.7	94.1	82.0
ST	100.0	94.1	NA	95.5
Others	75.0	91.7	90.5	87.8

Source: Field Survey, 2013-14.

Around 42 per cent of SC women who are eligible to get the benefit don't have a JSY card. In the West, only 38 out of 100 SC women have the card, the worst case among all other regions. The condition for STs in this respect is better as the percentage reached more than 80 per cent on the whole. However, for General Category and OBCs, this is a big reason to worry, especially in the East region.

Next, we focus on how the women come to know about the JSY and its beneficial components (Table 22.8). Generally, it is the ASHA works, better known as local ASHA *didi* who are responsible for informing the women about the scheme. They are supposed to keep a track of the newly married couples in her area and make them aware about the scheme and its uses. In some cases, the Anganwari Workers (AWW) also provides the information about the scheme. However, in absence of ASHA, the responsibility comes to the Auxiliary Nursing Midwifery (ANM) at SHC. Therefore, as expected, ASHA being the prime source of information had informed 52 per cent of women about the scheme on the whole. Apart from being informed by the ASHA/ANM/AWW, nearly 11 per cent came to know about the scheme from the neighbours.

Table 22.7

Possession of Janani Suraksha Yojna Card Among Eligible Women

Percentage of Eligible Mothers and Pregnant Women Having JSY Card	*Burdwan*			
	West	*Central*	*East*	*Aggregate*
Across Religio				
Hindu	44.2	70.2	76.3	61.7
Muslim	100.0	87.5	58.8	69.2
Across Caste				
SC	38.5	67.1	79.4	58.7
ST	80.0	88.2	NA	86.4
Others	75.0	75.0	57.1	65.9

Source: Field Survey, 2013-14.

This can be taken as remarkable point because if society is aware, then the pressure on health system reduces which is highly desired in a densely populated country like India where health institutions are overburdened with patient pressure.

Table 22.8

Sources of Information about JSY Among Eligible Women

Source of Information	*Burdwan*			
	West	*Central*	*East*	*Aggregate*
ANM	10.7	24.2	23.5	20.2
ASHA	57.1	56.0	41.2	52.5
AWW	19.6	15.4	15.7	16.7
Neighbour	12.5	4.4	19.6	10.6

Source: Field Survey, 2013-14.

Awareness About the Components of JSY

So far we looked at the general awareness about the scheme among eligible women. But it is important to know if people are aware about the specific components of JSY which are provided free of cost to the JSY card holders. Some common practices like incentive for institutional delivery, support for PNC (post natal care), helping the beneficiaries in their initial days after conceiving the baby to finding a doctor are known mostly by all women. In some sense, getting transportation support or 'Matriyan', the car stipulated for carrying pregnant women to hospital for delivery, is also quite commonly known. But knowledge about government accredited private hospitals where facilities can be obtained freely is significantly low. Only 11-16 per cent of the eligible women know about the selected private hospitals approved for free delivery services (Table 22.9). Same applies to the newly created centres for 24 hour delivery. About monetary incentive, more than 75 per cent of beneficiaries possess the information about getting money from SHC and/or from the hospital. However, regarding the knowledge about getting assistance to identify a doctor, the figure is low for backward communities and is moderate for 'others'. This component of JSY or the service is very important as the risk during pregnancy are identified and checked by the doctors.

Talking of PNC, even though it is really important for a child, the awareness about PNC is not satisfactory. 48 per cent of women are unaware of the proper PNC mechanisms. However, this doesn't mean that they never went for PNC checkup; they are generally ignorant about the importance of such medications and are prone to miss or ignore the daily checkup or scheduled immunisation of the child.

Impact and Participation

Having looked at the level of information and awareness about the scheme, we now look at the level of participation in the programme and consequent impact on outcome indicators like rise in institutional delivery and fall in infant mortality.

Place of Delivery

We classify the place of delivery into three groups, namely, government hospitals, private hospital and home delivery, and focus on the distribution across the two economic classes—APL and BPL. In earlier days poor people, generally categorised as BPL, used to prefer home delivery in comparison to bearing costly hospital expenses and this led to increase in maternal and infant mortality. The socially excluded communities like SCs and STs predominantly fall under the

Table 22.9

Awareness About Components of JSY Among Eligible Women

Zone	Caste	Percentage awareness about different components of JSY					
		Doctors are identified by health worker where pregnant women can visit for complications	Centres are created for delivery any time	Private hospitals have been approved for free delivery services	Money is given to mothers for delivering in the institutions	Money is paid / free car is provided for transportation to the health facility	Support is provided for post natal care
West	SC	55.4	35.4	12.3	69.2	47.7	49.2
	ST	100.0	60.0	20.0	80.0	100.0	60.0
	Others	62.5	25.0	0.0	87.5	62.5	62.5
Central	SC	57.5	57.5	12.3	75.3	63.0	58.9
	ST	52.9	47.1	29.4	82.4	70.6	52.9
	Others	58.3	50.0	25.0	75.0	58.3	66.7
East	SC	85.3	91.2	11.8	94.1	76.5	76.5
	ST	NA	NA	NA	NA	NA	NA
	Others	66.7	90.5	14.3	85.7	90.5	61.9
Aggt.	SC	59.0	35.9	11.5	71.8	52.6	51.3
	ST	56.9	54.9	16.7	76.5	63.7	58.8
	Others	78.2	90.9	12.7	90.9	81.8	70.9

Note: # there was no ST beneficiaries in the area.

Source: Field Survey, 2013-14.

BPL category. Therefore, they are targeted and incentivised to get their pregnant woman to hospitals so that with proper facilitation the risk of mortality is reduced and sound health can be ensured.

Discussing across economic status, it is important to see how many home deliveries have occurred still now. As shown in Table 22.10, 10 per cent of women from APL families and 14 per cent from BPL families reported delivering at home. Incidence of home delivery has significantly come down in East Burdwan, whereas it is too high in West and is highest among BPL families in the Central part of the district. Delivery in private hospital is high among APL families, which is not surprising as they have the potential to afford or bear such cost. It is important to note that the delivery in government hospital is substantial enough and is highest for BPL women. This is mere indication of the fact that the scheme has had an effect on the poor so far.

Table 22.10

Place of Delivery by Economic Status

Zone	*Economic Status*	*Place of Delivery*		
		Govt. Hospital	*Private Hospital*	*Home*
West	APL	58.1	23.3	18.6
	BPL	73.5	14.7	11.8
Central	APL	66.1	26.8	7.1
	BPL	76.1	2.2	21.7
East	APL	69.2	25.6	5.1
	BPL	83.9	9.7	6.5
Aggt.	APL	64.5	25.4	10.1
	BPL	77.5	8.1	14.4

Source: Field Survey, 2013-14.

Truncating across social groups, home delivery is observed to be dominant in SC families followed by STs in almost all regions of the district (Table 22.11). Once again to find, health administrators in the East could successfully reduce the incidence of home delivery across backward classes while West has severe problem; especially for SCs.

Table 22.11

Place of Delivery by Social Group

Zone	*Economic Status*	*Place of Delivery*		
		Govt. Hospital	*Private Hospital*	*Home*
West	SC	65.5	13.8	20.7
	ST	80.0	20.0	0.0
	Others	57.1	42.9	0.0
Central	SC	74.2	11.3	14.5
	ST	87.5	0.0	12.5
	Others	50.0	37.5	12.5
East	SC	83.3	6.7	10.0
	ST	NA	NA	NA
	Others	70.0	27.5	2.5
Aggt.	SC	72.7	16.0	11.3
	ST	85.7	9.5	4.8
	Others	61.5	5.1	33.3

Note: # there was no ST beneficiaries in the area.

Source: Field Survey, 2013-14.

It seems from the finding that STs are better targeted compared to the other backward communities. It is good to see that the delivery in government hospital has increased overall and is highest among STs, private hospital is being used for delivery by the upper class families regardless of their caste as they are economically better off in relative sense. In the earlier section, we noticed that the awareness about free delivery services at government accredited private hospitals is pretty low. This might be the cause for less number of deliveries by SC/ST mothers at private hospitals. They are completely unaware of such accredited hospitals and are with the notion that delivery under private facility is highly expensive.

Effect of JSY on Institutional Delivery in Last 5 Years

In the earlier section, we looked at the distribution of place of delivery across surveyed women. Let's now look at the whole district and see the impact of JSY on the extent of institutional delivery i.e., delivery separately at Block Primary Health Centres (BPHC), Rural Hospitals (RH), Sub Divisional Hospitals (SDH) and District

Hospital. Though it would not be possible to get the exclusive or sole effect of introducing JSY on institutional delivery as there are several other factors like population, literacy, etc., which can cause number of institutional delivery to increase, we just want to have a glimpse of what has been the scenario after the introduction of JSY. As Table 22.12 shows, the absolute number of deliveries has been increasing in large number in all regions. Excluding Burdwan Medical College Hospital (BMCH) from central zone, the number of institutional deliveries is always higher in West zone. However, the comparison is difficult unless we control for the total number of pregnant women in the respective zones; for which we are constrained by the absence of data. However, number of deliveries at BMCH alone is highest for all time points.

Table 22.12

Institutional Delivery at Burdwan at a Glance

Zone	*2009-10*	*2010-11*	*2011-12*	*2012-13*	*2013-14*
Central	7838	8837	9989	8668	8936
West	17128	17892	21468	19498	20279
East	13992	14924	17910	15374	16007
BMCH	17233	18076	20573	20559	21905
Burdwan (Total)	56191	59729	69940	64099	67127

Source: Office of CMOH, Burdwan District.

It is significant to note that a single hospital is assisting more number of deliveries compared to the number being assisted in all BPHCs of a particular zone. This amplifies the failure of primary healthcare system and exemplifies the extent to which the entire health service is dependent on the tertiary health system. In other words, patients are transferred to district hospitals as primary health centres may not be able to handle the cases due to poor infrastructure, thereby basically increasing the risk of mortality. If these centres are properly facilitated, then the pregnant women can deliver locally without travelling far distances and this would also reduce pressure on the tertiary health service. Hence, it is important to see the distribution of deliveries across different tiers of health institutions i.e., we should decompose the number of deliveries taking place at different type of health centres/hospitals, namely, BPHCs, RH, SDH and DH. This would also help us to explore the health infrastructure at regional level.

Table 22.13

Institutional Delivery at Health Institutions of Different Tier

Zone	*Health Institutions*	*2009-10*	*2010-11*	*2011-12*	*2012-13*	*2013-14*
West	Asansol SDH	5376	6116	7837	7304	7979
		(31.4)	(34.2)	(36.5)	(37.5)	(39.3)
	Durgapur SDH	4934	4790	4889	4468	4770
		(28.8)	(26.8)	(22.8)	(22.9)	(23.5)
	BPHC and RH	6818	6986	8742	7726	7530
		(39.8)	(39.0)	(40.7)	(39.6)	(37.1)
Central	BMCH	17233	18076	20573	20559	21905
		(68.7)	(67.2)	(67.3)	(70.3)	(71.0)
	BPHC and RH	7838	8837	9989	8668	8936
		(31.3)	(32.8)	(32.7)	(29.7)	(29.0)
East	Kalna SDH	4469	4531	5070	3515	3729
		(31.9)	(30.4)	(28.3)	(22.9)	(23.3)
	Katwa SDH	5043	5682	6776	6154	6690
		(36.0)	(38.1)	(37.8)	(40.0)	(41.8)
	BPHC and RH	4480	4711	6064	5705	5588
		(32.0)	(31.6)	(33.9)	(37.1)	(34.9)

Note: Figures in parentheses are the percentage of total deliveries in the region for a particular year.

Source: Office of CMOH, Burdwan District.

Table 22.13 shows the percentage distribution of deliveries taking place in different tiers of health institutions. In West zone in 2013-14, only 37 out of 100 deliveries in the district took place at BPHCs, rest 63 deliveries took place at referral hospitals. The percentage of deliveries at primary level health centres is dropping year after year. Similarly, in the central zone in 2013-14, 71 per cent of total deliveries took place at the District Hospital i.e. BMCH. Here again a diminishing trend is noted in terms of deliveries being performed at BPHCs. East zone is not beyond this trend. Here again the pressure on secondary/tertiary health system is increasing continuously with lesser and lesser number of deliveries being performed locally. To highlight more on this, one may be interested to look at the numbers of child birth in BPHCs and RHs (Tables 22.14 and 22.15).

It is to be noted that, there has been a fall in the number of deliveries in almost all BPHCs in 2012-13, reason for which is typically unknown. However, keeping that aside, there has been an increasing trend though the rate of increase is negligible in comparison to the total number of deliveries being performed in the district. It would have been more prominent if we take the ratio of deliveries at BPHCs to total number of new born in the block for a particular year. The ratio would reveal as to what percentage of births in the CD Block has occurred in the respective BPHC. The scenario of number of deliveries at rural hospitals is quite similar to BPHC (Table 22.15) though a rural hospital is better equipped than a BPHC. Hence, it can be understood after looking at Tables 22.12, 22.13, 22.14 and 22.15 that the incidence of delivery at primary health centres and secondary/tertiary hospitals is inversely proportional. To conclude, if people feel insecure about delivering at their local hospital, any programme undertaken to enhance the institutional delivery is not going to work. Government should therefore focus on improving infrastructure at village level first, and then try to convince people to go in for institutional delivery locally through schemes like JSY. So, if the safe motherhood hasn't been ensured so far, then that's not the fault of JSY but is the fault of poor infrastructure at village or block level.

Impact of JSY on Infant Mortality

It is needless to mention that with rise in institutional delivery, the risk of infant mortality deceases. In fact, the key rationale behind the JSY programme is to reduce the NNM (neo-natal mortality) by promoting institutional delivery. We already have looked at the progress of institutional delivery so far. So, let's now move on to see the final outlay i.e., how far the NNM and overall infant mortality has reduced. However, we could not look into the mortality figures specifically for Burdwan as we are constrained by the absence of

Table 22.14

Institutional Delivery at Block Primary Health Centres

Zone	*CD Block*	*Institutional Delivery at Block Primary Health Centres*					
		BPHC/PHC	*2009-10*	*2010-11*	*2011-12*	*2012-13*	*2013-14*
Central	Burdwan-I	Kurmun	159	235	306	263	268
	Burdwan-II	Barsul	71	74	203	224	337
	Memari - II	Paharhati	611	645	669	661	907
	Jamalpur	Jamalpur	712	598	783	694	665
	Raina - I	Mahesbati	534	585	629	551	556
	Raina - II	Madhabdihi	555	549	650	513	455
	Ausgram -I	Bononabogram	714	840	1043	1049	912
	Ausgram -II	Jamtara	315	497	572	486	597
	Galsi - II	Adrahati	408	417	597	471	455
	Khandaghosh	Khandaghosh	304	336	235	156	146
Total (Central Zone)	4383	4776	5687	5068	5298		
West	Andal	Khandra(Ukhra)	881	865	1278	1232	1252
	Faridpur-Durgapur	Laudoha	225	261	567	563	566
	Kanksa	Panagarh	459	565	604	543	586
	Galsi - I	Pursha	620	764	862	921	1013
	Kulti Municipality	Barakar	1366	1259	1295	1105	1013

contd...

...contd...

	Raniganj	Raniganj	661	663	834	742	646
	Salanpur	Pithaikeary	416	378	528	453	484
	Jamuria	Akalpur	76	41	57	42	75
	Jamuria	Bahadurpur	523	502	719	633	577
	Baraboni	Kelejora	804	801	1129	777	685
Total (West Zone)	6031	6099	7873	7011	6897		
East	Kalna - I	Atghoria	655	726	735	670	638
	Kalna - II	Badla	298	314	350	306	327
	Monteswar	Monteswar	1199	1261	1650	1465	1598
	Purbasthali -II	Purbosthali	140	139	359	561	461
	Katwa - I	Srikhanda	444	405	466	398	221
	Katwa - II	Noapara	150	171	371	402	410
	Ketugram - I	Ramjibanpur	296	333	401	391	492
	Ketugram - II	Ketugram	443	323	396	365	416
	Mongolkote	Mongolkote	285	306	370	328	446
Total (East Zone)	3910	3978	5098	4886	5009		

Source: Office of CMOH, Burdwan District.

data for the said indicators at block level. As a proxy to that, we managed to get the figures for the desired variables for West Bengal as a whole; of which Burdwan is a district. As Table 22.16 portrays, both IMR and NNM rate has decreased over the span of 6 to 7 years i.e., since the time JSY has been in effect in the state. Reduction has been substantial especially in rural West Bengal compared to urban. Though there are several factor which may cause the infant mortality to reduce, JSY being a one of such factors, has to have some contribution in this fall in mortality or improvement in infant survival rate.

Table 22.15

Institutional Delivery at Rural Hospitals

			Institutional Delivery at Rural Hospitals (RH)				
Zone	*CD Block*	*RH*	*2009-10*	*2010-11*	*2011-12*	*2012-13*	*2013-14*
Central	Memari - II	Memari	2672	3223	3284	2666	2660
	Bhatar	Bhatar	783	838	1018	934	978
Total (Central Zone)			3455	4061	4302	3600	3638
West	Galsi -I	Mankar	563	652	632	514	452
	Raniganj	Ballavpur	224	235	237	201	181
Total (West Zone)			787	887	869	715	633
East	Purbasthali -I	Srirampur	267	327	421	286	269
	Mongolkote	Singot	303	406	545	533	310
Total (East Zone)			570	733	966	819	579

Source: Office of CMOH, Burdwan District.

Participation in Ante Natal and Post Natal Services

Let's now move on to see the status of immunisation among pregnant women and mothers. ANC (ante natal care) is a must during pregnancy with its main two components being Titanus injections and Iron tablets on a routine basis. We categorised the status of getting or having such medications into two groups—those who are regularly getting it and those who are not/are irregular in getting so. The reason why it is important to look at the status of immunisation among mothers and pregnant in context of the present study on JSY is that the ASHA workers are supposed to be responsible for keeping a track or to remind the mothers/pregnant about their medications and other such precautions. This would thus act as an evaluation mechanism for ASHA. In addition to that, in fact more importantly, it would reveal the extent of participation or utilisation of the scheme benefits by the beneficiaries.

Table 22.16

Impact of JSY on Infant Mortality and Neo-natal Mortality

Indicators	*Year*	*West Bengal*			*India*		
		Rural	*Urban*	*Combined*	*Rural*	*Urban*	*Combined*
Infant Mortality Rate	2005	40	31	38	64	40	58
	2006	40	29	38	62	39	57
	2007	39	29	37	61	37	55
	2008	37	29	35	58	36	53
	2009	34	27	33	55	34	50
	2010	32	25	31	61	37	47
	2011	33	26	32	48	29	44
	2012	33	26	32	46	28	42
Neo-Natal Mortality Rate	2005	32	20	30	NA	NA	37
	2006	30	20	28	NA	NA	37
	2007	30	19	28	NA	NA	36
	2008	28	19	26	NA	NA	35
	2009	27	19	25	NA	NA	34
	2010	24	19	23	36	19	33
	2011	23	17	22	34	17	31
	2012	18	12	17	33	16	29

Source: Health on March, 2012-13, Govt. of West Bengal.

Table 22.17 focuses on immunisation/medications during pregnancy i.e., receipt of ANC services. As we see, among pregnant women, immunisation has been a success as the percentage of women receiving the required medications is quite substantial, more than 95 per cent in almost all regions across all social groups. However, SCs in the East are little bit lagged in this respect.

Table 22.17

Receipt of Ante-natal Care by Pregnant and Mothers

Zone	*Caste*	*Tetanus Injection*		*Iron Tablets*	
		Yes	*Irregular/No*	*Yes*	*Irregular/No*
West	SC	97.3	2.7	95.9	4.1
	ST	100.0	0.0	94.1	5.9
	Others	96.0	4.0	100.0	0.0
Central	SC	96.9	3.1	95.4	4.6
	ST	100.0	0.0	100.0	0.0
	Others	100.0	0.0	100.0	0.0
East	SC	91.2	8.8	88.2	11.8
	ST	NA	NA	NA	NA
	Others	97.7	2.3	93.2	6.8
Aggregate	SC	95.9	4.1	94.2	5.8
	ST	100.0	0.0	95.5	4.5
	Others	97.6	2.4	96.5	3.5

Source: Field Survey, 2013-14.

Irregular immunisation is noted among substantial number of SC pregnant women in East zone. Like the ANC which helps the baby to be safe within her mother, it is also important to have post natal checkups including proper immunisations. Therefore, we now look at the status of receiving post natal service across different caste and region (Table 22.18). The main three components of PNC are: after birth health checkup, immunisation of the child like giving polio and measles vaccination and lastly, the growth monitoring which is done by the AWW at ICDS centre. ASHA workers in coordination with local SHC and AWW in ICDS centres are supposed to take care of the above mentioned post natal care requirements. It has been observed that the two of SHC, namely, health checkup and vaccination of the child, is being taken care of in all regions among all castes.

But people are still not receiving proper help from the ICDS centre; in some cases, they are completely unaware about what exactly are the facilities provided at ICDS centres. These centres are commonly known as 'Milo School' where Milo drink is freely provided. Another common knowledge that people possess is that the children are provided with one time meal per day. But they are sceptical about the poor quality of food being served. Consequently they feel the risk of their child falling sick after having the food. The services like providing nutritional supplements, preschool training, etc., are not known to many parents. Thus, they are not that serious or sometimes reluctant to send their child to ICDS centre.

Table 22.18

Receipt of Post-natal Care by Mothers

Zone	*Caste*	*After Birth Health Checkup of the Child*		*Immunisation of the child*		*Help from ICDS Centre*	
		Yes	*Irregular/No*	*Yes*	*Irregular/No*	*Yes*	*Irregular/No*
West	SC	89.7	10.3	98.3	1.7	87.9	12.1
	ST	100.0	0.0	100.0	0.0	100.0	0.0
	Others	100.0	0.0	100.0	0.0	71.4	28.6
Central	SC	93.5	6.5	98.4	1.6	87.1	12.9
	ST	100.0	0.0	100.0	0.0	100.0	0.0
	Others	91.7	8.3	100.0	0.0	79.2	20.8
East	SC	90.0	10.0	100.0	0.0	93.3	6.7
	ST	NA	NA	NA	NA	NA	NA
	Others	97.4	2.6	97.4	2.6	94.7	5.3
Aggt.	SC	91.3	8.7	98.7	1.3	88.7	11.3
	ST	100.0	0.0	100.0	0.0	100.0	0.0
	Others	93.6	3.8	96.2	1.3	83.3	16.7

Source: Field Survey, 2013-14.

Receipt of Cash Incentive under JSY

We now look at the status of receiving monetary incentive among JSY beneficiaries. Eligible women get the incentive in two phases. In the 1st phase, during pregnancy they receive ₹500 from the SHC and in the 2nd phase they receive another ₹500 from the hospital immediately after the delivery of the baby. In our study, we found 72 per cent of mothers have received such incentive; East zone being the best performer in every respect. 86 per cent of mothers in the

East zone have received monetary incentive, highest among all other zones (Table 22.19).

Table 22.19

Status of Receipt of Incentive Across Region

Per cent of mothers	*Burdwan*			
	West	*Central*	*East*	*Aggregate*
Received monetary incentive (%)	57.1	71.8	85.7	72.0
Avg. time to get incentive*	41	51	25	42

Note: * in number of days.

Source: Field Survey, 2013-14.

Average waiting time to receive the incentive is also lowest in the East but is long enough in the West and Central region also. Discussing across caste, on the average, 30 per cent of SCs, 52 per cent of STs and 50 per cent of General and OBCs have received incentive for delivering at institution (Table 22.20). Waiting time to receive incentive is longer for SC/STs. This may be because of their illiteracy and related inability to understand the procedure or make the administrators understand their problems. SCs have been neglected everywhere, worst in the West. There are many a problems in getting the cash incentive. Firstly, pregnant women do register their pregnancy at the nearest SHC and get the 1st instalment of their incentive. But some of them deliver at home or at private hospital (which is not accredited by the Govt.) for which the rest of the incentive is not paid as per rule. Secondly, according to Government instruction, incentive money has to be given as an account payee cheque in favour of the mother. So, it is important to have a bank account to get the cheque encashed. But a mother from a BPL family or a poor SC/ST family is not expected to maintain a bank account. The idea behind giving account payee cheque is quite novel in the sense that it encourages the family to open a bank account and cultivate the habit of saving. But the groups that are targeted in the scheme are not that financially sound enough to have money left for saving. Consequently, cheques get lapsed and money goes in vain.

Moreover, these people being unaware about the banking system are fearful about going to bank and opening savings account.

Table 22.20

Status of Receipt of Incentive Across Social Groups

Zone	*Caste*	*Percentage of mothers who received monetary incentive*	*Avg. time to get the incentive (in no. of days)*
West	SC	19.0	16
	ST	0.0	30
	Others	57.1	36
Central	SC	24.2	69
	ST	68.8	30
	Others	36.4	30
East	SC	66.7	42
	ST	NA	NA
	Others	44.4	32
Aggt.	SC	30.7	47
	ST	52.4	30
	Others	50.0	33

Source: Field Survey, 2013-14.

Role of ASHA in JSY

One of the key components of the National Rural Health Mission is to provide every village in the country with a trained female-community-health activist. The government has made efforts to identify such activists called ASHA from the village itself. They are being trained to work as an interface between the community and the public health system. The ASHA workers are entitled to receive a fixed monthly honorarium of ₹1,500 and performance-based incentives for motivating women and children to receive services. They have a vital role to play in implementing the JSY scheme at the village or community level.

The present study administered a questionnaire separately for ASHA workers in the selected villages to know garner relevant information in context to their role in implementing JSY. This included their background characteristics, their role in providing support to mothers for getting maternal care services, motivating them for institutional delivery and their field experiences. We have already discussed about the indicators related to providing support to mothers for getting maternal care services in the section where we discussed about awareness about JSY and its specialised services.

Background Characteristics of ASHA

During our field study, we interviewed a total of 16 ASHA workers from all the three zones. The background characteristics of ASHAs include their religion, caste, educational qualification and age together with the duration of their work as an ASHA (Table 22.21). On the average, 75 per cent of ASHA workers are Hindu and rest are Muslim. Number of ASHAs from Muslim community is higher in Central region of the district. As the ASHAs are to be selected from the community or the village itself, the religious dominance or caste dominance does play a role in selection of the candidate. Disaggregating across caste, there has been no ASHA worker from the ST community in any of the regions. However, there is substantial representation from the SC community. It is important to note that all the ASHA workers in the surveyed area under West region belong to SC community. As far as their educational status is concerned, the average years of schooling of the ASHA workers in the district is found to be 13 years. The selected ASHA workers are found to be educated enough to perform their responsibilities; over qualified in some respect. Only 31 per cent of total interviewed ASHA workers are noted to be secondary graduate i.e. left formal schooling after completing 10th standard, rest have either completed their higher secondary schooling or are college graduate. ASHAs in West Burdwan are relatively low educated compared to the other two regions.

It is interesting to see that there is no ASHA having qualification of less than higher secondary in the East Zone. This is good as it helps acquire the skills quickly and apply them properly. The average age of the ASHAs was around 35 years in three regions, except for East Burdwan where they were found to be relatively younger with average age close to 32 years. The respondents were found to be working as an ASHA for nearly two half years on the average having combined the three regions together. However, in the West, ASHAs are found to be relatively low experienced as the average for them is found to be 18 months.

Table 22.21

Background Characteristics of the ASHAs

Categories	*Burdwan*			
	West	*Central*	*East*	*Aggt.*
Aggregate Number of ASHAs	4	5	7	16
Religion				
Hindu (%)	75.0	60.0	85.7	75.0
Muslim (%)	25.0	40.0	14.3	25.0
Caste				
SC (%)	100.0	20.0	14.3	37.5
ST (%)	NA	NA	NA	NA
General (%)	NA	80.0	85.7	62.5
Years of Schooling				
Secondary Passed (%)	50.0	60.0	NA	31.3
Higher Secondary Passed (%)	50.0	20.0	42.9	37.5
Graduate and Above (%)	NA	20.0	57.1	31.3
Avg. Yrs. of Education	12	12	14	13
Average Age	38	37	32	35
Avg. No. of Months Working as ASHA	18	34	29	28

Source: Field Survey, 2013-14.

Availability of ASHA

How far the ASHA workers have been made available is a big question. There are several problems in recruiting ASHAs, managing fund for them, etc. One ASHA worker is supposed to cover 1,000 population. But, in almost all surveyed villages, we found them covering much more than that. Situation has been worst in West followed by Central region. Let's now look into the overall availability of ASHA workers in the district (Table 22.22).

The district has a total of 3,102 ASHA workers as of March 2014. They do serve across different villages of the district. However, the number of ASHA per 1,000 population in the district is 0.63 i.e., 1 ASHA for every 1,587 population. The situation is relatively better for East and Central region, but West has severe problem in this respect where 2,272 population is being served by 1 ASHA. This substantiates our finding about lack of awareness and participation in JSY scheme in West Burdwan. ASHA being the prime information provider for JSY, people are not receiving relevant information due to non-availability of ASHA in their area. In some cases, ASHA workers are being told informally by the *panchayat* officials to not serve beyond their stipulated area/population as that would signal towards adequacy of ASHA workers in the area. Consequently, Government won't sanction any post for ASHA worker in the area. As a result, some people are not being covered under the JSY programme. This is definitely impacting the infant and maternal mortality as well as the health of the children in an adverse way. The extreme case we saw at the Uchalan SHC under Raina–II CD Block in the Central region. There is no ASHA worker under this centre. Even though a SHC is supposed to cover 5,000 population, covered population in Uchalan centre is 11,926; much above the stipulated norm. More surprisingly, this huge number of population is being covered by only two formal health workers (one 1st ANM and one 2nd ANM). In addition, they have three link persons who are paid a monthly honorarium of ₹100 only. No ASHA workers could join the centre as there has been a court case against the selection panel. Consequently, the whole of nearly 12,000 populations is suffering, the implementation of JSY is disrupted and several other problems are being faced. It is obviously not possible for two health workers to perform the duties of 12 ASHA workers (1 in every 1,000 population for the total 12,000 people under the sub centre). The link persons are also not accountable to the Government as this is more of a voluntary service with a negligible amount of honorarium.

Therefore, if we don't have adequate number of ASHA and the proper local hospital infrastructure is also lacking, then how can Government think of ensuring safe motherhood only by introducing a conditional cash transfer is a questionable issue.

Table 22.22

Availability of ASHA Workers

Zone	*Block*	*No of ASHAs**	*ASHA per 1000 pop*	*Zone*	*Block*	*No of ASHAs**	*ASHA per 1000 pop*
West	Andal	35	0.21	East	Kalna I	122	0.64
	Barabani	63	0.57		Kalna II	98	0.64
	Faridpur -Durgapur	55	0.51		Katwa I	97	0.64
	Galsi I	149	0.86		Ketugram I	128	0.88
	Jamuria	56	0.50		Ketugram II	86	0.80
	Kanksa	88	0.58		Mongolkote	150	0.64
	Pandabeswar	19	0.13		Monteswar	138	0.65
	Ranigunj	16	0.16		Purbasthali I	129	0.70
	Salanpur	62	0.40		Purbasthali II	172	0.91
	West Total	543	0.44		East Total	1185	0.70
Central	Ausgram I	87	0.81	Central	Khandaghosh	162	0.95
	Ausgram II	75	0.55		Memari I	134	0.68
	Bhatar	113	0.48		Memari II	91	0.67
	Burdwan I	140	0.78		Raina I	115	0.71
	Burdwan II	89	0.64		Raina II	123	0.89
	Galsi II	73	0.54		Central Total	1374	0.69
	Jamalpur	172	0.71	District	Total	3102	0.63

Note: * in Position as on 2nd May, 2014

Source: Office of CMOH, Burdwan District.

Awareness about ASHA among Mothers

It is important to know about the local ASHA worker. The ASHA is supposed to maintain a complete list of families covered by her with detailed information about mothers, pregnant women and the children. We asked the women, during our field study, if they know their ASHA *didi* (local ASHA worker) personally and if she comes to inform about the regular immunisation courses. Table 22.23 provide the responses. It is surprising to see that 18 per cent of surveyed women in the district don't even know their local ASHA worker. However, they do know the local health centre and visit the centre because of their own interest in immunisation and other necessities. The worst possible scenario is in the Western region where only 71 per cent of women know the local ASHA worker, rests have no clue. In the Central region, it has been a moderate experience for us. If the ASHA worker is known by the interviewed woman, our second question was if the ASHA visits her home or not. 74 per cent of the women who knows their local ASHA replied saying yes. That means 26 in every 100 women who know about ASHA doesn't get service; in addition 18 doesn't know the local ASHA. Once again, West has major problem in this respect. To main reason identified for this problem is the scarcity of ASHA workers. The available ASHA workers do not want to serve beyond their area and want to work within their population limit only. The main cause for this reluctance is low payment. If the Government is unable to sanction more posts for ASHA, then the existing workers can be rewarded with a bit more money to cover extra population. Though this may not be a permanent solution to tackle this problem but it may bring in the desired result at least to some extent.

Table 22.23

Awareness about ASHA

	Burdwan			
	West	*Central*	*East*	*Aggt.*
Do you know your ASHA didi? (%)	71	81	94	82
If know, does she visits your home? (%)	59	73	89	74

Source: Field Survey, 2013-14.

Difficulties Faced by ASHA Workers

We asked ASHA workers about the difficulties they face during their field work. Firstly, there is a difficulty in getting 'Matriyan', the car stipulated to carry pregnant women to hospital for delivery. The ASHA worker is supposed to call the car from the BPHC over phone and take the woman for delivery. In most of the cases, drivers are found to be not responsive, especially during the night. This accentuates the incidences of home delivery. Successive reporting of this problem to the higher authority by the ASHAs and ANMs have not led to any solution to this problem as of now. Secondly, it is expected that if someone has a SDH nearer to her place compared to a BPHC, then for obvious reason the woman would try for delivery at the SDH. But as per the norm, to get 'Matriyan', the woman has to go to the BPHC first. She can go to SDH/DH if referred by BPHC doctors. In that case the 'Matriyan' will take her to SDH/DH. But, if the woman directly wants to go to the SDH/DH, then the car is not provided. In that case she has to go on her own with no ASHA and 'Matriyan' support. The third important problem is obviously the number of population to cover. Though each ASHA is supposed to cover 1,000 population, in reality they do cover a lot more than that. While doing so, they face the problem of medicine scarcity and other related issues. Fourth, though in our study Muslims are found to be participating in the scheme in a large extent, ASHAs find it difficult to convince them about the precautions and medications for safe motherhood. This is dominant especially in Central Burdwan.

Summary and Conclusion

The impact of JSY as a safe motherhood intervention policy has been mixed. The scheme has been able to motivate the women to come for institutional delivery. Along with promoting safe delivery, JSY is also observed to provide or make arrangement for quality services towards ante and post natal care. The most significant success of the programme is that most of the tribal women are now convinced about delivering at an hospital. Institutional delivery at Government hospitals has been substantial among families living below the poverty line. This has effectively led to not only promoting safe motherhood but also in reducing the infant mortality. This has happened because of close personal linkage and association between the community, personnel at primary health workers and ASHA workers. However, this success is not uniform across all castes. Though the tribal women are better targeted, women's belonging to SC are a bit lagged and so is the case for other communities having poor economic status.

In terms of the awareness about the overall programme and some of its exclusive benefits, the findings have been mixed. While JSY is commonly known by almost all the women, the knowledge about benefits given under the scheme is not that common. ASHA workers, the interface between community and health institutions, are scanty in number; resulting in information asymmetry about JSY scheme among mothers. Political intervention to recruit ASHA also seems to be a major problem. This results in court case with reference to the recruitment panel and consequent non-availability of ASHA worker.

Some religious barriers are still found to be prohibitive. A Hindu ASHA finds it difficult to convince a mother from Muslim community. Moreover, in some places Muslims are still stuck with their traditional rituals on the infants which cause the baby to fall sick and make them vulnerable to death. Successive efforts by ASHA or ANMs have not been effective in this case. Lastly, the infrastructure at BPHCfor delivery is poor which results in referral cases, increase in the risk of mortality due to delay in delivery and physical hazards during transport to referral hospital.

Based on the identified problems, following steps can be taken to generate better outcome from the programme.

Firstly, the infrastructure at block level health centres needs to be improved to increase the number of successful deliveries that can be performed without referring the patients to higher level of health institutions. This would be helpful for the mothers as they won't have to travel long distances thus reducing the risk.

Secondly, the problem regarding availability of ASHA needs to be resolved by providing more number of ASHA workers. It wouldn't be possible to serve such a large number of populations with limited number of ASHA workers. More posts should be sanctioned in order to have better coverage.

Thirdly, once the infrastructure for delivery at block level hospitals is developed and the required number of ASHA workers is in place, conscious drives should be taken to promote JSY. The awareness about the scheme among SC community and some other communities is still not that satisfactory. This may either be because of information asymmetry or due to non-availability of ASHA or for any other reason.

Fourthly, monitoring activity on ASHA workers needs to be introduced. It is observed that ASHA workers are not active enough in those villages which are a little far from the SHC and consequently it is difficult for ANMs to look after the activities of ASHA workers.

Fifthly, literacy, a common factor behind awareness needs to be enhanced somehow; especially among mothers. This will make them understand the importance of safe motherhood and related immunisation procedures.

In conclusion, a promotive scheme like JSY can only be effective in reducing infant and maternal mortality and ensuring safe motherhood if and only if supported by necessary health infrastructure. Only promotion doesn't mean anything; Government needs to ensure that preventive/curative mechanisms are also in place.

References

Dreze, J. and A. Sen (1995). *India: Economic Development and Social Opportunity.* New York: Oxford University Press.

Govt. of West Bengal (2011-12). *Health on the March.* Kolkata: State Bureau of Health Intelligence, Directorate of Health Services.

————. (2012-13). *Health on the March.* Kolkata: State Bureau of Health Intelligence, Directorate of Health Services.

National Health Mission. (2014). *Indian Public Health Standards.* 25 July. Retrieved from *http://nrhm.gov.in/*

————. (2014). *Janani Suraksha Yojana (JSY).* 2 June. Retrieved from *http://nrhm.gov.in/: http://nrhm.gov.in/nrhm-components/rmnch-a/maternal-health/janani-suraksha-yojana/background.html*

UNICEF (2013). *Committing to Child Survival: A Promise Renewed.*

23

NOMITA P. KUMAR

Outlays and Outcomes of ICDS as National Flagship Programme in Uttar Pradesh

Introduction

"People say hungry children are a shame for India. I don't give a damn whether it is shame for India. It is a question of well-being and opportunities for these children," said Nobel Laureate Amartya Sen expressing outrage at the state of India's children. He was speaking at Bal Adhikar Samvaad, organised by the Citizens' Initiative for Rights of Children Under Six. Sen released FOCUS, a report that highlights the startling contrasts in effectiveness of the Integrated Child Development Services (ICDS) programme—designed to meet the educational, health and nutritional needs of children under six through an Anganwadi centre for 1000 families—within different states. It adds to the findings of the National Family Health Survey (NFHS)-3 data, which has made the startling revelation that in the last eight years, there has been no change in child malnutrition levels, no progress on immunisation and no decline in the incidence of anaemia.

With the advent of Eleventh Five Year Plan (FYP), emphasis was made to carry forward growth until achieved with inclusiveness of social justice and empowerment amongst the weaker section of our society. This resulted in the introduction of several flagship programmes with focus on welfare of the poor. At the same time, certain ongoing programmes were revamped and altered to improve their efficiency with a broad objective of improving the living standard and to ensure that growth widely trickles and its benefits filter to the bottom of the layer. Hence we find that the coverage of

ICDS has increased ever since its inception in 1975, but only about half of the children are covered under the supplementary nutrition programme by 2012; and in Uttar Pradesh (UP), the present data shows that about 62 per cent children are covered. The government had very graciously universalised after the landmark judgment of the Supreme Court, on 13 December, directing the government to universalise ICDS and the result shows a positive trend. This translates into 14 lakh Anganwadis too, by the end of 2012. Accepting the order, the then Deputy Chairman of Planning Commission, Montek Singh Ahluwalia said, it was clear that the ICDS needed to be substantially expanded and that existing financial allocations were inadequate to be able to provide for all children under six. The findings show that ICDS can make a big difference to the lives of children, provided that the programme receives the attention and support it deserves. Hence, a study on its functioning was required in the present situation to assess its creditability. "ICDS thrives where it receives attention and care, adequate resources, regular training, proper facilities, monitoring and planning...creating these conditions is a matter of political choice," said Jean Dreze.

Report of the Inter-Ministerial Group on ICDS Restructuring stressed more on inclusive growth which begins with young children. The report states that:

> There is consensus that early years are the most vulnerable period-when there are the greatest risks of survival, healthy growth, development and vulnerability to a vicious cycle of malnutrition and disease/ infections. The pre-natal first three years are critical for preventing undernutririon, ...undermining their survival, development potential and active learning capacity.

These early years are also the most crucial years—because their impacts lasts a lifetime. More than 80 per cent of brain development is already complete by the first three years of life and the quality of nurturing impacts upon this significantly. These are the years when the foundation is laid for physical, cognitive, emotional, social and linguistic development—for the purpose of cumulative lifelong learning and human development. The basic premise of the programme revolves around the growing consensus among researchers and practitioners that child care and education are inseparable issues and must be considered as one. Based upon this fundamental assumption, the modus operandi of the programme has been designed in such an integrated manner so as to address these twin issues on a continuum basis adopting a holistic approach. The programme covers supplementary nutrition, immunisation, monitoring of weight and height, and in some cases, crèche facilities too, for a limited period. Its coverage, however, is limited and often the youngest children in the 0-3 years age group are left out of its ambit. The Eleventh Plan targeted to universalise ICDS and also find practical ways of reaching out to the children in the said age group. Strong efforts were made to improve accountability through greater involvement of PRIs (panchayati raj institutions).

The programme approaches a holistic child health comprising health, nutrition, and education components for pregnant women, lactating mothers, and children less than six years of age, and is implemented through a network of community-level Anganwadi Centres (AWCs). A range of services is targeted at young children and their mothers for growth monitoring, immunisation, health check-ups and supplementary feeding, as well as nutrition and health education in oerder to improve the child care and feeding practices that mothers adopt. Pre-school education is provided to children between three and six years of age.

Objectives of the Scheme

The broad objectives of the ICDS scheme are:

i) To improve the nutritional and health status of children in the age group 0-6 years;
ii) To lay the foundation for proper psychological, physical and social development of children;
iii) To reduce the incidence of mortality, morbidity, malnutrition and school drop-out;
iv) To achieve effective coordinated policy and its implementation amongst the various departments to promote child development; and

v) To enhance the capability of the mother to look after the normal health and nutritional needs of the child by providing nutrition and health education.

Programme Inception and Growth

ICDS was launched on 22 October 1975 in 33 CD (Community Development) blocks for early child development, which was an objective promoted by National Planning Committee (NPC) during the freedom struggle in 1939-40. The Constitution of India affirmed the state's commitment to the welfare of children in its Directive Principles of State Policy. Based on the Directive Principles, the Central Social welfare board was set up on 13 August 1953, which started the scheme for providing care and medical attention to children and pregnant women besides standing up for setting up child welfare centres under the CD blocks (PEO, 2011).

Later on, schemes related to nutritional awareness were taken up under Applied Nutrition Programme (1963) and the Special Nutrition Programme (1970-71). These programmes got implemented at the ground level through *balwadi*, *mahila mandal*, *panchayats* and municipalities. The Balawadi nutrition programme (1970-71) had the objective of providing nutrition rich food to children of 3-5 years of age from low income families under its fold. A study conducted by Planning Commission pointed out the fact that the benefits accrued reached only a small proportion of the target group. Besides this, the fact that emerged was that various health care, educational and social activities undertaken by different departments did not converge at the local level.

Keeping the above derivatives in mind, the Planning Commission formulated a National Policy for Children in 1974 and declared children as "supremely important asset". This policy provided the required framework for assigning priority to different needs of the child (PEO, 2011). In 1975 when ICDS was launched, the MMR (maternal mortality ratio) and IMR (infant mortality rate) were very high, i.e., 853/1,00,000 and 134/1,000 live births, due to severe drought in the country.

Table 23.1

Statement Showing Existing and Revised Population Norms under ICDS Scheme

Sl. No.	*Existing*	*Revised*
1	For Rural/Urban Projects Population	Anganwadi Centres (AWC)
2	500-1500—One AWC	For Rural/Urban projects Population:
		400-800—1 AWC
		800-1600—2 AWC
		1600-2400—3 AWC
		Thereafter in multiples of 800, 1 AWC
3	Mini AWC 150-500—One Mini AWC	Mini AWC 150-400—1 Mini AWC
4	For Tribal Projects Population	
	300-1500—One AWC	300-800—1 AWC
	150-300—One Mini AWC	150-300—Mini AWC

Source: Ministry of Women and Child Development.

ICDS Beneficiaries and Services

The beneficiaries under the programme include the following:

i) Children below six years.
ii) Pregnant and lactating women.
iii) Adolescent girls.
iv) Other women in the age group 15-45 years.

Towards achieving the above objectives, a package of integrated services comprising supplementary nutrition, immunisation, health check-up, referral services, nutrition and health education and non-formal education is provided in a comprehensive and cost effective manner to meet the multidimensional and interrelated needs of children. AWC is the focal point for delivery of services. Immunisation and health-check ups are provided at the AWC through the network of health services in the project area. The beneficiaries and services under the ICDS scheme are clearly depicted in Table 23.2.

Table 23.2

Services and Beneficiaries under ICDS

Services	*Beneficiaries*	*Services Rendered By*
Supplementary Nutrition@	Children (6-72 months); Pregnant and lactating mothers.	Anganwadi Worker (AWW) and Helper
Immunisation*	Children below 6 years; Pregnant and lactating mothers.	ANM/MO
Health Check-up*	-do-	ANM/MO/AWW
Referral Services	-do-	AWW
Pre-School Education	Children in the age group of 3-6 years	AWW/ANM/MO
Nutrition and Health Education	Women in age group of 15-45 years	

Note: @Adolescent Girls under Kishori Shakti Yojana (KSY) are also eligible; *AWW assists ANM in identifying the beneficiaries.

Source: Ministry of Women and Child Development.

Accordingly, the ICDS involves the setting up of AWCs, each of which is intended to cater to a population of around 1,000 in rural and urban areas and to around 700 in tribal areas. The Anganwadi Worker (AWW) and helper, the basic functionaries of the ICDS, run the AWC and implement the Scheme in coordination with the functionaries of health, education, rural development and other departments. They are called 'social workers' and are paid an honorarium of ₹1,000 per month for the worker and ₹500 for the helper. However, the supervisors and other higher officials are government employees.

The Anganwadis are meant to provide the following services:

i) Supplementary nutrition to children below six years of age, and nursing and pregnant mothers from low income families;
ii) Nutrition and health education to all women in the age group of 15-45 years;
iii) Immunisation of all children less than six years of age and immunisation against tetanus for all the expectant mothers;
iv) Health check-up, which includes ANC (antenatal care) of expectant mothers, PNC (postnatal care) of nursing mothers,

care of newborn babies and care of all children under six years of age;

v) referral of serious cases of malnutrition or illness to hospitals, upgraded PHCs (primary health centres)/CHSs (community health services) or DHs (district hospitals); and

vi) non-formal pre-school education to children of 3-5 years of age.

The Challenges Before ICDS in Uttar Pradesh

Sprawling over a land area of 2.41 lakh sq km across the heartland of India, UP is the most populous state of the country with a population of 19.96 crore as per 2011 Census. Its share in total area of the country is 7.3 per cent, while its share in country's population is 16.5 per cent. Nearly 80 per cent population of UP resides in rural areas spread over 97,942 inhabited villages. The state is organised into 75 districts, 313 *tehsils* and 822 development blocks. It is divided into four economic regions *viz.*, Western region, Central region, Eastern region and Bundelkhand. The first three regions fall in the Gangatic plains, while Bundelkhand forms part of the southern plateau.

High population growth has been witnessed in UP in the recent decades. The decadal increase in population during the period of 1971-2001 remained almost static at 26 per cent. As against this, the national population figures show a declining trend from 25 per cent in 1971-1981 to 23.8 per cent in 1981-1991, and further to 21.5 per cent in 1991-2001. However, population growth in UP came down to 20.09 per cent during 2001-2011, but remained above the national population growth of 17 per cent (Table 23.3). Among major states, birth rate is the highest in UP. The decline in birth rate has also been slow in the state. Birth rate stood at 38.6 in 1951. It moderately declined to 35.7 in 1991. As per the Sample Registration System (SRS) birth rate in UP stood at 28.3 in 2010 against 22.1 in India. As per NHFS-3, total fertility rate in the year 2005-06 was 3.82 in UP as against 2.68 in India.

Table 23.3

Important Demographic Indicators for Uttar Pradesh and India

Sl. No.	*Indicators*	*UP*	*India*
1	Total population (in million)*		
	2001	166.0	1029.0
	2011	199.6	1210.2
2	Decadal rate of population growth (Percentage)*		
	1981-1991	25.61	23.86
	1991-2001	25.85	21.53
	2001-2011	20.09	17.64
3	Average annual exponential growth rate (Percentage)*		
	1981-1991	2.27	2.14
	1991-2001	2.33	1.94
	2001-2011	1.85	1.64
4	Population density (per sq km)*		
	1991	548	267
	2001	690	325
	2011	828	382
5	Sex ratio (female per 1000 males) *		
	1991	876	927
	2001	898	933
	2011	908	940
6	Percentage of SCs (scheduled castes) and STs (scheduled tribes) population in total population (2011)*		
	SCs	20.69	16.63
	STs	0.56	8.61
7	Crude birth rate 2012**	27.4	21.6
8	Crude death rate 2012**	7.7	7.0
9	Natural growth rate 2012**	20.0	14.7
10	Infant mortality rate 2012**	53	42
11	Life expectancy at birth, 2001-2005**		
	Total	59.8	63.2
	Male	60.1	62.3
	Female	59.3	63.9

Sources: *Registrar General, India, Census of India; **Registrar General, India, Sample Registration System, October 2007.

Status of ICDS in Uttar Pradesh

The ICDS programme was launched in UP with assistance from the Government of India (GoI) in 1975 in three blocks, to protect pregnant, lactating women and children from malnutrition and to ensure their overall development. Since the beginning of 1990, the World Bank started providing credit for some components of the ICDS project in a few select states. ICDS-III Project was started in five states of Kerala, Maharashtra, Rajasthan, Tamil Nadu and UP in March 1999. The total cost of the project was about ₹1,000.11 crores for a period of five years from 1998-99 to 2003-04 (excluding country-wide training cost). The project was divided into two primary components—service delivery and programme support—which include service quality improvement, women empowerment, staffing and infrastructure development, management and institutional development, community mobilisation, monitoring and evaluation, etc.

As of 2011-12, the state has 1,87,517 AWCs and 22, 186 mini AWCs, sanctioned by the Central government in 897 ICDS projects, of which 1,86,447 of the AWCs are operational. In view of the objectives laid down for the programme, it is imperative to assess the nutrition and health status of women and children in the state before moving forward. The status of women and children in the state (as per NFHS-3, 2005-06) is summarised in Figure 23.1

Table 23.4 based on recent PSMS-IV survey in the state throws light on current status of the programme and utilisation of ICDS services in UP. The table reveals low awareness and poor utilisation of ICDS services in the state. About 18 per cent of the households had no idea about AWCs in their village. A proportion of 40.9 per cent households r as found to be slightly better in rural areas and among relatively better-off households as well as the SC/ST group. Hardly 10 per cent of rural children were attending AWCs. About three-fourth of the children attending the AWC reported receiving the food supplements regularly.

Figure 23.1

Health Status of Child and Women in UP

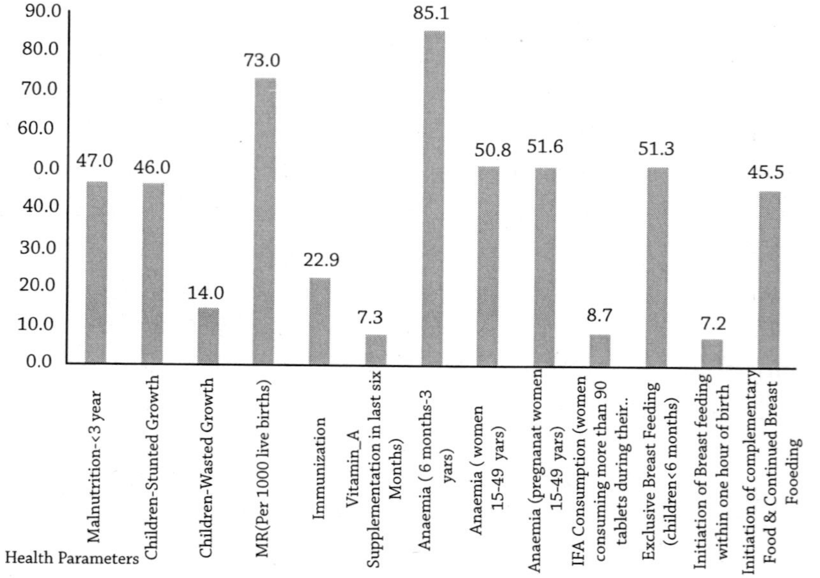

Source: *Twelfth Five Year Plan (2012-2017)*, UP.

Table 23.4

Percentage of Children Attending AWCs in Uttar Pradesh

Income Level and Social Group	*% of Children(0-6 Years) Attending Anganwadi in UP*		
UP overall	*Total*	*Rural*	*Urban*
2002-03	9.8	10	5.9
2007-08	9.4	10.8	1.7
2009-10	6.3	7.3	1.6
By Income	*Poor*	*Middle*	*Rich*
2002-03	11.4	9.8	7.4
2007-08	8.8	9.6	10.4
2009-10	6.8	6.4	5.2
By Social Group	*SC/ST*	*OBC*	*Other*
2002-03	12	9.1	8.5
2007-08	12.1	8.7	7.8
2009-10	8.8	5.5	4.6

Note: SC: Scheduled Caste; ST: Scheduled Tribe; OBC: Other Backward Classes.

Source: Government of U.P. (2014). *Monitoring Poverty in Uttar Pradesh-A Report on the Fourth Poverty and Social Monitoring Survey (PSMS-IV, 2009-10).*

Table 23.5

Percentage of Children (0-6 Years) Receiving Nutritional Supplement in Uttar Pradesh

	2002-03 PSMS II			2007-08 PSMS III			2009-10 PSMS IV		
	% of Children (0-6 Years) Receiving Nutritional Supplement			% of Children (0-6 Years) Receiving Nutritional Supplement			% of Children (0-6 Years) Receiving Nutritional Supplement		
Income Level & Social Group	*Always*	*Sometimes*	*Never*	*Always*	*Sometimes*	*Never*	*Always*	*Sometimes*	*Never*
UP Rural	77.2	17.7	5.1	88	11.9	0.1	82.6	17.1	0.4
By Income									
Poor	77.4	18.5	4.2	86.1	14	0	78.6	21.1	0.3
Middle	76.1	19.2	4.8	87.9	12	0	88.1	11.9	0
Rich	78.8	13.6	7.6	90.8	8.8	0.3	81.4	17.4	1.2
By Social Group									
SC/ST	81.3	12.1	6.6	85.3	14.8	0	84.2	15.7	0.1
OBC	73.8	20.4	5.8	88.8	11.2	0	82.6	16.9	0.5
Others	78.3	21.7	0	91.9	7.5	0.6	77.6	21.6	0.8
UP Urban	78.6	21.2	0.2	86.8	13.2	0	91.7	8.3	0
By Income									
Poor	80.5	19.3	0.3	80.9	19.1	0	91.5	8.6	0
Middle	74.7	25.3	0	95	5	0	92.7	7.4	0
Rich	100	0	0	100	0	0	86.8	13.2	0
By Social Group									
SC/ST	83.4	16.6	0	58.3	41.7	0	94.4	5.7	0
OBC	93.9	5.8	0.3	94.6	5.4	0	89.3	10.7	0
Others	10.1	89.9	0	88.3	11.7	0	94.3	5.7	0

Source: Government of UP (2014).

Physical Progress

Reasons for poor the performance/outcomes are questionable. An analysis of the physical and budgetary spending pattern of ICDS reveals two broad concerns, i.e., inadequate funds in terms of huge budgetary allocations and poor quality of fund utilisation.

Figure 23.2

Number of Sanctioned and Operational Projects in Uttar Pradesh

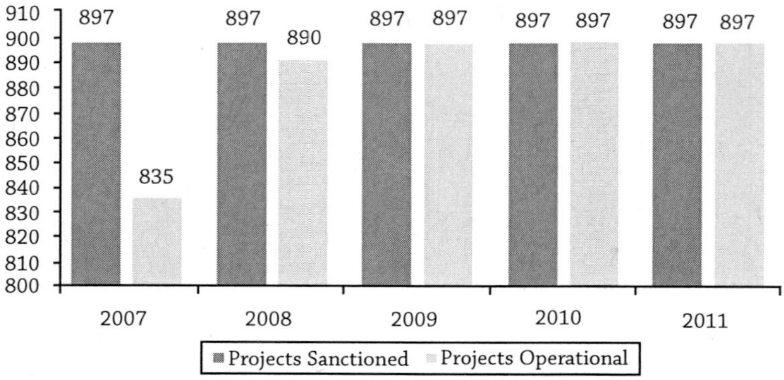

Source: Based on Ministry of Women and Child Development.

The well-being and rights of Indian children tend to receive little attention in public policy and democratic politics (Sen, 2006). An indicator of this state of affair is that only a minuscule share of public expenditure is allocated to child-related programmes. According to a recent estimate, out of every rupee spent by the Central government, less than five paise goes to child-related programme (HAQ, 2006a). Further, only a small proportion of this tiny amount is allocated to children under six (Sen, 2006). To our understanding ICDS is the only major programme addressed specifically to this age group. The total allocation of ICDS by the Central government in 2004-05 was mere ₹1,600 crores—less than one-tenth of a per cent of India's GDP (gross domestic product). By contrast, in the same year, the Central government spent ₹77,000 crores on defence (Sen, 2006).

Figure 23.3

Number of Sanctioned and Operational AWCs in Uttar Pradesh

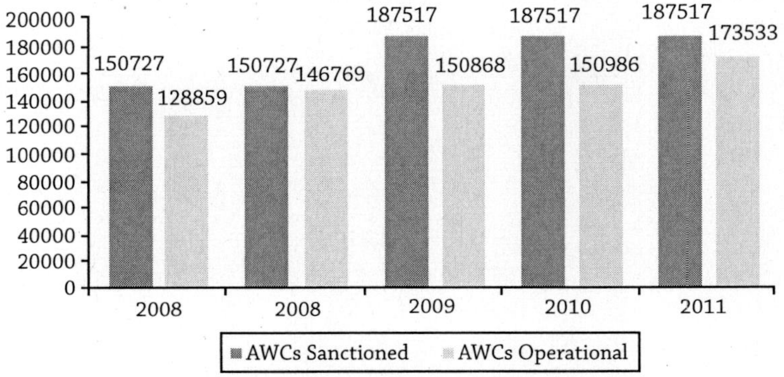

Source: Based on Ministry of Women and Child Development.

Calculations based on Census projections show that there were 17.4 crore children in the age group of 0-6 years during 2006-07, and our table (Table 23.6) show that 5.82 crores children benefitted as supplementary nutrition programme (SNP) beneficiaries in the same age group from ICDS. Similarly, the recent census indicates a decline in young population to 15.87 crores in 2011 and total beneficiaries reported are 7.51 crore at ICDS. In the Eleventh Plan period, ₹8,480 crore was allocated annually to ICDS. Allocations for the ICDS have seen a significant increase from ₹4,211 crore in 2006-07 to ₹15,850 crore in 2012-13. However, whether or not this amount is presently adequate to meet the needs of early childhood care and development of a burgeoning young population is difficult to say. To be more precise, the actual allocation during 2007-08 and 2008-09 was only ₹5,200 crore and ₹6,300 crore, respectively. Thus there was a shortfall of 39 per cent in 2007-08 and 26 per cent in 2008-09 (Borooah, Diwakar and Sabharwal, 2014). Further of the total amount released, ₹1,519 crore in 2007-08 (28.7%) and ₹2281 crore in 2008-09 (34.9%) were spent on SNP and the rest went for non-food components. As per the norms, 50 per cent of the cost was to be shared by the state government.

Table 23.6

Physical and Budgetary Performance of ICDS in Uttar Pradesh

Plan Period/ Indicators	*Unit*	*2007-08*	*2008-09*	*2009-10*	*2010-11*	*2011-12*	*2012-13*
SNP beneficiaries: Children	Lakh	185.91	194.42	193.45	203.99	187.03	187.25
SNP beneficiaries: Women	Lakh	36.78	37.94	42.64	47.93	49.41	49.33
Total SNP beneficiaries	Lakh	222.69	232.35	236.09	251.92	236.44	236.58
Budgetary Performance							
Annual outlays	(Lakh ₹)	847.00	672.00	844.06	2505.11	2683.11	4651.72
Fund released	(Lakh ₹)	371.89	543.49	515.43	486.31	901.65	1325.18
Budgeted cost per beneficiary per day (SNP and general)	₹	1.04	0.79	0.98	2.72	3.11	5.39
Fund released for SNP	(Lakh ₹)	479.69	570.91	867.78	1382.67	1316.00	1179.53
Fund released (SNP per beneficiary per day cost for 365 days).	₹	0.59	0.67	1.01	1.50	1.52	1.37
% spent on SNP	%	56.3	51.2	62.7	74.0	59.3	47.1

Source: Calculated from the data provided by Ministry of Women and Child Development and State Budget.

Table 23.6 shows that 185.91 lakh children in the age group of 0-6 years benefitted from the ICDS. Total beneficiaries of ICDS stood at 222.69 lakh, of which 36.78 lakh were women. Total outlays for ICDS was 847 crore, of which 371.89 crore was released in 2008-2009. However, the actual allocation made during 2008-09 to 2012-2013 was higher than the amount released. There was shortfall of funds due to non-release of funds, irrespective of declared outlays. Moreover, of the total amount released, ₹479.68 lakh in 2007-08 (56.3%), ₹570.90 lakh in 2008-09 (51.2%), ₹867.78 lakh in 2009-10 (62.7%), ₹1,382.67 lakh in 2010-11 (74.0%), ₹1,316.00 lakh in 2011-

2012 (59.3%) and ₹1,179.53 Lakh in 2012-13 (47.1%) were given to the SNP and the rest went for non-food components. In case of SNP, 50 per cent of the cost was to be shared by the Central government.

Figure 23.4

Beneficiaries of SNP in Uttar Pradesh

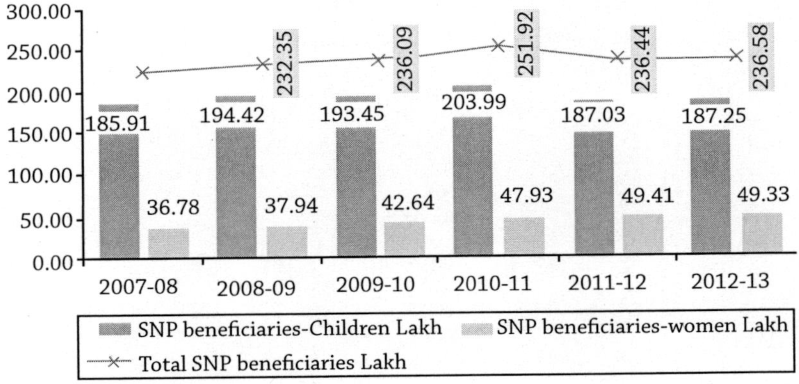

Source: Based on Ministry of Women and Child Development.

As per the prescribed norms, the government had to spent ₹2 per day on children and ₹2.30 per day on pregnant women and lactating mothers for the SNP until 2008. It was revised to ₹4 for children and ₹5 for mothers in 2009. The fund released for the SNP by the central and state government in UP shows that only ₹0.59 was provided per beneficiary per day in 2007-08, which increased to ₹1.01 in 2009-10 and to ₹1.50 and ₹1.52 in the subsequent years, i.e., 2010-11 and 2011-12. It clearly points to the fact that there was a huge shortfall in the financial allocation for children as per the norms prescribed.

Treading further we find that as per the norms, the government had to spend ₹2 per day on children and ₹2.30 per day on pregnant and lactating mothers for the SNP till 2008. But keeping the gaps in mind the government further revised it to ₹4 per day for children and ₹5 per day for mothers in 2009. The fund released for the SNP by the central government shows that only ₹0.59 was spent per beneficiaries per day in 2006-07 and it increased to ₹0.72 in 2008-09. It can be clearly understood that there was a huge shortfall in the financial allocation for children as per norms, and this was a major reason for the poor quality of food (Diwakar, 2011). Even under the revised norm, the gaps exist as per beneficiary cost, which even though was increased fell short of the prescribed norms in 2009-10, 2010-11 and 2011-12.

Figure 23.5

Beneficiaries of Pre-school Education in Uttar Pradesh

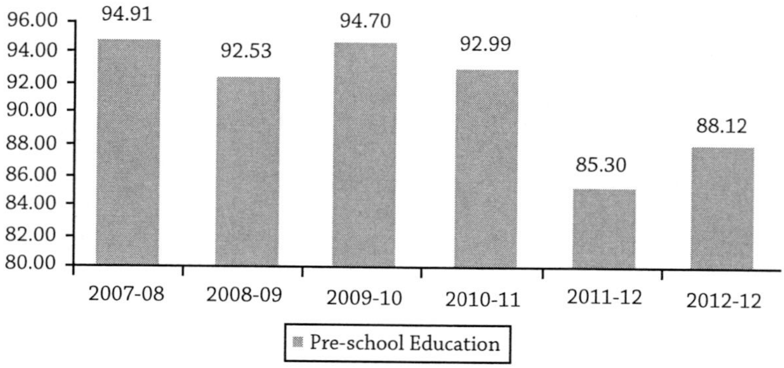

Source: Based on Ministry of Women and Child Development.

Table 23.7 highlights the outlays and expenditure incurred for achieving physical target of ICDS during the Eleventh Plan and subsequent Twelfth Plan. It has been targeted to execute 897 projects all over the state, along with 62 additional projects, which will cover 47.19 lakh additional beneficiaries, besides 194.5 lakh beneficiary children in the age group 0-6 years and pregnant women and lactating mothers. Table 23.7 shows that the approved outlays during the Eleventh Plan period was less than the actual expenditure incur for supplementary nutrition in UP. The Budget approved of ₹4,12,483.57 lakh for the total Plan period, i.e., 2007-2012 and the actual expenditure incurred stands at ₹4,39,249.17 lakh. The approved outlays further increased to ₹10,65,794.27 lakh for the entire period of 2012-2017 (Twelfth Plan) and anticipated expenditure in the approved amount approximately.

Table 23.7

Outlays and Expenditure on Supplementary Nutrition for Achieving Physical Targets of ICDS

Years	*Supplementary Nutrition Programme (Financial in Lakh ₹)*		*Unspent Balance*	
	Approved Outlay	*Actual/Anticipated Expenditure*	*Amount in Lakh ₹*	*% Unspent*
Eleventh Plan (2007-2012)	412,483.57	439,249.17	—	—
2007-08	43,638.0	40,032.8	7,935.9	16.54
2008-09	39,143.0	38,044.8	19045.9	33.36
2009-10	49,739.6	76,710.5	10,067.6	11.60
2010-11	133,272.0	142,949.3	-4,682.3	-3.39
2011-12	146,690.9	141,481.7	-9,881.5	-7.51
Twelfth Plan (2012-2017)	1065,794.27	—	—	—
2012-13	154,102.8	138,004.3	-20,051.2	-17.00
2013-14	138,004.3	—	—	—

Source: *Twelfth Five Year Plan*, UP.

Financial Allocations and Outcomes

ICDS is a Centrally-sponsored scheme that is implemented through the State Government/Union Territory administration with 100 per cent financial assistance for all inputs other than supplementary nutrition, which the states have to provide out of their own resources. Since 2005-06, the centre is meeting 50 per cent of the financial norms or of the expenditure incurred by states on supplementary nutrition, whichever is less.

The approved outlay for the programme was ₹84,700 lakh during 2007-08 and ₹67,200 lakh for 2008-09 (Table 23.9). The proposed outlay for the year 2009-10 was ₹84,406 lakh. As for as the utilisation of funds is concerned, the state had utilised more than 90 per cent of the funds made available during the year 2007-08, whereas the reported utilisation was 113 per cent for 2008-09, 167 per cent in 2009-10, 108 per cent in 2010-11 and 99.89 per cent in 2011-12. Surprisingly in Eleventh Plan period, total utilisation calculated for 2007-12 was 196.12 per cent in UP. This reflects upon sincere efforts made by the government to push funds in order to uplift the neglected mass (children and pregnant and lactating mothers) from the morass of poverty and malnutrition.

Table 23.8

Outlay and Expenditure for ICDS in Uttar Pradesh (in ₹ crore)

Period	Approved Outlay			Actual Expenditure			% Utilisation
	Total	Central share	State	Total	Central share/	State	
2007-08	847.0	423.5	423.5	754.2	377.1	377.1	89.0
2008-09	672.0	336.0	336.0	760.9	380.4	380.4	113.2
2009-10	844.1	422.0	422.0	1,410.6	705.3	705.3	167.1
2010-11	2,505.1	1,252.6	1,252.6	2,719.6	1,359.8	1,359.8	108.6
2011-12	2,683.1	1,341.6	1,341.6	3,708.1	2,155.7	1,552.4	138.2
2012-13	4,651.7	3,016.3	1,635.4	5,515.9	3,997.8	1,518.2	118.6
2013-14	3,284.6	1,589.3	1,695.3	—	—	—	—

Source: Statement 17 and 19, Five Year Plans, UP.

Figure 23.6

Outlays and Expenditures on ICDS in UP

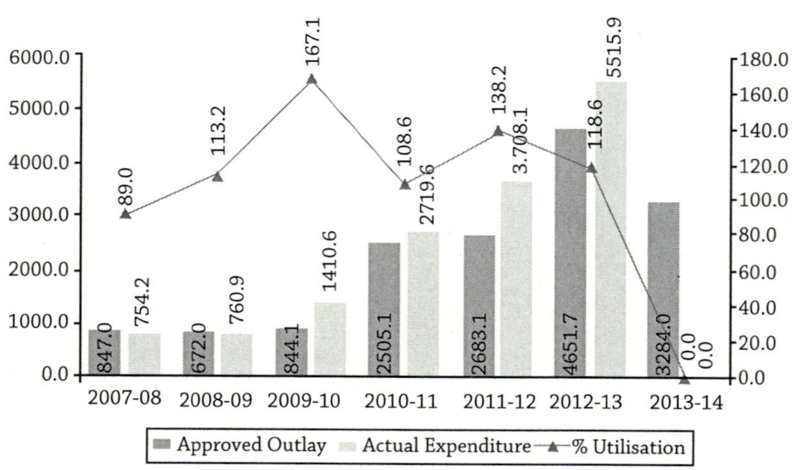

Source: Based on Ministry of Women and Child Development.

Table 23.9

Share of ICDS Allocations in GDP and Annual Budget in Uttar Pradesh

Expenditure Heads	*2008-09*	*2009-10*	*2010-11*	*2011-12*	*2012-13*	*2013-14*
Expenditure on ICDS (Cr. ₹)	482.26	2347.60	657.61	3,352.37	3,808.78	4,595.20
Total State Budget (Cr. ₹)	105,898.0	123,075.28	136,299.71	154,722.31	174,470.21	206,547.97
Expenditure as % of State Budget	0.46	1.91	0.48	2.17	2.18	2.22
GSDP at Current Prices(Cr. ₹)	444,684.86	523,394.18	600,285.72	685,291.83	782,285.34	890,265.14
Expenditure as % of GSDP	0.11	0.45	0.11	0.49	0.49	0.52

Note: GSDP: Gross State Domestic Product.

Source: Calculated from the data provided by Ministry of Women and Child Development and State Budget.

Table 23.9 shows that expenditure incurred on the ICDS was only 0.44 per cent of the state budget and 0.11 per cent of the GSDP in 2008-09. The subsequent years, i.e., 2009-10, 2010-11, 2011-12, 2012-13 and 2013-14, have seen increases in these shares, but not much. The share of ICDS expenditure to state budget, increased to 2.18 per cent in 2012-13 and 2.22 per cent of the state budget, which highlights the fact that state government realised the worth of ICDS project in culmination of hunger and malnutrition.

Status of the Utilisation of Funds Made Available by GoI

Table 23.10 shows the status of utilisation of the funds made available by GoI in the last three years. During 2007-08, out of the available funds of ₹1,181.22 crore, a sum of ₹1,101.9 crore (93%) was utilised. During 2008-09, the corresponding figures were ₹1,736.39 crore and ₹1,254.21 crore respectively. Thus, 72 per cent of the available funds could be utilised. Similarly for 2011-12, available funds stood at 3,928.66 crore and expenditure was ₹2,844.46 crores, thereby utilising only 72.4 per cent of the available funds.

Figure 23.7

Share of ICDS Allocations in GSDP and Annual Budget in UP

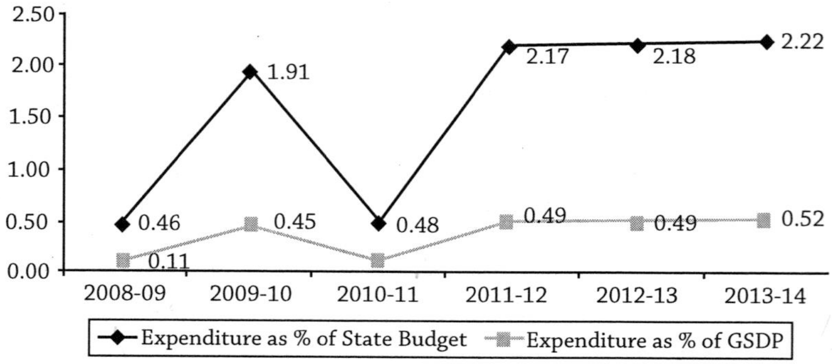

Source: Based on Statement 17 & 19, Five Year Plans, Uttar Pradesh.

The Twelfth FYP is ambitious in the context of child development. The delivery of essential services under the programme will be ensured, considering the following objectives—to prevent the incidence of low birth weight babies and to eliminate wasted and stunted growth of children. In order to achieve the aforementioned objectives, efforts would be made to control the incidence of anaemia in women. Further, efforts would be made to:

i) Reduce incidence of malnutrition from 47 to 23.5 per cent by 2012.
ii) Reduce incidence of severe malnutrition from 22 to 10 per cent by 2012.
iii) Reduce the incidence of malnutrition in children by 50 per cent.
iv) Reducing the incidence of stunted and wasted growth in children by 50 per cent.
v) Increasing the rate of exclusive breast feeding (children up to 6 months) by 60 per cent.

vi) Increasing the rate of use of appropriate complementary food by 50 per cent.
vii) Ensuring 100 per cent coverage of children (0-3 years) against all 6 vaccine preventable diseases (including measles vaccine at 9 months of age).
viii) Ensuring Vitamin-A supplementation for 80 per cent children (9 months-3 years) and eliminating clinical cases of vitamin-A deficiency by the year 2010.
ix) Ensuring provision of the recommended doses of micronutrient fortified supplementary foods to all children in the age group of 7 months to 3 years, adolescent girls and pregnant and lactating mothers.
x) Ensuring consumption of iodised salt with minimum 15-ppm iodine content in 80 per cent households.

Key Approaches

In order to achieve the above noted objectives, effective measures have been undertaken. Also, the Union Government has attempted restructuring of ICDS on the same track as of NRHM. In this regard, the state governments would be implementing the directives of the Union government. For achieving the objectives of ICDS, the activities to be implemented under the Twelfth FYP and the concerned implementation plans are presented below.

ICDS General

The Twelfth FYP reports that GoI has revised the funding pattern for ICDS general scheme since 2008. Now the share of GoI is 90 per cent and that of state government is 10 per cent. The estimated budget on ICDS general scheme for 2012-13 is ₹157,301.14 lakh, where in the state share proposed is ₹17,417.91 lakh.

ICDS Training

Since 2008, GoI has revised the funding pattern for ICDS training scheme too. Now once again, the GoI shall fund 90 per cent of the expenses and the share of state government will be 10 per cent. The

Table 23.10

Utilisation of Funds on ICDS by GoI (₹ in crore)

Year	Outlay			Release by GoI (Central Share)	Amount Available				Expenditure	% Utilised
	GoI Share	State	Total		Unspent Balance as on 1 April	GoI Share	State Share	Total		
2007-08	762.77	401.98	1,164.75	851.58	16.47	762.77	401.98	1,181.22	1,101.9	93.3
2008-09	895.72	382.17	1,277.89	1,114.4	24.69	895.72	382.17	1,736.39	1,254.21	72.2
2009-10	1,352.48	778.18	2,130.66	1,376.32	18.99	1,352.48	778.18	2,149.65	1,999.3	93.0
2010-11	2,005.76	1,433.48	3,439.24	1,863.69	0	2,005.76	1,433.48	3,439.24	3,384.41	98.4
2011-12	2,462.55	1,466.11	3,928.66	2,209.64	**	2,462.55	1,466.11	3,928.66	2,844.46	72.4
2012-13 Proposed	3,096.1	1,692.86	4,788.96	**	**	**	**	**	**	

Source: Twelfth Five Year Plan, Annexure 31.

estimated budget for ICDS Training scheme for 2012-13 was ₹800 lakh, where the state share proposed is ₹80 lakh.

Supplementary Nutrition Norms

Under the directives of Supreme Court, the decision to cover all children up to the age of 6 years and pregnant and lactating mothers under the programme was taken up by the state government in May 2006. Earlier 100 beneficiaries per centre were covered, but after the universalisation of the programme, the number of beneficiaries per centre has now increased to 160-170. After this policy decision, the number of beneficiaries should have been 2.20 crore, but according to the departmental sources (Performance Budget 2008-09), under target and achievement details, only 1.65 crore beneficiaries were listed (p.43). On page 45, it is stated that at present, the attendance of beneficiaries at the AWCs ranges from 65-70 per cent. In the year 2007-08, efforts were made to make the programme more effective and attractive so as to improve the attendance of beneficiaries at the centres up to 90 per cent.

Which year, 80 grams of weaning food to the children in the age group of 7 months-3 years, 80 grams of nutrition rich food to children in the age group of 3-6 years and 160 grams of the same are being provided to pregnant and lactating women. In compliance with the directives of the Supreme Court, complementary food would be made available to children (7 months to 3 years) and pregnant and lactating women, in a phased manner under a decentralised arrangement.

The activity of providing hot cooked meal at AWCs through mothers committees has already been initiated on pilot basis in 270 projects across 65 districts of the state. Work plan for providing hot cooked food in the remaining projects in the state had been devised. It was proposed to provide hot cooked meal to children (3-6 years) at AWCs under all projects in the state by the end of year 2008-09. The estimated expenditure was ₹1,224.48 crore which is to be shared equally by central and the state government.

The effort is to provide, on an average, daily nutritional supplements to the extent as indicated in Table 23.11.

Table 23.11

Nutritional Norms Revised

Beneficiaries	*Calories (cal)*	*Protein (g)*
Children below 3 years*	300	8-10
Children 3-6 years	300	8-10
[Severely malnourished children on medical advice after health check-up]	(double of above)	
Pregnant and Lactating (P and L) Mothers	500	20-25

Note: * Provisions regarding promotion of breast-feeding as recommended in Infant and Child Feeding (IYCF) guidelines are relevant.

The financial norms for supplementary nutrition revised by the GoI are presented in Table 23.12.

Table 23.12

Nutrition: Revised Rates for Beneficiaries

Category	*Revised rates for beneficiary per day*
Children (06-72 months)	₹4.00 per child/Per day.
Severely malnourished children (6-72 months)	₹6.00 per beneficiary per day.
Pregnant woman and Nursing mothers	₹5.00 per beneficiary per day.

Rajiv Gandhi Kishori Sashaktikaran Yojana (SABLA)

This scheme was launched by GoI Kishori Shakti Yojana and Nutrition Program for Adolescent Girls (NPAG), and is operated in two parts, i.e., training and supplementary nutrition. The training part conforms to being 100 per cent CSS (Centrally Sponsored Schemes) scheme, and for 2012-13 financial year, ₹972.80 lakh was proposed for budget provision. Regarding the other part of the scheme, i.e., the nutrition part, 50 per cent is centrally sponsored and 50 per cent is state sponsored. For that matter in 2012-13 financial year, ₹19,000.00 lakh was proposed for budgetary provision. Thus outlays proposed under planned expenditure was to the tune of ₹9,500.00 lakh.

Construction of AWC Buildings

The Twelfth Plan document reports that in the first financial year 2012-13, it was proposed to have rental premises in the middle of the villages for running AWCs so that the AWWs can deliver services to the beneficiaries independently without any hassles. Besides this, even under the national rural self-employment scheme and other similar programmes, priorities would be given to the construction of AWC buildings. In 2012-13, 5000 AWCs were sanctioned in UP. The proposed outlay of ₹30.00 crore for the construction of AWC buildings includes the facility of kitchen set and child—and mother—friendly toilets. Availability of AWC buildings will be helpful not only for nutrition and ECE (early childhood education) scheme, but also in extending information, education and communication to children, adolescent girls, pregnant and lactating mothers. Certainly, the centre will evolve as one for social awareness and change.

Construction of CDPO Offices (NABARD)

The Twelfth Plan noted that presently 897 POs (project offices) are operational under the ICDS in the state of UP including World Bank assisted ICDS-III projects and ICDS General. In total 231 projects have been constructed. The new proposal is of constructing another 666 Project Offices-cum-godowns in a phased manner under the Twelfth Five Year Plan. For 2012-13 the proposal is to construct 150 Project Offices–cum-godowns and the estimated cost on the construction of 150 Project Offices–cum-godowns is ₹18.05 crores which works out as ₹12.00 lakh per office. Thus for the construction of CDPO offices proposal is to have a proposed outlay of ₹10.00 crores.

Where Do the Hurdles Stand

ICDS, which was initiated in response to the evident problems of persistent hunger and malnutrition especially among children, has grown to become India's largest early child development programme. The coverage of the Scheme has expanded rapidly, especially in recent years. There are almost 13.7 lakh AWWs and nearly equal number of Anganwadi helpers providing services to beneficiaries throughout the country. According to the government, the programme has reach 79.01 million children and 18.2 million pregnant and lactating women by March 2012.

By many accounts, the scheme has been a success so far. Nevertheless, it is also clear that for a scheme that has been in operation for almost four decades, the benefits remain as the far too limited, and maternal and child health and nutrition remain as the areas of major concern for policy formulators. Even today, around one-third of Indian children—and more than half in rural areas—are born with low birth weight. Data indicate the extent of severe stunting and severe under-nutrition among young children in UP, both of which are still unacceptably high.

It is a fact that high incidence of premature births, low birth weight and neonatal and infant mortality can be attributed to poor nutritional conditions of the mothers. Yet majority of the women do not get proper nutrition and health care during their pregnancy. In some areas, 60-75 per cent of pregnant women receive no antenatal care at all. More than 85 per cent of women in rural areas and 95 per cent in the remote areas give birth at home. Only 16 per cent of women in UP have access to safe delivery facilities (NFHS-3). In addition, surveys indicate that even the immunisation services were well below minimally acceptable norms.

What explains this continuing dismal picture even 38 years after the launch of one of the more successful government schemes, specifically to address these problems, needs to be studied. To find the prevailing situation, study was conducted to capture the extent of resources devoted to this scheme in order to meet the huge requirement. Quite simply, an in-depth study for such a large state as UP was called forth so as to help eradicate shortcomings in the policy formulation and its implementation thereof.

Above analysis suggests that the prime factor involved in effective utilisation of funds under ICDS programme in UP lies in budgetary and institutional hurdles. The structure of cost sharing between the centre and the state puts forth major constraints related to the programme. Although the centre bears the major share in the

ICDS fund, the state is also required to contribute certain mandated amount for few specific components.

Conclusion

This study has considerable academic relevance because the issues such as maternal and child health and nutrition are still areas of major concern for policy. Even in the present, around one-third of Indian children—and more than half in rural areas—are born with low birth weight. Data indicate the extent of severe stunting and severe undernutrition among young children in our states, both of which remain unacceptably high. It is noteworthy that these indicators are particularly poor and the situation could be best assessed with the help of sample survey. This study will evoke better debate on the problems at hand which was a neglected arena of study. The study will throw light on the socio-economic factors which promote or retard efficacy of the government schemes in social sector. It would further highlight the specific problems and discrimination faced by women and children. Finally, the study will evaluate effectiveness of the existing programmes, and will help in formulating a better programme in the future for the development of women and children in UP.

References

Adhikari, Saroj K. and Bredenkamp Caryn (2009). "Moving Towards an Outcomes-Oriented Approach to Nutrition Program Monitoring: The India ICDS Program", *Health, Nutrition and Population (HNP) Discussion Paper*, June. Washington: World Bank.

Agnihotri, Satish B. (1999). "Eliminating Severe Malnutrition in Orissa: Profile of a Campaign" *Economic and Political Weekly* 34(51): 3616-21, 18-24 December.

Boroah Vani, Dilip Diwakar and Nidhi S. Sabharwal (2014). "Evaluating the Social Orientation of the Integrated Child Development Services Programme", *Economic and Political Weekly* XLIX(12): 52-62, 22 May.

Chaturvedi, B.K. (2000). *Integrated Child Development Services Scheme: A Compendium of Guidelines.* Department of Women and Child Development, Government of India.

Chandrasekhar, C.P. and Jayati Ghosh (2005). "The Unfulfilled Potential of the ICDS", *www.macroscan.com.* 21 March.

Dainik Jagran (2009a). "Aath Mah se Nahi Jala Mid-Day Meal ka Chulaha", *Dainik Jagran,* Lucknow edition, 28 October.

———. (2009b). "Koposhit hain Aaganwadi Kendra", *Dainik Jagran,* Lucknow edition, 27 October.

———. (2009c). "Chatak bhar Daliya se Nahi door hoga .. kooposhan", *Dainik Jagran,* Lucknow edition, 1 November.

Dhuru, Arundhati (2009). *ICDS in Uttar Pradesh: An Abandoned Vehicle.* Supported by CARE, Uttar Pradesh.

Diwakar, G.D. (2011). "Relevance of ICDS Programme in Post-liberalisation Period in Addressing the Malnutrition among 0-6 Years Children: A Case Study of Kancheepuram District, Tamil Nadu" in Sigamani and N.U. Khan (ed.), *Reinventing Public Management and Development in Emerging Economies, Advanced Research Series.* New Delhi: Macmillan. pp.55-74.

Dreze, Jean (2006). "Universalisation with Quality: ICDS in Rights Perspective" in *Economic and Political Weekly* 41(34): 3706-15, 26 August-1 September.

Dreze, Jean and Shonali Sen (2004). *Universalisation with Quality: An Agenda for ICDS.* Report prepared for the National Advisory Council, 7 September.

Ghosh Shanti (2004). "Child Malnutrition" , *Economic and Political Weekly* 36(40): 4412-13, 2-8 October.

———. (2006). "Food Dole or Health Nutrition and Development Programme?", *Economic and Political Weekly* 41(34): 3364-66, 26 August-1 September.

Gill, Kaveri (2012). "Promoting 'Inclusiveness'': A Framework for Assessing India's Flagship Social Welfare Programmes", *Social Policy Working Paper Series*-2, UNICEF, India.

Government of U.P. (2006). *Monitoring Poverty in Uttar Pradesh-A Report on the Second Poverty and Social Monitoring Survey (PSMS-II), Joint Report.* Directorate of Economics and Statistics Planning Department, Government of Uttar Pradesh and the World Bank.

———. (2014). *Monitoring Poverty in Uttar Pradesh-A Report on the Fourth Poverty and Social Monitoring Survey (PSMS-IV), Joint Report.* Directorate of Economics and Statistics Division, State Planning Institute, Planning Department, Government of Uttar Pradesh

HAQ (2006a). *Union Budget 2006-07 and Children.* New Delhi.

Krishnaraj, Maithreyi (2005). "Evaluating ICDS", *Economic and Political Weekly* 40(22/23): 2210-368, 28 May-10 June.

Khullar, Vandana (1998). "Integrated Child Development Services: A Critique of Evaluation Technique", *Economic and Political Weekly* 33(10): 537-45, 7-13 May.

Kumar, Nomita P. (2008). *Baseline Survey of Minority Concentrated Districts of Uttar Pradesh: A Study in Lucknow District.* Lucknow: Giri Institute of Development Studies.

Mahrotra, Santosh (2007). "Killing its Children Slowly" in *Seminar* 571, March.

Nayak, Nandini and N.C. Saxena (2006). "Implementation of ICDS in Bihar and Jharkhand, *Economic and Political Weekly* 41(34): 3680-84, 26 August-1 September.

National Advisory Council (2011). *Recommendation for a reformed and Strengthened ICDS.* June.

Planning Commission (2012). *Three Decades of ICDS: An Appraisal.*

Programme Evaluation Organisation (2011). *Evaluation Scheme on Integrated Child Development Scheme.* PEO Report 218. Vol. I. March. Planning Commission.

———. (2011). *Evaluation Scheme on Integrated Child Development Scheme.* PEO Report 218, Vol. II, March. Planning Commission.

Ramachandran, Vimla (2005). "Reflections on the ICDS Programme" in Seminar, No. 546, February.

Rajivan, Anuradha Khatri (2006). "ICDS with a Difference", *Economic and Political Weekly* 41(34): 3684-94, 26 August-1 September.

Sen, Amartya (2006). *Focus on Children under Six.* Abridged Report. December.

Sinha, Dipa (2006). "Rethinking ICDS: a Rights Based Perspective", *Economic and Political Weekly* 41(34): 3689-94, 26 August-1 September.

Shekar, Meera (2006). "ICDS and Persistent undernutrition: Strategies to Enhance the Impact", *Economic and Political Weekly* 41(12); 1193-201, 25-31 March.

Society for Economic Development and Environmental Management (2005). *Quick Review of Working of ICDS in Rajasthan.* New Delhi: Department of Women and Child Development, Ministry of Human Resources.

Sundaraman, T. (2006). Universalisation of ICDS and Community Health Worker Programme: Lessons from Chattisgarh", *Economic and Political Weekly* 41(34): 3374-79, 26 August-1 September.

UNICEF (2011). *Integrated Child Development Services (ICDS): Budgeting for Change Series.*

UPVAN (2008). *U.P. Social Watch Report 2008*. Lucknow: Uttar Pradesh Voluntary Action Network.

Working Group on Children Under Six (2007). "Strategies for Children Under Six" *Economic and Political Weekly* 42(52): 87-101, 29 December 2007-4 January 2008.

World Bank (1998). *Project Appraisal Document.* Report No. 17052-IN. Washington

24

SANJUKTA DAS AND MUKTARANI MISHRA

NRHM and the Status of Maternal Health in Rural Odisha
A Micro Study

Introduction

Worldwide, nearly half a million women die each year from complications during pregnancy and childbirth, and about 99 per cent of these women belong to the developing world, with over 90 per cent concentrated in Africa and Asia. India accounts for nearly 17 per cent of the global burden of both maternal and child death (WHO, 2013). In developing nations, one in every 11 women dies of pregnancy-related complications compared to 1 in 5000 in developed countries (WHO, 2004). The MMR (maternal mortality ratio) (which is an indicator of status of maternal health) in India is 190 (*World Health Statistic 2013*), which is high in comparison to other developing countries. While maternal mortality is related to a variety of health, social and economic factors, a majority of the deaths are directly caused by a limited number of complications such as haemorrhage, hypertensive disorders, sepsis, and obstructed labour which require access to emergency obstetric care. The most tragic fact is that deaths and episodes of ill-health that occurred mostly in rural areas, could have been prevented even with existing knowledge and means of prevention. Despite incorporating several programmes and policies, maternal health status of India particularly in the rural area is not satisfactory. To solve the problem of rural people in general and maternal health in particular, National Rural Health Mission (NRHM) was launched on 12 April 2005 for the period of seven years (2005-2012) and subsequently extended to

2017 in the Twelfth Five Year Plan (FYP). It is one of the biggest integrated health initiatives ever taken in the health sector in the last 50 years. With the objectives of reduction in maternal death and improvement in maternal health, the core motto of NRHM is to increase institutional delivery and comprehensive obstetric care in rural area. The programmes under NRHM to improve the status of maternal health are Janani Surakshya Yojana (JSY), Janani and Sishu Surakshya Karyakrama (JSSK), Mamata scheme, Free Drugs scheme, appointment of Accredited Social Health Activists (ASHA), fixed village health and nutrition day (VHND/*Mamata Diwas*), Yoshada scheme, maternity waiting homes in difficult blocks, 24/7 hospitals facility and referral transport. As maternal health situation is dire in rural area, maternal healthcare is the focused aspect in NRHM.

Background

Maternal health has been defined as safe motherhood, ensuring all women to receive the care they need to be safe and healthy through pregnancy, childbirth and after delivery (Family Care International, 2000). The preventive and protective measures taken to save the mother from the problems arising from pregnancy, child birth (also abortion) and in post-partum period are termed as maternal healthcare. It thus, covers ANC (antenatal check-up), provision of Tetanus Toxide (TT) vaccine during pregnancy, consumption of Iron and Folic Acid (IFA), institutional delivery, assistance of health personnel during delivery and PNC (postnatal care). There are some indicators through which maternal healthcare status of an area is generally measured. Those indicators are: level of availing of antenatal, intranatal and postnatal care, delivery assisted by a doctor/nurse/ ANM (Axillary Nurse Midwife)/other health personnel, institutional births, women BMI (Body Mass Index), infant death, stillbirth, neonatal death, anaemic and MMR. MMR, which is mostly used to describe the maternal health status, is defined as the number of maternal deaths per 100,000 live births.

A Review of Literature on the Impact of NRHM on the Status of Maternal Healthcare

Ample of studies has been done on NRHM and its impact on maternal healthcare. Here we have reviewed some of the studies conducted and tried to assess the impact of NRHM on maternal healthcare. Lahariyan (2009) in his study described the role of JSY emphasising on, ways in which well-thought government programmes bring about improvement in health of the people in short period of time. The change in delivery preference behaviour in India is mainly due to the implementation of JSY under NRHM. Incentive payments under JSY (Mother Protection Programme) encourages women to deliver in institutions (Ministry of Health and Family Welfare, 2011). The JSY is the most important factor that has increased the rate of institutional delivery in Uttar Pradesh (UP) (Khan *et al.*, 2010). A number of national surveys and provincial data sources have demonstrated a steep rise in institutional deliveries, both nationally and in Madhya Pradesh (MP) since the JSY programme (DLHS-2 and 3, NFHS-3). Considering the awareness prealant among people, a study on slum people in Delhi mention a need to improve the perception of the urban slum population about the utilisation of JSY scheme. Targeting difficult-to-access areas with special measures and encouraging more antenatal visits were essential prerequisites to improve the impact of JSY (Vikram *et al.*, 2013). Village women trained as ASHAs and integrated with existing health staff would provide antenatal, intrapartum and postnatal care (Rajalakshmi, 2005), motivate women to seek institutional deliveries and accompany other labouring women to the relevant facilities. A study by Nair *et al.* (2011) found that the public health machinery is not successful in generating awareness and creating a cadre of functional frontline workers in the form of ASHA. ANC services at the village level were affected due to lack of participation of ASHA in VHND and that of clarity in their roles in healthcare provision. The HMIS (Health Management Information Statistic) report, states that after introduction of NRHM in 2005, a low performing state like Odisha has started showing signs of improvements in various health indicators, e.g., institutional delivery (increased from 35.6% in 2006 to 75% in 2009-10); immunisation (increased from 52% in 2005-06 to 85% in 2009-10)[1]; positive malaria cases reduced to 359,619 in 2008 from 396,573 in 2005.[2] (HMIS Report, NRHM, Odisha, 2008-09); Malaria deaths reduced to 226 in 2008 from 255 in 2005[3] Leprosy prevalence reduced from 2.05 in 2005 to 0.87 in 2008; etc. There is a decentralised planning of programme implementation in NRHM. It depends largely on PRIs (Panchayati Raj Institutions) for effective implementation of proposed interventions and utilisation of resources. In most parts of our country, State Governments have not empowered PRIs with real devolution of power. Therefore, much needs to be done locally in order to build the capacity of PRIs and develop state-specific guidelines in operational terms to implement interventions under NRHM for reducing maternal mortality ratio (Kumar, 2005). A study by Pritam (2014) concluded that there is a little and marginal impact of the Mission on healthcare facilities even after so many years of implementation. It that there is Some progress in manpower has also been noticed, like that of doctors, specialists, staff nurse, ANMs and AYUSH medical personnel; but no such advancement is noted in construction of new medical institutions and other facility such as beds, laboratory and residential quarters, etc., under NRHM. The question of good governance—transparency, accountability, community-level participation and a committed government—comes into play in ensuring better healthcare facilities to the common man. The NRHM will not bear fruitful results until and unless a committed government is in place to ensure that the goals set forth are achieved (Priyanka, 2012). A study on Odisha (Patra *et al.*, 2013) shows that, although the poor health status (ANC, Institutional delivery, PNC) of the area is gradually improving in quality as owing to implementation of NRHM, the progress is not as much as that in other states. The reasons for this tendency are—low income, illiteracy, shortage of doctors, unwillingness of

1. HMIS Report, NRHM, Odisha, 2009-10.
2. HMIS Report, NRHM, Odisha, 2008-09 and 2005-06.
3. Ibid.

doctors to visit remote areas and lack of healthcare facilities as well as production of laboratory technicians and radiographers.

Conceptual Framework

The past studies show that the impact of NRHM on the utilisation of maternal healthcare is positive, but there are some political, infrastructural and socio-economic bottlenecks that create a huddle in maximising influence of the mission. The studies are mostly based on secondary data and has neglected the output variables like miscarriage, abortion, stillbirth, neonatal death and infant death as indicators of maternal health status. NRHM has completed its nine years of implementation in Odisha. It hence becomes necessary to assess the impact of NRHM on the maternal health indicators in order to know how the schemes under NRHM are working in Odisha and to assess the transition in the state's health status. The present paper is an attempt to evaluate the effectiveness of NRHM in Odisha considering two districts—one is a high focused district (Nuapada) where maternal health indicators score low and the other one is high performance district (Sambalpur) where maternal health status is quite good.

This paper attempts to examine the maternal health status of rural mothers and the change in this status due to inception of NRHM.

Study Area and Data Collection

Odisha is an eastern state of India with a total population of 41,947,358, where 83 per cent is the rural population (Census 2011). In term of human development indicators namely health, education and income, the state is lagging compared to other states of India. NRHM has consider Odisha as a high focused state due to its low health indicator. So the state is purposefully selected. The study is conducted in four villages of two districts, Sambalpur (developed) and Nuapada (underdeveloped) from April to June 2014. This study includes eligible mothers of the age group 15-49 years from the selected villages who have had children after 2010. For a comparative analysis of the impact of NRHM on maternal health, data are collected from the mothers with children before initiation of NRHM, as well as after NRHM. Pregnant women are knowingly avoided to get a complete data on maternal healthcare utilisation. For the study of pre-NRHM period, data are collected from the mother who delivered in the year 2003-04. Here the data are gathered from secondary sources as the primary ones could not give us the correct information. On the other hand, the information from mothers who delivered after 2010 is taken for post-NRHM analysis. Our sample size is 81 mothers (age 15-49), where 20 women have children before NRHM (2005) and 61 with children after 2010. The relevant information from AWCs and *padiabahal* PHC (primary health centre) (which is near to the village) is obtained to get the maternal health status for the period of pre-NRHM, and Field Survey (2014) data are used for post-NRHM analysis.

Methodology

The output indicators such as miscarriage, abortion, stillbirth, neonatal death, infant death and haemoglobin level are considered to evaluate the maternal health status of the area. The mentioned variables are taken as dependent variable and Education (mother and husband), economic index, caste and age at pregnancy are taken as independent variables. The various indicators such as abortion/ miscarriage, ANC, place of delivery, PNC taken, use of contraceptive and anaemic condition are considered to compare the maternal health status in pre-and post-NRHM period. Using the various statistical tools, the data are analysed in SPSS.

Maternal Health Status of the Study Area

A sound, healthy woman will produce a sound baby. Poor maternal health status of an area results in abortion/miscarriage, stillbirth, neonatal death and infant death. Here keeping in mind the abortion/miscarriage, stillbirth, neonatal death, postnatal death, infant death and anaemic condition of the children of these mothers, the situation of ill-health of the mother is examined.

Table 24.1 presents the maternal health status of the study area. Among 61 mothers, 19 mothers have experienced miscarriage who constitute 31 per cent of the total selection. Generally, miscarriage happened due to poor health status of the pregnant women, rendering her incapable of carrying the child up to the due date. Similarly, 23 per cent mothers have experienced stillbirth and about 15 per cent have faced neonatal death. More serious problems are noticed when the same mother has experienced multiple disadvantages, i.e., stillbirth, miscarriage, neonatal death. Three per cent of the mothers have experienced both stillbirth and miscarriage, 5 per cent have both stillbirth and neonatal death, and about 10 per cent have experienced more than these disadvantages.

Table 24.1

Mothers Experiencing Disadvantages

Disadvantages	*Number*	*Percentage*
Miscarriage	19	31.15
Stillbirth	14	22.95
Neonatal death	9	14.75
Post-neonatal death	11	18.03
Infant death	14	23
Both neonal and post-neonatal death	3	4.9

Note: Number of observation is 61.
Source: Field data.

Table 24.2

Mothers according to Haemoglobin Level

Haemoglobin level	*Code*	*No.*	*Percentage*	*Cumulative Percentage*
Normal	0	18	29.5	29.5
Mildly anaemic	1	21	34.4	63.9
Severely anaemic	2	22	36.1	100
	Total	61	100	

Note: Number of observation is 61.
Source: Field data.

Haemoglobin (Hb) level is another indicator of maternal health status, defining the anaemic situation of the mother. On the basis of Hb level, mothers are categorised as severely anaemic (Hb level<9mg/decelitre), mild anaemic (Hb level=9-11mg/decelitre),and not anaemic (Hb level >11mg/decelitre). We have used codes 2,1, and 0 for severely anaemic, mild anaemic,and not anaemic respectively. In the study area, 36 per cent severely anaemic mothers are found, along with 70 per cent of them suffering from haemoglobin level less than 11mg/de. Only 30 per cent have normal haemoglobin level. This shows the severity of anaemic situation in the study area.

Table 24.3

Maternal Health Status Index of Mothers

Type	*Code*	*Frequency*	*Percentage*	*Cumulative Percent*
Good	0	41	67.2	67.2
Bad	1	17	27.9	95.1
Worse	2	3	4.9	100

Note: Number of observations is 61.
Source: Field data.

Among all the indicators, stillbirth and neonatal death are directly and closely connected with health of the mother. Most miscarriages and stillbirth are the result of undernourishment of the child in the mother's womb. All other situations may occur due to other external factors. Hence to realise the maternal health status of the study area, we have taken Stillbirth and neonatal death as the index for maternal health status. Experiencing stillbirth/miscarriage is coded as '1' and absent of it is coded as '0'. In Table 24.3, '0' refer to good maternal health, implying absent of both miscarriage and stillbirth, while bad indicates presence of one of the ill health conditions and is coded as '1' On the other hand, present of both the situations is taken as worst and is coded as 2. Table 24.3 explains the maternal health status of study area, after nine years of implementation of NRHM. Yet five per cent of the mothers are found to have undergone both miscarriage and stillbirth and 30 per cent has suffered from one of the ill health situations. The aim of bringing about total absence of ill health among mothers has not yet materialised sixty seven per cent mothers are experiencing good health, implying an improvement, but there is still a long way to achieve the target.

Variables Associated with Maternal Health Status

Socio-economic variables like caste, education, economic status, religion, culture, age, location, etc., influence the maternal health status. Socio-economic and health system factors are the best predictors for availing maternal health scheme. The study tries to examine five socio-economic variables, such as caste, mother's education, husbands education, economic condition of the household and age of mother at pregnancy, for understanding the maternal health status of underpriviliged populations such as poor rural mothers. Table 24.4 shows the relationship between caste and maternal health status. Mothers belonging to ST (scheduled tribe) and SC (scheduled class) communities together constitute 89 per cent of abortions, 78 per cent of stillbirth, 88 per cent of neonatal death, 100 per cent infant death and 95 per cent of severely anaemic persons. On the other hand, in case of OBC (other backward classes) and General caste, the incidence of ill health of mothers is very low. Only 11 per cent have undergone abortion and neonatal death, 21 per cent have undergone stillbirth, 4 per cent of the mothers are anaemic and no cases of infant death are found. The probable cause of such caste differences in case of maternal health status may be due to the working environment of ST and SC mothers. As in case of SC and ST households, women contribute a significant portion of the household income. Even during pregnancy, they do strenuous physical work (fetching water from well, carrying heavy loads, etc., which are generally avoided during this time, the result is generally severe ill health of the mother.

The influence of mother's education over the maternal health status is also tested in the study. Table 24.5 reveals the relationship education of mothers and maternal health status. As per the table the percentages of abortion, stillbirth, neonatal death, the infant death and severely anaemic individuals are higher in case of illiterate mothers in comparison to the literate over.

Table 24.4

Caste and Maternal Health Status

	Abortion/ Miscarriage		Stillbirth		Neonatal death		Infant death		Anaemic	
Caste	*No.*	*%*	*No.*	*%*	*No.*	*%*	*No.*	*%*	*No*	*%*
ST	7	37	5	26	3	16	4	20	10	53
SC	10	42	6	28	5	21	7	29	11	46
OBC	1	20	2	40	0	0	0	0	0	0
General	1	8	1	8	1	8	0	0	1	8
Total	19		14		9		11		22	

Note: Number of observation is 61.
Source: Field data.

Table 24.5

Mother's Education and Maternal Health Status

	Abortion/ Miscarriage		Still-birth		Neonatal death		Infant death		Anaemic	
Education	*No*	*%*	*No*	*%*	*No*	*%*	*No*	*%*	*No*	*%*
Illiterate	6	37.5	6	40	3	20	7	47	10	67
1 to 4	5	50	3	30	1	10	1	10	6	60
5 to 9	4	24	2	18	4	24	3	18	5	29
10 to 14	4	24	3	18	1	6	0	0	1	6
15 to 20	0	0	0	0	0	0	0	0	0	0
Total	19		14		9		11		22	

Note: Number of observations is 61.
Source: Field data.

Out of the mothers with 10 and above 15 years of education, 24 per cent have had abortion, 18 per cent have had stillbirth, 6 per cent have had neonatal death, no one has experienced infant death and no anaemic situation is seen; whereas in the case of mothers with education less than 9 years, around 70 per cent have had abortion, stillbirth and neonatal death. The situation is worst in case of infant death and anaemic conditions. Above 90 per cent of them have had infant death and are severely anaemic. There are no cases of ill health found in case of mothers with education level of more than 15 years, indicating the significance of maternal education in better utilisation of the maternal healthcare services.

Table 24.6

Husband Education and Maternal Health Status

	Abortion/ Miscarriage		*Stillbirth*		*Neonatal death*		*Infant death*		*Anaemic*	
Education	*No*	*%*	*No*	*%*	*No*	*%*	*No*	*%*	*No*	*%*
Illiterate	3	50	1	20	1	20	1	20	4	80
1 to 4	5	62	4	50	1	13	3	37	5	62
5 to 9	6	32	4	21	4	21	6	31	10	52
10 to 14	5	18	5	18	3	11	1	4	3	11
15 to 20	0	0	0	0	0	0	0	0	0	0
Total	19		14		9		11		22	

Note: Number of observations is 61.

Source: Field data.

The role of husband's education in maternal health status is presented in Table 24.6 Education creates awareness and provides knowledge about maternal health. Similar to education of the mother, increase in education level of the husband shows a decline in ill health of mothers. When the husband is illiterate, the percentage of abortion is 40 per cent and 80 per cent of the wives of illiterate husbands are anaemic. At a higher level of education of the husband, the wives do not show any kind of ill health. In case of illiterate husbands the count of stillbirth, neonatal death and infant death is 20 per cent which reduces to 18 per cent, 11 per cent and 4 per cent when the education level rise to 10 years and above.

Table 24.7 reveals the link between maternal health status and economic status of the households. Economic status and availability of asset play a very important role in determining the maternal health status. The income and assets are considered to be the indicators of economic standard of the households. In the rural area, land is the most important asset. Besides that, people also possess productive assets like cattle, and consumer durables like ornaments, utensils, etc. Here due to the lack of information on other assets, by taking land holding and type of house into consideration, we have tried to assess the economic standard of the study area. Houses from lowest to highest quality are coded from 1 to 5. Similarly, land is assigned values like 0 (landless), 1 (land up to 3acres), 2 (3-5acres), 3 (5-8acres), 4 (8<acres). Total number of mothers in each index is given in the table. Index 4 to 8 clubbed together as number of mothers in single index was very low. It is found that landless households living in the lowest quality of houses with code 1 in economic status have all forms of problems while households with relatively high economic status (with code 4 to 8) have these problems in smaller proportions. However, in still birth the percentage is very high (27.3%) which needs further pondering. Similarly, in neonatal death and infant death higher percentages are found with economic index 2 and 3. These decline again when economic index rises to 4 and above. This implies that besides households economic condition other factors have influential role in child mortality. However, in anaemia, which is also an indicator (and direct indicator) of maternal health we see continuous decline in the percentage with rise in economic index of household. The mothers belonging to the economic index of less

Table 24.7

Economic Index and Maternal Health Status

Economic Index	*No. of mothers*	*Abortion/ Miscarriage*		*Stillbirth*		*Neonatal death*		*Infant death*		*Anaemic*	
		No.	*%*	*No.*	*%*	*No.*	*%*	*No.*	*%*	*No.*	*%*
1	11	8	72.7	3	27.3	2	18.2	1	9.1	9	81.8
2	13	8	61.5	3	23.1	3	23.1	6	46.2	6	46.2
3	15	0	0	2	13.3	3	20	3	20	6	40
4--8	22	3	13.6	6	27.3	1	4.5	1	9.1	1	9.1

Note: Number of observations is 61.

Source: Field data.

than 6 experience all forms of ill health; on the other hand, mothers belonging to economic index of more than 6 experience only abortion and neonatal death.

Table 24.8 assesses the age of mother at first pregnancy and the consequent maternal health situation. The ideal period to have a child is 20-25 years (MoHFW, 2012). The age 15-19 years is too early to conceive; at this age the woman's body is not fully developed to be pregnant. In our study area, there are 49 per cent of mothers who had been pregnant at the age of 15-19, among them 43 per cent experienced abortion, which is 23 per cent in case of mothers who had been pregnant after 25 years. Stillbirth, neonatal death, infant death and anaemic condition is 33 per cent, 23 per cent, 33 per cent and 53 per cent respectively in case of early pregnancy, but the same falls to 8 per cent, 15 per cent, 8 per cent and 15 per cent respectively in case of marriage after 25 year.

Table 24.8

Age at Pregnancy and Maternal Health Status

	Abortion/ Miscarriage		*Stillbirth*		*Neonatel death*		*Infact death*		*Anaemic*	
Age	*No.*	*%*	*No.*	*%*	*No.*	*%*	*No.*	*%*	*No.*	*%*
15-19	13	43	10	33	7	23	10	33	16	53
20-24	3	17	3	17	0	0	0	0	4	22
25-29	3	23	1	8	2	15	1	8	2	15
Total	19		14		9		11		22	

Note: Number of observation is 61.

Source: Field data.

Improvement in the Maternal Health Status

The present status of maternal health in the study area shows that the situation still needs policy attention. Undoubtedly, inception of NRHM has had positive effect on maternal health status, but the level of effect is not even for all regions. Here by considering certain indicators, an attempt has been made to realise the effect of NRHM on our study area by comparing the maternal health status in two periods, i.e., in pre and post NRHM. As information is unavailable for stillbirth, neonatal death and infant death, we have taken miscarriage and haemoglobin level to draw the comparison. Table 24.9 shows that the percentage of mothers experiencing miscarriage was 60 per cent in pre-NRHM period, which is reduced to 31 per cent in post-NRHM period. This shows that maternal health status has improved in post-NRHM period.

Table 24.9 shows that before implementation of NRHM, 30 per cent of pregnant women in the study area are found to be severely anaemic that increased to 36 per cent in post-NRHM; but the situation is better in case of mild anaemic and no anaemic level. There is fall of 10 per cent seen in case of mild anaemic and 5 per cent in case of severely anaemic situation. Among these, mothers who have taken two or more ANC are less anaemic in comparison to those have not taken any. Field survey shows that in pre-NRHM period, mothers who have taken no ANC experience 33 per cent severe anaemia, but those who have taken two or more ANC experienced no anaemia. In

Table 24.9

Miscarriage

	Pre-NRHM	*Post-NRHM*
Sample size	20	61
% of miscarriage	60	31

Source: Field data, Aaganwadi centre and *Padiabahal* PHC.

Table 24.10

Distribution of Mothers in Term of Hemoglobin Level

		Pre-NRHM		*Post-NRHM*	
Hemoglobin Level		*No.*	*%*	*No.*	*%*
11 and above	0= good	5	25	18	29.5
9.0--10.99	1= mild anaemic	9	45	21	34.4
<9	2= severely anaemic	6	30	22	36.1
	Total	20	100	61	100

Source: Field data, Aaganwadi centre and *Padiabahal* PHC.

post-NRHM period, mothers who have missed ANC are 71 per cent; anaemic, but among those who have taken full ANC, only 15 per cent are found anaemic.

Improvement in Service Utilisation

Maternal health status not only depends upon the socio-economic factors, but also on utilisation of various maternal healthcare services. Here we have compare service utilisation in pre-and post-NRHM and inferred the impact of NRHM on utilisation of services such as ANC, institutional delivery, PNC and the use of contraceptive.

Table 24.11

Distribution of Mothers in Terms of ANC Visits

	Pre-NRHM		*Post-NRHM*	
Times	No.	%	No.	%
0	9	45	0	11
1	8	40	2	27
2	2	10	10	39
3	1	5	8	21
Total	20	100	61	100

Source: Field data, Aaganwadi centre and *Padiabahal* PHC.

In Table 24.11 the range from no ANC to full ANC is coded as 0 to 3. The mothers who have not consumed any Iron and Folic Acid (IFA) tablets, not taken TT or any check-ups are coded as '0', 30 IFA with one TT and some check-ups is coded as 1,60 IFA with two TT and some check-ups is coded as 2 and 100 IFA with two TT and all check-ups is coded as 3 in the table. Full ANC on which the health status of both the mother and child depends increase from 5 to 21 per cent in post-NRHM, No ANC in pre-NRHM period was 45 per cent, which comes down to 11 per cent post NRHM implementation. The use of ANC depend upon several factors and awareness is one of them. Due to lack of awareness, people are unable to use the available services. The awareness level for ANC was 55 per cent in pre-NRHM period that increased to 70 per cent in post-NRHM period (field data); and here the role of ASHA is important for bringing about improvement (respondent's response).

Table 24.12

Delivery Place

	Pre-NRHM		*Post-NRHM*	
Place	*N*	*%*	*N*	*%*
Home	12	60	8	13.1
SBA	4	20	6	9.8
Government Hospital	3	15	44	72.1
Private Hospital	1	5	3	4.9
Total	20	100	61	100

Note: SBA-Skilled Birth Attendant.
Source: Field data, Aaganwadi centre and *Padiabahal* PHC.

Place of delivery and assistance during delivery determine delivery care of the mother, and it shows that in pre-NRHM period home delivery was 60 per cent, which reduced to 13 per cent in Post-NRHM period. Table 24.12 indicates that although 40 per cent of the home deliveries were done by unskilled persons in pre-NRHM, it reduced to 3 per cent in post-NRHM period. Institutional delivery (government hospitals and nursing home) increased from 20-77 per cent of which, delivery in government hospitals increased from 15-72 per cent. This high preference for hospital delivery is mainly due to the impact of NRHM created by providing various financial assistance to the family of the mother inform of JSY, JSSK, Mamata scheme and counselling of ASHA (respondents).

Seven visit in 42 days after delivery is regarded as full PNC as per the Ministry of Health and Family Welfare (MoHFW) guidelines. Table 24.13 shows that there was no percentage of full PNC in pre-NRHM period and only 2 per cent in post-NRHM period, which reveals that PNC level is still low in the catter period. Before NRHM, all mothers had visited only thrice, but after NRHM, even though the percentage is low, mothers have made up to seven visits.

Use of contraceptives saves the mother from unwanted pregnancy, thereby protecting her from abortion. It mostly depends upon the prevalent awareness and practice (which to a large extent depend upon counselling). In the study area ASHAs and other health workers are found active in counselling the mothers, but the cultural barriers to use contraceptives are still strong. Hence, the use of contraceptive has increased marginally from 30 (pre-NRHM) to 35 per cent (post-NRHM).

Table 24.13

Distribution of Mothers in Terms of PNC Visits

	Pre-NRHM		*Post-NRHM*	
Time	*No.*	*%*	*No.*	*%*
0	16	80	2	3
1	1	5	5	8
2	2	10	21	34
3	1	5	10	16
4			7	11
5			1	2
6			8	13
7			1	2
Total	20	100	55	100

Source: Field data, Aaganwadi centre and *Padiabahal* PHC.

Table 24.14

Use of Contraceptives

	Pre-NRHM		*Post-NRHM*	
	No.	*%*	*No.*	*%*
Notused	14	70	41	67
Used	6	30	20	35
Total	20	100	61	100

Source: Field data, Aaganwadi centre and *Padiabahal* PHC.

Conclusion

NRHM has created state-and country-wide belief that progress in health indicators is possible. Most importantly, engagements are made at grass-roots level in form of ASHAs, ANM, etc., in order to increase the maternal health status. However, the study findings reveal that maternal health status has substantially in post-NRHM period, but the rate of improvement in certain indicators are not acceptable. In the present situation, after nine years of implementation of the programme, socially and economically deprived mothers are still found to face multiple health risks. Hence, the paper concludes that although the effect of NRHM is positive, it alone cannot significantly enhance the maternal health status. The desired changes can be facilitated only through an improvement in their socio-economic status, which would enable mothers to use the maternal healthcare services available extensively, thereby boosting the maternal health status.

References

Family Care International (2000). *Sexual and Reproductive Health.* New York, USA. Also available at *http:www.familycareintl.org*

Government of Meghalaya (2010). *Evaluation of National Rural Health Mission (NRHM) in Meghalaya.* Directorate of Programme Implementation and Evaluation.

International Institute for Population Sciences (IIPS) (2006). *District Level Household and Facility Survey (DLHS-2), 2002-04: Madhya Pradesh, India.* Mumbai. Available from *http://www.rchiips.org/pdf/state/Madhya_Pradesh.pdf*

————. (2008). *National Family Health Survey (NFHS-3), India, 2005-06: Madhya Pradesh.* Mumbai. Available from *http://www.nfhsindia.org/NFHS-3Data/madhya pradesh_state_report_for_web site_17feb09.pdf*

————. (2010). *District Level Household and Facility Survey (DLHS-3), 2007-08: Madhya Pradesh, India.* Mumbai. Available from *http://www.rchiips.org/pdf/rch3/report/MP.pdf*

Khan, M.E, Avishek Hazra and Isha Bhatnagat (2010). "Impact of Janani Suraksha Yojana on Selected Family Health Behaviours in Rural Uttar Pradesh",*The Journal of Family Welfare* 56 (Special Issue).

Kumar, S. (2005). "Challenges of Maternal Mortality Reduction and Opportunities Under National Rural Health Mission: A Critical Appraisal", *Indian Journal of Public Health* 49(3): 163-67.

Lahariyan, Chandrakant (2009). "Cash Incentives for Institutional Delivery: Linking with Antenatal and Postnatal Care May Ensure 'Continuum of Care' in India", *Indian J Community Med.* 34(1): 15-18, Jan.

Ministry of Health and Family Welfare (2012). *Annual Report 2011- 12.* Government of India. Department of Health and Family Welfare.

Rajalakshmi, T.K. (2005). "Healthcare: Gaps in a Mission", *Frontline* 22(10).

Nair, Harish and Rajmohan Panda (2011). "Quality of Maternal Health Care in India: Has the National Rural Health Mission Made a Difference", *Journal of Global Health* 1(1), June.

Priyanka, K. Nongkynrih (2012). *Governance and Provision of Health Security: A Case Study of the Implementation of the National Rural Health Mission Programme in East Khasi Hills District of Meghalaya.* Research paper.

Patra, Suresh Kumar, L. Annam and M. Ramadass (2013). *National Rural Health Mission (NRHM) & Health Status of Odisha: An Economic Analysis.* Language in India. *www.languageinindia.com* April

Pritam (2014). "Impact of National Rural Health Mission (NRHM) on the Health Sector in Haryana", *American International Journal of Research in Humanities, Arts and Social Sciences* 5(2): 201-05.

Thind, A., A. Mohani, K. Banerjee and F. Hagigi (2008). "Where to Deliver? Analysis of Choice of Delivery Location from a National Survey in India", *BMC Public Health* 8: 29.

Vikram, K., A.K. Sharma and A.T. Kannan (2013). "Beneficiary Level factors Influencing Janani Suraksha Yojana Utilisation in Urban Slum Population of Trans-Yamuna Area of Delhi", *Journal of Humanities and Social Science* (IOSR-JHSS) 8(1): 1-6 (Jan.-Feb.).

Websites:

World Health Organisation (WHO), Geneva (2013). Available: *www.who.int/mediacentre/ factsheets/fs348/en/index.html*

World Health Organisation (WHO), Geneva (2004). Available: *www.who.int/mediacentre/ factsheets/fs348/en/index.html.*

25

BHAGABATA PATRO and SABITRIBALA DAS

Changing Dropout Scenario in Sarva Siksha Abhiyan

A Study of Situation in Odisha

Introduction

Ensuring provision of a minimum formal education to all children within a specific age group has been an area of lively debate throughout the world. But sadly, Universalisation of Elementary Education (UEE) is still a distance prospect in major parts of the globe, including India. Even in developed countries like the United States (US), it is estimated that loss of income due to dropout of a student in 2007 is approximately to the tune of 329 billion dollar in his lifetime (Smink and Reimer, 2013). Since the beginning of the 21st century, importance of five to eight years of schooling for all children has been recognised as a societal non-negotiable goal. Two important obstacles in the UEE in India has been a matter of serious concern. One is the discontinuity in studies before completing a stage of education and the second one is repetition in the same grades due to quality deficiencies (TNS India, 2013). Gone are the days when people, at least in the more educationally backward regions of the country, questioned the relevance of primary education in their daily battle for survival. In the last five years, more and more people have been publicly voicing concerns about the situation of primary education in a our country. However, providing right type of education to the right people in right manner is the biggest challenge with our policymakers so as to benefit from human capital formation. (Basumatary, 2012).

Education constitutionally belongs to the state governments, but the quantum of resources necessary to achieve UEE necessitates intervention of the centre in a big way, and this has happened in the country since beginning of the 21st century. The Central government have initiated many CSS (centrally sponsored schemes) to influence non-pedagogical and pedagogical areas of elementary education. The measures taken to enhance enrolment and prevent dropouts at the elementary stage are: (a) legislations for free and compulsory primary education; (b) provision of schooling facilities within easy walking distance from the homes of children; (c) creation of necessary infrastructure facilities in schools; (d) incentive schemes for students; and (e) introduction of 'no detention policy' at the primary stage. The central government initiated schemes like non-formal education (1982), Operation Blackboard (1986) and Total Literacy Campaign (1988) in order to provide minimum elementary education to the people since the Sixth Plan. But a quantum jump in the effort has taken place in 1993-94 with the introduction of District Primary Education Programme (DPEP) scheme by the central government. The scheme aimed to provide access for all children to primary school or its equivalent non-formal educational institutions; reduce overall dropout rates; increase average learning achievement levels; reduce gaps in enrolments, dropouts, learning among gender and social groups; and establish capacity at the district, state and national level to plan, manage and monitor the programme.

The 86th Constitutional Amendment Act, 2002, made education a Fundamental Right for children in the age group of 6-14 years by stating "the State shall provide free and compulsory education to all children of the age of six to fourteen years in such manner as the state may, by law, determine". The Act further provides under Article 51-A (k) that it shall be a fundamental duty of every citizen of India who is a parent or guardian to provide opportunities for education to his child/ward between the age of 6 and 14 years. The flagship scheme of Government of India (GoI) the Sarva Shiksha Abhiyan (SSA), had laid the foundation of universalising elementary education in the country. The SSA was conceived as a CSS at the end of the Ninth Five Year Plan to improve the educational status in the country through interventions designed to improve accessibility, reduce gender and social gaps and improve the quality of learning. The SSA established a framework for achieving the goals of universal enrolment through time–bound targets and was conceived in a mission mode.

The objectives of SSA were (Planning Commission, 2010):

i) All children in school, Education Guarantee Centre, Alternate School, 'Back-to-School' camp by 2003; extended to 2005.
ii) Bridge all gender and social category gaps at primary stage by 2007 and at elementary education level by 2010.
iii) Universal retention by 2010.
iv) Focus on elementary education of satisfactory quality with emphasis on education for life.

In the initial years of the scheme, beginning 2001 until 2003-04, the programme was under-resourced. In 2004-05, access to 2 per cent cess on income tax was introduced. Thereafter, the funding problem of the scheme has improved substantially.

Issues Related to Dropout of School Children

The enrolment rates at primary level is stated to be nearing 100 per cent. The 8th All India Education Survey (AIES) concluded that enrolment in the classes from I to XII have increased by 14 per cent between 2002 and 2009. In some states, the primary level enrolment has decreased in the same period. The number of schools as well as teachers has also increased by 26.77 and 30 percentage during the same period.

The problem, however, continues to remain to some extent with regard to checking of dropouts. The issue of dropout appears to be a quite complex problem in the country because of the socio-economic faced by the families in India. Further, the country has a history of structural divides—in terms of castes and gender. UEE intends to put all 6-14 age group children in schools in the day time. But visibility of such children in shops, business establishments, streets (as rag pickers) and in homes (to take care of the younger siblings) defies the objective of universalisation. Leakages of the children from the school stream to other activities may be for several reasons. Thus, with positive achievement in enrolment, the quality of teaching and retention of the students in school have been the two major concerns for the planners. Here dropout refers to those who leave school for any reason before completion of the minimum formal schooling up to 8th standard. Out-of-School children are those who do not attend any educational centres (formal or informal) on a regular basis. Cambridge Advanced Learner's dictionary described dropout as, "if a student dropout, they stop going to classes before they have finished their course." In Macmillan dictionary, dropout means, "to leave something such as an activity, school or competition before you have finished what you intended to do." Oxford dictionary presents it in another way saying dropout means, "a person who has abandoned a course of study or who has rejected conventional society to pursue an alternative life style." Many other researchers gave several other definitions of drop out of a student from the school. Major hurdles in analysing drop out situation are two-fold. The first one is related to the environmental factors and the second one is the social attitude towards education. Prominent factors are, poverty and search for income generating activities for male children and/or marriage of girls. This is mostly associated with disadvantaged groups. There is a feeling in the society that education is least relevant for earning livelihood.

There has been wide variation in dropout statistics across the states. This is evident from Table 25.1 (Planning Commission, 2010). The table shows a slight rise in the dropout rate for the whole country in the year 2009-10 over 2008-09. Karnataka, Bihar and Odisha are the three states with significantly high dropout rate compared to all–India figure.

Quantifying the number of dropouts appears to be a very difficult task given the situation in the schools in the country. Most of the schools are not willing to reveal the correct data in the fear that it may adversely indicate their performance. As a result they are harming the student community as it becomes difficult to find out the truth. In a study in 2010, Reddy and Sinha stated that of the more than 27 million children in India who joined in Class I in 1993, only 10 million reached Class X, which is only about 37 per cent of those who had entered the school system and in more than half the states, only 30 per cent of the children reached Class X. All India Indo-Asian News Service (2013) has reported 40 per cent dropout rate at the elementary level in India. A study report of Ministry of Human Resource Development (MHRD) states that from 1999-2000 to 2010-11, 28 per cent of boys and 25 per cent of girls in primary level and 40 per cent of boys and 41 per cent of girls in elementary level have dropped out from school in India.

Various rounds of National Sample Survey (NSS) and other studies have also brought out substantial insights into the issue of dropouts which are as follows:

i) The main reasons of dropout include lack of interest of parents or children, economic needs, and looking after siblings. Further, poor school infrastructure, curriculum, unfriendly school environment, and lacking confidence on the need of schooling were also important reasons (52nd round of NSS, 1995-96; NSSO, 1998)
ii) The economic needs and children supporting parents in household activities, such as child care, were further highlighted by 61st round of NSS (NSSO 2005).
iii) Unattractiveness of school environment and teaching process; lack of playground, toilet, library, teaching and learning materials; and involvement of teachers in non-teaching activities were highlighted by the PROBE report (Public Report on Basic Education in India, 1999).
iv) Lack of pre-school education that incorporates the school–going habits was also stressed upon by a number of studies (Faith, 2009).

Many other studies tried to find out the causes of dropout in the Indian economy and in other countries. This paper intends to present the magnitude of officially calculated dropout rate and link it with other important economic variables 'sp' as to understand the exact causes behind students quitting school before completion of the course. The work is done for Odisha state and for all the 30 districts separately.

Table 25.1

State–wise Average Repetition and Dropout Rate among States in India

States	*Primary Stage*				*Upper Primary Stage*			
	Repetition Rate		*Dropout Rate*		*Repetition Rate*		*Dropout Rate*	
	2008-09	*2009-10*	*2008-09*	*2009-10*	*2008-09*	*2009-10*	*2008-09*	*2009-10*
Andhra Pradesh	3.4	3.6	3.0	2.9	1.4	1.6	3.4	2.4
Assam	11.2	8.0	3.2	2.6	9.4	6.7	4.6	3.3
Bihar	14.0	13.3	3.4	3.0	4.8	3.7	1.1	1.2
Chhattisgarh	6.8	5.8	3.0	4.4	5.4	3.0	1.5	3.4
Delhi	1.8	2.1	2.7	4.3	1.8	0.9	0.3	0.3
Gujarat	7.6	8.2	1.0	1.0	6.2	5.7	3.5	3.0
Haryana	4.9	3.0	2.1	1.8	6.8	3.1	0.4	0.2
Himachal Pradesh(HP)	2.2	0.6	1.4	1.4	5.8	1.8	1.4	0.9
Jammu and Kashmir	4.9	4.4	1.3	1.3	6.3	3.1	0.7	0.5
Jharkhand	15.7	14.7	3.5	3.0	10.1	7.3	2.1	2.8
Karnataka	1.1	0.5	1.6	1.5	0.4	0.4	6.8	5.7
Kerala	1.1	1.1	2.7	4.2	0.9	0.5	2.9	3.7
Madhya Pradesh (MP)	12.9	10.3	3.2	2.8	9.1	5.7	1.5	2.2
Maharashtra	3.6	1.5	1.8	2.0	2.4	3.1	1.7	1.5

Contd...

Contd...

Odisha	7.2	4.7	2.7	1.3	6.3	2.5	4.1	5.0
Punjab	11.3	7.5	3.4	3.9	15.3	11.9	0.5	1.4
Rajasthan	14.9	13.4	3.2	3.1	14.2	10.8	2.7	2.2
Tamil Nadu	1.5	1.2	2.6	1.7	1.8	2.2	1.3	1.9
Uttar Pradesh	3.3	3.3	2.4	4.6	1.6	1.6	1.5	1.5
Uttarakhand	1.9	1.0	2.6	1.7	1.8	0.3	1.2	0.8
West Bengal	15.8	14.0	3.9	2.5	12.2	10.6	0.4	0.3
All States	7.5	6.6	2.7	3.1	5.4	4.0	2.1	2.2

Source: TNS Report (2013), *Survey for Assessment of Dropout Rates at Elementary Level in 21 States.*

Status of Elementary Education and Dropout Scenario in Odisha

Odisha happens to be one of the most backward states in the country with substantial population BPL (below poverty line). Education and health are the two basic infrastructures necessary for the citizens to improve their capability. The Government of Odisha (GoO) has been implementing the different central sector plans to improve the access and quality of elementary education in the state. As a result, primary and upper primary education have been expanding in the State, especially in rural and backward areas. The State aims at providing primary schools within an kilometre and upper primary schools within 3 kilometres of habitations, which have population of more than 300 and 500 respectively. In 1947-1948, there were only 6,814 primary schools with 16,520 teachers and 2.55 lakh students in the state. By 2011-12, there were 55,106 functional primary schools/sections. This includes 51,163 schools of government and local bodies; 346 aided schools and 3,597 other schools. These schools have 1.33 lakh teachers and 44.33 lakh students. In 2011-12, there was one primary school per 2.8 sq km on an average. The average teacher–pupil ratio is 1:30, which is better than the national norm of 1:40. In addition, the state government has engaged 42,747 sikhya sahayaks and 22,421 gana sikhyaks. With the view of building and improving their teaching capabilities and assuring reasonable career growth, GoO has introduced a career advancement policy for these teachers. There were only 286 upper primary schools with 1,483 teachers and 32,000 enrolments in the State in 1947-48. Due to sustained efforts of the government, the number of upper primary schools/sections increased to 23,239. This includes 19,302 government and local body schools, 1,649 aided schools and 2,288 other schools. These schools had 53,264 teachers and 20.87 lakh enrolment made by the end of 2011-12. In 2000-01, there were 27 primary and about 8 upper primary schools per 100 sq km of area. The respective numbers increased to 35 and 16 in 2010-2011. The teacher-pupil ratio for upper primary schools was 1:39 during 2011-12. However, the ratio is still lower than the national norm of 1:25. The major initiatives for promotion of elementary education in the state are given below.

- In order to improve access to elementary education and to achieve 100 per cent enrolment, the government has relaxed the norm for opening new primary schools.
- The government provides block grant to the 916 eligible upper primary schools.
- Block grant for the teaching staff of 74 *madrasas* at the primary level has been provided.
- Grant-in-aid released to 1,866 teaching and non-teaching staff of 691 privately–managed, aided upper primary schools.
- Free text books have been supplied to all students in the primary level.
- Under SSA/National Programme for Education of Girls at Elementary Level (NPEGEL)/Kasturba Gandhi Balika Vidyalya (KGBV), a total of 8,713 new primary schools were opened, 9,319 primary schools where upgraded to UP level and 9,412 UP (ME) schools have been upgraded to those with Class VIII.
- A total number of 17,232 sikhya sahayaks who have completed six years of continuous service have been regularised as primary school teachers under *zilla parishads*.
- Recruitment of 14768 sikhya sahayaks has been made.
- About 9.13 lakh children in 1,518 UP schools have been included in Computer Aided Learning (CAL) programme under SSA.
- Under SSA, 15,942 primary and UP school buildings have been constructed and that of 1,585 school buildings is in progress. Also 8,946 new primary schools have been opened and 10,711 primary schools have been upgraded to UP level.
- Through home based education, 2,735 out–of-school children–addressed.
- To enhance knowledge in various subjects, 137,823 teachers have been trained.
- School uniforms are provided to all girl students of government schools from classes I-VIII.

- There are 182 KGBVs that have been operationalised and 16,631 girls enrolled in these schools are availing benefits of the scheme.
- 3,159 model cluster schools are functioning in 27 districts of Odisha.
- 385 centres of Early Childhood Care and Education (ECCE) under SSA are functioning, while under NPEGEL, 779 centres are functioning with 24,280 enrolments.
- Mother tongue based education is operational in 544 schools of 8 tribal districts, covering 61 blocks of Odisha in 10 tribal languages.
- A community–based child cantered drive has been taken up in 180 blocks covering 2,264 Cluster Resource Centre (CRC) in the state.
- Out of 1.31 lakh Children With Special Need (CWSN), 1.26 lakh were enrolled and 1.05 lakh CWN where provided with aids and appliances. 5,476 sets of Braille books were supplied to the visually impaired children.
- Also under SSA, 46,241 ACRs (additional classrooms) have been completed and construction of 7,410 ACRs is in progress.

Regardless of all these initiatives, out of 55,106 functional government elementary schools in the state, 12,621 (23.8%) schools did not have common toilets, 31,824 (59.9%) had no girls toilets, 2,922 (5.50%) schools had no drinking water facilities and 8,570 (16.14%) schools had no electricity. Besides, 521 government elementary schools do not even have buildings. The government has taken considerable initiatives to improve school infrastructure facilities.

All children in schools do not complete their grades. However, dropout rates have significantly fallen over the years. At the primary level, the dropout rate declined from 41.80 per cent in 2000-01 to 0.37 per cent in 2012-13. The dropout rates of boys fell from 42.30 per cent to 0.25 per cent and those for girls from 41.40 per cent to 0.62 per cent over this period. Although the dropout rates at the primary level have fallen, such rates remain high among SC (scheduled caste) and ST (scheduled tribe) communities at 2.41 per cent and 3.36 per cent respectively. It is the highest (9.3%) in Jagatsinghpur district and lowest (0.01%) in Cuttack, Bolangir and Bargarh districts. Infrastructure facilities in schools have a direct bearing on the enrolment and dropout rates. The overall dropout rate in UP schools of the state declined substantially from 28.39 per cent in 2005-06 to 2.36 per cent in 2012-13, but it is higher than that in case of primary schools (0.43%). The dropout rates for SC, ST and girl students were relatively higher. The dropout rate of SC students has gone down to 1.72 per cent in 2011-12 but again increased to 2.41 per cent in 2012-13. The overall dropout rate at the UP level is the highest in Koraput district (16.98%) and the lowest in Nayagarh district (1.11%).

Table 25.2

Drop-out Rate in Primary and Upper Primary Schools of Odisha, 2005-06 to 2012-13

	Primary			*Upper Primary*		
Year	*All Categories*	*SC*	*ST*	*All Categories*	*SC*	*ST*
2005-06	18.49	19.46	23.32	28.39	29.33	37.07
2006-07	10.53	16.97	22.88	18.05	25.59	32.44
2007-08	7.79	12.54	16.89	13.27	18.80	23.82
2008-09	4.95	7.96	10.69	8.42	11.92	15.12
2009-10	2.83	4.21	6.46	8.19	8.89	9.72
2010-11	2.60	3.38	4.85	7.23	6.24	7.86
2011-12	0.43	2.41	3.10	3.07	1.73	4.70
2012-13	0.37	2.39	2.97	2.36	2.41	3.36

Source: Government of Odisha, Planning and Coordination Department, *Economic Survey, 2013-14.*

Causes of Dropout: An Econometric Analysis

The reasons for drop out of school children depend upon various factors, which play very crucial role in the education system of the country and in the state. According to researchers and educationists, the social, educational and environmental factors cause drop out of a child from a school. In this section, there is an attempt to explain the behaviour of drop out variable over a time. The SSA implementation has started in 2001, and this model uses information for the period from 2002 to 2010. Dropout variable is regressed on many other economic variables in one model. A multivariate relationship is assumed for this purpose. District–wise regression equations are estimated by including five independent variables in Model-I. After that, district–wise information is presented zone-wise to explain the dropout rate variation behaviour in the three revenue divisions of the state. Finally, the relationship between dropout rates with other variables is discussed in the context of Odisha in Model-II.

The variable chosen for the multivariate model and the justification for the same is discussed below. Normally, dropout rate is assumed to have a declining trend when the government undertakes different incentive programmes to attract the students. Similarly, over a period, many other economic variables have also influenced the dropout rate of the state.

(a) Dependent Variable: School dropout (DROPOUT): Dropout rate data is taken for 8 years from 2002-03 to 2009-10.

(b) Independent variables: Here 5 variables are used.

- Number of Schools (NOS):- Lack of accessibility to a school is a major reason for dropout of school children. Particularly, as parents are reluctant to send their girl child to a distant place, the education stops untimely. The existence of a school inside a habitation is thus most suitable for a student's continuity therein. Even schools located in outskirts of a village students required passing through lonely places, as well as prohibits the parents from taking the risk of sending a girl child. After implementation of SSA, the number of school facilities have increased, which in turns helps to increase the enrolment in school and reduce dropout rate.
- Number of Teachers (NOT): Besides the number of schools, the teacher in a school also determines the willingness of a student there. There is an unusual craze for the teachers to get appointed in roadside schools leaving those far off with lesser number of teachers. In

Odisha, for 51,000 schools, there are 1.33 lakh teachers which means on an average, per school has 2.6 teachers. If this many teachers are supposed to handle five classes, there will definitely be indiscipline and disturbance. This is the second independent variable in our model.

- Net District Domestic Product (NDDP): In the recent years, district domestic product data is available and it indicates the economic strength of families in a district. Low incomes of the population leads to withdrawal of the kids from schools engaging them in some income–earning activities. This is more visible for families belonging to the BPL category and to SC/ST categories.
- Female Literacy Rate (FLR): An educated mother may support the education of kids. Assuming so, female literacy of the district is taken as an independent variable. The data for this is collected from the Census figures.
- Rural Population (RUP): A district constitutes of both rural and urban areas. Less urbanisation reflects low income of the people because of the dependence on agriculture activities. So rural population of a district is considered as the fifth independent variable.

Source of Data and Model Structure

The secondary data is collected in the context of Odisha for 8 years and is processed through a multiple regression model using Gretl econometrics package. The data of the study is based on the situation in 30 districts of Odisha for the years from 2002-03 to 2009-10. Data are drawn from the Census reports, Economic Survey, Selected Educational statistics, MHRD report and Directorate of Elementary Education followed by District Information System For Education (DISE) reports. The major points related to the methods of data collection and research design are described below.

- The district and year wise counts of schools as well as teachers are collected from the Directorate of Economics and Statistics, GoO.

- The NDDP data is collected from the Economic Survey published by the Planning and Coordination Department, GoO, Bhubaneswar.
- Information on literacy rate and rural population is collected from the Census reports of 2001 and 2011. Considering the average growth rate, the year–wise figures are derived.

The structure of the model is,

(Drop out)i = b0+b1(NOS)i+b2(NOT)i+ b3(NDDP)i+b4(FLR) i+b5(RUP)i+ Ui ....1.

where i represent the districts in Model I and the whole state in Model II.

The model is a simple one and does not include rigorous testing for the existence of multicollinearity, heteroscedasticity and auto-correlation problems.

Findings of the Study

Model I

The results for the three revenue divisions are presented below. The regressions results and the data is given in Annexures A-25.1 and A-25.2.

Situation in Central Zone

The central zone consists of 10 districts. These are: Cuttack, Jagatsinghpur, Jajpur, Kendrapada, Khordha, Nayagarh, Baleswar, Bhadrak, Mayurbhanja and Puri. The detailed relationship between the incidence of dropout and the five independent variables is given below.

- NOS: Rise in the number of schools in the district is supposed to reduce the dropout rate indicating a negative relationship between the two variables. Six districts, i.e, Cuttack, Jagatsinghpur, Jajpur, Kendrapada, Khordha and Nayagarh exhibit this relationship. For the rest four districts there exists a positive link reflecting the reverse situation.
- NOT: Dropout rate is supposed to be negatively related with the number of teachers in a school. This trend is visible for

only four districts of Jagatsinghpur, Jajpur, Mayurbhanja and Puri. For other six districts, the regression coefficients are positive.

- NDDP: The dropout rate and NDDP is negatively related for four districts of Baleswar, Bhadrak, Jagatsinghpur, and Mayurbhanja only. For others, the situation is different. Here, NDDP and dropout rate coefficients are of positive sign.
- FLR: In Baleswar, Jagatsinghpur, Jajpur and Mayurbhanja districts, the dropout rate is negatively related to female literacy rate. In other districts, there exists an opposite relationship between the two variables. These districts are Bhadrak, Cuttack, Kendrapada, Khordha, Nayagarh and Puri.
- Rural Population: In the districts of Bhadrak, Cuttack, Kendrapada, Khordha, Nayagarh and Puri, the rural population variable and dropout rates are negatively related. In other districts of this zone, there exists positive relationship between dropout rate and rural population. These districts are Baleswar, Jagatsinghpur, Jajpur and Mayurbhanja.

The R^2 value is more than 0.70 for Baleswar, Cuttack, Jagatsinghpur, Kendrapada and Puri districts. Some districts of the central zone have R^2 value less than 0.70. These districts are Bhadrak, Jajpur, Khordha, Mayurbhanj and Nayagarh. Examination of individual regression coefficients for all the districts indicate that except Puri, none of the coefficients are significant for the other districts.

Situation in Northern Zone

The detailed explanation of the district-wise coefficient value of the variables for the Northern zone is described below.

- NOS: Dropout rate is negatively related to the number of schools in only three northern districts. These are Angul, Dhenkanal and Subarnapur. For other districts of this zone, there exists positive relationship between dropout and the number of schools. These other districts are Balangir,

Bargarh, Deogarh, Jharsuguda, Keunjhar, Sambalpur and Sundargarh.

- NOT: Dropout rate and the number of teachers also show negative relationship in only one district, i.e, Balangir. Other districts like Angul, Bargarh, Deogarh, Dhenkanal, Jharsuguda, Keunjhara, Sambalpur, Subarnapur and Sundargarh reveals positive relationship between dropout and the number of teachers employed.
- NDDP: Dropout is negatively related to NDDP in only three districts of the northern zone. These are Balangir, Sambalpur and Sundargarh. But other districts of this zone have positive relationship between these two variables. They are Angul, Bargarh, Deogarh, Dhenkanal, Jharsuguda, Keunjhara and Subarnapur.
- FLR: Dropout is negatively related to female literacy rate (FLR) in six districts of the northern zone. These are Angul, Balangir, Bargarh, Jharsuguda, Sambalpur and Sundaragarh. Positive relationship exists for the other four districts, i.e, Deogarh, Dhenkanal, Keunjhara and Subarnapur.
- Rural Population: For four districts in the northern zone, dropout rate and rural population are negatively related. These are, Deogarh Dhenkanal, Keunjhara and Subarnapur. Dropout is positively related to rural population in other districts of this zone. The districts are Angul, Balangir, Bargarh, Jharsuguda, Sambalpur and Sundragarh.

The R^2 value is more than 0.70 in Angul, Deogarh and Dhenkanal districts. Some districts of the northern zone have R^2 value less than 0.70. These districts are Balangir, Bargarh, Jharsuguda, Keunjhara, Sambalpur, Subarnapur and Sundargarh. Examination of the significance of the regression coefficients indicate, that it is almost significant for all variables for the districts of Dhenkanal and Deogarh and partly for Keunjhar. For other districts, the independent variables are not too significant.

Situation in Southern Zone

The southern division of the state consists of 10 districts. The detailed explanation of the district–wise regression coefficient values of the variables of southern zone is described below

- NOS: Dropout is negatively related to the number of schools in four districts of the Southern zone. They are Bouda, Ganjam, Gajapati and Koraput. For other districts of this zone, there is positive relationship between these two variables. These districts are Kalahandi, Kandhamal, Malkanagiri, Nabarangpur, Nuapada and Rayagada.
- NOT: For only two districts in the southern zone, this regression coefficient is negative. The districts are Ganjam and Rayagada. Positive relationship between the two variables exists in the districts of Bouda, Gajapati, Kalahandi, Kandhamala, Koraput, Malkanagiri, Nabarangpur and Nuapada.
- NDDP: Dropout is negatively related to NDDP in nine districts, except Nabarangpur. Probably, the slow growth of NDDP in Nabarangpur is the reason for this exception.
- FLR: Dropout is negatively related to female literacy rate (FLR) in majority of the districts in the southern zone. These are Bouda, Ganjam, Kalahandi, Kandhamal, Koraput, Malkanagiri, Nabarangpur and Nuapada. The exception of having positive relationship is associated with the districts of Gajapati and Rayagada.
- Rural population: Rural population and dropout rate is negatively related only in two districts of Gajapati and Rayagada. For other districts, it is positively related.

Higher R^2 value of more than 0.70 is associated with the districts of Bouda, Ganjam, Gajapati, Kalahandi, Kandhamal, Koraput and Rayagada. For other districts of the southern zone, it is less than 0.70. The regression coefficients are significant for the district of Koraput and partially for the districts of Gajapati and Kandhamal. The female literacy, rural population and independent variables are significant in most of the districts.

Model II

Overall Situation in Odisha

- Dropout is positively related with three variables—number of schools, number of teachers and rural population; but negatively related with only NDDP and female literacy rate.
- The absolute value of female literacy rate is the highest, followed by NDDP. This means female literacy has greater impact on the dropout situation.
- All the five variables taken together explain 0.48 per cent of variation in the dependent variable, which is not very satisfactory.
- None of the variables qualify the significance test. This implies that some other variables are required to be included in the model to explain behaviour of the dependent variable.
- This signifies that as many of the assumed variables are not showing the desired signs, fall in the dropout rate is probably due to none of the education provisioning variables like number of schools or number of teachers. But it is more due to general improvement in the awareness of families with regard to the need for education.

Table 25.3

Regression Results in Explaining Dropout Rate in Odisha
Dependent Variable Rate

R-square-0.48

Variables	*Coefficient*	*Std. Error*	*t-ratio*	*p-value*
const	-1.03E+09	5.85E+09	-0.1756	0.8768
Number of schools	1.28518	93.7951	0.0137	0.99031
Number of Teacher	7.44031	14.6573	0.5076	0.66216
NDDP	-0.174573	0.711111	-0.2455	0.82897
Female literacy rate	-2.19E+07	1.24E+08	-0.1763	0.8763
Rural population	68.4632	389.106	0.1759	0.87654

Source: Computed.

Suggestions for Policy Making

There is no denying that student dropout rates are a major social and economic problem in the state of Odisha. The burden of uneducated children is costly not only for the individual, but also for the entire society. In order to prevent dropouts and encourage drop-in, education policy should focus on measures to counter the disadvantages that pupils face, particularly of the weaker sections. Some suggestions are given below for effective policy making within the state and eliminate regional difference in the dropout situation.

- It is observed that in each of the three revenue divisions of the state, one or two districts adhere to the assumed pattern and all others show it differently. This means the dependent and independent variables have wide fluctuations without any particular trend.
- In case of the number of schools, there exists confusion regarding all–India pattern and the pattern followed in Odisha. Due to massive reorganisation there is no authentic count of the number of the schools.
- In case of the number of teachers, there is large–scale vacancy for the regular teachers because of retirement. Ischia Sahara appointment is mostly done in times of approaching election and when the government wants to take political mileage out of this exercise.
- The exercise clearly establishes the advantage of female literacy in the state. This suggests the more girl child oriented policies need to be undertaken to improve female literacy.
- The uneven situation in explaining dropout rate among the different district calls for further research into the matter. Some variables included in the model are Census data which is not do not reflect true ground time-series pattern. Hence, the same needs to be changed for deriving meaningful conclusion.

References

Basumatary, Rupon (2012). "School Dropout across Indian States and UTs: An Econometric Study", *International Research Journal of Social Sciences* 1(4): 28-35.

FAITH (2009). *Study of Dropout Rates of School Children in Punjab.* New Delhi: Faith Healthcare Private Ltd and Consulting Engineering Services (I) Ltd.

Government of Odisha (2009). *State Plan of Action for Children 2009-12.* Bhubaneswar: Department of Woman and Child Development.

————. (2013). *Economic Survey (2013-14).* Bhubaneswar: Planning and Coordination Department.

————. (various years). *Districts at a Glance.* Odisha, Bhubaneswar: Directorate of Economics and Statistics.

Govindaraju, R. and S.Venkatesan (2010). "A Study on School Drop-outs in Rural Settings", J. *Psychology* 1 (1):47-53.

Jalan, J. and E. Glinskaya (n.d.). *Improving Primary School Education in India: An Impact Assessment of DPEP I.*

Mehta, Arun C. (2005). *Dropout Rate at Primary Level: A Note Based on DISE 2003-04 and 2004-05 Data.* New Delhi: National University of Educational Planning and Administration and Department.

NSSO (1998). *Attending on Educational Institutions in India: Its Level, Nature and Cost.* NSS 52nd Round, 1995-96. Department of Statistics, Government of India.

————. (2005). *Unit Level Records on Seventh Quinquennial Survey on Employment and Unemployment in India 2004-05.* NSS 61st Round July 2004-June 2005. Government of India.

NUEPA (2013). *Elementary Education in India: Progress towards UEE, DISE 2011-12.* New Delhi: National University of Educational Planning and Administration and Department of School Education and Literacy, Government of India.

Panda, B.K. (2012). "Participation in Schooling and Household Work: A Study of Scheduled Caste Girls in Mewat District of Haryana", *NUEPA Occasional Paper* 39.

Patra, Ritwik (2005). *A Collection of Case Studies of Good Practices Adopted by States for Different Categories of Out-Of-School Children Under AIE Component of Sarva Shiksha Abhiyan.* New Delhi: CYBERART Information Pvt. Ltd.

PROBE (1999). *Public Report on Basic Education in India.* Probe Team and Oxford University.

Programme Evaluation Organisation (2010). *Evaluation Report on Sarva Shiksha Abhiyan.* New Delhi: Planning Commission Government of India.

Smink, Jay and Mary Reimer (2013). *Rural School Dropout Issues Implications for Dropout Prevention: Strategies and Programs.* A Publication of the National Dropout Prevention Center/Network.

TNS India (2013). *Survey for Assessment of Dropout Rates at Elementary Level in 21 States.* New Delhi .

UNESCO (1984). *Towards Universalization of Primary Education in Asia and the Pacific: The Drop Out Problem in Primary Education, Some Case Studies.*

Vaswani, L.K. (2012). *Cohort Dropout Study and the Issue of Out of School Children.* Bhubaneswar: KIIT School of Rural Management, KIIT University.

Websites:

All India Indo-Asian News Service, 2013. IANS India Pvt Ltd, Noida, U.P.

DISE, District Information System for Education, State Report Cards, NUEPA, *http://www.dise.in/src.htm*

DISE, District Information System on Education, Retrieved from *http://www.opepa.in/website/DISE.aspx* (accessed on 7 December 2012).

Annexure Table A-25.1

Regression Results

Central Zone

Independent variable	*Coefficient*	*Std. Error*	*t-ratio*	*p-value*
Baleswar (R^2=0.73)				
const	-1.84E+07	1.14E+08	-0.1615	0.88654
Number of schools	9.05794	38.0606	0.238	0.83405
Teacher	3.67209	7.04921	0.5209	0.65436
NDDP	-0.208231	0.361677	-0.5757	0.62294
Female literacy rate	-651418	4.16E+06	-0.1568	0.88982
Rural population	31.7214	200.361	0.1583	0.88874
Bhadrak (R^2=0.67)				
const	9.75E+07	8.16E+07	1.1946	0.35471
Number of schools	49.9545	148.003	0.3375	0.76786
Teachers	7.41878	8.21969	0.9026	0.46202
NDDP	-0.105485	0.299355	-0.3524	0.75822
Female literacy rate	1.91E+06	1.60E+06	1.1925	0.35537
Rural population	-183.77	154.01	-1.1932	0.35513
Cuttack (R^2=0.86)				
const	6.93E+07	8.72E+07	0.7953	0.50985
Number of schools	-57.9536	50.4936	-1.1477	0.36984
Teachers	0.140556	7.43737	0.0189	0.98664
NDDP	0.0257539	0.149345	0.1724	0.87896
Female literacy rate	1.26E+06	1.61E+06	0.781	0.51659
Rural population	-89.5932	113.908	-0.7865	0.51395
Jagatsinghpur (R^2=0.72)				
const	-3.06E+07	7.91E+07	-0.3871	0.73596
Number of schools	-9.24106	25.1889	-0.3669	0.7489
Teachers	-1.35575	4.36181	-0.3108	0.78534
NDDP	-0.014762	0.140403	-0.1051	0.92586
Female literacy rate	-383294	979646	-0.3913	0.73336
Rural population	60.2785	154.868	0.3892	0.73464
Jajpur (R^2=0.60)				
const	-1.90E+07	1.40E+08	-0.1362	0.9041
Number of schools	-22.7104	74.4858	-0.3049	0.78925
Teachers	-1.31559	10.146	-0.1297	0.9087
NDDP	0.0360247	0.248717	0.1448	0.89811
Female literacy rate	-280201	2.01E+06	-0.1394	0.90189
Rural population	23.417	169.583	0.1381	0.90282

contd...

Kendrapada (R^2=0.82)				
const	4.67E+07	6.00E+07	0.7786	0.5177
Number of schools	-55.7925	93.0462	-0.5996	0.60964
Teachers	5.2202	8.69788	0.6002	0.60934
NDDP	0.712362	0.597691	1.1919	0.35557
Female literacy rate	1.02E+06	1.39E+06	0.7336	0.53951
Rural population	-93.9514	125.128	-0.7508	0.53107
Khordha (R^2=0.68)				
const	1.63E+07	1.02E+08	0.1591	0.88824
Number of schools	-21.4552	48.7677	-0.4399	0.70295
Teachers	5.3686	6.86625	0.7819	0.51615
NDDP	0.154684	0.299787	0.516	0.65725
Female literacy rate	299785	2.19E+06	0.1367	0.90381
Rural population	-35.0617	240.888	-0.1456	0.89762
Mayurbhanja (R^2=0.63)				
const	-5.12E+08	5.32E+08	-0.9624	0.4374
Number of schools	37.0018	126.446	0.2926	0.79737
Teachers	-15.4892	46.3618	-0.3341	0.77009
NDDP	-0.128653	0.562216	-0.2288	0.84027
Female literacy rate	-6.66E+06	6.88E+06	-0.9671	0.43553
Rural population	370.773	384.711	0.9638	0.43685
Nayagarh (R^2=0.63)				
const	1.92E+08	3.81E+08	0.5038	0.66442
Number of schools	-32.6517	129.692	-0.2518	0.82473
Teachers	2.92222	23.7237	0.1232	0.91323
NDDP	0.414758	1.49038	0.2783	0.80692
Female literacy rate	1.27E+06	2.54E+06	0.5013	0.6659
Rural population	-321.225	638.539	-0.5031	0.66485
Puri (R2=0.95)				
const	6.75E+07	2.21E+07	3.0554	0.0925
Number of schools	167.189	52.3511	3.1936	0.08564
Teachers	-9.97041	2.95675	-3.3721	0.07782
NDDP	0.623527	0.222297	2.8049	0.10707
Female literacy rate	1.97E+06	653437	3.0201	0.09437
Rural population	-155.298	51.2044	-3.0329	0.09369

contd...

Northern Zone

Independent variable	*Coefficient*	*Std. Error*	*t-ratio*	*p-value*
Angul (R^2= 0.78)				
const	-2.24E+08	1.29E+08	-1.7389	0.22418
Number of schools	-19.0559	55.1468	-0.3455	0.76264
Teachers	4.05019	2.80927	1.4417	0.28612
NDDP	0.0270389	0.0843785	0.3204	0.77901
Female literacy rate	-2.52E+06	1.45E+06	-1.7394	0.22409
Rural population	372.594	214.205	1.7394	0.22409
Balangir (R^2= 0.67)				
const	-4.43E+07	5.25E+07	-0.8447	0.48723
Number of schools	74.9321	86.8431	0.8628	0.47916
Teachers	-7.25822	9.91437	-0.7321	0.54028
NDDP	-0.46955	0.510992	-0.9189	0.45515
Female literacy rate	-1.88E+06	2.23E+06	-0.8401	0.48926
Rural population	99.6765	118.388	0.8419	0.48845
Bargarh (R^2= 0.67)				
const	-1.67E+08	3.00E+08	-0.556	0.6341
Number of schools	39.6123	53.8164	0.7361	0.53831
Teachers	5.76133	9.8408	0.5855	0.6175
NDDP	0.307405	0.378705	0.8117	0.5022
Female literacy rate	-1.02E+06	1.81E+06	-0.5606	0.63147
Rural population	174.994	314.187	0.557	0.63356
Denkanal (R^2=0.98)				
const	1.74E+08	2.75E+07	6.3048	0.02425
Number of schools	-23.0101	14.4011	-1.5978	0.25118
Teachers	16.2676	3.14363	5.1748	0.03537
NDDP	0.31637	0.104723	3.021	0.09432
Female literacy rate	2.18E+06	346519	6.2888	0.02437
Rural population	-309.348	49.1183	-6.298	0.0243
Deogarh (R^2=0.91)				
const	3.65E+07	1.85E+07	1.9664	0.18816
Number of schools	52.8567	26.1715	2.0196	0.18086
Teachers	12.0119	3.91364	3.0692	0.09178
NDDP	0.769815	0.299042	2.5743	0.12355
Female literacy rate	579519	297641	1.947	0.1909

contd...

Rural population	-252.268	128.791	-1.9587	0.18924
Jharsuguda (R^2=0.47)				
const	-1.16E+09	4.22E+09	-0.2737	0.80999
Number of schools	32.2516	94.1973	0.3424	0.7647
Teachers	2.75356	8.45767	0.3256	0.77566
NDDP	0.117411	0.354839	0.3309	0.77218
Female literacy rate	-1.22E+07	4.45E+07	-0.2738	0.80994
Rural population	5797.93	21181.4	0.2737	0.80997
Keunjhara (R^2=0.69)				
const	1.09E+08	5.34E+07	2.0468	0.17728
Number of schools	7.61594	38.9697	0.1954	0.86311
Teachers	2.53679	10.1017	0.2511	0.82516
NDDP	0.0388853	0.0958384	0.4057	0.72423
Female literacy rate	3.47E+06	1.69E+06	2.0529	0.17649
Rural population	-201.281	98.1616	-2.0505	0.1768
Sambalpur (R^2= 0.36)				
const	-1.41E+08	3.33E+08	-0.422	0.71405
Number of schools	14.5609	57.1324	0.2549	0.82264
Teachers	7.78277	22.4714	0.3463	0.76213
NDDP	-0.515044	0.687832	-0.7488	0.53207
Female literacy rate	-1.15E+06	2.75E+06	-0.418	0.71658
Rural population	298.435	709.247	0.4208	0.71482
Subarnapur (R^2=0.59)				
const	5.61E+06	5.36E+07	0.1046	0.92627
Number of schools	-5.02187	24.639	-0.2038	0.85735
Teachers	3.12748	5.16079	0.606	0.60613
NDDP	0.00813813	0.293009	0.0278	0.98036
Female literacy rate	57002.9	556124	0.1025	0.92771
Rural population	-16.5354	159.221	-0.1039	0.92676
Sundaragarh (R^2=0.60)				
const	-3.92E+07	1.08E+08	-0.3647	0.75031
Number of schools	41.4453	87.1642	0.4755	0.68131
Teachers	4.8448	12.5027	0.3875	0.73574
NDDP	-0.0697707	0.174137	-0.4007	0.72742
Female literacy rate	-1.17E+06	3.23E+06	-0.3622	0.75188
Rural population	85.3436	235.179	0.3629	0.75145

contd...

Southern Zone

Independent variable	*Coefficient*	*Std. Error*	*t-ratio*	*p-value*
Bouda (R^2=0.70)				
const	-3.86E+07	4.72E+07	-0.8159	0.50026
Number of schools	-57.8953	58.1382	-0.9958	0.42426
Teachers	8.95706	9.59875	0.9331	0.44925
NDDP	-0.566905	0.39898	-1.4209	0.29123
Female literacy rate	-556465	688516	-0.8082	0.50382
Rural population	170.908	210.061	0.8136	0.50133
Ganjam (R^2=0.70)				
const	-1.23E+09	1.30E+09	-0.9423	0.4455
Number of schools	-2.2057	131.473	-0.0168	0.98814
Teachers	-11.3668	28.0811	-0.4048	0.72482
NDDP	-0.373425	0.859704	-0.4344	0.70639
Female literacy rate	-6.96E+06	7.39E+06	-0.9421	0.4456
Rural population	598.117	634.621	0.9425	0.44543
Gajapati (R^2=0.78)				
const	1.34E+08	8.18E+07	1.6426	0.24217
Number of schools	-13.3064	12.0779	-1.1017	0.38544
Teachers	11.5611	5.38954	2.1451	0.16511
NDDP	-0.0294032	0.203177	-0.1447	0.8982
Female literacy rate	1.01E+06	612396	1.6457	0.24156
Rural population	-350.772	213.497	-1.643	0.2421
Kalahandi(R^2=0.88)				
const	-1.50E+07	3.90E+07	-0.3842	0.73781
Number of schools	20.408	32.7055	0.624	0.59632
Teachers	6.36092	4.87238	1.3055	0.3217
NDDP	-0.389319	0.119828	-3.249	0.0831
Female literacy rate	-215518	584219	-0.3689	0.74759
Rural population	17.2793	45.5708	0.3792	0.74103
Kandhamala (R^2=0.94)				
const	-9.66E+07	3.23E+07	-2.9922	0.0959
Number of schools	72.0035	19.7361	3.6483	0.0676
Teachers	2.56677	1.76343	1.4556	0.28278
NDDP	-0.00823496	0.0351101	-0.2345	0.83639
Female literacy rate	-742450	246672	-3.0099	0.09493

contd...

Rural population	204.251	68.222	2.9939	0.0958
Koraput (R^2=0.86)				
const	-6.86E+08	2.25E+08	-3.0467	0.09295
Number of schools	-172.829	66.6658	-2.5925	0.12212
Teachers	40.0579	18.5209	2.1628	0.16304
NDDP	-2.21011	0.758079	-2.9154	0.10027
Female literacy rate	-1.25E+07	4.12E+06	-3.0458	0.093
Rural population	1015.38	333.274	3.0467	0.09295
Malakanagiri (R^2=0.43)				
const	-2.80E+09	6.87E+09	-0.408	0.72283
Number of schools	23.6769	88.6114	0.2672	0.81435
Teachers	0.545587	26.4771	0.0206	0.98543
NDDP	-0.55402	0.916556	-0.6045	0.60698
Female literacy rate	-4.43E+07	1.09E+08	-0.408	0.72284
Rural population	7978.4	19556.6	0.408	0.72283
Nabarangpur (R^2=0.37)				
const	-1.11E+08	3.30E+08	-0.3365	0.76851
Number of schools	4.22173	335.713	0.0126	0.99111
Teachers	19.2203	45.1822	0.4254	0.71195
NDDP	0.114086	3.3093	0.0345	0.97563
Female literacy rate	-1.73E+06	5.10E+06	-0.3386	0.76713
Rural population	152.523	452.429	0.3371	0.76812
Nuapada (R^2=0.31)				
const	-3.58E+07	1.86E+08	-0.1926	0.86505
Number of schools	63.672	156.635	0.4065	0.72375
Teachers	11.62	24.5958	0.4724	0.68315
NDDP	-0.255907	0.974545	-0.2626	0.81744
Female literacy rate	-364913	1.88E+06	-0.1936	0.86434
Rural population	90.3229	468.942	0.1926	0.86505
Rayagada (R^2=0.72)				
const	1.93E+08	1.29E+08	1.4949	0.27356
Number of schools	45.4338	57.6813	0.7877	0.51342
Teachers	-0.497459	10.8861	-0.0457	0.9677
NDDP	-0.478481	0.447456	-1.0693	0.39687
Female literacy rate	2.52E+06	1.68E+06	1.4989	0.27264
Rural population	-354.909	237.27	-1.4958	0.27335

Annexure Table A-25.2

A. District–wise Dropout Data from 2002-03 to 2011-12

Sl. No	District	2002-03	2003-04	2004-05	2005-06	2006-07	2007-08	2008-09	2009-10	2010-11	2011-12
		1	2	3	4	5	6	7	8	9	10
1	Angul	37990	10486	7136	10422	14092	7248	7490	6704	1345	77
2	Balasore	35799	18471	12645	39311	30987	16287	8104	5813	207	297
3	Baragarh	25598	7684	6183	12022	7486	7988	2196	4425	3045	1332
4	Bhadrak	32416	8291	5845	15910	16680	11690	6221	4538	830	185
5	Bolangir	38876	11408	8945	22244	36340	10793	6954	4994	472	326
6	Boudh	6564	3774	3147	14809	6519	3543	2289	1817	190	90
7	Cuttack	42817	16532	11392	12270	11718	4382	4382	844	913	187
8	Deogarh	7746	2320	2122	2653	2021	1669	2650	2147	1305	835
9	Dhenkanal	30152	3100	2557	14946	5554	3353	3938	2317	209	107
10	Gajapati	14040	10050	8223	14113	11530	13552	12367	5406	909	821
11	Ganjam	160630	38511	30425	77814	63546	15855	21422	3529	548	920
12	Jagatsinghpur	16903	6737	4127	4960	5443	2850	2471	1493	355	52
13	Jajpur	30311	11028	7823	15550	8245	7747	6483	4462	783	206
14	Jharsuguda	12639	3563	2224	3363	5713	2745	2295	1680	124	157
15	Kalahandi	22546	23675	16102	33654	29425	21613	17142	12858	5155	1039
16	Kandhamal	12320	9095	7124	14968	5475	5251	5155	6148	1561	853
17	Kendrapara	33454	9139	6323	7803	4169	5940	6727	4122	265	170

contd...

contd...

18	Keonjhar	34477	8823	6203	27409	33869	22128	20856	17948	10735	1521
19	Khurdha	39059	10866	7124	14859	10461	10211	6652	5493	595	372
20	Koraput	53592	12951	9956	32815	41642	24760	9056	7783	4908	3724
21	Malkangiri	27485	10932	9924	21317	17402	18235	14263	4732	2519	2170
22	Mayurbhanj	80444	19553	14423	50406	16410	36081	23948	22642	16351	5019
23	Nawarangpur	66558	15246	13114	41227	39264	19842	15132	12586	2056	2165
24	Nayagarh	36757	9936	6324	10252	5978	4207	3106	1989	278	189
25	Nuapada	24185	1622	1573	20480	10502	11371	8787	7748	2201	695
26	Puri	28271	11165	9263	8022	12454	3191	3079	1097	433	327
27	Rayagada	16324	7311	5115	25357	34039	30273	29917	18985	8190	4319
28	Sambalpur	12276	4434	2920	12797	26349	6872	5417	3344	1647	169
29	Sonepur	7410	3122	2844	4749	2928	2583	2633	2245	296	239
30	Sundergarh	57187	6654	5723	16788	21600	18443	9651	6949	3623	2028
	Total	1044826	316479	236849	603290	537841	350703	270783	186838	72048	30591

Source: Director, Odisha Primary Education Promotion Authority (for different years), Bhubaneswar.

B. District-wise Number of Schools in Odisha from 2002-03 to 2009-10

Sl. No	*District*	2002-03	2003-04	2004-05	2005-06	2006-07	2007-08	2008-09	2009-10	2010-11	2011-12
		1	*2*	*3*	*4*	*5*	*6*	*7*	*8*	*9*	*10*
1	Angul	1568	1568	1798	1824	1962	2045	1968	2014	2079	2252
2	Balasore	2729	2729	2982	3021	2741	3334	3166	3205	3298	3588
3	Baragarh	1844	1844	2018	2122	2462	2252	2301	2318	2335	2528
4	Bhadrak	1766	1766	1928	1949	1982	2096	2185	2274	2536	2483
5	Bolangir	2347	2347	2542	2393	2690	2854	2891	2923	3200	3227
6	Boudh	682	682	875	872	896	945	995	1033	1025	1132
7	Cuttack	2827	2827	3089	2925	2990	3009	2969	2992	2996	3448
8	Deogarh	532	532	629	636	702	730	747	781	780	860
9	Dhenkanal	1339	1339	1681	1740	1777	1848	1879	1895	1918	2084
10	Gajapati	1041	1041	1459	1498	1467	1618	1629	1692	1733	1827
11	Ganjam	3578	3578	4226	4260	4546	4542	4401	4496	4904	5056
12	Jagatsinghpur	1606	1606	1776	1796	1548	1708	1737	1814	1826	2099
13	Jajpur	2165	2165	2503	2511	2592	2613	2673	2767	2810	3054
14	Jharsuguda	808	808	843	861	916	1001	928	942	947	1083
15	Kalahandi	2061	2061	2190	2314	2357	2678	2687	2799	2995	3232
16	Kandhamal	1764	1764	1921	2026	2060	2111	2218	2324	2527	2616
17	Kendrapara	2040	2040	2217	2224	2369	2367	2370	2411	2403	2627
18	Keonjhar	2439	2439	2817	2818	2891	3103	3071	2997	3211	3476

contd...

contd...

19	Khurdha	1625	1625	2064	2043	1966	1996	1902	1944	1983	2663
20	Koraput	2112	2112	2549	2543	2569	2974	2937	3001	3078	3394
21	Malkangiri	1006	1006	1252	1232	1258	1451	1581	1603	1607	1768
22	Mayurbhanj	3767	3767	4097	4092	4477	4514	4645	4802	4988	5465
23	Nawarangpur	1450	1450	1644	1653	1835	2094	2261	2290	2461	2569
24	Nayagarh	1067	1067	1289	1321	1428	1470	1507	1521	1682	1635
25	Nuapada	935	935	1071	1128	1121	1261	1357	1439	1445	1554
26	Puri	1977	1977	2152	2343	2416	2436	2477	2511	2526	2785
27	Rayagada	1670	1670	2017	2012	2089	2211	2160	2245	2364	2715
28	Sambalpur	1274	1274	1596	1695	1701	1790	1900	1850	1724	2021
29	Sonepur	946	946	1161	1172	1211	1260	1215	1220	1221	1334
30	Sundergarh	2649	2649	2685	2603	3025	3251	3376	3434	3441	3770
	Total	53614	53614	61071	61627	64044	67562	68133	69537	72043	78345

Source: Directorate of Economics & Statistics, GoO.

C. District–wise Number of Teachers in Odisha from 2002-03 to 2009-10

Sl. No	*District*	*2002-03*	*2003-04*	*2004-05*	*2005-06*	*2006-07*	*2007-08*	*2008-09*	*2009-10*	*2010-11*	*2011-12*
		1	*2*	*3*	*4*	*5*	*6*	*7*	*8*	*9*	*10*
1	Angul	3810	3649	3914	5003	9714	5572	6066	4834	5133	5443
2	Balasore	6438	6178	6287	8150	11993	9950	10845	8607	9128	9883
3	Baragarh	4179	4165	4160	5109	4841	5422	5891	5383	5351	5960
4	Bhadrak	4386	3896	4257	5322	4635	5252	6649	5977	6675	6967
5	Bolangir	5585	5830	5603	5772	4744	7049	7008	6211	6786	7537
6	Boudh	1390	1482	1943	2193	2054	2510	2371	2189	2230	2502
7	Cuttack	7293	7627	7190	8583	7801	8938	9381	8226	8579	9348
8	Deogarh	1255	1120	1073	1533	1315	1786	1968	1841	1784	1925
9	Dhenkanal	3645	3330	3854	4804	4126	4675	5026	4613	3811	5658
10	Gajapati	1826	2460	2659	3227	2664	3753	3788	3330	3541	3795
11	Ganjam	8665	10102	9690	10674	10060	12058	12240	10528	13489	13861
12	Jagatsinghpur	3035	3593	3631	5030	3724	4349	4492	4185	5124	5251
13	Jajpur	5525	6909	5729	7161	5928	8111	8918	6451	7260	7847
14	Jharsuguda	2279	2211	1557	2426	1880	2704	2325	1998	2137	2420
15	Kalahandi	5084	5053	4821	5969	5242	5844	6802	6361	6609	7178
16	Kandhamal	3728	3679	3776	4791	4457	5277	5849	5011	5271	5596
17	Kendrapara	4420	4079	4717	5483	8066	6008	6199	5951	5755	6600
18	Keonjhar	5638	6052	6086	6951	6177	7316	8455	6574	6862	7488

contd...

contd...

19	Khurdha	4167	3976	4822	6689	5006	6274	6255	5279	5630	6292
20	Koraput	4794	4687	4921	5636	5122	5643	6771	6219	6469	6388
21	Malkangiri	2106	2316	2118	2612	2280	2953	3329	3007	3294	3171
22	Mayurbhanj	7980	7657	8915	10002	9823	10121	11787	12149	12061	13893
23	Nawarangpur	2755	3012	2811	4111	3758	4858	5437	4776	5212	5266
24	Nayagarh	2045	2555	2879	3832	3343	4100	4468	4252	4138	4556
25	Nuapada	2231	2242	2303	2936	2744	2781	3593	3194	3316	3372
26	Puri	4369	4706	5005	6345	5100	6709	6958	6095	6584	7094
27	Rayagada	3103	3133	3764	4792	4066	5167	5883	5496	5698	5143
28	Sambalpur	2994	3179	3227	4028	3548	4459	5375	4246	4210	4428
29	Sonepur	1973	1904	2121	2364	2162	2715	2722	2521	2594	2733
30	Sundergarh	8750	7237	5787	6600	6564	8333	9883	7842	8570	8931
	Total	125448	128019	129620	158128	152937	170687	186734	163346	173301	186526

Source: Directorate of Economics & Statistics, GoO.

D. District–wise Net District Domestic Product (NDDP) since 2001-02 to 2009-10

SL No	*District*	*2001-02*	*2002-03*	*2003-04*	*2004-05*	*2005-06*	*2006-07*	*2007-08*	*2008-09*	*2009-10*
1	Anugul	240139	271092	347251	446350	448021	525946	659879	783547	723330
2	Baleswar	183676	197227	234953	283124	299407	358836	458407	519912	566044
3	Baragrah	138173	133083	153174	181903	194331	227914	288647	332109	360631
4	Bhadrak	103413	120201	144644	167872	183137	212192	265620	302625	350044
5	Bolangir	135304	137538	175613	220378	241047	286458	372184	411106	477556
6	Bouda	38632	42279	53961	59643	68121	80198	104207	111462	127348
7	Cuttack	306891	333378	382321	513335	537538	631780	764416	873141	979552
8	Deograh	33098	28710	36737	43898	49498	57902	69750	78811	90672
9	Dhenkanal	111210	119281	148790	179645	197516	232814	297045	324949	367244
10	Gajapati	53817	58726	71543	86831	92147	108716	135383	153584	174671
11	Ganjam	321095	330785	393833	501033	547684	655984	802594	922694	1063765
12	Jagatsinghapur	124089	146354	163751	209035	217548	268560	332087	385918	372410
13	Jajpur	144751	163382	197891	288344	324540	390886	500889	576030	529635
14	Jharsuguda	112308	115625	140508	183708	198371	227853	283270	346862	364868
15	Kalahandi	126824	123314	156774	186241	208193	233761	311327	356873	403786
16	Kandhamala	82938	95651	115144	164293	177711	216151	278634	313148	399578
17	Kendrapara	101751	110056	130309	162079	175901	197176	244173	272408	311058
18	Kenojhara	177106	206510	326049	411949	481720	587669	867604	1027378	953502
19	Khordha	300468	321168	375014	472595	527327	639496	749536	871262	952477

contd...

contd...

20	Koraput	149556	152424	184413	223391	243841	303805	362324	405635	457492
21	Malkangiri	47848	49147	61333	74454	76207	91768	116530	121069	136843
22	Mayurbhanja	194074	207689	255255	307231	330107	388824	501156	558205	613701
23	Nabarangapur	84734	86376	97014	124219	130001	157020	185794	208285	237566
24	Nayagrah	69827	72219	90216	104937	114867	135056	162245	175728	202614
25	Nuapada	56323	51564	65168	76567	82241	98795	129408	138301	156642
26	Puri	143352	158942	190787	217806	239926	253029	305980	342794	400872
27	Rayagada	87951	94070	116646	140657	152657	187596	238004	262881	289558
28	Sambalpur	138584	136476	163766	218114	240113	285120	354391	413505	428865
29	Subarnapur	45463	48329	56992	69946	78125	93308	118724	129703	160233
30	Sunderagada	247187	271878	343472	479123	497114	657512	850716	1031694	931123
	Total	4100580	4383475	5373321	6798702	7354959	8792126	11110925	12751620	13583679

Source: *Economic Survey*, Planning & Coordination Department, Bhubaneswar.

E. District–wise Percentage of Female Literacy Rate (FLR) from 2001 to 2011

SL No	District	2001	2002	2003	2004	2005	2006	2007	2008	2009	2010	2011
1	Anugul	56.01	57.273	58.536	59.8	61.062	62.325	63.588	64.851	66.114	67.377	68.64
2	Baleswar	59.6	60.841	62.112	63.38	64.654	65.925	67.196	68.467	69.738	71.009	72.28
3	Baragrah	50.03	51.565	53.1	54.64	56.17	57.705	59.24	60.775	62.31	63.845	65.38
4	Bhadrak	63.62	64.841	66.062	67.28	68.504	69.725	70.946	72.167	73.388	74.609	75.83
5	Bolangir	39.27	40.693	42.116	43.54	44.962	46.385	47.808	49.231	50.654	52.077	53.5
6	Bouda	39.78	41.781	43.782	45.78	47.784	49.785	51.786	53.787	55.788	57.789	59.79
7	Cuttack	66.19	67.526	68.862	70.2	71.534	72.87	74.206	75.542	76.878	78.214	79.55
8	Deograh	47.56	49.109	50.658	52.21	53.756	55.305	56.854	58.403	59.952	61.501	63.05
9	Dhenkanal	58.55	59.977	61.404	62.83	64.258	65.685	67.112	68.539	69.966	71.393	72.82
10	Gajapati	28.91	30.337	31.764	33.19	34.618	36.045	37.472	38.899	40.326	41.753	43.18
11	Ganjam	47.7	49.043	50.386	51.73	53.072	54.415	55.758	57.101	58.444	59.787	61.13
12	Jagatsinghapur	69.94	71.009	72.078	73.15	74.216	75.285	76.354	77.423	78.492	79.561	80.63
13	Jajpur	61.45	62.634	63.818	65	66.186	67.37	68.554	69.738	70.922	72.106	73.29
14	Jharsuguda	59.23	60.38	61.53	62.68	63.83	64.98	66.13	67.28	68.43	69.58	70.73
15	Kalahandi	29.56	31.272	32.984	34.7	36.408	38.12	39.832	41.544	43.256	44.968	46.68
16	Kandhamala	36.19	37.765	39.34	40.92	42.49	44.065	45.64	47.215	48.79	50.365	51.94
17	Kendrapara	67.29	68.457	69.624	70.79	71.958	73.125	74.292	75.459	76.626	77.793	78.96
18	Kenojhara	46.71	47.867	49.024	50.18	51.338	52.495	53.652	54.809	55.966	57.123	58.28
19	Khordha	71.06	72.115	73.17	74.23	75.28	76.335	77.39	78.445	79.5	80.555	81.61

contd...

contd...

20	Koraput	24.81	26.184	27.558	28.93	30.306	31.68	33.054	34.428	35.802	37.176	38.55
21	Malkangiri	21.28	22.98	24.68	26.38	28.08	29.78	31.48	33.18	34.88	36.58	38.28
22	Mayurbhanja	38.28	39.723	41.166	42.61	44.052	45.495	46.938	48.381	49.824	51.267	52.71
23	Nabarangapur	21.02	22.498	23.976	25.45	26.932	28.41	29.888	31.366	32.844	34.322	35.8
24	Nayagrah	58.1	59.495	60.89	62.29	63.68	65.075	66.47	67.865	69.26	70.655	72.05
25	Nuapada	26.01	27.885	29.76	31.64	33.51	35.385	37.26	39.135	41.01	42.885	44.76
26	Puri	67.8	68.848	69.896	70.94	71.992	73.04	74.088	75.136	76.184	77.232	78.28
27	Rayagada	24.31	25.798	27.286	28.77	30.262	31.75	33.238	34.726	36.214	37.702	39.19
28	Sambalpur	54.79	56.104	57.418	58.73	60.046	61.36	62.674	63.988	65.302	66.616	67.93
29	Subarnapur	47.28	48.956	50.632	52.31	53.984	55.66	57.336	59.012	60.688	62.364	64.04
30	Sunderagada	54.25	55.373	56.496	57.62	58.742	59.865	60.988	62.111	63.234	64.357	65.48
	Odisha	50.97	52.119	53.268	54.42	55.566	56.715	57.864	59.013	60.162	61.311	62.46

Source: Census Survey, 2001 and 2011.

F. District–wise Percentage of Rural Population since 2001 to 2011

SL No	*District*	*2001*	*2002*	*2003*	*2004*	*2005*	*2006*	*2007*	*2008*	*2009*	*2010*	*2011*
1	Anugul	981587	990128	998670	1007211	1015752	1024294	1032835	1041376	1049917	1058459	1067000
2	Baleswar	1804140	1830426	1856712	1882998	1909284	1935570	1961856	1988142	2014428	2040714	2067000
3	Baragrah	1242795	1251616	1260436	1269257	1278077	1286898	1295718	1304539	1313359	1322180	1331000
4	Bhadrak	1192678	1205410	1218142	1230875	1243607	1256339	1269071	1281803	1294536	1307268	1320000
5	Bolangir	1182871	1209784	1236697	1263610	1290523	1317436	1344348	1371261	1398174	1425087	1452000
6	Bouda	355347	361912	368478	375043	381608	388174	394739	401304	407869	414435	421000
7	Cuttack	1699964	1718768	1737571	1756375	1775178	1793982	1812786	1831589	1850393	1869196	1888000
8	Deograh	254012	257611	261210	264808	268407	272006	275605	279204	282802	286401	290000
9	Dhenkanal	973964	984068	994171	1004275	1014378	1024482	1034586	1044689	1054793	1064896	1075000
10	Gajapati	465949	470054	474159	478264	482369	486475	490580	494685	498790	502895	507000
11	Ganjam	2604276	2619948	2635621	2651293	2666966	2682638	2698310	2713983	2729655	2745328	2761000
12	Jagatsinghapur	953180	959962	966744	973526	980308	987090	993872	1000654	1007436	1014218	1021000
13	Jajpur	1551361	1565425	1579489	1593553	1607617	1621681	1635744	1649808	1663872	1677936	1692000
14	Jharsuguda	323831	326248	328665	331082	333499	335916	338332	340749	343166	345583	348000
15	Kalahandi	1235275	1257248	1279220	1301193	1323165	1345138	1367110	1389083	1411055	1433028	1455000
16	Kandhamala	604107	609796	615486	621175	626864	632554	638243	643932	649621	655311	661000
17	Kendrapara	1227868	1240781	1253694	1266608	1279521	1292434	1305347	1318260	1331174	1344087	1357000
18	Kenojhara	1348967	1368970	1388974	1408977	1428980	1448984	1468987	1488990	1508993	1528997	1549000
19	Khordha	1071689	1081220	1090751	1100282	1109813	1119345	1128876	1138407	1147938	1157469	1167000
20	Koraput	982188	999269	1016350	1033432	1050513	1067594	1084675	1101756	1118838	1135919	1153000

contd...

contd...

21	Malkangiri	469582	479024	488466	497907	507349	516791	526233	535675	545116	554558	564000
22	Mayurbhanja	2067756	2093680	2119605	2145529	2171454	2197378	2223302	2249227	2275151	2301076	2327000
23	Nabarangapur	966496	983146	999797	1016447	1033098	1049748	1066398	1083049	1099699	1116350	1133000
24	Nayagrah	827450	833005	838560	844115	849670	855225	860780	866335	871890	877445	883000
25	Nuapada	500652	508187	515722	523256	530791	538326	545861	553396	560930	568465	576000
26	Puri	1298654	1312189	1325723	1339258	1352792	1366327	1379862	1393396	1406931	1420465	1434000
27	Rayagada	715702	726232	736762	747291	757821	768351	778881	789411	799940	810470	821000
28	Sambalpur	681835	686952	692068	697185	702301	707418	712534	717651	722767	727884	733000
29	Subarnapur	501767	507590	513414	519237	525060	530884	536707	542530	548353	554177	560000
30	Sunderagada	1201479	1216831	1232183	1247535	1262887	1278240	1293592	1308944	1324296	1339648	1355000
	Odisha	31287422	31655480	32023538	32391595	32759653	33127711	33495769	33863827	34231884	34599942	34968000

Source: Census Survey, 2001 and 2011.

26

KRISHNA PRASAD MUKHERJEE

Midday Meal Scheme

Operational Issues, Gaps and Recommendations

Poverty, Human Capital and Midday Meal Scheme

Education and nutrition are non-negotiable factors in relation to human capital, which in turn is indispensable as far as growth of a nation is concerned. Extreme poverty can be figured out as the single most important factor as to why, poor households have to involve their children in earning in whatsoever manner. This results into non-attainment of elementary and thereby higher education; and finally they continue to be in the poverty trap. Access to education is an entitlement to citizens and a vital instrument to accelerate social change through qualitative enhancement of human capital. As stressed in the Millennium Development Goals (MDGs) by the United Nations (UN), all boys and girls should complete a full course of education by 2015 (Choudhury, 2006). Kingdon (1999), taking clue from the World Bank Report (1997) finds a positive association between female education and decline in fertility, infant as well as child mortality. Colclough (1982) indicated that labour productivity is positively associated to the amount of schooling received. He further stresses that, higher education raises cognitive development and also contributes to economic betterment. Rumberger (2001) finds that, school-dropouts are less likely to find and maintain quality jobs that pay them enough to keep them off public assistance. Even if dropouts find a job,they earns substantially less than high school graduates; and as a whole such high unemployment and low earnings translate into suboptimum production and low tax income, deteriorating overall economic health of the state. Choudhury (2006) observes that school dropouts in many ways, affects society negatively. Apart from involvement in crime, dropouts have poorer health, low rates of inter-generational mobility and lower rates of political participation. Therefore, target-oriented policy measures need to be put in place so that effective transition along the route of education, employability and poverty reduction may be achieved in a time bound manner.

Hati and Majumdar (2012) observes that India is doing better than most of the low income countries with respect to gross enrolment as well as school dropouts. But in respect of high income countries, we are lagging behind. Hundred per cent net enrolment coupled with less than 5 per cent dropout have been evident in case of high income countries; while the same in India, in 2009-10, were 89.5 per cent and 6.4 per cent respectively. Moreover, in case of West Bengal, although enrolment rate is almost comparable to that of national one, in the same reference period, dropout was found to be far worse with 19.6 per cent for boys and 15.4 per cent for girls. Jayachandran (2007) defines dropout as an estimation made from official statistics as ratio of enrolment in class V to that in class I. According to him, lack of interest of children as well as that of parents, inability to cope with academic demands, need to work for wages to supplement family income, and for girl-children to perform domestic duties appear to be the major reasons of dropout. Ramchandran and Saihjee (2002) have identified factors like income, caste, occupation and educational level of parents to be critical in respect of schooling, attendance, completion of education and from learning point of view. For West Bengal, factors like parental schooling, household income as well as occupation, caste and religion were found to be influential by Sengupta and Guha (2002).

Poverty directly impacts the nutritional requirement of an individual negatively and thereby impedes their physical and intellectual growth. Ramchandran *et al.* (2004) observed that malnutrition is rampant among children of poor households. Laxamaiah *et al.* (1999) pointed that, poverty not only results into poor nutritional status of children, but leads to higher dropout and less school enrolment. Lack of education, apart from many other adverse effects, affects personality development at later stage of life.

With a view to enhance enrolment, retention and attendance, as well as to improve the nutritional levels among children, the Government of India, in collaboration with State governments is running one primary and upper-primary level school-lunch programme, known as, Mid Day Meal Scheme (MDMS) in the country for last 18 years. MDMS was launched in 1995 with the aim of universalisation of primary education by increasing enrolment, retention, attendance, and simultaneously creating a positive impact on nutrition of the children concerned. MDMS has been to a considerable extent successful in containing abject hunger among children of the age group 6-14. Dreze and Goyal (2003) have termed the initiative as nutritionist's dream, as the initiative has potential to tackle illnesses due to protein or micronutrient deficiencies. Anyway, Dreze and Goyal (2003) opined that MDMS has potential beyond containing classroom hunger, and its scope of imparting nutrition education and personal hygiene are yet to be explored. According to them, MDMS can be visualised from three distinct perspectives: educational achievements, nutritional advancements and social equity.

Present Study

With a view to understand the operational and outcome issues related to MDMS, an evaluation study was conducted along coal mine dominated rural areas of Asansol subdivision, West Bengal, during January-May 2014. In this study, from 37 primary schools and Sishu Shiksha Kendra (SSKs), 370 students (exactly half being girls; and 41%, 24%, 12% and 8% of sample students belonged to SC [scheduled caste], ST [scheduled tribe], OBC [other backward class] and minority categories respectively) and equal number of parents (50% were women; representation of SC, ST, minority and OBC categories were respectively 48%, 19%, 10% and 7%) were part of the sample. Responses of teacher-in-charges of MDMS and cooks were also recorded. Evaluation system, if any, in respect of human capital status was also explored in this study.

MDMS and Social Equity

Many researchers have found that implementation of MDMS has narrowed down social distances in terms of caste, class and gender through sharing a common meal, at a common place and cooked by a common cook, who often belongs to the so called backward or Dalit class. This has directly impacted the enrolment, retention and attendance of the socially disadvantaged children positively. MDMS has also enabled parents of the weaker sections to participate in the process of schooling and nutrition of their children through 'Parent Teacher Association' or 'School Management Committee' or 'School Development and Monitoring Committees to a considerable extent. Dreze and Kingdon (2001) found that the provision of MDM has halved the proportion of girls being excluded from the schooling system. They figured out that MDMS has been meaningful to overcome social barriers and class prejudices prevalent in Indian society. Moreover, by facilitating to sit together to share a common meal irrespective of caste, gender and economic background, i.e., by instilling the feeling of sharing and togetherness at the budding age, the evils of feudal social norms have been successfully minimised without any so-called mass movement.

In the present study it was observed that, 96 per cent of the parents encourage their children to take MDM in schools, however, parents from general category and higher income group constitute a significant chunk of those who do not allow their children to take MDM. More than two third of the parents opined that, MDM has contributed to get the children more sociable. It was observed that 94 per cent of the students take MDM; while 91 per cent take it on regular basis, 92 per cent eat whatever they are offered. It was informed by 84 per cent of the institutes that more than 90 per cent students are taking MDM in schools, while 89 per cent reported that the students eat together. Similar trend has been reported for Tamil Nadu, where it has been noticed that MDM has been effective to overcome class and caste feeling among children (Khera, 2006). Also, Garg and Mandal (2013) have noticed that MDM intervention has positively influenced the participation of girl children both in terms of enrolment and attendance following 2005. i.e., after introduction of cooked MDM. Afridi (2005) further noticed that the socialisation benefits of MDMS have proved to be substantial; although there happens to be other side of the coin also. Two distinct forms of caste discriminations have been reported in respect of MDMS. First one being discrimination against children on the basis of their caste or religion; and discrimination against cooks being the other one. However, in the present study, it was observed that majority (84%) of the cooks belong to either SC (49%), ST (22%), minority (8%) and OBC (5%) category. Moreover, in one of the wildest attempt to discriminate school children on the basis of caste, plates were labelled with the initial of the children's cast in Bihar. In Rajasthan, children from Dalit communities had no right to water themselves, wherein children from other communities had. Also, Afridi (2005) makes an important observation that, a section of parents is dissatisfied with MDMS, as they feel that this initiative necessitates intermingling of children from different castes.

MDMS and Education Quality

Poverty leaves little alternative but to utilise the manual labour of children to supplement the household economy to ensure minimum sustenance. As older boys and girls are meaningful in labour market, dropout at those stages is quite common in poverty stricken regions. Ramchandran *et al.* (2000) underlined that school absenteeism is an outcome of poor economic condition of parents. Shiva Kumar (2003) indicates that the problem of child labour has its origin in economic as well as food insecurity of households; and therefore enrolment of children belonging to SCs and STs has increased following the implementation of MDMS. Parents of such financially disadvantaged households rate MDMS as an incentive, and therefore influential factor in relation to schooling decision of their children. As observed in the present study, 78 per cent of the parents consider MDM to be the most important contributing factor in respect of active participation in classroom and therefore better academic performances. Ninety-four (94) per cent of the teacher-in-charges consider the role of MDMS to be most influential in respect of increase in enrolment and rise in attendance level. Moreover, PROBE

(1999) found that although apparently no tuition fees are charged for schooling in Government schools, parents have to incur costs towards uniform, stationery and sometimes travel. Further, there should be no room for undermining the opportunity cost of sending children to schools for such households. In this context, free meal on regular basis, acts as a direct subsidy for parents (Garg and Mandal, 2013). Studies further found that the disadvantaged parents send their children at an early age so as to become entitled for free meal earlier. And this has brought down the average enrolment age to 5-6 years from 8-10 years. However, as per the present study, one fifth of the parents, chiefly from general and higher income category, opine that implementation of MDM affect teaching adversely.

MDMS and Nutrition

Garg and Mandal (2013) made an interesting observation that, in ST children, nutritional intake is more on a school day than on a holiday. For all other social strata including SC, OBC and General, the scenario is opposite. Though, in SC students, the gap between the two is extremely low. Another major issue is: whether MDM is a substitute or supplement for home food. Garg and Mandal (2013) have found that for the poorest households, MDM is a better substitute to home meal in terms of nutritional content. In the current study, as much as 74 per cent of the students reported that they eat before coming to school, 62 per cent do not eat after reaching home from school, before dinner; while 73 per cent ask for a second serving. Nevertheless, in case MDM acts as substitute, there remains a chance of negative nutritional impact, if it is suboptimum in terms of quality or quantity. Some studies reflect that the quantity of food offered by schools under MDMS does not meet the norms prescribed by the Supreme Court (Khera, 2006). Further, the nutritional need differential among students across classes in primary section has not been taken into account while fixing the quantity norms across classes. Twenty-six per cent of the parents, interacted during the present study, irrespective of socio-economic strata, do not consider MDM as substitute for home made food. Although, a good majority (62%) of them feel that the intervention has resulted into weight gain of their children, while almost one third of the parents are dissatisfied with the quality of MDM and do not consider it to be nutritious. No systematic arrangement however was noticed in institutes to make any empirical inference about health-impact of MDMS. The research team found that the appearance of food cooked under MDMS was good only in 27 per cent of the cases observed, while it was found to have good taste and good smell in only 18 per cent of the institutes. As far as menu preference is concerned, 65 per cent of the students were found to like either egg, chicken, *posto*[1] or soybean; and 57 per cent dislike anything among brinjal, cauliflower, papaya, pumpkin, soybean and radish. Only 3 per cent of the students were observed to bring lunch ox to school; while, only 13 per cent of the students have ever been asked about their choices of menu by the school authorities.

MDMS and Hygiene

In the present study, presence of source of drinking water was found to be there in 86 per cent of the institutes, while in 27 per cent, the supply was found to be irregular. Tube well is the source in 75 per cent, followed by piped supply in 9 per cent of the cases. Although drinking water is stored in 60 per cent of the institutes, it was found to be properly covered in 70 per cent of the cases, where it is stored. As much as 49 per cent institutes informed about irregularity in the practice of hand wash before taking meals. It was observed that in as much as 89 per cent of the cases students themselves wash the utensils; of which use of detergent or clean water was found in only 57 per cent of the cases, while rest 43 per cent wash utensils by dirty pond water only. No garbage bins were noticed in 83 per cent of the institutes, and the sad practice of throwing around left over foods was observed in 41 per cent of the institutes. In respect of 'clean and dry' only 22 per cent institutes were rated good, whereas light and ventilation were found to be good in 24 per cent of the institutes. Only 3 per cent institutes were found to be free from insects or pests, overall cleanliness of kitchen was found to be good in only 24 per

1. *Posto*: A food-preparation extremely common in West Bengal made up of poppy seeds.

cent of the institutes covered under this study. Around two third of the parents were unhappy about the cleanliness aspect of kitchen or serving area.

Children falling ill after taking MDM have been reported a number of times in different parts of the country, indicating inadequate screening of food quality. As observed, 46 per cent of the institutes, either teachers or cook eat the meal before students, as a screening measure, to avoid student-health-hazards.

MDMS and Cost Norms

Khera (2006) found that the assumptions regarding prices of vegetable and *dal* while fixing the budget are absurd resulting into suboptimum quality of meals apparently at no one's fault. As found by Afridi (2005), a varied menu perform much better in terms of meeting recommended daily allowances, though there remains little room to substitute monotonous and unappetising meals due to inadequacy of fund. The current study reflects that only 11 per cent of the institutes are fully satisfied with MDMS. This is largely due to inadequate cost in respect of pulses, vegetable and fuel, as felt by 78 per cent of the institutes.

MDMS and Foodgrain (Supply, Quality and Storage)

Ninety-two per cent of the institutes informed that they receive monthly supply while weekly supply was reported by 5 per cent. Supply of ration was reported to be regular in 62 per cent of the institutes; further in 77 per cent of the cases no prior information was provided for any irregularity. Foodgrains were supplied at the institute in 92 per cent of the cases; and in 84 per cent of the cases, quantity had always been just adequate. Although the quality was found to be good in only 43 per cent of the cases, it was returned back, at least once, by only 16 per cent of the institutes studied. More than one third of the institutes lack an ideal storage facility for foodgrains.

MDMS and Grievance Redressal

It was found that, 12 per cent of the parents have at least once lodged complaints to the school authority regarding MDM. However, none of them felt it was useful. While in respect of institutes, the matter of irregularity of supply of foodgrain was brought to the notice of higher authority by 43 per cent of the institutes, yet only 29 per cent of them feel a positive change as an impact of such complaint.

Evaluation of MDMS in Respect of Human Capital Formation

In the current study, frequency of monitoring was found to be only once annually in 41 per cent of the institutes, while quarterly in 43 per cent of the cases. In 82 per cent of the institutes an inspection book was noticed. Moreover, only 67 per cent of the institutes have arrangement to display vital MDMS related information on public domain. Anyway, it was found that empirical evaluation mechanism of human capital status (achievements in terms of health and education) is outdated, and do not provide any real time as well as specific information about important parameters of health and education, be at level of individual or collective. However, it was argued in the Working Group Report on Elementary Education and Literacy for the 12th Five Year Plan (2011), that under MDMS, children should be regularly weighed and height should be measured for identification followed by counselling of the weaker ones. The report apart from recommending material support to carry out such measures, advocates for school health card and incorporation of the same within academic progress report to assess progress of an individual both in terms of selected health-indicators and education through a common report. Keeping in view the interrelation among education, employability and poverty, and absence of any formal instrument to gauze human capital status of individual children, this recommendation may serve as a pointer. In context of no-detention till class VIII level, the moot issue appears to be: how much correction or improvement of human capital is possible if deficiencies are detected at an age of 15 years or more; i.e., during or after class IX level. In 60th Central Advisory Board of Education (CABE) meeting[2] held on 8 November 2012 in New Delhi, Arun Kapur, Member CABE

2. *http://mhrd.gov.in/sites/upload_files/mhrd/files/document-reports/ATR%2060th%20CABE_0.pdf*

& Director, Vasant Valley Foundation indicated that "society is becoming over-schooled yet under-educated, so emphasis on quality is also crucial".

Recommendations

Operational Issues

In operational part, following recommendations are drawn from observations and analysis, for efficient implementation of the scheme:

i. Fund is to be released timely. Advance release of funds may be considered for hassle free implementation of MDMS.
ii. Door step as well as timely availability of quality foodgrain is to be ensured. There should be some central 'quality certifying authority' for foodgrains, apart from teachers, to minimise the unjustified burden on them. Stringent action for non-maintenance of quality norms may be considered as the issue is related to the future of the nation.
iii. Present cooking cost which includes cost of pulses, vegetable, oil & fat, salt & condiments, and fuel[3] on per child per day basis for primary and upper primary was found to be ₹3.59[4] and ₹5.38 respectively. Most of the teachers interacted urged an upward revision of the same.
iv. It was largely observed that the task of procurement of vegetable and fuel is being performed by teachers, without any apparent incentive. Some incentives may be considered for teachers responsible for procuring vegetable, fuel etc.
v. Regular assessment of drinking water quality is to be made sine qua non.
vi. Adequate infrastructure for drinking water and storage of raw ingredients are to be provided.
vii. Drinking water should not be allowed to be stored for more than 10-12 hrs under any circumstances. Utensils where water is stored are to be cleaned regularly, and stored water

3. *http://mdm.nic.in/Files/Guidelines/6.Rifision%20of%20norns%20MDM1_.pdf*
4. *http://mdm.nic.in/Files/OrderCirculars/2014/Revision-of-Cooking-Cost-2014-15.pdf*

is to be kept covered. Regular inspection to ensure water hygiene is strongly recommended.

viii. Students are to be encouraged to practice hand hygiene and keeping surrounding environment clean. Use of dust-bins within school premises is strongly urged.

ix. Awareness of parents is to be strengthened on de-worming and nutrition education with special emphasis on micro nutrients. It has to be stressed that medicines provided through school should be properly taken by students.

x. Opinion of students regarding menu may be taken once weekly, and the same may be implemented in the best possible economical form.

xi. Cooks are required to be trained on hygiene, variety as well as screening of cooked food so as to minimise possibilities of health hazards from consuming MDM.

xii. Remuneration ₹1,000 per month,[5] offered to cooks seems to be extremely inadequate, particularly in an era of skyrocketing prices for essential commodities. Rationalisation of the same may be considered. This activity may be incorporated under MGNREGA in rural areas, as suggested by Sri Manoj Kumar Singh, Commissioner (RD) Uttar Pradesh in the meeting[6] of the taskforce to review and suggest inclusion of more works under MGNREGA, on 27 May 2009. Wage may be offered on the basis of special schedule of rates in this regard.

xiii. The practice of kitchen garden and commercial poultry keeping may be encouraged to ensure provision of adequate vegetable and animal protein in MDMS. Convergence with MGNREGS, RKVY, etc. may be envisaged in this regard.

xiv. Eastern Coalfields Limited (ECL) and other major local enterprises may be approached to adopt institutes for provision of animal protein periodically in the menu of MDMS. Stress may be given to prioritise institutes on the

---

5. *Point 6, http://mdm.nic.in/Files/Guidelines/6.Rifision%20of%20norns%20MDM1_.pdf*

6. *http://nrega.nic.in/circular/Minutes_TaskForce_270509.pdf*

basis of presence of students from socially disadvantaged categories.

xv. Absenteeism of cooks and non-preparation of MDM owing to that is to be provided due as well as strict attention. Habitual absentees may be terminated.

Evaluation of 'National Human Capital Status' through 'Student Specific Health cum Academic Performance Record" & HCI

It has been felt that there should be some smart evaluation mechanism to periodically assess the status of outcome in terms of human capital. This study recommends use of 'student specific health cum academic performance record" to capture micro-data related to health, education and employability of individual students quarterly. Periodic evaluation of students from Class I onwards, by some reputed independent agency, having close industry interface, may be put in place to ensure proper and market linked evaluation of individual students. Such mechanism is likely to have the sole motto of detecting human capital status from an age of five years, so that issues related to employability are properly taken care of. The said card would reflect individual and collective status on body mass index, parasitic loads, eye-sight, gender sensitivity, hygiene-awareness, academic performance, computer proficiency, communication ability, etc., as suggested in Table 26.1. Further, separate score card for institutes may be there as per Table 26.2, to understand the degree of preparedness at that level.

The weighted average of parameters within 'student health cum academic performance card' may give rise to 'Human Capital Index (HCI)'. Such index as well as parameter specific scores, are likely to provide realistic as well as empirical information on strengths and weaknesses from individual to national level in respect of human capital from Class I level onwards. Such information may be used as vital policy-ingredient for effective targeting of individuals and judicious use of resources in an outcome oriented framework. By sharing the entire student specific information, along with the index placed on public domain, the whole mechanism can be made more accountable and transparent. The student specific report may be shared with parents in a mandatory 'monthly parent-teacher-student meeting'. Government officials may attend such meetings to manage shortfalls identified in these meetings; mothers wherever feasible may be facilitated to attend such meeting by providing some incentive.

Concluding Remarks

In order to combat poverty, employability within individual is to be raised substantially. Therefore, market driven indicators of education and health of individual children are required to be carefully monitored from the level of Class I onwards for detection of deficiencies at the budding stage and correction thereof. This paper therefore suggests improvement of operationalisation of MDMS on one hand, and argues in favour of development of student specific HCI at the entry level, and assessing the same quarterly, on the other. The HCI is likely to provide real time status of human capital at any given point of time, and thereby would assist policy makers to identify priorities in respect of human capital. This would also facilitate concurrent evaluation of ongoing human capital oriented interventions from primary level onwards, and would help formulation and implementation of demand driven region specific policies.

Table 26.1

Model Format of the Proposed Student Specific Academic Cum Health Progress Report

State: West Bengal (WB), District: Burdwan (02)*, Location: Rural (R), Block: Jamuria (31), GP: Shyamla (01)

Institute: .... (Institute code: 06), Class: I, Roll No.: 21

Name: ...., Unique Identification Code: WB/02/R/31/01/06/I/21/2013-14

Session: 2013-14, Age ....yrs.

		Academics						Health								HCI
Quarter	Date	Arithmetic	English	Computer	Presentation & Communication	Ethics & Values	Academics Total (I+II+III+IV+V)	BMI			Eye sight	Personal hygiene + Nutrition & deworming	Community hygiene	Gender sensitivity	Health Total (I+II+III+IV+V)	Academics + Health
		I	II	III	IV	V		Weight	Height	BMI I	II	III	IV	V		
1																
2																
3																
4																

Note: * *Figures in parenthesis are hypothetical codes for respective subjects, conceptualised to codify individual students with unique identity code (UIC).*

Table 26.2

Institutional Score of Student Health

Quarter	*Date*	*Calorie*		*Protein content*		*Deworming in current quarter*		*Health camp in current quarter*		*Eye sight*		*Score*
		Content	*Score*	*Content*	*Score*	*Y/N*	*Score*	*Y/N*	*Score*	*Y/N*	*Score*	
1												
2												
3												
4												

References

Afridi, F. (2005). "Mid-Day Meals in Two States: Comparing the Financial and Institutional Organisation of the Programme", *Economic and Political Weekly*: 1528-34, 9 April.

Choudhury, Amit (2006). "Revisiting Dropouts: Old Issues, Fresh Perspectives", *Economic and Political Weekly:* 5257-63, 23 December.

Colcough, C. (1982). 'The Impact of Primary School on Economic Development: A Review of Evidence", *World Development* 10(3): 167-85.

Drèze, J. and A. Goyal (2003). "The Future of Mid-Day Meals", *Economic and Political Weekly:* 4673-82, 1 November.

Drèze, Jean and Geeta Kingdon (2001). "School Participation in Rural India", *Review of Development Economics* 5 (1).

Garg Manisha and Mandal Kalyan Sankar (2013). "Mid day Meal for the Poor, Privatised Education for the Non-Poor", *Economic and Political Weekly* 155-63, 27 July.

Hati, Koushik Kumar and Rajarshi Majumdar (2012). "Proximate Determinants of School Dropout: A Study on Rural West Bengal", *MPRA Paper* No. 49764. accessed from: *http://mpra.ub.uni-muenchen.de/49764/*

Jayachandran, Usha (2007). "How High are Dropout Rates in India", *Economic and Political Weekly:* 982-83, 17 March.

Khera, Reetika (2006). "Mid day Meals in Primary Schools, Achievements & Challenges", *Economic and Political Weekly* 4742-49, 18 November.

Kingdon, G.G. (1999). "Gender Gap in Indian Schools: Is Labour Market a Factor?" *Id21 Insights* 29.

Laxmaiah, A., K.V. Sarma, D.H. Rao, G. Reddy, M. Ravindranath, M.V. Rao and K. Vijayaraghavan (1999). *"Impact of Mid Day Meal Program on Educational and Nutritional Status of School Children in Karnataka"*, *Indian Pediatrics* 36: 1221-28, December.

Planning Commission (n.d.) *Working Group Report on Elementary Education and Literacy for the 12th Five Year Plan 2012-2017*. New Delhi: Department of School Education and Literacy, Ministry of Human Resource Development, Government of India. pp.188-89. *http://planningcommission.gov.in/ aboutus/committee/wrkgrp12/ hrd/wgelementary1708.pdf*

PROBE (1999). *Public Report on Basic Education in India.* New Delhi: Oxford University Press.

Ramchandran, V. and A. Saihjee (2002). "The New Segregation: Reflections on Gender and Equity in Primary Education", *Economic and Political Weekly* 37(17): 1600-13, 27 April.

Ramachandran Vimala, Kameshwari Jandhyala and Aarti Saihjee (2000). "Through the Life Cycle of the Children: Factors that Facilitate and Impede Successful Primary School Completion", *Economic & Political Weekly*, July.

Ramachandran, Vimala, Periodi Vani, Jandhyala Kameshwari, Patni Bharat, Pal Madhumita, Mehrotra Nishi, Saxena Niti and Pankaj Bhavana (2004). *Analysis of Positive Deviance in ICDS Programme: Rajasthan and Uttar Pradesh.* New Delhi: World Bank. p.27.

Rumberger, R. (2001). "Why Students Dropout of School and What Can Be Done", Paper presented at the conference *Dropouts in America: How Severe Is the Problem? What Do We Know about Intervention and Prevention.* Harvard University.

Sengupta, P. and J. Guha (2002). "Enrolment Dropout and Grade Completion of Girl Children in West Bengal", *Economic and Political Weekly* 37(17): 1621-37, 27 April.

Shiva Kumar (2003). *Food Security and Child Rights.* A UNICEF publication.

World Bank (1997). *Primary Education in India.* Washington DC.

Websites:

Mid-day Meal Scheme, Physical Progress, Status of Kitchen-cum-Store as on 31-03-2012; http://mdm.nic.in/Files/Physical%20Progress/KS_AS_ON31-3-2012. pdf

27

P.K. KULKARNI

Impact of Training Programmes on Teachers to Improve Quality of Education under Sarva Shiksha Abhiyan Programme

Introducion

Sarva Shiksha Abhiyan (SSA) is Government of India's flagship programme for achievement of Universalisation of Elementary Education (UEE) in a time bound manner, as mandated by 86th amendment to the Constitution of India making free and compulsory education to the children of 6-14 years age group, a Fundamental Right. It is an effort to universalise elementary education through community-ownership of the school system.

SSA is being implemented in partnership with State governments to cover the entire country to address the needs of 192 million children in 1.1 million habitations. The programme seeks to open new schools in those habitations which do not have schooling facilities and strengthen existing school infrastructure through provision of additional class rooms, toilets, drinking water, maintenance grants and school improvement grants. Existing schools with inadequate teacher strength are provided with additional teachers, while the capacity of existing teachers is being strengthened through extensive training, grants for developing teaching-learning materials and strengthening of the academic support structure at a cluster, block and district level.

SSA seeks to provide quality elementary education including life skills. It focuses specially on girl's education and children with special needs. SSA also seeks to provide computer education to bridge the digital divide. The programme is also an attempt to provide an opportunity to all children, through provision of community-owned quality education in a Mission mode, for improving human capabilities. The main features of SSA are:

i. A programme with a clear time frame for universal elementary education.
ii. A response to the demand for quality basic education all over the country.
iii. An opportunity for promoting social justice through basic education.
iv. An effort at effectively involving the PRIs (panchayati raj institutions), School Management Committees, Village and Urban Slum Level Education Committees, Parents' Teachers' Associations, Mother Teacher Associations, Tribal Autonomous Councils and other grass root level structures in the management of elementary schools.
v. An expression of political will for universal elementary education across the country.
vi. A partnership between the Central, State and the local government.
vii. An opportunity for States to develop their own vision of elementary education.

Vision

Let us all learn—Let us all grow

Provision of relevant and useful Elementary Education of satisfactory quality for all children with full concern for social and gender equity and regional parity and with vibrant participation of the community in the management of schools.

Mission Statement

To provide access and to enrol and retain all the children between 6 to 14 years of age in schools including speciallyabled and to impart quality education imbued with universal human values equipping them to contribute constructively to society through empowering teachers and enlighten communities.

Objective

- Universalisation of 'access' to elementary education from 1st to 8th standards to all children up to the age of 14 years.
- Universalisation of enrolments and retention in elementary education and completion of 8th standard by all children.
- Universalisation means age-specific enrolment and full retention of all enrolled children.
- Provision of education of satisfactory quality with emphasis on life-skills and meaningful schooling.
- Complete attention to equity by sex and across social groups and parity across regions in educational development.

Karnataka State Educational Profile

As of March 2013, Karnataka had 60,036 elementary schools with 3,13,008 teachers and 8.39 million students, and 14,195 secondary schools with 1,143,50 teachers and 2.09 million students (*http://en.wikipedia.org/wiki/ Karnataka-cite_note-school-99*). There are three kinds of schools in the state, viz., government-run, private aided (financial aid is provided by the government) and private unaided (no financial aid is provided). The primary languages of instruction in most schools are Kannada apart from English, Urdu and other languages. The syllabus taught in the schools is by and large the state syllabus (SSLC) defined by the Department of Public Instruction of the Government of Karnataka, and the CBSE, ICSE in case of certain private unaided and Kendriya Vidyalayas (KVs). In order to provide supplementary nutrition and maximise attendance in schools, the Karnataka Government has launched a MDMS (mid-day meal scheme) in government and aided schools in which free lunch is provided to the students. A pair of uniforms and all text books are given to children; free bicycles are given to VIIIth standard children. Statewide board examinations are conducted at the end of the period of Xth standard and students who qualify are allowed to pursue a two-year pre-university course; after which students become eligible to pursue under-graduate degrees. There are two separate Boards of Examination for class X and class XII. There are 652 degree colleges (March 2011) affiliated with one of the universities in the state, viz. Bangalore University, Gulbarga University, Karnataka University, Kuvempu University, Mangalore University and University of Mysore. In 1998, the engineering colleges in the state were brought under the newly-formed Visvesvaraya Technological University headquartered at Belgaum, whereas the medical colleges are run under the jurisdiction of the Rajiv Gandhi University of Health Sciences. Some of these baccalaureate colleges are accredited with the status of a deemed university. There are 187 engineering, 289 polytechnic, 39 medical and 44 dental colleges in the state. Udupi, Sringeri, Gokarna and Melkote are well-known places of Sanskrit and Vedic learning. There is a women's university as well as a Kannada University in the state, apart from 3 agricultural universities. A veterinary university has been set up during 2009-10.

Status of Schools in Karnataka

i) Elementary education is provided in Karnataka through LPS (lower primary school) with 1 to 5 standards, HPS (higher primary school) with 1 to 7 standard and 1 to 8 standard, which also have 1 to 5 LPS attached to them. At the HPS stage, there are schools offering 6 and 7 standards as well as 6 to 8 standards only. In addition, 8th standard facility is provided to children in the high schools of the State for all children who complete the HPS in 1 to 7 and 6 to 7 standard.

ii) There is a separate State Board for 1 to 10 standard schools. There are 60,036 schools under the State Board. 25,950 Government sector schools provide elementary schooling at 1 to 5 LPS stage only, and 34,086 Government sector schools are at the HPS stage, which also include the LPS sections.

iii) When a count is taken of schools managed by the Department of Education (including those which are begun under SSA patronage), the schools of the Department of Social Welfare, schools run by Local Self Government Institutions, schools under government patronage for Grant-in-aid (the private aided schools) which is all government and government aided schools are taken into consideration. Leaving out Kasturba Gandhi Balika Vidyalaya (KGBV) and Children with Special Needs (CWSN) schools, it is observed that there is a decrease/increase of 393 schools in the State. The increase in the private unaided sector is 972 schools. The decrease in State sector schools from 2011-12 to 2012-13 is around 0.69 per cent while the increase is 6.27 per cent in case of private unaided schools.

In-service Teacher Training

Karnataka is well known for its capacity for having qualified teachers in its schools. There are no para or untrained teachers in the state. Keeping in view the frequent changes in the society, it is important to update and incorporate positive changes in the education system. Change in the curriculum and text is not an easy job. But they can be achieved through in service training to the teachers.

SSA training recognises the critical and central role of teachers and advocates a focus on their academic, professional and technical needs. Setting up of Block Resource Coordinators (BRC) and Cluster Resource Coordinators (CRC), recruitment of qualified teachers, opportunities for teacher development through participation in curriculum related material development, focus on classroom process and exposure visit for teachers are positive steps towards developing human resource among teachers.

All teachers are trained. But there is a need to regularly update and enhance their knowledge in relation to content and methodology. Therefore, in-service training needs to be an integral part of any quality based project like SSA. Under SSA, all the in-service trainings are conducted through a module for resource persons as well as the teachers.

In-Service Teachers Training 2013-14

State-level Training Background

The SSA aims to provide quality education to all the children in the 6 to 14 age group across the nation. It has several features that seek to improve the quality of elementary education. These essentially pertain to: a) ensuring basic provisioning to enable improvement in the quality of classroom transactions, b) large scale capacity building of States, for undertaking and evaluating interventions for quality enhancement, and c) focus on assessment of learning outcomes and their improvement, as key indicators of the quality of learning.

The programme places great emphasis on building the capacity of teachers through regular training programmes. All trainings funded from SSA cover several pedagogical issues, including content and methodology, improving teaching learning transactions at classroom level. States have started exploring several innovative means of imparting these trainings, including use of distance, self-learning mode and use of educational technology. Teacher training under SSA emphasises child-centred pedagogy and activity based teaching learning.

Review of Literature

Sarada (1996) conducted a study on effectiveness of strategies used in developing information processing skill involving thinking in teaching of history. The following conclusion may be drawn on the basis of findings. The strategies used in developing information processing skill are more effective than using traditional approach in teaching history. These strategies deepen the imagination and understanding of the students. These strategies also help the student in processing and organising information in a meaningful compact structure which are in easily readable from. Agarwal and Kamlesrao (1997) conducted an appraisal study on the quality of in-service teacher training programme for primary school teacher. In his study he found that considerable amount of content was not transacted in the training programmes for resource persons under District Primary Education Programme (DPEP) and Special Orientation Programme of Primary Teachers (SOPT) programmes. Further loss was observed at teachers' level as more content were left out. Emphasis was on transmission of information and knowledge rather than on instructional strategies and activities. Transactions during training were mainly through lecture and discussions. Groups work activities were too less. The loss of information was more in SPOT than in DPEP training programme. DPEP training programme compared to the SOPT programme provided better quality of training in terms of more coverage and adoption of child centred activities, and less loss of information.

Paranjpe and Sandhya (1997) conducted a study on developing partnership for teacher's empowerment. He found that most of the INSET programmes did not use partnership as a strategy for promoting education and training of primary school teachers either as a part of the overall training strategy or specific INSET programmes. For the realisation of INSET inputs, a support system of teacher peer groups along with an expert facilitation guide for achieving continuity and applicability of new INSET practices needed to be viewed as a continuous ongoing activity and not a one time input. Venkataiah (1997) conducted a study on impact or inputs provided in District Institutes of Education and Training (DIETs) on teaching competency.

Objectives of the Research Paper

i) To assess the impact of in-service teacher education programmes on class room activities.
ii) To make suggestions based on the findings of the study.

Research Methodology

The study is a micro study and has been confined to Yadgir district in Karnataka state. The primary data and other relevant information were collected from 258 respondents. The respondents were given a questionnaire. The researcher also conducted interview in this regard and has used necessary statistical techniques to conduct the study.

Scope and Limitations of the Study

i) The study has considered only four training programmes attended by teachers and the training was done at only two levels: Block level: 5 days and Cluster level: 2 days. The training programmes included: a) British Council Training, b) Nali-Kali Training, c) Nali-Kali Urdu Training, and d) CCE Training.

ii) The study has been conducted in Yadgir district only.

British Council English Training—3 Days

Training Objectives

- To develop the skills and knowledge of the teachers to use appropriate interactive and child centred teaching methodology to teach English.
- To develop an understanding of the progression of developing learners' writing skills from Standard 1 to 8.
- To develop the writing skills of learners' appropriate to age and level.

SSA had planned to train all 2,18,697 teachers of the State and have trained 1,80,554 teachers during the academic year 2013-14.

Training Impact

- Understood the principles and practices of being 'good' writing teachers.
- Teach learners the mechanics of writing including prewriting activities, the formation, size and spacing of letters and hand writing development.
- Teach punctuation appropriate to the age and level of the learners.
- Teach sentence and paragraph writing appropriate to the age and level of the learners.
- Teach learners about genre, so they are able to compose appropriately.
- Implement the stages of the writing process in the class rooms.
- Provide positive and constructive feedback to learners on their writing skills.

CCE Training—2 days

Objectives

- To know the importance of integration of 'evaluation' in the teaching-learning process.

- To identify 'evaluation' as a self-assessment tool in rationalisation of learning.
- To know the child's achievement in all dimensions.
- To mould the child's individuality in all respects.
- To identify the child's achievements and drawbacks, and help the child to overcome the obstacles in achieving the goals.
- Use evaluation outcomes in self-realisation by learners, imparters & parents.

SSA had planned to train 1,59,577 teachers of the State and have trained 1,59,970 teachers during the academic year 2013-14.

Training Impact

- The teachers are capable of evaluating the different domains of learning.
- They are well versed in using different tools and techniques of evaluation.
- They can record the behaviour and progress of each child in different situations.
- They are able to inculcate the competencies in the children.
- They are capable of identifying the learning gaps.
- They can maintain child portfolio.

Nali-Kali Kannada Training–2 Days

Objectives

- To transform the rigid system of teaching in government schools to an enjoyable, participative system focusing on the 'Joys of Learning'.
- Systematic learning in accordance with age wise competency in an interactive situation.
- To familiarise with the use of revised learning materials like cards and exercise books for classes 1, 2 and 3.
- To know and understand the Nali-Kali materials generated for class 3.
- To understand the techniques of classroom process and management incorporating the children of classes 1, 2 and 3 together.

- To train teachers on revised Nali-Kali learning materials generated for class 3. Training target was 59,120 teachers; 57,267 teachers were trained during the academic year 2013-2014.

Training Impact

- Teachers were trained in teaching methodology on the basis of the level of competency of the students.
- Enabled the teachers to acquaint with changes brought in Nali-Kali.
- Teachers were familiarised with the Nali-Kali kit.

Nali-Kali Urdu Training—5 days

Objectives

- To familiarise with the use of Urdu Nali-Kali learning materials, like cards, for class 1 and 2.
- To know and understand the Nali-kali materials generated for class 1 and 2.
- To understand the techniques of classroom process and management incorporating the children of classes 1 and 2 together.
- To make learning joyful, fearless and child centred.
- To encourage peer learning.

During the academic year 2013-14, 7,468 teachers were trained out of the target group of 7,927 teachers.

Training Impact

- Teachers were familiarised with the Nali-Kali kit.
- Helped Urdu Teachers to develop positive attitude towards Nali-Kali methodology.
- Teachers were trained in designing teaching methodology on the basis of the level of competency of students.
- The importance of Nali-Kali methodology was understood by the Urdu Teachers.

Result and Analysis

To attain the objective, 258 teachers gave their perception regarding the impact of in-service teacher education programmes on the class room transactions through 16 items stated in the questionnaire. None of these items was negative. The detailed summary of item wise result is given in Table 27.1.

The table indicates that 75-80 per cent teachers can always ensure class room learning by asking questions, encourage students to ask questions, diagnose the learning difficulties of the students, sustain the attention of the students, to resolve class room difficulties by interacting with students whereas 65-75 per cent teachers found themselves always capable to arrange the class room for activities, to equip themselves with theoretical as well as practical knowledge of activity based methods of teaching and modern teaching aids, to initiate discussions in staff meeting for the improvement in teaching learning process, to ensure class room learning by asking questions, to bring competency to evaluate students comprehensive through class tests (written) and by checking their note books & activity books, to remedify the diagnosed learning difficulties of the students, to enjoy teaching, to resolve class room difficulties by discussion in staff meeting and to resolve the problems of drop-outs and absenteeism through parent-teacher meeting. 50-60 per cent teachers recognise the competencies to ensure class room learning through class test and by giving home work, conducting multiple learning activities, giving home-assignment related to real life situations, receiving immediate feedback, bringing competency to evaluate students comprehensively by giving assignment (written) and through half yearly examination, resolving class room difficulties by consulting with colleagues. But only 39 per cent were able to resolve class room difficulties by consulting various sources such as print material, audio-visual material and the Internet.

Further, it could be concluded that most of the teachers always find themselves competent enough to encourage students to ask questions and resolve class room difficulties by interacting with students. Whereas reasonably high number of teachers said that these programmes were helpful to ensure class room learning by asking

Table 27.1

Impact of In-service Teacher Education Programmes on Class Room Activities

Sl. No	*Impact*	*Always (%)*	*Occasionally (%)*	*Never (%)*
1	To arrange the class room for activities	186 (72.427)	58 (22.524)	13 (5.049)
2	To equip ourselves with theoretical as well as practical Knowledge of activity based methods of teaching.	183 (71.068)	67 (26.602)	6 (2.330)
3	To equip ourselves with theoretical as well as practical knowledge of modern teaching aid	181 (70.291)	70 (27.184)	7 (2.524)
4	To handle audio-visual aids effectively	175 (67.961)	69 (26.796)	14 (5.243)
5	To initiate discussions in staff meeting for the improvement in teaching learning process	168 (65.049)	75 (28.932)	15 (6.019)
6	To conduct multiple learning activities	149 (57.864)	86 (33.398)	23 (8.738)
7	To introduce interesting learning activities	188 (72.816)	65 (25.049)	5 (2.136)
8	To give home-assignment related to real life situations	139 (53.786)	81 (31.456)	38 (14.757)
9	To receive immediate feedback	139 (53.981)	86 (33.204)	33 (12.816)
10	To encourage students to ask questions	205 (79.417)	48 (18.641)	5 (1.942)
11	To give clear instructions to the students.	159 (61.748)	75 (28.544)	25 (9.709)
12	To diagnose the learning difficulties of the students.	198 (76.893)	54 (20.971)	6 2.136
13	To remedify the diagnosed learning difficulties of the students	186 (72.233)	61 (23.689)	11 4.078
14	To sustain the attention of the students.	196 (76.117)	57 (22.136)	5 1.748
15	To make us enjoy teaching.	187 (72.621)	51 (19.612)	20 7.767
16	To resolve the problems of drop-outs and absenteeism through parent-teacher meeting.	172 (68.155)	72 (27.767)	11 4.078

Source: Primary data.

questions, diagnose the learning difficulties of the students, sustain the attention of the students, to arrange the class room for activities, to equip themselves with theoretical as well as practical knowledge of activity based methods of teaching and modern teaching aids, to initiate discussions in staff meeting for the improvement in teaching learning process, to ensure class room learning by asking questions, to bring competency to evaluate students comprehensively through class tests (written) and by checking their note books & activity books, to remedify the diagnosed learning difficulties of the students, to enjoy teaching, to resolve class room difficulties by discussion in staff meeting and to resolve the problems of drop-outs and absenteeism through parent-teacher meeting. Majority teachers recognise the competencies to ensure class room learning through class test and by giving home-work, to conduct multiple learning activities, to give home-assignment related to real life situations, to receive immediate feedback, to bring competency to evaluate students comprehensively by giving assignment (written) and through half yearly examination, To resolve class room difficulties by consulting with colleagues. But only marginal number of teachers were able to resolve class room difficulties by consulting various sources such as print material, audio-visual material and the Internet.

Observations of the Teachers

Observations of some teachers regarding different aspects of in-service training are reproduced below:

i) Training programmes must be conducted by well equipped and skilled persons in the concerned subject or else these are useless.

ii) Resource persons should take personal interest in order to make their interaction well and meaningful.

iii) We want to learn some new things in training programmes like attractive methods of teaching and how to make working models, puppets etc.

iv) What we are learning in the training programme is not possible to use in the school situation.

v) Trainings under SSA are not useful to highly experienced teachers because they know how to teach lessons to students. So BRC and CRC trainings are not helpful to teachers as well as to students. The effectiveness of trainings needs to be improved by giving proper training related to the subject.

Suggestions

i) While selecting teachers for training, number of training programmes attended by them should be taken into account.

ii) Training needs to imparted in the beginning of the academic session.

iii) Training programmes should lay a great deal of emphasis on developing skills among teachers' such as preparing working models and puppets and life skills.

iv) Sometimes teachers are asked through mobile phone a day before the commencement of the training programme to participate. In such a situation, teachers come to the training programme unprepared to gain experiences from training situation. They need to be informed well in advance about their participation in the training programme

v) Training programmes are conducted in working days. This reduces the teaching hours in schools. Therefore, training should not be conducted during working days. School based training programmes need to be launched

vi) Teachers should be motivated to attend more training programmes by giving both monetary and non-monetary benefits.

vii) Practical applicability of training programmes should be carefully evaluated qualitatively and not quantitatively.

viii) In-service teacher education programmes make teachers more confident in planning and preparing for their classroom interaction.

ix) Training should focus on handling of print material, audio-visual material and the Internet.

x) Every year education department should not wait for the Central government for funds. But as soon as it gets the green signal from the government, it should start working and should work very fast.

xi) Before implementing any plans, government has to see that there is no shortage of funds.

Conclusion

The impact clearly indicates a high level of satisfaction among teachers in imparting knowledge through training programmes. Teachers have gained clarity and confidence in planning and preparing for their classroom interaction. They have become more empowered to handle the classes effectively. However, only a few teachers were capable to resolve class room difficulties by consulting various sources such as print and audio-visual material. Undoubtedly the efforts made by the SSA are highly appreciated and found to be inspiring. But there is scope for improvement.

References

Aggarwal, V.P. and G. Kamalesaro (1997). *The Quality of In-Service Teacher Programme for Primary School Teachers An Appraisal Study*. NCERT.

Aiholli, V.D. and K. Sahoo (1995). *Nature and Forms of In-Service Education for Secondary School Teachers in the Karnataka State by 2005 A.D.* Vol.31(3).

Bhatawdekar, M.V. (1986). *Evaluation of Training and Development*. Pune: NIBM.

Flippo, Edwin B. (1982). *Principles of Personnel Management*. New York: McGraw Hill.

Gupta, A.K. (1984). *Teacher Education: Current Status and Prospects*. New Delhi: Sterling Publications.

Khader, M.A. (1997). *A Model for Strategic Planning of In-Service Training Inputs for Teachers*. NCERT.

Kothari, C.R. (2004). *Research Methodology Methods and Techniques*. Second Edition. New Age International (P) Ltd.

Kulkarni, V.G. (1997). *An Investigation into the Classroom Management Behaviours of Teacher and its Implication for the Teacher Training: PhD Education*. Shivaji University.

Manjunath, S.V. (2014). "Sarakari Shalegala Ulivige Kerala Madari (Kerala Model for Survival of Government Schools)", *Prajavni Newspaper* 6. 29 September.

Mishra and Kishore (1997). *Teacher Empowerment Issues Related to Development of Local Specific Competencies Based Curriculum at Primary Level*. NCERT.

Paranjpe and Sandhya (1997). *Developing Partnership for Teacher Empowerment: A Focus on INSET*. New Delhi: NCERT.

Phillips, Jack (1990). *Hand Book Training and Development Evaluation and Management Methods*. Houston, Texas, USA: Kogan Page, Crulf Publishing Company.

Pigors, Paul (1976). *Case Methods in Training and Development and Development Handbook*. New York: Mc Graw Hill Book Company.

Prasad and Prasad (2005). "Towards Professionalisation in Education", *University News* 43(18), May. New Delhi.

Ranganathan, V. (1992). *Research Project on Developing a Plan for In-Service Education of Elementary Teachers at District level*. New Delhi: NIEPA. Planning and Management.

Sarada, K. (1996). *Effectiveness of Strategies used in Developing Information Processing Skill Involving Thinking in Teaching of History, Innovative Experiments and Practices in Education.* New Delhi: NCERT.

Virmani, B.R. and Pemila Seth (1985). *Evaluation Management Training and Development and Development*. New Delhi: Vision Books Pvt Ltd.

Venkathaiah, N. (1997). *Impact of Inputs Provided in District Institute of Education and Training (DIET) on Teaching Competency*. New Delhi: NCERT.

Yadav, Bhupendra and Pooja Bhardwaj (2012). *Impact of In-service Teacher Education Programmes on Class Room Transactions*. Educationia Confab.

Websites and other:

http://nerie.nic.in/ip.html

http://www.ssa.tn.nic.in/Docu/Inservice%20teacher%20training%20%202011%20proof.pdf

http://www.britishcouncil.in/programmes/englishpartnerships/state/karnataka

http://www.indg.in/india/sitemap-1/primaryeducation/improvement_in_quality_of_elementary_education.pdf

Attainment of the Goal: Education for All—A study of effectiveness of in service education of teachers-2008 All India Primary Teachers', New Delhi.

State Analytical Report 2011-12 of U-DISE data and U-DISE Data 6f 2012-13

28

GAURAV SINGH and M.S. KHAN

Public Private Partnership in Infrastructure Development of Rural India

Opportunities and Challenges

Introduction

The term PPP (public private partnership) implies a collaborative agreement between public and private sector organisation to deliver infrastructure and social services to the society in a clearly defined and specific time frame. In other words, PPP can be seen as shared responsibilities with innovative methods that enables the private sector to participate in nation-building and sustainable development activities. It fosters the delivery of public infrastructure like means of transportation (roads, airports, seaports, railways, etc.) and services (health, education, sanitation, portable water, skill development, etc.) of supreme quality through collaboration between of public and private sector. Government of India (GoI), Ministry of Finance, Department of Economic Affairs (2007) defines PPP as:

> A partnership between a public sector entity (sponsoring authority) and a private sector entity (a legal entity in which 51 per cent or more of equity is with the private partner/s) for the creation and/ or management of infrastructure for public purpose for a specified period of time (concession period) on commercial terms and in which the private partner has been procured through a transparent and open procurement system.

PPP model across the globe in general and within India in particular is gaining huge appreciation and popularity due to its invaluable contribution towards infrastructure development and national growth and prosperity. It is also a well-accepted truth and reality that when an economy is deprived and is devoid of adequate and optimum infrastructure, it reflects a lackluster performance in terms of economic and social growth. For overall growth of a nation, the development of urban infrastructure must be clubbed with a focus on rural infrastructure as these two together will provide impetus to economic growth on a much faster and sustainable rate. The development of rural infrastructure is very crucial as it helps in developing and bettering the performances of agriculture, agro-industries and overall economic development of rural areas. It also helps in providing basic amenities that goes a long way in improving the quality of life and bringing rural folk at par with the mainstream. In a rapidly growing economy like India, which suffers from paucity of capital, PPP is the most potent and viable option of public funding by way of harnessing private sector efficiencies for infrastructure development, which traditionally has been the government domain. The linkages between infrastructure, economic growth and poverty alleviation are now a proven fact, and therefore the focus is shifting towards more and more use of PPP model.

Good quality infrastructure provides pace and force to economic growth and also helps in improving economic growth that, in turn, renders investment in infrastructure projects more attractive and rewarding. As per the opinions of economic experts, India is very sound and self-sufficient as fas as institutional infrastructure is concerned, but is very fragile in terms of physical infrastructure. The case of rural infrastructure is even worse and needs immediate attention. The rural infrastructure must be built at the earliest so that the contribution of rural economy in development of the country may increase. However, the challenges before the policy makers as far as rural infrastructure is concerned are huge. Rural infrastructure plays a significant role in the overall infrastructure development of a country. Even today, 70 per cent population of India is living in rural areas and a vast majority is still dependent on agriculture for their livelihood. The viability of basic and fundamental infrastructure in rural areas is far away. At the time of independence, Government and Planning Commission initiated various plans for infrastructure development of rural India. In the First Five Year Plan (FYP), the highest priority was given to agriculture development, including irrigation and power, as it was recognised that large areas of the country have remained underdeveloped due to the lack of basic services, such as transport, communication, irrigation and power. Now, although the Twelfth FYP is under progress, a lack of basic infrastructure, both social and physical, continues to be a major constraint in the progress of many villages and their habitations. The Twelfth Plan encourages participation and investment in infrastructure by private sector directly as well as through various forms of PPPs, wherever desirable and feasible. The share of private sector in infrastructure investment will have to be increased substantially from about 36.61 per cent anticipated in the Eleventh Plan to about 48 per cent in the Twelfth Plan. It is expected that competition and private investment will not only expand capacity, but also improve the quality of service provided, besides minimising cost and time overruns in the implementation of infrastructure projects.

The total public sector investment in infrastructure envisaged in the Twelfth Plan is ₹16,01,061 crore by the Centre and ₹12,89,762 crore by the states. Investment by the private sector, which includes PPP projects, makes up the balance of ₹26,83,840 crore, which is 48.14 per cent of the required investment during the Twelfth Plan—a much higher share than the anticipated 36.61 per cent during the Eleventh Plan.

Objectives of the Study

The basic objectives of this study are:

i) To assess the PPP models and explain the present scenario of PPP projects, particularly in the infrastructure development sector.

ii) To analyse various opportunities and issues related to PPP, specially with regard to Indian rural infrastructure development.

Literature Review

Rural India needs business to invest in industries such as finance and insurance; in ventures that bring new infrastructure

Table 28.1

Projected Investment in Infrastructure: Twelfth Five Year Plan

(₹ *Crore at Current Prices)*

Sectors	*Total Eleventh Plan*	*Twelfth Plan Projections*					*Total Twelfth Plan*
		2012-13	*2013-14*	*2014-15*	*2015-16*	*2016-17*	
Grand Total	24,24,277	7,51,012	8,87,454	10,61,316	12,85,573	15,89,308	55,74,663
Centre	8,56,717	2,50,758	2,80,662	3,15,217	3,54,296	4,00,129	16,01,061
States	6,80,056	2,06,944	2,30,045	2,55,645	2,83,201	3,13,928	12,89,762
Private	8,87,504	2,93,310	3,76,747	4,90,455	6,48,077	8,75,251	26,83,840
Grand Total	24,24,277	7,51,012	8,87,454	10,61,316	12,85,573	15,89,308	55,74,663
Public	15,36,773	4,57,702	5,10,707	5,70,862	6,37,497	7,14,057	28,90,823
Private	8,87,504	2,93,310	3,76,747	4,90,455	6,48,077	8,75,251	26,83,840
GDP	3,36,04,450	1,01,50,618	1,16,45,987	1,33,58,028	1,53,47,089	1,76,61,48	6,81,63,208
Investment as % of GDP	7.21	7.40	7.62	7.95	8.38	9.00	8.18

Source: Volume I, *Twelfth Five Year Plan (2012–2017): Faster, More Inclusive and Sustainable Growth,* Planning Commission (Government of India), 2013.

such as telephony and roads (Chambers, 2006). This is where telecommunications can help. Where physical infrastructure may not reach easily, the Internet can. Broadband access is the ideal platform to connect a geographically diverse country, such as India. The high-speed Internet technology holds tremendous potential for sectors such as distance learning, telemedicine, supply chain management and customer relationship management (Desai, 2006). In some cases, even though PPP models allow for exclusive right over public assets, it can be free from the evil of monopolistic features such as high user charges or low service quality. To ensure this, the government follows competitive bidding process to decide on lowest user charges or provide viability gap funding to safeguard consumer interests. Contracts are designed to ensure service quality.

Smita and Sangita (2008) suggested that the PPP as an alternative service delivery model can be used achieve efficiency and address shortages. Although it is unlikely that PPP model will fully replace the traditional services delivered by governments. Efficiency level of service delivery has improved over time and has shown positive result in some of the public utilities in the rural area. Mahalingam (2008) stated that given India's infrastructural needs, PPPs are a necessity and not just an option. However, there is a myriad of issues that needs to be addressed and resolved in order to facilitate a better understanding of ways to develop infrastructure efficiently and seamlessly via PPPs. Gopal *et al.* (2009) in the wake of increasing challenges to deliver quality public services in developing countries like India, mentions that PPPs seems to address some of the major problems faced by the governments, such as investment needs and trained manpower capacity constraints.

Research Methodology

The present study is the culmination of both primary and secondary data. The primary data are drawn through questionnaire, personal interview, telephonic interview; and the secondary data are derived from journals, books, internet and from GoI's official website on PPP (*http://www.pppinindia.com*), the official website of the committee on infrastructure, Planning Commission and Investment

Commission of India. The data available on these websites are regularly updated and is directly under the control of Ministry of Finance, GoI.

Result and Discussion

The study shows the state level distribution of PPP and its impact-directly or indirectly-on various schemes. The results of the study reveal that PPP approach has a very crucial and strong positive influence on infrastructure and sustainable development of a country. The influence of carrying out PPP work is positive as it helps in growth and progress of the society in particular, and nation in general.

Table 28.2

Various PPP Models in Indian States

	Concession
	Build-Own-Operate
	Design-Build-Finance-Operate-Maintain
	Design-Build-Finance-Operate
	Design-Build-Finance-Maintain
	Design-Build-Operate
Degree of Private Sector Risk	Lease-Develop-Operate
	Build-Finance-Maintain
	Build-Finance
	Operation and Maintenance
	Design Build
	Degree of Private Sector Involvement
	The Scale of Public-Private Partnerships

Sources: Ghosh and Gope (2011).

PPPs Models in Infrastructure Sectors

Ghosh and Gope (2011) described models like (a) Buy-Build-Operate (BBO), (b) Build-Own-Operate (BOO), (c) Build-Own-Operate-Transfer (BOOT), (d) Build-Operate-Transfer (BOT), (e) Build-Lease-Operate-Transfer (BLOT), (f) Design-Build-Finance-Operate (DBFO), (g) Finance Only, (h) Operation and Maintenance Contract (O & M), (i) Design-Build (DB) and (j) Operation License.

They also plotted a graph between degree of private sector involvement and that of private sector risk. BOT provides consortia with a concession to finance, build, operate and maintain a facility. During the life of the concession, investors collect user fees to cover the costs of construction and debt servicing and operations, and to realise a return on investment. At the end of concession, the facility is returned to the government agency, which had awarded the contract. BOT model is by far the most extensively used technique in roads and highway sectors. BOO is similar to BOT model, but without a clause for transfer of ownership. BOO is commonly used in developing telecom, power and social infrastructure, for example, wastewater treatment facilities. Design-build-finance-operate is very similar to BOO, but with the main difference that the former is more applicable for high-tech engineering projects, such as a petroleum refinery where considerable design engineering is involved. BOOT is very similar to BOT, but with the difference that in the former the project is transferred to the government agency, which controls the project after a negotiated period. This model is commonly used for financing road projects, port infrastructure, power utilities, etc.

Government's Plans in Rural Infrastructure Development

The second most important finding of study highlights the government's initiatives with regard to infrastructure development of the rural areas in order to improve the standard of living of rural people. The programmes were initiated for the development of roads, water supply and sanitation, power, housing, irrigation, ICT (information and communication technology). The various programmes are briefly discussed under the following heads.

- Mahatma Gandhi National Rural Employment Guarantee Act (MNREGA) (2006): This scheme enhanced livelihood security in rural areas by providing at least 100 days of guaranteed wage employment in a financial year and in turn strengthening natural resource management.
- Bharat Nirman (2005): Bharat Nirman helps in building rural infrastructure, mainly roads, water supply, power,

housing, irrigation, telecommunication and information technology (IT).

- Indira Awaas Yojana (IAY) (1985-86): This scheme provides financial assistance for construction/upgradation of dwelling units to BPL (below poverty level) rural household belonging to SCs (scheduled castes), STs (scheduled tribes) and free-bonded labourers, which was later extended to other groups.
- Rajiv Gandhi Grameen Vidyukranthi Yojana (RGGVY) (2005): This provides access to electricity to all rural households in five years.
- National Rural Health Mission (NHRM) (2005): This provides accessible, affordable and accountable quality health services to the poorest households in the remotest rural regions.
- Provision of Urban Amenities in Rural Areas (PURA) (2004): The primary objective of this scheme is to provide good quality infrastructure and associate services in rural areas. Urban amenities that are essential for fulfilment of the scheme include drinking water, sewerage, drainage, solid waste management, skill development, and enhancement of economic activities, in addition to electricity distribution, street lighting through non-conventional energy sources, etc. For the first time, a uniquely designed PPP model is being tested for creation and maintenance of rural infrastructure assets with pre-determined service delivery standards, almost akin to urban standards While most of the capital expenditure needs would be met from the existing central schemes where the service charges are determined by the government, the construction and maintenance of assets and service delivery for a pre-determined period would be under the private partner on commercial basis. To attract the private sector, the scheme is designed to be project based with well-defined risks, sound measures for risk mitigation and allocation of risk between the sponsoring authority (*panchayats*), the Centre/states and the private developer clearly spelt out.

- Central Rural Sanitation Programme (1986): This scheme aims at improving the quality of life of rural people and to provide privacy and dignity to women in rural areas. It led to the formulation of Total Sanitation Campaign approach in 1999.
- Rural Infrastructure Development Fund (RIDF) (1995-1996): This was set up by National Bank for Agriculture and Rural Development (NABARD), owing to the shortfall of commercial banks in lending to agricultural/priority sectors, with the primary aim of providing low cost funds to the governments so as to undertake infrastructure development projects in rural areas. Since the commencement of this fund, NABARD has allowed initiation of the PPP model to access these funds for infrastructure development projects in irrigation, housing, water supply, rural electrification and construction of roads and bridges.
- Pradhan Mantri Gram Sadak Yojana (PMGSY): This plan provides connectivity to all unconnected habitations in rural areas, having a population of more than 500 persons in rural areas (250 persons in the hills and desert areas), by good quality all-weather roads.

Opportunities in Rural Infrastructure Development

The major areas that have huge potential for the growth in rural infrastructure through PPP are discussed under the following heads.

- Rural Roads: The demand for rural roads is increasing day by day. In the rural areas, we still have low population in the villages, and there is no connectivity. The demands for good quality of roadways are huge and increasing. As per the Tenth Plan document, there are around 100,000 unconnected habitations with population of more than 500 persons. The average distance from a village to an all-weather road is 2 kms, and on an average 52 per cent people living away from the main village do not have access to such roads (Bery *et al.*, 2004). Over the last few years, the demand of vehicles in rural area has reach its peak. The requirement of high quality road network is also important in rural areas. Such facilities would enhance the physical, economical and social development of rural areas. This sector has most of the projects in India that are under various stages of implementation. Most of the road projects have been confined to development, maintenance and operation of the national and state highways, expressways, bridges and bypasses under the BOT-Toll, Annuity, BOOT, and DBFOT type model. Private sectors are not interested in making investment in rural, backward and remote areas due to poor ROI (Return on Investment). Only those rural areas are benefitted, which has national highway, state highway and district/local level road pass. This reflects that there are vast opportunities for PPP to operate and maintain the rural roads.

- Rural Electrification: The availability of electricity in rural areas is still a distant dream for the villagers across the country and it poses another big challenge for the government. The farmers do not get assured supply during peak cultivation periods. The government has put in various efforts for generation and distribution of power in rural areas. The rural areas often suffer from shortages in power. Installed capacity has greatly increased since Independence, but the gap between supply and demand remains wide due to inadequacies in generation, transmission and distribution as well as inefficient use of electricity. The access of individual households to electricity is questionable even if these targets are met. The RGGVY has done effective work for enabling electrification in rural and BPL areas. Many states have undertaken PPP projects to reduce the power deficit, such as GVK Jegurupadu Combined Cycle Power Project (BOO), Jegurupadu, Andhra Pradesh (AP) is under operation, 1000-1320 MW coal-based power plant (BOO), Karnataka, and 2 MW Hydel Power (BOT), Assam, are under bidding. The 60 MW thermal power project (BOT), Assam; Mahatma Gandhi Thermal Power Project (BOT), Jhajjar, Haryana, Ringyang Hydro power plant, Kissim Khola HEP power Plant, Hee

Khola HEP Power Plant, Kalez Khola HEP power plants, all under BOOT in Sikkim, are under construction (Amirullah, 2014). This infrastructure would serve the requirements of agriculture and other activities in the rural areas, including irrigation pump sets, small and medium industries, local industries, warehousing, healthcare, education and information technology in order to facilitate overall rural development, generate employment opportunities and alleviate rural poverty.

- Storage and Cold Chain: Over the last few years, the production of crop has reached a high level. However due to improper facility for storage, wheat, rice, potato and other food grains are getting wasted. The farmers are not able to earn sufficient profit. Keeping in mind the huge shortage of storage facilities, the need of storage and cold chain has increased manifold, which can be met through PPP.
- Drinking Water: The provision of clean drinking water in rural areas is another most basic infrastructural requirement. Naandi Foundation, a non-profit organisation promoted by Dr Reddy's Laboratories in association with Satyam Computer, has targeted 20,000 villages by 2011, offering safe drinking water to the villagers. A unique collaboration between ACCESS Development Services, a microfinance technical service non-profit organisation, and Hindustan Unilever Limited, one of the country's largest producers of fast moving consumer goods, has plans to provide safe drinking water to rural areas. Apart from that, a SHG (self-help group) and a private player have together financed a safe drinking water venture (based on community purification units). Here the power of private public partnership can be seen in a project because executives of the private player will manage the enterprise operations for some years, after which the management will also be handed over to the SHG. Above discussion shows the strategic role of players in public private partnership regarding provision of drinking water in rural area.

- Education: There is a huge opportunity in the education sectors too. The infrastructure expansion and improvement in quality education in rural area is not satisfactory. This can only be solved by attracting private capital through PPP route. Central and all state governments are encouraging private sectors to take the task for building infrastructure so as to promote quality education. PPP can deliver high- quality education at a low cost, increase the enrolment ratio, provide quality education and upgrade and establish new elementary and secondary schools, Industrial Training Institutes (ITIs), polytechnics and libraries, thereby improving the standard of education in rural areas through synergy between private players. The Eleventh FYP termed as "India's educational plan," launched a scheme in November 2008 for setting up 6000 model schools as the benchmark of excellence at block level with one school per block for providing quality education to talented rural children. Of these, 2500 schools are to be set up under PPP mode in blocks that are not educationally backward and will commence from the Twelfth FYP. The revised centrally sponsored vocationalisation of secondary education scheme aims to address weaknesses of the earlier scheme in order to strengthen vocational education in classes XI-XII, and assistance is provided to 500 vocational schools under the PPP mode. The government has approved setting up of 20 new Indian Institute of Information Technology (IIIT) on a PPP basis.
- Rural Healthcare: The GoI has decided to increase healthcare expenditure to 2.5 per cent of the GDP (gross domestic product) by the end of the Twelfth FYP. However, the government alone cannot meet the infrastructure, capacity and delivery shortages existing in the current healthcare system. There has to be increased participation of private sector through PPP route. The NRHM was launched in 2005 to provide accessible, affordable and accountable quality health services to the poorest households in the remotest rural regions. Its strategy includes promoting PPP for

gaining managerial efficiency and ensuring achievement of public health goals. The government has allowed the private sector to invest in manufacturing of medical equipment, and setting up of training centres for medical professionals (nurses, paramedics, etc.) in rural areas. Some of the successful PPP involves laboratory services (pathology, radiology, CT scan, MRI, etc.), mobile medical units, primary health centre (PHC) management and telemedicine services (Amirullah, 2014). The private sector is the most important source of healthcare services in India, providing close to 80 per cent of all services, according to the government's reckoning. At independence, the private sector in India had only 8 per cent of the healthcare facilities (World Bank, 2004); but recent estimates indicate that 93 per cent of all hospitals, 64 per cent of beds, 85 per cent of doctors, 80 per cent of outpatients and 57 per cent of inpatients are in the private sector (World Bank, 2001).

Challenges Before PPP in India

Although, there are various opportunities for PPP in rural infrastructure development in India, at the same time it faces huge challenges and hurdles in its way. These challenges have slowed down the success of PPP projects in India. The biggest hurdle being that the government has not framed an appropriate policy for the PPP. Many states have framed their own policies and guidelines creating great confusion for private sectors. Some of the challenges that were investigated during the study are discussed as under:

- Lack of clear PPP policies and guidelines in the states.
- Private sectors do not want to invest in rural areas due to low ROI and low literacy level.
- Absence of extra incentives by the government for private players in rural area.
- Unwillingness on part of rural people to pay toll charges and create chaos through protests.
- Lack of proper coordination between central, state and local level governments.

- Unclear roles of public and private sectors in PPP projects with regard to rural areas.
- The biggest challenge is the slow process of PPP projects approval.
- Governments are not willing to recognise the importance of project development activities, such as detailed feasibility study, environmental/forest clearances, etc., of PPP projects in rural areas.

Suggestions

On the basis of above discussion, we can say that PPP projects are an excellent mean of value addition as it lays the platform for exchange of skills, knowledge, and expertise between the public and private sector organisations. There are huge opportunities for private sector to invest in rural areas under the PPP model. The need to develop basic infrastructure and fundamental facilities is a top priority in rural, backward and remote areas. Improvement in sectors like power, healthcare and drinking water are good examples where private sector investment has been effective. It has been seen that central or state government are now focusing more on the improving education sector through PPP model.

Majority of the private sector is reluctant to invest in rural area fearing low return on investment and unstructured working environment. The government wants to facilitate basic infrastructure development and fundamental facilities in the remote areas of the country. But there is no enabling policy environment which facilitates additional benefit for the private sector for making investment in the rural areas. For the development of rural infrastructure, the private sector requires assurance of proper return on investment from the government. The government should initiate and arrange some additional benefit policy for investment by private sector in rural areas through PPP mode. There is also a need for fast track PPP projects approval system, emphasis on environment, forest clearance, land acquisition and arrangement of finance facility under PPP projects.

Conclusion

The expansion of PPP projects in India in various sectors, such as road, port, urban development, health, education and others is a good sign for the country. However, the number of PPP projects in rural infrastructure or services is very less. The government has to accord top priority to rural infrastructure development and must start schemes for facilitating the same at the earliest possible. The government needs to follow a pro-active approach that will encourage private sector to invest in rural development, along with the public sector. Both the public and private sectors have to collaborate and strive together to bring about the development of rural economy and social upliftment.

References

Amirullah (2014). "Public Private Partnership in Infrastructure Development of Rural Areas: Opportunities and Challenges in India", *The International Journal of Humanities & Social Studies.*

Bery *et al.* (2004). 'The Nature of Rural Infrastructure: Problems and Prospects', *Working Paper* 94. New Delhi: National Council of Applied Economic Research.

Chambers, J. (2006). "An Emerging 'Interactions Economy'", *The Economics Times*, 18 September.

Desai, J. (2006). "Perspectives: Public-Private Partnership in Infrastructure", *The Economic Times*, 4 July.

Mahalingam, A. (2010). "PPP Experiences in Indian Cities: Barriers, Enablers, and the Way Forward", *Journal of Construction Engineering and Management,* April.

Mahajan, V. et al. (2007). "Financing of Rural Infrastructure", *India Infrastructure Report: Public Private Partnership and Social Infrastructure* .

Mital, K.M. and V. Mital (n.d.). *Public Private Partnership and Social Infrastructure*. Computer Society of India.

Naik, G. *et al* (n.d.). "Public Value Creation Through Private Partnership: Lessons from Public Service Delivery in Karnataka India", *Working paper* No. 315. Indian Institute of Management-Bangalore.

Smitha, K.C. and S.N. Sangita (2008). "Urban Government and Service Delivery in Bangalore: Public-Private Partnership", *Working Paper* 189. Bangalore: Institute for Social and Economic Change.

Sharma, V. (2009). "Public Private Partnerships for rural Development through Creating Business Opportunities", *JOAAG* 4(1).

Sinha, A.B. (2011). *Public Private Partnership in Building Rural Infrastructure in India*. JM Academy.

Other:

National Rural Health Mission (2005-12), Mission Document.

Ministry to Woo Pvt Sector, Rural Infrastructure, 2010.

29

S.K. NAYAK

Economic Analysis of the Impact of Pradhan Mantri Gram Sadak Yojana on the Economy of Arunachal Pradesh

Introduction

Arunachal Pradesh (AP) is a northeastern state with a total area of 83,743 sq km and a population of 13.8 lakh. It borders three countries, namely China, Bhutan and Myanmar, having international border of 1,680 kms. Out of the total area, 95 per cent of the area is hilly. Density of population is 17, which is very low compared to other states of India. The state is a late starter in development. After the China war of 1961, the process of development was initiated. The state is mainly agrarian as 65 per cent of the population is engaged in agriculture. As only 5 per cent of the land is plain land, there is heavy pressure on land and scope of plain cultivation is very limited. The literacy of the state is fast moving and is one of the fastest in the country. With the limited resources and growth of education, people are fast migrating from traditional agriculture to other forms of employment. Due to lack of industrialisation, the demand for government jobs is increasing.

In this context, infrastructure acts as the driver of the economy. Road connectivity plays a crucial role in generation of income in rural areas. Initially at the implementation of Pradhan Mantri Gram Sadak Yoyana (PMGSY), the road density of the state was 18.02, which increased to 25.74 in 2010-11. In fact through this programme alone, an incremental road density of 4.49 took place in the state.

Table 29.1

Road Density in Arunachal Pradesh

Year	*Road Length (in km)*	*Road Density in km/100 sq km*
1960-61	505.54	0.60
1965-66	1,486.93	1.78
1970-71	2,315.13	2.76
1975-76	3,100.76	3.70
1980-81	3,572.42	4.27
1985-86	5,362.36	6.40
1990-91	8,344.77	9.96
1994-95	11,037.88	13.18
2000-01	15,091.32	18.02
2003-04	15,712	18.76
2004-05	17,751	21.20
2005-06	17,216	20.56
2006-07	17,430	20.81
2007-08	16,494	19.70
2008-09	20,384	24.34
2009-10	21,122	25.22
2010-11	21,555	25.74

Source: *Human Development Report of Arunachal Pradesh (2005)* and Basic Road Statistics of India (various issues).

Hence, it is important to examine the impact of this programme on different sectors of the economy. In this context, the main objectives of the presentation paper are to analyse: a) the economy of Arunachal Pradesh; b) the status of infrastructure, particularly road; c) the role of PMGSY in improving road connectivity; and d) the impact of increasing road density on income generation.

Implementation PMGSY in the State

PMGSY was implemented in the state in 2000-01. Table 29.2 reveals connectivity status of the habitation as on 1 April 2000 and 01 April 2014. In April 2000, out of 3,880 habitations in the state

68.81 per cent were unconnected by road. After implementation of the programme, the percentage of unconnected habitation is reduced to 40 per cent. Thus, in the span of 14 years, 1,106 habitation were connected by road through this programme.

Table 29.2

Connectivity Status of Habitations Initially the implementation of PMGSY

	Eligible				*Not Eligible*	
	1000+	*999-500*	*499-250*	*Total Eligible*	*Less Than 250*	*Total Habitations*
As on 1-04-2000						
Total Habitations	172	266	480	918	2,962	3,880
Unconnected Habitations	49	112	274	435	2,235	2670
% of Unconnected Habitations	28.49	42.11	57.08	47.39	75.46	68.81
As on 1-04-2014						
Unconnected Habitations	0	0	47		1,517	1564
% of Unconnected Habitations	0	0	9.79		51.22	40.31

Source: Computed from *http://pmgsy.nic.in/*

In the category of habitation with 1000+ population, out of 172,49 were unconnected in 2000 and in 2014, all habitations were connected by road. In habitation with population of 999-500, out of 266, 112 were unconnected in 2000. In 2014, all habitations were connected. In the category 250-499, out of 480, 274 were unconnected. By 2014, 227 were connected. In the category of less than 250 population, out of 2,962, 2,235 were unconnected in 2000. By 2014, 1,718 habitations were connected and 1,564 of them are yet to be connected. This is mainly because the unconnected habitations do not satisfy the population norms of the programme. The state government through own resources also connected around 301 habitations. State-wise performance of PMGSY as given in Table 29.3 reveals that 736 habitations in the state were connected through road and 3,760 kms of rural road was constructed therein. This increased road length contributes to greater road density (4.49 km/sq km) between 2000 and 2014, which is substantial.

Table 29.3

Status Regarding Finance of PMGSY

	Total No. of Proposals	*Total Length*	*Sanctioned Cost*	*Maintenance Cost*	*Total Payment Made*	*Payment per One Km*
2000-01	202	317.97	4,095.00	5	4,095.00	12.88
2001-02	137	728.76	8,643.27	0	8,562.01	11.75
2002-03	0	0	0.00	0	0.00	
2003-04	0	0	0.00	0	0.00	
2004-05	64	337.95	9,798.67	557.19	10,524.96	31.14
2005-06	43	395.355	19,034.65	463.3	20,346.49	51.46
2006-07	69	433.56	15,832.04	1,625.84	16,894.55	38.97
2007-08	101	807.691	45,061.03	1,655.24	47,457.01	58.76
2008-09	60	490.642	28,854.93	922.88	27,447.04	55.94
2009-10	29	287.578	18,594.98	268.21	11,197.88	38.94
2010-11	0	0	0	0	0	
2011-12	0	0	0	0	0	
2012-13	1	0	123.52	0	0	
2013-14	1	3.752	267.28	0	0	

Source: Computed from *http://pmgsy.nic.in/*

Some Salient Features of PMGSY in the State

Tables 29.3 and 29.4 point out some important aspects of the programme in AP. In the hilly terrain, due to landslide during the rainy season, maintenance cost becomes substantial. From 2000 to 2004, under the heading of maintenance cost, even though proposals were submitted by the state, not a single rupee was sanctioned. The proposal of maintenance cost was accepted in 2004-05 and maintenance was accepted as a component of PMGSY for the state.

For two years, 2002-03 and 2003-04, no new project was sanctioned. However, from 2004-05 to 2009-10, 366 proposals were sanctioned. Then again, from 2010-11 to 2013-14, only two proposals were sanctioned. This is mainly because habitations did not satisfy the population norms as prescribed by the programme.

Table 29.4

Status of PMGSY in India (State-wise)

State	*Habitations Benefitted*	*Length Completed (Roads)*	*Total Expenditure (Roads) in ₹Lakh*	*Cost of 1 KM of Road in ₹*	*Road Length Per Habitation*
Andhra Pradesh	7272	11938.515	241298.22	20.21	1.64
Arunachal Pradesh	736	3760.018	173313.71	46.09	5.11
Assam	8758	12841.71	797868.25	62.13	1.47
Bihar	8361	26803.601	1363392.89	50.87	3.21
Chhattisgarh	10343	22315.971	10472796.7	469.30	2.16
Goa	101	155.85	1147.64	7.36	1.54
Gujarat	3492	10145.492	249149.27	24.56	2.91
Haryana	1554	4546.351	139656.2	30.72	2.93
Himachal Pradesh	3891	8863.144	194968.38	22.00	2.28
Jammu & Kashmir	1324	3610.405	258145.93	71.50	2.73
Jharkhand	5445	8910.228	290865.8	32.64	1.64
Karnataka	8214	16171.735	366642.71	22.67	1.97
Kerala	913	1826.272	80941.85	44.32	2.00
Madhya Pradesh	18523	53824.743	1347130.76	25.03	2.91
Maharashtra	8790	22445.91	518643.3	23.11	2.55
Manipur	706	3459.181	88993.05	25.73	4.90
Meghalaya	206	1022.22	29355.01	28.72	4.96
Mizoram	161	2178.36	63248.22	29.03	13.53
Nagaland	194	2839.07	56279.62	19.82	14.63
Odisha	12248	28218.411	1174471.97	41.62	2.30
Punjab	3685	5505.72	213018.51	38.69	1.49
Rajasthan	16153	52699.333	942951.05	17.89	3.26
Sikkim	65	2518.721	73057.39	29.01	38.75
Tamil Nadu	8152	11392.372	246487.57	21.64	1.40
Telangana	4303	9134.537	166446.68	18.22	2.12
Tripura	3324	2956.699	175162.13	59.24	0.89
Uttar Pradesh	22570	42561.678	1093861.4	25.70	1.89
Uttarakhand	982	3943.815	143875.09	36.48	4.02
West Bengal	12169	16098.866	584983.44	36.34	1.32
Total	172635	392688.928	21548152.74	54.87	2.27

Source: Computed from *http://pmgsy.nic.in/*

Unit Cost of Construction

Table 29.5 reveals unit cost of construction across the states in India. During 2000-14, the unit cost of construction at the all India average was ₹54.87 lakh. This is mainly because, in many of the hilly states, unit cost of construction was substantially high. For example, in Chhattishgarh, it was ₹469 lakh and in Jammu and Kashmir, ₹71.5 lakh. It was lowest in Goa (₹7.36 lakh) and Rajasthan (₹17.89 lakh). Surprisingly in the northeastern hilly states, unit cost of construction is comparable with that of Madhya Pradesh (MP), Karnataka and Haryana. Unit cost in Manipur, Meghalaya, Mizoram was in the range of ₹25 to ₹29 lakh. In AP, it is ₹46.09 lakh, which is less than that of Bihar (₹50.87 lakh) and Chhattishgarh (₹469.30 lakh).

Road Length per Habitation

The all-India average of road length created per habitation through this programme was 2.27 km. In the northeastern hilly states, it is substantially higher. In AP, it was 5.11 km, and in Sikkim, 38.75 km. In Manipur and Meghalaya, it was around 5 km, whereas in Mizoram and Nagaland it was around 13-14 km. Generally in the hilly terrain, the total cost of road connectivity should have been more. Considering cost per km of road, as given in Table 29.5 it may be inferred that the northeastern states have out-performed many of these in mainland India.

Changing Structure and Growth of GDP and its Different Sector

The growth rate is analysed from 1980 to 2014. The time period is divided as—Pre-liberalisation (1981-1991); Post-liberalisation, Phase I (1991-1999); Post-liberalisation Phase II (1999-2007) and post-liberalisation Phase III (2007-2014).

Agriculture

In the pre-liberalisation period, agriculture in the state grew at a rate of 7.65 per cent per annum, which was higher than the national average. During 1991-1999, there was negative growth, which was mainly due to Supreme Court restriction of timbering. During 1999-2007, the growth rate was 0.75 per cent. In the recent period, it has gone up to 3.7 per cent per annum. In terms of contribution to overall growth of the economy, there was substantial decline from 44 per cent in 1980-1991 to -49.72 per cent in 1991-1999 and to 2.83 per cent in 1999-2007. During 2007-2014, it has gone up to 17.09 per cent.

Table 29.5

Growth Rate of SDP, its Different Sector and Population

		AP	*India*
Agriculture	Pre-Liberalisation	7.65	3.03
Agriculture	Post-Liberalisation, Phase-I (1991-1999)	-3.53	3.16
Agriculture	Post-Liberalisation, Phase-II (1999-2007)	0.75	2.73
	Post-Liberalisation, Phase-III (2007-2014)	3.7	3.7
Industry	Pre-Liberalisation	7.44	6.84
Industry	Post-Liberalisation, Phase-I (1991-1999)	12.46	7.46
Industry	Post-Liberalisation, Phase-II (1999-2007)	19.01	6.84
Industry	Post-Liberalisation, Phase-III (2007-2014)	6.7	5.4
Service	Pre-Liberalisation	8.76	6.25
Service	Post-Liberalisation, Phase-I (1991-1999)	5.66	8.06
Service	Post-Liberalisation, Phase-II (1999-2007)	8.39	8.69
Service	Post-Liberalisation, Phase-III (2007-2014)	8	8
SDP/GDP	Pre-Liberalisation	7.95	5.23
SDP/GDP	Post-Liberalisation, Phase-I (1991-1999)	2.75	6.53
SDP/GDP	Post-Liberalisation, Phase-II (1999-2007)	7.26	7.06
SDP/GDP	Post-Liberalisation, Phase-III (2007-2014)	6.2	6.7
PCSDP	Pre-Liberalisation	2.74	3.24
PCSDP	Post-Liberalisation, Phase-I (1991-1999)	0.41	4.58
PCSDP	Post-Liberalisation, Phase-II (1999-2007)	5.82	5.44
PCSDP	Post-Liberalisation, Phase-III (2007-2014)	3.7	4.8

Note: SDP-State Domestic Product; PCSDP-Per capita State Domestic Product.
Source: Computed from *www.mospi.nic.in/*

Industry

Growth rate during pre-liberalisation period was 7.44 per cent. In the post-liberalisation period, Phase I and II, it was 12 per cent and 19 per cent respectively. It decelerated during Phase III (2007-2014).

Contribution to the growth by industry was 21.7 per cent in pre-liberalisation period, which increased to 39 per cent in 1991-1999 and declined to 24.5 per cent in Phase II, further rising to 34.6 per cent in 2007-2014.

Table 29.6

Contribution of Different Sectors to the Growth of GSDP of Different States

		AP	*India*
Agriculture	Pre-Liberalisation	43.92	20.02
	Post-Liberalisation, Phase-I (1991-1999)	-49.72	13.65
	Post-Liberalisation, Phase-II (1999-2007)	2.83	8.06
	Post-Liberalisation, Phase-III (2007-2014)	17.09	8.14
Industry	Pre-Liberalisation	21.72	26.28
	Post-Liberalisation, Phase-I (1991-1999)	38.85	25.45
	Post-Liberalisation, Phase-II (1999-2007)	24.5	18.87
	Post-Liberalisation, Phase-III (2007-2014)	34.6	22.35
Service	Pre-Liberalisation	34.32	53.66
	Post-Liberalisation, Phase-I (1991-1999)	110.87	60.9
	Post-Liberalisation, Phase-II (1999-2007)	72.67	73.07
	Post-Liberalisation, Phase-III (2007-2014)	48.3	68.69

Source: Computed from *www.mospi.nic.in/*

Service

The growth rate of service sector was 7.95 per cent in the pre-liberalisation period, which declined to 2.75 per cent in 1991-1999. Then it increased to 7.26 per cent in Phase II (1999-2007) and declined further to 6.2 per cent during 2007-2014. In term of contribution to growth, this sector's contribution was 34.32 per cent in 1980-1991, which heightened to 110.87 per cent in 1991-1999. Then, it declined to 72.67 per cent in 1991-2007 and further to 48.3 per cent in recent times.

Thus, the growth process which was inequitious during 1980-1991 and 1991-2007, seemed to be more equitious during 2007-2014. This is mainly owing to the better performance of agriculture and industrial sector in recent times, as 65 per cent of the population is dependent on it.

Hence, in a nutshell, we can say that the growth performance of AP's economy is becoming more equitious in recent times.

Impact of PMGSY on GSDP of Arunachal Pradesh

There was substantial increase in road length after the implementation of the programme. In order to realise the impact of this programme indirectly on different components of GSDP (gross state domestic product), the present attempt has considered the following relationship.

GSDP	=	f(ROAD_DEN)	(1)
GSDP_ALLI	=	f(ROAD_DEN)	(2)
GSDP_AGRI	=	f(ROAD_DEN)	(3)
GSDP_IND	=	f(ROAD_DEN)	(4)
GSDP_MIN	=	f(ROAD_DEN)	(5)
GSDP_MAN	=	f(ROAD_DEN)	(6)
GSDP_SER	=	f(ROAD_DEN)	(7)

The description of the variables are as follows.

GSDP_MIN	=	GSDP from Minerals
GSDP	=	Gross State Domestic Product
GSDP_ALLI	=	GSDP from Agriculture and Allied Services
GSDP_IND	=	GSDP from Mining
GSDP_MAN	=	GSDP from Manufacturing
GSDP_ SER	=	GSDP from Service
ROAD_DEN	=	Road Density

Sources of Data: Time series data is available for all the variables. For GSDP and its components, Planning Commission data is used. For road density, Basic Road Statistics of India (various issues), published by Ministry of Road Transport and Highways, GoI is used.

Discussion

We then follow the now established three-step procedure for assessing the properties of a time series relationship—find out whether the variables are stationary or non-stationary; if they are non-stationary, carry out a co-integration test to identify if there is any long run relationship among the variables; and if co-integration holds, apply the ECM (error correction mechanism).

We apply Augmented Dickey-Fuller (ADF) test to our variables in order to assess their stationary (or non-stationary) property. The results of the test are shown in Appendix Table A-29.1 and A-29.2.

Our test reveals that all the variables possess' unit root, that is, they are non-stationary. However, first difference of GSDP, GSDP_ALLI, GSDP_AGRI, GSDP_IND, GSDP_MIN, GSDP_SER and ROAD_DEN is stationary. For the variable GSDP_MANU, second difference is stationary. Thus, the variables GDSP, GSDP_ALLI, GSDP_AGRI, GSDP_IND, GSDP_MIN, GSDP_SER and ROAD_DEN are integrated of order one, that is, I (1). GSDP_MANU is integrated of order two, that is, (II).

Next, we examine whether the relationships expressed by the equations are characterised by a cointegrating relationship. For this, we apply the Engle and Granger (1987) test of cointegration. This test requires, assessing the residuals of cointegrating equations for stationary. Applying ADF test on the residuals of the regression equations, we found that all the residuals, except for the equation (6), are non-stationary. Thus, the variables specified in equation (6) are cointegrated. This means that the regression is not spurious and there is long run relationship between the variables. To reconcile the long run changes with short run ones, we try to re-establish the model through an Error Correction Model as shown in Appendix Table A-29.17. The sign of Ut-1 is negative which is expected. The coefficient of the cointegrating term Ut-1 indicates that about 41 per cent of the disequilibrium divergence tends to be eliminated in one year.

From above discussion of the regression result, it is clear that equation (6) has the problem of cointegration and others are free. Hence, from OLS results as given in Appendix, we infer the followings:

- Road density explains 80 per cent of the variation in GSDP.
- Road density explains 50 per cent of the variation in GSDP from Allied sector.
- Road density explains 49 per cent of the variation in GSDP from Agriculture sector.

- Road density explains 80 per cent of the variation in GSDP from Industry.
- Road density explains 52 per cent of the variation in GSDP from Minerals sector.
- Road density explains 29 per cent of the variation in GSDP from Manufacturing sector.
- Road density explains 83 per cent of the variation in GSDP from Service sector.

Thus, we can say that PMGSY has tremendously contributed towards the equitable growth process of the economy of Arunachal Pradesh.

References

Engle, R.F. and C.W.J. Granger (1987). "Cointegration and Error Correction: Representation, Estimation, and Testing", *Econometrica* 55: 251-27.

Appendix

Table A-29.1

Augmented Dickey-Fuller test of Stationary of Variables in Equations

Variable	*Lag*	*OLS Estimate*	*t-value*	*Null*	*Result*
GSDP	1	-0.0227	-0.3991 (0.91000)	Unit root	Not rejected•
GSDP_ALLI	0	-0.0955	-0.4585 (0.90000)	Unit root	Not rejected•
GSDP_AGRI	0	-0.1075	-0.4929 (0.89000)	Unit root	Not rejected•
GSDP_IND	0	-0.0287	0.1954 (0.94000)	Unit root	Not rejected•
GSDP_MIN	0	-0.4429	-1.9968 (0.29000)	Unit root	Not rejected•
GSDP_MANU	1	-0.1813	-1.6661 (0.44000)	Unit root	Not rejected•
GSDP_SER	0	-0.0784	-0.4942 (0.89000)		
ROAD_DEN	0	-0.1924	-0.8488 (0.800000		

Note: • at 10 per cent level of significance; parentheses include p-value.

Table A-29.2

Augmented Dickey-Fuller Test of Stationary of First Difference of Variables

Variable	*Lag*	*OLS Estimate*	*t-value*	*Null*	*Result*
ΔGSDP	0	-0.9194	-2.9410(0.04000)	Unit root	Rejected**
ΔGSDP_ALLI	0	-1.1587	-3.0614(0.03000)	Unit root	Rejected**
ΔGSDP_AGRI	0	-1.1682	-3.0928(0.03000)	Unit root	Rejected**
ΔGSDP_IND	0	-1.3512	-3.5759(0.01000)	Unit root	Rejected**
ΔGSDP_MIN	0	-0.9951	-2.6267(0.09000)	Unit root	Rejected•
ΔGSDP_MANU	0	-1.0072	-2.3709(0.15000)	Unit root	Not Rejected*
ΔGSDP_SER	0	-1.4392	-3.9566(0.00000)	Unit root	Rejected**
ΔROAD_DEN	0	-1.1951	-3.0840(0.03000)	Unit root	Rejected**
Δ2GSDP_MANU	0	-1.2936	-3.0947	Unit root	Rejected**

Note: * at 10 per cent level of significance ** at 5 per cent level of significance; parentheses include p-value.

Regression Results of Equation

Table A-29.3

OLS Estimates of Equation (1)

Dependent Variable: GSDP

Variables	*Constant*	*t-value*	*p-value*
Constant	-3035.4633	-2.209	0.027
ROAD_DEN	330.8432	5.697	0.00000

F(1,8) = 32.46 sig:-0.00046

R^2 = 0.8023

D-W = 1.4578, N=10

Table A-29.4

ADF Test on the Residuals of Regression Equation (1)

Lag	*OLS Estimate*	*t-value*	*Null*	*Result*
0	-0.8579	-2.1650 (0.22000)	Unit root	Not rejected**

Note: **at 5 per cent level of significance

Table A-29.5

OLS Estimates of Equation (2)

Dependent Variable: GSDP_ALLI

Variables	*Constant*	*t-value*	*p-value*
Constant	278.4101	0.677	0.4983
ROAD_DEN	49.5377	2.850	0.00437

F(1,8) = 8.12 sig:- 0.02147

R^2 = 0.5038

D-W = 1.38021, N=10

Table A-29.6

ADF Test on the Residuals of Regression Equation (2)

Lag	*OLS Estimate*	*t-value*	*Null*	*result*
0	-0.7474	-1.9454 (0.3100)	Unit root	Not rejected*

Note: *at 10 per cent level of significance

Table A-29.7

OLS Estimates of Equation (3)

Dependent Variable: GSDP_AGRI

Variables	*Constant*	*t-value*	*p-value*
Constant	-315.2466	-0.800	0.42400
ROAD_DEN	46.2800	2.777	0.00549

F(1,8) = 7.71 sig:-0.02404

$R^2 = 0.4908$

D-W = 1.417789, N=10

Table A-29.8

ADF Test on the Residuals of Regression Equation (3)

Lag	*OLS Estimate*	*t-value*	*Null*	*Result*
0	-0.7639	-1.9769 (0.30000)	Unit root	Not rejected*

Note: *at 10 per cent level of significance

Table A-29.9

OLS Estimates of Equation (4)

Dependent Variable: GSDP_IND

Variables	*Constant*	*t-value*	*p-value*
Constant	-1256.7788	-2.546	0.01091
ROAD_DEN	118.8013	5.693	0.00000

F(1,8) = 32.41 sig:- 0.00046

$R^2 = 0.8020$

D-W = 1.321249, N=10

Table A-29.10

ADF Test on the Residuals of Regression Equation (4)

Lag	*OLS Estimate*	*t-value*	*Null*	*Result*
0	-0.7383	-1.8847 (0.34000)	Unit root	Not rejected*

Note: *at 10 per cent level of significance.

Table A-29.11

OLS Estimates of Equation (5)

Dependent Variable: GSDP_MIN

Variables	*Constant*	*t-value*	*p-value*
Constant	-16.0985	-0.376	0.70684
ROAD_DEN	5.4319	3.002	0.00268

F(1,8) = 9.01 sig:- 0.01701

$R^2 = 0.5298$

D-W = 1.574983, N=10

Table A-29.12

ADF Test on the Residuals of Regression Equation (5)

Lag	*OLS Estimate*	*t-value*	*Null*	*Result*
0	-0.8998	-1.2478 (0.65000)	Unit root	Not rejected*

Note: *at 10 per cent level of significance.

Table A-29.13

OLS Estimates of Equation (6)

Dependent Variable: GSDP_MANU

Variables	*Constant*	*t-value*	*p-value*
Constant	-50.9744	-1,342	0.17956
ROAD_DEN	6.7230	4.188	0.00003

F(1,8) = 17.54 sig:- 0.00305

$R^2 = 0.6867$

D-W = 1.355048, N=10

Table A-29.14

ADF Test on the Residuals of Regression Equation (6)

Lag	*OLS estimate*	*t-value*	*Null*	*Result*
0	-0.8334	-2.6486 (0.09000)	Unit root	rejected*

Note: *at 10 per cent level of significance.

Table A-29.15

OLS Estimates of Equation (7)

Dependent Variable: GSDP_SER

Variables	*Constant*	*t-value*	*p-value*
Constant	-2098.9851	-3.389	0.00070
ROAD_DEN	164.4931	6.284	0.00000

$F(1,8) = 39.48$ sig:- 0.00024

$R^2 = 0.8315$

D-W = 2.248913, N=10

Table A-29.16

ADF Test on the Residuals of Regression Equation (7)

Lag	*OLS Estimate*	*t-value*	*Null*	*Result*
1	-1.5755	-1.8483 (0.35000)	Unit root	Not rejected*

Note: *at 10 per cent level of significance.

Table A-29.17

Error Correction Model of Equation (6)

Dependent Variable: ΔGSDP_MANU

Variable	*Parameter*	*St. Error*	*t-value*	*Significance*
Constant	7.4958	2.528551	2.965	0.00303
ΔROAD_DEN	-1.59989	1.24848	-1.281	0.20003
ΔUt-1	-0.4128886	1.2549	-0.329	0.74214

$R^2=0.2911$

Adj.$R^2=-0.0633$

N=7 $F(2,4) = 0.82$

Sig.=>0.50253

D-W=> 1.651218

30

SARASWATI UNNI and ANISH NAIR

Rural Electrification

A Flawed Approach

In the 21st century, electricity is undoubtedly more than a mere utility. It sustains livelihoods and improves one's standard of living. It is a important driver of economic growth and industrial progress. But electricity is yet to be treated as a public common or as a resource essential to one's livelihood, especially so in a country like India, where about a third of the households do not have regular access to electricity. In India, the policy discourse surrounding electricity is such that continuous supply of electricity for domestic use is still regarded as a luxury. While electricity as a utility and as a tool to drive change in industry and in the economy was considered as necessary, electricity as resource for smooth functioning of households as a notion came rather late in the government's policy discourse. This differential policy standard contextualises our understanding of the rural electrification policies and programmes.

Access to electricity is considered a basic indicator of rural development. It affects all aspects of development including livelihoods, access to water, agricultural productivity, health, and education. Energy services are essential to both social and economic development and much wider and greater access to energy services is critically important in achieving all of the Millennium Development Goals (MDGs). Both the Government of India (GoI), Planning Commission's strategy for the development of rural India as well as the United Nation's MDGs, are inherently dependent on the integration of electricity services to achieve a set of varied development goals.

India has 5,97,464 villages[1] as per the 2011 census, of which 5,71,742 villages are electrified as of August 2014. This puts the village electrification rate of the country at an impressive 95.7 per cent (Central Electrical Authority, 2014). However, census data on rural household electrification is not so impressive. Only a little more than half (52.5%) of rural Indian households have access to electricity (Census of India, 2011). The discrepancy between both the figures reveals the magnitude of the problem of access to electricity of rural India, as compared to urban India.[2] A closer look at the rural electrification policy is hence needed to put these issues in perspective.

Evolution of the Electricity Sector: A Brief Overview

The Constitution of India lists 'power' as a subject in the concurrent list; both GoI and state governments can make laws on the subject. Designated a basic and capital-intensive sector, its future became the exclusive responsibility of the state. Since Independence, the growth of the power sector in India has been predominantly in the public sector—either through SEBs (state electricity boards) or central government-owned generating and transmissions companies. This aspect was accentuated by the fact that after independence, India adopted the Mahalanobis model of economic development with focus on planned growth. Right from the First Five Year Plan itself, high priority was given to the expansion of infrastructural facilities. The plans have generally allocated over 50 per cent of the total plan outlay for infrastructure development (Datt and Sundaram, 2007).

The outlay on power in the various plans has been rising each year but expenditure has lagged behind Plan provisions (Ministry of Information and Broadcasting, 1980: 172). It has been observed that

1. All places that do not have a minimum population of 5,000, with 75 per cent of the male working population in agriculture, and a population density of at least 400 per sq. km. (i.e. 1000 per sq. mile).
2. The rate of unelectrified urban households stands at 6.9 per cent, according to the 2011 Census of India.

there is a positive co-relation between economic growth and demand for energy because growth is an index of increasing productive activity which requires larger quantity of energy. A 3 per cent rise in industrial production in the world is accompanied by a 2 per cent increase in energy consumption. A similar relationship has been observed in India. Consumption of energy in domestic use and public lighting also increases with growing affluence. At the world level, per capita consumption of energy is much higher in high income countries as compared to India (Mishra and Puri, 2006).

The Industrial Policy Resolutions as well as subsequent policy statements of the GoI sought state participation to accelerate the process of industrialisation in the country. Given its high sunk costs and wide social and environmental impacts and the recognition that electricity supply is a core industry and of strategic importance in industrial development, the policy for power was carefully formulated. But over the years, several forms of government intrusiveness that beset the Indian public sector quite naturally enveloped electric utilities as well. Utilities increasingly became financially non-viable and incapable of meeting demand—qualitatively and quantitatively (Rao, 2004).

In 1973, the Organisation of Petroleum Exporting Countries (OPEC) announced a cut-back in oil production and a four-fold increase in oil prices (Reddy and Prasad, 1995: 104). The implications of such a crisis were profound. The oil price hike had severe repercussions on petroleum importing countries like India. It also seriously impacted the economies of developed countries. It was a clear manifestation of an energy crisis. The pattern of energy development that occurred over a 30 year period from 1950 to 1980 led to the harmful growth of urban islands of energy affluence amidst vast oceans of rural energy deprivation (Reddy and Prasad, 1995).

Between 1960-61 and 1970-71, oil consumption doubled from 6.02 million tonnes to 15.31 million tonnes (Reddy and Prasad, 1995: 52). It was believed that energy crisis would undermine India's efforts to eradicate poverty. However, even as late as 1973, nearly 60 per cent of the Indian population did not have the purchasing power to enter the market for commercial energy. In other words, the oil-price hike was not a problem of immediate relevance to the vast majority of the Indian people because they neither used cars nor did they cooked with LPG (liquefied petroleum gas), and they also did not buy many energy-intensive products. The real problem was that an Indian village has been in an 'area of darkness' in many senses; there was a serious inadequacy of electricity which is a clear indicator of the low levels of energy use in rural India (Reddy and Prasad, 1995: 111).

In urban India, by the 1990s, failures in the electricity sector developed into a crisis-like situation, pushing the electricity sector to the brink of collapse. It was at this time that structural changes, such as the increased role of the private sector and the introduction of Independent Regulatory Commissions (IRCs), were initiated, apparently to solve the crisis. Electricity was now considered as a commodity that could be bought and sold in the market, unlike its traditional role as a development input. Private participation, the increased role of market forces and the reduced role of the state are key aspects of this policy shift (Baijal, 1999). The power sector was no longer expected to be an instrument of public policy and the emphasis on self-reliance in fuel and related technology became less important. Subsidies for the poor consumers (as cross subsidy from rich consumers and directly through state budget support) began to be questioned. As part of the structural changes, many new players came up in the place of one big electricity board. In the place of direct regulation of the sector by the government, regulation by an IRC was introduced. The Electricity Act 2003, enacted by the Central Government consolidated this approach (D'Sa *et al.*, 2005).

Some of the changes in the electricity sector have resulted in improvements, whereas some have worsened the situation. There is an increased and direct consumer orientation in the acts and policies. Regulatory Commissions and Consumer Grievance Forums have made it easier for consumers to understand the working of these utilities and pursue their complaints. On the other hand, high emphasis on making utility operations profitable has resulted in the neglect of power supply to the poor and low attention to environmental sustainability. The sector operation has become more complex with many more players like distribution companies, private generating companies, power traders, franchisees, grievance forums and Regulatory Commissions.

With recurring power cuts and worsening quality of supply, the situation is not far from a crisis like situation. 47 per cent of rural households do not have access to electricity (Census of India, 2011). The remaining do not get electricity when they want it, due to heavy load shedding. Thus, about half the rural population get very limited benefits from electricity. Agricultural consumers get highly subsidised (or at times free) electricity supply. But the duration and reliability of supply are rapidly decreasing (The Energy Research Institute, 2005).

A History of India's Rural Electrification Efforts

One of the early flagship programmes of GoI was the Minimum Needs Programme (MNP), which began in Fifth Year Plan (1974-1979) with rural electrification being given separate allocation in the national programme. The MNP while laid out a significant blueprint for rural development, came at a time when the glaring inequity between rural and urban India came into focus. Funds were provided as Central assistance to the states in the form of grants and loans. The areas covered under MNP for the purposes of rural electrification were remote, far flung and difficult villages with low load potential. For identifying the beneficiaries and beneficiary areas, certain all-India norms were taken as benchmarks at various points of time and the MNP assistance was directed to the population/area with low level of achievement below respective benchmark level (Ernst and Young, 2007).

In the beginning, loans were made available at interest rates lower than the funds provided under the budgetary support for rural electrification by GoI. However, over a period of time, rate of interest charged under the MNP and the normal budgetary support became equal with the result that State Electricity Boards (SEBs) had to bear the burden of higher rate of interest for these uneconomical programmes. No funds were released under the scheme from 2004-05 onwards in view of it being merged with the new scheme Rajiv Gandhi Grameen Vidyutikaran Yojana (RGGVY) (Ernst and Young, 2007: 17).

The Kutir Jyoti Yojana (KJY) was launched in 1988 to provide connections to BPL (below poverty line) households. The beneficiaries of this programme were Dalits and tribals having annual income below ₹27,000. The main focus of the KJY was to extend single point light connections to households of rural BPL families. Grants for the same were provided by the Rural Electrification Corporation (REC). However, increasing T&D (transmission and distribution) losses and rising costs of initial connections hampered KJY's effectiveness in rural electrification (Ernst and Young, 2007).

In the KJY, the outlay used to be allocated amongst the states based on two indicators i.e. size of rural population below the poverty line and level of village electrification obtained in the state in a manner that higher weightage is given to states with larger population of rural poor and with low electrification level. Under this programme, one-time cost of internal wiring and service connection charges was provided by way of 100 per cent grant to the states. The norm for grant per connection was changed from time to time. In 1988-1990 it was ₹180, which was increased to ₹400 in 1992-1994. For 1996-1998, the grant was ₹800 for unmetered connections and ₹1,000 to the metered ones. In March 2002, the grant amount was again increased to ₹1,500 and ₹1,800 for special category of states (which included Jammu & Kashmir, Himachal Pradesh, Uttaranchal, and the North-Eastern States). According to an evaluation study set up by Ministry of Power, one of the reasons for low willingness on the part of beneficiaries to go for this programme was unreliable and poor quality of supply. For instance in states like Uttar Pradesh and Bihar, it was found that because of interrupted power supply beneficiaries did not pay the bills as they found little use of the connection. In May 2004, it was merged into the programme for "Accelerated Electrification of One Lakh Villages and One Crore Households" (Ernst and Young, 2007: 17-18).

Until 2003, the electricity supply industry in India was governed by three enactments: the Indian Electricity Act 1910, the Electricity (Supply) Act 1948 and the Electricity Regulatory Commissions Act 1998. The 1910 Act gave the basic framework for the industry. It envisaged growth through private licensees and provided for licensees to supply a specified area. The 1948 Act mandated the creation of SEBs with the responsibility of managing electricity supply in the state. The 1998 Act created the Central Regulatory Commission (CRC) and provided the legal framework for creating State Regulatory Commissions (SRCs). State Acts related to reform have been passed in eight states—Orissa (1996), Haryana (1997), Andhra Pradesh (1998), Uttar Pradesh (1999), Karnataka (1999), Rajasthan (1999), Delhi (2000), and Madhya Pradesh (2000). The Electricity Act 2003 replaced all these laws (Ministry of Power, 2003).

The Electricity Act 2003 (E-Act) is a watershed in the reform calendar. The E-Act and related policies were meant to usher competition into the power sector. After nearly three years of drafting, the Electricity Bill was passed in the Parliament in April 2003 and enacted in June 2003. The E-Act had fundamental and far-reaching impact. The Act consolidates the laws relating to generation, transmission, distribution, trading and use of electricity. But more importantly, the Act revised the then existing definition of an electrified village,[3] which currently dictates and directs the rural electrification policy of India. According to the E-Act a village would be declared as electrified if:

i. Basic infrastructure such as Distribution Transformer and Distribution lines are provided in the inhabited locality as well as the Dalit *basti*/hamlet where it exists.
ii. Electricity is provided to public places like schools, *panchayat* office, health centres, dispensaries, community centres etc., and
iii. The number of households electrified should be at least 10 per cent of the total number of households in the village.

The E-Act led to creation of two major programmes dedicated towards rural electrification, viz., the Accelerated Rural Electrification Programme (AREP) and Remote Village Electrification (RVE) programme.

---

3. The pre-2003 definition of an electrified village was, "A village will be deemed to be electrified if electricity is used in the inhabited locality, within the revenue boundary of the village, for any purpose whatsoever". See: *http://www.rggvy.gov.in/rggvy/rggvyportal/def_elect_vill.htm*

The AREP was introduced in the year 2003-04. Interest subsidy of 4 per cent was provided on loans availed by state governments and power utilities from financial institutions like REC, Power Finance Corporation (PFC), Rural Infrastructure Development Fund (RIDF), and National Agricultural Bank and Rural Development (NABARD) for carrying out rural electrification programme. The assistance was limited to electrification of un-electrified villages, electrification of hamlets, Dalit *bastis*, and tribal villages and electrification of households in villages through both conventional and non-conventional sources of energy. Funds were provided on the basis of NPV (net present value)[4] of the interest subsidies applicable on disbursement. 'Accelerated Electrification of One lakh Villages and One Crore Households' was introduced in the year 2004-05 by merging AREP and KJY (Ernst and Young, 2007: 18-20).

While the KJY, AREP, and later the Accelerated Electrification concentrated on villages where centralised grid connectivity was feasible, the E-Act necessitated the formation of a programme for remote hamlets and villages where centralised gird connection was not feasible. The Remote Village Electrification (RVE) programme was initiated by the Ministry of New and Renewable Energy to electrify all the remote villages and remote hamlets through non-conventional energy sources such as solar energy, small hydro power, biomass and wind energy. The programme was meant to provide electricity to un-electrified remote villages by 2007, un-electrified remote hamlets by 2012, and all households in remote villages and hamlets by 2012 (Ernst and Young, 2007: 20). As of September 2014 these aims were yet to be achieved (Ministry of New and Renewable Energy, 2014).

Rajiv Gandhi Grameen Vidyutikaran Yojana (RGGVY) : An Appraisal

Established in the year 2005 with an aim to provide "electricity for all", the RGGVY is a flagship programme administered by the Ministry of Power's nodal agency the REC. Under the RGGVY, 90 per cent capital subsidy for overall cost of the project is provided by the Central government, with the states being given the major

4. The NPV is defined as the sum of the PVS (present values), both incoming and outgoing, of the individual cash flows of the same entity, within a time series of cash flows.

responsibility of the arranging for electricity supply equally (in terms of hours of supply) to all rural and urban households, while bearing the rest of 10 per cent of the project cost. The grant for BPL households was different as they were given 100 per cent subsidy for electrification, including for setting up a connection (Ministry of Power, 2005).

RGGVY provides capital subsidy for strengthening the rural electricity distribution backbone, i.e., constructing distribution lines and sub-stations in places where these do not exist, creating a village electrification infrastructure and electrification of unelectrified villages and habitations, and setting up decentralised distributed generation and supply, i.e. supply from conventional sources for villages where grid connectivity is either not feasible nor cost effective. However, this is only for those villages which have not been electrified by the RVE programme of the Ministry of New and Renewable Energy (Ministry of Power, 2005).

The RGGVY also caters to the requirements of agriculture, *khadi* and village industries, cold chains, healthcare, education, and small and medium industries. The original outlay for RGGVY when the scheme was formulated was approximately ₹16,000 crore making it the largest run electrification programme in the country. At that time (2005), approval had been given to forward a capital subsidy of ₹5,000 for the implementation of the first phase of the programme. According to a Ministry of Power Report (2011), ₹28,148.88 crore was sanctioned for the project, out of which ₹7,021.95 crore was disbursed to various states for the Eleventh Five Year Plan (Unni, 2013). For the Twelfth Five Year Plan, the capital subsidy provided by the project currently stands at ₹35,447 crore (Ministry of Power, 2013).

Yet, the government's target of "Lifeline Consumption of 1 unit per day by all households by 2012" under the RGGVY has led to a very low consumption threshold for consumers of subsidised tariff. The underlying assumption is that the poor consume less electricity because they have fewer appliances in their homes. A consumption of 30 units per month implies the use of two 60 watt bulbs in the house operating daily for 8 hours (Kanitkar and Sreekumar, 2008).

While it has been easy to certify villages as being electrified by the establishment of rural feeders, distribution lines and transformers under the RGGVY, household electrification has proved to be a challenge. This can be attributed to the faulty definition of "electrified village", which states that "the number of households electrified should be at least 10 per cent of the total number of households in a village." This means that in villages with more than 10 per cent of BPL population, many BPL families have not got the connections whereas the scheme mandates free connection to all BPL families (Udupa, 2011).

It was also observed that even the specified limit of covering 10 per cent of the BPL families was not achieved in many villages. Additionally, low awareness about the scheme and centralised system coupled with low confidence on the grid meant that in some villages even the APL families did not apply for connections despite village electrification. Further, a large number of APL families in many villages illegally hooked to main distribution lines, which in turn led to overloading and damage to transformers. Another reason for such damage was attributed to installation of low capacity transformers under the scheme (Udupa, 2011).

Between the two programmes, RGGVY and RVE, of the Central government, there is potential to actually provide access to many of the 47.5 per cent rural households in India who do not have access. The fact that very little progress was made under RGGVY, even after disbursement of funds, is a cause for concern. There is a gap between the programme and the actual implementation. The principle behind the planning of this scheme, which is to build a centralised electricity network to ensure access to power, is flawed. Also, the focus towards village electrification instead of household electrification remains to be the major flaw afflicting our policy implementation and that needs to change.

Sustaining Access to the Poor: Problems and Suggestions

Although the rural poor constitute a majority, little attention and resources are devoted towards providing quality and affordable electricity due to whole host of reason, for instance, the low political bargaining power, low awareness of pro-poor provisions due to information asymmetry, lack of credibility of political promises, and the unviability of providing subsidised electricity to the poor by the utilities (Prayas Energy Group, 2005). Access to electricity depends on many factors: affordability, quality of supply, awareness, and participation. Although access, affordability, quality of supply, awareness and participation are mentioned separately here, all these are interconnected. For example, domestic consumers using less than 100 units per month in Maharashtra, contribute only 4 per cent of the total revenue. These consumers are subsidised—they do not pay the entire cost that is required to supply them with electricity. However, even if they did, their contribution would only increase to 9 per cent (Nakhooda and Dubash, 2000: 279). The poor get inferior quality of supply and services because the utilities view them as "non-profitable". Thus, the issue of prices for electricity and quality of supply and service are related (Kanitkar and Sreekumar, 2008: 14).

One of the most critical aspects of any basic service (like water supply, healthcare, education, public transport or electricity) is its affordability. There is money to be paid while getting new connections —service connections charges, service line charges, security deposits and monthly electricity bills. In many states, agricultural consumers and some domestic consumers are not metered. The actual amount of electricity used is not measured. Consumers pay a fixed amount each month based on the connected load and estimated hours of use. The high cost for getting a new connection is the first hurdle preventing the poor from getting electricity (Prayas Energy Group, 2003: 31).

The next hurdle is the high charge for the use of electricity. In Maharashtra for instance, the service connection charge for a small domestic consumer with a connected load of less than 500 watts is ₹500. The total amount that the consumer has to pay to the utility after including registration charges and security deposits is ₹1,460. In a state where 30 per cent of the population has a per capita expenditure of about ₹360 per month, ₹1,460 is a considerable amount to be paid for an electricity connection (Ministry of Power, 2007).

Electricity access to poor households while being unprofitable is also not so significant for the SEBs and electricity distributors.

Industrial and urban use gets priority over domestic and rural use. The case of Akshay Prakash Yojana (APY) is illustrative of this fact. An innovative attempt to provide villages with a stable and reliable supply of electricity, APY was implemented in Maharashtra in an attempt to regulate power use through consumer-utility-partnerships. Villagers were asked to regulate electricity use during peak hours, using it only for residential lighting during these times. Electricity used for agricultural pumps, flour mills, and lights required in schools was scheduled for use only during the necessary hours. Theft was also checked and people were asked to give up appliances consuming extremely high amounts of electricity, e.g., hot plates and heaters. The demand in these villages dropped, sometimes by as much as 50-70 per cent. In return, they were given 22 hours of assured electric supply in a day. This scheme had been implemented in 4,611 villages and according to Maharashtra State Electricity Distribution Company Limited (MSEDC), the peak demand has reduced by 960 MW. But the programme was discontinued in 2007. Official reasons given for this were extreme shortage of power which made it difficult to supply electricity for 22 hours to the Akshay Prakash villages, and lower benefits than expected from the scheme (Reddy and Dixit, 2010) It can be argued that Maharashtra government's neglect of decentralised systems and its over reliance on the centralised energy system is to be blamed for the failure of APY. When electricity shortage became acute in the state, electrification of the APY villages became non-essential for policymakers who cited low remunerative potential as the primary reason for abandoning the project.

Recommendations

Considering the fact that access to poor, especially the rural poor, is mostly dependant on the overall feasibility and profitability of the utility companies, measures need to be taken to safeguard their needs and demands. One step towards this direction would be to institutionally or legally 'ring-fence' the money intended for the poor i.e., ensure its usage exclusively to improve services to the poor. While the RGGVY has capital dedicated solely for rural electrification, no part of it is specifically dedicated for sustaining electricity for poor households which may not be able to survive the commercial energy market right after gaining access to electricity. The ring-fenced money can then be used to offer fee-waivers and subsidies on bills for the poor.

Table 30.1

Service Connection Charges in Select States

State	*Rajasthan*	*Maharashtra*	*Uttar Pradesh*	*Orissa*
Initial Cost (₹)	2500	1500	700-1000	600-800
% Rural Population with Per Capita Expenditure less than ₹12/day (₹365/month)	17	30	33	57
% Urban Population with Per Capita Expenditure less than ₹19/day (₹580/month)	36	25	44	50

Source: Ministry of Power, 2007.

The rationale behind subsidising electricity is to encourage its use as an agent for development. The areas which require use of electricity by the poor are domestic use, livelihood activities and community services. Lighting is the most important of these. In India, around 66 per cent of all poor rural households use kerosene for lighting which is nearly 5 times more expensive than electricity. As a percentage of total expenditure, an average BPL household spends more on lighting than a non-BPL household (Kanitkar and Sreekumar, 2008: 12).

The other step to secure steady and reliable electricity supply to the rural poor would be for the RGGVY and the government to move towards decentralised grids for rural electrification. One of the commonly cited official reasons for unequal and disparate supply of electricity to the rural areas is lack of profitability due to extension of grids, coupled with T&D losses. For instance, the MSEDC released a series of circulars in 2012 that detailed allocation of longer hours of load shedding to areas that returns greater loss to the company (MSEDC, 2012). A decentralised network of grids for rural clusters may have a positive effect on the electrification of rural areas where grid extension causes more loss to the supplier.

The other way in which access to the rural poor can be facilitated is by making the utilities answerable to the consumers. Institutionalising not just public participation, but also public deliberation is important for a transparent functioning of the public sector utilities. Right to Information Act tools could be used for direct intervention by the public leading to better accountability and in turn better service delivery. The Regulatory Commission also provides a forum for the public, in particular, the poor to bargain for lowering costs of new connections. Through the orders given to fix the 'Schedule of Charges', the Commission determines the amount that the utility can demand from a consumer while giving a new connection. The Commission also holds a public hearing before passing this order. Such existing measures can be further developed to democratise the governance of electricity.

The Underlying Flaw

Rural electrification is a flawed approach because it is an afterthought in the larger discourse of national development, where the rural rarely ever existed as anything more than the tool to facilitate the electoral ambitions of the political class. The first major attempt to bring the issue within the discourse was as late as 1974 with the MNP, when rural electrification was given separate allocation in the national programme. The very fact that rural aspects of infrastructure had to be defined, segregated, and categorised shows the problem with the then existing discourse and praxis of development, where the focus was the urban and the industrial and not the rural and the agrarian.

Also, the discourse of rural electrification is paternalistic, because the state decides the benchmark of electrification and even the feasibility and availability of timely supply of electricity. This can be seen by the low consumption threshold set by the government in the Electricity Act of 2003, for an electrified village and an electrified household. The failure of the APY in Maharashtra too is illustrative of this paternalistic nature of rural electrification.

Post-liberalisation, several state supplies started to treat the rural population as non-priority, something that was aggravated by the restructuring of SEBs. The neglect of rural India is reflected in the significantly disparate electricity supply, both in terms of hours of supply and the quality (D'Sa *et al.*, 2005). The fact that rural development is still not a priority, especially post-liberalisation, can be seen with the sudden stagnation of rural electrification rates. There was high focus on village electrification in the first few decades after independence. It can be seen from Figure 30.1 that the decades of 1961-71, 1971-81 and 1981-91 witnessed a high pace of village electrification. The definition of village electrification was changed in 2003 and as per the new definition, a much lower number of villages are treated as electrified which explains the fall in the graph after 2001 (Ministry of Power, 2010). Despite the adjustments there is a noticeable slowdown in the rate of village electrification.

Figure 30.1

Rise and Slow Down of Village Electrification

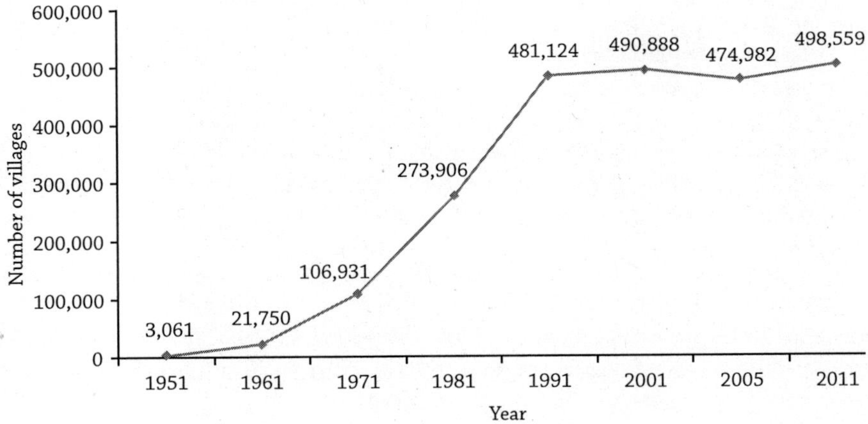

Source: Kalra and Shrivastava, 2007 and Ministry of Power, 2012.

Power sector reforms, in the post-liberalisation era, have concentrated on issues of utility finances, capacity addition and reducing tariffs to industry but have neglected the issue of electricity access to the poor. In many states, village electrification programmes slowed down and household electrification was neglected after privatisation (Hoonihal, 2004).

Access to electricity in rural areas has been regarded synonymous with rural electrification, implemented through the extension of a centralised grid. This is consequently accompanied by the problems of high T&D losses; frequent disruption in supply of grid power, and financial non-viability of extending grid to remote and inaccessible areas. While the RGGVY scheme has raised expectations of people with no access to electricity, lack of quality and unreliable electricity supply has underlined that the scheme has failed to deliver so far and has also failed to match the expectations created.

Electricity should no longer be treated as a commodity or even as a utility. The dynamics associated with considering it as a commodity leads to 'citizens as consumers' approach. The commodification of electricity was reinforced in the post-liberalised economic discourse, adversely affecting access to the poor in general and the rural poor in particular. The focus needs to change so that electricity will be viewed as an entitlement.

References

Baijal, P. (1999). "Restructuring Power Sector in India: A Base Paper", *Economic and Political Weekly* XXXIV(39): 2795-803, 5 September.

Bell, J. (2007). *Security Via Decentralized Energy.* Washington, DC: WADE Publications.

Census of India (2011). *Houses, Households Amenities and Assets.* Retrieved 15 March 2012 from: *http://www.censusindia.gov.in/2011census/hlo/Data%20sheet/HLO%20All%20Indicators.pdf*

Central Electrical Authority (2014). *Progress Report of Village Electrification.* August. Retrieved 10 October 2014 from: *http://www.cea.nic.in/reports/monthly/dpd_div_rep/village_electrification.pdf*

———. (2013). *Highlights of the Power Sector.* December. Retrieved from Central Electricity Authority website: *http://cea.nic.in/reports/monthly/executive_rep/dec13.pdf*

Datt, R. and K. Sundaram, K. (2007). *Indian Economy* (55th ed.). New Delhi: S. Chand and Company.

D'Sa, A., N. Murthy and A. Reddy (2005). "India's Power Sector Liberalisation: An Overview", *Economic and Political Weekly* XL(24): 1427-34, 5-11 June.

Ernst and Young (2007). *Models of Rural Electrification: Report to the Forum of Indian Regulators: Final Report.* 5 March. Retrieved 10 October 2014 from Forum of Regulators website: *http://www.forumofregulators.gov.in/Data/Reports/Final_Foir_Report_5th_March07_Models_of_RE_E&Y%5B1%5D.pdf*

Hoonihal, S. (2004). "Estimating Power Consumption in Agriculture", *Economic and Political Weekly* XXXIX(8): 790-92, 12-26 May.

Kalra, P., R. Shekhar and V. Shrivastava (2007). *India Infrastructure Report 2007: Rural Infrastructure.* New Delhi: Oxford University Press.

Kanitkar, T. and N. Sreekumar (2008). *Awareness and Action for Better Electricity Service.* Pune: Prayas Publication.

Ministry of Information and Broadcasting. (1980). *India: Reference Annual.* New Delhi: Government of India Press.

Ministry of New and Renewable Energy (2014). *Remote Village Electrification Programme.* Retrieved 10 October 2014, from: *http://mnre.gov.in/mission-and-vision-2/achievements/*

Ministry of Power (2003). *Electricity Act 2003.* New Delhi: Government of India Press.

———. (2005). *Ministry of Power Office Memorandum No. 44/19/2004-D(RE). 18* March.

———. (2007). *Report of the Rajiv Gandhi Grameen Vidyutikaran Yojana.*

———. (2010, April). *Rise and Slowdown of Village Electrification.* Retrieved 9 July 2012 from: *http://powermin.nic.in/village-electrification/rise-slowdown.htm*

———. (2012). *Annual Report 2011-12.* Retrieved an 15 March 2014 from: *http://www.powermin.nic.in/reports/pdf/Annual_Report_2011-12_English.pdf*

———. (2013). *Ministry of Power Office Memorandum No. 44/10/2011-RE.* 2 September.

———. (2014). *Bharat Nirman: A Business Plan.* 31 May. Retrieved 10 October 2014 from: : *http://powermin.nic.in/bharatnirman/bharatnirman.asp*

———. (n.d.). *Rural Electrification Corporation (REC).* Retrieved 10 October 2014 from: *http://www.powermin.nic.in/funds_for_power_sector/rural_electrification_corp.htm*

Mishra, S. and V. Puri (2006). *Indian Economy* (24th ed.). Mumbai: Himalaya Publishing House.

MSEDC (2012). *Maharashtra State Distribution Corporation Circular 43 (No. SE/LM/LS/30183) and Circular 44 (SE/LM/10472).* 21 April. Retrieved 20 August 2013 from: *http://www.mahadiscom.in/consumer/cir%2043_21_04.zip*

Nakhooda, S., S. Dixit and N. Dubash (2000, June). "Least-Cost Power Planning: Case Study of Maharashtra State-Energy for Sustainable Development", *The Journal of International Energy Initiative* IV(1): 275-94.

Pachauri, R. (1995). *Energy Policy for India: An Interdisciplinary Analysis.* New Delhi: MacMillan India.

Prayas Energy Group (2003). *A Good Beginning But Challenges Galore.* Pune: Prayas Publication.

————. (2005). *Privatisation or Democratisation: The Key to the Crisis in the Electricity Sector—The Case of Maharashtra.* Pune: Prayas Publication.

Rao, S.L. (2004). *Governing Power: A New Institution of Governance: The Experience With Independent Regulation of Electricity.* New Delhi: TERI Press.

Reddy, A. and K. Prasad (1995). "Technological Alternatives and the Indian Energy Crisis", in R. Pachauri (ed.), *Energy Policy for India: An Interdisciplinary Analysis.* New Delhi: MacMillan India. pp.44-149.

Reddy, T. and S. Dixit (2010). *Clean Energy Regulation and Civil Society in India: Need and Challenges to Effective Participation.* Pune: Prayas Publication.

The Energy and Resources Institute. (2013). "Indian Energy Sector: An Overview", in *TERI Energy Data Directory and Yearbook 2012/13.* pp.1-14.

————. (2005). *Regulatory Issue* 25: 4-11, March.

Udupa, A. (2011). *Failed Aspirations: An Inside View of the RGGVY.* Greenpeace India.

Unni, S. (2013). "Electricity Services: Issues and Linkages", in S. Unni, *Energy Policy of India.* Unpublished PhD thesis. University of Mumbai. pp.193-261.

31

SRIKANTHA NAYAKA, V. RAMAKRISHNAPPA
AND VISHWANATHA

Housing Status of Scheduled Tribes in Mysore District of Karnataka

A Study of Integrated Tribal Development Programme (ITDP) and Indira Awaas Yojana (IAY)

Introduction

Housing, water supply, sanitation and electricity are important indicators for measuring the physical quality of life and status of settlements where humans congregate and live. These aspects are fairly easy to measure and are also the secondary parameters to compute HDI (human development index). These indicators have intimate relationships with the state of health, education and with primary aspects of human development. House is one of the basic requirements for human survival. Housing is much an economic need as it is a social need not only it an indicator of social and economic status, but it is also an important determinant of development participation. The most challenging problem India faces today is housing problem. The STs (scheduled tribes) become more vulnerable than other social groups in access housing facilities. Though there is an attempt by the Central and State governments to fulfil the huge demands of both the urban and rural areas, the problems of housing and other infrastructural facilities persist still in different settlements.

India has been land of the tribes since time immemorial and recognised as second largest concentration of STs in the world after Africa. The ST population represents one of the most economically impoverished and marginalised groups in India. Although STs are a minority, they constitute about 8.6 per cent of the total population in India (Census of India, 2011). Out of their total population in the country, 91.7 per cent were living in rural areas, whereas, only 8.3 per cent from urban areas. STs have traditionally been concentrated in about 15 per cent of the country's geographical areas, mainly forests, hills, undulating inaccessible areas. The fact that most of them live in isolated groups in relatively remote areas has made it more difficult to deliver essential services to them and has also made it much more difficult for them to benefit from the acceleration of overall growth than is the case with SCs. The housing status of STs at all India level is worst than compare to others (Table 31.1). The STs are lagging behind the general population in access basic amenity of housing facilities. According to Census 2011, across India, 40.6 per cent of STs live in good condition houses compared to 53.1 per cent of that of the all social groups. The data shows that at the All India level only 46.9 per cent of all households out of which 22.6 per cent of ST households have latrine facility within the premises.

Table 31.1

Housing Status of Scheduled Tribes in India (2011 Census)

Sl.No		*No. of Total Houses*	*Good Houses (%)*	*% Having Latrine Facility Within the Premises*	*% Having Separate Kitchen Inside*
1	All social groups	246,692,667	53.1	46.9	61.3
2	ST	23,329,105	40.6	22.6	53.7

Sources: *Tribal Profile at a Glance*, May 2013, Ministry of Tribal Affairs, Govt of India.

Objectives and Database of the Study

The objectives of the present study are:

1. To analyse the housing status among STs in Karnataka and Mysore.
2. To study the progress of ITDP in Mysore district.
3. To review the progress of IAY in providing housing infrastructure for STs.

The paper is based on the secondary data collected from the State government and Central government reports and other published documents and journals.

Housing Status of STs in Mysore District of Karnataka

The ST population in the Karnataka has increased from 34,63,986 in 2001 Census to 42,48,987 in 2011, registering a decennial growth rate of 22.66 per cent. The proportion of the ST population to total population of the State is 6.95 per cent. In Karnataka, the tribal population varies from one district to another district in response to the geographical character of the region. The highest proportion of ST population is returned from Raichur district (19.03%) and the least proportion is returned from Mandya district (1.24%). The proportion of ST population is less than 5 per cent in 12 districts, between 5 to 9 per cent in 7 districts and above 10 per cent in the remaining 11 districts. About 85 per cent of the STs are living under the poverty line.

According to the Human Development Report 2005 (KHDR, 2006), the percentage of STs Living in permanent houses (43.7%) is lower than the corresponding figures for SCs (51.1%) and all households (54.9%). About 39 per cent dwell in semi-permanent houses compared with 35.6 per cent for all households and 36.6 per cent for SCs (scheduled castes). A higher percentage of rural STs live in semi-permanent houses (43.4%) than urban STs (23.1%) who live predominantly in permanent houses (66.9%). There is little difference between STs and all households, with reference to building material used. A high percentage of STs (84.4%) owned their houses, compared with 78.5 per cent for all households. House ownership is highest in rural areas (91.9%).

Mysore district consists of seven revenue taluks such as H.D.Kote, Hunsur, K.R.Nagar, Nanjangud, Periyapatna, T.Narasipura, Mysore Urban and Mysore Rural. For administration purpose, Mysore district comprises two subdivisions, which are Hunsur and Mysore; it consists of 1,216 villages, 11 statutory towns, 235 Gram Panchayats and 226 Wards. H.D. Kote and Nanjangud blocks have vast geographical areas because of the forests. Nanjangud block has a large number of Gram

Panchayats in the district and this is due to larger population of the block compared to the remaining blocks of the district.

The socio-economic imbalances amidst the marginalised STs are reflected in the types of housing they live in. The district data for the STs are 16.57 per cent for permanent, 49.83 per cent for semi-permanent and 33.6 per cent for temporary housing (Table 31.2). Permanent housing in regard to STs are 33.63 per cent in T. Narasipura taluk and 7.42 per cent in H.D. Kote taluk. There is also a repeat of the patterns in regard to semi-permanent (K.R. Nagar taluk 57.61%, Nanjangud taluk 43.26%; K.R. Nagar 68.40%, H.D. Kote 39.57%) and temporary housing (H.D. Kote taluk 48.11%, Hunsur taluk 24.59%; H.D. Kote taluk 53.01%, K.R. Nagar taluk 19.05%), for the tribes of the district.

Table 31.2

House Types of Scheduled Tribes of Mysore District (Percentage)

Sl.No	*Taluks*	*Permanent*	*Semi-Permanent*	*Temporary*
1	H.D. Kote	7.42	39.57	53.01
2	Hunsur	20.09	59.58	20.33
3	K.R. Nagar	12.55	68.40	19.05
4	Mysore	16.98	56.77	26.25
5	Nanjangud	14.35	42.43	43.22
6	Periyapatna	13.45	58.27	28.28
7	T. N. Pura	33.63	44.69	21.68
	District	16.57	49.83	33.60

Source: *Mysore Human Development Report, 2008.*

Most of SCs and STs are poor and percentages of site-less population of those categories are 27.5 per cent and 13.24 per cent respectively (Table 31.3). Among the taluks, H.D. Kote (35.45%) and T.N. Pura (35.69%) show the highest percentages of site-less SC population. Among STs, Hunsur (28.86%) and H.D. Kote (18.2%) taluks shows highest percentages of site-less population. The least proportions of site-less population are found in K R. Nagar taluk at 15.98 per cent for SCs and 8.09 per cent for STs.

Table 31.3

Site-less Population of Mysore District by Taluks (Percentage)

		Site-less		
Sl.NO	*Taluks*	*SC*	*ST*	*Others*
1	H.D. Kote	35.45	18.20	46.35
2	Hunsur	20.09	28.86	18.05
3	K.R. Nagar	15.98	9.13	74.89
4	Mysore	20.50	8.09	71.40
5	Nanjangud	26.63	11.71	61.64
6	Periyapatna	27.23	9.29	63.46
7	T. N. Pura	35.69	17.54	46.76
	District	27.5	13.24	59.25

Source: *Mysore Human Development Report, 2008.*

Housing among the ST communities has shown a significant record of activity as the *District Human Development Report 2008* reveals 32.22 per cent ST household have houses *pucca* in Mysore district. K.R. Nagar alone hast he highest per cent of the households (70.34%) have *pucca* house. Periyapatna taluk records the least of 9.95 per cent of households with *pucca* housing and the rest of 90.05 per cent of the households with semi *pucca* houses and *katcha* houses. Among the 90.05 per cent, about 46 percent of the total surveyed households are in semi-*pucca* conditions. It was in Periyapatna taluk where 87.40 per cent of the ST households are in semi-*pucca* and it happens to be the highest in the district. Among the kutcha housing it is only 21.69 per cent of the surveyed households with the highest number in Hunsur taluk (Table 31.4).

There are 50 STs inhabiting the State. The ST population of the district as per Census 2011 was 271,351 constituting 10.3 per cent of the total population. Among the STs, Jenukuruba, Kadukuruba, Soliga, Hakkipikki, Dongigarasia, Yerava andYerava's are indigenous who lived in colonies or hamlets. They are groups or tribes with different historical and social backgrounds, language families ethnic stocks. The government has taken initiatives to bring the primitive tribes (STs) from remote forest area to the main streams of living and provide the facilities like housing, health, education and other infrastructure facilities in the rehabilitation centres. There are 201 ST colonies/Hamlets in Mysore with 8472 families (Table 31.5).

Table 31.4

House Types of Scheduled Tribes of Mysore District (percentages)

Sl.NO	Taluks	Katcha Semi	Pucca Pucca	Katcha Semi
1	H.D. Kote	36.15	45.51	18.33
2	Hunsur	44.26	37.85	17.89
3	K.R. Nagar	14.27	15.39	70.34
4	Mysore	16.58	30.53	52.89
5	Nanjangud	9.78	71.79	18.43
6	Periyapatna	2.65	87.40	9.95
7	T. N. Pura	9.62	34.17	56.21
	District	21.69	46.10	32.22

Source: Mysore Human Development Report, 2008.

Table 31.5

Sub Caste-wise Distribution of Indigenous among ST Population in Mysore District

Sl.No	Taluks	No. of Colonies	No. of Families	Indigenous Population					
				Jenu kuruba	Kadu ku-ruba	Yerava	Haki Pikki	Dongri Gerasa	Soliga
1	H.D. Kote	111	4433	10952	1667	1573	407	-	1268
2	Hunsur	52	2651	10385	535	143	1378	1787	1529
3	K.R. Nagar	-	-	-	-	--	-	-	-
4	Mysore	1	72	-	-	-	-	-	286
5	Nanjangud	5	225	472	275-	-	-	-	151
6	Periyapatna	32	1091	2809	149	971	-	164	-
7	T. N. Pura	-	-	-	-	-	-	-	-
	District	201	8472	19246	2626	2687	1785	1951	3234

Source: Mysore District Statistics at a Glance, 2005-06.

Table 31.6

House Types of Scheduled Tribes of Mysore District (percentage)

Sl.No	*Taluks*	*Katcha Semi*	*Pucca Pucca*	*Katcha Semi*
1	H.D. Kote	36.15	45.51	18.33
2	Hunsur	44.26	37.85	17.89
3	K.R. Nagar	14.27	15.39	70.34
4	Mysore	16.58	30.53	52.89
5	Nanjangud	9.78	71.79	18.43
6	Periyapatna	2.65	87.40	9.95
7	T. N. Pura	9.62	34.17	56.21
	District	21.69	46.10	32.22

Source: Mysore Human Development Report, 2008.

Housing among the ST communities has shown a significant record of activity as the sample survey reveals 32.22 per cent ST household have houses *Pucca* in Mysore district. K.R. Nagar alone has the highest per cent of the households (70.34) have *pucca* house. Periyapatna taluk records the least of 9.95 per cent of households with *Pucca* housing and the rest of 90.05 per cent of the households with semi *pucca* houses and *katcha* houses. Among the 90.05 per cent, about 46 percent of the total surveyed households are in semi-*pucca* conditions. It was in Periyapatna taluk where 87.40 per cent of the ST households are in semi-*pucca* and it happens to be the highest in the district. Among the *Katcha* housing it is only 21.69 per cent of the surveyed households with the highest number in Hunsur taluk (Table 31.6).

Policy Interventions in Housing Sector under Tribal Sub-Plan and ITDP in Mysore district

The concept of the Tribal Sub-Plan (TSP) emerged in the National Fifth Five-Year Plan. The Tribal Sub-Plan was first introduced in 1976-77 when it was implemented in six ITDP in the districts of Mysore, Chamarajanagar, Chikmaglur, Kodagu Dakshina Kannada and Udupi. The long term objective of the TSP approach has been to narrow gap between the levels of development of tribal and other area while improving the quality of life the tribal communities. A number of measure s has been introduced under the TSP which can help the tribal's to reach economic and social benefit. The imbalance between the demand for and supply of housing has steadily been increasing with the massive growth of population along with the purchasing power of the individuals. Imbalances are more commonly found among poorer populations. Both the State and Central governments have introduced many schemes for both house-less and site-less households, especially the BPL (below poverty line) households. Different housing schemes operating under the State government for rural areas are Ashraya, Matsya Ashraya, Ambedkar and Basava Schemes. These housing schemes are extended to poorer people of scheduled castes and STs under special priority programmes. Similarly, housing schemes sponsored by the Central Government are the IAY for rural areas.

Addressing housing shortage is thus an important strategy of poverty alleviation. To meet the growing demand of housing, the State government has been pro-active in its housing progammes and is likely to bring out the draft Karnataka Housing and Habitat Policy. To provide an affordable shelter to the needy people, the State government has set up Rajiv Gandhi Rural Housing Corporation Limited (RGRHCL), Karnataka Housing Board (KHB) and Karnataka Slum Development Board (KSDB), The Government is also successfully implementing Rural Ashraya, Rural Ambedkar, IAY, and Urban Ashraya with a view to provide quality houses to the families living below poverty line and for weaker sections in the rural areas.

Indira Awaas Yojana

The Government of India is implementing IAY the year 1985-1986 with the objective of providing assistance primarily to the below poverty line rural households belonging primarily to SC, STs and freed bonded labour categories. From the year 1993-94, the scope of the scheme was extended to cover non-SCs/STs rural BPL poor subject to the condition that the benefits to non-SC/ST households would not be more than 40 per cent of tile total IAY allocation. IAY, which used to be a components of Jawahar Rozgar Yojana became an independent scheme from 1997-98 onwards. Beneficiaries are selected From the BPL list approved by the Gram Sabha (Village Meeting). Government of India have also asked the States to earmark 15 per cent of the beneficiaries from amongst the Minorities. New house as well up gradation of *kutcha* houses are being taken up under the scheme. It is funded by the Central and State in the ratio of 75:25. Under the IAY, Gram Sabha is empowered to select the beneficiaries. Further, the allotment of dwelling units should be. In the name of female member of the beneficiary household. Alternatively, it can be allocated in the name of both husband and wife. Sanitary latrine and smokeless *chulha* (cooking stoves) are the integral part of an IAY house.

The total expenditure on EWS housing schemes has increased significantly from 2000-01 to 2010-11. The Government has spent a total amount of ₹5,599.24 crore, of which ₹1,723.61 crore (30.8%) is from centrally sponsored schemes and ₹3,875.63 crore (69.2%) from the State government sponsored housing schemes for economically weaker section. The details are given in Table 31.7. Since 2000-01 to 2010-11, the Corporation has constructed 20,72,044 houses under various housing schemes and 1,69,446 sites have been distributed for needy people (*Economic Survey of Karnataka, 2011-12*).

Conclusions

The social, economic and educational deprivation of this community is a common and unifying characteristic. Housing is an important basic need and it indicates socio-economic status of the family. To meet the growing demand of housing, the State government has been implementing housing progammes. Housing and amenities schemes need to be participatory, involving and engaging local people and tribal communities. Since independence a number of housing schemes have been introduced for the tribals. Accordingly, several steps have been undertaken by central and State governments for framing appropriate policies and implementing various welfare programmes for achieving the objective of ensuring the rapid socio-economic development of the STs. But still majority of the STs are house-less. In rural or tribal hamlets housing, immediate action must be taken that the rural poor and the marginalised who are unable to have permanent or semi permanent housing may be greatly helped to provide for themselves reasonably good housing. In this environment, the STs the forest area indigenous people must be taken care of in the stipulation. A large number of tribal population in rural areas of India is still dependent on forests for their livelihood, and therefore provisions for basic necessities like food, fuel, housing material, etc. are made from the forest produce in this forest based tribal economy.

Table 31.7

Expenditure Incurred on Housing Schemes in Karnataka from 2000-01 to 2010-11

(₹in Crore)

Year	*Housing Schemes in Rural and Urban Areas*				
	Rural Ashraya	*Rural Ambedkar*	*Indira Awaas Yojana*	*Urban Ashraya*	*Total*
2004-05	174.76	18.11	68.21	30.46	291.54
2005-06	156.01	13.01	128.35	22.64	320.01
2006-07	255.90	13.47	119.45	14.08	402.90
2007-08	617.15	23.26	99.14	3.63	743.18
2008-09	558.69	36.34	325.46	5.79	926.28
2009-10	373.04	38.11	545.10	7.53	963.78
2010-11	210.40	13.88	437.90	5.17	667.35
Total	3211.33	313.78	1723.61	350.52	5599.24

Source: Economic Survey of Karnataka (2011-12), Government of Karnataka.

References

Government of Karnataka (2006). *Karnataka Human Development Report-2005.* Bangalore: Planning, Program Monitoring & Statistics Department.

———. (2012). *Economic Survey of Karnataka-2011-12.* Bangalore: Planning, Program Monitoring & Statistics Department.

———. (n.d.). *Mysore District Statistics Glance (2005-06).* Directorate of Economics and Statistics

———. (n.d.). *Mysore Human Development Report (2008).* Bangalore: Planning and Statistics Department.

Government of India (2013). *Tribal Profile at a Glance.* May. New Delhi: Ministry of Tribal Affairs.

———. (n.d.). *Census Reports (2001 & 2011).* New Delhi: The Office of the Registrar General & Census Commissioner.

Nayaka, Srikantha G. (2013). "Integrated Tribal Development Programme and Human Development: A Study of Mysore District in Karnataka". Unpublished Thesis. University of Mysore.

Yadav, Lalit (2011). *Panchayti Raj Institutions and Rural Development.* New Delhi: Anmol Publication.

32

NARAYANA BILLAVA and NAYANATARA NAYAK

Impact of Poor Water Supply and Sanitation on Households in Rural Areas

A Case Study from Karnataka, India

Introduction

The provision of safe and adequate drinking water supply and sanitation facility is a prerequisite for human resource development to maintain clean environment and also fundamental in building blocks in the development process, influencing economic development, employment, agriculture, housing, health and numerous other sectors. These benefits are spread broadly across societal concerns. Often, the role of drinking water is neglected in the health indices. Reflecting on this, Dr Halfdan Mahler (1984), former Director-General of the World Health Organization (WHO) said, "The number of water taps per 1000 persons is a better indicator of health than the number of hospital beds".

Images of big dams, bridges, roads, power plants, airports, etc., evoke the word 'infrastructure'. But only a few think of the toilet bowl or the water tap in the house as infrastructure, which remain as the most commonly needed items of basic infrastructure. Recent studies have shown that investing in infrastructure will improve health of the people, which in turn will increase productivity (Mavalankar and Shankar, 2004). The demand for water supply and sanitation services is growing fast owing to the interactive effects of demographic growth, economic development and improvement in living standards.

Since the beginning of Sixth Five-Year Plan (FYP) (1980-1985), and launch of the international drinking water supply and sanitation decade, India has substantially increased its commitment to the water supply and sanitation sector. The provision of safe drinking water supply and sanitation facilities is a basic necessity of life and a crucial input in achieving the goal of 'Health for All'. The Ninth FYP envisaged provision of potable drinking water to every settlement in the country on a sustainable basis and pursued all possible measures for the rapid expansion and improvement of sanitation facilities in rural and urban areas. The 2002 National Water Policy of the Government of India (GoI) states that "provision for drinking water should be a primary consideration" in water resource development projects and that "drinking water needs of human beings and animals should be the first charge on any available water" (GoI, 2002).

> Water and sanitation are one of the primary drivers of public health, which means that once we can secure access to clean water and to adequate sanitation facilities for all people, irrespective of the difference in their living conditions, a huge battle against all kinds of diseases will be won (Dr Le Jong-wook, former Director-General, WHO).

One-sixth of the world's population, approximately 1.1 billion people, do not have access to safe drinking water, and 2.4 billon lack basic sanitation. Six thousand children die every day from diarrhoeal diseases alone and a large proportion of diarrhoel diseases in the developing world stems from poor water, sanitation and hygiene (UNICEF, 2003). The most affected people are in developing countries, living in extreme conditions of poverty, normally peri-urban dwellers or rural inhabitants. Among the main problems that are responsible for this situation are: lack of priority given to water supply and sanitation facilities, lack of financial resources, lack of sustainability of water supply and sanitation services, poor hygiene behaviours, inadequate sanitation in public places including hospitals, health centres and schools. Providing access to sufficient quantity of safe water, provision of facilities for a sanitary disposal of excreta, and introducing sound hygiene behaviour are of capital importance to reduce the burden of disease caused by these risk factors.

Health benefits result from the provision of improved quality and increased quantity of water, adequate sanitation facilities, and changes in hygiene behaviour. For a number of waterborne diseases, transmission occurs as a direct result of draining the contaminated water. In other cases, transmission cycle is through stagnant water, which provides a breeding site for disease carrying vectors (e.g., malaria-bearing mosquitoes). Inadequate water for washing hands and cooking utensils and poor sanitation practices often result in diarrhoeal diseases. Disease and poor health are a heavy burden on the economy, the community, the family and the industry. Improvements in water supply and sanitation can reduce the incidence of severl recurring diseases or eliminate them entirely. A safe and sustainable water supply, basic sanitation and good hygiene are fundamental for a healthy, productive and dignified life. Yet, many of the world's rural poor lack access to an improved water supply (900 million), and improved sanitation facilities (2 billion) (Joint Monitoring Programme for Water and Sanitation, 2006).[1] As put forth by Kofi Annan, United Nations' former Secretary-General:

> We shall not finally defeat AIDS, tuberculosis, malaria, or any of the other infectious diseases that plague the developing world until we have also won the battle for safe drinking water, sanitation and basic health care.

While rural drinking water supply and sanitation will continue to face many challenges, a lot can be done socially and collectively in order to ensure both equitable access and economic viability in Karnataka. Many studies conducted by Das (2000), Rajsheker *et al.* (2006) and Raju *et al.* (2006) indicate the benefits from improvements made in water supply and sanitation. Improved water supply and sanitation practices are instrumental in reducing infant mortality, preventing diarrohea, and improving nutrition and overall health; and this fact can be used as a powerful lever in garnering support for improvement in water supply and sanitation.

The main purpose of the study is to understand the current status of water supply and sanitation in rural areas of Dharwad district

1. Improved' water supply refers to a household connection, standpipe, and borehole, protected dug well, protected spring or rainwater collection. 'Improved' sanitation facilities refer to a simple latrine, ventilated improved pit latrine or pour-flush latrine and connection to a septic system or public sewer.

and identify the impact of poor water supply and sanitation on rural households.

Methodology and Data Source

The study covers four gram panchayats (GPs) in the state of Karnataka for understanding the nature of rural water supply and sanitation services in general. Dharwad district has been selected in particular. There are five taluks in the district. They are Kundagol, Navalgund, Kalaghatagi, Dharwad and Hubli. According to High Power Committee Report (2002), Dharwad and Hubli taluks are relatively developed ones and Kundagol, Navalgund, and Kalaghatagiare backward taluks (HPC, 2002). Among the taluks of Dharwad district, Kalaghatagi is the most backward taluk, while Dharwad talukis relatively developed. We have selected these two taluks for the study purpose. On similar grounds, we have selected two GPs from each taluk. Based on objectives of the study, we have chosen one developed and one less developed GP from each taluk so as to be able to identify factors that influence performance. To identify the developed and less developed GP, seven indicators relating to demographical, social and economic factors were considered. These include density of population, sex ratio, percentage of SC (scheduled caste) and ST (scheduled tribe) population to the total population, per capita income of the GP, and proportion of villages with safe drinking water facility (Litres per Capita per Days); After listing out all the villages of four GPs, two villages were randomly selected from each of the two GPs. on the whole eight villages are covered in the study to collect village level and household information. The study is based on five-stage systematic sampling method with households as basic unit of survey. To elicit household level information on water and sanitaion, we have interviewed 10 per cent of the households from each selected village. Accordingly, the total sample size amounted to 235 households in eight villages of four GPs.

The study is based on both secondary and primary sources of information. The required secondary data is obtained from the Department of Rural Development and Panchayat Raj, Government of Karnataka (GoK). For health scenario (water and sanitation related disease) of Dharwad at the district level, published as well unpublished accounts of District Health Office (DHO) have been referred. The primary data is collected from GP records and through survey of the households in selected villages. The information from households was collected through administration of pilot-tested schedules. Descriptive statistics are used in analysis of the data in the study.

Status of Rural Water Supply and Sanitation

Rural Water Supply and Sanitation Situations in Karnataka

Karnataka is selected for the study and is a progressive state in many respects. The state of Karnataka is one of the largest in the country, having an area of 1.91 lakh sq. km. The High Power Committee for Redressal of Regional Imbalances divides the entire 27 districts (excluding newly reorganised districts like Ramanagar, Yadgiri and Chikkaballapur) of Karnataka into four divisions using district-level Cumulative Deprivation Index (CDI), viz., Gulbarga, Belgaum, Bangalore and Mysore. As per 2001 Census, approximately 3.48 crore people live in rural areas of Karnataka, spread over 56,682 habitations. Currently, water is being provided to rural areas through 18,919 Piped Water Supply (PWS), 24,813 Mini Water Supply (MWS) and 19,9556 hand pump borewells. In Karnataka, about 35 per cent are partially served by borewell with hand pumps and open well, 9 per cent by MWS schemes and 56 per cent by a mix of piped water supply and hand pump schemes (Saleth and Sastry, 2004: 163).

There are many fundamental rights of citizens in the constitution. Access to clean drinking water is one fundamental right as enunciated in the right to life under Article 21 of the Constitution of India judgments delivered in December 2000 (Ramachandraiah, 2001). The centrally-sponsored Minimum Needs Programme (MNP) and the Accelerated Rural Water Programme (ARWP) have increased access to safe water sources within 1.6 km and the desired quantity of water per day to at least 40 litres per person. The GoK aims at providing 55 lpcd to the rural inhabitations. The norms also prescribe water quality standard that is free from bacterial and chemical contamination and specify the distance of availability of water to be within 500 metres from the place of residence. The service level of water supply stands at 55 lpcd in 37,886 (67%) habitations, and below 45 in 18,796 habitations. Thirty seven per cent of the people are facing problems of quality drinking water and insufficient supply of water in rural Karnataka. Many schemes like Rajeev Gandhi Drinking Water Supply Scheme, Rain Water Harvesting, externally-aided Rural Drinking Water Supply and Sanitation Projects, World Bank Assisted Jal Nirmal Project, Swajaldhara Project, etc., are being implemented through the GPs in Karnataka.

Further, according to Census the state-level coverage of sanitation was increased from 37.5 per cent to 51.3 per cent over 2001 to 2011 in Karnataka. As per 2011 Census, only 28.4 per cent of rural households was covered by toilets facility as against 17.4 per cent in 2001, while 84.9 per cent urban households had access to toilet facility in 2011 as against 75.2 per cent in 2001. It is clear that there is high disparity in access to sanitary facility between urban and rural areas. In this context, the GoK implemented many schemes, like Nirmala Karnataka, SwachaGrama etc., to improve the sanitation facility therein. As a result, there is slow improvement in the access to toilet facility in rural areas. The provision of sanitary facility not only depends on government schemes or programmes, but also requires greaters individual effort and awareness in rural areas.

Rural Water Supply and Sanitation Situations in Selected District

Status of Drinking Water

Dharwad district depends mainly (about 90%) on ground water resources for water supply in rural areas, where water is supplied the villages through piped water supply (PWS) schemes, MWS schemes, and borewell with hand pumps (Table 32.1). About 76 per cent of households depended on hand pump/borewell, while 11.66 per cent and 12.43 per cent households depended on MWS water supply and PWS respectively in the year 2008.

The availability of drinking water in Dharwad district and selected taluks as per a Zilla Panchayat report is given in Table 32.2. According to the report, only 52 per cent of the rural habitations in Dharwad district are getting more than 55 LPCD.

Table 32.1

Percentage of Households by Principal Source of Drinking Water (2008)

Water Sources	*Dharwad*	*Kalghatagi*	*Total*
Piped water supply	11.61	9.61	12.43
Mini water supply	12.69	11.33	11.66
Hand pump/Borewell	75.70	79.06	75.91
Total	100	100	100

Source: ZP Annual Reports.

Table 32.2

Percentage of Villages by LPCD Norms (2008)

LPCD	*Dharwad*	*Kalghatagi*	*District Total*
Total no of villages	119	93	371
0-30	0	0	0
31-40	7.6	10.7	14.3
41-55	27.73	32.3	33.7
55 and above	64.71	57.0	52.0

Source: ZP Annual Reports.

Rural Sanitation Facility

Accessibility to latrine facility, drainage and garbage disposal is poorer in rural areas than that in urban areas. Many economists [Bijlani and Rao (1990); Saleth and Sastry (2004); Raju *et al.*, (2006)] have studied rural sanitation facilities and found that less than 20 per cent households in rural areas, and 75 per cent of households in urban areas have latrine facility. Dharwad had less coverage of latrine facility (19.28%) compared to the state-level situation (22.19%) in the year 2007.

Accessibility and Adequacy of Rural Water Supply in Selected GPs

The survey undertaken at the micro-level confirms the picture emerging at the taluk level and district level. A majority of the households depend on modern sources (public sources like MWS, PWS and handpump/borewell) for water supply (See Table 32.3). Also

Table 32.4 shows that, nearly 56.6 per cent of the households gather water from outside their dwelling, but within their premises.

Table 32.3

Details about Rural Water Sources

	GP Name	*Drinking Water*		*Cooking*		*Washing/Bathing*		*Total*
		Modern	*Traditional*	*Modern*	*Traditional*	*Modern*	*Traditional*	
Developed GPs	Madakihonnihalli	100.0	-	100.0	-	87.5	12.5	100.0
	Yarikoppa	97.8	2.2	100.0	-	91.3	8.7	100.0
Backward GPs	Galagi	100.0	-	100.0	-	77.2	22.8	100.0
	Kanakur	100.0	-	100.0	-	100.0	-	100.0
Total of GPs		99.6	0.4	100.0	-	86.0	14.0	100.0

Source: Primary Data.

People's Perception on Availability and Quality of Water Supply

Adequacy, in this context, refers to people's opinion on whether availability of water is sufficient or insufficient in order to meet the needs of all households in rural areas. The opinion of the people on satisfaction varied between taluks and even between households within a GP. Figure 32.1 shows households' opinion on adequacy of water supply. More than 73 per cent of the households are satisfied with their access to drinking water supply. The rate of satisfaction is higher in developed GPs like Yarikoppa (95%) and Madakihonnihalli (100%) where people are more satisfied than the backwards GPs Kanakur (69.6%) and Galagi (54.4%).

The quality of the available water is another major problem faced by the drinking water sector in the state. According to the National Sample Survey Organisation (NSSO) report on Drinking Water and Sanitation 1999 in Karnataka, 97.2 per cent of the households reported that they received satisfactory quality of water. However, this is not the scenario at the empirical level. Percentages of households with access to a satisfactory quality of drinking water in rural areas provided by public water supply sources is given in Figure 37.2. Only about 51.5 per cent of households reported receiving water with satisfactory quality. The households in the developed GPs appear to be more satisfied about the quality of water than those in the backward GPs.

Table 32.4

Distance of Dwelling from Drinking Water Supply Source

	GP Name	*Within Premises /Dwelling*	*Outside Dwelling but Within Premises*	*Outside Premises at Distance <0.25 km*	*Distance 0.25 km to 0.50 km*	*Distance 0.50 km to 1 km*	*Total*
Developed GPs	Madki-honnihalli	31.3	58.3	10.4			100
	Yarikoppa	32.5	47.5	17.5	2.5		100
Backward GPs	Galagi	27.7	61.4	7.9	2.0	1.0	100
	Kanakur	32.6	52.2	13.0	2.2		100
Total		30.2	56.6	11.1	1.7	0.4	100

Source: Primary Data.

Figure 32.1

Households Satisfaction with Access to Safe Drinking Water Supply

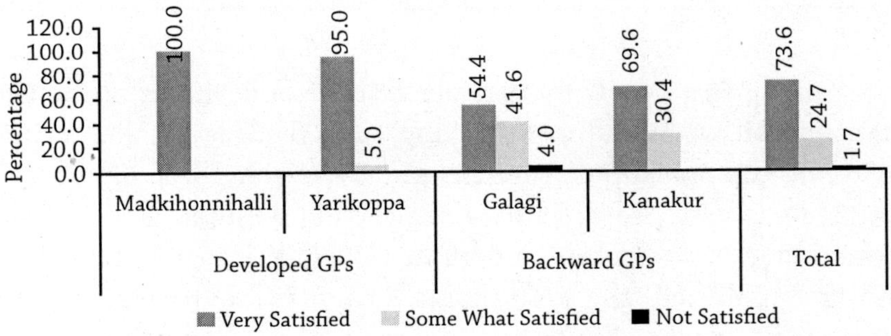

Source: Primary Data.

Figure 32.2

Households' Opinion about Quality of Drinking Water

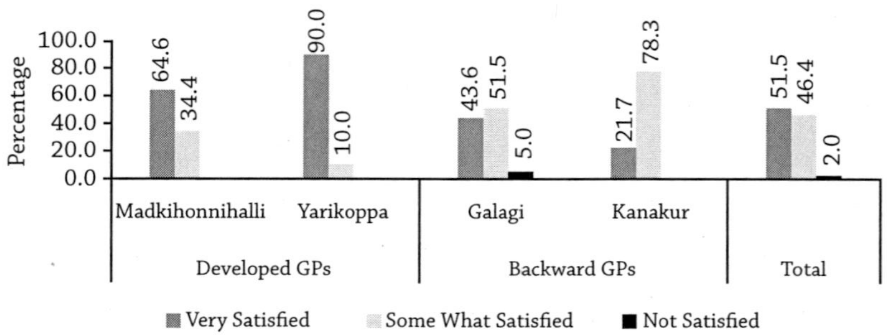

Source: Primary Data.

Table 32.5

Distribution of Households according to Reasons of Dissatisfaction with Water Quality

	GP Name	*Known to be Polluted*	*Clean but Contains Excess of Iron or Other Mineral*	*Bad Taste Due to Unknown Causes*
Developed GPs	Madkihonnihalli	70.6	29.4	-
	Yarikoppa	-	75.0	25.0
Backward GPs	Galagi	94.7	1.8	3.5
	Kanakur	52.8	33.3	13.9
Total		74.6	18.4	7.0

Source: Primary Data.

Among the four GPs, 49.5 per cent of households are not very satisfied with the quality of drinking water made available for various reasons, the breakup of which is given in Table 32.5. About 93 per cent households feel that they are getting polluted water or water containing excess of iron and other minerals. Despite knowing that water is polluted, the households do not treat the water in rural areas. This speaks about their low awareness and little concern for health (see Table 32.5).

Table 32.6 presents the fact that more than 80 per cent of the households are not using treated water in rural areas. They think that fluoride water is tastier without filtering and lack awareness about its effects or seriousness of poor water quality.

Table 32.6

Usage of Water Treatment

	GP Name	*Filtering by Plain Clothes*	*Boiling of Water*	*No Treatment*
Developed GPs	Madkihonnihalli	12.5	2.1	85.4
	Yarikoppa	-	-	100.0
Backward GPs	Galagi	27.7	7.9	64.4
	Kanakur	2.2	2.2	95.7
Total		14.9	4.3	80.9

Source: Primary Data.

Rural Sanitation Facility in Selected GPs: Individual Latrine Facility

A preliminary idea of the extent to which households have access to latrine facility in the selected GPs can be seen from the table below. Under the Section 1 Act 29 of 1997, one of the important functions of the GP is to provide latrines to atleast 10 per cent of the households every year.

Community Latrine Facility

Community latrines are useful for those who are facing scarcity of place and have too little income to construct latrines. Table 32.10 shows the number of GPs with community latrine facility; only Kanakur GP has received grant for community latrine facility among the four GPs. Although Kanakur GP had constructed community latrine facility 5 years ago, people have not been using it due to lack of maintenance by the GP. Other GPs have also received grants for community and women's latrine; however, due to scarcity of place, GPs have sent back the money to taluk panchayat. So literally none of the GPs have community latrines.

Table 32.7 indicates that only 21.3 per cent of rural households are covered with latrine facility in selected GPs. The GPs in Kalaghatagia, a backward taluk, have fewer latrine facilities as compared to those in Dharwad, a developed taluk. Among four GPs, galagi has the least latrine facilities. One of the villages, Hasarambi does not have any latrine facilities among the selected sample households from Galagi GP. About 37 per cent of households have been covered by individual latrine facility in Kanakur GP, which received money under the Swacha Gram scheme for three villages in the year 2005-06. One of the villages Kavalageri has utilised Swacha Grama scheme properly and constructed around 150 individual latrines under this scheme with a subsidy of ₹3500. The other two villages including GP headquarter, Kanakur, have not used the funds so far. According to Kanakur GP secretary, the fund has not been utilised because people do not cooperate in construction of drainage and latrine. The major reasons for not constructing latrine are economic problem and scarcity of place in the rural areas.

Table 32.7

Sanitary Facility in Selected Households

	GP Name	*Yes*
Developed GPs	Madkihonnihalli	25.0
	Yarikoppa	32.5
Backward GPs	Galagi	7.9
	Kanakur	37.0
Total		21.5

Source: Primary Data.

Usage of Latrine Facility

Table 32.8 shows that around 50 (21%) rural households have latrine facility, but not all of them are using them. Rural people often find it very convenient to defecate in the open fields. It is usual for them to carry a small tin of water, which hardly suffices for proper cleaning. Table 32.8 reveals that only 66.0 per cent of households are using latrine facility and it indicates their poor awareness and negligence for personal hygiene and public health.

Children (Below 6 Years Old) Using Latrine Facility

Here, we have examined about the children's sanitation facility in rural areas in selected GPs. Sanitation-related illnesses affect young children heavily, not only because of their lower immunity to pathogens, but also because of their carelessness for hygiene. This means that they are more likely to come into contact with excreta, the primary cause of diarrhoeal disease and intestinal parasites, as well as other pathogens. A study conducted by UNICEF's India office found that only 1 per cent of children below the age group six use latrine (UN-HABITAT, 2003). As presented in Table 32.9 none of the children use latrines in rural households from selected GPs. Usually rural children go for open defecation nearby their houses. Table 32.9 shows that about 97 per cent of the children go outside their dwelling, but within the premises for open defecation.

Table 32.8

Distribution of Households according to Use of Latrine Facility

	GP Name	*Yes*
Developed GPs	Madkihonnihalli	75.0
	Yarikoppa	46.2
Backward GPs	Galagi	87.5
	Kanakur	64.7
Total		66.0

Source: Primary Data.

Table 32.9

Percentage of Children Using Latrine Facility

	GPs Name	*Outside Dwelling but Within Premises*	*Outside Premises at Distance <0.25 km*
Developed GPs	Madkihonnihalli	100	-
	Yarikoppa	83.3	16.7
Backward GPs	Galagi	100	-
	Kanakur	85.7	14.3
	Total	96.2	3.8

Source: Primary Data.

Table 32.10

Community Latrine Facility in Selected GPs

	GP Name	*Community Latrine*
Developed GPs	Galagi	-
	Madakihonnihalli	-
Backward GPs	Yarikoppa	-
	Kanakur	1*
	Total	1

Note: * Households not using latrine.
Source: Primary Data.

Households' Perceptions on Village Sanitation Services

Figure 32.3 shows households' opinion about the village sanitation service in selected GPs. More than 73 per cent of the households are not satisfied with their village sanitation services. The percentage of households satisfied with village sanitation services is higher in developed GPs. More than 95 per cent of households are dissatisfied with these services in backward GPs. The main reason being poor maintenance of village sanitation by the GP.

Figure 32.3

Households Satisfaction over Village Sanitation Services (% of HHs)

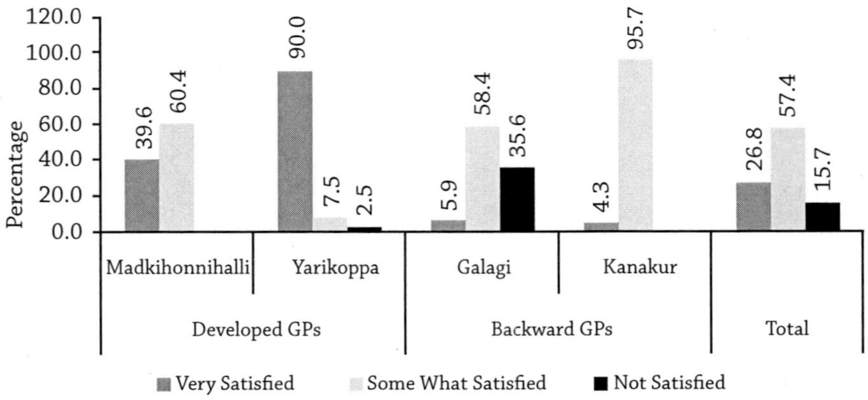

Impact of Poor Water Supply and Sanitation

In this section, we have tried to explain the household burden of water and sanitation related diseases in rural Dharwad, which is due to unsafe water supply and poor sanitation. Also an attempt is made to register the extent of waterborne and sanitation related illness as reported by villagers during the reference period of 2008-09 and account for the burden of these diseases in terms of treatment cost incurred by the households. These should be taken as rough estimates as they are based on self-perceived morbidity.

Incidence of Waterborne and Sanitation Related Diseases

Sixty-six million people in India are assumed to be consuming ground water with unsafe levels of fluoride. Nearly 30 million people in the eastern states are estimated to be at the risk of consuming water with arsenic content higher than the acceptable levels (Kolavalli and Raju, 2003). As discussed in earlier section, 37 per cent of the rural habitations in Karnataka are affected by water quality problems and only 22 per cent of the households have latrine facility in rural areas. The common diseases occurring due to unsafe water are gastroenteritis, malaria, cholera, typhoid, and viral hepatitis. Table 32.11 presents the incidence of these diseases in the state. Gastroenteritis is an acute disease with nearly 24,000 reported cases and 200 deaths in 2001. Although the numbers of reported cases are very high for malaria followed by typhoid, the death cases are higher in gastroenteritis. So it can be said that the ultimate burden appears to be higher in the case of gastroenteritis than other waterborne diseases. In all the cases, households have to face the burden of treatment cost, loss of income, heavy expenditure on prolonged treatment, absence in schools/colleges and reduced productive capacity on account of these diseases. It should be noted that the figures presented in Table 32.11 is gross underestimates as the data on incidence of waterborne disease is obtained from the Department of Health and Family Welfare, which does not include the cases reported in private health centres.

Table 32.12 depicts the incidence of waterborne and sanitation related diseases in Dharwad district. Gastroenteritis, cold and fever and chikungunya were major water and sanitation related diseases in this district during the year 2006. Although more than 37,500 chikungunya cases were registered, there were no reported deaths associate with it. Malaria imposed a heavy burden as out of 479 registered cases, 10 deaths were reported.

Table 32.11

Distribution of Waterborne and Sanitation-related Diseases in Karnataka (2002)

Water and Sanitation Related Disease	*Cases (Nos.)*	*Death (Nos.)*	*Cases (%)*	*Death (%)*	*Cases/ Death Ratio*
Gastroenteritis	23893	198	37.91	84.97	0.83
Cholera	342	1	0.54	0.43	0.29
Malaria	197625	21	75.82	8.27	0.01
Viral Hepatitis	5438	28	8.63	12.02	0.51
Typhoid	33346	6	52.91	2.58	0.02
Total	63019	233	100.00	100.00	0.37

Source: Department of Health and Family Welfare, GoK.

Table 32.12

Waterborne and Sanitation Related Diseases in Dharwad (2006)

Water and Sanitation Related Disease	*Cases (Nos.)*	*Death (Nos.)*	*Cases (in %)*	*Death (in %)*	*Cases/Death Ratio*
Gastroenteritis	1746	-	4.2	-	-
Cholera	5	-	0.0	0.0	-
Viral Hepatitis	120	1	0.3	7.1	0.83
Typhoid	-	-	-	-	-
Cold and Fever	1881	03	4.5	21.4	0.16
Malaria	479	10	1.1	71.4	2.09
Chikungunya	37568	-	89.9	-	-
Total	41799	14	100.0	100.0	0.03

Source: Report of Communication Diseases, District Health Office (DHO), Dharwad.

Individual health and hygiene is largely dependent on adequate availability of drinking water and proper sanitisation; therefore, there exists a direct relationship between water, sanitation and health.

Table 32.13 presents the level of households' satisfaction in terms of water supply and sanitation in the study area. Only 26.8 per cent are satisfied with sanitation facility, while around 51 per cent are satisfied about the quality of water supply. This indicates that over half of the population is deprived of safe drinking water, and three-fourth do not have proper sanitation in selected GPs. Around 36 per cent of people are affected from water and sanitation related diseases in selected GPs in the last one year; and besides that, people have incurred a direct expenditure of around 6.7 per cent (₹589) of their annual per capita income on water and sanitation related diseases. The burden is higher if we include indirect cost (loss of income), resulting in a loss of 18.5 per cent of their per capita annual income.

Table 32.14 shows details of the incidences of water and sanitation related diseases in selected GPs. Incidence of water and sanitation related diseases is 94 cases per 1000 person in the year 2008-09. The rate of incidence is highest in Kanakur GP (179 cases per 1000), and lowest in Galagi GP (62 cases per 1000). The table also shows disease-wise cases for cholera, cold-Fever, dysentery, joint pain, skin problems, chikungunya, etc. The incidence of these diseases is higher in Kanakur GP, which is one of the backward ones. Households in Kavalgere village in the Kanakur GP have been affected by filthy water supplied through pipes. The villagers are unhappy on account of this poor quality of water. Further, Kanakur GP does not have a primary health centre (PHC), and people have to go to hospitals in Dharwad or Hebballi, which are far (more than 10 km) from the village. The zilla panchayat has arranged for a medical camp once in a month for a duration of one week in this village. Two doctors and 4 nurses are made available for service in that week. As the quality of water is poor, most of the people treat the water by filtering with plain clothes or boiling the water before drinking. People suffer from multiple diseases in backward GPs (Galagi and Kanakur GP). Chikungunya is one of the common diseases in all selected GPs. This disease spreads from mosquitoes and is a communicable disease. Poor sanitation facility including inadequate drainage, poor disposable of garbage, and lack of latrine facility and improper storage of water are some of the reasons for the occurrence of this disease. Only Galagi

GP has a PHC among the selected GPs. More than 79 per cent of the people from this *panchayat* who suffered from water and sanitary related diseases have visited this government hospital.

Table 32.13

Water and Sanitation Facility and Health Impacts in Selected GPs (As Reported by the Households)

Details	*Backward GPs*		*Developed GPs*		*Total*
	Galagi	*Kanakur*	*Madikihon-nalli*	*Yerikoppa*	
Satisfaction about water supply	54.4	69.6	100.0	95.0	73.6
Satisfaction about water quality	43.6	21.7	64.6	90.0	51.5
Satisfaction about sanitation facility	5.9	4.3	39.6	90	26.8
Access to drainage facility	77.2	13.0	47.9	56.2	56.2
Possession of individual Latrine facility	7.9	37.0	25.0	32.5	21.5
Reporting of water and sanitation related diseases (% of HHs)	24.8	56.5	35.4	42.5	36.2
Annual per capita amount spent for treatment of water and sanitation related diseases (in ₹/as %) [direct cost]	460 (6.0)	750 (7.4)	391 (4.4)	765 (7.4)	589 (6.7)
Annual per capita amount spent for treatment of water and sanitation related diseases (in ₹/as %) [indirect cost]	679 (8.9)	1367 (13.5)	872 (9.7)	1358 (13.1)	1052 (11.9)
Annual per capita amount spent for treatment of water and sanitation related diseases (in ₹/as %) [total cost]	1139 (14.9)	2117 (20.9)	1264 (14.1)	2122 (20.4)	1640 (18.5)
Average annual per capita income of the sample population (₹)	7649	10139	8961	10388	8871

Source: Primary Data.

Table 32.14

Details of Incidence of Waterborne and Sanitation Related Diseases and their Impact in Selected GPs (2008-09)

Particulars	*Backward GPs*		*Developed GPs*		*Total*
	Galagi	*Kanakur*	*Madikihonnalli*	*Yerikoppa*	
HH members reporting illness due to poor quality of water and sanitation (per 1000)	62	179	71	107	94
Male	62.5	63.4	41.2	36.4	54.5
Female	37.5	36.6	58.8	63.6	45.5
Type of diseases (reported) (per 1000)					
Cholera	8	48	--	--	13
Cold and Fever	12	13	4	--	9
Dysentery	21	9	--	19	14
Joint Pain*	--	4	--	--	1
Skin Problem	2	9	--	--	3
Chikungunya	19	96	71	87	56
Others	--	4	--	5	2
Frequency of hospital visits (Average) (Nos.)	2.0	3.5	1.8	1.9	2.4
Type of hospitals visited					
Government	79.0	36.6	55.5	4.3	31.3
Private	21.0	63.4	44.5	95.7	68.7
Average distance to hospital (% of HHs)					
Less than 0.50 km	40.6	14.6	--	24.3	21.1
0.51 km to 1 km	6.3	2.4	--	21.6	6.1
1.01 km to 5 km	15.6	17.1	--	21.6	15.8
5 km to 10 km	0.0	4.9	100.0		17.5
More than 10 km	37.5	61.0	--	32.4	39.5
Expenditure (direct and indirect) on water and sanitation related diseases as share of per capita income (%)	14.9	20.9	14.1	20.4	18.5

Note: HH-Household; *Joint pain due to excess of fluoride content in the water (respondent's opinion in Kanakur GP).

Source: Primary Data.

The major burden of ill health is borne by the rural areas, where access to basic infrastructure services (water and sanitation) is poor (World Bank, 2001:2). Adverse health impacts of contaminated water and poor sanitation include disorder of bones, skin allergies, birth defects, premature infant death, waterborne and sanitary related diseases, etc. A study on Bangalore's rural and peri-urban areas reveals occurrence of health problems, such as skin irritation, throat infection, vomiting and jaundice among children on account of poor quality of water and an increased health expenditure of about Rs 3000 per year per family (Diwakar and Nagaraj, 2002).

Unsafe water and poor sanitation results in countless deaths and huge burden of disease among young children. We have tried to present a rough estimate of direct and indirect costs of water and sanitation related diseases based on households reporting of treatment costs. The direct costs include the cost of consultation, medicine and hospitalisation. The indirect costs include loss of wages on account of absence from work and transport costs incurred by the patients and the accompanying persons for visiting the health care centres. Table 32.15 presents the account of direct and indirect burden from water and sanitation related disease in selected rural areas. People spend more than 18.5 per cent of their per capita income over water and sanitation related diseases. The indirect burden is higher than the direct burden, because the former includes loss of income/wages due to ill health and transport costs. The Galagi and Madakihonnihalli GPs have government hospital facilities near to their GPs, so households' expenditure on treatment of water and sanitation related diseases is less than that of those in Yarikoppa and Kanakur GPs. As explained in Table 32.14, households in Yarikoppa and Kanakur GPs visit private hospitals. Obviously, a private hospital charges more than the government hospital. If GP provides safe water and good sanitation facilities in the villages, rural people will be able to save money spent on treatment of above-mentioned diseases.

Major Findings and Conclusions

Dharwad district depends mainly (about 90%) on ground water resources for water supply in rural areas. The percentage of

Table 32.15

GP-wise Direct and Indirect Burden from Water and Sanitation Related Diseases

	GP Name	Direct Burden (₹)	(% to Per Capita)	Indirect Burden (₹)	(% Per Capita)	Total (₹)	(% Per Capita)	Average Per Capita Income (₹)
Developed GPs	Madkihonnihalli	391	4.4	872	9.7	1264	14.1	8961
	Yarikoppa	765	7.4	1358	13.1	2122	20.4	10388
Backward GPs	Galagi	460	6.0	679	8.9	1139	14.9	7649
	Kanakur	750	7.4	1367	13.5	2117	20.9	10139
Total		589	6.6	1052	11.9	1640	18.5	8871

Source: Primary Data.

households satisfied with access to drinking water supply is higher in developed GPs than those in less developed *panchayats*. Above 37 per cent of rural habitations in Karnataka are affected by water-quality problems due to presence of excess iron, followed by excess fluoride, excess TDS (total dissolved solids) and nitrate.

Table 32.16 shows disease-wise direct and indirect burden from water and sanitation related diseases. Water and sanitation related diseases like cholera, dysentery and Chikungunya appear to be dangerous than the other diseases in selected GPs. People affected by these diseases have taken on an average 6-9 days for recovery. If each GP provides safe drinking water and improves sanitation facility under their jurisdiction, people can save their income as well as maintain good health, which can in term enhance a person's ability to work and earn.

Table 32.16

Disease-wise Direct and Indirect Burden from Water and Sanitation Related Diseases

S.No.	*Disease/Illness*	*No. of Cases*	*Average No. of Days of Illness*	*Direct Burden Per Case (₹)*	*Indirect Burden Per Case (₹)*
1.	Cholera	15	6	345	673
2.	Cold and fever	9	3	278	473
3.	Dysentery	17	6	523	396
4.	Skin problem	3	2	305	358
5.	Vomiting	1	2	200	400
6.	Joint pain	1	4	1500	400
7.	Chikungunya	64	9	400	959

Source: Primary Data.

Our field study shows that about 51 per cent of households reported satisfaction over quality of drinking water, and only 21 per cent of rural households are provided with latrine facility in selected GPs. Further among these 21 per cent, only 67 per cent of the households are using latrine facility, although it exists in the house. This indicates poor awareness and negligence for personal hygiene and public health. Although all GPs received grant for community latrines, only Kanakur GP has a community latrine facility which was constructed 5 years ago. But due to lack of maintenance, the GP households are not using the latrine now. Other GPs have returned the grant because of the scarcity of space to build the latrines.

Gastroenteritis, cold and fever and Chikungunya were the major water and sanitation related diseases reported in Dharwad district for the year 2006. More than 37,500 Chikungunya cases were registered in the district in 2009. Around 36 per cent people reported illness due to water and sanitation related diseases in selected GPs during 2008-09. The burden of such diseases like cholera, dysentery and Chickungunya appears to be greater than other diseases, given that the direct and the indirect costs are higher for the former—an average of 6-9 days is taken for recovery. People have spent more than 18.5 per cent of their annual per capita income for the treatment of water and sanitation related diseases. The indirect burden is higher than the direct burden.

In addition to three-fourth of the households without individual latrines, the fact that half of the households are dissatisfied with the quality of water and three-fourth with sanitation facility explains the risk factors associated with occurrence of waterborne and sanitation-related diseases. These also indicate the necessity for appropriate intervention by GP to provide hygienic environment for the better health of the people. The health effects of poor water, sanitation and hygiene have been underemphasised because people are not serious about poor quality of water supply and sanitation in rural areas. The government in the interest of public has to continue the implementation of various programmes and introduce new schemes to facilitate the provision of safe water and sanitation facility in the rural areas. Fluoride content in water can result in long-term harmful effects, which the people have not yet realised. Therefore, there is a need for trained local personnel to maintain and manage the treatment plant at village level. Quality problem as a whole should be handled with a planned approach, beginning from identification to completion. It is the responsibility of GP to create awareness about safe drinking water, uphold the importance of sanitation among villagers and provide safe drinking water to them. GPs can play a major role in reducing the disease burden by facilitating improved water supply and sanitation. Such improvements reduce child mortality and, water and sanitation related diseases in rural areas.

Reference

Bijlani H.U. and P.S.N. Rao (1990). *Water Supply and Sanitation in India*. New Delhi: Oxford and IBH Co Pvt Ltd.

Das, Keshab (2000). "Rural Drinking Water Supply in India; Issues and Strategies", *Working Paper* No 120. Ahmedabad: Gujarat Institute of Development Research.

Diwakar, H. and N. Nagaraj (2002). "Impact of Water Pollution and Food Security and Environment: Bearing the Brunt", *Wasteland News*, August-October.

GoI (2002). *National Water Policy 2002*. New Delhi: Ministry of Water Resource. April. *http://www.wrmin.nic.in/writereaddata/linkimages/nwp20025617515534.pdf*

Halfdan, Mahler (1984). "Water Taps, before Hospitals Bed", *Social Welfare* XXXXI(3): 11, June.

HPC FRRI (2002). *High Power Committee on Redressal of Regional Imbalances*. Government of Karnataka.

Kolavalli, S. and K.V. Raju (2003). "Protecting Drinking Water Sources: A Sub-Basin View", *Working Paper* No. 126. Bangalore: Institute for Social and Economic Change.

Maria Saleth R. and G.S. Sastri (2004). "Water Supply and Sanitation Sector of Karnataka, India: Status, Performance and Change", *Water Policy Issue* 6: 161-83.

Mavalankar, D. and M. Shankar (2004). *http://www.3inetwork.org/reports/IIR-2004/Chap%2013%20 2003.pdf*.

Panda, Pradeep Kumar (1997). "The Effects of Safe Drinking Water and Sanitation on Diarrhoeal Diseases among Children in Rural Orissa", *Working Paper* No. 278. Thiruvananthapuram: Centre for Development Studies.

Rajasekhar D., R. Manjula, K.H. Anantha (2006). "Charges for Rural Drinking Water: Gram Panchayats in Karnataka", in K.V. Raju (ed.), *Elixir of Life*. Bangalore: Books for Change. pp.257-83.

Raju K.V., S. Manasi and Veershekarappa (2006). "Perception and Politics: Grey Zones in Rural Water Supply", in K.V. Raju (ed.), *Elixir of Life*. Bangalore: Books for Change. pp.173-91.

Ramachandraiah, C. (2001). "Drinking Water as a Fundamental Right", *Economic and Political Weekly* 36(8): 619-21, Feb.24-March 2.

WHO/UNICEF (2006). *Meeting the MDG Drinking-water and Sanitation Target: The Urban and Rural Challenge of the Decade, Joint Monitoring Programme for Water and Sanitation*. Geneva: World Health Organization.

World Bank (2001). *Environmental Health in India Priorities in Andhra Pradesh*. Environment and Social Development Unit, South Asia Region. October. *http://siteresources.worldbank.org/INDIAEXTN/Resources/Reports-Publications/APHealth.pdf* Accessed on May 2012.

33

PRADIP KUMAR NATH

Institution Building in NREGS at the Village Level

A Study of Gaon Sathi in Odisha

> In a unique protest, Gaon Sathis sold more than five quintals of vegetables at the rate of one per kg here on Wednesday. They were protesting against the notification of the State Government changing Gaon Sathi nomenclature to 'mate'. As per the recent notification by the State Government, the 'mate' for every village will be selected by the Palli Sabha and not necessarily based on merit. "Earlier, the educated people of the village were rightfully recruited as the Gaon Sathis but with the latest notification, the Palli Sabha will have all power to appoint 'mates', irrespective of their educational qualifications," said Gaon Sathi Mahasangha member Manmohan Panda. The members have also demanded regularisation of jobs. Currently, they are paid on the basis of number of days they have worked ("Gaon Sathis Go Green Over Government's 'Mate' Move", *Express News Service*, Bhubanesswar, 10 October 2013).

The above piece caught the attention of the writer immediately as a Google tweet on Mahatma Gandhi National Rural Employment Guarantee Scheme (MGNREGS). Way back in 2008-09, the author had the occasion to undertake a quick study with another colleague Dr V. Suresh Babu (CWEPA, NIRD&PR) on the Institution of Gaon Sathi and had a serious look into this innovative idea of the State Government in Odisha. Much water has flown down the river Mahanadee, since 'Gaon Sathi' concept has come into vogue and after a long journey of seven years, one is bewildered to see the progress of this kind of institution building process in Odisha.

Looking at the literature one finds a book *Gaon Sathi: Experiment in Extension* (OUP, 1956). The book was prepared as a textbook by members of the staff of the Extension Project being carried on at the Allahabad Agriculture Institute with funds made available by Ford Foundation. The book was limited to a description of Extension as was practised in the Jamuna-par Punarnirman, the Allahabad Pilot Extension Project. Extension workers were called by several names like Gram Sevaks, village level workers etc. In the Jamuna-par Punarnirman, an expression conveying a warmer meaning and describing the conceived role of the extension worker was coined—Gaon Sathi—the Companion of the Village.

Creed of a Gaon Sathi

I believe in village life and that it can be rich & wholesome.

I believe in village families founded on mutual affection and respect.

I believe in village youth; in their longings for opportunity, and in the fulfilment of their right for trained minds, healthy bodies and clean hearts.

I believe in village people, in their ability to solve their own problem, and in their power to develop their own lives.

I believe in my own work; in the opportunity it affords to be of service to others; and this because:

All men need self respect.

All men need friendship.

All men need recognition.

All men need opportunity.

And therefore in all my work:

I shall seek at all times to be friendly.

I shall seek at all times to be honest.

I shall seek at all times to be sincere.

I shall seek at all times to be humble.

I shall, with sincerity of purpose, work with village men, women, and children, for better family living, by helping them to make their fields and livestock more productive, their homes more comfortable and beautiful and their community more satisfying.

And because I believe in all this, and I shall to the best of my ability endeavour to fulfil them.

I AM A GAON SATHI.

Source: *Gaon Sathi: Experiment in Extension*, p.54.

"Economists like North and Thomas (1973) and Landes (1998)[1] have argued that the rich world is rich today because, over the centuries, it has devised institutions that have enabled people to

1. *Source: Selected Paper of Partha Dasgupta*, Vol-II. p.451.

improve their material conditions of life. On the other hand the people in today's rich country were able to fashion their institutions in ways that enabled those proximate causes of prosperity to explode there. One can safely ask whether it was the institutions or whether it was the enlightened policies of rulers that were responsible for the explosion. But then, policies are not plucked from the air, they emerged from consultations and deliberations within institutions" (Partha Dasgupta).

The Gaon Sathi nomenclature has been given to an institution created by MGNREGS in Odisha. One of the mandates in MGNREGS was to usher in an era of new ways of doing business, as a model of governance anchored on the principles of transparency and grass root democracy. This calls for establishment of new and sustainable institutions. Acemoglu writes "Nations fail because they have extractive Institutions". Are we creating institutions which are extractive in nature? In the light of this, the present paper explores the efficacy of Gaon Sathi as an institution in Odisha.

Extractive Institutions: The Case of Zimbabwe

It was January 2000 in Harare, Zimbabwe, Master of Ceremonies Fallot Chawawa was in charge of drawing the winning ticket for the national lottery organised by a partly state-owned bank, the Zimbabwe Banking Corporation (ZIMBANK). The lottery was open to all clients who had kept five thousand or more Zimbabwe dollars in their accounts during December 1999. When Chawawa drew the ticket, he was dumfounded. As the public statement of Zimbabwe put it, "Master of Ceremonies Fallot Chawawa could hardly believe his eyes when the ticket drawn for the Z$100,000 prize was handed to him and he saw His Excellancy R.G. Mugabe written on it. President Robert Mugabe, who had ruled Zimbabwe by hook or crook, and usually with an iron fist, since 1980, had won the lottery, which was worth a hundred thousand Zimbabwe dollars, about five times the annual per capita income of the country. Zimbank claimed that Mr Mugabe's name had been drawn from among thousands of eligible customers. What a lucky man! Needless to say he did not really need the money. Mugabe had in fact only recently awarded himself and his cabinet salary hikes of up to 200 per cent.

The lottery ticket was just one more indication of Zimbabwe's extractive institutions. One could call this corruption, but it is just a symptom of the institutional malaise in Zimbabwe. The fact that Mugabe could even win the lottery if he wanted showed how much control he had over matters in Zimbabwe, and gave the world a glimpse of the extent of the country's extractive institutions.

The most common reason why nations fail today is because they have extractive institutions.

Source : Acemoglu and Robinson, 2013: 368-69.

What is an Institution

Writing on the challenges involved in studying institutions Elinor Ostrom writes that, "The term institutions is to refer to many different types of entities including organisations as well as the rules, norms, and strategies used to structure patterns of interaction and across organisation.

"Rules are the shared prescriptions (must, must not, or may) that are mutually understood and enforced in particular situations by agents responsible for monitoring conduct physical and for imposing sanctions.

"Norms are the shared prescriptions known and accepted by most of the participants themselves involving intrinsic costs and benefits rather than material sanctions or inducements.

"Strategies are meant to connote the regularised plans that individuals make within the structure of incentives produced by rules, norms, and expectations of the likely behaviour of others in a situation affected by relevant physical and material conditions."

Source: *Framework of Institutional Analysis*. pp.828-29.

National Rural Emplyment Guarantee Act (NREGA): A Paradigm Shift

Amongst the unprecedented enactments in the post independent era, NREGS and Right to Information (RTI) happen to stand very tall in terms of making an attempt to fulfil the dictates of the fundamental rights as enshrined in the Constitution. Almost a decade has passed by with attempts to ensure 100 days of work to the rural households volunteering for unskilled work. The enactment of these laws has brought in a sea change in the mind set of the Indian villagers. What many a laws could not achieve in half a century, these two enactments have made it possible in imparting that minimum information to the rural masses by virtue of which they are empowered to assert their rights as enshrined in the Constitution (viz., Minimum Wages Act of 1948).

Goals of NREGA

NREGA was notified on 7 September 2005, with the objective to enhance livelihood security in rural areas by providing at least 100 days of guaranteed wage employment in a financial year to every household whose adult members volunteer to do unskilled manual work.

i) It aimed to provide a strong social safety net for the vulnerable groups by providing a fall-back employment source, when other employment alternatives are scarce or inadequate,

ii) It will act as the growth engine for sustainable development of an agricultural economy. Through the process of providing employment on works that address causes of chronic poverty such as drought, deforestation and soil erosion, the act seeks to strengthen the natural resources base of rural livelihood and create durable assets in rural areas. Effectively implemented, NREGA has the potential to transform the geography of poverty.

iii) It will catalyse the process of empowerment of rural poor through the process of a rights-based law.

iv) It will usher in an era of new ways of doing business, as a model of governance anchored on the principles of transparency and grass root democracy.

NREGA was expected to foster conditions for inclusive growth, ranging from basic wage security and recharging rural economy to a transformative empowerment process of democracy.

After completion of almost a decade, each pockets in the country has a different story to tell about the implementation of this workfare programme in it's own specific way compelling any discernible thinker to come out with some solution to face the age old social hierarchy and deep rooted stratification based on caste, religion and ethnicity. The 100 days agenda of the Ministry of Rural Development has brought in significant changes in this flagship programme in the form of NREGA-2 calling for serious debate amongst the academicians, policy planners and the members of the civil society. The nomenclature of NREGS has also been changed by prefixing it with the name of Father of the Nation, Mahatma Gandhi. It is a fact that for the first time an act has brought in real inclusiveness of all the stakeholders and perhaps has largest ever population coverage in the post independent India. The RTI sin quo non with this act on "Right to Employment" has brought in new hopes and challenges in the *genre-de-vie* of the rural masses. Apart from the PRI (panchayati raj institution) members, the entire government machinery, the CBO (community-based organisation) and the civil society have faced the daunting task of fulfilling the hopes and aspirations of the teeming millions who still remain outside the benefit realms of a planned development growth path followed very meticulously in this country

The MGNREGA is a legal guarantee that the sovereign authority of this country makes with it's people to provide work when it is demanded. The right to work automatically follows from the right to life. It holds the government responsible for making this employment and it's equivalent income available to each of it's citizen. The MGNREGA transfers power to the people. It is a legal instrument in the hands of the poor based on the demand of the worker. The obligation to respond to demand is a legal compulsion. In this context, the implementation of MGNREGA offers the countryman an opportunity to strengthen the democratic processes.

Coming down to the question of devolution of power as per the 73rd Amendment, it is a fact that it is still in the statute book and yet to be translated into action with much gimmick by the respective states to make laws to transfer that power to the three-tier PRIs. In the policy implementation of MGNREGA, the same lacuna is with the state legislatures and their whims and caprices in terms of developing the structure of governance at the village level. It has pan Indian variation depending upon the legacy of administration carried on by the respective state governments. Gaon Sathi (GS) is such a concept which brought much debate in implementation of NREGS in Orissa. Actually, this happened to be a concept equivalent of the 'mate' introduced through the NREGA Operational Guidelines 2008 (3rd Edition) of Ministry of Rural Development, GoI. The process of selection of GS and the responsibility earmarked for in NREGS work was such that it created a sort of internal conflict within the very structure of village governance in terms of decision making by the Gram Sabha. Accordingly, after the election when Biju Janata Dal (BJD) government came to power for the third time (in 2009), it went with a policy change of engaging seven Gram Sanjojaks in each Revenue Village for monitoring the NREGS works.

In 2013, the whole concept was reverted back to the original legislation vide it's circular No. 24897 dated 05-10-2011, stating the abolition of the concept of GSs/Gram Sanjojaks. Both the nomenclatures of GS and Gram Sanjojaks have also been dropped and engagement of mate as work site supervisor was issued vide this letter. Eligibility for selection of mate was limited to permanent residency of the concerned Revenue Village, more than 18 years of age and minimum education qualification was limited to fifth pass. The mate would get the wage for unskilled worker under MGNREGS or semi-skilled labour as per Labour & Employees' State Insurance Department, Government of Odisha. It was decided that every Revenue Village will have two mates.

Orissa Rural Employment Guarantee Scheme, 2006

Orissa Rural Employment Guarantee Scheme, 2006 (OREGS) was implemented in 2006 in 19 districts of the state with the basic objective to enhance the livelihood security in rural areas by providing at least 100 days of guaranteed wage employment in a financial year to every household whose adult members volunteer to do unskilled manual work. In 2007-08 the scheme was extended to five more districts and in 2008-09 it was extended to the remaining six districts of the state. With a view to keeping a village level functionary exclusively for NREGS works the Government of Orissa decided to deploy two GSs in every Revenue Village for helping the Government Engineers/Officials concerned in smooth execution of NREGS work. Earlier, i.e. in the first two years of implementation of NREGS, there were Village Labour Leaders (VLLs) who looked after the NREGS works at the village level. VA VLL was selected for each work taken up in the village by the Panchayat Raj Department. There were three agencies/mechanisms at the disposal of the Block for doing any development work: a) through tender, b) through any Line Department, c) through the VLL.

A VLL was basically a labourer coming from the labour class and his duty was to supervise the works in the field, arrange labourers, looking after the materials at the work site, work as per the instruction/order of the JEs (Junior Engineers) of the Block, maintaining the muster roll etc. Through the Operational Guidelines of MoRD, Government of India, the concept of Mate came into force since 2008. With VLL concept already in force since the days of Sampoorna Grameena Rozgar Yojana (SGRY) and the system of Mate coming into picture in 2008, Government of Orissa abolished both the system of VLL and Mate in NREGS and introduced the system of GS in each NREGS work. The institution of GS came into being since April 2008. But nowhere formal engagement of Mate was made for NREGS works in Orissa. The VLL system in vogue since long was also abolished and it was made clear that it would not continue beyond 30th June 2008. Actually, at the block level the VLL was popularly known as Mate. But the terminology of Mate was not in official/formal use.

Since 2006 Government of Orissa has gone in for engagement of Multi Purpose Assistants (Gram Rozgar Sevak) in the Gram Panchayat (GP) where there was no GP Secretary. The GP where Secretary was there, it was decided in 2006 that he would perform the work of GRS. He would be responsible for maintenance of accounts, database in the computer and discharge the duties and responsibilities under NREGS. Since 2007 Government of Orissa went in for engagement of Gram Rozgar Sevak in each GP whether the GP secretary post was vacant or not. The qualification and the selection process for Gram Rozgar Sevak remained the same. The job chart for the Gram Rozgar Sevak was same as mentioned in the NREGA Operational Guidelines 2007. In 2008, the nomenclature of GRS was changed from Gram Rozgar Sevak to Gram Rozgar Sahayak (GRS). Accordingly in Orissa also they are known as GRS. Currently, in Orissa we have GRS at the GP level and GS at each Revenue Village for NREGS works. For each *panchayat* there is a GRS and a number of GS depend upon the number of Revenue Villages attending to the NREGS works.

The present paper analyses the innovative measures in institution building in the process of implementation of NREGS in Orissa. It studies the structure of village governance existing in Orissa and it's implication in carrying out this demand driven workfare programme. The paper is based on a field study conducted during December 2008

The Objectives

The purpose of the present study was to examine the institution of GSs in execution of NREGS works in the light of following points.

i. Whether the procedure of appointment of GS was in consonance with the provisions of NREGS.
ii. Whether the work distribution between GRS and the GS in any way leads to a duplication of work.
iii. In what way the institution of GS is different from the pan Indian Mate concept

Table 33.1

Sample Area of the Study (District, Block, Gram Panchayat, Villages)

State	*District*	*Block*	*Gram Panchayat*	*Village*
Orissa	Balangir	Puintala	Bairasar	Bhadrapali
			Chhatamakhana	Padiabahal
			Bahalpadar	Burobhadi
		Deogaon	Sikuan	Sikuan
			Sarasmal	Sarasmal
			Jarasingha	Barkani
	Sambalpur	Maneswar	Bargaon	Bhardol
			Huma	Karanjola
			Baduapali	Mahulpali
		Dhankauda	Kalamati	Kalamati
			Chaunpur	Chaunpur
			Sankarma	Dhankauda
			A.Katapali	A.Katapali

Source: Primary Data.

The Scope of the Study

i. To find out the perceptions about GS from different stakeholders in NREGS.
ii. To examine the utility of deployment of GS in every Revenue Village.

iii. To look into the institutional mechanism after the deployment of GS at the village level for effective execution of NREGS work.
iv. To find out the sustainability of such institutions (GS) in the light of the appointment procedure and the payment of incentive to GS.
v. To find out the conflict/clash of interest, if any, between the GS and the GRS.
vi. To ascertain whether in reality GS contributes significantly in NREGS work in terms of mobilising more number of workers.
vii. To ascertain whether the engagement of GS has led to any increase in the level of awareness about NREGS in the villages.
viii. Whether the institution of GS vis-à-vis others has significantly contributed to overall increase in the demand for work and consequent development in the rural area.

Data Analysis

Seven Schedules of questionnaires were prepared for the following:

i. Additional Secretary of PR Department of Orissa who is in charge of NREGS.
ii. DPCs of the District.
iii. POs of the block.
iv. *Sarpanch* or the PRI member of the GP.
v. Focus Group Discussion (FGD) with the NREGS workers.
vi. GRS of the GP.
vii. GS of the Revenue Village where NREGS work was in progress.

Simple statistical measures are used to collate the data collected from the State and District offices and from the Villages. For easy interpretation, the tables are prepared based on the issues/questions asked to different respondents. Opinions of the respondents are treated separately and analysed.

Institutional Arrangements for Execution of NREGS

In the initial phase of NREGS implementation, there were no clear cut guidelines about the institutional arrangements to be made at the grass root level. Accordingly, the State utilised the existing institutional setup for implementation of the scheme at the *panchayat* and the village level. Some of the institutional arrangements made for execution of the scheme are mentioned under different sub-heads.

Institution of Gaon Sathi

Panchayat Raj Department, Government of Orissa, vide it's official order on 30.01.2008 decided to deploy GS in every Revenue Village for smooth execution of NREGS works. The salient features of the institution of Gaon Sathi are:

Qualification

a. For every Revenue Village of the state there will be two GSs out of which at least one will be a woman.
b. He/she should be permanent resident of the same Revenue Village where applies for this assignment.
c. He/she should be within 18 to 35 years of age.
d. The minimum educational qualification is 5th pass. However, the most educated (highest qualified and securing highest marks) applicants will be selected as GS.
e. In scheduled areas of the state, only ST (scheduled tribe) persons shall be deployed as GSs. However, in scheduled areas where the tribal population is less than 5 per cent of the total village population, both ST and non-ST candidates shall be considered.

Both husband and wife cannot be selected as GSs in the same Revenue Village. Persons engaged as Gram Rakhi/PRI representatives/ ASHA Worker/Anganwadi worker/Helper/Swechhasebi Siksha Sahayak (SSS)/Watershed or Pani Panchayat Association President/Secretary etc., and similar other assignments, cannot be selected as GS.

Role

The institution of GS was created by abolishing the concept of engagement of Mate in every NREGS work with effect from 01/01/2008. Even the system of VLL was discontinued with GS system coming into effect since 01/04/08.

GSs are basically representatives of the villagers whose main role is to function as a link between wage seekers and NREGS programme administrators. It is a sort of voluntary work for the benefit of the wage seekers of his/her own village.

The function of GS is the same as that of a Mate (as given in the Operational Guidelines)—organising job card holders for work, bringing them to the work site for execution of work, formation of groups, marking out the task required to earn minimum wage, maintaining muster rolls, helping in measurement of work, helping in payment of wages and ensuring work site facilities.

Financial Incentive

Being a voluntary sort of work there is no salary/honorarium for GSs. However an incentive of ₹4 per wage seeker per day will be paid to the GS for the entire duration of the work. Further, when a GS is engaged for the first time in any NREGS work, the first 15 days of his engagement shall be treated as on-the job training for which the GS will be paid an incentive @ ₹80 per day for 8 hours of work as per his attendance.

Selection of GS

GS is selected by the selection committee comprising the BDO, Sarpanch, ABDO (or any extension officer in his absence). Selection to the GS is made on merit with highest qualification. Two merit lists will be prepared: i) a common merit list and ii) a separate merit list of woman applicants. The common merit list will contain the names of all the applicants in descending order of their qualification and marks irrespective of their sex or caste.

The number one candidate of the common merit list (whether male or female) will be selected as First GS and the other from the merit list of woman applicants who will be selected as the Second GS. In such a selection process there may be two woman GSs in a Revenue Village, in case a woman top the list in both the merit list.

Engagement Order for Gaon Sathi

No engagement order will be issued to the GSs. However when works under NREGS are to be taken up, the GS will be deployed on turn basis for which appropriate order will be passed in the case record by the concerned JE/Asst. Engineer/*Sarpanch*/BDO. GSs may also be engaged in line department work as and when need arises.

Study Findings

Study Area Profiles

District-wise and block-wise profile of the study area is given in Table 33.2 and Table 33.3 respectively. It is evident from Table 33.3, that in Maneswar and Dhankauda blocks the share of SCs and STs is very high.

Table 33.2

District Profile at a Glance

Administrative set up	*Balangir*	*Sambalpur*
Sub-divisions	3	4
Blocks	14	9
Tehasils	6	5
Gram Panchayats	285	148
Revenue Villages	1761	1247
Population (Lakhs)	13.37	9.35
Male	6.74	4.75
Female	6.63	4.60
Rural	11.82	6.82
Urban	1.54	2.54
SC	2.26	1.59
ST	2.76	3.23
Literacy Rate	54.93%	67.01%

Source: District Collectorate.

Table 33.3

Block Profile at a Glance

Details	*Blocks*			
	Puintala	*Deogaon*	*Maneswara*	*Dhankauda*
Total Population	86571	84491	90288	90185
SC	18415 (21.3 %)	14240 (16.9 %)	27071 (30.0 %)	22509 (25.0 %)
ST	5733 (6.62 %)	17882 (21.2 %)	26261 (29.0%)	30580 (34.0 %)
Literacy rate	42.17 %	49.17 %	47.39 %	47.93 %

Source: Block office.

The GRS, GS Engaged at Block, GP, Revenue Village

Almost every village in the state has a GS in place. It is informed that there are nearly 62,000 GS all over the State. The latest figures were not available with the State office. But the data in the study area reveal that there are hardly any Revenue Village without a GS. For deployment of GS there was advertisement at the State level twice in newspapers.

Further, there was advertisement at the District level twice for deployment of GS. Still all the villages could not deploy two GSs.. There are nine (9) villages in the Puintala Block where GS are yet to be deployed. The PO (Puintala Block) informed that after four rounds of advertisement there are no applicants. In the rest three Blocks no Revenue Village was found without at least one GS.

The vacancy position of GS could be furnished only by the BDO Puintala. The other three BDOs could not furnish the same. Only from their statements it is recorded that there is no village in their Block without at least one GS. As is the case in the state office, there is no proper maintenance of record about the deployment of GS at the Block office also.

"The engagement of GS was basically to mobilise the job seekers for NREGS programme. After the engagement of GS the demand for work in NRREGS has significantly increased. We have at least one representative at the Revenue Village level to exclusively look after the NREGS work and other works also", opines the NREGS Head of the State. GS has been very helpful in identifying the job seekers.

Table 33.4

State-wise, Selected District-wise GPs , GRS and GS (As on July 2008)

State	*No./Name of District*	*No./Name of Block*	*No. of GPs*	*No. of Revenue Villages*	*No. of Gram GRS*	*No. of GS*
Orissa	30	314	6234	52025	5455	53946
Districts	Balangir	14	285	1792	271	2678
	Sambalpur	9	148	1320	148	1947
Blocks	Balangir	Puintala	24	134	24	201
		Deogaon	23	127	21	236
	Sambalpur	Maneswar	17	105	16	169
		Dhankauda	16	85	16	151

Source: Panchayat Raj Department, Government of Orissa.

Education of GRS and GS

It is found that most of the GSs are +2 passed or having more qualification. Amongst the GRS only 23.07 per cent were +2 Pass which is the minimum qualification for the GRS. 61.53 per cent are graduates and 15.38 per cent are post graduates. Out of 13, only 3 GRS are from Commerce stream even though as per the selection criteria they were to be given preference. Only 1 out of 13 is having computer proficiency while applying for GRS.

Only 12.5 per cent of GS are with minimum qualification i.e. 5th pass. 6.25 per cent of GS have passed the 10th class. The percentage of GS with +2 qualifications is 31.25; graduates 37.5 per cent and Post Graduate 12.5 per cent. Accordingly, +2 graduate and post graduates constitute 81.25 per cent. Table 33.5 provides the necessary details about the educational levels of GRS and GS.

The selection of GS on mark basis has led to deployment of GS with higher educational qualification than the minimum qualification of 5th class. This has curbed the opportunities of wage seekers to represent their community to become GS. The highest qualification criterion has affected the interest of the institution of

GS at grass root level. Highest qualification has overlooked the true representation of real poor wage seekers. In two cases, the GS got better appointment and left sooner. Again excepting two GS in the study areas all others belong to higher economic strata in comparison to the wage seekers. It is manifested from the living condition and the residential structure they live in; also, the locality where his/her house is located. Being of higher economic group as well as with higher education, they do not represent the wage seekers truly. Most of the GS have aspiration to shift to better job with higher income.

Table 33.5

Educational Qualification of GRS and GS

	5th Pass	*10th Pass*	*+ 2 Pass*	*Graduate*	*Post Graduate*
GS	--	--	3 (24.0 %)	8 (61.0 %)	2(15.0 %)
GRS	2 (12.5%)	1(6.25%)	5 (31.2 %)	6 (37.5 %)	2 (12.5 %)

It is observed that maximum number of GRS are having graduate (37%) degrees followed by +2 pass (31%). In the 3 villages (Chhatamakhana, Karanjola, A. Katapali) the GS are having higher educational qualification than their GRS. During the study the GS in these villages were found to be well versed with the NREGS guidelines and works, and are more vocal than their respective GRS.

Caste and Gender Status of GS and GRS

Out of the 16 GS, 6 (5 males and one female) belonged to SC (scheduled caste), one belonged to ST, 7 (2 males and 5 females) belonged to OBC (other backward class), 2 (1 male and 1 female) belonged to Other Castes. And out of the 13 GRS, 4 (3 male and 1 female) belonged to SC, none belonged to ST, 7 (all males) belonged to OBC and 2 belonged to Other Castes (1 male and 1 female).

Works Rendered by GS

Out of the 16 NREGS assignments, the works rendered by GS as per their own information is recorded in Figure 33.1. The percentage varies with reference to works rendered by the GS. Above 80 per cent respondents reported of doing the works of formation of wage seekers, marking of works for wage seeker groups, maintenance of muster roll, payment of wages, ensuring provision of work site facilities, overseeing of job cards, providing information and advice to REGs workers and residents of Revenue Villages. Around 60-75 per cent of respondents informed about furnishing of dated receipts against job applications and ensuring of holding of Gram Sabha. However for measurement of works and ensuring flow of information within GP, being the most important aspect of NREGS, less than 35 per cent of the respondents have responded. Maintaining of REGs related documents/accounts, furnishing information to PO and payment of unemployment allowance were not rendered by the GS.

Figure 33.1

Works Rendered by Gaon Sathi for Wage Seekers in Gram Panchayat

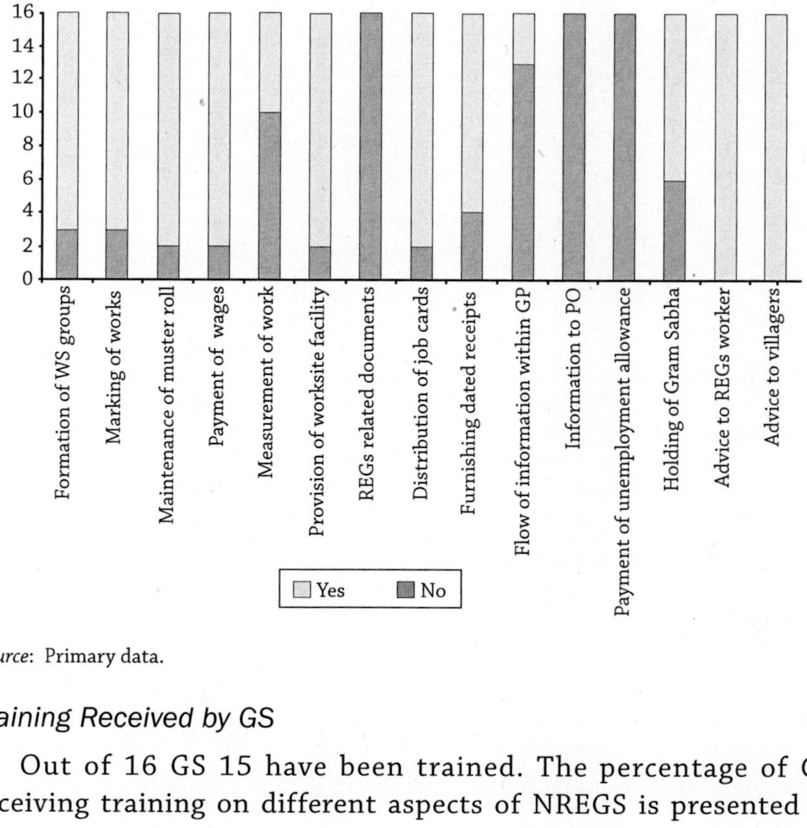

Source: Primary data.

Training Received by GS

Out of 16 GS 15 have been trained. The percentage of GS receiving training on different aspects of NREGS is presented in

Figure 33.2. 100 per cent of GS have been trained on the main provision of NREGS, entitlement of NREGS workers and work site facilities, followed by mobilisation of wage seekers (86.67%) and measurement of works (53.33%). Transparency safeguards at work site, and maintaining of muster rolls were given least importance while imparting training to GS.

Figure 33.2

Topics Covered in Training Received by Gaon Sathi

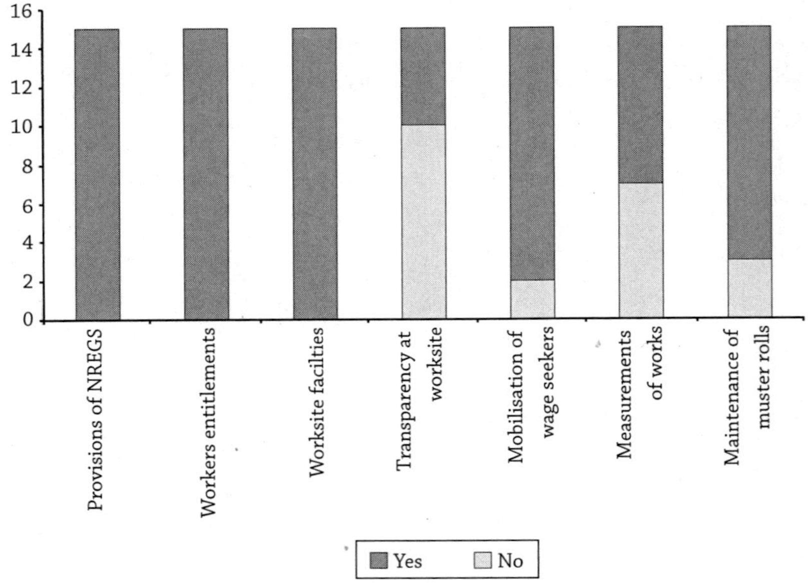

Source: Primary data.

Kits Given to GS

The basic tool kit requirements for a GS are tape, calculator, first aid box and diary to record daily measurement. 18.75 per cent of the GS have been provided with tapes, 31.25 per cent have been provided with first aid box and 37.5 per cent with diary, while none have been provided with calculators.

Works by GRS

Out of the 16 works related to NREGS, the GRS have indicated the types of works attended to by them and the details are presented in Figure 33.3. Among the sampled GRS, 80-100 per cent of them informed that they render works such as ensuring of holding of Gram Sabha, overseeing process of registration, furnishing dated receipts against job applications, overseeing of job cards, ensuring holding of social audit, ensuring flow of information within GP, providing information and advice to REGS workers and residents of Revenue Village/GP, maintaining of REGS related documents/accounts and furnishing information to PO. About 60-70 per cent of GRS informed that they have been maintaining muster roll, payment of wages and measurement of works as well. About 23 per cent of respondents have been forming wage seekers groups and marking of works for wage seekers. About 46 per cent of respondents have been providing work site facilities. None of the respondents have paid any unemployment allowance to wage seekers.

Training Received by GRS

Out of 13 GRS, 10 have been trained. The percentage of GRS receiving training on different aspects of NREGS is presented in Figure 33.4. 90 per cent of GRS have been trained on awareness generation, book keeping, mobilisation of job seekers and accounts, 100 per cent on supervision of NREGS works, maintaining of muster rolls and work site facilities, measurement of works (60%) and none on social audit.

Help Received by GRS from GS in NREGS works

The GRS were asked about the activities in which the GS have been rendering help to them. There is some disagreement between the responses of GS and GRS with regard to the support provided by the GS to GRS in NREGS. The percentage of responses in the functional linkage between the GRS and GS is presented in Figure 33.5.

Figure 33.3
Works Rendered by GRS

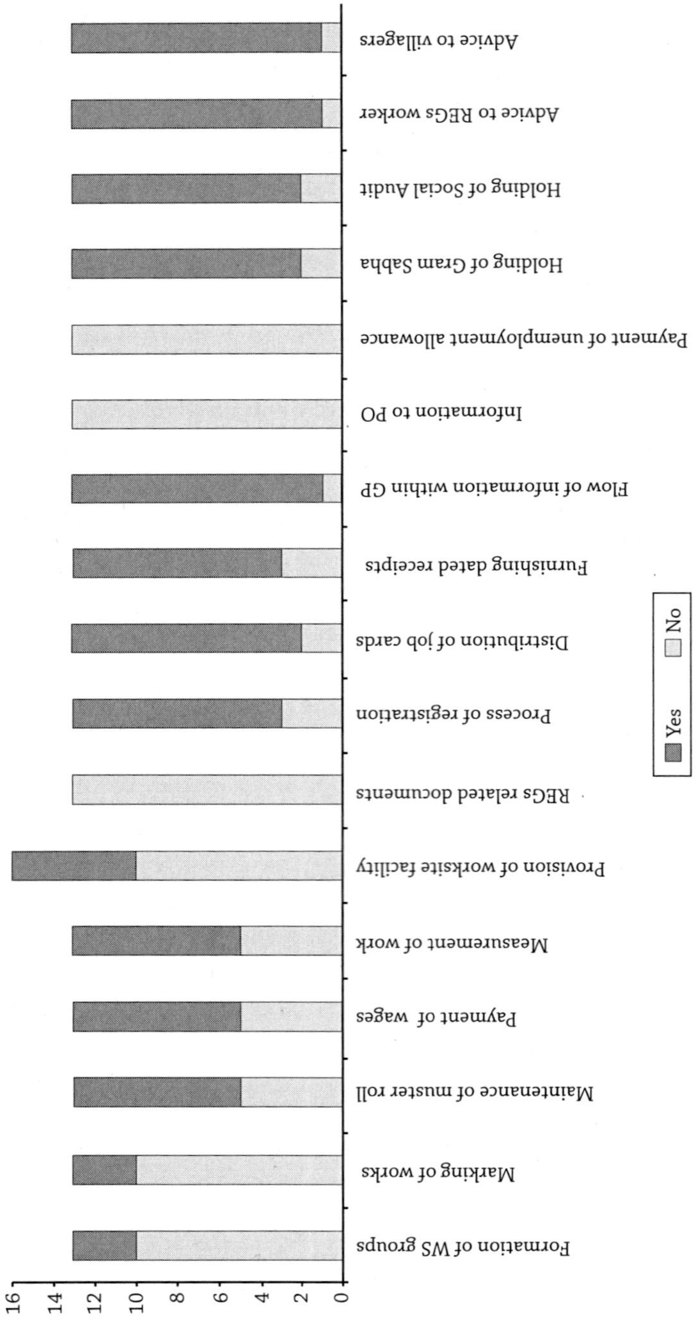

Source: Primary data.

Figure 33.4

Topics Covered in Training Received by GRS

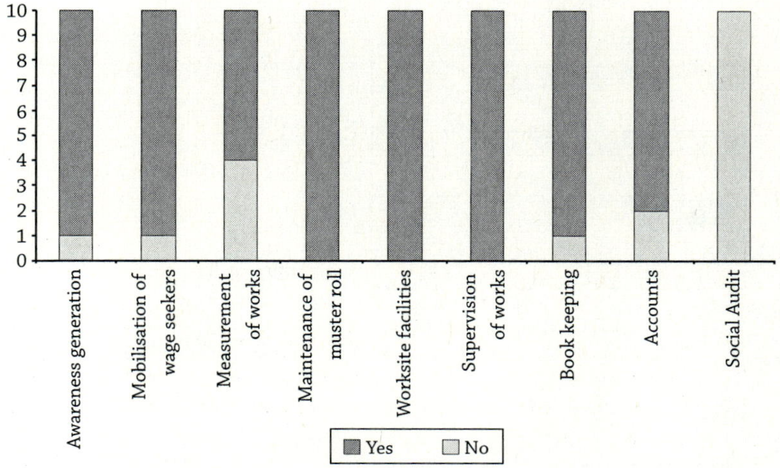

Source: Primary data.

Views of Sarpanches on Functional Linkages between GS and GRS

The PRI representatives have a significant role in NREGS work. Even though the *sarpanch* (i.e. the GP head) has very limited role in the appointment or deployment of GRS and GS, he/she has a prime role in overall supervision of NREGS work meant for the total development of his/her GP. The *sarpanches* have their own perceptions about the works rendered by GS as a helping hand to the GRS (see Figure 33.6).

The 12 *sarpanches* have been asked about their views in the works wherein the GS renders help to the GRS. Hundred per cent of the *sarpanches* informed that the GS helps the GRS in mobilisation of job card holders, in maintaining of muster roll (83%), payment of wages (92%), maintenance of accounts (33%), in overseeing process of registration (75%), overseeing distribution job cards (83%), flow of information within GP (19%), furnishing information (42%), payment of unemployment allowance (0%), holding of Gram Sabha (75%), conduct of social audit (33%).

Figure 33.5

Functional Linkage between GRS and GS: Works in which GS Helps the GRS

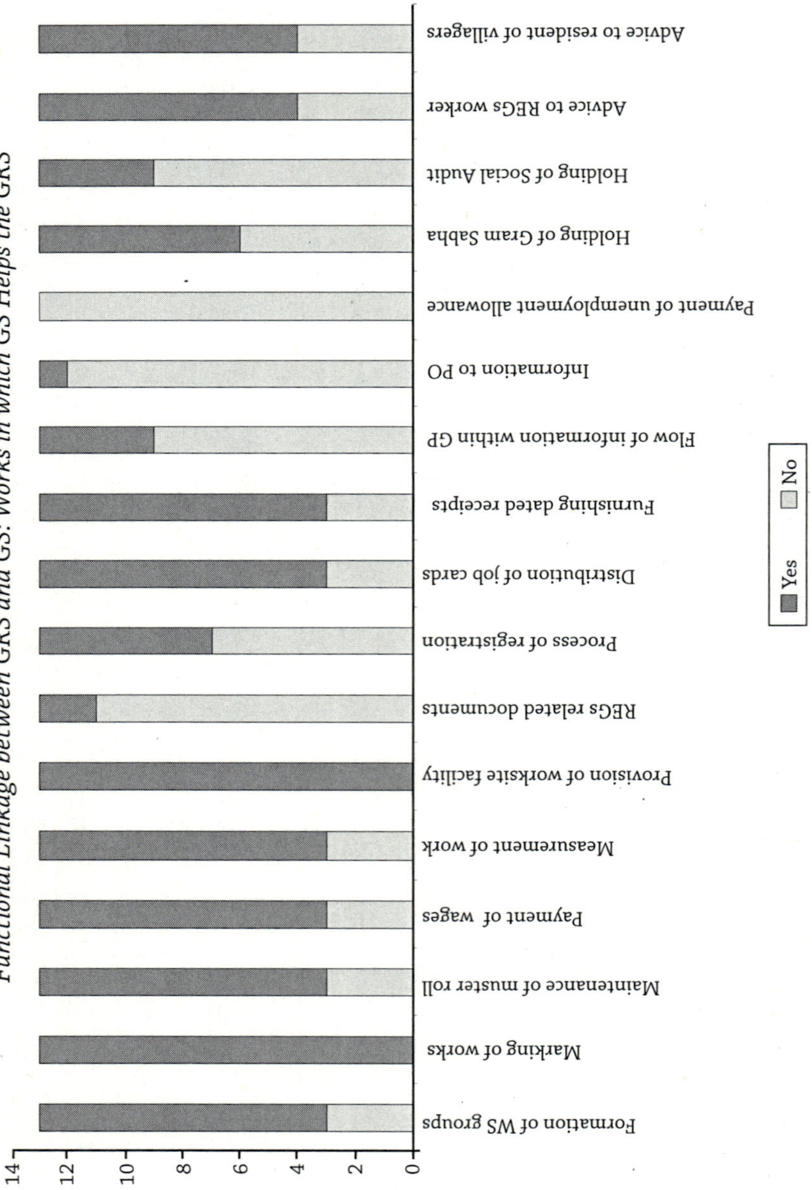

Source: Primary data.

Interactions with Various Stakeholders

The study team has not only collected the information from the various stakeholders at the grass root level, but also interacted with the wage seekers, villagers and PRI members by personnel interview. During the interactions, views about the roles and responsibilities of GS, GRS and other functionaries in NREGS were elicited. This highlighted the real problems and possible solutions in implementation of this scheme. Some of them are presented here under.

Figure 33.6

Views of Sarpanches on Activities where GS Renders Help to GRS

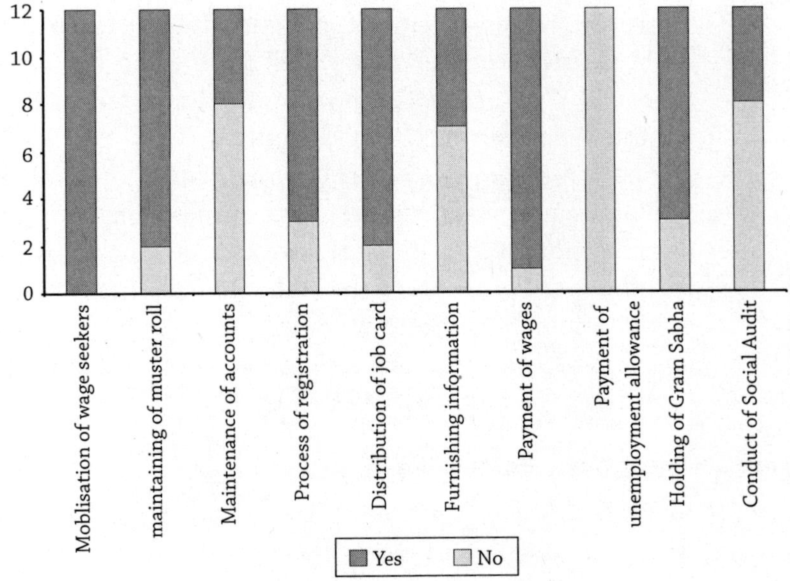

Source: Primary data.

Utility of the GS in Effective Implementation of Works in NREGS

- The GS being a native of the Revenue Village knows the job seekers personally so that he/she are capable of identifying the job seekers easily & unmistakably.
- The GS helps the job seekers in opening the pass books and also in filling up the forms for withdrawing the cash from the pass book. As claimed by the GS in every village, more

number of wage seekers are coming to works in NREGS each year than the previous year. But this is not reflected as per the percentage of wage seekers coming to NREGS work in different villages. This is because the actual job seekers in NREGS represent a low percentage compared to the total number of persons holding the job cards.

- There is incentive to GS to bring more number of wage seekers per day, since it will help him/her in getting more incentives.
- GS is assisting the GRS and the JEs in measurement of works. He/she takes daily measurement (even though it is heuristic) and informs the wage seekers about the performance of their work. The wage seekers get some idea about the work done each day and whether that would fetch them the minimum wages. There is, however, no training imparted to them for accurately measuring the work done.
- Formation of group (particularly formation of combination of male/female wage seekers) has been very important in soil digging (pond etc.). The male workers do the earth digging and the female carry it to the embankment. The combination of male/female workers working together in one work on piece rate basis and sharing the wages with out any problem has been done by the GS very smoothly.

Management of Work Site Facilities by GS

- In all the work sites visited in the villages the GS has ensured water and shade only. Very few had first aid box and none have the crèche facilities.
- In the study area, children of the wage seekers were not found in the work site. Even though the customary practice in the area of study is not to bring the children to the work site, the wage seekers than also expressed the problem of bringing food for the children. The wage seekers generally leave behind their children in the care of their kith and kin or the neighbour with who the child is familiar with.

- There is no facility available like provision of baby food or breakfast for children. It was informed by the wage seekers that woman with child of a few months generally could not come to work. In the absence of crèche facility, women with infant children cannot bring them to the work site. Women insist on privacy at the time of feeding their children. The role of GS in this aspect is discouraging. In the absence of awareness of the rights and entitlements, workers cannot insist such facilities.
- In the study area, GS have no notion as to how to provide crèche facilities. GS and wage seekers are also not aware about who will bear the cost and provide food in case the children are brought to the work site. This is irrespective of the fact that Government of Orissa (vide letter No 16842, dt 21-08-2006) has issued instruction about the crèche facility in the NREGS work site (there is provision of ₹7 per child per day towards baby food and ₹2 towards soaps and disinfectants for children below three years). Expenditure of ₹1,500 may be made towards purchase of buckets, mats for five children.
- During the study it was found that neither the District head (Additional District Project Coordinator) nor the Block head (Programme Officer) of the OREGS was aware of any such instructions from the government. It is a fact that Orissa has been a pioneer in making laws of all kinds on governance but is one of the worst in policy implementation. This is basically due to wrong and inadequate data base resulting in wrong appraisal of the ground reality and faulty prioritisation.

Difficulties Faced by Women GS in Rendering Support to the Works of NREGS

- There is no problem as such faced by the women GS in particular. But some POs and GRS inform that the women GS do not remain at the work site all through the day. Also, the women GS find it difficult to mobilise the workers daily by going to their residences. Here the male members of the family help them out in going to different households.

- The married women GS with small children find it difficult to go to the work site which is farther away from their residence i.e., more than one km. The husband/any other family member takes them to the work site. If male person is to accompany the women GS to the work site, then it is not at all remunerative—opines the family members of the women GS. The educated (particularly graduate or more) spinster women GS however find no difficulty in going to the work site either by cycle or mopeds.

Duplication of Works Between the GRS and GS

- Before the deployment of GS, the GRS was doing all works related to NREGS along with the VLL at the village level apart from the works to be done at the GP level. Now he/she is concerned more with GP level work and over all supervision of NREGS works in different villages. After the deployment of GS the workload of the GRS has been reduced.
- Now the GRS is exclusively concerned with the works of maintaining REGS related documents/accounts, overseeing the process of registration, ensuring flow of information within GP, furnishing information to PO, ensuring holding of social audits etc.
- The GS is exclusively concerned with the tasks of formation of wage seeker groups, marking of works for wage seeker groups, ensuring work site facilities etc.
- The works which both the GRS and GS claim to do is maintenance of muster-roll, measurement of works, payments of wages, overseeing the distribution of job cards, furnishing dated receipts against job application, ensuring holding of Gram Sabha, providing information to REGS workers and residents of the Revenue Village and the GP etc.
- The day-to-day work supervision, helping the wage seekers in opening up their Pass Books, ensuring work site facilities, formation of wage seeker groups, marking of works to wage seeker groups, taking daily attendance of the wage seekers at the work site and accordingly maintaining the muster roll are

exclusively done by GS and the GRS make overall supervision of all works done by different GS. So the GRS is finding time to maintain the NREGS record properly and update all the information in MIS on a weekly basis. Every Block has its own fixed day of the week (EGS day) when all the GRS of the Block come to the Block office and furnish all the information related to NREGS. When the works are going on in more than one village in a GP, the GRS doesn't find time to go to each work site daily. Here the GS is in a position to smoothen the process of NREGS work without any problem.

- However, during the field study it was found that wage seekers are not convinced with the measurement of word by GS or GRS. They fully rely on the measurement work done by the JEs of the Block. During the study it was found that JEs were finding it difficult to go to each NREGS work site (irrespective of the fact that Orissa Government has gone in for appointment of one or two Gram Panchayat Technical Assistant i.e. GPTA in each Block exclusively for NREGS works). The newly recruited GPTAs are also not well versed with the measurement of works. They are also learning from the JEs in the Block and accordingly the JEs find it difficult to go to each work site in each village. Some JEs are of the opinion that the GS should be trained to take measurement of simple nature of work and should also be made responsible for the works. The BDO-cum-PO of Puintala Block opines that GRS should be empowered for reporting on whether GS has any contribution in mobilising wage seekers for work. If not then the GS should not be paid ₹4 per day per wage seeker.

Adequacy and Sufficiency of Training Received by GS for Rendering the NREGS Works

- Most of the GS have received training for at least one day in the Block Office, and some for even five days. When the GS is engaged for the first time in any NREGS work, the first 15 days of his engagement shall be treated as on the job training for which GS will be paid incentive at the rate of ₹80 per day. During this period, he/she is given training on main provisions of NREGS, awareness generation, entitlement of NREGS wage seekers, mobilising the job seekers, work site facilities, measurement of work, maintaining of muster roll, Gram Sabha etc.

- During the study it was revealed that none of the GS have been trained about the transparency safeguards to be maintained in the NREGS works. During the study in all the work sites the muster rolls were found to be with the GS. The GS have rolling note books either supplied by the GP office or of their own to maintain the daily attendance of the wage seekers. It was revealed that the GS have no idea about social audit. None of the GS have not been supplied with tool kits like tape, calculator, first-aid box, daily measurement record books etc. The GS take the measurement tape of the GP from the GRS. Out of the 14 Revenue Villages studied only 5 GS had first aid box.
- Most of the GSs wanted more training at the GP level on the NREGS. They asked for training specifically on measurement of works, conduct of Gram Sabha and social audit.
- None of the GS was aware of the amount of unemployment allowance to be paid in case work could not be provided within 15 days of demand by the wage seeker. No where in the study area unemployment allowances had been paid.

Views of the Elected Representatives Towards the Institution of GS

- The *sarpanches* have been very casual in their responses. They have expressed happiness about the deployment of GS in each village in their GPs. But their involvement in NREGS in planning for the overall development of the village in a stipulated time frame seems to be very minimal. Except for two *sarpanches* (of Chaurpur and Katapali) others did not have any idea about developing a village perspective plan within the framework of the NREGS. Aprat from these two *sarpanches* all complained about lack of fund in the NREGS work and delay in allotment of fund. They still have a notion of NREGS as a supply driven programme and not a demand driven.

- Most of the villages have been engaged in digging ponds or road connectivity works. There is complete lack of vision as to what other works can be taken up under the NREGS. Works related to irrigation facility, plantation, horticulture, land development have been taken up.
- Based on the field observations, it is clear that less number of wage seekers are coming for NREGS works. Since most of the works taken up demand hard physical labour (like digging of soil), people have less interest to come and work in NREGS. *Sarpanches* opine that people are not used to doing such hard work.

The Positive Contribution of GS in the Implementation of NREGS

- 12 GP *sarpanches* out of the 13 under the study knew the procedure of selection of GS. But no one has taken any active participation in the same since it was done on the marks basis. Everyone expressed the view that they had no involvement of any kind in the deployment of GS except signing the final selection list prepared by the block staff. 11 GP *sarpanches* had no idea about the training given to GRS or GS.
- Most of the *sarpanches* (10 out of 12) were in the favour of deployment of one male and one female GS. Two *sarpanches* were against the deployment of woman GS and one *sarpanch* was of the view that under no circumstances both the GS should be women.

Wage Seekers' Opinion about the Utility of GS to them

- In every Revenue Village and at the work site, the wage seekers were informed about the beneficial effect of GS. They are also duly informed about NREGS and the works to be taken up under NREGS in their village or nearby villages.
- In all the Revenue Villages under study, the wage seekers informed that the GS was responsible for opening their Pass

Book and timely payment of their wages. In most of the cases, the GS accompanies the wage seekers to the banks or post offices and helps them in filling up the withdrawal form and informs them about the balance amount. The wages seekers strongly rely on the GS on all accounts except the measurement of work. The GS have taken ample interest initially and are doing these works more out of hope of more number of wage seekers to come forward to work in future in the NREGS than out of compulsion of the job chart.

Table 33.6

Work Distribution of NREGS from the District Level Onwards

District level	*Block level*	*GP level*	*Village level*
Collector-cum DPC	BDO-cum-PO	Panchayat Executive Officer	Gaon Sathi/ Gram Sanjojak/ Mate
PD DRDA-cum-Additional DPC	ABDO-cum-APO	Secretary	
Additional PD (Administration) and Additional PD (Technical)	Assistant Engineer	Gram Rozgar Sahayak	
Assistant Engineer	Two JEs and two GPTA		
Junior Engineer			

- The wage seekers have strong faith in the measurement of JE of the Block as he possesses power of some level of flexibility in recording measurement. With his measurement the wage seekers think they get little more wages. But it was also revealed that slowly the GS have started learning the exact measurement of earth digging work and it is hoped that the wage seekers would develop faith in them in the future.
- In all the Revenue Villages under study, the wage seekers are satisfied with the work site facilities in NREGS works. For the first time they say they were provided with drinking water and a rest shade (in most cases made up of green leaves and wooden poles). But their ignorance about other

work site facilities like crèche and first aid was also revealed. It also came to light that no where any injury was reported till this time.

- No where the wage seekers made any kind of complaints against the GS.

Conflict between the GRS and GS: Observations of PO, *Sarpanch* and Wage Seekers

- PO, *sarpanch* or wage seekers are yet to find any conflict between the GRS and GS in the NREGS work. But it is too early to say because only one or two works have been taken up under the NREGS in the villages under the study.

Suggestion for the Sustainability of the Institution of Gaon Sathi

- Selection criteria of GS based on higher educational qualification has defeated the purpose of engagement of a mate in every NREGS work as enunciated in the operational guidelines. It is a tall claim that Government of Orissa has attempted to solve the problem of unemployment of educated persons in rural areas through deployment of them as GS.
- Decision to put up at least one woman GS in every village has been very encouraging. But the woman GS need to be specially trained to render services effectively as seen in Rajasthan in the NREGS works.
- Government needs review the decision regarding the incentive of ₹4 to be paid to the GS. Provision of such low amount that too involving all uncertainty, will certainly dilute the institution of GS and forcing them to take the role of a labour contractor in the future as was the case with VLL earlier.
- The incentives paid to GS till now has already convinced the GS that they are simply hoodwinked. Therefore, they have been going on for strikes/*dharanas*. They have also started organising themselves by making registered associations

thus preparing to go to court of law for their permanent absorption in Government jobs.

- Updated information about GS is not available either at State NREGS cell or at Block level. It is suggested that the information about GS be put in the MIS system, so that one can easily locate who is the GS for a specific work in any village at any point of time and monitor the work and rectify the discrepancies if any.
- It is high time that provisions need be made to supply the tool kits to the GS.
- Training on different aspects of NREGS to all the stakeholders is urgently called for.
- Rigorous training on a regular basis need to be imparted to GS as is the case in Rajasthan.
- Without proper planning in the last three years (2005 to 2008), at least one work every year in each village is also not taken up. In such a situation, the institution of GS is highly unsustainable. Without any certainty of works to be undertaken the GS in all probability will never stay in the village. It is suggested that village perspective plan along with seasonality of labour demand be prepared in each village in right earnestness to ensure adequate monetary incentive to GS and for effective implementation of NREGS.

Gram Sanjojaka in Lieu of Gaon Sathi

In 2009 after the election, Government came out with the concept of Gram Sanjojak vide it's circular No. PR2439 dated 29/07/2009 and Letter No. 26555 dated 18/08/2009. Herein a long 12 page guidelines on Gram Sanjojak was issued by the government (duely signed by Aparajita Sarangi, IAS, Director (special project and additional secretary to Govt.-Panchayati Raj Department, Odisha) dt 18/08/2009). In order to supplement the efforts of Gaon Sathis, the concept of Gram Sanjojak has been formulated. Each Revenue Village would have a panel of 7 Gram Sanjojaks selected by Palli Sabha including the 2 GSs. The labour leader selected by MGNREGS wage seekers and SHG members will be in this 7 member 'empanelled

Gram Sanjojaks'. Qualification was limited to residents of the Revenue Village, more than 18 years of age, and class fifth pass. The Gram Sanjojaks are entitled to get the wage of a semi skilled labour while rendering work.

Government of the day, on the election eve, went on to the extent of claiming that thousands of jobs had been given to Gaon Sathi. Even during the election campaign many politicians of BJD took credit for creation of jobs that too of educated youth in rural areas vide Gaon Sahti in 2009. The fundamental question is whether engagement of a person—the equivalent of a Mate as per the Central Govt. act—a job? Can it be called as employment/recruitment? People have gone to the court on the issue of engagement of Gaon Sathi/Gram Sanjojaka. Looking/referring to the court case No W.P.(C)/16847/20098, of Odisha High Court, one gets surprised how this workfare programme has been utterly misinterpreted/misunderstood in Odisha. In the writ referred, a question was raised as to whether both husband and wife could be listed as the two Gaon Sathis in a particular Revenue Village if they are selected on merit.

The people in Odisha are embroiled with issues of getting employment (*Sarkari Naukari*) through MGNREGS without understanding the basic ethos of this employment Guarantee Act. In other states like Rajasthan and Andhra Pradesh, the qualification for mate is completion of MGNREGS work of a specific number of days in the previous year. Necessarily the mate himself/herself is a MGNREGS wage seeker. But in the context of Odisha Gaon Sathis were not MGNREGS wage seekers and it was another cadre of *Sarkari Babu* monitoring MGNREGS work sites. Central government funding of even up to 90 per cent in MGNREGS, could not sustain institutions like Gaon Sathis/Gram Sanjojaks due to gross misunderstanding of the same by the bureaucracy in Odisha.

Reference

Acemoglu, Daron and James A. Robinson (2013). *Why Nations Fail: The Origins of Power, Prosperity, and Poverty.* Profile Books Ltd.

Allahabad Agricultural University (1956). *Experiment in Extension: The Gaon Sathi.* Oxford University Press.

Dasgupta, Partha (2010). *Poverty, Population and Natural Resources: Selected Paper of Partha Dasgupta.* Vol 2. Oxford University Press.

Nath, Pradip Kumar and V. Suresh Babu (2008). *A Quick Study on Gaon Sathi in Orissa.*

Ostrom, Elinon (2005). "Doing Institutional Analysis: Digging Deeper than Markets and Hierarchies", in Claude Menard and Mary M. Shirley (eds.), *Handbook of New Institutional Economics.* Springer.

Note: The present paper is based on a quick study taken up by P.K.Nath & V. Suresh Babu during 2008-09.